W9-BHF-031

ANNALS OF ENGLISH DRAMA

For nearly fifty years, starting with the Alfred Harbage first edition, *Annals of English Drama, 975–1700* has been a standard reference text for scholars and specialists in the field of English pre- and post-Renaissance drama. This new, third edition supersedes the 1964 edition, taking account of the profusion of new scholarship with more than 1,000 new entries, clarifications, and corrections.

As in previous editions, the *Annals* provides a chronological listing as complete as knowledge permits of plays, masks, and similar forms of entertainment, devised in England (or by Englishmen abroad) from the time of the earliest *Quem Quaeritis* trope in the tenth century until the death of Dryden in 1700. It gives details of articles, monographs, full-length dramatic studies, comprehensive collections, separately published editions, anthologies, facsimiles, and doctoral dissertations.

For this edition, a Selective List of Medieval Texts has been added, and the Index of English Playwrights now contains bibliographical citations on definitive, comprehensive collections encompassing the complete dramatic works of pre-Restoration dramatists. Entries in the Index of English Plays now show recent publications of the plays in collected form, in individual editions as part of a scholarly series, in facsimile reprints, and as dissertations. Suggestions are made about alternative possibilities in date and authorship, based on the latest work of the most reliable authorities.

The new *Annals* will be an invaluable addition to public and private scholarly collections throughout the world, and an essential tool for all students of the medieval, Renaissance, and Restoration drama.

ANNALS
OF ENGLISH DRAMA

975–1700

AN ANALYTICAL RECORD
OF ALL PLAYS, EXTANT OR LOST,
CHRONOLOGICALLY ARRANGED AND INDEXED
BY AUTHORS, TITLES, DRAMATIC COMPANIES &C.

BY ALFRED HARBAGE
REVISED BY S. SCHOENBAUM

THIRD EDITION

REVISED BY SYLVIA STOLER WAGONHEIM

ROUTLEDGE

LONDON AND NEW YORK

Second edition published 1964
by Methuen & Co. Ltd
11 New Fetter Lane, London EC4
© *1964 by the Trustees of the University of Pennsylvania*

Third edition published 1989
by Routledge
11 New Fetter Lane, London EC4P 4EE
29 West 35th Street, New York, NY 10001
© *1989 Sylvia Stoler Wagonheim*

Typeset in 10/12 Baskerville by
Colset Private Ltd, Singapore
Printed in Great Britain by Richard Clay Ltd, Bungay, Suffolk

British Library Cataloguing in Publication Data

Wagonheim, Sylvia Stoler
Annals of English drama, 975–1700: an analytical record of all plays,
extant or lost, chronologically arranged and indexed by authors, titles,
dramatic companies, etc. – 3rd ed.
1. Drama in English – Bibliographies
I. Title II. Harbage, Alfred. Annals of English drama, 975–1700
016.822'008

ISBN 0 415 01099 3

Library of Congress Cataloging in Publication Data
applied for

CONTENTS

PREFACE TO THIRD EDITION

In the two decades since Professor Sam Schoenbaum revised the original Alfred Harbage edition of the *Annals of English Drama, 975–1700* the roster of articles, monographs, and full-length dramatic studies – not to mention comprehensive collections, separately published editions, anthologies, facsimiles, and doctoral dissertations – has swelled significantly. As I became more involved in the project of updating the *Annals* and increasingly aware of the magnitude and importance of the energetic scholarly activity of the past twenty years, I also awakened to the need for an enlarged and somewhat revised third edition.

Following the precedent set in the previous editions, I have tried to include the results of recently published research and to suggest alternative possibilities in date and authorship. At the same time, I have attempted, in all decisions, to maintain the conservative nature of the text by recording opinions, particularly on the subject of authorship and date, that reflect, as Professor Schoenbaum stated in the Introduction to the previous edition, 'the most conservative opinions of the most reliable authorities'. Consequently, among the approximately four dozen alterations in attribution, most have occurred in the form of confirmation of a favoured author, deletion of a doubtful contributor, or the reconsideration of an anonymous entry. There are few surprises. In the Limits column, approximately one hundred performance dates have been altered. About one-third of these changes record more specific limits of season, month, day or year; in other cases, when new facts warranted it, an entire entry has been moved to indicate a year of performance different from that noted in the previous edition of the *Annals*.

To record the scholarly editions that have seen print primarily since 1964, the new *Annals* has made, in round figures, more than one thousand new entries, clarifications, corrections, and deletions. For example, more than 150 comprehensive scholarly dramatic collections; approximately the same number of individual editions in a scholarly series; a dozen Shakespeare Variorum editions and Supplements completed since 1964; and more than 250 thesis editions have been added. The Supplementary Lists have increased by more than two dozen entries, and a like number of names has been added to the Index of English Playwrights. Approximately seventy additions or changes have been entered in the List of Extant Play Manuscripts and a number of substantive additions and alterations reflecting new knowledge have augmented the entries in the Lists of Theatres, Foreign Plays, Foreign Playwrights, and Dramatic Companies.

Though omissions and oversights are unavoidable in a reference compilation of this type, no effort has been spared in the attempt to cover the productivity of the period. In addition to scholarly prefaces, journal articles, bibliographies, checklists, and surveys published since 1964 on the drama of the period covered by the *Annals*, almost 200 publishers of dramatic literature have been consulted for information on pertinent scholarship and editions issuing from their presses. The flood of new information which these inquiries produced required certain changes and additions to the format of the *Annals* which could accommodate and adapt to the overflow. For example *A Selective List of Medieval Drama Texts* was added to the new *Annals* in order to recognize the growing store of pre-Renaissance drama collections which is currently available.

To facilitate the use of the new *Annals*, the Index of English Playwrights now includes bibliographical citations of collections encompassing the dramatic works of pre-Restoration dramatists. Similarly, the Index of English Plays now includes entries showing 'last editions' of the plays in a variety of shapes: in collected form, in individual editions as part of a scholarly series, in facsimile reprints, and as thesis or dissertation editions. These data are indicated in the Chronology and Information section through coded entries in the seventh, Latest Edition, column. Because publication information has been incorporated into the Index of English Playwrights and the Index of English Plays, the separate Lists of Editions and Dissertations, which appeared in the second edition of the *Annals*, were no longer necessary.

At this point, I would like to continue the tradition begun by Professor Harbage in the 1940 edition and request that colleagues and friends continue to share the fruits of their research as they have in the past by bringing to my attention errors, omissions, and new findings so that the future usefulness of the *Annals* may be assured.

My debts for this volume are, to be sure, many and almost beyond my ability to record. I take particular pleasure, however, in thanking Professor Schoenbaum whose Supplements to the revised *Annals*, whose correspondence with scholars throughout the world, and whose personal notes and annotations gave me an incalculable advantage in beginning this project. I would be remiss if I did not also express my gratitude to him publicly for his indispensable guidance and counsel throughout the project.

I would also like to give special thanks to Professor A.H. Scouten, who encouraged me throughout this project and was uncommonly generous with his time and expertise; Professor Robert Hume, who has been unceasingly gracious in sharing his opinions and his research in the area of Restoration drama; Professor Richard Hosley, who painstakingly reviewed and liberally contributed to the new data throughout this edition; Professor Herbert Berry, who contributed his expertise in the theatres of the period and made the List of Theatres quantitatively and qualitatively better than it would have been without his help; and Professor Trevor H. Howard-Hill who frequently shared the fruits of his meticulous scholarship to add to and correct the entries in the List of Extant Play Manuscripts.

A number of other scholars have shared their recent research so that the *Annals* could reflect new findings in literary research and outdated entries could be corrected, among them: William J. Burling, for new information on four lost Restoration plays found in musical sources; Georges Groussier, for refining this edition with his meticulously compiled corrigenda; Carolyn Kephart, for new dating information on Thomas Durfey's masque *Cinthia and Endimion*; Nancy Klein Maquire for calling attention to a potential source of information on old plays found in a Folger Shakespeare Library manuscript; C. Edward McGee for sharing new findings on Stuart entertainments; and Marvin Spevack for correcting several entries in the List of Extant Play Manuscripts.

Throughout the six years that I have worked on the new edition I have been constantly reminded of the generosity of literary scholars. In the last days of this project, I was privileged to have the help of Professor Alan H. Nelson of the University of California, Berkeley, who confirmed many of the new entries and shared with me dozens of items unknown to me that he had uncovered in the course of his research in manuscripts and printed texts of plays in preparation for the publication of the Cambridge volumes of *Records of Early English Drama*. At the same time, I was fortunate to hear from Professor John Elliott for Syracuse University. Professor Elliott supplied valuable information gleaned from his research on plays performed at Oxford, all of which will appear in expanded form in his forthcoming publication of *Records of Early English Drama: Oxford*.

Among the numerous librarians who freely offered their assistance I would especially like to recognize R. Geraint Gruffydd and D.B. Lloyd of the National Library of Wales, T.I. Rae, Keeper of Manuscripts at the National Library of Scotland, Mary L. Robertson, Curator of

Manuscripts at the Huntington Library, and the librarians and staff of the Folger Shakespeare Library and the Library of Congress.

To verify the hundreds of new bibliographical entries considered for this edition, it was my good fortune to have the meticulous assistance of Dr Lillian Doherty whose efforts were untiring and exacting. I am also grateful for the assistance of Marjorie P. Crain, Thomas Dughi, and Douglas Evans for their diligence during the final stages of this compilation.

Words are insufficient to thank my family. For the encouragement, support, and inexhaustible patience of my husband, Ira, and our children, Ruth, Eliot, and Howard, only my debt surpasses my appreciation.

Sylvia Stoler Wagonheim
Baltimore, Maryland

May 1988

PREFACE TO SECOND EDITION

Six years ago, while in London on a Guggenheim Fellowship, I was invited by Professor Alfred Harbage to undertake a revision of his *Annals of English Drama*. The book had been, in my own experience, one of the most useful of reference works: remarkable for the way in which comprehensiveness was allied with economy of presentation. Yet it had been out of print for some years, and was almost impossible to come by on the secondhand-book market; several great reference collections were without a copy. Moreover, since 1940, when the book was published, there had appeared the monumental works of Greg, on the English printed drama to the Restoration, and Bentley, on the Jacobean and Caroline stage. For the Restoration period, Woodward and McManaway's *Check List of English Plays* was now available. A number of important editions, monographs, and articles had been published. Brought up to date with the aid of these new tools, the *Annals* would, I felt, be even more helpful than before. So I did not hesitate to set aside for a year (as I then thought) my own work on Thomas Middleton, and begin at once the labour of revision.

The task has proved more arduous than I anticipated, and one year has stretched to six. The original plan to reprint by photo-offset, with such corrections as could not be made in the text relegated to an appendix, had ultimately to be abandoned, along with the apparatus I had devised for the purpose. As my work progressed, several ways of including additional information without sacrifice of conciseness occurred to me, and these innovations were adopted. The titles listed in the second column of the Chronology now appear in more complete form, without omission of articles, etc. In the Limits column the month and day of first performance are provided in a great many instances where formerly only the year was given; here, too, I have used Henslowe's *Diary* to fuller advantage, and supplied dates for the purchase of plays. In the Type column I have not exempted from classification translated or adapted works. I have made the bibliographically important distinction between edition and issue in the Earliest Texts column. The final column (Last Edition) is now documented, and I have appended a list of doctoral thesis editions. Approximately one hundred new entries, including about a dozen plays extant in manuscript, have been added to the Chronology and Supplements. The indexes have been made fuller and more detailed (there are some 600 additions to the Index of English Plays). In the Appendix I have given the new catalogue numbers assigned by the Folger Shakespeare Library to their manuscripts. Where necessary, I have described these changes more fully in the Introduction.

In a book of this scope, extending as it does from the Middle Ages to the close of the Restoration period, errors and omissions on my part are inevitable, although I have not spared myself effort to avoid them. Moreover, scholarly investigation will not cease, of course, to bring to light facts previously unnoted, or to replace old interpretations with new. It is my expectation, as it was that of the original compiler, to take note of advances in knowledge, and also to record mistakes and omissions brought to my attention. I hope to assemble this information from time to time, and to make it freely available, in the form of supplements, to users of this book, who need only inform me of their wish to be recipients.

Friends and colleagues have once again demonstrated the essential unselfishness of scholarly enterprise by generously sharing their knowledge, and it is a pleasure for me to express my appreciation. Professor Harbage supplied me at the outset with a number of corrections, and he was a faithful correspondent as problems arose. Professor Arnold Williams looked at the medieval section, and made a number of suggestions from which I have, I trust, profited. Dr James G. McManaway was good enough to show me his own annotated copy of the *Check List of English Plays*, and also his personally corrected copy of the *Annals*. Professor Emmett L. Avery not only examined my notes for the Restoration years but also placed at my disposal a draft of his forth-coming volume for *The London Stage, 1660–1800*; as a result, I was able to provide more accurate limits for a number of Restoration plays. Many others have helped by volunteering information, or by answering queries. I wish particularly to thank W. A. Armstrong, Lester A. Beaurline, Arthur Brown, Giles Dawson, G. Blakemore Evans, Mrs Inga-Stina Ewbank, R. A. Foakes, Arthur Freeman, Richard Hosley, George Hunter, S. F. Johnson, R. J. Kaufmann, J. W. Lever, Robert J. Lordi, James M. Osborn, William A. Ringler, Jr, I. A. Shapiro, and John Hazel Smith. With characteristic generosity, the late Professor F. P. Wilson offered several corrections and suggestions. I am obliged to Mrs Ann G. Larson, my typist, for excellent work on a difficult assignment. Mr Clive Burch assisted with the proof-reading. My wife, as always, gave invaluable support from beginning to end.

Work on this book has been facilitated by a leave of absence from Northwestern University for the autumn of 1960, and by grants for summer study from the Huntington Library and the Newberry Library. To the staffs of these institutions, as well as to the librarians and assistants at the British Museum, the University of London Library, the Folger Shakespeare Library, and the English College in Rome, I am grateful for many courtesies. Northwestern University helped also to defray clerical and other research costs. Mr A. P. Riemer saved me many hours of labour by assisting with the compilation of the list of editions in Section IV. To Mr Peter Wait at Methuen I am much indebted for his unfailing kindness and patience.

S. S.

12 *August* 1963

PREFACE TO FIRST EDITION

The nature of this book – its method, purpose, and defects – is explained in the Introduction. I wish to reserve this space for a request that I be sent notice of errors and omissions. It is part of my plan to bring together, a year or two after my list has been exposed to view, as much corrective material as possible, and to publish it, with acknowledgements, in the 'Comment and Criticism' section of *PMLA*. Such material, transferred to individual copies, should increase the usefulness of the book. Its pages are intended for marginal notation, and I have petitioned for paper that would take ink.

For their interest and encouragement I am deeply indebted to Dr Joseph Quincy Adams and to Professor Albert C. Baugh. I wish also to thank, for their good offices, the Secretary and the Committee of Research Activities of the Modern Language Association, and the Secretary for Grants and the Jury of Award of the American Council of Learned Societies.

A. H.

July 1940

INTRODUCTION

> This Introduction follows closely in language and format the Introductions in the previous editions of the *Annals*. Changes are noted in the explanation of format and abbreviations.

Following, for the most part, the soundly conceived fundamental intent and basic structure of the previous editions, the present volume is designed to supply a ready and quick reference to essential information on English drama from the tenth century's first recorded *Quem Quaeritis* to the birth of the eighteenth century. The book is intended not only for the historian, but also for the librarian, the teacher, the student, and the ordinary reader of early English drama. The fact that subtitles and alternative titles are included in it should make the index of plays a useful finding list. The author index should prove helpful to those anxious to discover quickly what attention some poet or scholar conceded to drama. Foreign influences are suggested by later indexes, some of the relations between early and late drama by the method of indicating adaptations. Where extensive reference facilities are not available, the *Annals* should provide the necessary clue as to the accessibility of a play and whether the particular edition available may have been superseded.

Finally, and it was for this purpose that the book was originally planned, the *Annals* will aid the student in determining immediately the approximate *environment* of any given play – what other new plays were being performed at the same time, the few years before and the few years after, by the same company, by a competing company or by all companies.

Included are plays in Latin and French as well as in English, lost as well as extant, unacted as well as acted, translated or adapted as well as original. Works of unknown title and the barest hint of subject matter or character designation are, if recordable, included in the Supplementary Lists. Also listed are descriptions of royal receptions and entertainments although such descriptions as Henry Roberts' two accounts of the reception of Christian IV of Denmark in 1606 are themselves narrative rather than dramatic. Intentionally excluded are revisions of known works entered earlier in the *Annals* under original titles and dates of performance.

The items are arranged chronologically, first by centuries, later by years. Medieval pieces, until the last decade of the fifteenth century, are categorized by centuries rather than by years, since the chronology of early medieval drama is vague and the records fragmentary. The play titles listed in Column 3 include both the abbreviated (commonly used) titles and, parenthetically, the full versions of the titles, as listed in the Table of Contents of the 1987 Oxford edition of *William Shakespeare: The Complete Works*, edited by Stanley Wells, Gary Taylor, *et al.* Thus, the entry for *Romeo and Juliet* parenthetically cites the Oxford edition's version, *The Most Excellent and Lamentable Tragedy of Romeo and Juliet*. Column 7 of the Chronology, that is, Latest Texts, is expanded in scope and now includes coded bibliographical information, fully explained below.

A series of indexes and lists gives access to the main listing. The data in the book are compiled chiefly from authoritative historical works, from articles in scholarly journals, from introductory data in modern editions, and through professional contributions from literary scholars. In the course of preparing this volume, primary materials such as manuscripts, early editions, etc., have been consulted frequently and have provided corrections, new facts, and other valuable information. In one such instance, through the aid of an alert and helpful librarian, Mr Philip Wyn Davies of the National Library of Wales, it was possible to add to the *Annals* the location of the extant manuscript of *The Elizabethan Jig* not previously noted.

This edition, like its predecessors, does not attempt to present original interpretation of contemporary evidence. Its purpose is to render a service solely through inclusiveness, condensation, and arrangement. When discretionary powers concerning authorship and dating must be exercised, as when old records are incomplete and modern scholars disagree, the conclusions reflect, as much as possible, the most conservative opinions of the most reliable authorities. Through the liberal use of interrogation marks in the Author column of the Chronology and information section, and through the indication of alternative possibilities of date, an attempt has been made to suggest divergent opinions and to give flexibility to an arrangement otherwise too rigid. Since ultimate refinement of facts cannot be achieved in a book of this kind, frequently only an interrogation mark signals the place where learned conflicts have been waged.

The list is unannotated and undocumented, and it may seem that a large measure of trustfulness on the part of the reader is implied. Such is not the intent. The lack of documentation limits the usefulness of the book but was unavoidable if its present scope and arrangement were to be retained. A great deal of time and care have been expended on the list, and I believe that it is trustworthy in the main. Yet, it must contain errors – not only in respect to the preponderance of the best current opinion, but also, in respect to clearly demonstrable fact. In extenuation, one can say only that many thousands of facts have been recorded and that these facts have been extracted from a copious and confusing body of literary discussion. Analytical lists of this kind have limitations that are too well known to require enumeration here, and the research worker will seek his information in more detailed works than this; but he may find this book useful sometimes in assisting his memory in the peripheral regions of his immediate problem. The chronological and tabular arrangement of the main list and the alphabetical arrangement of the appended indexes have the advantage of making related bodies of information quickly accessible.

Sources of the information

Certain older play-lists cover the entire period treated in this volume; although superseded in the main, they have not entirely lost their usefulness. They are: Gerard Langbaine, *An Account of the English Dramatick Poets*, 1691; *Biographia Dramatica*, ed. D.E. Baker, I. Reed, S. Jones, 4 vols, 1812; J.O. Halliwell [-Phillipps], *A Dictionary of Old English Plays*, 1860; W.C. Hazlitt, *A Manual for the Collector and Amateur of Old English Plays*, 1892.

For medieval and early Tudor drama, particularly useful references have been E.K. Chambers, *The Mediaeval Stage*, 2 vols, 1903; F.S. Boas, *University Drama in the Tudor Age*, 1914; G.C. Moore Smith, *College Plays*, 1923; *A Short-Title Catalogue of Books . . ., 1475–1640*, comp. A.W. Pollard, G.R. Redgrave, *et al.*, 1926; A.W. Reed, *Early Tudor Drama*, 1926; A.J. Mill, *Mediaeval Plays in Scotland*, 1927; K. Young, *The Drama of the Medieval Church*, 2 vols, 1933 (reprinted in 1951); G.M. Sibley, *The Lost Plays and Masques, 1500–1642*, 1933; E.K. Chambers, *English Literature at the Close of the Middle Ages*, 1945; C.J. Stratman, C.S.V., *Bibliography of Medieval Drama*, 1945; H. Craig, *English Religious Drama of the Middle Ages*, 1955; G. Wickham, *Early English Stages, 1300 to 1660*, vol. I (to 1576), 1959; N. Davis, *Non-Cycle Plays and Fragments*, 1970; Alan H. Nelson, *The Medieval English Stage*, 1974; Albert E. Hartung, *A Manual of the Writings in Middle English: 1050–1500*, 1975, based upon John Edwin Wells' book of the same name originally published in 1916 and supplemented from 1919–51; and Trevor N.S. Lennam's *Sebastian Westcott, the Children of Paul's, and 'The Marriage of Wit and Science'*.

Also useful were three Malone Society *Collections* volumes: III (1954), *A Calendar of Dramatic*

Records in the Books of the Livery Companies of London, 1485–1640, and V (1959 [1960]) containing extracts from the records of the academic drama in Oxford, and IX (1970 [1977]) containing J.M. Nosworthy's edition of *An Elizabethan Jig* as well as G.R. Proudfoot's edition of 'Five Dramatic Fragments from the Folger Shakespeare Library and the Henry E. Huntington Library'.

For the medieval and Tudor periods as well as for the Elizabethan, articles in scholarly journals have proven indispensable for new facts and as a source of valuable bibliographical materials and historical checklists. One such article which deserves acknowledgement is C.E. McGee and John C. Meagher's 'Preliminary Checklist of Tudor and Stuart Entertainments: 1485–1558' in *Research Opportunities in Renaissance Drama* XXV (1982): 31–114.

For the Elizabethan period, the basic reference texts have been: F.E. Schelling, *Elizabethan Drama, 1558–1642*, 2 vols, 1908; E.K. Chambers, *The Elizabethan Stage*, 4 vols, 1923; E.K. Chambers, *William Shakespeare*, 2 vols, 1930; and W.W. Greg, *A Bibliography of English Printed Drama to the Restoration*, 4 vols, 1939–59. The surveys and bibliographies of T.P. Logan and D.S. Smith have been very helpful for the Elizabethan, Jacobean, and Caroline dramatists: *The Predecessors of Shakespeare*, 1973; *The Popular School*, 1975; *The New Intellectuals*, 1977; and *The Later Jacobean and Caroline Dramatists*, 1979.

In compiling the data for the Jacobean and Caroline periods, editions of individual playwrights have been frequently consulted and particularly helpful. The principal single work used was G.E. Bentley, *The Jacobean and Caroline Stage*, 7 vols, 1941–68. Other general works – aside from Greg's *Bibliography* previously cited were W.W. Greg, *A List of English Plays, written before 1643 and printed before 1700*, 1900; W.W. Greg, *A List of English Masques, Pageants, &c.*, 1902; W.W. Greg, *Pastoral Poetry and Pastoral Drama*, 1906; P. Reyher, *Les Masques anglais*, 1909; J.W. Adams, *The Dramatic Records of Sir Henry Herbert*, 1917; M.S. Steele, *Plays and Masques at Court*, 1926.

For the period of the Restoration, the reference texts include: M. Summers, *A Bibliography of Restoration Drama*, n.d.; M. Summers, *The Playhouse of Pepys*, 1935; *A Check List of English Plays, 1641–1700*. comp. G.L. Woodward and J.G. McManaway, 1945, suppl. F. Bowers, 1949; A. Nicoll, *Restoration Drama, 1660–1700* (*A History of English Drama*, vol. II), 4th ed., rev., 1952. Other indispensable works are H.B. Wheatley, *The Diary of Samuel Pepys*, 2 vols, n.d.; and the new and complete transcription of *The Diary of Samuel Pepys*, 11 vols, 1970–83 under the general editorship of R. Latham and W. Matthews. A continually valuable article for the dating of first performances is S. Rosenfeld, 'Dramatic Advertisements in the Burney Newspapers, 1660–1700', *PMLA* LI (1936), 123–52. Restoration adaptations are noted in H. Spencer, *Shakespeare Improved*, 1927, and A.C. Sprague, *Beaumont and Fletcher on the Restoration Stage*, 1926. More recent and highly useful references include *The London Stage, 1660–1800*, edited by W. Van Lennep, E.L. Avery and A.H. Scouten, 1965; E.A. Langhans, *Restoration Promptbooks*, 1981; and P. Danchin, *The Prologues and Epilogues of the Restoration*, part I, 1981.

For the Index of dramatic companies, besides the works already cited, I have used: J.T. Murray, *English Dramatic Companies*, 2 vols, 1910; L. Hotson, *The Commonwealth and Restoration Stage*, 1928; E. Nungezer, *A Dictionary of Actors*, 1929; and *A Biographical Dictionary of Actors, Actresses, Musicians, Dancers, and other Stage Personnel in London, 1660–1800*, compiled by P.H. Highfill, Jr, K.A. Burnim, and E.A. Langhans, 2 vols, 1973.

For the information in the List of theatres, besides the works previously cited, J.Q. Adams, *Shakespearean Playhouses*, 1917, retains its usefulness. In this case, however, special mention should be made of Herbert Berry's, *The Boar's Head Playhouse*, 1986, and his earlier edition of essays on *The First Public Playhouse: The Theatre in Shoreditch, 1576–1598*. In general, the lengthier entries in the List of Theatres are largely the result of these two works, independent scholarly contributions, and the large number of articles which have recently appeared on the subject in scholarly journals and proceedings.

The works listed above represent a small fraction of those I have actually consulted. Most of them are comprehensive in nature and themselves contain play-lists. Omitted, but noted elsewhere in the *Annals*, are many recent works on individual authors and the many editions of individual plays with their informative prefaces. Omitted also are the periodical articles which supplied new and fresh insights into and facts about royal entertainments, receptions, and children's companies.

Primary sources of information necessarily consulted frequently during the preparation of this edition include: the *Stationers' Register* transcribed by Arber and Eyre, and (in extract) by Greg; the *Term Catalogues*, transcribed by Arber; the Revels documents, edited by Feuillerat; and Henslowe's *Diary* and papers, edited by Greg (1904–8) and by Foakes and Rickert (1961). A list of all the works consulted in preparing the play-list would be long, yet inadequate, as a bibliography of early English drama and, in view of the bibliographical facilities already available, not very useful. Authors of works used but not cited will forgive the omission.

Changes in the third edition

The third edition of the *Annals* has removed the need for a separate List of Editions in favour of incorporating the information that the List contained in the Index of English playwrights and the Index of English plays. To augment the information on early dramatic collections which appeared in the List of editions, a Selective list of medieval drama texts has been added. Moreover, to inform the reader of the availability of recent editions of the plays (particularly those published since 1964, the date of the second edition of the *Annals*), updated and more complete information on Last Editions has been provided in abbreviated form in the seventh column of the Chronology and information section and in more detailed form in the Index of English plays. The coded entries, explained below, are intended to alert the reader to the forms in which an edition of a play has been published: in collected form, such as the Yale *Ben Jonson*; in an individual edition in a scholarly series such as the Revels plays; in facsimile reprint; or as a doctoral thesis. Since nearly a thousand potential entries were considered for inclusion in the listing, certain limitations had to be imposed. At the same time, it is unavoidable that eligible entries have been missed. I would appreciate hearing about corrections and additions to the new listings.

Arrangement and abbreviations

The chronology and tabulation is arranged after 1495 according to modern calendar years, with each play placed in that year when it was most probably first presented. Using 1 January as the point of division creates an awkward split in several instances, since winter festivities at the Court and in the schools tended to extend from before Christmas until after Twelfth Night. However, no other arrangement was practical in this edition. Within each year the plays are listed alphabetically by author; where there is more than one entry for the same author within a given year, the sequence is alphabetical by title. Anonymous plays are listed alphabetically by title at the end of each year.

The Chronology contains seven columns, and for each of these a word of explanation will be necessary.

FIRST COLUMN: This column is devoted to the names of authors. When the play is a work of collaboration the collaborators are indicated simply thus: *Day; Dekker; Chettle*. To indicate that Fletcher had the main hand in a play on which Beaumont collaborated and on which Massinger may have collaborated, the arrangement might be thus: *Fletcher, with Beaumont (and Massinger?)*. The term 'Anonymous' is used in all cases where authorship is unknown, whether or not the author's name was consciously withheld. Authors assigned to anonymous plays and generally accepted are indicated thus: *Fletcher, J.; Massinger, P.*; authors assigned and pretty generally accepted, thus: *Heywood, Thomas (?)*; authors assigned and not generally accepted, thus: *Anon. (Peele, G.?)*, or *Anon. (Marlowe? Kyd? Greene?)*, or simply *Anon.* Inverted commas about an author's name indicate that a contemporary attribution of authorship is now held in question. In a few instances of Tudor and Stuart entertainments, where more than one description is extant, the names of the describers are separated by a diagonal (/) rather than a semicolon, to distinguish these entries from collaborations; for example, *The Queen's Visit to Tilbury* (1588), described independently by Aske and by Deloney, is entered thus: *Aske, James/Deloney, Thomas (describers)*.

SECOND COLUMN: This column is devoted to titles. (A number of the designations, such as those for early Tudor entertainments known only from Revels documents and contemporary descriptions, are of course not true titles, but merely convenient descriptive phrases.) Beside the title, in round brackets, are placed full versions of titles as listed in the 1987 edition of *William Shakespeare: The Complete Works* as well as alternative titles, from licensing records, running-titles, etc. Most titles are given in modern spelling.[1] At the expense of strict logic, advantage has often been taken of the space afforded by this column, the widest of the seven, to give cross-references, to provide information about revival or revision, to cite the author and title of parent plays in cases of adaptation or translation, and to supply other kinds of miscellaneous information which otherwise could not have been included.

THIRD COLUMN: This supplies the limits of date. When the year of first performance is conclusively known there will be in this column a single date coinciding with that of the year in which the play is grouped. Where greater refinement is possible a more exact date is given – the licensing date for all plays where the licensing record has survived, the day of first performance for many masks, entertainments, and civic pageants, and the month or day of first performance for most of the Restoration plays. When the date of first performance of a Restoration play derives from Pepys's *Diary* it is followed by his name in round brackets. Where the date supplied for a Restoration play is that of the licence for printing, the abbreviation *imprim.* for *imprimatur* follows in round brackets. When the date of first performance is not conclusively known the forward and backward limits are indicated thus: *1622–30*, or thus: *c. 1600–10*, the latter meaning that the play in all probability was performed first before 1610 but not much before 1600. Henslowe's plays presented special problems. Where Henslowe gives the date of first performance, this information is supplied, but where he is wrong, Greg's corrections are inserted in square brackets[2]; thus the date given for *The Tanner of Denmark* (1592) is *23 [26] May*. For a number of other Henslowe plays, where the date of first performance is unavailable, the dates of payments to dramatists or of expenditures for properties have been provided. An initial *P* in round brackets follows dates of payments made to playwrights; the abbreviation *prop.* for *property*, also in round brackets, signifies the purchase of stage properties. For example, the entry for *Damon and Pythias* (1600) is *16 Feb.–27 Apr./6 May (P)*, and means that Henslowe made his first payment to Chettle for the play on 16 February and his last between 27 April and 6 May. (Sometimes the year in which a play has been placed is merely a median point between a forward and a backward limit, but usually there are better reasons for its chronological position than this.)

FOURTH COLUMN: This supplies a rough classification of the play: *Mask, History, Tragedy, Latin Comedy*, etc. Unless otherwise indicated, the play is in English.

FIFTH COLUMN: This supplies the auspices of first production; that is, the name of the professional company performing the play, such as *Strange's, Queen's Revels*, or *King's*: or the place where the play was performed if the production was amateur or by an unknown company, such as *London; King's College, Camb.; Middle Temple*; or *Court*. Plays not intended for performance are here marked *Closet*; those possibly intended for performance but evidently not performed are marked *Unacted*; a few early Elizabethan interludes printed with such legends as 'Six may easily play' are marked *Offered for acting*; the word *Unknown* needs no explanation.

SIXTH COLUMN: This gives the date of the first edition of printed plays, or the information that the play has come down to us in manuscript, or both. For medieval plays, the approximate date of the manuscript is supplied in this column. The present location of any play manuscript may be determined by consulting the catalogue in the Appendix. Square brackets about a date mean that the title page of the edition is undated. A single asterisk (*) after the date means that the first is the only early edition. By 'early' is meant before 1700 for plays written before 1660, and before about 1750 for plays written between 1660 and 1700. A double asterisk (**) following the date signifies that there was only one early edition, but two or more issues of that edition. (For an explanation of the distinction between edition and issue, see Greg, *Bibliography*, IV, xxxv–xxxvi.) An initial *F* in this column means that a manuscript or early edition, usually the first, has been reproduced in photographic facsimile. To illustrate: *1594 & MS* should be interpreted thus: the first edition of the play appeared in 1594, but there are later early editions, and also an early manuscript copy. Or, to take an impossibly complicated case: [*c. 1580*]**F & MSS* (*frags.*) should be interpreted thus: the play was published in a single early edition, of which there was more than one issue, about the year 1580 with no date on the title page; this edition has been reproduced in photographic facsimile, and there exist in addition two or more early manuscript fragments, for the location of which see the Appendix. (It is necessary only to add that such entries as *Hall, 578*, which appear a number of times in the sixth column for the early Tudor period, refer to a page number in the 1809 edition of Hall's *Chronicle*, where a description of the entertainment in question may be found; citations – less frequent – of the *Great Chronicle* refer to *The Great Chronicle of London*, ed. A. H. Thomas and I. D. Thornley, 1938.)

SEVENTH COLUMN: This gives the date of the latest modern editions of the play. (It is perhaps unnecessary to caution the reader that although the most satisfactory edition is very often the most recent, this is not always the case.) Paperback editions, even when they represent works in scholarly series, are not recorded. The editions prepared by French scholars for Aubier's *Collection bilingue* have been included. Initials serve two purposes in the new *Annals*. First, initials are used to indicate certain nineteenth- and twentieth-century standard collections usually found in college libraries: *D* (W.C. Hazlitt's edition of Dodsley's *Old English Plays*, 15 vols, 1874–6); *B (Materialien zur kunde des alterem englischen Dramas*, W. Bang, gen ed.; New Series, H. de Vocht, gen.ed.); *G* (the Malone Society Reprints under the general editorship of W.W. Greg, 1906–39; F.P. Wilson, gen. ed., 1948–61; Arthur Brown, gen.ed., 1960–). More recent *Malone Society Reprints* are indicated by the initial *S* which represents an edition of a play published as part of a scholarly series, several of which are now represented in the Index of English plays. What to do with the seventh column in the case of Shakespeare's plays continues to present a problem. As Professor Schoenbaum wisely noted, 'simply to give the latest edition would be pointless, but to discriminate would be dangerous.' Consequently, the new *Annals* provides information on the

Variorum editions of Shakespeare, indicated by the initial *V* and on Supplements to the Variorums, indicated by *VS*.

Second, among the changes implemented in this edition of the *Annals* is the expanded use of initials to provide useful bibliographical information. Thus, in addition to the initial code explained above: *C* indicates that the work is included in a recent comprehensive collection of the playwright's works; *S* indicates that the work has been published as part of a series of scholarly editions using authoritative texts and usually including a discussion of the background of the work and detailed notes; *F* indicates that the work has been reproduced in facsimile; *E* indicates a unique edition of the play not found in a comprehensive collection or as a part of a scholarly series; and *T* indicates that the play has been edited as a doctoral dissertation. The reader is referred to the Index of English playwrights where comprehensive collections are listed under the names of the playwright. Some collections, however, are also to be found in the Index of English plays. If the editor of a dissertation edition subsequently publishes the same play, the thesis citation is omitted.

OTHER ABBREVIATIONS: Abbreviations not mentioned in the foregoing explanation are, for the most part, self-explanatory. Generally used are *a*. for *after*; *adapt*. for *adaptation*; *add*. for *addenda* (referring to additional plays grouped in the fifteenth century and in the years 1570 and 1599); *b*. for *before*; *c*. for *circa*; *C*. or *Col*. for *College*; *Co*. for *Company*; *d*. for *died*; *descrip*. for description; *ed*. for *edition*; *Epil*. for *Epilogue*; *Lat*. for *Latin*; *lic*. for *licensed*; *ment*. for *mentioned*; *perf*. for *performance*; *poss*. for *possibly*; *prob*. for *probably*; *prog*. for *progress*; *Prol*. for *Prologue*; *Pt*. for *Part*; *pub*. for *published*; *S.R*. for *Stationers' Register*; *Supp. I*, or *Supp. II*, *a*, etc. (referring to the supplementary lists following the Chronology); *t.p*. for *title page*; and *trans*. for *translation*. Several of these abbreviations, not ordinarily admitted, have been employed in the interest of conciseness.

NOTES

1 Exceptions are made for certain proper names where a difference in pronunciation is implied, e.g. *Bistowe* (rather than Bristol).

2 But see Henslowe's *Diary*, ed. R.A. Foakes and R.T. Rickert (Cambridge, 1961), pp. xxvi–xxix.

CHRONOLOGY AND INFORMATION

DATE	AUTHOR	TITLE	LIMITS
Tenth century			
	Aethelwold, Bishop of Winchester (adapter).	*Quem Quaeritis* (of Easter), or *Visitatio Sepulchri* (Included in the *Regularis Concordia*, appended to the *Rule* of St Benedict. The *Concordia* contains also directions for the quasi-dramatic ceremonies, *Adoratio Crucis, Depositio Crucis*, and *Elevatio Crucis*. Directions for, or descriptions of, these ceremonies at Sarum and Durham occur between the 13th and the 16th centuries, and examples are printed severally by Chambers, Adams, and Young.)	965–975(?)
	Anon.	*Quem Quaeritis* (of Easter) in the *Winchester Troper*, otherwise known as the *Aethelred Troper*. (For the relations of this trope with the more advanced form in the *Regularis Concordia*, see Chambers, *M.S.*, II, 12–15.)	978–980(?)
Eleventh century			
	Geoffrey, afterwards Abbot of St Albans	*St Katherine (Ludus de Sancta Katerina)*	*c*. 1090–*c*. 1119
Twelfth century			
	Hilarius (poss. English)	*The Raising of Lazarus (Suscitacio Lazari)*	*c*. 1120–*c*. 1130
	Hilarius (with others)	*Daniel (Historia de Daniel Repraesentanda)*	*c*. 1120–*c*. 1130
	Hilarius	*St Nicholas (The Image of St Nicholas. Ludus super Iconia Sancti Nicolai)*	*c*. 1120–*c*. 1130
	Anon.	*Adam (Le Mystère d'Adam. Repraesentatio Adamae)* (Poss. Norman rather than Anglo-Norman.)	*c*. 1146–*c*. 1174
	Anon.	'Lundonia . . . ludos habet sanctiores, repraesentationes miraculorum quae sancti confessores operati sunt, seu repraesentationes passionum quibus claruit constantia martyrum.'	*c*. 1170–1182 (ment. by Fitzstephen)
	Anon.	*Pastores*; *Quem Quaeritis* (of Easter); *Peregrini*	1188–*c*. 1300
Thirteenth century			
	Anon.	'. . . et verbis et actu fieret repraesentatio Dominicae resurrectionis.'	*c*. 1220 (ment.)
	Anon.	*Stella* (?) ('coronae ad repraesentationes faciendas')	1222 (ment.)
	Anon.	'Actiones' at the churches of the parish	1220–1228 (ment.)

TYPE	AUSPICES	EARLIEST TEXTS	LATEST TEXTS
Latin Liturgical Drama	Winchester Cathedral	MS (*c.* 1025) & MS (*c.* 1000?)	
Latin Trope	Winchester Cathedral	MS (978–80?) & MS (*c.* 1050)	
Latin or French Miracle	Dunstable, Bedfordshire	Lost	
Latin and French Semi-liturgical Drama	France	MS (12th cent.)	
Latin Semi-liturgical Drama	France	MS (12th cent.)	
Latin and French Semi-liturgical Drama	France	MS (12th cent.)	
Anglo-Norman or Norman Mystery	Unknown	MS (12th cent.) (frag.)	
Miracles and Mysteries	London	Lost	
Latin Liturgical Dramas	Lichfield Cathedral	Lost	
Latin Liturgical Drama (?)	Beverley Minister, Yorkshire	Lost	
Latin Liturgical Drama (?)	Salisbury Cathedral	Lost	
Miracles and Mysteries (?)	Shipton, Oxfordshire	Lost	

DATE	AUTHOR	TITLE	LIMITS
	Anon.	'Miracula' ordered suppressed by Bishop Grosseteste	c. 1244
	Anon.	The Harrowing of Hell (Non-dramatic, but apparently influenced by mystery plays.)	c. 1200–c. 1250
	Anon.	St Nicholas Play	c. 1250 (ment.)
	Anon.	Pastores; Stella, or Tres Reges	c. 1255 (ment.)
	Anon.	'. . . comedendo, bibendo, ludendo, ioculando seu quod cumque ystrionatus officium exercendo . . .'	1286 (condemned by Bishop of Hereford)
	Anon.	La Seinte resureccion (La Résurrection du Sauveur)	b.c. 1275

Fourteenth century

DATE	AUTHOR	TITLE	LIMITS
	Anon.	Dux Moraud (One speaker's part in a play on the story of the Incestuous Daughter.)	c. 1300–c. 1400
	Anon.	Caiphas (Ceremonial verses, in Latin and English, for Palm Sunday.)	c. 1300–c. 1325
	Anon.	Interludium de Clerico et Puella	c. 1290–c. 1335
	Anon.	Shrewsbury Fragments: Pastores (Officium Pastorum); Quem Quaeritis (of Easter), or Visitatio Sepulchri (Officium Resurrectionis); Peregrini (Officium Peregrinorum) (Fragments, consisting of one actor's part and cues in the three plays.)	Late 13th–early 14th cent.
	Anon.	Stella, or Tres Reges	1317–1318 (1st ment.)
	Anon.	St Thomas (from Peregrini?)	1321–1322 (1st ment.)
	Anon.	Origo Mundi; Passio Domini; Resurrexio Domini (The Creation of the World) (Fifty episodes divided into three groups, for performance on three separate days.) See also 1611, 1695.	c. 1300–c. 1325
	Anon.	Ipswich Corpus Christi Procession (and Plays?) (In charge of Corpus Christi Guild.)	1325 (Guild formed); laid aside, 1531
	Anon.	Quem Quaeritis (of Easter), or Visitatio Sepulchri (Included in the MS are directions for the quasi-dramatic ceremonies, Depositio Crucis and Elevatio Crucis.)	1300–1400
	Anon.	Bury St Edmunds Fragment (French and English versions of a single stanza.)	Early 14th cent.
	Anon.	Ludi Domini Regis (First recorded disguising at Court.)	Xmas, 1347
	Anon.	Ludus Filiorum Israelis	1350 (ment.)
	Anon.	York Plays (Corpus Christi Plays) (Forty-eight plays and a fragment in present form, at	c. 1352–b. 1376 (originated);

TYPE	AUSPICES	EARLIEST TEXTS	LATEST TEXTS
Miracles or Mysteries, or both	Lincoln Diocese	Lost	
Dialogue	Unacted	MSS (*c.* 1325)	
Miracle	Unknown	Lost	
Latin Liturgical Dramas	York Minster	Lost	
Festival Play (?)	Hereford, Herefordshire	Lost	
Anglo-Norman Mystery	Unknown	MSS (frags.)	
Miracle (of Virgin?)	Unknown	MS (*c.* 1300–25)	
Latin and English Dramatic Monologue and Song	Wells Cathedral	MS (*c.* 1300–25)	
Interlude (?)	Unknown	MS (*c.* 1290–1335) (frag.)	
Liturgical Plays in Latin and English	Lichfield Cathedral (?)	MS (*c.* 1400–25) (frag.)	
Latin Liturgical Drama	Lincoln Cathedral	Lost	
Latin Liturgical Drama	Lincoln Cathedral	Lost	
Cornish Cosmic Cycle of Mystery Plays	Penrhyn (?), Cornwall	MS (1400–1500)	
Procession, and later a Play	Ipswich, Suffolk	Lost	
Latin Liturgical Drama, and Ceremonials	Church of St John the Evangelist, Dublin	MSS (1300–1400)	
Mystery	East Midlands	MS (1370) (frag.)	
Disguising or Mumming	Court	......	
Mystery (?)	Cambridge, Cambs.	Lost	
Cosmic Cycle of Mystery Plays	York, Yorkshire	MS (*c.* 1475 & 1558)	

DATE	AUTHOR	TITLE	LIMITS
		one time fifty-seven; acted on pageants at stations in the city.)	1376 (1st ment.); played until *c.* 1568
	Katherine of Sutton (adapter?)	*Quem Quaeritis* (of Easter), or *Visitatio Sepulchri*; also *Depositio Crucis*; *Elevatio Crucis*	1363–1376
	Anon. ·	*The Visit to Richard II* (First Court disguising recorded in detail.)	1 Feb. 1377
	Anon.	*Beverley Plays* (*Corpus Christi Plays*) (Consisted in 1490 of thirty-eight plays.)	1377 (1st ment.); played until *c.* 1555
	Anon. (conceivably Higden, R.)	*Chester Plays* (*Whitsun Plays. Corpus Christi Plays*) (Consist of banns and twenty-five plays, acted on pageants at stations in the city.)	*c.* 1377–1382(?) (originated); 1462 (1st ment.); played until 1575
	Anon.	*Pater Noster Play* (On the triumph of the virtues over the vices, performed at stations in the city by a guild formed to perpetuate it.)	1378 (1st ment.); played until 1572
	Anon.	*St Paul's Old Testament Plays*	1378 (ment.)
	Anon.	*Skinners' Well Plays* (Of a cyclical character, given by the London clerks in minor orders.)	1384 (1st ment.); played until a. 1442
	Anon.	*St Thomas the Martyr*	1385–1386
	Anon.	*Pater Noster Play*	1397 (1st ment.); played until 1521
	Anon. (revised by Croo, R., 1534)	*Coventry Plays* (*True Coventry Plays. Corpus Christi Plays*) (Of the cycle, only two plays survive: the *Shearmen and Tailors' Pageant* of the Annunciation, Nativity, and Shepherds; and the *Weavers' Pageant*, of the Magi, Herod, the Massacre, and the Flight to Egypt. Cycle was acted on ten or twelve pageants at stations in the city.)	1392 (1st ment.); played until 1580
	Anon.	*Abraham and Isaac* (Brome)	*c.* 1375–*c.* 1400
	Anon.	*Interludium de Corpore Christi* (Performed by the Corpus Christi Guild.) Pageants (for mysteries?) by the craft guilds are mentioned below, 15th cent.	1389 (ment.)
	Anon.	*Hedon Plays*	1389–1390 (1st ment.)
	Anon.	*Annunciation Play* (?) ('pro Salutacione')	1390–1391 (1st ment.)

TYPE	AUSPICES	EARLIEST TEXTS	LATEST TEXTS
Latin Liturgical Drama, and Ceremonials	Nunnery of Barking, near London	MS (1363–76)	
Disguising or Mumming	Court	......	
Cosmic Cycle of Mystery Plays	Beverley, Yorkshire	Lost	
Cosmic Cycle of Mystery Plays	Chester, Cheshire	MS (1475–1500) (frag.) Other MSS, 1591, etc.	
Morality	York, Yorkshire	Lost	
Mysteries	St Paul's, London	Lost	
Mysteries	Skinners' Well, London	Lost	
Miracle	King's Lynn, Norfolk	Lost	
Morality	Lincoln, Lincolnshire	Lost	
Cosmic Cycle of Mystery Plays	Coventry, Warwickshire	MS (1534) (*Shearmen Pageant* destroyed 1879)	
Mystery	Unknown	MS (*c.* 1470–80)	
Mystery	Bury St Edmunds, Suffolk	Lost	
Mysteries (?)	St Augustine's Church, Hedon	Lost	
Latin Liturgical Drama	Lincoln Cathedral	Lost	

DATE	AUTHOR	TITLE	LIMITS
	Maydiston, Richard (describer)	*Richard II's Reconciliation with the City of London*	21 Aug. 1392
	Anon.	*St Katherine*	1393
	Anon.	*Wells Plays*	1394 (1st ment.)
	Anon.	*Wakefield Plays* (*Towneley Plays. Woodkirk* or *Widkirk Plays. Corpus Christi Plays*) (Consists of thirty-two plays, including the *Suspencio Iude*, which is in a different hand and may not be a play. Several of the plays are taken from the *York Cycle*, others resemble York plays, especially a homogeneous group usually credited to an unknown 'Wakefield Master'; in the latter group is the play variously called *Secunda Pastorum*, *The Second Shepherd's Play*, or *Mak.*)	*c.* 1390–1410(?) (originated); work of Wakefield Master may have begun *c.* 1435 and extended to *c.* 1450
	Anon.	*The Pride of Life*	Late 14th cent.

Fifteenth century

DATE	AUTHOR	TITLE	LIMITS
	Anon.	*Corpus Christi Procession* (and *Plays?*)	*c.* 1400–*c.* 1462
	Anon.	*The Castle of Perseverance* (One of the *Macro Morals.*)	1405–1425
	Anon.	*St George, St Thomas à Becket*, and *Corpus Christi Processions*	15th and 16th cent.
	Anon.	*The Reception of Henry V, Returning from France*	23 Nov. 1415
	Chamberleyn, Thomas	*Rubum Quem Viderat* (Part of an *Ordo Prophetarum?*)	1420
	Anon.	*Noah Play* (By Guild of Master Mariners and Pilots.)	1421(?)–*c.* 1529
	Anon.	*Newcastle Plays* (*Corpus Christi Plays*) (Consisted of twenty-two plays, of which only one, *Noah's Ark*, is extant.)	1426 (1st ment.); played until 1567–1568
	Anon.	*St Clotilda*	1429
	Lydgate, John	*A Mumming at Eltham*	1427–1430
	Lydgate, John	*A Mumming at Hertford*	*c.* 1430(?)
	Lydgate, John	*The Mumming at Bishopswood*	*c.* 1430(?)
	Lydgate, John	*A Mumming at London* (*A Mumming before the Great Estates of the Land*)	1427–1430
	Lydgate, John	*A Mumming at Windsor*	1427–1430
	Lydgate, John	*A Mumming for the Goldsmiths of London*	1427–1430
	Lydgate, John	*A Mumming for the Mercers of London*	1427–1430
	Lydgate, John (describer)	*The Reception of Henry VI, Returning from France*	21 Feb. 1432
	Anon.	*Passion and Resurrection Play*	*c.* 1428–*c.* 1560
	Anon.	*The Burial and Resurrection of Christ* (*Christ's Burial and Resurrection*) (In two parts: I for Good Friday, II for Easter.)	*c.* 1430–*c.* 1450

TYPE	AUSPICES	EARLIEST TEXTS	LATEST TEXTS
Pageants and Speeches	London	MSS	
Miracle	London	Lost	
Liturgical Plays	Wells	Lost	
Cosmic Cycle of Mystery Plays	Wakefield, Yorkshire	MS (1450–1500)	
Morality	Kent (?)	MS (1400–25) (frag.)	
Cosmic Cycle (?)	King's Lynn, Norfolk	Lost	
Morality	Lincolnshire (?)	MS (*c.* 1440) F	
Guild Processions	Norwich, Norfolk	......	
Royal Reception	London	*Great Chronicle*, 93–4	
Liturgical Drama (?)	Lincoln Cathedral	Lost	
Mystery	Hull, Yorkshire	Lost	
Cosmic Cycle of Mystery Plays	Newcastle-on-Tyne	Lost MS (1425–50)	
Miracle	Acted at Court	Lost	
Verses, for Mumming	Court	MSS	
Verses, for Mumming	Court	MSS	
Verses, for Mumming	Court	MS	
Verses, for Mumming	London	MSS	
Verses, for Mumming	Court	MSS	
Verses, for Mumming	London	MSS	
Verses, for Mumming	London	MSS	
Pageants and Speeches	London	MS	
Mysteries	New Romney, Kent	Lost	
Liturgical Drama	Unknown (Northern)	MS (*c.* 1430–50)	

DATE	AUTHOR	TITLE	LIMITS
	Anon.	*Hereford Plays* (*Corpus Christi Plays* or *Dumb Shows.*)	1440 (1st ment.); ceased b. 1548
	Anon.	*Aberdeen Plays* (*Haliblud* or *Passion Play* on Corpus Christi Day, *Nativity Play* on Candlemas Day, and also *St Nicholas Day Ride*, with Robin Hood, Maid Marian, etc.)	1440–1442 (1st ment.); played until early 16th cent.
	Anon.	*Ludus Coventriae* (*Corpus Christi Plays. Hegge Plays. N. Town Plays*) (Consists of forty-two plays, variously considered an amalgam for reading, a travelling cycle, or an adaptation for acting on a fixed stage.) See *The Assumption or Coronation of the Virgin*, and *Lincoln Plays*, below.	*c.* 1400–*c.* 1450
	Anon.	*St Laurence*	1441–1442 (ment.)
	Anon.	*The Welcome for Margaret of Anjou* (Pageant of St Margaret.)	28 May 1444
	Anon.	*Eglemour and Degrebelle*	30 June 1444 (acted)
	Anon.	'a knight cleped Florence'	Aug. 1444 (acted)
	Anon.	*Corpus Christi Procession*	*c.* 1444–*c.* 1544
	Anon.	*Creed Play* (Stationary play, acted about 1 Aug., every tenth year.)	1446 (1st ment.); played until 1535
	Anon.	*St Susannah*	1447–1448 (ment.)
	Anon.	*Abraham and Isaac* (Dublin.)	*c.* 1445–*c.* 1450
	Anon.	*King Robert of Sicily*	1447–1453 (ment.)
	Laingby, Robert (?)	*St Dionysius*	1455 (ment.)
	Anon.	*St Clara*	1455–1456 (ment.)
	Anon.	*St George*	1456 (ment.)
	Anon.	*The Assumption or Coronation of the Virgin* (Prob. represented in Play XLI of *Ludus Coventriae*, above.)	(1st ment.)
	Anon.	*Mankind* (One of the *Macro Morals*.)	1465–1470
	Anon.	*Worcester Plays* (*Corpus Christi Plays*) (Consisted of five plays.)	1467 (1st ment.); played until a. 1559
	Anon.	*Pater Noster Play* (Consisted of eight pageants devoted severally to eight vices, presented by craft guilds at stations in the city.)	1469 (ment.)

TYPE	AUSPICES	EARLIEST TEXTS	LATEST TEXTS
Cosmic Cycle	Hereford, Herefordshire	Lost	
Processions with Mystery and Folk Plays	Under direction of Abbot of Bon Accord, Aberdeen	Lost	
Cosmic Cycle of Mystery Plays	Lincoln (?)	MS (1468)	
Miracle	Lincoln, Lincolnshire	Lost	
Royal Reception	London	*Great Chronicle*, 177–8	
Romance (?)	St Albans	Lost	
Romance (?)	Bermondsey	Lost	
Guild Procession	Coventry, Warwickshire	......	
Morality	York, Yorkshire	Lost	
Miracle	Lincoln, Lincolnshire	Lost	
Mystery	Northampton (?)	MS (*c.* 1458)	
Miracle	Lincoln, Lincolnshire	Lost	
Miracle	York, Yorkshire	Lost	
Miracle	Lincoln, Lincolnshire	Lost	
Miracle	Lydd, Kent	Lost	
Latin and English Semi-liturgical Drama	Lincoln Cathedral	Lost (?)	
Morality	Norfolk (?)	MS (1450–1500) F	
Mystery Cycle	Worcester, Worcestershire	Lost	
Morality	Beverley, Yorkshire	Lost	

DATE	AUTHOR	TITLE	LIMITS
	Anon.	*Belial* (*Ludus de Bellyale*)	1471 (ment.)
	Anon.	*Lincoln Plays* (*Corpus Christi Plays*, so called, but acted on St Anne's Day [26 July]. In 1483 Lincoln Cathedral Chapter voted to add *The Assumption of the Virgin* [in vernacular?] to the citizens' plays [a new departure?]. The *Assumption*, perhaps all the plays, to be performed in the nave of the Cathedral. See *The Assumption or Coronation of the Virgin*, and *Ludus Coventriae*, above.)	1472 (1st ment.); played until 1555
	Anon.	*Mind, Will, and Understanding* (*The Wisdom That Is Christ*) (One of the *Macro Morals*.)	1450–1500
	Anon.	*Robin Hood Plays*	1473
	Anon.	*Robin Hood and the Sheriff of Nottingham*	*c.* 1473
	'R.C.' (scribe?)	*The Sacrament* (*The Croxton Play of the Sacrament*)	1461–1500
	Anon.	*Bury St Edmunds Plays* or *Dumb Shows*	Old in 1477
	Anon.	*Leicester Passion Play*	1477 (ment.)
	Anon.	*Corpus Christi Play*	1478, 1482 (ment.)
	Anon.	*Norwich Plays* (*Whitsun Plays*) (Consisted of at least twelve plays; only the Grocers' play survives: *Adam and Eve*, or *The Creation of Eve*, with the *Expelling of Adam and Eve out of Paradise* [two versions].)	1478 (1st ment.); played until *c.* 1565
	Anon.	*Coronation of Henry VII*	30 Oct. 1485
	Anon.	*Sleaford Ascension Play*	1480 (ment.)
	Anon.	*Quem Quaeritis*	1482 (ment.)
	Anon.	*Henry VII's Provincial Progress*	1486
	Anon.	*Descensus Christi ad Inferos*	1486
	Anon.	*Quem Quaeritis*	1487 and later
	Anon.	*St Katherine*	1490–1491
	Anon.	*St George*	1490–a. 1497
	Anon.	*The Conversion of St Paul* (A Digby 'Mystery'.)	*c.* 1480–1520
	Anon.	*Mary Magdalene* (A Digby 'Mystery'.)	*c.* 1480–1520
	Parfre, John (scribe?)	*The Massacre of Innocents* (*Candlemas Day and the Killing of the Children of Israel*) (A Digby 'Mystery', part of a cycle.)	*c.* 1480–*c.* 1490
	Anon.	*Quem Quaeritis* (*Play* or *Puppet Show*.)	1491 (1st ment.)
	Anon.	*Abraham and Isaac*	1491–1520
	Anon. (Cornish, W.?)	*St George and the Castle*	6 Jan. 1494
	Anon.	*Canterbury Plays* (*Corpus Christi Plays*) Additional lost plays of traditional character	1500 (revived)

TYPE	AUSPICES	EARLIEST TEXTS	LATEST TEXTS
Mystery, or Morality (?)	Aberdeen	Lost	
Mysteries	Lincoln, Lincolnshire	Lost	
Morality	West Midlands (?)	MSS (1450–1500) F	
Folk Plays	At Sir John Paston's	Lost	
Folk Play	At Sir John Paston's (?)	MS (*c.* 1475–6) (frag.) F	
Miracle	Croxton (Norfolk?)	MS (1461–1500) F	
Cosmic Cycle (?)	Bury St Edmunds	Lost	
Mystery	Leicester, Leicestershire	Lost	
Mystery	Stamford, Lincolnshire	Lost	
Cosmic Cycle of Mystery Plays	Norwich, Norfolk	Lost MSS (1533 & 1565)	
Joust	London (?)	MS (descrip.)	
Mystery	Sleaford, Lincolnshire	Lost	
Liturgical Play (?)	Bath, Somersetshire	Lost	
Pageants	York, Hereford, Worcester, and Bristol	MS (descrip.)	
Mystery	Court	Lost	
Liturgical Play (?)	Magdalen Col., Oxford	Lost	
Miracle	Coventry, Warwickshire	Lost	
Miracle	New Romney, Kent	Lost	
Miracle-Mystery	East Midlands (?)	MS (*c.* 1480–1520)	
Miracle-Morality	Lynn, Norfolk (?)	MS (*c.* 1480–1520)	
Mystery	East Midlands (?)	MS (1512)	
Liturgical Play (?)	Leicester Churches	Lost	
Mystery	St Dunstan's Church, Cant.	Lost	
Disguising	Court	*Great Chronicle*, 251–2	
Cosmic Cycle	Canterbury, Kent	Lost	

DATE	AUTHOR	TITLE	LIMITS

mentioned at various times after 1495: *St James* (15th cent., Lincoln); *Shrewsbury Plays* (1st ment. 1495; *Sts Feliciana and Sabina*, 1516, *Three Kings of Cologne*, 1518); *Midsummer Show* (1498–1678, Chester); *Robin Hood Procession* or *Play* (ment. 1498, Wells, Somerset); *Corpus Christi Procession*, including shows on *Arthur and His Knights* and *Nine Worthies* (1st ment. 1498, Dublin); *St George Pageant* (contemporary with preceding?, Dublin); *Adam and Eve, Kings of Cologne*, etc. (1499–1535, Reading); *Three Kings of Cologne* (ment. 1503, Canterbury); *St Thomas à Becket Pageant* (1st ment. 1504, Canterbury); *St Mary Magdalene* (ment. 1503–4, Thetford Priory, Norfolk); *St Christian* (ment. 1504–5, Coventry); *Easter Play* (1505–65, Kingston-on-Thames); *Corpus Christi Pageant* (1514–91, Bungay, Suffolk); *Easter Play* (16th cent., Morebath, Devonshire); *Corpus Christi Play* (1516–32, Heybridge, Essex); *Corpus Christi Play* (1526–46, Dunmow, Essex); *Noah* Play (ment. 1518–19, Boston, Lincolnshire: sponsored by St Mary's guild); *Corpus Christi Play* (ment. 1519–20 and later; Louth, Lincoln-shire); *Holy John of Bower Play* (1527, Grimsby: sponsored by Mariners' Guild?); *St Erasmus* (1518, Aberdeen); *St Christina* (1522, Bethersden, Kent); *Nativity Play* and *Resurrection Play* (played until at least 1522, Earl of Northumberland's Chapel); *St Swithin* (1523, St Michael's Church, Braintree, Essex); *St Andrew* (1525, same as preceding); *St Eustace* (1534, same as preceding); *King Robert of Sicily* (1529, Chester); *Corpus Christi Play*, distinct from Chester cycle (1544–7, Chester); *Midsummer Watch* (played until 1538, and once revived in 1548, London); '*Fisher Play*' (recorded 1540 in Court Rolls of Doncaster, Rossington, Hexthorpe, and Long Sandall); *Three Kings of Cologne* (1548, Holbeach, Lincolnshire); *St George Riding* (old in 1554, York); *Passion Play* (1557, Greyfriars, London); *St Olave's*

TYPE	AUSPICES	EARLIEST TEXTS	LATEST TEXTS

DATE	AUTHOR	TITLE	LIMITS
		Play (1557, St Olave's Church, London); *Corpus Christi Play* (1562–74, Chelmsford, Essex: wardrobe of this play was hired by the following towns: Baddow; Billericay, Boreham, Braintree, Brentford, Burnham, Colchester, Hanningfield, High Easter, 'Lanchire', Little Baddow, Maldon, Nayland, 'Sabsford', Saffron Walden, Stapleford, Woodham, Walter, Witham, Writtle); *Tobias* (1564, Lincoln); *Corpus Christi Play* (1575–1612, Kendal, Westmorland); *Corpus Christi Play* (played until *c.* 1576, Doncaster); 'King Play' (1579, Hascombe, Surrey); *Manningtree Moralities* (played until 1612, Manningtree, Essex); *St Tewdricus* (ment. 1701, Carnarvon, Bangor); *St Obert* (b. 1575, Perth, Scotland).	
1495	More, Thomas	'Comoediolae'	*c.* 1491–*c.* 1499
	More, Thomas	*King Solomon*	*c.* 1495
1496	Medwall, Henry	*I & II Nature*	*c.* 1496
1497	Medwall, Henry	*I & II Fulgens and Lucrece* (*Fulgens, Senator of Rome*) (Adapt. of a tale by Bonaccorso through French and English intermediaries.)	1497
1498			
1499			
1500			
1501	Cornish, Wm, Sr, and others	*The Marriage of Prince Arthur* (Pageants of castle, ship, and mount, prob. by Cornish, on 19 Nov.)	Nov.
	Cornish, Wm, Sr, and others (Fox, R.?)	*The Welcome for Katherine of Aragon* (Pageants, with speeches, of St Katherine, and St Ursula; the Castle of Portcullis, with Policy, Nobleness, and Right; Raphael, Alphonso, Job, and Boethius; the Sphere of the Sun; the Temple of God; Honour and the Seven Virtues.)	12 Nov.
	More, Thomas	*Solomon*	1501 (ment.)

TYPE	AUSPICES	EARLIEST TEXTS	LATEST TEXTS
Interludes (?)	Unknown	Lost	
Comedy	Magdalen Col. School (?)	Lost	
Moral Interlude	Morton's House (?)	[1530–4?]* F	C
Romantic Interlude	Morton's House (?)	[c. 1512–16]* F	C
Tilt and Disguising	Westminster and Richmond	MS (descrip.); cf. also Hall, 493–4	C
Pageantry	London	MSS (descrip.); cf. also Great Chronicle, 297–310, & Hall, 493	C
Latin Comedy	Unknown	Lost	

DATE	AUTHOR	TITLE	LIMITS
1502			
1503	Dunbar, William (?)	*The Droichis [Dwarf's] Part of the Play* (*The Manner of the Crying of a Play*) (A part of the following?)	1503(?)
	Anon.	*The Welcome for Princess Margaret*	7 Aug.
1504	Skelton, John	*The Nigramansir* [*Necromancer*] (Poss. a fabrication, by Warton.)	*c.* 1504
	Ton, Ralph (and another?)	*The Life of St Meriasek, Bishop and Confessor*	1504
1506			
1507	Burgess, John	*St Mary Magdalene*	1507
	Anon.	*The Joust of the Wild Knight and the Black Lady*	June
	Anon.	*The Jousts of the Months of May and June*	May, June
1508	Cornish, Wm, Jr and others (?). Carmelianus, Petrus (describer)	*Betrothal of Mary and Archduke Charles* (also, *The Entertainment of the Flemish Ambassadors*)	Dec.
	Anon.	*The World and the Child* (*Mundus et Infans*)	*c.* 1500–1522
1509	Anon.	*The Coronation Triumph of Henry VIII*	24 June
	Anon.	*The Scholars of Dame Pallas and Knights of Diana*	June
1510	Anon.	*Almains and Spaniards*	14 Nov.
	Anon.	*The Entertainment of the Ambassadors*	10 Feb.
	Anon. (Rastell, J.?)	*The Nine Hierarchies of Angels*	1510
	Anon.	*Robin Hood's Men*	1510
1511	Hobarde, John	*St George* (For other miracles of 16th cent., see 15th cent. add.)	20 July
	Anon.	*The Four Chevaliers of the Forest Salvigny*	13 Feb.
	Anon.	*The Garden of Pleasure*	14 Feb.
	Anon.	*A Pageant of a Mountain*	6 Jan.
	Anon.	*The Ship of Fame*	1 May
	Anon.	*The Welcome for Queen Margaret*	May
1512	Anon.	*The Castle Dangerous*	1 Jan.
	Anon.	*The Dolorous Castle*	June
	Anon.	*An Epiphany Mask*	6 Jan.
1513	Arduenna, Remaclus	*Palamedes* (By a foreigner, living in London.)	*c.* 1513 (pub.)
	Anon.	*Beauty and Venus*	1513–1514
	Anon.	*Hick Scorner* (*Hycke Scorner*)	*c.* 1513–1516
	Anon.	*The Rich Mount*	6 Jan.

TYPE	AUSPICES	EARLIEST TEXTS	LATEST TEXTS
Banns for May Game	Edinburgh	MSS	C
Pageantry	Edinburgh	MS (descrip.)	
Interlude	Court at Woodstock	Lost	
Cornish Miracle	Camborne (?), Cornwall	MS	E
Miracle Play (?)	Magdalen Col., Oxford	Lost	
Tilt	Scottish Court	......	
Tilt	English Court	[c. 1508]* (descrip.)	C
Disguisings	Court	MS (ment.) Public Record Office	
Moral Interlude	Unknown	1522* F	(D),C
Pageantry	London and Westminster	Hall, 507–13	
Disguising and Tilt	Court	Hall, 511–12	
Disguising	Court	Hall, 516	
Disguising	Court	Hall, 513–14	
Pageant for King	Coventry	......	
Disguising	Court	Hall, 513	
Miracle	Bassingbourne, Cambridgeshire	Lost	
Disguising and Tilt	Court	Hall, 517	
Disguising	Court	Hall, 518–19	
Entertainment	Court	Hall, 516–17	
Setting for Tilt	Court	Hall, 520	
Pageants	Aberdeen	......	
Disguising and Tilt	Court	Hall, 526	
Disguising and Tilt	Court	Hall, 533–4	
Mask	Court	Hall, 526	
Latin Comedy	Closet	[c. 1513]	
Interlude	Court	Lost	
Moral Interlude	Unknown	[1515–16?] F	(D),S
Disguising	Court	Hall, 535	

DATE	AUTHOR	TITLE	LIMITS
1514	Cornish, Wm, Jr	*The Triumph of Love and Beauty* (Prob. a Collier forgery.)	6 Jan.
	Medwall, Henry	*The Finding of Troth* (Prob. a Collier forgery.)	6 Jan.
	Anon.	*The Mask at Tournay*	18 Oct.
	Anon.	*Youth, The Interlude of*	1513–1514
1515	Skelton, John	*Achademios*	*c.* 1504–1523
	Skelton, John	*Good Order* (*De Bono Ordine*) (Poss. same as *Old Christmas*, 1533.)	*c.* 1504–1529
	Skelton, John	*Magnificence*	1515–1526
	Skelton, John	*Virtue* (*De Virtute*)	*c.* 1504–1523
	Anon.	*The Place Perilous* (*Wild Men*)	6 Jan.
	Anon.	*Robin Hood's Feast*	1 May
1516	Cornish, Wm, Jr (producer)	*Entertainment at Greenwich* (held by Henry VIII in honour of Mary, Queen of Scots)	20 May (acted)
	Cornish, Wm, Jr (?)	*The Eltham Pageant of a Castle*	6 Jan.
	Cornish, Wm, Jr (?)	*Troilus and Pander*	6 Jan.
1517	Cornish, Wm, Jr	*The Garden of Esperance*	6 Jan.
	Rastell, John	*The Nature of the Four Elements* (*Natura Naturata*)	*c.* 1517–*c.* 1518
1518	Anon.	*The Entertainment of the French Ambassadors*	Oct.
	Anon.	*A Mask of Palmers*	1518
	Anon.	*The Rock of Amity* (With speeches in French.)	5 Oct.
	Anon.	*St Erasmus*	1518 (acted)
1519	Heywood, John (?)	*The Pardoner and the Friar, the Curate, and Neighbour Pratte*	1513–1521
	Anon.	*The Summoning of Every Man* (*Every Man, A Treatise How the High Father of Heaven Sendeth Death To Summon Every Creature*) (Adapt. Elckerlije of Dorlandus?)	*c.* 1519
	Anon.	*The Entertainment of the Hostages*	7 Mar.
	Anon.	'Revels called a Maskalyn'	1519
	Anon.	'Summer and Lust', etc.	1519
1520	Heywood, John	*The Four P's*	*c.* 1520–1522
	Heywood, John (?)	*Johan Johan the Husband, Tib, His Wife, and Sir Johan the Priest* (*Johan Johan*) (Adapt. *Farce du Pasté*.)	1520–1533
	Anon.	*Andria* (Terence in English)	1516–1533
	. . . . . .	*The Field of the Cloth of Gold*	9–14 June
	Anon.	*Johan the Evangelist*	*c.* 1520–*c.* 1557
	Anon.	*A Pageant of a Wagon*	1 Feb.

TYPE	AUSPICES	EARLIEST TEXTS	LATEST TEXTS
Interlude	Chapel at Court	'Lost'	
Interlude	Court Interluders	'Lost'	
Mask	Court at Tournay	Hall, 566	
Moral Interlude	Unknown	[1530–5] F	(DB),E,C
Comedy	Unknown	Lost	
Moral Interlude (?)	Unknown	Lost (?)	
Moral Interlude	Unknown	[1530?]★ F	S
Moral Interlude	Unknown	Lost	
Disguising	Court	Hall, 580	
Maying	Court	Hall, 582	
Disguising (?)	Children of the Chapel (in Queen's Chamber)	Hall, 584–5 (ment. Chambers Accounts MS)	
Disguising	Court	Hall, 583	
Romantic Interlude	Chapel at Court	Lost	
Disguising	Court	Hall, 585–96	
Didactic Interlude	Unknown	[c. 1526–30]★ (frag.) F	(D)
Mask	Wolsey's House	Hall, 594–5	
Mask	Court	Lost	
Allegorical Show	Court	Hall, 595 *State Papers Venetian* II, No. 1088	
Miracle	Aberdeen	Lost	
Comic Interlude	Unknown	1533★ F	(D)
Morality	Unknown	[1510–19?] F	(DP)
Disguising	Court	Hall, 597	
Mask	Court	Lost	
Interlude	Chapel at Court	Lost	
Comic Interlude	Unknown	[1541–7] F	(D)
Comic Interlude	Unknown	1533★ F	
Comedy	Closet	[1516–33]★	
Disguising and Tilt	Court at Guisnes	Hall, 610–20	
Moral Interlude	Unknown	[c. 1550?]★ F	(G)
Disguising and Tilt	Court	Hall, 600–1	

DATE	AUTHOR	TITLE	LIMITS
1521	Anon.	*The Entertainment of the Emperor's Ambassadors*	1521–1522
1522	Cornish, Wm, Jr	*Friendship, Prudence, and Might* (*The Triumph of Amity*)	15 June
	Lyly, W.; Rastell; and others	*The Welcome for Emperor Charles V* (Pageants, with Latin verses, of Jason and Medea; Charlemagne; John of Gaunt; the Four Cardinal Virtues; King Alphonsus; the Apostles [by Rastell?].)	6 June
	Anon.	*The Conquest of Lady Scorn*	4 Mar.
1523			
1524	Anon.	*The Entertainment of the Scottish Ambassadors*	28 Dec.
1525	Artour, Thomas	*Microcosmus*	1520–1532
	Artour, Thomas	*Mundus Plumbeus*	1520–1533
	Bourchier, John	*Ite in Vineam, or The Parable of the Vineyard*	1525
	Anon.	*The Golden Fleece*	2 Feb.
1526	Roo (or Rho), John	*Lord Governance and Lady Public Weal*	Xmas (acted)
1527	Rastell, John	*Love and Riches* (*The Father of Heaven*)	5 May
	Rastell, John (?)	*Calisto and Melebea* (*Celestina. The Beauty and Good Properties of Women*) (Adapt., through Italian intermediary, of part of the *Celestina* of de Rojas.)	*c.* 1527–1530
	Rastell, J. (?) (Heywood, J., also suggested)	*I & II Gentleness and Nobility*	*c.* 1527–1530
	Ritwise, John	*Dido*	1522–1532
	Ritwise, John (?)	*Heretic Luther* (*The Deliverance of the Pope*) (In Latin and French.)	10 Nov.
	Anon.	*Godly Queen Hester*	1525–1529
	Anon.	*The Mask for the French Ambassadors*	10 Nov.
	Anon.	*A Mask of Venus, Cupid, Six Damsels, and Six Old Men*	3 Jan.
	Anon.	*The Visit of Henry VIII to Wolsey*	5 May
1528	Heywood, John	*The Play of the Weather*	1519–1528
	Anon.	*Adam and Eve* (by Tailors), *Bacchus* (by Vintners), *Ceres* (by Bakers), *Crispin and Crispinianus* (by Shoemakers), *The Deaths of the Apostles* (by Priors), *Joseph and Mary* (by Carpenters), *The Passion of the Saviour* (by Priors), *Vulcan* (by Smiths)	1528 (ment.)
	Anon.	*Religion, Peace, and Justice*	7 Jan.

TYPE	AUSPICES	EARLIEST TEXTS	LATEST TEXTS
Disguising	Court	Hall, 628	
Political Moral	Boys at Court	Cf. *State Papers Spanish*; also Hall, 641 MS (descrip.) & Hall, 641	
Royal Entertainment	London	MS (descrip.)* Hall, 637–40	
Disguising and Tilt	Wolsey's House	Hall, 631	
Mask and Tilt	Court	Hall, 688–90	
Latin Tragedy or Comedy	St John's Col., Cambridge	Lost	
Latin Tragedy or Comedy	St John's Col., Cambridge	Lost	
Interlude	At Calais	Lost	
Pageant or Interlude (?)	Cappers of Canterbury	Lost	
Political Moral	Gray's Inn	Lost	
Pageant and Dialogue	Chapel at Court	Lost	
Romantic Interlude	Rastell's stage (?)	[*c.* 1527–30]* F	G,D
Dialogue	Rastell's stage (?)	[*c.* 1527–30]* F	G
Latin School Play	Paul's at Wolsey's	Lost	
Anti-Protestant Interlude	Paul's at Court	Lost	
Biblical Interlude	Unknown	1561*	B
Mask	Court at Greenwich	Hall, 735	
Mask (Latin Speeches)	At Wolsey's	Cf. *State Papers Venetian*	
Mumming	At Wolsey's	Hall, 724	
Comic Interlude	Unknown	1533 F	S,D
Popular Plays on classical and religious subjects	Guilds of Dublin	Lost	
Latin Political Interlude	At Wolsey's (by Paul's?)	Cf. *State Papers Venetian*	

DATE	AUTHOR	TITLE	LIMITS
1529			
1530	Anon.	*Pater, Filius, et Uxor, or The Prodigal Son* (Adapt. Textor's *Juvenis, Pater, Uxor.*)	*c.* 1530–1534(?)
1531			
1532	Anon.	*The Triumph at Calais and Boulogne*	11–29 Oct.
1533	Heywood, John	*Witty and Witless* (*Wit and Folly*)	*c.* 1520–*c.* 1533
	Udall, N., with Leland, J.	*The Coronation Triumph of Anne Boleyn*	31 May
	Anon.	*Against the Cardinals*	1533
	Anon. (Skelton, J.?)	*Old Christmas, or Good Order* (Poss. same as *Good Order*, 1515.)	1533 (pub.)
	Anon.	*Old Custom*	*c.* 1520–1550
1534	Heywood, John	*A Play of Love* (Perf. during Xmas 1528–9, conjectured.)	1533–1534 (pub.)
	Udall, Nicholas (?)	*Placidas, alias Sir Eustace*	1534
	Anon.	'. . . *Interpretation of a chapter of the Apocalypse . . . [showing Henry VIII] cutting off heads of the clergy.*'	23 June
1535	Anon.	*Temperance and Humility* (*Disobedience, Temperance, and Humility*)	*c.* 1521–1535
	Anon.	*The Lord Mayor's Show* (Installation ceremonies were revived in or just before this year, after suppression since 1481. Shows will be listed below when descriptions are extant.)	29 Oct.
1536	Bale, John	*The Life of John the Baptist,* in 14 books (*Vitam D. Ioannis Baptistae*); *Christ and the Doctors* (*De Christo Duodenni*); *I & II The Baptism and Temptation* (*De Baptismo et Tentatione*); *The Raising of Lazarus* (*De Lazaro Resuscitato*); *The Council of Bishops* (*De Consilio Pontificum*); *Simon the Leper* (*De Simone Leproso*); *The Lord's Supper and Washing the Feet* (*De Coena Domini et Pedum Lotione*); *I & II The Passion of Christ* (*De Passione Christi*); *I & II The Burial and Resurrection* (*De Sepultura et Resurrectione*)	*c.* 1530–1539
	Bale, John	*On the Seven Sins* (*De Septem Peccatis*) (Distinct from following?)	*c.* 1530–1539
	Bale, John	*Pater Noster Play* (?) (*Super Oratione Dominica*)	*c.* 1530–1539

TYPE	AUSPICES	EARLIEST TEXTS	LATEST TEXTS
Interlude	Unknown	[1530–4?]* (frag.)	G
Pageantry and Mask	Court abroad	[1532] (descrip.) & Hall, 793–4	C
Dialogue	Closet (?)	MS (frag.) F	C
Pageantry	London	[1533] (descrip.) & MS (frag.)	C
Anti-Catholic Interlude	Court	Lost	
Moral Interlude	Unknown	1533 (frag.) F	G
Interlude	Unknown	Lost	
Disputation	Inns of Court (?)	1534 (i.e. 1533/)	S
Neo-Miracle	Braintree, Essex	Lost	
Anti-Catholic Interlude	Outside London	Lost (cf. *Letters* *& Papers, Henry* *VIII* item 949)	
Moral Interlude	Unknown	[1521–35]*	G
Civic Pageant	London	Lost	
Mystery Cycle adapted to anti-Catholic purposes (?)	Thorndon, Suffolk (?); later (1538–40) St Stephen's, Canterbury (?). The plays were written, says Bale, for the Earl of Oxford.	Lost	
Anti-Catholic Moral (?)	Same as above (?)	Lost	
Anti-Catholic Moral (?)	Same as above (?)	Lost	

DATE	AUTHOR	TITLE	LIMITS
	Anon.	*St Thomas the Apostle* (subject)	23 Aug. (1536?)
1537	Bale, John	*Against Adulterators of the Word of God* (*Contra Adulterantes Dei Verbum*)	*c.* 1536–1539
	Bale, John	*I & II Against Momi and Zoili* (*Erga Momos et Zoilos. Against Scoffers and Backbiters*)	*c.* 1536–1539
	Bale, John	*I & II On Sects among the Papists* (*De Sectis Papisticis*)	*c.* 1538–1548
	Bale, John	*I & II Treacheries of the Papists* (*Proditiones Papistarum*)	*c.* 1538–1548
	Bale, John	*I & II Upon Both Marriages of the King* (*Super Utroque Regis Coniugio*)	1533–1539
	Udall, Nicholas (?)	*Thersites* (Adapt. Textor.)	12–24 Oct.
	Wylley, Thomas	*Against the Pope's Councillors*	1535–*c.* 1537
	Wylley, Thomas	*A Reverent Receiving of the Sacrament*	1537
	Wylley, Thomas	*A Rude Commonalty*	1537
	Wylley, Thomas	*The Woman on the Rock*	1537
	Anon.	*Albion Knight*	*c.* 1537–1566
	Anon.	*Of a King How He Should Rule His Realm*	1 May
1538	Bale, John	*God's Promises* (*The Chief Promises of God unto Man. De Magnis Dei Promissionibus*)	1538
	Bale, John	*The Image of Love* (*Amoris Imago*)	*c.* 1538–1548
	Bale, John	*John Baptist's Preaching in the Wilderness* (*De Predicatione Ioannis*)	1538
	Bale, John	*I & II King John* (*De Ioanne Anglorum Rege*)	A-version: 1538; B-revision: 1558–1562(?)
	Bale, John	*The Knaveries of Thomas Becket* (*De Imposturis Thomae Becketi*)	*c.* 1536–1539
	Bale, John	*I, II, III, & IV Pammachii* (Adapt. Kirchmayer's *Pammachius.*)	1538–1548
	Bale, John	*The Temptation of Our Lord and Saviour Jesus Christ by Satan* (*De Christi Tentatione*)	1538
	Bale, John	*Three Laws of Nature, Moses, and Christ, Corrupted by the Sodomites, Pharisees, and Papists* (*Corruptiones Legum Divinarum*)	1538; revised *c.* 1547; again in 1562
	Lindsay, David	*The Welcome for Marie de Lorraine*	10 June; July
	Anon.	*A Pretty Complaint of Peace that was Banished out of Divers Countries*	*c.* 1538 (pub.)

TYPE	AUSPICES	EARLIEST TEXTS	LATEST TEXTS
Anti-Catholic Interlude	York (acted)	Lost (see *Letters of the Kings of England*, ed. J.O. Halliwell [-Phillips], I, 354)	
Anti-Catholic Interlude	Unknown	Lost	
Anti-Catholic Interlude	Unknown	Lost	
Anti-Catholic Interlude	Unknown	Lost	
Anti-Catholic Interlude	Unknown	Lost	
Anti-Catholic Interlude	Thorndon, Suffolk (?); later (1538–40) St Stephen's, Canterbury (?). The play was written, says Bale, for the Earl of Oxford	Lost	
Interlude	Eton Boys (?)	[1561–3]* F	D
Anti-Catholic Moral	Yoxford (?)	Lost	
Lenten Play	Before Cromwell	Lost	
Moral Interlude (?)	Yoxford (?)	Lost	
Unknown	Closet	Lost	
Moral Interlude	Unknown	[*c.* 1565]* (frag.)	G
Political-Moral Interlude	Suffolk (acted)	Lost (cf. *Letters and Papers, Henry VIII*, xii (1), items 1212, 1284)	
Anti-Catholic Mystery	St Stephen's, Canterbury	[*c.* 1547–8] F	D,C
Didactic Interlude (?)	Unknown	Lost	
Anti-Catholic Mystery	St Stephen's, Canterbury	[*c.* 1547–8]* (now lost)	C
Anti-Catholic History	St Stephen's, Canterbury	MS (1560–3) F	G,C,D
Anti-Catholic History	Unknown	Lost	
Anti-Catholic Neo-moral	Closet (?)	Lost	
Anti-Catholic Mystery	St Stephen's, Canterbury	[*c.* 1547–8]* F	C
Anti-Catholic Moral	St Stephen's, Canterbury	[*c.* 1547–8] F	C
Pageants	St Andrews, and Edinburgh	Lost	
Dialogue	Unknown	*c.* 1538*	

DATE	AUTHOR	TITLE	LIMITS
	Anon.	*Rex Diabole*	Oct.
1539	Heywood, John	*King Arthur's Knights*	1539
	Hoker, John	*Piscator sive Fraus Illusa*	1535–1543
	Redford, John	*Courage, Kindness, Cleanness*	1531–1547
	Redford, John	*D, G, and T[om]*	1531–1547
	Redford, John	*Wit and Science*	1531–1547
	Spencer,—	*The Sacrament of the Altar*	*c.* 1539
	Udall, Nicholas	*De Papatu* (Poss. identical with following.)	*c.* 1537–1548
	Udall, Nicholas	*Ezekias* (Poss. same as above.)	1537–1556
1540	Buchanan, George	*Baptistes sive Calumnia* (prob. same as *John Baptist* acted at Trinity Col., Camb., in 1562–3.)	1540–1545
	Buchanan, George	*Medea* (Trans. Euripides.)	1539–1542
	Grimald, Nicholas	*Christus Nascens*	*c.* 1540(?)
	Grimald, Nicholas	*Christus Redivivus*	*c.* 1540–1541
	Lindsay, David	*A Satire of the Three Estates* (The following titles have sometimes been assigned to separate parts: *The Poor Man and the Pardoner*; *The Three Vices Overcome Truth and Chastity*; *The Sermon of Folly*; *The Punishment of the Vices*: *Humanity and Sensuality*; *Auld Man and His Wife*; *Flattery, Deceit, and Falsehood Mislead King Humanity*.)	6 Jan. (Version I); 7 June 1552 (Version II); 12 Aug. 1554 (Version III)
	Palsgrave, John	*Acolastus* (Trans. de Volder.)	1540
	Radcliff, Robert (trans.)	*Ecclesia; or A Governance of the Church*, work of Ravisius Textor	1540
	Watson, Thomas	*Absalom* (Prob. same as Absalom of MS Stowe 957.)	*c.* 1535–1544
	Wedderburn, James	*The Beheading of John the Baptist*	1539–1540
	Wedderburn, James	*Dionysius the Tyrant*	1539–1540
1541	Buchanan, George	*Alcestis* (Trans. Euripides.)	1539–1542
	Buchanan, George	*Jephthes sive Votum*	1539–1545
	Anon.	'An Interlude wherein Priests were Railed On and Called Knaves'	1541
	Anon.	*The Nine Worthies*	1541
1542	Anon.	*Battle between the Spirit, the Soul, and the Flesh*	June (?)
	Anon.	*The Four Cardinal Virtues* (Related to *Temperance and Humility*, 1530.)	1537–1547

TYPE	AUSPICES	EARLIEST TEXTS	LATEST TEXTS
Interlude	Acted before Lady Lisle	Lost (cf. *Letters and Papers, Henry VIII*, Add., 1362)	
Mask	Court	Lost	
Latin Play	Magdalen Col., Oxford	Lost	
Moral Interlude	Paul's (?)	MS (frag.)	G
Interlude	Paul's (?)	MS (frag.)	G
Moral Interlude	Paul's (?)	MS (frag.) F	G
Anti-Catholic Moral	Unknown	Lost	
From a Latin Tragedy	Trans. for Katherine Parr	Lost	
Biblical Interlude	Eton Boys (?) (King's Col., Camb., in 1564)	Lost	
Latin Political Allegory	Guyenne Col., Bordeaux	1577	E (trans.), T
Latin Tragedy	Guyenne Col., Bordeaux	1544	
Latin Neo-miracle	Brasenose Col., Oxford (?)	Lost	
Tragicomedy	Brasenose Col., Oxford	1543★ (Cologne, printed text)	1925 (text & trans.), C,F
Political-religious Moral	Before James V at Linlithgow (Version I); Castle Hill, Cupar, Fifeshire (Version II); Calton Hill, Edinburgh (Version III)	MS (Version I, descrip. only); MS (Version II, extracts); 1602★★ (Version III)	C (all versions) E (Version III) F
Neo-moral	Closet	1540★	E
Dialogue	Jesus College, Cambridge	MS	
Latin Biblical Play	St John's Col., Cambridge	MS (?)	S,T,F
Anti-Catholic Tragedy	Playfield, Dundee	Lost	
Anti-Catholic Tragedy	Playfield, Dundee	Lost	
Latin Tragedy	Guyenne Col., Bordeaux	1550	
Latin Biblical Play	Guyenne Col., Bordeaux	1554	
Anti-Catholic Interlude	Shoreditch	Lost (cf. Foxe, *Acts and Monuments*)	
Pageant (?)	Dublin	Lost	
Moral Interlude	Suffolk's Men (London?)	Lost (cf. *Letters and Papers, Henry VIII*, Add. 1547)	
Moral Interlude	Unknown	[1541–7]★ (frag.)	

DATE	AUTHOR	TITLE	LIMITS
1543	Ascham, Roger	*Philoctetes* (Trans. Sophocles.)	1543
	Anon.	*A Mask of Almains*	1543
	Anon.	*A Mask of Mariners*	1543
	Anon.	*A Mask of Women*	1 Jan.
1544	Christopherson, John	*Jephthah*	*c.* 1539–*c.* 1544
1545	Foxe, John	*Titus et Gisippus* (Latin)	1544–1545
	Anon.	*A Mask of Egyptian Women*	1545–1546
	Anon. (Bale, J.?)	*The Resurrection of Our Lord* (*Christ's Resurrection*) (Poss. a part of Bale's *Burial and Resurrection*, 1536.)	*c.* 1530–*c.* 1560
1546	Radcliffe, Ralph	*De Ioannis Huss Bohemie Noti Condemnatione*; *De Iobi Iusti Affictionibus*; *De Iona a Deo ad Niniuitas Ablegati Defectione*; *De Iudith Bethuliensis Incredibili Fortitudine*; *De Lazaro a Diuitis aedibus Abacto*; *De Sodomo et Gomorre Incendio*; *De Susanne per Iudices Iniquos ob Lese Pudicitie Notam Diuini Liberatione*	1546(?)–1556 (Bale gives 1538 for Radcliffe's plays, but Radcliffe went to Hitchin in 1546)
	Radcliffe, Ralph	*The Melibeus of Chaucer* (*De Melibaeo Chauceriano*)	1546(?)–1556
	Radcliffe, Ralph	*The Most Firm Friendship of Titus and Gisippus* (*De Titi et Gisippi Firmissima Amicitia*)	1546(?)–1556
	Radcliffe, Ralph	*The Rare Patience of Chaucer's Griselda* (*De Griseldis Chauceriane Rara Patientia*)	1546(?)–1556
	Anon.	*The Market of Mischief*	1546–1547
1547	Grimald, Nicholas	*Archipropheta* (Adapt. Schoepper's *Decolatus.*)	1546–1547
	Grimald, Nicholas	*Athanasius sive Infamia*	*c.* 1540–*c.* 1547
	Grimald, Nicholas	*Fama*	*c.* 1540–*c.* 1547
	Grimald, Nicholas	*Protomartyr*	*c.* 1540–*c.* 1547
	Grimald, Nicholas	*Troilus, from Chaucer* (*Troilus ex Chaucero*)	*c.* 1540–*c.* 1547
	Grimald, Nicholas	'De Puerorum in Musicis Institutione'	*c.* 1540–*c.* 1547
	Anon.	*The Coronation of King Edward VI*	19 Feb.
	Anon.	*Impatient Poverty*	*c.* 1547–1558
	Anon.	*A Mask of Prester John*	Xmas, 1547–1548
	Anon.	*The Story of Orpheus*	9 Mar.
1548	Edward VI	*De Meretrice Babylonica* (*The Whore of Babylon*)	1548
	Punt, William	*The Indictment Against Mother Messe*	1548 (pub.)
	Anon.	*A Mask of Men*	1548
	Anon.	*A Mask of Young Moors*	12 Feb.

TYPE	AUSPICES	EARLIEST TEXTS	LATEST TEXTS
Latin Tragedy	Closet (?)	Lost	
Mask	Court	Lost	
Mask	Court	Lost	
Mask	Court	Lost	
Latin version of Greek Biblical play	St John's Col. or Trinity Col., Camb.?	MSS	E (text & trans.)
Latin Comedy	Unacted	MS	F
Mask	Court	Lost	
Protestant Mystery	Unknown	MS (frag.)	G
Tragedies (except for *De Lazaro*, a Comedy). Prob. in Latin and poss. anti-Catholic	Radcliffe's School at Hitchin	Lost	
Comedy (English?)	Radcliffe's School at Hitchin (?)	Lost	
Comedy (English?)	Radcliffe's School at Hitchin (?)	Lost	
Comedy (English?)	Radcliffe's School at Hitchin (?)	Lost	
Moral Interlude (?)	Queen's Men at Norwich	Lost	
Latin Biblical Tragedy	Christ Church or Exeter, Oxford	1548★ & MS	C (text & trans.), F
Latin Play	Brasenose, Merton, or Christ Church, Oxford	Lost	
Latin Play	Same as above	Lost	
Tragedy (Latin?)	Same as above	Lost	
Comedy	Same as above	Lost	
Comedy	Unknown	Lost	
Pageantry and Masks	London and Westminster	MS (descrip.)	C
Moral Interlude	Offered for acting	1560 F	B,S
Mask	Court	Lost	
Play or Mask	Court	Lost	
Anti-Catholic Interlude	Unknown	Lost	
Dialogue	Unknown	1548	F
Mask	Court	Lost	
Mask	Court	Lost	

DATE	AUTHOR	TITLE	LIMITS
	Anon.	*The Tower of Babylon*	Xmas, 1547–1548
	Anon.	*Two Masks of Women*	1548
1549	Anon.	*Jube the Sane* (i.e. *Job the Saint?*)	1547–1553
	Anon.	*A Mask of Almains*	Xmas, 1548–1549
1550	Hoby, Thomas	*Free-Will* (Trans. Francesco Negri's *Tragedia del libero arbitrio.*)	1550
	Key, or Caius, Thomas	*Tragedies of Euripides* (Trans. Euripides.)	*c.* 1540–1572
	Wever, R.	*Lusty Juventus*	1547–1553
	Anon.	*Love Feigned and Unfeigned*	*c.* 1540–*c.* 1560
	Anon. (Sebastian Wescott?)	*Nice Wanton* (Adapt. Macropedius's *Rebelles.*)	1547–1553
	Anon.	*Somebody, Avarice, and Minister* (*Somebody and Others, or The Spoiling of Lady Verity*) (Trans. *La Verité Cachée.*)	1547–1550(?)
1551	Anon.	*A Mask of Amazons, Women of War*	Xmas, 1551–1552
	Anon.	*A Mask of Argus*	Xmas, 1551–1552
	Anon.	*A Mask of Moors and Amazons*	Xmas, 1551–1552
1552	Chaloner, Thomas (?)	*Riches and Youth*	6 Jan.
	Udall, Nicholas	*Ralph Roister Doister* (*Roister Doister*)	1552–54?
	Anon.	*Aesop's Crow*	Xmas, 1552–1553
	Anon.	*A Drunken Mask*	2 Jan.
	Anon.	*A Mask of Babions* (i.e. *Baboons*)	Xmas, 1552–1553
	Anon.	*A Mask of Covetous Men*	Xmas, 1552–1553
	Anon.	*A Mask of Matrons*	Xmas, 1552–1553
	Anon.	*A Mask of Men*	6 Jan.
	Anon.	*A Mask of Polanders*	Xmas, 1552–1553
	Anon.	*A Mask of Soldiers*	Xmas, 1552–1553
	Anon.	*A Mask of Women of Diana*	Xmas, 1552–1553
	Anon.	*Self-Love*	1551–1553
1553	Baldwin, William (?) ('set out' by)	*The State of Ireland*	Easter & May Day

TYPE	AUSPICES	EARLIEST TEXTS	LATEST TEXTS
Biblical Interlude	Court	Lost	
Masks	Court	Lost	
Biblical Interlude (?)	Court (?)	Lost	
Mask	Court	Lost	
Anti-Catholic Moral	Closet	Lost	
Latin Tragedies	Closet (?)	Lost	
Anti-Catholic Moral Interlude	Offered for acting	[c. 1565?] F	D,S,T
Interlude	Unknown	MS (frag.)	
Unknown	Paul's at Court (?)	1560 F	D,S
Anti-Catholic Moral Interlude	Unknown	[c. 1547–50?]* (frag.) F	G
Mask	Court	Lost	
Mask	Court	Lost	
Mask	Court	Lost	
Dialogue	Court	Lost •	
Comedy	Unknown (Windsor Boys?)	[c. 1567]	D,B,G,C,S
Anti-Catholic Interlude	Court Interluders	Lost	
Mask	Court	Lost	
Mask	Court	Lost	
Mask	Court	Lost	
Mask	Court	Lost	
Mask	Court	Lost	
Mask	Court	Lost	
Mask	Court	Lost	
Mask	Court	Lost	
Moral Interlude (?)	Court Interluders	Lost	
Interlude	Court	Lost	

DATE	AUTHOR	TITLE	LIMITS
	Howard, G. (?) or Ferrers, G. (?)	*Cupid, Venus, and Mars*	6 Jan.
	Robinson, Nicholas	*Strylius*	1553
	Stevenson, W. (?) (revised by Bridges, J.?)	*Gammer Gurton's Needle (Diccon of Bedlam, etc.)*	*c.* 1552–1563
	Anon.	*Anglia Deformata et Anglia Restituta*	Xmas, 1553–1554
	Anon.	*Genus Humanum*	Xmas, 1553–1554
	Anon.	*A Mask of Bagpipes*	Easter & May Day
	Anon.	*A Mask of Cats*	Easter & May Day
	Anon.	*A Mask of Greek Worthies*	Easter & May Day
	Anon.	*A Mask of Medioxes*	Easter & May Day
	Anon.	*A Mask of Tumblers*	Easter & May Day
	Anon.	*Coronation Entry of Queen Mary*	30 Sept.
	Anon. (Udall, N.?)	*Respublica*	Xmas
1554	Grafton, Richard & others	*Entry of Philip and Mary*	18 Aug.
	Lauder, William	*The Entertainment for Queen Mary*	Dec.
	Udall, N. (?) or Hunnis, W. (?)	*Jacob and Esau*	*c.* 1550–1557
	Anon.	*A Mask of Arcules* (i.e. Hercules), *with Mariners*	St Andrew's Tide
	Anon.	*A Mask of Mariners* (Same as above?)	Hallowtide
	Anon.	*A Mask of Venetian Senators*	Xmas, 1554–1555
	Anon.	*A Mask of Venuses with Cupids*	Xmas, 1554–1555
	Anon. (Mey, John?)	'Theano' (Character's name)	*c.* 1540–1559
	Anon.	*Wealth and Health*	1553–*c.* 1555
1555	Hutton, Matthew (?) (Oxenbridge, A., co-author or co-producer?)	*De Crumena Perdita (Crumenaria)*	1555
	Worseley, Ralph	*Synedrii sive Concessus Animalium* (and *Synedrium*, an incomplete prose version of *Synedrii*.)	1554–1555
	Anon.	*Jack Juggler* (Adapt. Plautus's *Amphitruo*.)	*c.* 1553–*c.* 1558
	Anon.	*A Mask of Goddesses, Huntresses, with Turkish Women*	24–26 Feb.
	Anon.	*A Mask of Turks Magistrates with Turks Archers*	24–26 Feb.

TYPE	AUSPICES	EARLIEST TEXTS	LATEST TEXTS
Comedy (?)	Court	Lost	
Latin Comedy	Queens' Col., Cambridge	Lost	
Comedy	Christ's Col., Cambridge	1575 F	(D),E,S
Show	Trinity Col., Cambridge	Lost	
Moral Interlude	Chapel at Court	Lost	
Mask	Court	Lost	
Mask	Court	Lost	
Mask	Court	Lost	
Mask	Court	Lost	
Mask	Court	Lost	
Royal Entertainments	London	MSS & Holinshed	
Anti-Protestant Moral Interlude	Boys, at Xmas, London	MS F	E
Royal Entry	London	MSS	
'Farce and Play'	Edinburgh	Lost	
Biblical Interlude	Unknown (boys)	1568* F	G (D)
Mask	Court	Lost	
Mask	Court	Lost	
Mask	Court	Lost	
Mask	Court	Lost	
Latin (?) Tragedy	Queens' Col., Camb.	Lost	
Moral Interlude	Court Interluders (?)	[c. 1565?]* F	G,S
Latin Play	Trinity Col., Camb.	Lost	
Latin 'Beast Drama'	Closet (?)	MS	
Comedy	Offered for acting	[c. 1562] F	G,D
Mask	Court	Lost	
Mask	Court	Lost	

DATE	AUTHOR	TITLE	LIMITS
1556	Baldwin, William	*The Way to Life* (*A Discourse of the World*)	1556–1557
	Foxe, John	*Christus Triumphans*	1556
	Anon.	*The Hatfield Mask for the Princess Elizabeth* (See following.)	1554 or 1556
	Anon.	*Holophernes* (Authenticity of these Hatfield performances is questioned.)	1554 or 1556
1557	Anon.	*A Great Mask of Almains, Pilgrims, and Irishmen*	25 Apr.
	Anon.	*The Passion of Christ*	7 June
	Anon.	*The Sackful of News*	Aug. (suppressed)
	Anon.	*The Six Worthies* (See *The Nine Worthies*, 1541.)	1557
1558	Browne, Thomas	*Thebais* (Trans. Seneca.)	*c.* 1550–1563
	Fisher, John	*Three Dialogues Between Gelasimus and Spudaeus, Eda and Agna, and Wisdom and Will*	1557–1558 (S.R.)
	Lauder, W.; Adamson, W.	*The Marriage of Queen Mary*	July
	Lumley, Jane	*Iphigenia in Aulis* (Trans. Euripides.)	1549–1577
	Wager, Lewis	*The Life and Repentance of Mary Magdalene*	*c.* 1550–1566
1559	Heywood, Jasper	*Troas* (Trans. Seneca.)	1559
	Phillip, John	*Patient and Meek Grissil*	1558–1561
	Wager, W.	*The Longer Thou Livest the More Fool Thou Art*	*c.* 1559–1568
	Anon.	*The Coronation Triumph of Queen Elizabeth*	14 Jan.
	Anon.	*A Mask of Almains and Palmers*	1559(?)
	Anon.	*A Mask of Astronomers*	24 May
	Anon.	*A Mask of Conquerors*	1558–1559
	Anon.	*A Mask of Fishermen, Fishwives, and Market-wives*	7 Feb.
	Anon.	*A Mask of Hungarians*	1558–1559
	Anon.	*A Mask of Mariners* (same as above?)	1558–1559
	Anon.	*A Mask of Moors*	1558–1559
	Anon.	*A Mask of Nusquams, with Turkish Commoners*	1559–1560
	Anon.	*A Mask of Shipmen and Country Maids*	Aug.
	Anon.	*A Mask of Swart Rutters*	5 Feb.
	Anon.	*A Mask of Turks*	1558–1559
	Anon.	*Papists*	6 Jan.
1560	Alley, William (?)	*Aegio*	*c.* 1560–1565
	Heywood, Jasper	*Thyestes* (Trans. Seneca.)	1560
	Ingelend, Thomas	*The Disobedient Child*	*c.* 1559–1570
	Wager, W.	*Enough Is as Good as a Feast*	*c.* 1559–*c.*1570
	Anon.	*Juli and Julian*	*c.* 1560–1570
	Anon.	*A Mask of Actaeons*	1559–1560

TYPE	AUSPICES	EARLIEST TEXTS	LATEST TEXTS
Moral Comedy	Inns of Court, or Court	Lost	
Latin Religious Play	Trinity Col., Camb., in 1562-3	1556 & MS	F
Mask	Hatfield	Lost	
Interlude	Hatfield	Lost	
Mask	Court	Lost	
Biblical Play	Grey Friars, London	Lost	
Popular Comedy	Boar's Head Inn	Lost	
Popular Show	Dublin	Lost	
Tragedy	King's Col., Cambridge (?)	Lost	
Dialogues	Unknown	1558*	
'Triumph and Play'	Edinburgh	Lost	
Tragedy	Closet (?)	MS	G,C
Moral-Biblical Interlude	Offered for acting	1566-7* F	
Tragedy	Closet	1559	B,C
Comedy	Offered for acting	[1566?]*	G,T
Protestant Moral	Offered for acting	[*c.* 1569]* F	E,S
Pageant	London	1558[59] (descrip.) F	C
Mask and Tilt	Court	Lost	
Mask	Court	Lost	
Mask	Court	Lost	
Mask	Court	Lost	
Mask	Court	Lost	
Mask	Court	Lost	
Mask	Court	Lost	
Mask	Court	Lost	
Mask	West Horseley	Lost	
Mask	Court	Lost	
Mask	Court	Lost	
Anti-Catholic Farce	Court Interluders (?)	Lost	
Interlude	Unknown	1565* (frag.)	
Tragedy	Closet	1560	B,C
Interlude	Offered for acting	[*c.* 1569?]* F	D,C
Protestant Moral	Offered for acting	[*c.* 1565-70]* F	
Comedy	Unknown	MS	G,S
Mask	Court	Lost	

DATE	AUTHOR	TITLE	LIMITS
	Anon.	*A Mask of Barbarians*	1 Jan.
	Anon.	*A Mask of Clowns*	1559–1560
	Anon.	*A Mask of Diana and Six Nymphs Huntresses*	1560
	Anon.	*A Mask of Italian Women*	6 Jan.
	Anon.	*A Mask of Patriarchs*	6 Jan.
	Anon.	*Robin Hood* (*Robin Hood and the Friar. Robin Hood and the Potter*)	1560
	Anon.	*Sapientia Solomonis* (Adapt. Sixt Birck.)	1560
1561	Ashton, Thomas	*The Passion of Christ*	25 May
	Buchanan, George	*Apollo et Musae Exules*	Oct. (?)
	Elizabeth I	*Hercules Oetaeus* (Trans. pseudo-Seneca; second chorus only.)	1561–*c*. 1570
	Heywood, Jasper	*Hercules Furens* (Trans. Seneca.)	1561
	Preston, Thomas	*Cambises* (Same as *Huff, Suff,* and *Ruff,* below?)	*c*. 1558–1569
	Anon.	*Huff, Suff* [sic]*, and Ruff* (Same as *Cambises,* above?)	Xmas, 1560–1561
	Anon.	*A Mask of Wise and Foolish Virgins*	25–28 Oct.
	Anon.	*The Pedlar's Prophecy*	1561–*c*. 1563
	Anon.	*Romeo and Juliet*	*c*. 1560–1562
	Anon.	*Tom Tyler and His Wife*	*c*. 1561
	Anon.	*The Welcome for Queen Mary*	2 Sept.
1562	Norton, T.; Sackville, T.	*Gorboduc* (*Ferrex and Porrex*)	18 Jan.
	Anon.	*Devices for Nottingham Castle*	May
	Anon.	*Julius Caesar* (Poss. not a play.)	1562
	Anon.	*The Marriage Entertainment for Lord James Stuart*	8 Feb.
	Anon.	*The Two Sins of King David*	1562 (S.R.)
1563	Croston, W.; Man,—	*Aeneas and Queen Dido*	27 June
	Neville, Alexander	*Oedipus* (Trans. Seneca.)	1563
	Wager, W.	*'Tis Good Sleeping in a Whole Skin*	*c*. 1560–*c*. 1565
	Anon.	*Barbarous Terrine*	1563 (acted)
	Anon.	*Six Shepherds*	11 Jan.
1564	B[lower?], R[ichard?]	*Appius and Virginia*	1559–1567
	Buchanan, G., & another	*Cupid, Chastity, and Time*	13–15 Feb.
	Edwards, Richard	*Damion and Pithias*	1564–1568
	Halliwell Edward	*Dido*	7 Aug.
	Jeffere, John (?)	*The Bugbears* (Adapt. Grazzini's *La Spiritata.*)	1563–*c*. 1566
	Anon.	*Ajax Flagellifer* (Trans. Sophocles.)	9 Aug. (projected)

TYPE	AUSPICES	EARLIEST TEXTS	LATEST TEXTS
Mask	Court	Lost	
Mask	Court	Lost	
Mask	Court	Lost	
Mask	Court	Lost	
Mask	Court	Lost	
May Game Play	Offered for acting	[c. 1560]	G
Latin Biblical Play	Trinity Col., Cambridge	Lost	
Biblical Play	Shrewsbury	Lost	
Latin Mask	Scottish Court	1584 (verses)	
Tragedy	Closet	MS	C,E
Tragedy	Closet	1561	B,C
Tragedy	Court (?)	[c. 1569] F	D,T
Comedy (?)	At Court	Lost (?)	
Mask	Court	Lost	
Protestant Moral	Unknown	1595* F	G,T
Tragedy	Unknown	Lost	
Domestic Interlude	Chapel (?) Paul's (?)	1661** F	G
Royal Reception	Edinburgh	MSS (descrip.)	C
Tragedy	Inner Temple	1565 F	S,F
Moral Mask	Projected for meeting of Elizabeth and Mary	MS (design)	C
Classical History (?)	At Court (?)	Lost	
Mask (?)	Scottish Court	Lost	
Biblical History	Unknown	Lost	
Show	Chester	Lost	
Tragedy	Closet	1563	C
Interlude (?)	Unknown	Lost	
Tragedy (?)	Ipswich (Co. unknown)	Lost	
Pastoral Mask (?)	Scottish Court (Marriage of Commendator of St Colm's Inch)	Lost	
Classical Moral	Westminster Boys (?)	1575* F	G,D
Banquet Show	Scottish Court	MS (Ital. & Lat. verses)	C
Tragicomedy	Merton Col., Oxford	1571 F	G,D,T
Latin Tragedy	King's Col., Cambridge	Lost	
Comedy	By 'Boys'	MS	S
Latin Tragedy	Cambridge	Lost	

DATE	AUTHOR	TITLE	LIMITS
	Anon.	*Holofernes* (Prob. a traditional play.)	*c.* 1563–1565
	Anon. (Ikytton, W.?)	'Mock Mass' (before Queen Elizabeth I)	10 Aug.
1565	Buchanan, George	*Pompae Deorum in Nuptiis Mariae*; *Pompae Equestres*	29 July
	Wager, [W.?]	*The Cruel Debtor*	*c.* 1560–1565
	Anon.	*Juno and Diana* (*Diana, Pallas*)	4–6 Mar.
	Anon.	*King Darius*	1565 (pub.)
	Anon.	*A Mask of Hunters and the Nine Muses*	18 Feb.
	Anon.	*A Mask of Satyrs and Tilters*	4–6 Mar.
	Anon.	*Massinissa and Sophonisba*	1565
1566	Ashton, Thomas	*Julian the Apostate*	1556–1566
	Buchanan, George	*Pompae Deorum Rusticorum*	17 Dec.
	Calfhill, James	*Progne* (Adapt. Corraro.)	5 Sept.
	Edwards, Richard	*I & II Palamon and Arcite* (Trans. from Latin?)	Pt. I: 2 Sept.; Pt. II: 4 Sept.
	Gascoigne, George	*Supposes* (Trans. Ariosto's *I Suppositi*.)	1566
	Gascoigne, G.; Kinwelmershe, F.	*Jocasta* (Trans. Dolce's *Giocasta*.)	1566
	Mathews, Toby (?)	*Marcus Geminus*	1 Sept.
	Nuce, Thomas	*Octavia* (Trans. Seneca.)	1566 (S.R.)
	Pound, Thomas	*The Radcliffe Wedding Mask*	1 July
	Pound, Thomas	*The Southampton Wedding Mask*	Feb.
	Studley, John	*Agamemnon* (Trans. Seneca.)	1566
	Studley, John	*Hercules Oetaeus* (Trans. pseudo-Seneca.)	1566 (S.R.)
	Studley, John	*Medea* (Trans. Seneca.)	1566
	Anon.	*Far Fetched and Dear Bought Is Good for Ladies*	1566 (S.R.)
	Anon.	*Sapientia Solomonis* (Adapt. Sixt Birck.)	17 Jan.
1567	Pickering, John	*The Interlude of Vice* (*Horestes*)	1567 (S.R.)
	Studley, John	*Hippolytus* (Trans. Seneca.)	1567 (S.R.)
	Wager, W. (?)	*The Trial of Treasure*	1567 (pub.)
	Wilmot, R.; Stafford; Hatton; Noel; Al., G.	*Gismond of Salerne* (Revised by Wilmot in 1591 as *Tancred and Gismund*.)	1567–1568
	Anon.	*As Plain as Can Be*	1567–1568
	Anon.	*The College of Canonical Clerks*	1566–1567 (S.R.)
	Anon.	*Jack and Jill*	1567–1568
	Anon.	*The Painful Pilgrimage*	1567–1568
	Anon.	*Prodigality* (Same as *The Contention between Liberality and Prodigality*, 1601?)	1567–1568
	Anon.	*Samson*	1567
	Anon.	*Six Fools*	1567–1568
	Anon.	*Wylie Beguylie*	3 Jan.
1568	Fulwell, Ulpian	*Like Will to Like*	1562–1568
	Anon. (Hunnis, W.?)	*The King of Scots*	1567–1568

TYPE	AUSPICES	EARLIEST TEXTS	LATEST TEXTS
Interlude	Donington, Lincolnshire	Lost	
Anti-Catholic Burlesque	Cambridge students at Hinchinbrook	MS.	E
Latin Masks	Scottish Court	1584 (verses)	
Interlude	Unknown	[c. 1566]* (frag.)	G
Disputation	Gentlemen of Gray's Inn	Lost	
Protestant Moral	Offered for acting	1565 F	C
Mask	Court	Lost	
Mask	Court	Lost	
Latin (?) Tragedy	At Court	Lost	
Neo-miracle	Shrewsbury	Lost	
Latin Mask	Scottish Court	1584 (verses)	
Latin Tragedy	Christ Church, Oxford*	Lost	
Comedy	Christ Church, Oxford*	Lost	
Comedy	Gray's Inn	1573	T
Tragedy	Gray's Inn	1573 & MS	S
Latin Comedy	Christ Church, Oxford	Lost	
Tragedy	Closet	[c. 1566]	C
Wedding Mask	Before Elizabeth	MS (frag.)	
Wedding Mask	Before Elizabeth	MS (frag.)	C
Tragedy	Closet	1566	B,C
Tragedy	Closet	1581*	C
Tragedy	Closet	1566	B,C
Comedy (?)	Unknown	Lost	
Latin Biblical Play	Westminster Boys	MSS	E (text & trans.)
Moral Interlude	Rich's, or Boys, at Court (?)	1567* F	G,T
Tragedy	Closet	1581*	C
Moral Interlude	Offered for acting	1567* F	D,C
Senecan Tragedy	Inner Temple	MSS F &	C
Comedy (?)	Rich's, or Boys, at Court	Lost	
Interlude	Unknown	Lost	
Comedy (?)	Rich's, or Boys, at Court	Lost	
Moral Interlude (?)	Rich's, or Boys, at Court	Lost	
Moral Interlude (?)	Rich's, or Boys, at Court	Lost (?)	
Biblical History (?)	At Red Lion Inn	Lost	
Moral Interlude (?)	Rich's, or Boys, at Court	Lost	
Comedy	Merton Col., Oxford	Lost	
Moral Interlude	Offered for acting	1568 F	D,W
Tragedy	Chapel at Court	Lost	

* Newly discovered accounts by Windsor in Elliott, *ELR*, 1988, Corpus Christi MS 257.

DATE	AUTHOR	TITLE	LIMITS
	Anon.	*The Marriage of Wit and Science* (Same as following?)	b. 1569 (S.R.)
	Anon.	*Wit and Will* (Identical with above?)	1567–1568
1569	Garter, Thomas	*The Most Virtuous and Godly Susanna*	1563–1569 (S.R.)
	Anon.	*The Destruction of Thebes* (*The Contention between Eteocles and Polynices*)	15 May (projected)
1570	Anon.	*The Castle* (or *Cradle*) *of Security*	1565–1575
	Anon. (Preston, T.?)	*Clyomon and Clamydes*	*c.* 1570–1583
1570 ADDENDA	Anon.	The following plays cannot be dated with any approximation to accuracy, but all seem to belong to the period of the popularity of the moral interlude: *Dives and Lazarus*, *The Dialogue of Dives*, and *The Devil and Dives* are titles mentioned satirically in Greene's *Groatsworth of Wit*, in *Sir Thomas More*, and in *Histriomastix*, all referring perhaps to a popular moral stemming from Radcliffe's *Dives and the Devil*; *Delphrygus and the King of Fairies*, *The Highway to Heaven*, *Man's Wit*, and *The Twelve Labours of Hercules* are mentioned in *Groatsworth of Wit*; *Hit Nail o' the Head*, in *Sir Thomas More*; *Craft upon Subtlety's Back*, in S.R., 1609; *Joseph's Afflictions*, *Manhood and Misrule* (*Manhood and Wisdom*), *Susanna's Tears*, and *Nineveh's Repentance*, in the play-lists of 1656 and 1661.	. . . . . .
1571	Davidson, John	*The Siege of Edinburgh Castle*	July

	Rudd, Anthony
	   Richards, T. (?)
	   Johnson, L. (?)
		Misogonus ('Laurentius Barjona' on t.p.; prob. Laurence Johnson)	1564–77

	Anon.	*Iphigenia*	28 Dec.
	Anon.	*Lady Barbara*	27 Dec.
	Anon.	*New Custom* (*Nugize*, (i.e. *New Guise*)	1570(?)–1573
1572	Gascoigne, George	*The Mask for Lord Montacute* (*The Montague Mask*)	1572
	Goldingham, William	*Herodes*	*c.* 1570–*c.* 1575
	Woodes, Nathaniel	*The Conflict of Conscience*	1570–1581
	Anon.	*Ajax and Ulysses*	1 Jan.
	Anon.	*Chariclea* (*Theagenes and Chariclea*)	1572–1573
	Anon.	*Cloridon and Radiamanta*	17 Feb.
	Anon.	*A Double Mask* [*of Fishermen and Fruit-wives*?]	1572–1573

TYPE	AUSPICES	EARLIEST TEXTS	LATEST TEXTS
Moral Interlude	At Court (?)	[*c.* 1569]★ F	G,D,S,E
Moral Interlude	Paul's at Court	Lost (?)	
Moral Interlude	Offered for acting	1578★	G
Latin (?) Play	Christ Church, Oxford	Lost	
Moral Interlude	At Gloucester	Lost	
Heroical Romance	Revived by Queen's (?)	1599★ F	G
......	Unknown	Lost	
Polemical Show	St Leonard's Col., St Andrews	Lost	
Comedy	Trinity Col., Camb. (?)	MS	S
Tragedy	Paul's at Court	Lost	
Romance (?)	Lane's at Court	Lost	
Protestant Moral	Offered for acting	1573★ F	D,C
Wedding Mask	At Lord Montacute's	1573	C
Latin Tragedy	Trinity Col., Camb. (?)	MS	F
Protestant Moral	Offered for acting	1581★★ F	G,D
Classical Legend	Windsor Boys at Court	Lost	
Heroical Romance (?)	At Court	Lost	
Heroical Romance (?)	Lane's at Court	Lost	
Mask	Court	Lost	

DATE	AUTHOR	TITLE	LIMITS
	Anon.	*Fortune*	Xmas, 1572–1573
	Anon.	*A Mask of Apollo, the Nine Muses, and Lady Peace*	15 June
	Anon.	*Narcissus*	6 Jan.
	Anon.	*Paris and Vienne*	19 Feb.
1573	Anon.	*Alcmaeon*	27 Dec.
	Anon.	*Mamillia*	28 Dec.
	Anon.	*A Mask of Janus*	1 Jan.
	Anon.	*A Mask of Lance Knights*	27 Dec.
	Anon.	*Predor and Lucia*	26 Dec.
1574	Authinleck, Patrick	*The Forlorn Son*	1 Aug.
	Churchyard, T.; Roberts, J.	*The Queen's Entertainment at Bristow*	13–21 Aug.
	Anon.	*Herpetulus the Blue Knight and Perobia*	3 Jan.
	Anon.	*An Interlude of Minds* (Trans. Niclaes's *Ein Gedicht des Spels van Sinnen.*)	*c.* 1574
	Anon.	*A Mask of Foresters, or Hunters* [*with Wild Men?*]	1 Jan.
	Anon.	*A Mask of Hobby-Horses*	25 Dec. (?) 1574–1575
	Anon.	*A Mask of Mariners* (Same as above?)	25 Dec. (?) 1574–1575
	Anon.	*A Mask of Pilgrims*	25 Dec. (?) 1574–1575
	Anon.	*A Mask of Seven Ladies*	23 Feb.
	Anon.	*A Mask of Seven Warriors*	23 Feb.
	Anon.	*A Mask of Six Pedlars*	1574–1575
	Anon.	*A Mask of Six Sages*	6 Jan.
	Anon.	*A Mask of Six Virtues*	2 Feb. (projected)
	Anon.	*Panecia*	Xmas, 1574–1575
	Anon.	*Perseus and Andromeda*	23 Feb.
	Anon.	*Phedrastus*	Xmas, 1574–1575 (projected)
	Anon.	*Phigon and Lucia*	Xmas, 1574–1575 (projected)
	Anon.	*Philemon and Philecia*	21 Feb.
	Anon.	*Pretestus*	Xmas, 1574–1575
	Anon.	*Quintus Fabius*	6 Jan.
	Anon.	*Timoclea at the Siege of Thebes by Alexander*	2 Feb.
	Anon.	*Truth, Faithfulness, and Mercy*	1 Jan.

TYPE	AUSPICES	EARLIEST TEXTS	LATEST TEXTS
Moral Interlude (?)	At Court	Lost	
Mask	Court	Lost	
Classical Legend	Chapel at Court	Lost	
Heroical Romance (?)	Westminster at Court	Lost	
Classical Legend (?)	Paul's at Court	Lost	
Romance (?)	Leicester's at Court	Lost	
Mask	Court	Lost	
Mask	Court	Lost	
Romance (?)	Leicester's at Court	Lost	
Biblical Interlude	St Andrew's School	Lost	
Royal Reception	Bristol	1575	C
Heroical Romance	Clinton's at Court	Lost	
Protestant Moral	Closet	[c. 1574]*	
Mask	Court	Lost	
Mask	Court	Lost	
Mask	Court	Lost	
Mask	Court	Lost	
Mask	Court	Lost	
Mask	Court	Lost	
Mask	Court	Lost	
Mask	Court	Lost	
Mask	Court	Lost	
Romance (?)	Leicester's at Court	Lost	
Classical Legend	Merchant Taylors Boys at Court	Lost	
Romance (?)	Sussex's at Court	Lost	
Romance	Sussex's at Court	Lost	
Romance	Leicester's at Court	Lost	
Romance (?)	Clinton's at Court	Lost	
Classical History	Windsor Boys at Court	Lost	
Classical History	Merchant Taylors Boys at Court	Lost	
Moral Interlude	Westminster at Court	Lost	

DATE	AUTHOR	TITLE	LIMITS
1575	Gascoigne, George	*The Glass of Government*	1575
	Gascoigne; with Hunnis; Ferrers; Goldingham, H.; Badger; Paten (?); Mulcaster (?)	*The Princely Pleasures at Kenilworth* (*Zabeta* [projected]; *Silvanus* [27 July]; *The Savage Man and Echo* [1 July], by Gascoigne: *The Lady of the Lake* [18 July], by Hunnis, Ferrers, Goldingham: Speeches, by the others: Hock-Tuesday play also performed [17 July].)	9–27 July
	Gascoigne, G. (?) or Lee, H. (?)	*The Queen's Entertainment at Woodstock* (Consisted of various 'conceiptes', some poss. by Lee; an extant allegorical tale, *Hemetes the Hermit*, later translated into Latin, Italian, and French by Gascoigne; and as sequel to the tale, an extant brief comedy of Occanon and Caudina [acted 20 Sept.], poss. by Gascoigne.)	Sept.
	Golding, Arthur	*Abraham's Sacrifice* (Trans. Beza's *Abraham Sacrifiant*.)	1575
	Wyatt, R.; Heywood, T.	*The Entertainment at Worcester*	Aug.
	Anon.	*King Xerxes*	6 Jan.
	Anon.	*Processus Satanae*	*c.* 1570–1575
	Anon.	*Prodigality* (Revival of surviving version of *The Contention Between Liberality and Prodigality?*)	2 Feb.
1576	Wapull, George	*The Tide Tarrieth No Man*	1576 (pub.)
	Anon.	*The Collier*	30 Dec.
	Anon.	*Common Conditions*	1576 (S.R.)
	Anon.	*The Painter's Daughter*	26 Dec.
	Anon.	*The Red Knight*	25 July– 5 Aug.
	Anon.	*Tooly*	27 Dec.
1577	Campion, Edmund	*King Saul*	1577
	Gosson, Stephen	*Captain Mario* (First acted in 1581–2.)	1576–1577
	Gosson, Stephen	*Praise at Parting* (First acted in 1581–2.)	1576–1577
	Lupton, Thomas	*All for Money*	1559–1577
	Anon.	*Cutwell*	1576–1577
	Anon.	*The Cynocephali* (*The History of the Cenofalles*)	2 Feb.
	Anon.	*The History of Error* (Adapt. Plautus's *Menaechmi?*)	1 Jan.
	Anon.	*The Irish Knight*	18 Feb.
	Anon.	*A Mask of Boys*	19 Feb.
	Anon.	*Mingo* (or *Myngs*)	13–19 Oct.
	Anon.	*Mutius Scaevola*	6 Jan.
	Anon.	*The Solitary Knight*	17 Feb.
	Anon.	*Titus and Gisippus*	19 Feb.

TYPE	AUSPICES	EARLIEST TEXTS	LATEST TEXTS
Moral Allegory	Closet	1575** F	C
Royal Entertainment	Host: Leicester	1576* (lost) & 1587*	C
Royal Entertainment	Court	1579 (& MSS) & 1585* (frag.)	C,E
Tragedy	Closet	1577*	E
Royal Entertainment	Worcester	Lost	
Classical History (?)	Windsor Boys at Court	Lost	
Neo-miracle	Unknown	MS (actor's part)	G
Moral Interlude (?)	Paul's Boys at Court	Lost (?)	
Moral	Offered for acting	1576* F	E
Comedy (?)	Leicester's at Court	Lost	
Heroical Moral	Offered for acting	[c. 1576]	E
Romance (?)	Warwick's at Court	Lost	
Heroical Romance	Sussex's at Bristol	Lost	
Unknown	Howard's at Court	Lost	
Latin Tragedy	At Prague	Lost	
Comedy	Leicester's at Theatre (?)	Lost	
Moral	Leicester's at Theatre	Lost	
Satirical Moral	Unknown	1578* F	E
Unknown	Tried at Court	Lost	
Pseudo-history (?)	Sussex's at Court	Lost	
Comedy (?)	Paul's at Court	Lost	
Heroical Romance	Warwick's at Court	Lost	
Mask	Court	Lost	
Unknown	Leicester's at Bristol	Lost	
Classical Legend	Chapel and Windsor at Court	Lost	
Heroical Romance	Howard's at Court	Lost	
Comedy	Paul's at Court	Lost	

DATE	AUTHOR	TITLE	LIMITS
1578	Campion, Edmund	*Nectar et Ambrosia* (*St Ambrose and Emperor Theodosius*)	1578
	Churchyard; Garter, B.; Goldingham, H.	{ *The Entertainment at Norwich* { *The Entertainment in Norfolk and Suffolk*	Aug. Aug.
	Gosson, Stephen	*Catiline's Conspiracies*	1576–1579
	Sidney, Philip	*The Lady of May* (*The Entertainment at Wanstead*)	1578–1582
	Whetstone, George	*I & II Promos and Cassandra*	1578
	Anon.	*The Blacksmith's Daughter*	1576–1579
	Anon.	*The Court of Comfort*	1578 (acted)
	Anon.	*The Cruelty of a Stepmother*	28 Dec.
	Anon.	*The Jew* (*The Practice of Parasites*)	1576–1579
	Anon.	*Ptolome* (Same as *Telemo* of 1583?)	1576–1579
	Anon.	*The Queen of Ethiopia* (*Chariclea* of 1572?)	1578 (acted)
	Anon.	*Quid pro Quo*	1578–1579
	Anon.	*The Three Sisters of Mantua*	26 Dec.
	Anon.	*What Mischief Worketh in the Mind of Man*	6–12 July
1579	Churchyard, Thomas	'The devices of war and a play at Osterley'	1579(?)
	Fraunce, A. (?) or Hickman, H. (?)	*Hymenaeus*	1578–1580
	Merbury, Frances	*A Marriage between Wit and Wisdom* (Date on MS may be interpreted as either 1570 or 1579. Same as *The Marriage of Mind and Measure*, below?)	1571–1579
	Peele, George	*Iphigenia* (Trans. Euripides.)	1576–1580
	Wilson, Robert	*Short and Sweet* (Poss. descrip. rather than title.)	*c.* 1578–1579
	Anon.	*Alucius*	27 Dec.
	Anon.	*The Duke of Milan and the Marquis of Mantua*	26 Dec.
	Anon.	*A Greek Maid*	4 Jan.
	Anon.	*The Knight in the Burning Rock*	1 Mar.
	Anon.	*Loyalty and Beauty*	2 Mar.
	Anon.	*The Marriage of Mind and Measure*	1 or 4 Jan.
	Anon.	*A Mask of Amazons*	11 Jan.
	Anon.	*A Mask of Knights*	11 Jan.
	Anon.	*A Morris Mask*	3 Mar.
	Anon.	*Murderous Michael*	3 Mar.
	Anon.	*The Rape of the Second Helen*	6 Jan.
	Anon.	*The Welcome for James VI*	30 Sept.
1580	Legge, Thomas	*Richardus Tertius*	Mar. 1578(?)–1580
	Puttenham (Rich.?, or George?)	*Gynaecocratia*	*c.* 1570–1589
	Puttenham (Rich.?, or George?)	*Lusty London*	*c.* 1570–1589
	Puttenham (Rich.?, or George?)	*The Wooer*	*c.* 1570–1589

TYPE	AUSPICES	EARLIEST TEXTS	LATEST TEXTS
Latin Tragedy	At Prague	Lost	
Entertainment	Norwich	[c. 1578]	C
Entertainment	Norfolk and Suffolk	[c. 1578]*	
Didactic History	Leicester's at Theatre (?)	Lost	
Royal Entertainment	Host: Leicester	1598 & MS	C,E
Comedy	Unacted (?)	1578* F	C,T
Heroical Romance	Leicester's at Theatre (?)	Lost	
Moral (?)	Sheffield's at Bristol	Lost	
Tragedy (?)	Sussex's at Court	Lost	
Satirical Comedy (?)	At the Bull Inn	Lost	
Pseudo-history (?)	At the Bull Inn	Lost	
Heroical Romance	Howard's at Bristol	Lost	
Comedy or Moral (?)	Bath's at Bristol	Lost	
Comedy (?)	Warwick's at Court	Lost	
Moral	Berkeley's at Bristol	Lost	
Royal Entertainment	Host: Thomas Gresham	Lost	
Latin Comedy	St John's Col., Cambridge	MSS	E,F
Moral Interlude	Offered for acting	MS F	S
Latin (?) Tragedy	Christ Church, Oxford (?)	Lost	
Classical History (?)	Unknown	Lost	
Unknown	Chapel at Court	Lost	
Romance (?)	Sussex's at Court	Lost	
'Pastorell'	Leicester's at Court	Lost	
Heroical Romance (?)	Warwick's at Court	Lost	
Moral (?)	Chapel at Court	Lost	
Moral	Paul's at Court	Lost	
Mask	Court	Lost	
Mask	Court	Lost	
Mask	Prepared for Court	Lost	
Realistic Tragedy (?)	Sussex's at Court	Lost	
Classical Legend (?)	Sussex's at Court	Lost	
Royal Reception	Edinburgh	MS (descrip.)	C
Latin Tragedy	St John's Col., Cambridge	MSS	C,F
Comedy	Unknown	Lost	
Interlude	Unknown	Lost	
Interlude	Unknown	Lost	

DATE	AUTHOR	TITLE	LIMITS
	Robinson, Gwiliam (?)	*The Sailor's Mask*	*c.* 1570–1590
	Sidney, Philip	*A Dialogue between Two Shepherds* (*Pastoral Dialogue*)	1577–1583
	Anon.	*Calistus* (Same as *Calisto and Melebea*, 1527? *Celestina*, S.R., 1598?)	*c.* 1576–1580
	Anon.	*Delight* (Same as *The Play of Plays and Pastimes*, 1582?)	26 Dec.
	Anon.	*The Four Sons of Fabius* (*The Fabii*)	1 Jan.
	Anon.	*Portio and Demorantes*	2 Feb.
	Anon.	*Publii Ovidii Nasonis Meleager*	1570–1590
	Anon.	*Reception for Queen Elizabeth at Greenwich*	*c.* 1580
	Anon.	*Sarpedon*	16 Feb.
	Anon.	*Scipio Africanus*	3 Jan.
	Anon.	*The Soldan and the Duke of—*	14 Feb.
1581	Forsett, Edward	*Pedantius* (Formerly attrib. to A. Wingfield.)	6 Feb. (?)
	Goldwell, Henry (describer)	*The Fortress of Perfect Beauty*	15–16 May
	Newton, Thomas	*Thebais* (Trans. Seneca.)	1581
	Peele, George	*The Arraignment of Paris*	*c.* 1581–1584
	Watson, Thomas	*Antigone* (Trans. Sophocles.)	1581 (pub.)
	Wilson, Robert	*The Three Ladies of London*	*c.* 1581
	Anon.	*Caesar and Pompey* (Poss. same as *Pompey*, below.)	1576–1582
	Anon.	*Cupid and Psyche*	*c.* 1580–1582
	Anon.	*Hugh Aston's Mask*	1581(?)
	Anon.	*London against the Three Ladies*	1581–1582
	Anon.	*Pompey* (Poss. same as *Caesar and Pompey*, above.)	6 Jan.
1582	Edes, Richard	*Caesar Interfectus* (Epil. extant.)	Feb.
	Fraunce, Abraham	*Victoria* (Adapt. Pasqualigo's *Il Fedele*.)	1580–1583
	Gager, William	*Meleager*	Feb.
	Hutton, Leonard (?)	*Bellum Grammaticale sive Nominum Verborumque Discordia Civilis*	*c.* 1582–1592(?)
	Murgetrode, Michael (?)	*Puer Vapulans*	1581–1582
	Anon.	*Beauty and Housewifery*	27 Dec.
	Anon.	*A Game of the Cards*	26 Dec.
	Anon. (poss. Lodge, T.)	*The Play of Plays and Pastimes* (Same as *Delight*, 1580?)	1580–1582
	Anon.	*The Rare Triumphs of Love and Fortune*	30 Dec.
	Anon.	*Solymannidae*	5 Mar.
	Anon.	*A Virgin Play*	22 Feb. (acted)

TYPE	AUSPICES	EARLIEST TEXTS	LATEST TEXTS
Wedding Mask	Leicester	MS (descrip.)	
Dialogue	In show at Wilton	1613	C
'Tragical comedie'	At the Theatre (?)	Lost (?)	
Comedy	Leicester's at Court	Lost	
Classical Pseudo-history (?)	Warwick's at Court (and Theatre?)	Lost	
Romance (?)	Sussex's at Court	Lost	
Tragedy	Paul's	Lost	
Royal Entertainment	Children of the Chapel Royal	MS	
Classical Legend	Sussex's at Court	Lost	
Classical History	Paul's at Court	Lost	
Heroical Romance	Derby's at Court	Lost	
Latin Satirical Comedy	Trinity Col., Cambridge	1631* & MSS	B,E,F
Tilt and Entertainment	Court	[1581]*	C,T
Tragedy	Closet	1581*	C
Classical Legend (Pastoral)	Chapel at Court	1584*	G,T
Latin Tragedy	Cambridge in c. 1583 (?)	1581*	F
Moral	Unknown	1584 F	D,T
Classical History	At the Theatre (?)	Lost	
Classical Legend	Paul's (?)	Lost	
Mask	Unknown	Lost	
Moral	Unknown	Lost	
Classical History	Paul's at Court and at Paul's Theatre	Lost	
Latin Tragedy	Christ Church, Oxford	MS (Epil. only)	
Latin Comedy	St John's Col., Cambridge (?)	MS	B,F
Latin Tragedy	Christ Church, Oxford	1592*	F
Latin Comedy	Christ Church, Oxford, in 1592	1635*	E,F
Latin Comedy	Jesus Col., Cambridge	Lost	
Comedy	Hunsdon's at Court	Lost	
Moral (?)	Chapel at Court	Lost	
Moral (defending plays)	At the Theatre	Lost	
Mythological Moral	Derby's at Court	1589*	G,D,T
Latin Tragedy	Unknown	MS	
Unknown	Unknown	Lost	

DATE	AUTHOR	TITLE	LIMITS
1583	Gager, William	*Dido*	12 June
	Gager, William	*Rivales* (Prol. extant.)	11 June
	Lyly, John	*Campaspe* (*Alexander, Campaspe, and Diogenes*)	*c.* 1583
	Lyly, John	*Sappho and Phao*	*c.* 1583
	Anon.	*Ariodante and Genevora*	12 Feb.
	Anon.	*A History of Ferrar*	6 Jan.
	Anon.	*A Mask of Ladies and Boys*	5 Jan.
	Anon.	*A Mask of Six Seamen*	1583
	Anon.	*Telomo* (Poss. same as *Ptolome*, 1578.)	10 Feb.
1584	Gager, William	*Oedipus*	*c.* 1577–1592
	Grafton, John	*Midsummer Show*	23 June 1584 & 1585
	Harrison, John	*Philomathes' Dream* (Title assigned.)	11 Feb.
	Legge, Thomas	*Solymitana Clades, or The Destruction of Jerusalem*	*c.* 1580–1598
	Munday, Anthony	*Fedele and Fortunio* (*Two Italian Gentlemen*) (Trans. Pasqualigo's *Il Fedele*.)	1579–1584
	Smythe, John	*The Destruction of Jerusalem*	1584
	Anon. (poss. De Vere, E.)	*Agamemnon and Ulysses*	27 Dec.
	Anon.	*Phyllida and Corin*	26 Dec.
1585	Lyly, John	*Gallathea* (*Titirus and Galathea*, S.R., 1585)	1583–1585
	Peele, George	*The Pageant before Woolstone Dixie*	29 Oct.
	Anon.	'Antic Play and a Comedy'	23 Feb.
	Anon.	*Felix and Philiomena*	3 Jan.
	Anon. (Tarlton, R.?)	*Five Plays in One* (Revived as *I The Seven Deadly Sins*, *c.* 1590?)	6 Jan.
	Anon. (Tarlton, R.?)	*Three Plays in One* (Revived as *II The Seven Deadly Sins*, by Strange's, *c.* 1590, and as *Four Plays in One*, 6 Mar. 1592?)	21 Feb. (projected)
1586	Harrison, John	*Philomathes' Second Dream* (Title assigned.)	Feb.
	Marlowe, C.; Nashe, T.	*Dido, Queen of Carthage* (1591 recently urged.)	*c.* 1585–1586
	Nashe, T. (?) & another	*Terminus et Non Terminus*	1586–1588
	Peele, George	*The Hunting of Cupid*	1581–1591
	Wotton, Henry	*Tancredo*	1586–1587
	Anon.	*Duns Furens*	1580–1587
	Anon. (Tarlton? Rowley, S.?)	*The Famous Victories of Henry V*	1583–1588

TYPE	AUSPICES	EARLIEST TEXTS	LATEST TEXTS
Latin Tragedy	Christ Church, Oxford	MS & MS (frag.)	C,T,F
Latin Comedy	Christ Church, Oxford	Lost	
Classical Legend (Comedy)	Oxford's Boys	1584	G,T
Classical Legend (Comedy)	Oxford's Boys	1584	C
Romance (?)	Merchant Taylors Boys at Court	Lost	
Unknown	Sussex's at Court	Lost	
Mask	Court	Lost	
Mask	Prepared for Court	Lost	
Unknown	Leicester's at Court	Lost	
Latin Tragedy	Christ Church, Oxford (?)	MS	E,F
Show	York, Yorkshire	Lost	
Dialogue	St Paul's School	MS	G
Tragedy	Unacted (?)	MS	F
Comedy	At Court	1585*	G,T,E
Biblical History	Coventry	Lost	
Classical Legend	Oxford's Boys at Court	Lost	
Pastoral	Queen's at Court	Lost	
Classical Legend (Comedy)	Paul's (revived 1588?)	1592	C,S
Civic Pageant	London	1585*	C
Comedy	Queen's at Court	Lost	
Romance	Queen's at Court	Lost	
Moral	Queen's at Court	Lost	
Moral	Queen's at Court	MS ('plot' of *The Seven Deadly Sins*, *c.* 1590) F	C
Dialogue	St Paul's School	MS	G
Classical Legend (Tragedy)	'Chapel'	1594* F	C,S,T
Satirical Show	St John's Col., Cambridge	Lost	
Pastoral (Play?)	Unknown	(Lost ed., *c.* 1591)	G,C (frags.)
Latin (?) Tragedy	Queen's Col., Oxford	Lost	
Latin Satirical Comedy	Peterhouse, Cambridge	Lost	
History	Queen's at Bull Inn	1598 F	T,C

DATE	AUTHOR	TITLE	LIMITS
	Anon.	*The Forces of Hercules*	23 Apr.
	Anon.	*Tararantantara turba*	*c.* 1581–1586
	Anon.	*Timon*	*c.* 1581–1590(?)
1587	Churchyard, Thomas	*Leicester's Service in Flanders*	1587(?)
	Greene, Robert	*Alphonsus, King of Aragon*	1587–1588
	Greene, Robert (?)	*Job*	1586–1593(?)
	Kyd, T.	*The Spanish Tragedy (Hieronimo is Mad Again)* (Revised *c.* 1597? and 1601–2.)	1585–1589
	Marlowe, Christopher	*I Tamburlaine the Great*	1587–1588
	Anon.	*The Mad Priest of the Sun* (Same as *Heliogabalus*, 1594?)	1587–1588
1588	Aske, James/Deloney, Thomas (describers)	*The Queen's Visit to Tilbury (Elizabetha Triumphans)*	8–9 Aug.
	Greene, R.; Lodge, T.	*A Looking Glass for London and England*	1587–1588
	Hughes, T.; with Bacon; Trotte; Fulbeck; Lancaster; Yelverton; Penroodock; Flower	*The Misfortunes of Arthur (Certain Devices and Shows Presented to Her Majesty)*	28 Feb.
	James I	*An Epithalamion on the Marquis of Huntly's Marriage*	21 July
	Kyffin, Maurice	*Andria* (Trans. Terence.)	1588
	Kyffin, Maurice (?)	*Eunuchus* (Trans. Terence.)	1587–1597
	Lateware, Richard	*Philotas*	*c.* 1588–1596
	Lodge, Thomas	*The Wounds of Civil War, or Marius and Scilla* (i.e. *Sulla*)	1586–1591
	Lyly, John	*Endymion, the Man in the Moon*	2 Feb. (?)
	Marlowe, Christopher	*II Tamburlaine the Great*	1587–1588
	Peele, George	*The Pageant for Martin Calthrop*	29 Oct.
	Peele, George	*The Turkish Mahomet and Hiren the Fair Greek* (Poss. same as *Mahomet*, or *The Love of a Grecian Lady* [*The Grecian Comedy*]; see 1599 add.)	1581–1594
	Wilson, Robert	*The Three Lords and Three Ladies of London*	1588–1590
	Anon.	*Sylla Dictator* (*Catiline*)	16 Jan.
	Anon.	*The Wars of Cyrus* (based on play by Farrant, *c.* 1578?)	1587–1594
1589	Greene, Robert	*Friar Bacon and Friar Bungay*	1589–1590
	Kempe, William	*Rowland (Rowland and the Sexton)*	*c.* 1589
	Lyly, John	*Midas*	1589
	Marlowe, C. (revised by Heywood, T., *c.* 1632?)	*The Jew of Malta*	*c.* 1589–1590
	Munday, Anthony	*John a Kent and John a Cumber*	*c.* 1587–1590
	Peele, George	*The Battle of Alcazar* (Poss. same as *Muly Molloco*, 1599 add.)	1588–1589
	Anon. (poss. Kyd, T.)	*Hamlet*	*c.* 1587–*c.* 1590
	Anon.	*King Ebrauk with All His Sons*	1589

TYPE	AUSPICES	EARLIEST TEXTS	LATEST TEXTS
Athletic Show	For Leicester at Utrecht	Lost	
Satirical Comedy	Clare Hall, Cambridge (?)	Lost	
Tragedy	Cambridge (?) Inner Temple?	MS	C
Show	Unknown	Lost	
Heroical Romance	Queen's (?)	1599*	G,M,T
Biblical History	Unknown	Lost	
Tragedy	Strange's (by 1592)	[c. 1592]	D,G,S,F
Heroical Romance	Admiral's	1590	M,C,S,F
Romance (?)	Unknown	Lost	
Royal Entertainment	Tilbury Camp	1588/[1588]	C
Biblical Moral	Queen's (?)	1594 F	G,M,T
Tragedy	Gray's Inn at Court	1587[88]* F	C,D
Wedding Mask	Scottish Court	MSS	C
Comedy	Closet	1588*	
Comedy	Closet	Lost	
Tragedy	St John's Col., Oxford	Lost	
Classical History	Admiral's (by 1594)	1594*	G,D,S
Classical Legend (Comedy)	Paul's at Court	1591	C,T
Heroical Romance	Admiral's	1590	C,M,S
Civic Pageant	London	Lost	
Heroical Romance	Unknown (Admiral's in 1594?)	Lost	
Moral	Queen's (?)	1590* F	D
Classical History	Gray's Inn	Lost	
Classical History	'Chapel'	1594* F	E
Comedy	Strange's (by 1592)	1594 F	E,S,M,G
Jig	Unknown	Lost	
Comedy	Paul's	1592	C,S
Tragedy	Strange's (by 1592)	1633*	M,C,S,F
Pseudo-history	Admiral's (?) Strange's (?)	MS F	G,T
Foreign History	Admiral's (by 1594)	1594* & MS ('plot') F	G,C
Tragedy	Chamb.'s & Adm.'s (by 1594)	Lost	C (plot)
Show	Chester	Lost	

DATE	AUTHOR	TITLE	LIMITS
1590	Greene, Robert	*The Scottish History of James IV*	*c.* 1590
	Greene, Robert (?)	*George a Greene, the Pinner of Wakefield*	1587–1593
	Greene, R.; Lodge T.	*A Looking Glass for London and England*	1587–1591
	Herbert, Mary	*Antonius* (*Antony*) (Trans. Garnier's *Marc-Antoine.*)	1590
	Lee, H.; Peele, G.	*Polyhymnia* (Directed by Lee; described by Peele.)	17 Nov.
	Lyly, John	*Love's Metamorphosis*	*c.* 1588–1590
	Nelson, Thomas	*The Pageant for John Allot*	29 Oct.
	Peele, George	*The Old Wives Tale* (Revised for provincial perf.?)	*c.* 1588–1594
	Salterne, George	*Tomumbeius sive Sultanici in Aegypto Imperii Eversio*	*c.* 1580–1603
	Shakespeare, William	*I Henry VI*	1590
	Shakespeare, William	*II Henry VI* (*I The First Part of the Contention of the Two Famous Houses of York and Lancaster*)	*c.* 1590
	Wilson, Robert	*The Cobbler's Prophecy*	*c.* 1589–1593
	Anon.	*The Dead Man's Fortune*	*c.* 1590–1591
	Anon. (Shakespeare in part?)	*Edward III, The Reign of King* [Shakespeare Apocrypha]	*c.* 1590–1595
	Anon. (Wilson, R.?)	*Fair Em, the Miller's Daughter* [Shakespeare Apocrypha]	*c.* 1589–1591
	Anon.	*King Leir, The True Chronicle of*	*c.* 1588–1594
	Anon.	*Mucedorus* (*and Amadine*) [Shakespeare Apocrypha]	1588–1598 (revised 1610)
	Anon.	*Rowland's Godson*	*c.* 1590
	Anon.	*The Welcome for Queen Anne*	19 May
1591	Fraunce, Abraham	*Phillis and Amyntas* (*Ivychurch, Amyntas' Pastoral*) (Trans. Tasso.)	1591
	Greene, R. (& Rowley, S.?)	*Orlando Furioso* (Same as *Brandimer,* 1599 add.?)	1591
	Lyly, John	*Mother Bombie*	1587–1590
	Peele, George	*Descensus Astraea*	29 Oct.
	Peele, George	*Edward I*	1590–1593
	Shakespeare, William	*III Henry VI* (*The True Tragedy of Richard Duke of York and the Good King Henry the Sixth*)	*c.* 1591
	Shakespeare, William	*The Life and Death of King John*	1590–1591
	Anon. (Kyd, T.?)	*Arden of Faversham* [Shakespeare Apocrypha]	1588–1592
	Anon. (Lyly, J.?)	*The Entertainment at Cowdray*	14 Aug.
	Anon. (Breton, N.; Lyly, J.; Johnson, J.?)	*The Entertainment at Elvetham*	20–23 Sept.
	Anon.	*A Fig for a Spaniard* (Poss. not a play title.)	*c.* 1578–1592
	Anon.	*Jack Straw*	1590–1593

TYPE	AUSPICES	EARLIEST TEXTS	LATEST TEXTS
Romantic Comedy	Queen's (?)	1598*	G,M,S,T
Romantic Comedy	Sussex's (by 1593)	1599* F	G,M,T
Biblical Moral	Queen's (?)	1594	F
Tragedy	Closet	1592	
Tilt	Court	1590 & MS	C
Pastoral	Paul's	1601*	C,T
Civic Pageant	London	1590*	C
Romance	Queen's	1595*	C,E
Latin Tragedy	Unknown	MS	G,S,F,T
History	Strange's	1623 F	V (in prog.)
History	Pembroke's (poss. offshoot of Strange's)	1594 F	F
Comedy	At Court (?)	1594* F	G,T
Romantic Comedy	Admiral's (?)	MS ('plot') F	C
History	Admiral's (?)	1596 F	C,S,T
Romantic Comedy	Strange's	[1593?] F	G,C,T
Legendary History	Queen's (?)	1605* F	G,F,C,T
Romantic Comedy	Unknown (King's in 1610)	1598 F	D,C,T
Jig	Unknown	MS	C
Royal Reception	Edinburgh	1590* (descrip.)	C
Pastoral	Closet	1591*	
Romantic Comedy	Queen's and Strange's	1594 & MS (frag. of Orlando's part) F	G,M,G (Orlando's part)
Comedy	Paul's	1594	G
Civic Pageant	London	[1591]*	C
History	Queen's (?)	1593	G,C
History	Pembroke's (poss. offshoot of Strange's)	1595 F	V (in prog.)
History	Chamberlain's	1623 F	V
Realistic Tragedy	Unknown	1592 F	G,F,C,S,F
Royal Entertainment	Host: Anthony Browne	1591 (2nd ed. lost)	C
Royal Entertainment	Host: Edward Seymour	1591 (2nd ed. lost)	C
Unknown	At the Bull Inn	Lost	
History	Unknown	1593 (coloph. 1594) F	G,D

DATE	AUTHOR	TITLE	LIMITS
	Anon.	*Octavia*	1590(?)–1591
	Anon.	*The Troublesome Reign of King John* (A play in two parts; may be derived from Shakespeare's *Life and Death of King John*.)	1591
	Anon.	*The True Tragedy of Richard III*	1588–1594
1592	Alabaster, William	*Roxana* (Adapt. Groto's *La Dalida*.)	1590–*c.* 1595
	Edes, R. (& Lee, H.?)	*The Second Woodstock Entertainment*	20 Sept.
	Gager, William	*Panniculus Hippolyto Assutus*	8 Feb.
	Gager, William	*Ulysses Redux*	6 Feb.
	Greene, Robert (?)	*I Selimus* (Second part unknown.)	1591–1594
	Greene, R. (?); Chettle, H. (prob. reviser rather than collab.)	*John of Bordeaux, or The Second Part of Friar Bacon*	1590–1594
	Herbert, Mary	*Thenot and Piers in Praise of Astraea* (*The Royal Entertainment at Ramsbury*)	1592(?)
	Marlowe, C. (& Rowley, S.?)	*Doctor Faustus* (Additions by W. Bird and S. Rowley in 1602.)	1592–1593
	Marlowe, Christopher	*Edward II*	1591–1593
	Nashe, Thomas	*Summer's Last Will and Testament* (Expansion of entertainment written by Lyly for Queen's progress in 1591?)	1592
	Shakespeare, William	*The Comedy of Errors*	*c.* 1590–1593
	Shakespeare, William	*The Tragedy of King Richard III*	1591–1592
	Shakespeare, William	*The Taming of the Shrew*	*c.* 1590–1604
	Warner, William	*Menaechmi* (Trans. Plautus.)	1592(?)–1594
	Anon. (Lyly, J.?)	*The Entertainment at Bisham*	21 Aug.
	Anon. (Lyly, J.?)	*The Entertainment at Rycote*	10, 11 Sept.
	Anon. (Lyly, J.?)	*The Entertainment at Sudeley*	28 Sept.; 1, 2 Oct.
	Anon. (Kempe? Peele? Wilson?)	*A Knack to Know a Knave*	10 June
	Anon.	*I Richard II, or Thomas of Woodstock* (*Woodstock*)	1591–1595
	Anon. (Kyd, T.?)	*Soliman and Perseda* (*Zulziman*)	*c.* 1589–1592
	Anon.	*I Tamar Cham* (See 1596.)	1592–1593
	Anon.	*II Tamar Cham* (See 1596.)	28 April
	Anon. (poss. Shakespeare, W.)	*The Taming of a Shrew* (Poss. derived from Shakespeare's *The Taming of the Shrew*.)	*c.* 1592–1594
	Anon.	*The Tanner of Denmark* (i.e. *Tamworth*?) (Part basis of *Edward IV*, 1599?)	23 [26] May
	Anon.	*Titus and Vespasian*	11 Apr.
1593	Attowell, George	*Attowell's Jig* (*Francis and Richard*)	*c.* 1590–1595
	Daniel, Samuel	*Cleopatra*	1593 (revised 1607)
	Lyly, John	*The Woman in the Moon*	1590–1595
	Marlowe, Christopher	*The Massacre at Paris*	30/26/Jan.

TYPE	AUSPICES	EARLIEST TEXTS	LATEST TEXTS
Latin (?) Play	Christ Church, Oxford	Lost	
History	Queen's	1591 F	C,T
History	Queen's	1594★	G
Latin Tragedy	Trinity Col., Cambridge	1632 & MSS	T,F
Royal Entertainment	Court	MSS (frags.)	C
Latin Additions to Seneca	Christ Church, Oxford	1592★	F
Latin Tragedy	Christ Church, Oxford	1592★	T,F
Heroical Romance	Queen's	1594★★	G,C
Comedy	Strange's (?)	MS	G,E
Pastoral Dialogue	Host: Pembroke	1602	C
Tragedy	Admiral's (by 1594)	1604 F	M,S,F
History	Pembroke's	1594	M,G,S,W
Comedy	Whitgift's household (?)	1600★	D,C
Comedy	Strange's (?)	1623 F	V
History	Strange's (?) Pembroke's (?)	1597 F	1908 V new V (in prog.)
Comedy	Sussex's (?) Chamberlain's (?)	1623 F	
Comedy	Closet	1595★	C
Royal Entertainment	Host: Edward Hoby	1592★	C
Royal Entertainment	Host: Henry Lord Norris	1592★	C
Royal Entertainment	Host: Giles Brydges	1592★	C
Comedy	Strange's	1594★ F	D,S,T
History	Unknown (later Chamberlain's?)	MS (last leaf missing)	G,C,E
Tragedy	Unknown	[c. 1592] F	D,C,T
Heroical Romance	Strange's	Lost	
Heroical Romance	Strange's	Lost	
Comedy	Queen's (?) (Pembroke's on t.p., 1594	1594 F	C
Heroical Romance	Strange's	Lost	
Classical or British History	Strange's	Lost	
Jig	Strange's (?)	[1595?]★	C
Tragedy	Closet	1594	B,T
Comedy	Unknown	1597★	C
Foreign History	Strange's	[1594?]★ & MS	G,S

DATE	AUTHOR	TITLE	LIMITS
	Marlowe, C.; Day, J. (?)	*The Maiden's Holiday* (S.R., 1654, & Warburton.)	1586(?)–1593(?)
	Shakespeare, William	*The Two Gentlemen of Verona*	*c.* 1593–1594
	Anon.	*The Jealous Comedy* (See *Cosmo*, 1599 add. Also conjectured basis of *The Merry Wives of Windsor*, 1601.)	5 Jan.
	Anon. ('B.J.' on t.p.)	*Guy Earl of Warwick* (See also 1620.)	*c.* 1590–*c.* 1615
1594	Bacon (?); Campion; Davison; etc.	*Gesta Grayorum* (Narrative of a series of entertainments, including *The Amity of Graius and Templarius*, followed by speeches of six 'Councellors', prob. written by F. Bacon, 3 Jan. 1595; *Knights of the Helmet*, a Mask, 6 Jan. 1595; *Proteus and the Rock Adamantine*, a Mask, written by Campion and Davison, 3 Mar. 1595.)	1594 and 1595
	Cecil, Robert	*The Queen's Entertainment at Theobalds*	13–23 June
	Heywood, Thomas	*The Four Prentices of London* (Related to *Jerusalem*, 1599 add., and *II Godfrey of Boulogne*, 1594?)	1594
	Kyd, Thomas	*Cornelia* (*Pompey the Great His Fair Cornelia's Tragedy*) (Trans. Garnier's *Cornélie*.)	1594 (pub.)
	Kyd, Thomas	*Portia* (Trans. Garnier's *Porcie*.) (Projected only?)	1594
	Peele, George	*The Love of King David and Fair Bethsabe*	*c.* 1593–1594
	'W.S.' (Peele? Greene?)	*Locrine* (Collier [forgery?] calls *Elstrid* and assigns to G. Buck, and C. Tilney, who d. 1586.) [Shakespeare Apocrypha]	*c.* 1594
	Shakespeare, William (reviser?)	*Titus Andronicus* (*The Most Lamentable Tragedy of Titus Andronicus*) (Related to *Titus and Vespasian*, 1592?) (Poss. originally written in 1590–2.)	23 [24] Jan.
	Yarington, Robert	*Two Lamentable Tragedies*	1594–*c.* 1598
	Anon. (Peele, G.?)	*Alphonsus, Emperor of Germany* (Ascribed in S.R., 1653, to John Peele, and on t.p. to Chapman.)	b.1604(?) (revised, *c.* 1630?)
	Anon.	*The Baptism of Prince Henry*	30 Aug.
	Anon.	*Bellendon* (i.e. *Belin Dun*) (Same as *King Rufus* [i.e. *Henry*] *I, with the Life and Death of Belyn Dun*, S.R., 1595?)	8 [10] June
	Anon.	*I Caesar and Pompey*	8 Nov.
	Anon. (Dekker, T.?)	*Diocletian* (Basis of *The Virgin Martyr*, 1620?)	16 Nov.
	Anon.	*Galiaso*	26 [28] June
	Anon. (Heywood, T.?)	*I Godfrey of Boulogne*	1594–1595
	Anon. (Heywood, T.?)	*II Godfrey of Boulogne* (Related to *Jerusalem* 1599 add., and *The Four Prentices of London*, 1600? Prob. same as 'interlude'	19 July

TYPE	AUSPICES	EARLIEST TEXTS	LATEST TEXTS
Comedy	Unknown	Lost	
Comedy	Unknown (later Chamberlain's)	1623 F	
Comedy	Strange's	Lost	
Heroical Romance	'King's (II Derby's Men in 1618?)	1661*	
Royal Entertainment	Gentlemen of Gray's Inn	1688* & MSS (frags.)	G,C
Royal Entertainment	Host: Wm. Lord Burghley	MS (frag.)	C
Heroical Romance	Admiral's	1615	C,T
Tragedy	Closet (?)	1594**	D,C
Tragedy	Closet (?)	Lost	
Biblical History	Unknown	1599*	G,T
Pseudo-history	Unknown	1595 F	G,C,S,F
Tragedy	Pembroke's, Sussex's	1594 F & MS (frag.)	V (in prog.)
Tragedy	Admiral's (?)	1601* F	C,T
Tragedy	Unknown (later King's)	1654* F	C [Chapman]
Royal Entertainment	Stirling Castle	1594 (descrip.)	
History	Admiral's	Lost	
Classical History	Admiral's	Lost	
Classical History (?)	Admiral's	Lost	
Unknown	Admiral's	Lost	
Heroical Romance (?)	Admiral's	Lost	
Heroical Romance (?)	Admiral's	Lost	

DATE	AUTHOR	TITLE	LIMITS
		of *Godfrey of Boulogne, with the Conquest of Jerusalem*, S.R., 1594.)	
	Anon.	*Heliogabalus* (Same as *The Mad Priest of the Sun*, 1587?)	1594 (S.R.)
	Anon.	*John of Gaunt* (Poss. not a play.)	1594 (S.R.)
	Anon. (Munday? Heywood?)	*A Knack to Know an Honest Man*	22 [23] Oct.
	Anon.	*The Love of an English Lady*	24 [25] Sept.
	Anon.	*The Merchant of Emden*	30 July
	Anon.	*Palamon and Arcite*	17 [18] Sept.
	Anon. (poss. Dekker, T.)	*Philipo and Hippolito* (Basis of Massinger's *Philenzo and Hippolyta*, 1620?)	9 July
	Anon.	*Robin Hood and Little John*	1594 (S.R.)
	Anon.	*The Set at Maw*	14 Dec.
	Anon. (revised by Dekker, 1602)	*Tasso's Melancholy*	11 [13] Aug.
	Anon. (James I & Fowler, W.?)	*The Three Christians* (Part of baptismal celebrations.)	23 Aug.
	Anon.	*The Venetian Comedy*	25 [27] Aug.
	Anon.	*The Wise Man of West Chester* (Related to *John a Kent*, 1589?)	2 [3] Dec.
1595	Dekker, Thomas (?)	*Disguises, or Love in Disguise, a Petticoat Voyage* (Author and double title given by Hill; see Supp. II, m. Henslowe mentions only *The Disguises*, 1595, without naming an author.)	2 Oct.
	Kempe, William (?)	*The Broom-Man*	b.1595
	Kempe, William (?)	*The Kitchen Stuff Woman*	b.1595
	Kempe, William (?)	*Singing Simpkin* (*A Soldier, and a Miser, and Sym the Clown*)	b.1595
	Munday; Dekker; Chettle; Heywood (?); Shakespeare (?)	*Sir Thomas More* (Revision of play originally composed *c*. 1590-3; 1600 and later also urged for revision.) [Shakespeare Apocrypha]	*c.* 1593-*c.* 1601
	Peele, George (describer)	*Anglorum Feriae*	17 Nov.
	Phillips, Augustine (?)	*The Slippers*	b.1595
	Shakespeare, William	*Love's Labour's Lost*	*c.* 1595
	Shakespeare, William	*Richard II* (*The Tragedy of King Richard II*)	1595
	Anon.	*Barnardo and Fiammetta*	28 [30] Oct.
	Anon.	*II Caesar and Pompey*	18 June
	Anon.	*Caesar and Pompey, or Caesar's Revenge*	*c.* 1592-*c.* 1596
	Anon.	*Crack Me This Nut*	5 Sept.
	Anon.	*Edmond Ironside, or War Hath Made All Friends* [Shakespeare Apocrypha]	*c.* 1590-1600

TYPE	AUSPICES	EARLIEST TEXTS	LATEST TEXTS
Romance (?)	Unknown	Lost	
History	Unknown	Lost	
Tragicomedy	Admiral's	1596★ F	G
Comedy (?)	Admiral's	Lost	
Realistic Tragicomedy (?)	Admiral's	Lost	
Tragedy (?)	Admiral's	Lost	
Tragicomedy (?)	Admiral's	Lost	
'Pastoral Comedy'	Unknown	Lost	
Comedy (?)	Admiral's	Lost	
Tragedy (?)	Admiral's	Lost	
Mask	Stirling Castle	Lost	
Comedy	Admiral's	Lost	
Pseudo-history (?)	Admiral's	Lost	
Comedy (?)	Admiral's	Lost	
Jig	Strange's and Chamberlain's (?)	Lost	
Jig	Strange's and Chamberlain's (?)	Lost	
Jig	Strange's and Chamberlain's (?)	[1655?]	C
History	Unknown (Chamberlain's?)	MS F	G,C,T
Tilt	Court	MS	C
Jig	Strange's and Chamberlain's (?)	Lost	
Comedy	Unknown (later Chamberlain's)	1597 F	1904 V; 1966 V
History	Chamberlain's	1597 F	1955 V; 1977 VS
Romance (?)	Admiral's	Lost	
Classical History	Admiral's	Lost	
Tragedy	Trinity Col., Oxford	[c. 1606]★★ F	E
Comedy (?)	Admiral's	Lost	
History	Unknown	MS	G,T,C

DATE	AUTHOR	TITLE	LIMITS
	Anon.	*The French Comedy*	11 Feb.
	Anon.	*Henry V*	28 Nov.
	Anon.	*I Hercules*	7 May
	Anon.	*II Hercules*	23 May
	Anon.	*Judith* (Trans. Schonaeus's *Judithae Constantia.*)	1595–*c.* 1600
	Anon.	*Laelia* (Adapt. *Gl' Ingannati* through Estienne's *Le Sacrifice* [*Les Abusez*].) (Revival of play performed at Queen's Col., 1546?)	1 Mar.
	Anon.	*Long Meg of Westminster*	14(?) Feb.
	Anon.	*Longshanks* (Poss. a revision of Peele's *Edward I*; see also *The Welshman*, 1599 add.)	29 Aug.
	Anon. (Bacon? Essex?)	*Love and Self-Love* (*The Essex Entertainment*)	17 Nov.
	Anon.	*The Mack*	21 Feb.
	Anon.	*The New World's Tragedy*	17 Sept.
	Anon.	*Ninus and Semiramis* (Poss. not a play.)	1595 (S.R.)
	Anon.	*Seleo and Olympio* (Prob. same as *Olympio and Heugenyo* [*Eugenio*].)	5 Mar.
	Anon.	*I The Seven Days of the Week*	3 June
	Anon.	*A Toy to Please Chaste Ladies*	14 Nov.
	Anon.	*Valentine and Orson* (Basis of *Valentine and Orson*, 1598?)	1595 (S.R.)
	Anon.	*The Wonder of a Woman* (Poss. basis of *A New Wonder, a Woman Never Vexed*, 1611)	15 [16] Oct.
1596	Burton, William	*Amores Perinthi et Tyantes*	1596
	Chapman, George	*The Blind Beggar of Alexandria* (*Irus*)	12 Feb.
	Greville, Fulke	*Mustapha*	*c.* 1594–*c.* 1596
	Jonson, Ben	*A Tale of a Tub* (Substantially new when lic., 7 May 1633?)	1595–1598
	Shakespeare, William	*The Merchant of Venice* (*The Comical History of the Merchant of Venice, or Otherwise Called The Jew of Venice*)	1596–1598
	Shakespeare, William	*A Midsummer-Night's Dream*	1596
	Shakespeare, William	*Romeo and Juliet* (*The Most Excellent and Lamentable Tragedy of Romeo and Juliet*)	1594–1596
	Anon. (Heywood, T., in part?)	*Captain Thomas Stukeley* (Revised *c.* 1599?)	11 [10] Dec.
	Anon.	*Chinon of England*	3 Jan.
	Anon.	*Julian the Apostate*	29 Apr.
	Anon.	*Nebuchadnezzar*	19 [18] Dec.
	Anon.	*Paradox*	1 July
	Anon.	*Phocasse* (*Focas*)	19 [20] May
	Anon.	*Pythagoras*	16 Jan.
	Anon.	*II The Seven Days of the Week*	22 [23] Jan.
	Anon.	*I The Seven Days of the Week*	Feb., 1596
	Anon.	*I Tamar Cham* (New version of play? See 1592.)	6 [7] May

TYPE	AUSPICES	EARLIEST TEXTS	LATEST TEXTS
Comedy	Admiral's	Lost	
History	Admiral's	Lost	
Classical Legend	Admiral's	Lost	
Classical Legend	Admiral's	Lost	
Sacred Comedy	Closet	MS (frag.)	E
Latin Comedy	Queens' Col., Cambridge	MS	E,F
Comedy (?)	Admiral's	Lost	
History	Admiral's	Lost	
Royal Entertainment	Court	MSS (frags.)	C
Comedy (?)	Admiral's	Lost	
Tragedy	Admiral's	Lost	
'Tragedie'	Unknown	Lost	
Classical Legend	Admiral's	Lost	
Moral (?)	Admiral's	Lost	
Comedy	Admiral's	Lost	
Romance	Queen's	Lost	
Comedy (?)	Admiral's	Lost	
Latin Play	Unacted	Lost	
Comedy	Admiral's	1598*	G
Tragedy	Closet	1609 & MSS	C
Comedy	Admiral's (?)	1640	B,C
Comedy	Chamberlain's	1600 F	1888 V; 1965 V
Comedy	Chamberlain's	1600 F	1895 V; 1965 V
Tragedy	Chamberlain's (?)	1597 F	1871 V
History	Admiral's	1605* F	C,S
Heroical Romance	Admiral's	Lost	
Classical History	Admiral's	Lost	
Biblical History	Admiral's	Lost	
Comedy (?)	Admiral's	Lost	
Classical History (?)	Admiral's	Lost	
Classical Biography (?)	Admiral's	Lost	
Moral (?)	Admiral's	Lost	
Moral (?)	Admiral's	Lost	
Heroical Romance	Admiral's	Lost MS ('plot' of 1602)	C

DATE	AUTHOR	TITLE	LIMITS
	Anon.	*II Tamar Cham* (New version of play? See 1592.)	11 June
	Anon.	*That Will Be Shall Be*	30 Dec.
	Anon.	*The Tinker of Totness*	18 [23] July
	Anon.	*Troy*	22 [25] June
	Anon.	*Vortigern* (*Valteger*) (See *Hengist*, 1599 add.)	4 Dec.
1597	Chapman, George	*An Humorous Day's Mirth* (*The Comedy of Humours*)	11 May
	Jonson, Ben	*The Case is Altered* (Interpolations later.)	1597–1598
	Morrell, Roger (?) (Pratt, Henry or John?) (completed by Jonson, Ben)	*Hispanus*	Feb. or Mar.
	Nashe, T.	*The Isle of Dogs*	July
	Shakespeare, William	*I Henry IV* (*The History of Henry the Fourth*)	*c.* 1596–1597
	Shakespeare, William	*II Henry IV* (*The Second Part of Henry the Fourth*)	*c.* 1597–1598
	Shakespeare, William	*The Merry Wives of Windsor* (First perf. 23 Apr. 1597)	1597
	Wilburne, Nathaniel (?)	*Machiavellus*	9 Dec.
	Anon.	*Alexander and Lodowick*	14 Jan.
	Anon.	*Alice Pierce*	8–10 Dec. (prop.)
	Anon.	*Black Joan*	1597(?)
	Anon.	*Branhowlte* (*Brunhild*)	26 Nov.
	Anon.	*The Cobbler* (*of Queenhithe*)	21 (or 23) Oct. (P)
	Anon.	*Five Plays in One*	7 Apr.
	Anon.	*Frederick and Basilea*	3 June
	Anon.	*The French Comedy*	18 Apr.
	Anon.	*Friar Spendleton*	31 Oct.
	Anon.	*Guido*	19 [21] Mar.
	Anon.	*Henry I* (Basis of *The Famous Wars of Henry I*, 1598?)	26 May
	Anon.	*Martin Swart*	30 June
	Anon. (poss. Dekker, T.)	*Pontius Pilate* (Prol. and Epil. in 1601 by Dekker.)	*c.* 1597–1601
	Anon. (Rollinson, F.?)	*Silvanus*	1597–1598
	Anon.	*Uther Pendragon* (Basis of *Merlin*, 1608?)	29 Apr.
	Anon.	*A Woman Hard to Please*	27 Jan.
1598	Bernard, Richard	*Terence in English*: *Andria, Eunuchus, Adelphi, Heautontimorumenus, Hecyra, Phormio* (Trans. Terence.)	1598 (pub.)

TYPE	AUSPICES	EARLIEST TEXTS	LATEST TEXTS
Heroical Romance	Admiral's	Lost	
Unknown	Admiral's	Lost	
Comedy (?)	Admiral's	Lost	
Classical Legend	Admiral's	Lost	
History	Admiral's	Lost	
Comedy	Admiral's	1599*	G,C
Comedy	Unknown (later Queen's Revels)	1609	C
Latin Comedy	St John's Col., Cambridge	MS	F
Satirical Comedy	Pembroke's	Lost	
History	Chamberlain's	[1598] F & MS (frag.)	1936 V; 1956 V S
History	Chamberlain's	1600 F	1940 V; 1977 V S
Comedy	Chamberlain's	1602 F	V (in prog.)
Latin Comedy	St John's Col., Cambridge	MS	F
Romance (?)	Admiral's	Lost	
History	Pembroke's and Admiral's	Lost	
Tragedy (?)	Pembroke's (?) (Admiral's in 1598)	Lost	
Tragedy (?)	Pembroke's (?) and Admiral's	Lost	
Comedy (?)	Pembroke's and Admiral's	Lost	
Unknown	Admiral's	Lost	
Romance	Admiral's	MS ('plot') F	C
Comedy	Admiral's	Lost	
Comedy (?)	Pembroke's and Admiral's	Lost	
Unknown	Admiral's	Lost	
History	Admiral's	Lost	
History	Admiral's	Lost	
Biblical History	Pembroke's (?)	Lost	
Latin Comedy	St John's Col., Cambridge	MS	F
Pseudo-history	Admiral's	Lost	
Comedy	Admiral's	Lost	
Comedies	Closet	1598	

DATE	AUTHOR	TITLE	LIMITS
	Brandon, Samuel	*The Virtuous Octavia*	1598
	Chapman, George	*The Fount(ain) of New Fashions (The Ill [Jill]? of a Woman)*	16 May–12 Oct. (P)
	Chettle, Henry	*II The Conquest of Brute* (Prob. same as *Brute Greenshield*, 1599.)	12–22 Oct. (P)
	Chettle, Henry	*'Tis No Deceit to Deceive the Deceiver* (Not completed?)	25–28 Nov. (P)
	Chettle, Henry (reviser?)	*Vayvode* (An old play revised?)	29 Aug. (P)
	Chettle, Henry	*The Woman's Tragedy* (Not completed?)	14 July (P)
	Chettle; Dekker; Drayton	*The Famous Wars of Henry I and the Prince of Wales (The Welshman's Prize)*	13–13/20(?) Mar. (P)
	Chettle; Dekker; Drayton; Wilson	*I Black Bateman of the North*	2/9–22 May (P)
	Chettle; Dekker; Drayton; Wilson	*I & II Earl Godwin and His Three Sons*	25 Mar.–10 June (P)
	Chettle; Dekker; Drayton; Wilson	*Pierce of Exton* (Not completed?)	30 Mar./7 Apr. (P)
	Chettle; Drayton; Munday; Wilson	*The Funeral of Richard Coeur de Lion*	13–26 June (P)
	Chettle; Jonson; Porter	*Hot Anger Soon Cold*	18 Aug. (P)
	Chettle, H.; Munday, A.	*The Death of Robert, Earl of Huntingdon (II Robin Hood)*	20 Feb.–8 Mar. (P)
	Chettle, H.; Munday, A.	*The Downfall of Robert, Earl of Huntingdon (I Robin Hood)*	15 Feb. (P)
	Chettle, H.; Wilson, R.	*Catiline's Conspiracy (Catiline)* (Not completed?)	21–29 Aug. (P)
	Chettle, H.; Wilson, R.	*II Black Bateman of the North*	26 June–14 July (P)
	Chettle or Dekker; Drayton; Munday; Wilson	*Chance Medley*	19–24 Aug. (P)
	Day, J. (prob. completed by Chettle, H.)	*I The Conquest of Brute*	30 July–16 Sept. (P)
	Dekker, Thomas	*Phaeton* (Basis of *The Sun's Darling*, 1624?)	8–15 Jan. (P)
	Dekker, Thomas	*The Triangle* (or *Triplicity*) *of Cuckolds*	1 Mar. (P)
	Dekker, T.; Drayton, M.	*I, II, & III The Civil Wars of France*	29 Sept.–30 Dec. (P)
	Dekker, T.; Drayton, M.	*Connan, Prince of Cornwall*	16–20 Oct. (P)
	Dekker, T.; Drayton, M.	*[II] Worse (A) feared Than Hurt (II Hannibal and Hermes)*	30 Aug.–4 Sept. (P)
	Dekker; Drayton; Wilson	*[I] Hannibal and Hermes ([I] Worse (A) feared Than Hurt)*	17–27 July (P)
	Dekker; Drayton; Wilson	*The Madman's Morris*	31 June [1 July]–10 July (P)
	Dekker; Drayton; Wilson	*Pierce of Winchester*	28 July–10 Aug. (P)

TYPE	AUSPICES	EARLIEST TEXTS	LATEST TEXTS
Tragicomedy	Closet	[1598]** F	G
Comedy	Admiral's	Lost	
Pseudo-history (?)	Admiral's	Lost	
Comedy (?)	Admiral's	Lost	
Foreign History (?)	Admiral's	Lost	
Tragedy	Admiral's	Lost	
History	Admiral's	Lost	
Tragedy (?)	Admiral's	Lost	
History	Admiral's	Lost	
History	Admiral's	Lost	
History	Admiral's	Lost	
Comedy	Admiral's	Lost	
History	Admiral's	1601* F	D,S,T
History	Admiral's	1601* F	D,S,C,T
Classical History	Admiral's	Lost	
Tragedy (?)	Admiral's	Lost	
Comedy	Admiral's	Lost	
Pseudo-history (?)	Admiral's	Lost	
Classical Legend	Admiral's	Lost	
Comedy	Admiral's	Lost	
Foreign History	Admiral's	Lost	
History	Admiral's	Lost	
Unknown	Admiral's	Lost	
Unknown	Admiral's	Lost	
Comedy (?)	Admiral's	Lost	
Unknown	Admiral's	Lost	

DATE	AUTHOR	TITLE	LIMITS
	Drayton, M.; Munday, A.	*Mother Redcap*	22 Dec. 1597–5 Jan. 1598 (P)
	Hathway, Richard	*Arthur, King of England*	11–12 Apr. (P)
	Hathway, R.; Munday, A.	*Valentine and Orson* (Based on *Valentine and Orson*, 1595?)	19 July (P)
	Haughton, William	*Englishmen for My Money, or A Woman Will Have Her Will*	18 Feb.– 2/9 May (P)
	Jonson, Ben	*Every Man in His Humour*	1598
	Porter, Henry	*Love Prevented*	30 May (P)
	Porter, Henry	*I The Two Angry Women of Abingdon*	1598(?)
	Rankins, William	*Mulmutius Dunwallow* (Poss. an old play.)	3 Oct. (P)
	Shakespeare, William	*Love's Labour's Won* (Same as *The Taming of the Shrew*, 1594, or *Much Ado about Nothing*, below?)	*c.* 1590–1598
	Shakespeare, William	*Much Ado about Nothing*	1598
	Anon.	*Astiages*	1597–1598
	Anon.	*Celestina* (Trans. or adapt. de Rojas.)	1598 (S.R.)
	Anon.	*Dido and Aeneas* (Poss. an old play.)	8 Jan. (acted)
	Anon. (Lyly, J.?)	*The Entertainment at Mitcham* (*Poet, Painter, and Musician*)	13 Sept.
	Anon.	*The Fair Maid of London*	1598 (lic.)
	Anon.	*A Mask of the Nine Passions*	6 Jan.
	Anon. (Lee, Robert, payee)	*The Miller* (Poss. an old play.)	22 Feb. (P)
	Anon.	'*Pope, Cardinals, Friars*'	July
	Anon.	*Sturgflaterey* (i.e. *Stark Flattery*? *Strange Flattery*?)	1598 (listed)
	Anon.	*The Wooing of Nan*	*c.* 1590–*c.* 1600
1599	Chapman, George	*All Fools but the Fool* (Title altered from *The World Runs on Wheels*. Basis of *All Fools*, 1601.)	22 Jan.– 2 July (P)
	Chapman, George	*The Four Kings*	18/22 Mar. (lic.)
	Chapman, George	*A Pastoral Tragedy* (Not completed?)	17 July (P)
	Chettle, Henry	*Troy's Revenge, with the Tragedy of Polyphemus*	16–27 Feb. (P)
	Chettle, H.; Dekker, T.	*Agamemnon* (Same as *Orestes' Furies*, below?)	2(?)–30 May (P)
	Chettle, H.; Dekker, T.	*The Stepmother's Tragedy*	23 Aug.– 14 Oct. (P)
	Chettle, H.; Dekker, T.	*Troilus and Cressida*	7–16 Apr. (P)
	Chettle; Dekker; Jonson (& Marston?)	*Robert II, King of Scots* (*The Scot's Tragedy*)	3–27 Sept. (P)
	Chettle, H.; Haughton, W.	*Arcadian Virgin* (Not completed?)	13–17 Dec. (P)

TYPE	AUSPICES	EARLIEST TEXTS	LATEST TEXTS
Comedy (?)	Admiral's	Lost	
Pseudo-history	Admiral's	Lost	
Romance	Admiral's	Lost	
Comedy	Admiral's	1616 F	D,G,E
Comedy	Chamberlain's	1601 F	C,B,M,S
Unknown	Admiral's	Lost	
Comedy	Admiral's	1599 F	G,D,M,T
Pseudo-history (?)	Admiral's	Lost	
Comedy	Chamberlain's (?)	Lost (?)	
Comedy	Chamberlain's	1600 F	1899 V; 1966 V
Latin (?) Tragedy	St John's Col., Oxford	Lost	
Romance	Closet (?)	Lost	
Classical Legend	Admiral's	Lost	
Royal Entertainment	Host: Dr Julius Caesar	MS	E
Romance (?)	Unknown	Lost	
Mask	Middle Temple at Court	Lost	
Comedy (?)	Admiral's	Lost	
Protestant Comedy	High School, Edinburgh	Lost	
Unknown	Admiral's	Lost	
Jig	Unknown	MS	C
Comedy	Admiral's	Lost	
Unknown	Admiral's	Lost	
Tragedy	Admiral's	Lost	
Classical Legend	Admiral's	Lost	
Classical Legend	Admiral's	Lost	
Tragedy	Admiral's	Lost	
Classical Legend	Admiral's	MS ('plot' frag.) F	C
History	Admiral's	Lost	
Pastoral (?)	Admiral's	Lost	

DATE	AUTHOR	TITLE	LIMITS
	Chettle, H.; Porter, H.	*The Spencers*	4–22 Mar. (P)
	Day, J.; Haughton, W.	*Cox of Collumpton (John Cox)*	1–14 Nov. (P)
	Day, J.; Haughton, W.	*Thomas Merry (Beech's Tragedy)*	21 Nov.– 6 Dec. (P)
	Dekker, Thomas	*Bear a Brain* (Title altered from *Better Late Than Never*.) (Poss. same as *The Shoemaker's Holiday*, below; or *Look about You*, below.)	1 Aug. (P)
	Dekker, Thomas	*The First Introduction of the Civil Wars of France*	20 Jan. (P)
	Dekker, Thomas	*Old Fortunatus* (See *I Fortunatus*, 1599 add.)	9–30 Nov. (P)
	Dekker, Thomas	*The Shoemaker's Holiday, or The Gentle Craft*	15 July (P)
	Dekker, T. (& Chettle, H.?)	*Orestes' Furies (Furens?)* (Same as *Agamemnon*, above?)	2 May (P)
	Dekker, T.; Jonson, B.	*Page of Plymouth*	10 Aug.– 2 Sept. (P)
	Drayton, Michael	*William Longbeard* (i.e. *Longsword?*) (Not completed?)	20 Jan. (P)
	Drayton; Hathway; Munday; Wilson	*I Sir John Oldcastle* [Shakespeare Apocrypha]	16 Oct. (P)
	Drayton; Hathway; Munday; Wilson	*II Sir John Oldcastle* (Additions by Dekker in 1602.)	16 Oct.– 19/26 Dec. (P)
	Haughton, William	*The Poor Man's Paradise* (Not completed?)	20–25 Aug. (P)
	Hawkesworth, Walter	*Leander* (Adapt. Sforza Oddi, *Frofilomachia*, 1572) (Revised when revived in 1602.)	7 Jan. (MS date)
	Heywood, Thomas	*Joan as Good as My Lady*	10–12 Feb. (P)
	Heywood, Thomas	*War without Blows and Love without Suit (or Strife)*	6 Dec. 1598–26 Jan. 1599 (P)
	Heywood, T. (?), and others (?)	*I & II Edward IV* (See *The Siege of London*, 1599 add., and *The Tanner of Denmark*, 1592.)	1592–1599
	Jonson, Ben	*Every Man out of His Humour*	1599
	Marston, John	*Antonio and Mellida*	1599–1600
	Marston, J. (reviser?) and others (?)	*Histriomastix, or The Player Whipped* (Based on play of *c.* 1589?) (The following titles, some no doubt fictitious, are mentioned in the above play: *A Knot of Knaves, Lady Nature, The Lascivious Knight, The Prodigal Child, A Proud Heart and a Beggar's Purse, A Russet Coat and a Knave's Cap, The Widow's Apron Strings*.)	1598–1599
	Porter, Henry	*II The Two Angry Women of Abingdon* (See following.)	22 Dec. 1598–12 Feb. 1599 (P)
	Porter, Henry	*Two Merry Women of Abingdon* (Not completed? Or same as preceding?)	28 Feb. (P)

TYPE	AUSPICES	EARLIEST TEXTS	LATEST TEXTS
History	Admiral's	Lost	
Tragedy	Admiral's	Lost	
Tragedy	Admiral's	Lost	
Comedy	Admiral's	Lost (?)	
History	Admiral's	Lost	
Comedy	Admiral's	1600★	C,M
Comedy	Admiral's	1600	M,C,S,F
Classical Legend	Admiral's (?)	Lost	
Tragedy	Admiral's	Lost	
History	Admiral's	Lost	
History	Admiral's	1600 F	G
History	Admiral's	Lost	
Comedy (?)	Admiral's	Lost	
Latin Comedy	Trinity Col., Cambridge	MSS (both versions)	T,F
Comedy	Admiral's	Lost	
Comedy (?)	Admiral's	Lost	
History	Derby's	1599 F	C,T
Comedy	Chamberlain's	1600 F	C,B,G
Tragicomedy	Paul's	1602	C,S,D
Comedy	Paul's (?) Middle Temple	1610★ F	C
Comedy	Admiral's	Lost	
Comedy	Admiral's	Lost	

DATE	AUTHOR	TITLE	LIMITS
	Ruggle, George (?)	*Re Vera, or Verily*	*c.* 1598–1620
	Shakespeare, William	*As You Like It*	1598–1599
	Shakespeare, William	*Henry V* (*The Life of Henry the Fifth*)	1599
	Shakespeare, William	*Julius Caesar* (*The Tragedy of Julius Caesar*)	1598–1599
	Wilson, Robert	*II Henry Richmond* (No first part known.)	8 Nov. (P)
	Anon. (Ruggle, George?)	*Club Law*	1599–1600
	Anon.	*Friar Fox and Gillian of Brentford*	10 Feb. (P)
	Anon.	*A Larum for London, or The Siege of Antwerp*	*c.* 1594–1600
	Anon. (poss. Chettle, Dekker, or Wadeson)	*Look about You* (Poss. same as *Bear a Brain*, above.)	*c.* 1597–1599
	Anon. (Gwyn, O., in part?)	*The Pilgrimage to Parnassus*	1598–1599
	Anon. ('John Webster and William Rowley' on t.p. rejected)	*The Thracian Wonder*	1590–*c.* 1601
	Anon.	*Tristram de Lyons* (A revised older play?)	13 Oct. (P)
	Anon.	*Turnholt*	1598–1599
	Anon. (Heywood, T.?)	*A Warning for Fair Women*	1596–1600
1599 ADDENDA		The following plays are known only through revivals, in the years 1592–1600, by Henslowe's groups. The year of the revival is here given as the posterior limit, followed by the month and day in round brackets; the company is that of the revival.	
	Anon.	*Abraham and Lot*	*c.* 1580–1594 (9 Jan.)
	Anon.	*Antony and Vallia* (Poss. basis by Dekker of Massinger's *Antonio and Vallia*, S.R. 1660, and Warburton's list.)	*c.* 1590(?)–1595 (4 Jan.)
	Anon.	*Bendo* (or *Byndo*) *and Richardo*	1580(?)–1592 (4 Mar.)
	Anon.	*Brandimer* (Same as *Orlando Furioso*, 1591?)	1588(?)–1592 (6 Apr.)
	Anon.	*Buckingham* (Poss. same as *The True Tragedy of Richard III*, 1591.)	1591(?)–1593 (30 [29] Dec.)
	Anon.	*Burbon* (i.e. *Bourbon*?)	*c.* 1580–1597 (2 Nov.)
	Anon.	*Clorys and Orgasto* (i.e. *Ergasto*?)	*c.* 1580–1592 (28 Feb.)
	Anon.	*Constantine*	*c.* 1580–1592 (21 Mar.)
	Anon.	*Cosmo* (Poss. *The Jealous Comedy*, 1593.)	1593(?)–1593 (12 [11] Jan.)
	Anon.	*Cutlack* (i.e. *Guthlac*?)	*c.* 1580–1594 (16 May)

TYPE	AUSPICES	EARLIEST TEXTS	LATEST TEXTS
Satirical Comedy	Clare Hall, Cambridge (?)	Lost	
Comedy	Chamberlain's	1623 F	1890 V; 1965 V
History	Chamberlain's	1600 F	1977 V
Tragedy	Chamberlain's	1623 F	1913 V
History	Admiral's	Lost	
Satirical Comedy	Clare Hall, Cambridge	MS	E,T
Comedy	Admiral's	Lost	
History	Chamberlain's	1602* F	G
Comedy	Admiral's	1600* F	G,E,D
Satirical Comedy	St John's Col., Cambridge	MS F	C
Comedy	Unknown	1661*	C
Romance	Admiral's	Lost	
Topical Play	Unknown	Lost	C,E
Romantic Comedy (?)	Chamberlain's	1599* F	C,T,E
Biblical History	Sussex's	Lost	
Romance (?)	Admiral's	Lost	
Comedy	Strange's and Admiral's	Lost	
Romantic Comedy (?)	Strange's and Admiral's	Lost (?)	
History	Sussex's	Lost (?)	
Foreign History (?)	Admiral's and Pembroke's	Lost	
Pastoral (?)	Strange's and Admiral's	Lost	
Classical or English History	Strange's and Admiral's	Lost	
Comedy (?)	Strange's and Admiral's	Lost	
Tragedy (?)	Admiral's	Lost	

DATE	AUTHOR	TITLE	LIMITS
	Anon. (Kyd. T.?)	*Don Horatio* (*Jeronimo. Spanish Comedy*) (Same as *I Jeronimo with the Wars of Portugal*, 1604?)	*c.* 1584–1592 (23 Feb.)
	Anon.	*The Fair Maid of Italy*	*c.* 1580–1594 (12 Jan.)
	Anon.	*I Fortunatus* (Basis of *Old Fortunatus*, 1599?)	*c.* 1580–1596 (3 Feb.)
	Anon.	*The French Doctor* (Same as *The Venetian Comedy*, 1594?)	1594(?)–1594 (18 [19] Oct.)
	Anon.	*Friar Francis*	*c.* 1580–1594 (7 Jan.)
	Anon.	*God Speed the Plough*	*c.* 1580–1593 (27 [26] Dec.)
	Anon.	*Hardicanute* (Canute)	*c.* 1580–1597 (20–30 Oct.)
	Anon.	*Harry of Cornwall*	*c.* 1580–1592 (25 Feb.)
	Anon.	*Hengist* (Same as *Vortigern*, 1596, and basis of *Hengist, King of Kent*, 1618?)	1596(?)–1597 (22 June)
	Anon.	*Hester and Ahasuerus*	*c.* 1580–1594 (3 [5] June)
	Anon.	*Huon of Bordeaux*	*c.* 1580–1593 (28 [27] Dec.)
	Anon.	*Jerusalem* (Related to *Godfrey of Boulogne*, with the Conquest of Jerusalem, S.R., 1594, and *II Godfrey of Boulogne*, 1594?)	*c.* 1580–1592 (22 Mar.)
	Anon.	*King Lud*	*c.* 1580–1594 (18 Jan.)
	Anon.	*Like unto Like* (Same as *Like Will to Like*, 1568?)	*c.* 1568–1600 (28 Oct.)
	Anon.	*The Love of a Grecian Lady* (*The Grecian Comedy*) (Same as *The Turkish Mahomet*, 1588, and *Mahomet*, below?)	1588(?)–1594 (4 [5] Oct.)
	Anon.	*Machiavel*	*c.* 1580–1592 (2 Mar.)
	Anon.	*Mahomet* (Same as *The Love of a Grecian Lady*, above, and *The Turkish Mahomet*, 1588?)	1588(?)–1594 (14 [16] Aug.)
	Anon.	*Muly Molloco* (Poss. same as *The Battle of Alcazar*, 1589.)	*c.* 1588–1592 (20 [21] Feb.)
	Anon.	*Osric*	*c.* 1580–1597 (3 Feb.)
	Anon.	*Pope Joan*	*c.* 1580–1592 (1 Mar.)
	Anon.	*The Ranger's Comedy*	*c.* 1580–1594 (2 Apr.)
	Anon.	*Richard the Confessor*	*c.* 1580–1593 (31 Dec.)
	Anon.	*Roderick*	*c.* 1580–1600 (29 Oct.)

TYPE	AUSPICES	EARLIEST TEXTS	LATEST TEXTS
Comedy	Strange's and Admiral's	Lost	
Comedy (?)	Sussex's	Lost	
Romantic Comedy	Admiral's	Lost	
Comedy (?)	Admiral's	Lost	
Realistic Tragedy (?)	Sussex's	Lost	
Comedy (?)	Sussex's	Lost	
History	Pembroke's and Admiral's	Lost	
History	Strange's and Admiral's	Lost	
History	Admiral's	Lost	
Biblical History	Admiral's or Chamberlain's	Lost	
Romance	Sussex's	Lost	
Heroical Romance (?)	Strange's	Lost	
History	Sussex's	Lost	
Unknown	Pembroke's	Lost	
Heroical Romance (?)	Admiral's	Lost	
Foreign History (?)	Strange's and Admiral's	Lost	
Heroical Romance (?)	Admiral's	Lost	
Foreign History	Strange's	Lost	
Unknown	Admiral's	Lost	
Foreign Pseudo-history	Strange's and Admiral's	Lost	
Comedy	Queen's and Sussex's	Lost	
History	Sussex's	Lost	
History (?)	Pembroke's	Lost	

DATE	AUTHOR	TITLE	LIMITS
	Anon.	*The Siege of London* (Part basis of *Edward IV*, 1599?)	*c.* 1580–1594 (26 [27] Dec.)
	Anon.	*Sir John Mandeville*	*c.* 1580–1592 (24 Feb.)
	Anon.	*Time's Triumph and Fortus* (i.e. *Fortune's?*)	*c.* 1580–1597 (13 Apr.)
	Anon.	*Warlamchester*	*c.* 1580–1594 (28 Nov.)
	Anon.	*The Welshman* (Same as *Longshanks*, 1595?)	1595(?)–1595 (29 Nov.)
	Anon.	*William the Conqueror* (Same as *Fair Em*, 1590?)	*c.* 1590(?)–1594 (4 Jan.)
	Anon.	*The Witch of Islington*	*c.* 1580–1597 (14 July)
	Anon.	*Zenobia*	*c.* 1580–1592 (9 Mar.)
1600	Boyle, William	*Jurgurth, King of Numidia*	9 Feb. (P) (re-lic. 3 May 1624)
	Chettle, Henry	*Damon and Pithias*	16 Feb.– 27 Apr./ 6 May (P)
	Chettle, Henry	*The Wooing of Death* (Not completed?)	27 Apr.–6 May (P)
	Chettle; Day; Dekker	*Cupid and Psyche* (*The Golden Ass*)	27 Apr./ 6 May– 14 May (P)
	Chettle; Day; Dekker; Haughton	*The Seven Wise Masters*	1–8/10 Mar. (P)
	Chettle; Day (& Haughton?)	*I The Blind Beggar of Bednal Green* (*I Tom Strowd*)	26 May (P)
	Chettle; Dekker; Haughton	*Patient Grissil*	16 Oct./ 1 Nov.– 29 Dec. (P)
	Day, John	*The Italian Tragedy of —* (Not completed?)	10 Jan. (P)
	Day; Dekker; Haughton (& Marston?)	*The Spanish Moor's Tragedy* (Prob. same as *Lust's Dominion*, below.)	13 Feb. (P)
	Dekker, Thomas	*The Fortewn Tenes* (i.e. *Fortune's Tennis?*) (Revision of *II Fortune's Tennis*, 1597?)	6 Sept. (P)
	Dekker, Thomas	*Truth's Supplication to Candlelight* (Basis of *The Whore of Babylon*, 1606?)	18–30 Jan. (P)
	Dekker; Drayton; Hathway; Munday; Wilson	*I Fair Constance of Rome*	3–14 June (P)
	Drayton; Hathway; Munday; Wilson	*Owen Tudor* (Not completed?)	10/18 Jan. (P)
	Greville, Fulke	*Alaham*	*c.* 1598–*c.* 1600
	Hathway, R.; & others	*II Fair Constance of Rome* (Not completed?)	20 June (P)

TYPE	AUSPICES	EARLIEST TEXTS	LATEST TEXTS
History	Admiral's	Lost	
Romantic Comedy (?)	Strange's and Admiral's	Lost	
Moral (?)	Admiral's	Lost	
History (?)	Admiral's	Lost	
History (?)	Admiral's	Lost	
Romantic Comedy (?)	Sussex's	Lost (?)	
Realistic Tragedy (?)	Admiral's	Lost (?)	
Classical History	Strange's and Admiral's	Lost	
Tragedy (?)	Admiral's	Lost	
Tragicomedy (?)	Admiral's	Lost	
Tragedy (?)	Admiral's	Lost	
Classical Legend	Admiral's	Lost	
Tragicomedy (?)	Admiral's	Lost	
Comedy	Admiral's	1659* F	B
Comedy	Admiral's	1603* F	C
Tragedy	Admiral's	Lost	
Tragedy	Admiral's	1657** (?)	C,B,D (?)
Unknown	Admiral's	Lost	
Allegorical History (?)	Admiral's	Lost (?)	
Classical History (?)	Admiral's	Lost	
History	Admiral's	Lost	
Tragedy	Closet	1633* & MS	C
Classical History (?)	Admiral's	Lost	

DATE	AUTHOR	TITLE	LIMITS
	Haughton, William	*The English Fugitives* (Not completed?)	16–24 Apr. (P)
	Haughton, William	*Ferrex and Porrex*	18 Mar.–3/ 13 Apr. (P) 6 May (P)
	Haughton, William (revised for press by 'I.T.')	*The Devil and His Dame* (Prob. same as *Grim the Collier of Croydon, or The Devil and His Dame*, pub. 1662.)	1593?–*c.* 1601
	Haughton, W.; Pett, [Peter?]	*Strange News out of Poland*	17 May (P)
	Jonson, Ben	*Cynthia's Revels, or The Fountain of Self-Love*	1600–1601
	Marston, John	*Antonio's Revenge (II Antonio and Mellida)*	1600–1601
	Marston, John	*Jack Drum's Entertainment (Katherine and Pasquil)*	1600
	Anon.	*Cloth Breeches and Velvet Hose*	1600 (S.R.)
	Anon.	*Give a Man Luck and Throw Him into the Sea*	1600 (S.R.)
	Anon. ('Christopher Marlowe' on t.p.; by Day; Dekker; Haughton? [& Marston?])	*Lust's Dominion, or The Lascivious Queen* (Prob. same as *The Spanish Moor's Tragedy,* above.)	13 Feb. (P)(?)
	Anon. (Day? Lyly?)	*The Maid's Metamorphosis*	1599–1600
	Anon. (Gwyn, O., in part?)	*I The Return from Parnassus*	1599–1601
	Anon.	*The Tartarian Cripple, Emperor of Constantinople* (Poss. non-dramatic.)	1600 (S.R.)
	Anon. (by 'W.S.')	*Thomas Lord Cromwell* [Shakespeare Apocrypha]	*c.* 1599–1602
	Anon. (Dekker, T., in part?)	*The Weakest Goeth to the Wall*	*c.* 1595–1600
	Anon.	*The Wisdom of Doctor Dodypoll*	1600 (published and performed)
1601	Bird; Haughton; Rowley, S.	*Judas* (Prob. same as *Judas* begun in 1600 by Haughton.)	27 May 1600– 24 Dec. 1601 (P)
	Chapman, George	*All Fools* (See *All Fools but the Fool,* 1599.)	1601
	Chettle, Henry	*All Is Not Gold That Glisters*	31 Mar.– 6 Apr. (P)
	Chettle, Henry	*The Life of Cardinal Wolsey*	5 June– 18 Aug. (P)
	Chettle, Henry	*The Orphans' Tragedy* (Not completed?)	10 Nov. 1599–24 Sept. 1601 (P)
	Chettle, H.; Dekker, T.	*Sebastian, King of Portugal* (Poss. the basis of *Believe as You List,* 1631.)	1601
	Chettle; Drayton; Munday; Smith, Went.	*The Rising of Cardinal Wolsey*	24 Aug.– 12 Nov. (P)

TYPE	AUSPICES	EARLIEST TEXTS	LATEST TEXTS
Topical Play (?)	Admiral's	Lost	
Tragedy (?)	Admiral's	Lost	
Comedy	Admiral's (?)	1662* F (?)	C,D (?)
Foreign History	Admiral's	Lost	
Comedy	Chapel	1601 F	C,M,B
Tragedy	Paul's	1602	C,G,S
Domestic Comedy	Paul's	1601 F	C
Comedy (?)	Chamberlain's	Lost	
Jig (?)	Unknown	Lost	
Tragedy	Admiral's (?)	1657**	C,B,D
Comedy	Paul's	1600* F	C
Satirical Comedy	St John's Col., Cambridge	MS F	C
'Tragical History'	Unknown	Lost	
History	'Chamberlain's'	1602 F	C
Pseudo-history	Oxford's	1600 F	G,C,S
Comedy	Paul's	1600* F	C,S
Biblical History	Admiral's	Lost	
Comedy	Queen's Revels	1605*	C,S
Comedy (?)	Admiral's	Lost	
History	Admiral's	Lost	
Tragedy	Admiral's	Lost	
Foreign History	Admiral's	Lost	
History	Admiral's	Lost	

DATE	AUTHOR	TITLE	LIMITS
	Day, J.; Haughton, W.	*II The Blind Beggar of Bednal Green* (*II Tom Strowd*)	29 Jan.– 5 May (P)
	Day, J.; Haughton, W.	*III The Blind Beggar of Bednal Green* (*III Tom Strowd*)	21 May– 30 July (P)
	Day, J.; Haughton, W.	*Friar Rush and the Proud Woman of Antwerp* ('Mended' by Chettle, Jan. 1602.)	4 July– 29 Nov. (P)
	Day, J.; Haughton, W.	*The Six Yeomen of the West*	20 May– 8 June (P)
	Day, J.; Haughton, W.	*II Tom Dough* (*II The Six Yeomen of the West?*)	30 July– 11 Sept. (P)
	Day; Haughton; Smith, Went	*The Conquest of the West Indies*	4 Apr.– 1 Sept. (P)
	Dekker, T. (with Marston, J.?)	*Satiromastix, or The Untrussing of the Humorous Poet*	1601
	Dymock, John (?)	*Il Pastor Fido, or The Faithful Shepherd* (Trans. Guarini.)	1601 (S.R.)
	Dymock, Tailbois	*The Death of the Lord of Kyme*	31 Aug.
	Greville, Fulke	*Antony and Cleopatra*	*c.* 1600–1601
	Hathway; Haughton; Smith, Went.	*I The Six Clothiers*	12–22 Oct. (P)
	Hathway; Haughton; Smith, Went.	*II The Six Clothiers* (Not completed?)	3/8 Nov. (P)
	Hathway, R.; Rankins, W.	*The Conquest of Spain by John of Gaunt* (Not completed.)	24 Mar.– 16 Apr. (P)
	Hathway, R.; Rankins, W.	*Hannibal and Scipio*	3–12 Jan. (P)
	Hathway, R.; Rankins, W.	*Scogan and Skelton*	23 Jan.– 8 Mar. (P)
	Haughton, William	*Robin Hood's Pennyworths* (Not completed? Or completion of *The English Fugitives,* 1600?)	20 Dec. 1600–13 Jan. 1601(P)
	Jonson, Ben	*Poetaster, or The Arraignment*	1601
	Marston, John	*What You Will*	1601
	Mitchell, Francis	*Michael and Frances*	1601–1602
	Percy, William	*Arabia Sitiens, or A Dream of a Dry Year* (*Mahomet and His Heaven, or Epimethea, Grand Empress of the Deserts of Arabia, or A Dream of a Dry Summer, or The Weather-Woman*)	1601
	Percy, William	*The Cuckqueans and Cuckolds Errants, or The Bearing Down the Inn* (*Change Is No Robbery, or The Bearing Down of the Inn*)	1601
	Shakespeare, William	*Hamlet* (*The Tragedy of Hamlet, Prince of Denmark*)	1600–1601
	Shakespeare, William	*Twelfth Night, or What You Will*	1601–1602
	Wadeson, Antony	*The Humorous Earl of Gloucester, with His Conquest of Portugal* (Not completed?)	13 June– 23/25 July (P)
	Anon. (Dekker?)	*Blurt, Master Constable, or The Spaniard's Night Walk*	1601–1602

TYPE	AUSPICES	EARLIEST TEXTS	LATEST TEXTS
Comedy	Admiral's	Lost	
Comedy	Admiral's	Lost	
Comedy (?)	Admiral's	Lost	
Comedy (?)	Admiral's	Lost	
Comedy (?)	Admiral's	Lost	
History	Admiral's	Lost	
Comedy	Chamberlain's and Paul's	1602*	C,B
Pastoral	Closet (?)	1602	
Topical Satire	'May Pole Green', Lincoln	Lost	
Tragedy	Closet	Lost	
Unknown	Admiral's	Lost	
Unknown	Admiral's	Lost	
History	Admiral's	Lost	
Classical History	Admiral's	Lost	
Comedy (?)	Admiral's	Lost	
Comedy (?)	Admiral's	Lost	
Comedy	Chapel	1602	B,M,S
Comedy	Paul's (?)	1607	C
Jig	Strollers in Yorkshire	MS F	C
Tragicomedy	Privately acted (?)	MSS	
Comedy	Privately acted (?)	MSS	E
Tragedy	Chamberlain's	1603 F	1877 V, 1965 V, F,D
Comedy	Chamberlain's	1623 F	1901 V, 1966 V, 1984 VS
History	Admiral's	Lost	
Comedy	Paul's	1602* & MS (frag.)	C,S

DATE	AUTHOR	TITLE	LIMITS
	Anon.	*The Contention between Liberality and Pro-digality* (Revival of *Prodigality*, 1567?).	22 Feb. (acted)
	Anon.	*George Scanderbarge*	1601 (S.R.)
	Anon. (Heywood? Chettle?)	*The Trial of Chivalry* (*This Gallant Cavaliero Dick Bowyer*)	1599–1604
1602	Chapman, George	*The Gentleman Usher* (*Vincentio and Margaret*)	c. 1602–1603
	Chapman, George	*May Day*	1601–1602
	Chapman, George	*Sir Giles Goosecap*	Sept. 18
	Chettle, Henry	*A Danish Tragedy*	7 July (P)
	Chettle, Henry	*Hoffman, or A Revenge for a Father*	29 Dec. (P)
	Chettle, Henry	*Tobias*	16 May–27 June (P)
	Chettle; Dekker, Heywood; Smith, Went; Webster	*I Lady Jane* (*The Overthrow of Rebels*) (Parts of *I & II Lady Jane* may be incorporated in *Sir Thomas Wyatt*, 1604.)	15–21 Oct. (P)
	Chettle; Dekker; Heywood; Webster	*Christmas Comes but Once a Year*	2–26 Nov. (P)
	Chettle; Hathway; Smith, Went	*Too Good to Be True*	14 Nov. 1601–7 Jan. 1602 (P)
	Chettle, H.; 'Mr. Robinson'	*Felmelanco*	9–15/27 Sept. (P)
	Chettle, H.; Smith, Went.	*Love Parts Friendship*	4 May (P)
	Davies, J. (& Cecil, R.?)	*The Entertainment at Cecil House*	6 Dec.
	Davies, J. (& Lyly, J.?)	*The Entertainment at Harefield*	31 July–2 Aug.
	Day, John	*Bristow Tragedy* (Poss. same as *Baxter's Tragedy*, below.)	4–28 May (P)
	Day; Hathway; Smith, Went.	*As Merry as May Be*	9–17 Nov. (P)
	Dekker, Thomas	*A Medicine for a Curst Wife*	19 July–22 Sept. (P)
	Dekker; Drayton; Middleton; Munday; Webster	*Caesar's Fall* (*Two Shapes*)	22–29 May (P)
	Dekker, T. (& others?)	*II Lady Jane* (Not completed? Parts of *I & II Lady Jane* may be incorporated in *Sir Thomas Wyatt*, below.)	27 Oct.–12 Nov. (?) (P)
	Dekker, T., Munday, A.	*Jephthah*	5 May (P)
	Dekker; Webster (& others?)	*The Famous History of Sir Thomas Wyatt* (A version of *I & II Lady Jane?*)	1602
	Haughton, William	*William Cartwright* (Not completed?)	8 Sept. (P)
	Heywood, T. ('additions' by)	*Cutting Dick*	1602 (revised)
	Heywood, T. (?) ('Joshua Cooke' rejected)	*How a Man May Choose a Good Wife from a Bad*	c. 1601–1602

TYPE	AUSPICES	EARLIEST TEXTS	LATEST TEXTS
Moral Interlude	Chapel	1602★ F	G,D
Foreign History	Oxford's	Lost	
Pseudo-history	Derby's	1605★★ F	C
Comedy	Chapel or Paul's	1606★	C,S
Comedy	Chapel	1611★	C
Comedy	Chapel (?)	1606 F	C,F,T
Tragedy	Admiral's	Lost	
Tragedy	Admiral's	1631★ F	G,T
Biblical History	Admiral's	Lost	
History	Worcester's	Lost (?)	
Comedy (?)	Worcester's	Lost	
Comedy (?)	Admiral's	Lost	
Unknown	Admiral's	Lost	
Unknown	Admiral's	Lost	
Royal Entertainment	Host: Robert Cecil	1608/MSS (frags.)	C
Royal Entertainment	Host: Thomas Egerton	MSS (frags.)	C
Tragedy	Admiral's	Lost	
Comedy	Admiral's	Lost	
Comedy	Worcester's	Lost	
Tragedy	Admiral's	Lost	
History	Worcester's	Lost (?)	
Biblical History	Admiral's	Lost	
History	Queen Anne's	1607 F	C
Unknown	Admiral's	Lost	
Topical Play	Worcester's	Lost	
Comedy	Worcester's	1602 F	B,D

DATE	AUTHOR	TITLE	LIMITS
	Heywood, T.; Smith, Went.	*Albere Galles* (Same as *Nobody and Somebody*, 1605?)	4 Sept. (P)
	Heywood, T.; Smith, Went.	*Marshal Osric* (Same as following?)	20–30 Sept. (P)
	Heywood, T. (& Smith, Went.?)	*The Royal King and the Loyal Subject* (See play above.)	1602–1618
	Hobbes, Thomas	*Medea* (Trans. Euripides.)	1602
	Jonson, Ben	*Richard Crookback* (Not completed?)	22 June (P)
	Lyly, John	*The Entertainment at Chiswick*	28–29 July
	Massey, Charles (?)	*Malcolm, King of Scots*	18 Apr. (P)
	Middleton, Thomas	*Randall, Earl of Chester* (*Chester Tragedy*)	21 Oct.– 9 Nov. (P)
	Munday, Anthony	*The Set at Tennis* (Related to *The Fortewn Tenes*, 1600?)	2 Dec. (P)
	Percy, William	*The Aphrodisial, or Sea Feast*	1602
	Percy, William	*A Country Tragedy in Vacunium or Cupid's Sacrifice* (*A Forest Tragedy in Vacunium, or Love's Sacrifice*)	1602
	Rowley, Samuel	*Joshua*	27 Sept. (P)
	Shakespeare, William	*Troilus and Cressida*	1602–1603
	Smith, W[entworth?]	*The Freeman's Honour*	c. 1600–1603
	Smith, Wentworth	*The Three* (or *Two*) *Brothers* (Poss. same as *Absalom*, below.)	1–15 Oct. (P)
	Vennar, Richard	*England's Joy*	1602
	'Antony (Wadeson? Munday?) the poet'	*The Widow's Charm* (Not completed?)	9 July– 11 Sept. (P)
	Anon.	*Absalom* (Character's name.) (Poss. same as *The Three Brothers*, above.)	3/11 Oct. (prop.)
	Anon.	*Baxter's Tragedy* (Poss. same as *Bristow Tragedy*, above.)	1602
	Anon. (Chapman, G?)	*Biron* (*Berowne, Burone*) (Earlier version of the *Tragedy of Charles Duke of Byron*?)	25 Sept.– 2/3 Oct. (prop.)
	Anon.	*The Capture of Stuhlweissenburg*	13 Sept. (acted)
	Anon.	*De Humfredo Aulico Confessionem Repudiante* (See Supp. II, 1.)	1602
	Anon.	*The Earl of Hertford* (Poss. not title but name of company that sold play.)	15/27 Sept. (prop.)
	Anon. (Heywood, T.?)	*The Fair Maid of the Exchange*	1601–1602
	Anon.	*II Fortune's Tennis* (See *The Fortewn Tenes*, 1600.)	1597–1603
	Anon. (poss. Dekker, T.)	*The Merry Devil of Edmonton* [Shakespeare Apocrypha]	1599–1604
	Anon.	*Philip of Spain* (An old play.)	8 Aug. (bought)
	Anon.	*A Royal Widow of England*	18 Sept. (acted)
	Anon.	*Samson*	29 July (bought)

TYPE	AUSPICES	EARLIEST TEXTS	LATEST TEXTS
Pseudo-history (?)	Worcester's	Lost (?)	
Tragicomedy (?)	Worcester's	Lost (?)	
Tragicomedy	Worcester's (?) (Queen Henrietta's in 1637)	1637*	E
Tragedy	Unacted	Lost	
History	Admiral's	Lost	
Royal Entertainment	Host: William Russell	MS	
History	Admiral's	Lost	
History	Admiral's	Lost	
Unknown	Admiral's	Lost	
'Piscatory'	Essex House (?)	MSS	
Tragedy	Privately acted (?)	MSS	
Biblical History	Admiral's	Lost	
Tragedy	Chamberlain's	1609 F	V
Bourgeois Romance (?)	Chamberlain's	Lost	
Biblical History (?)	Worcester's	Lost	
Hoax Show	Unacted	1602* ('plot')	C
Comedy	Admiral's	Lost	
Biblical History	Worcester's	Lost	
Tragedy	Chapel	Lost	
Tragedy	Worcester's	Lost	
Foreign History	Unknown	Lost	
Latin Tragedy	St Omers	Lost	
History (?)	Admiral's	Lost	
Comedy	Unknown	1607	G,S
Comedy (?)	Admiral's	MS ('plot' frag.) F	C
Comedy	Chamberlain's	1608 F	C,D,E
Foreign History	Admiral's	Lost	
History (?)	Chapel	Lost	
Biblical History	Admiral's	Lost.	

DATE	AUTHOR	TITLE	LIMITS
	Anon.	*The Spanish Fig*	6 Jan. (bought)
	Anon.	*Timon*	*c.* 1602–1603
	Anon. (poss. Rowley, S.)	*Wily Beguiled* (Revision of *Wylie Beguylie,* 1567?)	1601–1602
1603	Alexander, William	*Darius*	1603 (pub.)
	Chapman, George	*The Old Joiner of Aldgate*	Feb.
	Chettle, Henry	*II The London Florentine*	12 Mar. (P)
	Chettle, H.; Day, J.	*[Jane] Shore* (Poss. based on *Edward IV,* 1599.)	9 May (P)
	Chettle, H.; Heywood, T.	*I The London Florentine*	18/21 Dec. 1602–7 Jan. 1603 (P)
	Day; Hathway; & another	*The Boss of Billingsgate*	1–12 Mar. (P)
	Day; Hathway; Smith, Went	*The Unfortunate General* (*The French History.*)	7–19 Jan. (P)
	Day; Hathway; Smith, Went; & 'the other poet'	*I & II The Black Dog of Newgate*	24 Nov. 1602–26 Feb. 1603 (P)
	Gwinne, Matthew	*Nero*	*c.* 1602–1603
	Hawkesworth, Walter	*Labyrinthus* (Adapt. Della Porta's *La Cintia.*)	1603–1606
	Heywood, Thomas	*The Blind Eats Many a Fly*	24 Nov. 1602–7 Jan. 1603 (P)
	Heywood, Thomas	*A Woman Killed with Kindness*	12 Feb.– 6 Mar. (P)
	Jonson, Ben	*The Entertainment of the Queen and Prince at Althorp* (*The Satyr*)	25 June
	Jonson, Ben	*Sejanus His Fall*	1603
	Massey, Charles	*The Siege of Dunkirk, with Alleyn the Pirate* (Not completed?)	7 Mar. (P)
	Middleton, T.	*The Family of Love*	*c.* 1603–1607
	Parkinson,—	*Speech to King James I at Berwick*	6 Apr.
	Percy, William	*The Fairy Pastoral, or Forest of Elves* (*The Fairy Chase, or A Forest of Elves*)	1603
	Savile, John (describer)	*The Entertainment at Theobalds*	3–7 May
	Shakespeare, William	*All's Well That Ends Well*	1603–1604
	Shaw, Robert (?)	*The Four Sons of Aymon* (An old play?)	Feb. (?)(P)
	Singer, John	*Singer's Voluntary*	13 Jan. (P)
	Smith, Wentworth	*The Italian Tragedy*	7–12 Mar. (P)
	Anon.	*Narcissus, a Twelfth Night Merriment*	6 Jan.
	Anon. (Montgomery?)	*Philotus*	1603 (pub.)
	Anon.	*Prince Henry's Welcome to Winchester*	20 Sept.– 17 Oct.
	Anon. (Gwyn, O., in part?)	*II The Return from Parnassus, or The Scourge of Simony* (*The Progress to Parnassus*)	Xmas 1601–1602
	Anon. ('T.M.', describer)	*The Welcome into England*	5 Apr.– 11 May

TYPE	AUSPICES	EARLIEST TEXTS	LATEST TEXTS
Unknown	Admiral's	Lost	
Comedy	Inner Temple (?)	MS	C,S
Comedy	Paul's (?)	1606 F	G,D,S
Tragedy	Closet	1603	C
Comedy	Paul's	Lost	
Comedy (?)	Admiral's	Lost	
History	Worcester's	Lost	
Comedy (?)	Admiral's	Lost	
Unknown	Admiral's	Lost	
Foreign History	Worcester's	Lost	
Topical Play	Worcester's	Lost	
Latin Tragedy	St John's Col., Oxford	1603	F
Latin Comedy	Trinity Col., Cambridge	1636★ & MSS	F
Comedy	Worcester's	Lost	
Tragedy	Worcester's	1607	S,F
Royal Entertainment	Host: Robert Spencer	1604	C
Tragedy	King's	1605	B,C,S
History	Admiral's	Lost	
Comedy	Admiral's (?) (King's Revels in 1607)	1608★	C,S,D
Royal Entertainment	Berwick, Northumberland	MS	
Pastoral	Syon House (?)	MS	E
Royal Entertainment	Theobalds and London	1603★	C
Comedy	Chamberlain's	1623 F	
Romance (?)	Admiral's (Prince's in 1624)	Lost	
Improvisation (?)	Admiral's	Lost	
Tragedy	Worcester's	Lost	
Farce	St John's Col., Oxford	MS	E
Comedy	Closet (?)	1603	C
Mask	Court	Lost	
Satirical Comedy	St John's Col., Cambridge	1606 F & MS	C,D
Royal Entertainment	Edinburgh to London	1603★	C

DATE	AUTHOR	TITLE	LIMITS
1604	Alexander, William	*Croesus*	1604
	Cary, Elizabeth	*Mariam, the Fair Queen of Jewry*	1602–1605
	Chapman, George	*Bussy D'Ambois (For The Revenge of Bussy D'Ambois,* see 1610.)	1604–1605
	Chapman, George	*The Widow's Tears*	1604–1605
	Daniel, Samuel	*Philotas* (Three acts written in 1600.)	1604
	Daniel, Samuel	*The Vision of the Twelve Goddesses (The Mask at Hampton Court)*	8 Jan.
	Day, J. (with Wilkins, G.?)	*Law Tricks, or Who Would Have Thought It*	1604–1607
	Dekker, T. (Zeal's speech by Middleton)	*The Magnificent Entertainment Given to King James* (Various descriptions of and verses from the entertainment appear in next item and below under Dugdale and Jonson.)	15 Mar.
	Dekker; Harrison; Webster	*Arches of Triumph*	15 Mar.
	Dekker; T., with Middleton, T.	*I The Honest Whore (I The Converted Courtesan)*	1604
	Dekker, T., with Webster, J.	*Westward Ho*	1604
	Dugdale, G. (describer)	*The Time Triumphant*	15 Mar.
	Heywood, Thomas	*I The Fair Maid of the West, or A Girl Worth Gold*	1597–1604
	Heywood, Thomas	*How to Learn of a Woman to Woo* (Same as *The Wise Woman of Hogsdon,* below?)	30 Dec. (acted)
	Heywood, Thomas	*I If You Know Not Me You Know Nobody, or The Troubles of Queen Elizabeth*	1604–1605 rev., *c.* 1632
	Heywood, Thomas	*The Wise Woman of Hogsdon* (Same as *How to Learn of a Woman to Woo,* above?)	*c.* 1604(?)
	Jonson, Ben	*The Coronation Triumph* (Part by Jonson.)	15 Mar.
	Jonson, Ben	*The Entertainment at Highgate (The Penates)*	1 May
	Jonson, Ben	*A Panegyre*	19 March
	Marston, J. (additions by Webster)	*The Malcontent*	1602–1604
	Marston, John	*Parasitaster, or The Fawn*	1604
	Middleton, Thomas	*The Phoenix*	1603–1604
	Rowley, Samuel	*When You See Me You Know Me (Henry VIII)*	1604
	Shakespeare, William	*Measure for Measure*	1604
	Shakespeare, William	*Othello (The Tragedy of Othello, the Moor of Venice)* (completed 1603–4)	*c.* 1603–1604
	Verney, Francis	*Antipoe*	1603–1608
	Anon.	*Alice and Alexis*	a. 1603
	Anon. (Bernard, Richard?)	*The Birth of Hercules* (Adapt. Plautus's *Amphitryon.*)	1600–1606
	Anon. (poss. Chapman, G.)	*Charlemagne, or The Distracted Emperor*	*c.* 1603–1622
	Anon.	*The Fair Maid of Bristow*	1603–1604
	Anon.	*Gowry*	Dec.

TYPE	AUSPICES	EARLIEST TEXTS	LATEST TEXTS
Tragedy	Closet	1604	C
Tragedy	Closet	1613**	G
Foreign History	Paul's	1607 or '8	E,M,C S
Comedy	Queen's Revels (?)	1612*	C,S
Tragedy	Queen's Revels	1605	E
Mask	Court	1604	C
Comedy	King's Revels	1608*	G
Coronation Entertainment	London	1604	C
Coronation Entertainment	London	1604	
Comedy	Prince Henry's	1604	C,M
Comedy	Paul's	1607* F	C
Coronation Entertainment	Westminster	1604*	C
Comedy	Anne's (?) (Queen Henrietta's in 1631)	1631*	M,S
Comedy	Queen Anne's	Lost (?)	
History	Queen Anne's	1605	G
Comedy	Queen Anne's	1638*	M,T
Coronation Entertainment	London	1604	C
Royal Entertainment	Host: William Cornwallis	1616	C
Royal Entertainment	London	1604	
Tragicomedy	Queen's Revels & King's	[1604]	C,S,F
Comedy	Queen's Revels	1606	C,S,T
Comedy	Paul's	1607	W,T
History	Prince Henry's	1605 F	G
Comedy	King's	1623 F	1980 V
Tragedy	King's	1622 F	1886 V; 1965 V
Tragedy	Trinity Col., Oxford (?)	MS	
Tragicomedy	Unknown	MS (frag.)	
Comedy	Christ's Col., Cambridge (?)	MS	G,S
Tragedy	Unknown	MS	G,S
Comedy	King's	1605* F	E
Tragedy	King's	Lost	

DATE	AUTHOR	TITLE	LIMITS
	Anon.	*Hippolytus*	13 Feb.
	Anon. (Kyd. T.?)	*I Jeronimo, with the Wars of Portugal* (Bad Quarto or revision of *Don Horatio*, 1599 add.?)	1600–1605
	Anon.	*Lady Amity*	1600–*c.* 1604 .
	Anon. ('William Shakespeare'; Dekker? Drayton? or Marston?)	*The London Prodigal* [Shakespeare Apocrypha]	1603–1605
	Anon.	*A Mask of the Knights of India and China*	1 Jan.
	Anon.	*A Mask of Scots*	6 Jan.
	Anon. (Quarles, W.?)	*Pastor Fidus* (Trans. Guarini's *Il Pastor Fido*.)	1590–1605
	Anon.		1 Jan.
	(Shakespeare, W.?)	*Robin Goodfellow* (Revival of *A Midsummer-Night's Dream*?)	(acted.)
	Anon.	*The Wedding Mask for Sir Philip Herbert* (*Juno and Hymenaeus*)	27 Dec.
	Anon.	*The Wit of a Woman*	1604 (pub.)
1605	Burton, R.; & others	*Alba*	27 Aug.
	Chapman, George	*Caesar and Pompey* (*The Wars of Pompey and Caesar*)	1602–1605 (present II. i written 1610–1611(?)
	Chapman; Jonson; Marston	*Eastward Ho*	1605
	Chapman, George	*Monsieur D'Olive*	1605
	Daniel, Samuel	*The Queen's Arcadia* (*Arcadia Reformed*)	30 Aug.
	Dekker, Thomas	*II The Honest Whore* (*II The Converted Courtesan*)	1604–*c.* 1605
	Dekker, T.; Webster, J.	*Northward Ho*	1605
	Gwinne, Matthew	*Tres Sibyllae*	29 Aug.
	Gwinne, Matthew	*Vertumnus sive Annus Recurrens*	29 Aug.
	Heywood, Thomas	*II If You Know Not Me You Know Nobody, with the Building of the Royal Exchange, and the Famous Victory of Queen Elizabeth* (Prob. same as *The Life and Death of Sir Thomas Gresham, with the Building of the Royal Exchange*, ment. in *The Knight of the Burning Pestle*, 1607.)	1604–1605 (rev. *c.* 1632)
	Jonson, Ben	*The Mask of Blackness* (*The Twelfth Night's Revels*)	6 Jan.
	Marston, John	*The Dutch Courtesan* (Cockle de Moye)	1603–1605
	Marston, John	*The Wonder of Women, or Sophonisba*	1605–1606
	Middleton, Thomas	*A Trick to Catch the Old One*	1605
	Munday, Anthony	*The Triumphs of Reunited Britannia*	29 Oct.
	Shakespeare, William	*King Lear* (*The Tragedy of King Lear*)	1605–1606
	Anon.	*Ajax Flagellifer* (Sophocles)	28 Aug.

TYPE	AUSPICES	EARLIEST TEXTS	LATEST TEXTS
Latin (?) Tragedy	St John's Col., Oxford	Lost	
Pseudo-history	King's (?), unknown (performed by children?)	1605★	C,D,S
Unknown	Inner Temple	Lost	
Comedy	King's	1605 F	C
Mask	Court	Lost	
Mask	Court	Lost	
Latin Pastoral	King's Col., Cambridge	MSS	F
Comedy (?)	King's	Lost (?)	
Wedding Mask	Wedding: Herbert-Vere	Lost	
Comedy	Unacted (?)	1604★ F	G
Latin (?) Pastoral	Christ Church, Oxford	Lost	C
Classical History	Unacted (?)	1631★★	C
Comedy	Queen's Revels	1605 F	C,S
Tragedy	Queen's Revels	1606★	C
Pastoral	Christ Church, Oxford	1606	C,T
Comedy	Prince Henry's	1630★	C,M
Comedy	Paul's	1607★ F	C
Latin Royal Entertainment	St John's Col., Oxford	1607★	F
Latin Play	St John's men at Christ Church, Oxford	1607★	F
History	Queen Anne's	1606	G
Mask	Court	[*c.* 1608] & MS	C
Comedy	Queen's Revels	1605	C,S
Tragedy	Queen's Revels	1606	C,T
Comedy	Paul's (S.R.: 'Chapel')	1608	C,M,S,F
Civic Pageant	London	[1605]★	C
Tragedy	King's	1608 F	1880 V; 1965 V
Latin Tragedy	Magdalen men at Christ Church, Oxford	Lost	

DATE	AUTHOR	TITLE	LIMITS
	Anon.	*'Locus, Corpus, Motus'*, etc.	*c.* 1604–*c.* 1605
	Anon.	*Lucretia*	11 Feb.
	Anon.	*Nobody and Somebody* (A play of *c.* 1592 revised? *Albere Galles*, 1602, revised?)	1603–1606
	Anon.	*Richard Whittington*	1605 (S.R.)
	Anon.	*The Spanish Maze*	11 Feb. (acted)
1606	Armin, Robert	*The Two Maids of More-Clacke*	*c.* 1606–1608 perf. 1606
	Barnes, Barnabe	*The Devil's Charter, or Pope Alexander VI*	pub. 2 Feb.
	Beaumont, Francis (?)	*Madon, King of Britain* (S.R., 1660.)	*c.* 1605–1616
	Beaumont, F.	*The Woman Hater (The Hungry Courtier)*	1606
	Beaumont, Francis; Fletcher, John (revised by Massinger)	*Love's Cure, or The Martial Maid*	*c.* 1606 (rev. 1625)
	Burton, Robert	*Philosophaster* (Revised 1615, acted 16 Feb. 1618.)	1606
	Day, John	*The Isle of Gulls*	1606
	Dekker, Thomas	*The Whore of Babylon* (Revision of *Truth's Supplication to Candle-light*, 1600?)	*c.* 1606–1607
	Fletcher, J. (with the help of another)	*The Noble Gentleman*	*c.* 1605–1606 extant version rev. by Fletcher b. 1625; lic. 3 Feb. 1626
	Heywood, Thomas	*The Bold Beauchamps*	*c.* 1600–1607
	Jonson, Ben	*The Entertainment of the Two Kings of Great Britain and Denmark (The Hours)*	24 July
	Jonson, Ben	*Hymenaei*	5 Jan.
	Jonson, Ben	*Volpone, or The Fox*	1605–1606
	Marston, John	*City Pageant*	31 July
	Middleton, Thomas	*A Mad World, My Masters*	1604–1607
	Middleton, Thomas	*Michaelmas Term*	1604–1606
	Middleton, Thomas	*The Viper and Her Brood*	1606
	Roberts, Henry (describer)	*England's Farewell to the King of Denmark*	16 July–11 Aug.
	Roberts, Henry (describer)	*The Honourable Entertainment of the King of Denmark*	16–31 July
	Shakespeare, William	*Macbeth (The Tragedy of Macbeth)*	1606
	Sharpham, Edward	*The Fleer*	1606
	Wilkins, George	*The Miseries of Enforced Marriage*	1605–1606
	Anon.	*Abuses*	30 July (acted)
	Anon.	*The King of Denmark's Welcome*	18 July
	Anon. (by Middleton, T.?)	*The Puritan, or The Widow of Watling Street* [Shakespeare Apocrypha]	1606
	Anon. (Middleton?)	*The Revenger's Tragedy*	1605–1606
	Anon.	*Solomon and the Queen of Sheba*	24–28 July

TYPE	AUSPICES	EARLIEST TEXTS	LATEST TEXTS
Moral (English)	Trinity Col., Cambridge	MS (frag.)	
Latin (?) Tragedy	St John's Col., Oxford	Lost	
Pseudo-history	Queen's (Anne's?)	[c. 1606]* F	C,S
Pseudo-history	Prince Henry's	Lost	
Tragedy	King's	Lost	
Comedy	King's Revels	1609* F	C,S
Tragedy	King's	1607** F	B,S
Pseudo-history	Unknown	Lost	
Comedy	Paul's	1607	C
Comedy	King's (?)	1647	C
Latin Comedy	Christ Church, Oxford	MSS	E (text & trans.)
Comedy	Queen's Revels	1606 F	C,T
Allegorical History	Prince Henry's	1607*	C,T
Comedy	King's	1647	C
History (?)	Unknown	Lost	
Royal Entertainment	Theobalds	1616	C
Mask and Barriers	Court	1606	C
Comedy	King's	1607	C,S,MB
Royal Entertainment	London	MS	C
Comedy	Paul's	1608	C,S,T
Comedy	Paul's	1607	C,S,T
Tragedy	Queen's Revels	Lost	
Royal Entertainment	London	1606*	C
Royal Entertainment	London	1606* & MS (?)	C
Tragedy	King's	1623 F	1903 V; 1963 V
Comedy	Queen's Revels	1607	B
Domestic Drama	King's	1607 F	D,S,T
Comedy and Tragedy	Paul's	Lost	
Royal Entertainment	Theobalds and London	1606*	C
Comedy	Paul's	1607 F	E,C,T
Tragedy	King's	1607 or '08*	D,M,S,E
Show (for King of Denmark)	Theobalds	Lost	

DATE	AUTHOR	TITLE	LIMITS
	Anon. ('W. Shakespeare'; Middleton with others unidentified)	*A Yorkshire Tragedy* (*All's One, or One of the Four Plays in One*) [Shakespeare Apocrypha]	1605–1608
	Anon. (Rollinson, F.?)	*Zelotypus*	1606
1607	Alexander, William	*The Alexandraean Tragedy*	1605–1607
	Alexander, William	*Julius Caesar*	1607
	Barnes, Barnabe	*The Battle of Hexham*	*c.* 1607–1609
	Beaumont, F. (with Fletcher, J.?)	*The Knight of the Burning Pestle*	1607
	Campion, Thomas	*The Mask at Lord Hay's Marriage*	6 Jan.
	Day; Rowley, W.; Wilkins	*The Travels of the Three English Brothers*	1607
	Heywood, Thomas	*The Rape of Lucrece*	1606–1608
	Jonson, Ben	*The Entertainment at Merchant Taylors* (Songs, and speech by Angel of Gladness.)	16 July
	Jonson, Ben	*The Entertainment at Theobalds* (*The Genius*)	22 May
	Marston, John	*The Entertainment at Ashby* (*Cynthia and Ariadne*) (*The Entertainment of the Dowager-Countess of Darby*)	Aug.
	Marston, J.; Barkstead, W. (rev. by Barkstead, William and Mackin, Lewis)	*The Insatiate Countess*	*c.* 1607–1608; rev. 1609–1613
	Mason, John	*The Turk* (*Mulleasses the Turk*)	1607–1608
	Middleton, Thomas	*Your Five Gallants* (*The Five Witty Gallants*)	1607
	Sansbury, J.; & others	*The Christmas Prince* (Included following; see also 1608.)	Xmas 1607–1608
	Anon.	*Ara Fortunae*	30 Nov.
	Anon.	*Philomela, or Tereus and Progne*	29 Dec.
	Vertue, Owen (?)	*Saturnalia*	25 Dec.
	Shakespeare, William	*Antony and Cleopatra* (*The Tragedy of Antony and Cleopatra*)	*c.* 1606–1608
	Shakespeare, William	*Timon of Athens* (*The Life of Timon of Athens*)	*c.* 1606–*c.* 1608
	Sharpham, Edward	*Cupid's Whirligig*	1607
	Tomkis, Thomas	*Lingua*, or *The Combat of the Tongue and the Five Senses for Superiority*	1602–1607
	Anon.	*Aeneas and Dido* (An earlier play revived?)	25 May (acted)
	Anon.	*Claudius Tiberius Nero*	1607 (pub.)
	Anon.	*Every Woman in Her Humour*	1599–1608
	Anon.	*The Jesuits' Comedy*	Oct.
1608	Barry, Lording	*Ram Alley or Merry Tricks*	1608 (–1610?)
	Chapman, George	*The Conspiracy and Tragedy of Charles Duke of Byron* (*The Tragedy*, a revision of *Biron*, 1602?)	1607–1608

TYPE	AUSPICES	EARLIEST TEXTS	LATEST TEXTS
Tragedy	King's	1608 F	C,S
Latin Comedy	St John's Col., Cambridge	MSS	F
Tragedy	Closet	1607	C
Tragedy	Closet	1607	C
History	Unknown	MS (lost?)	
Burlesque Romance	Queen's Revels (?)	1613	M,S,E
Wedding Mask	Court	1607*	E,F
Topical Play	Queen Anne's	1607**	C,T
Tragedy	Queen Anne's	1608	M,E
Royal Entertainment	Merchant Taylors	Lost	
Royal Entertainment	Host: Salisbury	1616	C
Mask and Speeches	At Lord Huntington's	MSS	C
Tragedy	Queen's Revels	1613	C,S
Tragedy	King's Revels	1610	B
Comedy	Paul's (?) (S.R.: 'Chapel')	[c. 1608]*	C,S,T
Dramatic Festival	St John's Col., Oxford	MS	G,F
Latin Mock Coronation			
Latin Tragedy			
Latin Interlude			
Tragedy	King's	1623 F	1907 V
Tragedy	Unacted (?)	1623 F	
Comedy	King's Revels	1607	E
Academic Moral	Trinity Col., Cambridge	1607 F	D
Tragedy	Earl of Arundel's Banquet	Lost (?)	
Tragedy	Closet (?)	1607* F	G,D
Comedy	King's Revels (?)	1609* F	C,T,S
Anti-Protestant Allegory	Jesuit Col., Lyons	Lost	
Comedy	King's Revels	1611 F	B,D
Tragedy	Queen's Revels	1608	C,T,M

DATE	AUTHOR	TITLE	LIMITS
	Day, John	*Humour out of Breath*	1607–1608
	Fletcher, John	*The Faithful Shepherdess*	1608–1609
	Fletcher, J., with Beaumont, F.	*Cupid's Revenge*	*c.* 1607–1608
	Jonson, Ben	*Entertainment at Salisbury House for James I*	5–11 May
	Jonson, Ben	*The Mask at Lord Haddington's Marriage* (*The Hue and Cry after Cupid*)	9 Feb.
	Jonson, Ben	*The Mask of Beauty*	10 Jan.
	Markham, G.; Machin, L.	*The Dumb Knight*	1607–1608
	Rowley, William	*A Shoemaker a Gentleman*	1607–1609
	Rowley, W. (& another?; 'William Shakespeare and William Rowley on t.p.)	*The Birth of Merlin, or The Child Hath Found His Father* (Based on *Uther Pendragon,* 1597?) (Date *c.* 1620 also proposed.) [Shakespeare Apocrypha]	1597–1621
	Sansbury, J.; & others	*The Christmas Prince* (Included following; see also 1607.)	Xmas 1607–1608
	Anon.	*The Creation of White Knights*	1608
	Anon.	*The Embassage from Lubber-Land*	1608
	Anon.	*The Five Bells of Magdalen Church*	1608
	Anon.	*Ira Seu Tumulus Fortunae*	9 Feb.
	Anon.	*Penelope's Wooers*	1608
	Sansbury, John	*Periander*	13 Feb.
	Anon.	*Philomathes*	15 Jan.
	Anon.	*The Seven Days of the Week*	10 Jan.
	Sansbury, J. (?); Alder, J. (?)	*Somnium Fundatoris*	10 Jan.
	Anon.	*Time's Complaint*	1 Jan.
	Sansbury, John	*The Triumph of All the Founders in Oxford*	1608
	Anon.	*Yuletide*	21 Jan.
	Shakespeare, William	*The Tragedy of Coriolanus*	1608
	Shakespeare, W. (reviser? collaborator? Wilkins, G., now rejected)	*Pericles, Prince of Tyre*	1606–1608
	Anon. (Marston, J.; Chapman, J.?)	*The Silver Mine* (Subject; title assigned.)	Feb.–Mar.
	Anon.	*Torrismount*	*c.* 1607–1608
1609	Beaumont, F., with Fletcher, J.	*Philaster, or Love Lies a-Bleeding*	May (?), 1609
	Fletcher, with Beaumont (revised by Massinger or Rowley, W.?)	*The Coxcomb*	1608–1610
	Field, Nathan	*A Woman is a Weathercock*	1609–1610
	Heywood, T.; Rowley, W.	*Fortune by Land and Sea*	*c.* 1607–1609
	Jonson, Ben	*Entertainment at Britain's Burse for James I*	11 April
	Jonson, Ben	*Epicoene, or The Silent Woman*	1609

TYPE	AUSPICES	EARLIEST TEXTS	LATEST TEXTS
Comedy	King's Revels	1608*	M
Pastoral	Queen's Revels	[c. 1609]	M,T, 1908 V
Tragedy	Queen's Revels	1615	C
Royal Entertainment	Host: Earl of Salisbury	Lost	
Wedding Mask	Court	[c. 1608]	C
Mask	Court	[c. 1608]	C
Comedy	King's Revels	1608	D
Comedy	Queen Anne's	1638*	E
Romance	Unknown	1662* F	C
Dramatic Festival	St John's Col., Oxford	MS	G,E,F
Show (intended)		(omitted)	
Show (intended)		(omitted)	
Wassail		(omitted)	
Latin Mock Dethronement			
Mask (intended)		(omitted)	
Tragedy			
Latin Comedy			
Comedy			
Latin Allegory		(omitted)	
Moral			
Show (intended)		(omitted)	
Burlesque of *Christmas Prince*	Christ Church, Oxford	Lost	
Tragedy	King's	1623 F	1928 V
Tragicomedy	King's	1609 F	
Comedy	Queen's Revels	Lost	
Tragedy (?)	King's Revels	Lost	
Tragicomedy	King's	1620	C,S,F,M,V
Comedy	Queen's Revels	1647	C
Comedy	Queen's Revels	1612*	C,D,M
Comedy	Queen Anne's	1655*	C,T
Royal Entertainment	Host: Earl of Salisbury	Lost	
Comedy	Queen's Revels	1616 (earliest extant)	M,C,S

DATE	AUTHOR	TITLE	LIMITS
	Jonson, Ben	*The Mask of Queens*	2 Feb.
	Munday, Anthony	*Campbell, or The Ironmongers' Fair Field*	30 Oct.
	Shakespeare, William	*Cymbeline, King of Britain*	*c.* 1608–1611
	Wren, Christopher, Sr.	*Physiponomachia*	*c.* 1609–1611
	Anon.	*Bonos Nochios*	1609 (S.R.)
	Anon.	*St Christopher*	1609 (acted)
1610	Amerie, R.; Davies, R.	*Chester's Triumph*	23 Apr.
	Beaumont, F., with Fletcher, J.	*The Maid's Tragedy*	*c.* 1610–1611
	Chapman, George	*The Revenge of Bussy D'Ambois*	*c.* 1610–1611
	Daborne, Robert	*A Christian Turned Turk (The Two Famous Pirates)*	1609–1612
	Daniel, Samuel	*Tethy's Festival, or The Queen's Wake*	5 June
	Heywood, Thomas	*The Golden Age, or The Lives of Jupiter and Saturn*	1609–1611
	Jonson, Ben	*The Alchemist*	1610
	Jonson, Ben	*Prince Henry's Barriers (The Lady of the Lake)*	6 Jan.
	Munday, Anthony	*London's Love to Prince Henry*	31 May
	Price, Daniel (describer)	*The Creation of Prince Henry*	4 June
	Shakespeare, William	*The Winter's Tale*	*c.* 1610–1611
	Anon.	*Belinus, Brennus (One play or two?)*	1610 (listed)
1611	Beaumont, F.; Fletcher, J.	*A King and No King*	1611
	Chapman, George	*The Twelve Months*	1608–1612
	Cooke, J[oshua?]	*Greene's Tu Quoque, or The City Gallant*	1611
	Dekker, Thomas	*Match Me in London*	*c.* 1611–*c.* 1613
	Dekker, T. (with Daborne, R.?)	*If It Be Not Good, the Devil Is in It (If This Be Not a Good Play, the Devil Is in It)*	1611–1612
	Dekker, T.; Middleton, T.	*The Roaring Girl, or Moll Cutpurse*	1611
	Field, Nathan	*Amends for Ladies*	*c.* 1610–1611
	Fletcher, John	*The Night Walker, or The Little Thief* (Revised by Shirley and lic. 11 May 1633.)	*c.* 1611(?)
	Fletcher, John	*The Woman's Prize, or The Tamer Tamed*	1611
	Heywood, Thomas	*The Brazen Age* (Revision of *I Hercules*, 1595?)	1610–1611
	Heywood, Thomas	*The Silver Age* (Revision of *II Hercules*, 1595?)	1610–1612
	Jonson, Ben	*Catiline His Conspiracy*	1611
	Jonson, Ben	*Love Freed from Ignorance and Folly*	3 Feb.
	Jonson, Ben	*Oberon, the Fairy Prince*	1 Jan.
	Jordan, William	*The Creation of the World, with Noah's Flood* (In Cornish; adapt. *Origo Mundi*, 14th cent.)	1611
	Middleton, T. (Chapman, G?)	*The Second Maiden's Tragedy*	lic. 31 Oct.
	Middleton, Thomas	*No Wit, No Help Like a Woman's* (Revised 1638; by J. Shirley?)	*c.* 1611
	Munday, Anthony	*Chryso-Thriambos*	29 Oct.

TYPE	AUSPICES	EARLIEST TEXTS	LATEST TEXTS
Mask	Court	1609 & MS	C
Civic Pageant	London	[1609]★ (frag.)	
Tragicomedy	King's	1623 F	1913 V
Latin Comedy	St John's Col., Oxford	MS	F
'Interlude'	Unknown	Lost	
Neo-miracle (?)	Strollers in Yorkshire	Lost	
St George's Day Show	Chester	1610★	E
Tragedy	King's	1619	S,T,E M,V
Tragedy	Queen's Revels	1613★	C,S,F,M
Tragedy	King's (?) Queen's Revels (?)	1612★	C
Mask	Court	1610★	C
Classical Legend	Queen Anne's	1611★	C
Comedy	King's	1612 F	B,M,C,S,F
Speeches at Barriers	Court	1616	C
Royal Entertainment	London	1610★ (descrip.)	C
Tilt and Pageant	Court	1610★	C
Tragicomedy	King's	1623 F	1898 V; 1966 V
Legendary History	Unknown	Lost	
Tragicomedy	King's	1619	C,S,M,V
Mask	Court (?)	MS (Lost?)	C
Comedy	Queen Anne's	1614 F	D
Tragicomedy	Queen Anne's (?)	1631★	C
Comedy	Queen Anne's	1612★	C
Comedy	Prince Henry's	1611★ F	C,M
Comedy	Queen's Revels (?)	1618	C,D,M
Comedy	Lady Elizabeth's (?)	1640	C
Comedy	Unknown (King's in 1633)	1647 & MS	C,T
Classical Legend	Queen's (and King's?)	1613★	C,T
Classical Legend	Queen's and King's	1613★	C
Tragedy	King's	1611	C,S
Mask	Court	1616	C
Mask	Court	1616	C
Cornish Mystery	Cornwall	MSS	E
Tragedy	King's	MS	G,D,T,S
Comedy	Lady Elizabeth's (?)	1657★	C,S,T
Civic Pageant	London	1611 F	C (extracts)

DATE	AUTHOR	TITLE	LIMITS
	Rowley, William	*A New Wonder, a Woman Never Vexed* (Based on *The Wonder of a Woman,* 1595?)	1611–1614
	Shakespeare, William	*The Tempest*	1611
	Tourneur, Cyril	*The Atheist's Tragedy, or The Honest Man's Revenge*	1607–1611
	Anon.	*The Almanac*	29 Dec. (acted)
	Anon.	*Priest the Barber*	6–7 Feb. (?) (performed)
	Anon.	*Richard II* (An older play revived?)	30 Apr. (acted)
	Anon.	*The Ship* (Misprint for *The Slip?*)	1611 (ment.)
1612	'R.A.' (Armin, R.? Anton, R.?)	*The Valiant Welshman* (*Caradoc the Great*)	1610–1615
	Chapman, George	*Chabot, Admiral of France* (Revised by J. Shirley, 1635.)	1611–1613
	Dekker, Thomas	*Troia Nova Triumphans*	29 Oct.
	Fletcher, J. (with Beaumont, F.?)	*The Captain*	1609–1612
	Heywood, Thomas	*I The Iron Age*	1612–1613
	Heywood, Thomas	*II The Iron Age*	1612–1613
	Jonson, Ben	*Love Restored*	6 Jan.
	Niccolls, [Richard]	*The Twins' Tragedy*	1 Jan. (acted)
	Parsons, Philip	*Atalanta*	1612
	Rowley, William	*Hymen's Holiday, or Cupid's Vagaries* (Revised 1633; by J. Shirley?)	24 Feb. (acted)
	Tourneur, Cyril	*The Nobleman* (Identified with following, S.R., 1653.)	23 Feb. (acted)
	Tourneur, Cyril (?)	*The Great Man* (See preceding; separately listed by Warburton.)	1612(?)
	Webster, John	*The White Devil* (*Vittoria Corombona*)	Winter 1612–1613
	Anon. (Ford, J.?)	*A Bad Beginning Makes a Good Ending* (Prob. same as *An Ill Beginning Has a Good End,* assigned to Ford in S.R. 1660.)	1612–1613 (acted)
	Anon.	*Boot and Spur*	1611–1620(?)
	Anon.	*Cancer* (Adapt. Salviati's *Il Granchio.*)	1611–1613
	Anon.	*Captiva Religio*	1612–1613
	Anon.	'Garlic' (Prob. player rather than title.)	1612 (1st ment.)
	Anon.	*The Knot of Fools*	1612–1613 (acted)
	Anon.	'Microcosmus'	1612(?)
	Anon.	*The Proud Maid's Tragedy*	25 Feb. (acted)
	Anon.	*Roffensis* (With 'Intermedium' of Sensus, Fronto, Somnium, etc. [frag.].)	1612–1613
	Anon.	*Thomas Morus* (With 'Intermedium' of Mercurius.)	1612

TYPE	AUSPICES	EARLIEST TEXTS	LATEST TEXTS
Comedy	Unknown	1632*	D,T
Comedy	King's	1623 F	1892 V; 1966 V
Tragedy	King's (?)	1611 or '12*	C,S,F,M
Comedy (?)	Prince Henry's	Lost	
Unknown	Unknown	MS	E
History	King's	Lost	
Jig (?)	Prince Henry's	Lost	
History	Prince's Men	1615 F	E
Tragedy	Lady Elizabeth's (?)	1639*	C
Civic Pageant	London	1612*	C
Comedy	King's	1647	C
Classical Legend	Queen's (and King's?)	1632**	C,T
Classical Legend	Queen's (and King's?)	1632*	C
Mask	Court	1616	C
Tragedy	King's	Lost	
Lastin Pastoral	St John's Col., Oxford	MS	S,F
Comedy (?)	Prince's (later Queen Henrietta's)	Lost	
'Tragicomedy'	King's	Lost	
'Tragedy'	King's (?)	Lost	
Tragedy	Queen Anne's	1612	M,S,F
Comedy	King's	Lost	
Entertainment	Unknown (Oxford?)	MS	S
Latin Comedy	Trinity Col., Cambridge	1648* & MS	F
Latin Tragicomedy	English Col., Rome	MSS	
Jig	Prince Henry's	Lost	
Comedy (?)	King's	Lost	
Latin Moral	Cambridge (?)	MS	F
Tragedy	Lady Elizabeth's	Lost	
Latin Tragedy	English Col., Rome	MS	
Latin Tragedy	English Col., Rome	MS	

DATE	AUTHOR	TITLE	LIMITS
1613	Beaumont, Francis	*The Mask of the Inner Temple and Gray's Inn*	20 Feb.
	Brooke, Samuel	*Adelphe* (Adapt. Terence.)	27 Feb.
	Brooke, Samuel	*Scyros* (Trans. Bonarelli's *Filli di Sciro*.)	3 Mar.
	Campion, Thomas	*The Entertainment at Cawsome*	27–28 Apr.
	Campion, Thomas	*The Lord's Mask*	14 Feb.
	Campion, Thomas	*The Mask at the Earl of Somerset's Marriage* (*The Mask of Squires*)	26 Dec.
	Chapman, George	*The Mask of the Middle Temple and Lincoln's Inn* (same as *The Memorable Mask*)	15 Feb.
	Chapman, George (?)	*A Yorkshire Gentlewoman and Her Son* (S.R., 1660, and Warburton.)	*c.* 1595–*c.* 1613
	Daborne, Robert	*Machiavel and the Devil*	1613
	Daborne, R.; Tourneur, C.	*The Arraignment of London* (Prob. same as *The Bellman of London*, listed by Henslowe.)	1613
	Ferebe, George	*The Shepherd's Song*	11 June
	Fletcher, John	*Bonduca*	1611–1614
	Fletcher, J. (with Field?)	*Four Plays, or Moral Representations, in One* (Induction by Field; *The Triumph of Honour*, by Field; *The Triumph of Love*, by Field; *The Triumph of Time* and *The Triumph of Death*, by Fletcher.)	*c.* 1613–1619
	Fletcher, J., with Beaumont, F.	*The Scornful Lady*	1613–1616
	Field, N. (with Fletcher, J. and poss. Massinger, P.)	*The Honest Man's Fortune* (Re-lic. 8 Feb. 1624.)	1613
	Jonson, Ben	*A Challenge at Tilt*	27 Dec. 1613, 1 Jan. 1614
	Jonson, Ben	*The Irish Mask*	29 Dec.
	Jonson, Ben	*The May Lord* (Poss. non-dramatic.)	1613–1619
	Middleton, Thomas	*A Chaste Maid in Cheapside*	Mar.–Aug. (?), 1613
	Middleton, Thomas	*The New River Entertainment* (*The Running Stream Entertainment*)	29 Sept.
	Middleton, Thomas	*The Triumphs of Truth*	29 Oct.
	Middleton, Thomas	*The Witch*	*c.* 1613–1616
	Middleton, T.; Rowley, W. (Fletcher, J.?)	*Wit at Several Weapons* (Assigned almost entirely to Middleton and Rowley.)	*c.* 1709–1620
	Naile, Robert (describer?)	*The Entertainment at Bristol*	June
	Rowley, William	*The Fool without Book* (S.R. 1653. Related to *I or II Knaves*, below?)	*c.* 1607–1626
	Rowley, William	*A Knave in Print, or One For Another* (S.R., 1653. Related to *I or II Knaves*, below? Alternative title may be independent play.)	*c.* 1607–1626
	Shakespeare, W. (& Fletcher, J.?)	*Henry VIII* (*All Is True*)	June
	Shakespeare; Fletcher (& Beaumont?)	*The Two Noble Kinsmen* [Shakespeare Apocrypha]	1613–1614

TYPE	AUSPICES	EARLIEST TEXTS	LATEST TEXTS
Mask	Court	[c. 1613]	C
Latin Comedy	Trinity Col., Cambridge	MSS	F
Latin Pastoral	Trinity Col., Cambridge	MSS	F
Royal Entertainment	Host: Lord Knolles	1613* (descrip.)	C
Wedding Mask	Court	1613*	C
Wedding Mask	Court	1614* (descrip.)	C,F
Mask	Court	[c. 1613]	C
Tragedy	Unknown	Lost	
Tragedy	Lady Elizabeth's	Lost	
Comedy (?)	Lady Elizabeth's	Lost	
Royal Entertainment (Pastoral)	In Wiltshire	Lost	
Tragedy	King's	1647 & MS	G,M
Moral	Unknown	1647	C
Comedy	Queen's Revels (?)	1616	C,V
Tragicomedy	Lady Elizabeth's	1647 & MS	C
Tilt	Court	1616	C
Mask	Court	1616	C
Comic Pastoral	Unknown	Lost	
Comedy	Lady Elizabeth's	1630*	M,T,C,S,F
Civic Entertainment	London	1613*	C
Civic Pageant	London	1613**	C
Tragicomedy	King's	MS	G,M,B
Comedy	Unknown	1647	C
Royal Entertainment	Bristol	1613*	C
Comedy (?)	Unknown	Lost	
Comedy (?)	Unknown	Lost	
History	King's	1623 F	
Tragicomedy	King's	1634	C,S,T,V

DATE	AUTHOR	TITLE	LIMITS
	'Shakespeare, William'	*Duke Humphrey* (S.R., 1660, and Warburton.)	*c.* 1591–1616(?)
	'Shakespeare, William'	*Iphis and Iantha, or A Marriage without a Man* (S.R., 1660.)	*c.* 1591–1616(?)
	'Shakespeare, William'	*King Stephen* (S.R., 1660.)	*c.* 1591–1616(?)
	'Shakespeare; Fletcher'	*Cardenio* (or *Cardenno*, S.R. 1653. Poss. the basis of Theobald's *Double Falsehood, or The Distressed Lovers*, 1728.)	1612–1613 (acted)
	Stephens, John	*Cynthia's Revenge, or Maenander's Ecstasy*	1613 (pub.)
	Tailor, Robert	*The Hog Hath Lost His Pearl*	21 Feb.
	Taylor, John	*Heaven's Blessing and Earth's Joy*	11, 13 Feb.
	Anon.	*Gigantomachia, or Work for Jupiter*	*c.* 1600–1620(?)
	Anon.	*Heteroclitanomalonomia*	1613
	Anon.	*I The Knaves* (Related to *The Fool without Book* or *A Knave in Print*, above?)	2 Mar. (acted)
	Anon.	*II The Knaves* (Related to *The Fool without Book* or *A Knave in Print*, above?)	10 Mar. (acted)
	Anon. (describer)	*The Marriage of Frederick and Elizabeth*	11–15 Feb.
	Anon.	*Raymond, Duke of Lyons*	1 Mar. (acted)
	Anon.	*S. Thomas Cantuariis* (With 'Intermedium' of Minutum.)	1613
	Anon.	*The Sycophant*	1613
	Anon.	*The Triumph of the Cross*	1613
1614	Daborne, Robert	*The Owl*	1614
	Daborne, Robert	*The She Saint*	1614
	Daniel, Samuel	*Hymen's Triumph*	2 Feb.
	Fletcher, John	*Valentinian*	1610–1614
	Fletcher, J.	*Wit without Money*	1614–1616
	Jonson, Ben	*Bartholomew Fair*	31 Oct.
	Middleton, Thomas	*The Mask of Cupid*	4 Jan.
	Munday, Anthony	*Himatia-Poleos*	29 Oct.
	Smith, W[entworth?]	*The Hector of Germany, or The Palsgrave, Prime Elector*	*c.* 1614–1615
	Webster, John	*The Duchess of Malfi* (Revised 1617–23?)	1612–1614
	Zouche, Richard	*The Sophister* (*Fallacy, or The Troubles of Great Hermenia*)	*c.* 1614–1620
	Anon.	*Cupid's Festival*	1614–1622
	Anon.	*Magister Bonus sive Arsenius*	14 Oct.
	Anon. (dedication signed 'I.G., W.D., T.B.')	*The Mask of Flowers*	6 Jan.
	Anon.	*The Noble Grandchild*	1614
1615	'Francis Beaumont and John Fletcher'	*A Right Woman* (S.R., 1660. Given as alternative title for *Women Beware Women*, S.R., 1653.)	*c.* 1608–1625
	Brooke, Samuel	*Melanthe*	10 Mar.
	Browne, William	*Ulysses and Circe* (*Circe and Ulysses*)	13 Jan.
	Cecil, T[homas?]	*Aemilia*	7 Mar.

TYPE	AUSPICES	EARLIEST TEXTS	LATEST TEXTS
Tragedy	Unknown	Lost	
Comedy	Unknown	Lost	
History	Unknown	Lost	
Tragicomedy (?)	King's	Lost	
Tragedy	Closet	1613*	T
Comedy	Apprentices at Whitefriars	1614*	S,D
Royal Entertainment	Westminster and London	1613	C
Academic Entertainment	Cambridge (?)	MS	T,S
Academic Moral	Cambridge (?)	MS	T,S
Comedy	Prince's Men	Lost	T
Comedy	Prince's Men	Lost	
Pageants, etc.	Court	1613 & MS	C
Foreign History	Lady Elizabeth's	Lost	
Latin Tragedy	English Col., Rome	MS	
Latin Comedy	Trinity Col., Cambridge	Lost	
Tragedy	St Omers	Lost	
Comedy	Lady Elizabeth's	Lost	
Unknown	Lady Elizabeth's	Lost	
Pastoral	Court (company unknown)	1615 & MS	C
Tragedy	King's	1647	V,M
Comedy	Lady Elizabeth's (?)	1639	C,V
Comedy	Lady Elizabeth's	1631	M,C,S
Mask	Merchant Taylors Hall	Lost	
Civic Pageant	London	1614*	
Pseudo-history	Tradesmen at Bull & Curtain	1615*	E
Tragedy	King's	1623	E,S,F,D,M
Moral	Oxford	1639* & MS	
Comedy	Unknown	Lost	
Latin Tragedy	St Omers	MS	
Mask	Gray's Inn at Court	1614* & MS	C
Unknown	Unknown	Lost	
Comedy	Unknown	Lost (?)	
Latin Pastoral	Trinity Col., Cambridge	1615* & MS	E,F
Mask	Inner Temple	MSS	C,E
Latin Comedy	St John's Col., Cambridge	Lost	

DATE	AUTHOR	TITLE	LIMITS
	Fletcher, John	*Monsieur Thomas* (*Father's Own Son*)	1610–*c.* 1616
	Fletcher, Phineas	*Sicelides*	13 Mar.
	Jonson, Ben	*The Golden Age Restored*	6 Jan.
	Kynder, Philip	*Silvia*	1615–1616
	Middleton, Thomas	*More Dissemblers Besides Women* (Re-lic. 17 Oct. 1623.)	*c.* 1615(?)
	Munday, Anthony	*Metropolis Coronata*	30 Oct.
	Ruggle, George	*Ignoramus*	1615
	'S.S.'	*The Honest Lawyer*	*c.* 1614–1615
	Tomkis, Thomas	*Albumazar* (Adapt. Della Porta's *L'Astrologo.*)	9 Mar.
	Webster, John	*Guise*	1614–1623
	Anon.	*Band, Cuff, and Ruff, or Exchange Ware at the Second Hand* (See also 1646.)	1615 (pub.)
	Anon.	*Romeus et Julietta*	1615
	Anon.	*Work for Cutlers* (*Sword, Rapier, and Dagger*)	1614–1615
1616	Chappell, John (?)	*Susenbrotus, or Fortunia*	12 Mar.
	Cruso, Aquila	*Euribates Pseudomagus*	1610–*c.* 1616
	Fletcher, J. (with Beaumont, F.?)	*Love's Pilgrimage* (Passages from Jonson's *New Inn*, incorporated in I.i.)	1616(?) (revised 1635)
	Jonson, Ben	*Christmas His Mask* (*Christmas His Show*)	Xmas
	Jonson, Ben	*The Devil Is an Ass*	Oct.–Nov. (?)
	Jonson, Ben	*Mercury Vindicated from the Alchemists at Court*	1 Jan.
	May, Thomas	*Julius Caesar*	*c.* 1613–*c.* 1630
	Middleton, Thomas	*Civitatis Amor*	4 Nov.
	Middleton, T., poss. with Fletcher, J.	*The Nice Valour, or The Passionate Madman*	*c.* 1615–1616
	Middleton, Thomas	*The Widow*	*c.* 1616
	Munday, Anthony	*Chrysanaleia: The Golden Fishing, or Honour of Fishmongers*	29 Oct.
1617	Bernard, Samuel	*Julius et Gonzaga*	23 Jan.
	Brewer, Anthony	*The Lovesick King* (Revived 1680 as *The Perjured Nun.*)	1607–1617(?)
	Daborne, Robert	*The Poor Man's Comfort*	1615–1617
	Fletcher, John	*The Chances*	*c.* 1617
	Fletcher, John	*The Mad Lover*	5 Jan. (acted)
	Fletcher, J.; Massinger, P. (rev. by Massinger)	*The Bloody Brother* (*Rollo, Duke of Normandy*)	1617; rev. 1627–1630
	Fletcher (& Massinger? Field?)	*The Queen of Corinth*	1616–*c.* 1618
	Fletcher; Field; Massinger	*The Jeweller of Amsterdam, or The Hague*	1616–1619
	Fletcher; Massinger	*Thierry and Theodoret*	1613–1621

TYPE	AUSPICES	EARLIEST TEXTS	LATEST TEXTS
Comedy	Lady Elizabeth's (?)	1639	V,T
'Piscatory'	King's Col., Cambridge	1631* & MSS	C
Mask	Court	1616	C
Latin Pastoral	Pembroke Col., Camb. (acted?)	Lost	
Comedy	King's	1657*	C,T
Civic Pageant	London	1615*	C
Latin Comedy	Trinity Col., Cambridge	1630 & MSS	E,F
Comedy	Queen Anne's	1616* F	
Comedy	Trinity Col., Cambridge	1615	E,D
Tragedy of Intrigue (?)	Unknown	Lost	
Comic Dialogue	Trinity Col., Cambridge	1615 & MSS	C,S
Latin Tragedy	Unacted	MS (frag.)	
Comic Dialogue	Trinity Col. (?), Cambridge	1615*	E
Latin Comedy	Trinity Col., Cambridge	MSS	F
Latin Play	Caius Col., Cambridge at Royston	MS	F
Tragicomedy	King's	1647	C
Christmas Show	Court	1641 & MSS	C
Comedy	King's	1631	C
Mask	Court	1616	C
Latin Tragedy	Sidney Sussex Col., Camb. (?)	MS (lost)	
Civic Pageant	London	1616*	C
Comedy	Unknown	1647	C
Comedy	King's	1652*	M,S
Civic Pageant	London	1616*	E
Latin Tragedy	Magdalen Col., Oxford	Lost	
Tragedy	Unknown (acted in Newcastle?)	1655* (1680 ed. a ghost?)	B
Pastoral Comedy	Queen Anne's	1655* & MS	G,T
Comedy	King's	1647	C,V
Tragicomedy	King's	1647	V
Tragedy	King's (?)	1639	E,F
Tragicomedy	King's	1647	C
Tragedy	King's	Lost	
Tragedy	King's	1621	C,M

DATE	AUTHOR	TITLE	LIMITS
	Goffe, Thomas	*Orestes*	*c.* 1613–*c.* 1618
	Heylin, Peter	*Spurius*	8 Mar.
	Jonson, Ben	*Lovers Made Men* (*The Mask at Lord Hay's*) (Called *The Mask of Lethe* by Gifford.)	22 Feb.
	Jonson, Ben	*The Vision of Delight*	6 Jan.
	Middleton, Thomas	*The Triumphs of Honour and Industry*	29 Oct.
	Middleton, T.; Rowley, W.	*A Fair Quarrel*	*c.* 1615–1617
	White, Robert	*Cupid's Banishment*	4 May
	Anon.	*Marquis d'Ancre* (subject)	22 June (ordered suppressed)
	Anon.	*The Mask at the Middle Temple*	17 Jan.
	Anon.	*Pathomachia, or The Battle of Affections* (*Love's Loadstone*)	*c.* 1616–*c.* 1617(?)
	Anon.	*Stonyhurst Pageants*	1610–1625
	Anon.	*The Younger Brother*	3 Oct. (acted)
1618	Atkinson, Thomas	*Homo*	1615–1621
	Belchier, Daubridgcourt	*Hans Beer-Pot* (*See Me and See Me Not*)	1618 (pub.)
	Bernard, Samuel	*Andronicus Comnenus* (*Alexis Imperator*) (See anon. play of same name, 1636.)	26 Jan.
	Fletcher, John	*The Loyal Subject*	lic. 16 Nov. (revised 1633?)
	Fletcher; Field; Massinger	*The Knight of Malta*	1616–1619
	Goffe, Thomas	*The Raging Turk, or Bajazet II*	*c.* 1613–*c.* 1618
	Heylin, Peter	*Theomachia*	1618
	Holiday, Barten	*Technogamia, or The Marriages of the Arts*	13 Feb.
	Jonson, Ben	*For the Honour of Wales* (Revision of *Pleasure Reconciled to Virtue*, below.)	17 Feb.
	Jonson, Ben	*Pleasure Reconciled to Virtue*	6 Jan.
	Middleton, T.	*Hengist, King of Kent, or The Mayor of Queenborough* (See *Hengist*, 1599 add. Following fictitious [?] titles are mentioned in this play: *The Carwidgeon*; *The Cheater and the Clown*; *Gull upon Gull*; *The Whibble*; *The Whirligig*; *The Wild Goose Chase*; *Woodcock of Our Side*.)	1615–1620(?)
	Middleton, T; Rowley, W.	*The Old Law, or A New Way to Please You* (Traditional date 1599 now rejected.)	1618(?)
	Munday, Anthony	*Siderothriambos, or Steel and Iron Triumphing*	29 Oct.
	Shirley, H. (& Heywood, T.?)	*The Martyred Soldier*	b.1627
	Anon.	*Antoninus Bassianus Caracalla*	1617–1619
	Anon.	*Christ's Passion*	1613–1622
	Anon.	*The Entertainment at Brougham Castle*	Aug.
	Anon. (Campion, T.?)	*The First Anti-Mask of Mountebanks* (*The Mask at Gray's Inn*)	2 and 19 Feb.
	Anon.	*The Marriage of a Farmer's Son* (Same as *Tom of Bedlam*, below?)	1617–1618

TYPE	AUSPICES	EARLIEST TEXTS	LATEST TEXTS
Tragedy	Christ Church, Oxford	1632	T
Latin Tragedy	Magdalen Col., Oxford	Lost	
Mask	House of Lord Hay	1617	C
Mask	Court	1641	C
Civic Pageant	London	1617*	C
Tragicomedy	Prince's	1617	C,M,S,T
Mask	Ladies' Hall, Deptford	MS	C
Topical Play	Unknown	Lost	
Mask	Middle Temple	Lost	
Moral	Trinity Col., Cambridge (acted?)	1630* & MSS	E
Old Testament Cycle	Closet (?)	MS	E
Comedy (?)	Prince's (?)	Lost	
Latin Tragedy	St John's Col., Oxford	MS	S,F
Dialogue	Unacted (?)	1618*	
Jesuit Neo-Latin Tragedy	Magdalen Col., Oxford	MS (?)	F
Tragicomedy	King's	1647	V
Tragicomedy	King's	1647	C,T
Tragedy	Christ Church, Oxford	1631	S,T
Latin Comedy	Unacted	Lost	
Moral/Comedy	Christ Church, Oxford	1618 F	E
Anti-mask	Court	1641	C
Mask	Court	1641 & MS	C
Tragedy	Unknown (King's in 1641)	1661** & MSS	M,E
Comedy	Unknown	1656*	C,S
Civic Pageant	London	1618*	C
Tragedy	Queen Anne's (?)	1638*	C
Latin Tragedy	Christ Church, Oxford	MSS	F
Neo-miracle	Ely House	Lost	
Entertainment	Brougham Castle	Lost	
Christmas Entertainment	Gray's Inn	MSS	C
Mask	Court	Lost	

DATE	AUTHOR	TITLE	LIMITS
	Anon.	*The Mask of Amazons, or The Ladies' Mask*	1 Jan. (projected)
	Anon. (Jonson, B.?)	*A Mask Presented at Coleoverton*	2 Feb. (?)
	Anon.	*The Part of Poor* (Title assigned.)	1617–1619
	Anon.	*Stoicus Vapulans*	1618–1619
	Anon.	*Swetnam the Woman-Hater Arraigned by Women*	1617–1619
	Anon.	*Tom of Bedlam* (Same as *The Marriage of a Farmer's Son*, above?)	9 Jan.
1619	Bernard, Samuel	*Phocas*	27 Jan.
	Carleton, Thomas	*Fatum Vortigerni* (Same as play acted at Cambridge *c.* 1595–6?)	22 Aug.
	Cumber, John (?) (or Cobber, James?)	*The Two Merry Milkmaids, or The Best Words Wear The Garland*	1619–1620
	Drury, William	*Aluredus sive Alfredus*	1619
	Drury, William	*Mors Comoedia*	1619(?)
	Drury, William	*Reparatus sive Depositum*	1619(?)
	Field, N.; Massinger, P.	*The Fatal Dowry*	1617–1619
	Fletcher, John	*The Humorous Lieutenant* (*Generous Enemies, Demetrius and Enanthe. The Noble Enemy*)	1619(?)–1625
	Fletcher, J.; Massinger, P.	*The Little French Lawyer*	1619–1623
	Fletcher, J.; Massinger, P.	*Sir John van Olden Barnavelt*	Aug.
	Ford, J.	*The Laws of Candy*	1619–1623
	Goffe, Thomas	*The Courageous Turk, or Amurath I* (Same as *The Tragedy of Amurath*, MS dated 1618.)	24 February 1619
	Goffe, Thomas	*Phoenissae* [subject]	*c.* 1613–1629
	Goffe, Thomas (?) (rev. by Brome, R.?)	*The Careless Shepherdness*	1618–1629 (revised *c.* 1638)
	Middleton, Thomas	*The Inner-Temple Mask, or Mask of Heroes*	6 Jan.–2 Feb.
	Middleton, Thomas	*The Triumphs of Love and Antiquity*	29 Oct.
	Rowley, William	*All's Lost by Lust*	*c.* 1619–1620(?)
	Stub, Edmund	*Fraus Honesta* (*Callidamus et Callanthia*)	10 Feb.
	Webster, John	*The Devil's Law Case* (*When Women Go to Law the Devil Is Full of Business*)	1617–1621
	Anon.	*'A Christmas Messe'*	Xmas
	Anon.	*Fool's Fortune*	*c.* 1619–1622
	Anon.	*A Mask of Warriors*	21 Apr.
	Anon.	*Nero* (Date? Text quoted in *The Little French Lawyer*, 1619.)	1624 (pub.)
	Anon.	*Perkin Warbeck* [subject]	1619 (ment.)
	Anon.	*Two Wise Men and All the Rest Fools* (Below are titles from fragments of Revels Office documents, prob. 1610–22.)	1613–1619 (1619 pub.)
	Anon.	*The Bridgegr[oom]* (Same as *The Bridegroom and the Madman* in King's list, 1641?)	*c.* 1610–1622
	Anon.	*The City*	*c.* 1610–1622

TYPE	AUSPICES	EARLIEST TEXTS	LATEST TEXTS
Mask	Court	Lost	
Mask	Coleoverton	MS	E
Moral	Christ Church, Oxford	MS (actor's part)	
Latin Moral	St John's Col., Cambridge	1648★	F
Comedy	Queen Anne's	1620★ F	E,F,T
Comic Show	Court	Lost	
Latin Tragedy	Magdalen Col., Oxford	Lost	
Latin Tragedy	English Col., Douai	MS	
Comedy	Red Bull Company	1620 F	S
Latin Tragicomedy	English Col., Douai	1620	
Latin Farce	English Col., Douai	1620	T
Latin Tragicomedy	English Col., Douai	1628	
Tragedy	King's	1632★	E,C,S
Tragicomedy	King's	1647 & MS	G,V,T
Comedy	King's	1647	V
Tragedy	King's	MS	E,S,T
Tragicomedy	King's	1647	V
Tragedy	Christ Church, Oxford	1632 & MS	S,T
Tragedy	Christ Church, Oxford (?)	Lost	
Pastoral	Christ Church, Oxford (?) (Queen Henrietta's in *c.* 1638)	1656★	
Mask	Inner Temple	1619★	C
Civic Pageant	London	1619★	C
Tragedy	Prince's (later Lady Elizabeth's)	1633★	E
Latin Comedy	Trinity Col., Cambridge	1632★ & MSS	F
Tragicomedy	Queen Anne's	1623★	S
Entertainment	Cambridge (?)	MS	T,S
Jig	Amateurs of Shropshire	MS	C
Mask	Merchant Taylors Hall	Lost	
Tragedy	Unknown	1624 & MSS	M,S,D
History	Unknown	Lost	
Dialogues	Privately acted (?)	1619★ F	C
Unknown	King's (?)	Lost	
Unknown	Unknown Company at Court	Lost	

DATE	AUTHOR	TITLE	LIMITS
	Anon.	*The False Friend* (Same as *The False One*, 1620?)	*c.* 1610–1622
	Anon.	*Henry the Una . . .*	*c.* 1610–1622
	Anon.	*The House is Haunte*[*d*]	*c.* 1610–1622
	Anon.	*Look to the Lady* (Same as play by 'J. Shirley', with ident. title, in S.R., 1640?)	*c.* 1610–1622
	Anon.	*The Scholar Turned to School Again*	*c.* 1610–1622
	Anon.	*Titus and Vespasian* (Same as 1592 play?)	*c.* 1610–1622
	Anon.	*A Turk's Too Good for* [*Him?*]	*c.* 1610–1622
1620	Carleton, Thomas	*Emma Angliae Regina*	8 Sept.
	Davenport, R.; Drue, T.	*The Woman's Mistaken* (S.R., 1653.)	*c.* 1620–*c.* 1624
	Day, J.; Dekker, T.	*Guy of Warwick* (Revision of *Guy of Warwick*, 1593?)	1620 (S.R.)
	Dekker, T.; Massinger, P.	*The Virgin Martyr*	lic. 6 Oct.
	Fletcher, John	*Women Pleased* (An earlier play revised?)	1619–1623
	Fletcher, J., Massinger, P.	*The Custom of the Country*	1619–1620
	Fletcher, J.; Massinger, P.	*The Double Marriage*	1619–1623
	Fletcher, J.; Massinger, P.	*The False One*	1619–1623
	Heylin, Peter	*Doublet, Breeches, and Shirt*	Jan.
	Jonson, Ben	*The Entertainment at Blackfriars* (*The Newcastle Entertainment*)	May (?)
	Jonson, Ben	*News from the New World Discovered in the Moon*	7 Jan.
	Jonson, Ben	*Pan's Anniversary, or The Shepherds' Holiday*	19 June (?)
	Massinger, Philip	*Antonio and Vallia* (S.R., 1660. Based on *Antony and Vallia*, 1599 add.?)	*c.* 1613–1640
	Massinger, Philip	*Philenzo and Hypollita* (Based on *Philipo and Hippolito*, 1594?)	*c.* 1613–1640
	May, Thomas	*The Heir* (Orig. perf. at a college?)	1620 (acted)
	Middleton, T.; Rowley, W.	*The World Tossed at Tennis*	1620 (pub.)
	Squire, John	*Tes Irenes Trophoea, or The Triumphs of Peace*	30 Oct.
	Anon.	*The Costly Whore*	*c.* 1619–1632
	Anon.	*Risus Anglicanus*	1614–1625
	Anon.	'*Running*' (or *Travelling*) *Mask* (Not a title but a type, also presented Xmas 1627–8.)	Feb.
	Anon.	*Sophomorus* (See Halliwell, *Dict.*, p. 233.)	1620(?)
1621	Dekker; Ford; Rowley, W.	*The Witch of Edmonton*	1621
	Fletcher, John	*The Island Princess*	1619–1621
	Fletcher, John	*The Pilgrim*	1621(?)
	Fletcher, John	*The Wild Goose Chase*	1621(?)
	Garnett, Jasper	*The Tenants' Complaint against the Landlords* (Title assigned.)	1621
	Jonson, Ben	*The Gypsies Metamorphosed* (*The Metamorphosed Gypsies*)	3, 5 Aug.; Sept.
	Massinger, Philip	*The Duke of Milan*	1621–1623

TYPE	AUSPICES	EARLIEST TEXTS	LATEST TEXTS
Unknown	Unknown Company at Court	Lost	
History (?)	Unknown Company at Court	Lost	
Unknown	Unknown Company at Court	Lost	
Comedy (?)	Unknown Company at Court	Lost	
Comedy (?)	King's (?)	Lost	
Classical or British History	Unknown Company at Court	Lost	
Tragedy	Unknown Company at Court	Lost	
Latin Tragedy	English Col., Douai	Lost	
Comedy (?)	Unknown	Lost	
Tragedy (?)	Unknown	Lost	
Tragedy	Red Bull Company (Revels)	1622	C,M
Tragicomedy	King's	1647	C
Comedy	King's	1647	C,V
Tragedy	King's	1647	C
Classical History	King's	1647	V
Christmas Show	Magdalen Col., Oxford	Lost	
Entertainment	Newcastle House, Blackfriars	MS	C
Mask	Court	1641	C
Mask	Court	1641	C
Comedy	Unknown	Lost	
Tragicomedy	Red Bull Company (Revels) (?)	Lost	
Comedy	Red Bull Company (Revels)	1622	D
Mask	Prince's Men	1620★	C
Civic Pageant	London	1620★	C
Pseudo-history	Red Bull Company (Revels) (?) King's Revels (?)	1633★	C
Latin Anti-Catholic Comedy	Cambridge (?)	MS	F
Mask	Court	Lost	
Latin Comedy	Cambridge (?)	Lost (?)	
Tragicomedy	Prince's Men	1658★	C,M,T
Tragicomedy	King's	1647	
Comedy	King's	1647	C
Comedy	King's	1652	C,M,F
Topical Play	Kendal Castle, Westmorland	Lost	
Mask	Burley, Belvoir, and Windsor	1640 & MSS	E,C
Tragedy	King's	1623	E,M,C

DATE	AUTHOR	TITLE	LIMITS
	Massinger, Philip	*The Maid of Honour* (prologue delivered on revival, 1629/30?)	1621–1622
	Massinger, Philip	*The Woman's Plot*	5 Nov. (acted)
	Middleton, T. (& Webster, J.)	*Anything for a Quiet Life*	*c.* 1620–*c.* 1621
	Middleton, Thomas	*Honourable Entertainments* (A collection of ten brief entertainments: *The Entertainment at Bunhill on the Shooting Day* [*The Archer*], *The Entertainment at Sir Francis Jones's at Christmas* [*The Triumph of Temperance*], *The Entertainment at Sir Francis Jones's at Easter* [*The Seasons*], *The Entertainment at Sir Francis Jones's Welcome* [*Comus the Great Sir of Feasts*], *The Entertainment at Sir William Cokayne's in Easter Week* [*The Cock*], *The Entertainment at Sir William Cokayne's upon Simon and Jude's Day* [*The Year's Funeral*], *The Entertainment at the Conduit Head* [*The Water Nymph*], *The Entertainment for the General Training* [*Pallas*], *The Entertainment of the Lords of the Council by Sheriff Allen* [*Flora's Welcome*], *The Entertainment of the Lords of the Council by Sheriff Ducie* [*Flora's Servants*].)	1620–1621
	Middleton, Thomas	*Women Beware Women* (*A Right Woman*, given as alternative title in S.R., 1653, prob. sep. piece; see 1615.)	*c.* 1620–1627
	Middleton, T. (& Munday, A.?)	*The Sun in Aries*	29 Oct.
	Anon. ('Francis Beaumont? Daborne? Massinger? Field?')	*The Faithful Friends*	1620–1628
	Anon.	*Gramercy Wit*	30 Dec. (acted)
	Anon.	*The Man in the Moon Drinks Claret*	27 Dec. (acted)
	Anon.	*A Mask of the Middle Temple*	13 Feb.
	Anon.	*The Woman Is Too Hard for Him* (Same as *The Woman's Prize*, 1611, or *The Wild Goose Chase*, above?)	26 Nov. (acted)
1622	Dekker, T. ('S.R.' [Samuel Rowley?] on t.p.)	*The Noble Spanish Soldier* (*The Noble Soldier, or A Contract Broken Justly Revenged*) (Revision of earlier play? Rewritten as *The Welsh Ambassador*, 1623)	1622 (revised?)
	Fletcher, J. (with Massinger, P.?)	*Beggars' Bush* (Prob. same as *Beggars* of King's list, 1641.)	*c.* 1615–1622
	Fletcher, J.; Massinger, P.	*The Prophetess*	lic. 14 May
	Fletcher, J.; Massinger, P.	*The Sea Voyage*	lic. 22 June

TYPE	AUSPICES	EARLIEST TEXTS	LATEST TEXTS
Tragicomedy	Red Bull Company (?) (later Queen Henrietta's)	1632★★	E,M,C
Comedy	King's	Lost	
Comedy	King's	1662★	T
Entertainments	London	1621★	G
Tragedy	King's (?)	1657★	M,T,S
Civic Pageant	London	1621★	C,T
Tragicomedy	Unknown	MS	C,S
Comedy (?)	Red Bull Company (Revels)	Lost	
Comedy	Prince's Men	Lost	
Mask	Court	Lost	
Comedy (?)	King's	Lost (?)	
Foreign Pseudo-history	Admiral's (?)	1634★ F	C
Comedy	King's	1647 & MS	C,V,E
Tragicomedy	King's	1647	C
Comedy	King's	1647	C

DATE	AUTHOR	TITLE	LIMITS
	Fletcher, J.; Massinger, P.	*The Spanish Curate*	lic. 24 Oct.
	Jonson, Ben	*The Mask of Augurs*	6 Jan.
	Markham, G.; Sampson, W.	*Herod and Antipater*	*c.* 1619–1622
	Mease, Peter	*Adrastus Parentans sive Vindicta*	1619–1626
	Middleton, Thomas	*An Invention for the Service of Edward Barkham*	1622
	Middleton, Thomas	*The Triumphs of Honour and Virtue*	29 Oct.
	Middleton, T.; Rowley, W.	*The Changeling*	lic. 7 May
	'W.R.' (& Middleton, T.?)	*A Match at Midnight*	1621–1623
	Anon.	*Ambitio Infelix sive Absalom*	28 Nov.
	Anon.	*The Black Lady*	lic. 10 May
	Anon.	*The Dutch Painter, and the French Branke* (i.e. *Brawle? Branle?*)	lic. 10 June
	Anon. (Carlell, L.?)	*Osmond, the Great Turk* (Same as *Osmond, the Great Turk*, 1637?)	lic. 6 Sept.
	Anon.	*The Two Noble Ladies and the Converted Conjurer*	1619–1623
	Anon.	*The Valiant Scholar*	lic. 3 June
	Anon.	*The Welsh Traveller*	lic. 10 May
1623	Bonen, William	*The Cra[fty?] Merchant, or Come to My Country House*	lic. 12 Sept.
	Bonen, William	*Two Kings in a Cottage*	lic. 19 Nov.
	Brewer, Thomas	*A Knot of Fools*	1623 (S.R.)
	Brome, R.; Jonson, 'Young'	*A Fault in Friendship*	lic. 2 Oct.
	Carleton, Thomas	*Henrico 8°*	10 Oct.
	Davenport, Robert	*The Fatal Brothers* (S.R. 1660.)	*c.* 1623–1636
	Davenport, Robert	*The Politic Queen, or Murder Will Out* (S.R., 1660.)	*c.* 1623–1636
	Day, J.; Dekker, T.	*The Bellman of Paris*	lic. 30 July
	Day, J. (& Dekker, T.?)	*Come See a Wonder* (Same as *The Wonder of a Kingdom*, 1631?)	lic. 18 Sept.
	Dekker, T.; Ford, J.	*The Spanish Gypsy*	lic. 9 July
	Dekker, T. (& Ford, J.)	*The Welsh Ambassador, or A Comedy in Disguises* (Reworking of *The Noble Spanish Soldier*, 1626. Related to *Connan, Prince of Cornwall*, 1598?)	*c.* 1623
	Dering, Edward (?)	*Henry IV* (Adapt. Shakespeare's *Henry IV, I & II*)	1613–*c.* 1624
	Fletcher, John	*The Devil of Dowgate, or Usury Put to Use*	lic. 17 Oct.
	Fletcher, J. (& Massinger, P.?)	*The Wandering Lovers* (*The Lovers' Progress, Cleander*)	lic. 6 Dec. (revised, 1634, by Massinger)
	Fletcher, J.; Rowley, W.	*The Maid in the Mill*	lic. 29 Aug. (revised 1 Nov.)
	Gunnell, Richard	*The Hungarian Lion*	lic. 4 Dec.

TYPE	AUSPICES	EARLIEST TEXTS	LATEST TEXTS
Comedy	King's	1647	C,M,V
Mask	Court	[1622]	C
Tragedy	Red Bull Company (Revels)	1622★	T
Latin Tragedy	Jesus Col. (?), Cambridge	MS	F
Dinner Entertainment	London	MS	C,T
Civic Pageant	London	1622★	C
Tragedy	Lady Elizabeth's	1653★★	S,M,T
Comedy	Red Bull Company (Revels) (?)	1633★	D
Latin Tragedy	St Omers	MS	
Comedy (?)	Lady Elizabeth's	Lost	
Unknown	Prince's	Lost	
Tragedy (?)	King's	Lost (?)	
Tragicomedy	Red Bull Company (Revels)	MS	G
Comedy (?)	Lady Elizabeth's	Lost	
Unknown	Red Bull Company (Revels)	Lost	
Comedy	Lady Elizabeth's	Lost	
Tragedy	Palsgrave's Men	Lost	
Semi-dramatic Dialogue	Unknown	1624	
Comedy	Prince's	Lost	
Latin Play	English Col., Douai	Lost	
Tragedy	King's (?)	Lost	
Tragedy	King's (?)	Lost (? see 1690)	
Tragedy	Prince's	Lost	
Comedy	'Strangers' at Red Bull	Lost (?)	
Tragicomedy	Lady Elizabeth's	1653	C,T,M,S
Pseudo-history	Lady Elizabeth's (?)	MS	C,G
History	Amateurs at Surrenden	MS	E,F
Comedy (?)	King's	Lost	
Tragicomedy	King's	1647	C
Comedy	King's	1647	C
Foreign History (?)	Palsgrave's	Lost	

DATE	AUTHOR	TITLE	LIMITS
	Hacket, John	*Loyola* (Revision, by E. Stub. of play written *c.* 1616?)	28 Feb. (acted)
	Jonson, Ben	*Time Vindicated to Himself and to His Honours*	19 Jan.
	Massinger, Philip	*The Bondman* (*The Noble Bondman*)	lic. 3 Dec.
	Maynard, John	*The Mask at York House* (Revived 5 Aug. 1624?)	18 Nov.
	Middleton, Thomas	*The Puritan Maid, Modest Wife, and Wanton Widow* (S.R., 1653, and Warburton.)	*c.* 1601–1627
	Middleton, Thomas	*The Triumphs of Integrity*	20 Oct.
	Rowley, Samuel	*Hard Shift for Husbands, or Bilboe's the Best Blade*	lic. 29 Oct.
	Rowley, Samuel	*Richard III, or The English Profit* [*Prophet*?]	lic. 27 July
	Rowley, William	*The Four Honourable Loves* (S.R., 1660, and Warburton.)	*c.* 1607–1626
	Rowley, William	*The Nonesuch* (S.R., 1660 and Warburton.)	*c.* 1607–1626
	Shirley, Henry	*The Duke of Guise* (S.R., 1653.)	b.1627
	Shirley, Henry	*The Dumb Bawd* (S.R., 1653. Prob. same as *The Dumb Bawd of Venice*, 1628.)	b.1627
	Shirley, Henry	*Giraldo, the Constant Lover* (S.R., 1653.)	b.1627
	'Henry Shirley' (Ford, J., also suggested)	*The Spanish Duke of Lerma* (S.R., 1653.)	b.1627
	Simons, Joseph	*Vitus sive Christiana Fortitudo*	13 May
	Simons, Joseph (?)	*King Robert of Sicily* (subject)	19 June
	Smith, –	*The Fair Foul One, or The Baiting of the Jealous Knight*	lic. 28 Nov.
	'Will, Smithe'	*St George for England* (Warburton.)	b.1642
	Ward, Robert (?)	*Fucus sive Histriomastix* (*Fucus Histriomastix*)	1622–1623
	Anon.	*The Buck Is a Thief*	28 Dec. (acted)
	Anon.	*Ghismonda* (*Tancred and Ghismonda*)	1623–1624
	Anon. (Speed, John?)	*Gown, Hood and Cap*	1623?
	Anon. ('P. Claretus')	*Innocentia Purpurata seu Rosa Candida et Rubicunda* (Henry VI)	26 Oct. (?)
	Anon.	*The Peaceable King, or The Lord Mendall* (An old play re-licensed.)	lic. 19 Aug.
	Anon.	*The Plantation of Virginia*	lic. Aug.
	Anon.	*S. Pelagius Martyr*	27 July
	Anon.	*A Vow and a Good One*	6 Jan. (acted)
1624	Barnes, –	*The Madcap*	lic. 3 May
	Davenport, Robert	*The City Nightcap, or Crede Quod Habes et Habes*	lic. 14 Oct.
	Davenport, R. ('Shakespeare, & Davenport', S.R., 1653, & Warburton)	*Henry I*	lic. 10 Apr.
	Davenport, R. ('Shakespeare, & Davenport', S.R., 1653)	*Henry II*	1624(?)

TYPE	AUSPICES	EARLIEST TEXTS	LATEST TEXTS
Latin Comedy	Trinity Col., Cambridge	1648★ & MSS	F
Mask	Court	[1623] F	C
Tragicomedy	Lady Elizabeth's	1624	E,C
Mask	Court	Lost	
Comedy (?)	Unknown	Lost	
Civic Pageant	London	1623★	C,T
Comedy	Palsgrave's	Lost	
History	Palsgrave's	Lost	
Comedy	Unknown	Lost	
Comedy	Unknown	Lost	
Foreign History (?)	Unknown	Lost	
Comedy (?)	King's (acted at Court 15 Apr. 1628) (?)	Lost	
Unknown	Unknown	Lost	
Foreign History	King's (listed as theirs, 1641)	Lost (? see 1668)	
Latin Tragedy	St Omers	1656	
Latin Tragedy	St Omers	Lost	
Comedy (?)	'Strangers' at Red Bull	Lost	
Heroical Romance (?)	Unknown	Lost	
Latin Comedy	Queens' Col., Cambridge	MSS	E,F
Comedy (?)	King's	Lost	
Tragedy	Unknown (private performance?)	MSS	
Play with Mask	Trinity Col., Cambridge?	MS	S
Latin Tragedy	St Omers	MS	
Unknown	Prince's	Lost	
Tragedy	Unknown	Lost	
Latin Tragedy	St Omers	MS	
Unknown	Prince's	Lost	
Comedy (?)	Prince's	Lost	
Comedy	Lady Elizabeth's	1661★	C,D,S
History	King's	Lost	
History	King's (?)	Lost (? see 1692)	

DATE	AUTHOR	TITLE	LIMITS
	Dekker, Thomas	*Joconda and Astols[f?]o* (S.R., 1660.)	b. 1632
	Dekker, T.; Ford, J.	*The Bristow Merchant* (Same as *The London Merchant*, below?)	lic. 22 Oct.
	Dekker, T.; Ford, J.	*The Fairy Knight*	lic. 11 June.
	Dekker, T.; Ford, J.	*The Sun's Darling*	lic. 3 Mar. (revised 1638–1639)
	Drue, Thomas	*The Duchess of Suffolk*	lic. 2 Jan.
	Fletcher, John	*Rule a Wife and Have a Wife*	lic. 19 Oct.
	Fletcher, John	*A Wife for a Month*	lic. 27 May
	Ford, J. (& Dekker, T.?)	*The London Merchant* (S.R., 1660, and Warburton. Same as *The Bristow Merchant*, above?)	1624(?)
	Gunnell, Richard	*The Way to Content All Women, or How a Man May Please His Wife*	lic. 17 Apr.
	Heywood, Thomas	*The Captives, or The Lost Recovered*	lic. 3 Sept.
	Jonson, Ben	*The Mask of Owls*	19 Aug.
	Jonson, Ben	*Neptune's Triumph for the Return of Albion*	6 Jan. (projected)
	Massinger, Philip	*The Renegado, or The Gentleman of Venice*	lic. 17 Sept.
	Massinger, Philip	*The Unnatural Combat*	1624–1625
	Massinger, P.	*The Parliament of Love*	lic. 3 Nov.
	Maynard, John	*The Mask at Burley* (Revival of *The Mask at York House*, 1623?)	5 Aug.
	Middleton, Thomas	*A Game at Chess*	lic. 12 June
	Rowley, Samuel (?) (or William?)	*A Match or No Match*	lic. 6 Apr.
	Shank, John	*Shank's Ordinary*	lic. 16 Mar.
	Simons, Joseph	*Mercia seu Pietas Coronata*	7 Feb.
	Simons, Joseph	*Theoctistus sive Constans in Aula Virtus*	8 Aug.
	Webster, John	*Monuments of Honour*	29 Oct.
	Webster, J.? (& others?)	*Appius and Virginia*	*c.* 1624–1634?
	Webster, J.; Ford, J. (and Dekker? Rowley?)	*The Late Murder in White Chapel, or Keep the Widow Waking* (*The Late Murder of the Son upon the Mother*)	lic. Sept.
	Anon.	*The Angel King*	lic. 15 Oct.
	Anon.	*The Fair Star of Antwerp*	lic. 15 Sept.
	Anon.	*Honour in the End*	lic. 21 May
	Anon. (Gunnell, R.?)	*The Mask* (Same as 'Govell's' *Mask*?; see Supp. II, g.)	lic. 3 Nov.
	Anon.	*The Parricide*	lic. 27 May
	Anon.	*The Spanish Contract*	1624 (acted)
	Anon.	*The Spanish Viceroy*	*c.* Dec. (acted)
	Anon.	*The Whore in Grain*	lic. 26 Jan

TYPE	AUSPICES	EARLIEST TEXTS	LATEST TEXTS
Comedy	Unknown	Lost	
Comedy (?)	Palsgrave's	Lost	
Mask (?)	Prince's (?)	Lost	
Moral Mask	Lady Elizabeth's	1656**	C
History	Palsgrave's	1631*	T
Comedy	King's	1640	C,V
Tragicomedy	King's	1647	C,E
Comedy	Palsgrave's (?)	Lost	
Comedy	Palsgrave's	Lost	
Tragicomedy	Lady Elizabeth's	MS	G
Entertainment	Court	1641	C
Mask	Court	[1624]	C
Tragicomedy	Lady Elizabeth's	MS (altered transcript of Quarto) 1630*	C
Tragedy	King's	1639*	E,C
Comedy	Lady Elizabeth's	MS (frag.)	G,C
Mask	Burley-on-the-Hill	Lost	
Political Satire	King's	[1625?] & MSS	E,T,S
Comedy	Palsgrave's	Lost	
Jig (?) Variety (?)	King's	Lost	
Latin Tragedy	St Omers	1648	
Latin Tragedy	St Omers	1653	
Civic Pageant	London	1624* F	
Tragedy	Unknown (Beeston's Boys in 1634)	1654**	
Comedy and Tragedy	Prince's (?)	Lost	
Unknown	Palsgrave's	Lost	
Tragedy	Palsgrave's	Lost	
Comedy	Palsgrave's	Lost	
Unknown	Palsgrave's	Lost	
Tragedy	Prince's	Lost	
Comedy	Lady Elizabeth's at Norwich	Lost	
Unknown	King's	Lost	
Tragedy	Palsgrave's	Lost	

DATE	AUTHOR	TITLE	LIMITS
1625	Beaumont, John	*The Theatre of Apollo*	1625
	'J.D.'	*The Knave in Grain, New Vamped* (See Supp.	*c.* 1625; rev.
	(author or reviser?)	II, m.)	*c.* 1632
	Davenport, Robert	*A New Trick to Cheat the Devil*	*c.* 1624–1639
	Fisher, Jasper	*Fuimus Troes* (*The True Trojans*)	*c.* 1611–1633
	Fletcher, J.	*The Elder Brother*	1625(?)
	(revised by Massinger?)		
	Heywood, Thomas	*The Escapades of Jupiter, or Calisto* (Episodes	*c.* 1625
		from *The Golden Age* and *The Silver Age*,	
		1610 and 1611.)	
	Jonson, Ben	*The Fortunate Isles and Their Union* (Revision	9 Jan.
		of *Neptune's Triumph*, 1624. Same as *Virtue*	
		and Beauty Reconciled [Hazlitt, *Manual*, p.	
		247]?)	
	Massinger, Philip	*A New Way to Pay Old Debts*	1625
	Sampson, William	*The Vow Breaker, or The Fair Maid of Clifton*	1625(?)–1636
	Sampson, William	*The Widow's Prize, or The Woman Captain*	lic. 25 Jan.
	Shirley, James	*St. Albans* (S.R., 1640.)	*c.* 1625–1640
	Shirley, James	*The School of Compliment* (*Love Tricks*)	lic. 11 Feb.
	Webster; Rowley, W.	*A Cure for a Cuckold*	1624–*c.* 1625
	(& Heywood?)		
	Anon.	*Clytophan*	*c.* 1620–*c.* 1630
	(Ainsworth, William,?)		
	Anon. (Davenport, R?)	*A Fool and Her Maidenhead Soon Parted*	*c.* 1624(?)–1639
	Anon.	*The Partial Law*	*c.* 1615–1630(?)
	Anon.	*Wine, Beer, and Ale Together by the Ears*	1624–1626(?)
		(Augmented in 1630 ed. as *Wine, Beer,*	
		Ale, and Tobacco Contending for Superiority.)	
1626	Bellamy, Henry	*Iphis*	1621–1623
	Beuil, Honorat de,	*L'Artenice* (*Les Bergeries, The Queen's Pas-*	21 Feb.
	Seigneur de Racan	*toral*) (Written by a foreigner, but often	(acted)
		attrib. to Henrietta Maria.)	
	Davenport, Robert	*The Pirate*	*c.* 1623–1640
	Fane, Rachel	*Dramatic Pastimes for Children* (Title ascribed	1626–1630?
		by later hand on MS.)	
	Fletcher (with Massinger?	*The Fair Maid of the Inn*	lic. 22 Jan.
	Rowley, W.? Webster,		
	J.? & Ford?)		
	Hemming, William	*The Jews' Tragedy*	*c.* 1622–1642
	Jonson, Ben	*The Staple of News*	Feb.
	Massinger, Philip	*The Painter* (S.R., 1653.)	*c.* 1613–1640
	Massinger, Philip	*The Roman Actor*	lic. 11 Oct.
	May, Thomas	*Cleopatra, Queen of Egypt*	1626
	Mewe, William	*Pseudomagia*	1618–*c.* 1627
	Middleton, Thomas	*The Conqueror's Custom, or The Fair Prisoner*	*c.* 1601–1627
		(Ment. by Hill; see Supp. II, m.)	
	Middleton, Thomas	*The Triumphs of Health and Prosperity*	30 Oct.
	Randolph, Thomas	*Aristippus, or The Jovial Philosopher*	1625–1626

TYPE	AUSPICES	EARLIEST TEXTS	LATEST TEXTS
Entertainment	Intended for Court	MS	E
Comedy	Red Bull Company at Fortune	1640*	G
Comedy	Queen Henrietta's (?)	1639**	C
History	Magdalen Col., Oxford	1633*	D
Comedy	King's	1637 & MS	V
Classical Legend	Unknown	MS	S
Mask	Court	[1625]	C
Comedy	Queen Henrietta's	1633*	E,M,C,S,F
Tragedy and History	Unknown	1636*	B
Comedy	Prince's	Lost	
Tragedy	Unknown	Lost	
Comedy	Lady Elizabeth's	1631	C,T
Comedy	Unknown	1661**	
Latin Comedy	Emmanuel Col., Cambridge (?)	MS	F
Unknown	Queen Henrietta's (?)	Lost	
Tragicomedy	Closet (?)	MS	E
Academic Entertainment	Cambridge (?)	1629 & MS	E
Latin Comedy	St John's Col., Oxford	MS	F
French Pastoral	Henrietta's Maids	1625	C
Unknown	Unknown	Lost	
Pastoral Mask	Private: Children of Apthorpe	MS	
Tragicomedy (?)	King's	1647	C
Tragedy	Unknown	1662*	B
Comedy	King's	1631	C,S
Unknown	Unknown	Lost	
Tragedy	King's	1629*	E,M,C
Tragedy	Unknown	1639** & MS	T
Latin Comedy	Emmanuel Col., Cambridge?	MSS	E,F
Tragicomedy (?)	Unknown	Lost	
Civic Pageant	London	1626*	C,T
Comic Show	Trinity Col., Cambridge	1630 & MS	C

DATE	AUTHOR	TITLE	LIMITS
	Shirley, James	*The Brothers*	lic. 4 Nov.
	Shirley, James	*The Maid's Revenge*	lic. 9 Feb.
	Shirley, James	*The Wedding*	1626
	Simons, Joseph (?)	*S. Damianus*	13 Feb.
	'J.W.'	*The Valiant Scot*	1625–1626 (pub. 1637)
	Anon. (Heywood? Davenport?)	*Dick of Devonshire*	1626
	Anon.	*Parthenia* (Trans. Groto's *Il Pentimento amoroso*.)	*c.* 1625– *c.* 1630(?)
	Anon.	*Queen Henrietta's Mask*	16 Nov.
1627	Crowther, Joseph	*Cephalus et Procris*	1626–1628
	Davenant, William	*The Cruel Brother*	lic. 12 Jan.
	Hawkins, William	*Apollo Shroving*	6 Feb.
	Heywood, Thomas	*The English Traveller*	*c.* 1627
	Massinger, Philip	*The Great Duke of Florence* (*The Great Duke*)	lic. 5 July
	Massinger, Philip	*The Judge*	lic. 6 June
	May, Thomas	*Antigone, the Theban Princess*	1627–1631
	Newman, Thomas	*The Andrian Woman* (*Andria*) (Trans. Terence.)	1627
	Newman, Thomas	*The Eunuch* (Trans. Terence's *Eunuchus*.)	1627
	Randolph, Thomas	*The Conceited Pedlar* (*The University Pedlar*) (Prob. same as *The Pedlar*, assigned to Davenport in S.R., 1630.)	1 Nov.
	Randolph, T. (revised by 'F.J.')	*Plutophthalmia Plutogamia* (*Hey for Honesty, Down with Knavery*) (Adapt. Aristophanes' *Plutus*.)	*c.* 1626–*c.* 1628 (revised 1648–*c.* 1649)
	Randolph, Thomas	*Thomas Randolph's Salting*	1627
	Simons, Joseph	*Leo Armenus* (*Ultio Divina*)	1624–1629(?)
	Anon.	*The Duke of Buckingham's Mask*	15 May
	Anon.	*Queen Henrietta's Mask*	14 or 15 Jan.
1628	Davenant, William	*Albovine, King of the Lombards*	1626–1629
	Davenport, Robert	*King John and Matilda*	*c.* 1628–1629
	Dekker, Thomas	*Britannia's Honour*	29 Oct.
	Ford, John	*The Lover's Melancholy*	lic. 24 Nov.
	Ford, John	*The Queen, or The Excellency of Her Sex*	*c.* 1621–1642
	Gomersall, Robert	*Lodovick Sforza*	1622–1628 (pub.)
	Massinger, Philip	*The Honour of Women* (Title coupled in S.R., 1653, with *The Spanish Viceroy*, 1624.)	lic. 6 May
	Massinger, Philip	*The Tyrant* (Identification with *The King and the Subject*, 1638, prob. incorrect.)	*c.* 1613–1640
	May, Thomas	*Julia Agrippina, Empress of Rome*	1628
	Reynolds, Henry	*Aminta* (Trans. Tasso.)	1628
	Shirley, James	*The Witty Fair One*	lic. 3 Oct.

TYPE	AUSPICES	EARLIEST TEXTS	LATEST TEXTS
Unknown	Queen Henrietta's (?)	Lost	C
Tragedy	Queen Henrietta's	1639★	C,T
Comedy	Queen Henrietta's	1629	C,T
Latin Play	St Omers	MSS	
Tragedy	Acted at Fortune in 1639(?) (by King's Provincial Company?)	1637★	S
Tragicomedy	Unknown	MS	G
Latin Pastoral	Cambridge(?)	MS	F
Mask	Court	Lost	
Latin Comedy	St John's Col., Oxford (?)	MS	F
Tragedy	King's	1630	C
Comedy	Hadleigh School, Suffolk	[c. 1627]★	E
Tragicomedy	Queen Henrietta's	1633★	M,F,T
Tragicomedy	Queen Henrietta's	1636★	E,M,C
Comedy (?)	King's	Lost	
Tragedy	Unacted	1631★	T
Comedy	For acting in schools	1627★	
Comedy	For acting in schools	1627★	
Monologue	Trinity Col., Cambridge	1630 & MSS	C
Comedy	Trinity Col., Cambridge (?)	1651★	C
Monologue	Trinity Col., Cambridge	MS	
Latin Tragedy	St Omers	1656 & MSS	
Mask	Court	Lost	
Mask	Court	Lost	
Tragedy	Unacted	1629	C
History	Queen Henrietta's	1655	C,T
Civic Pageant	London	1628★	C
Tragicomedy	King's	1629★	B,M,S
Tragicomedy	Unknown	1653★	B,T
Tragedy	Unacted (?)	1628	B
Comedy	Unknown	Lost	
Tragedy	Unknown	Lost	
Tragedy	Unknown	1639★★	B
Pastoral	Closet	1628★	
Comedy	Queen Henrietta's	1633★	M,T

DATE	AUTHOR	TITLE	LIMITS
	Vincent, Thomas	*Paria*	3 Mar.
	Anon. (Shirley, H.?)	*The Dumb Bawd of Venice* (Prob. same as H. Shirley's *The Dumb Bawd*, 1623.)	15 Apr. (acted)
	Anon.	*Philander, King of Thrace*	a. 1627
1629	Brome, Richard	*The Lovesick Maid, or The Honour of Young Ladies*	lic. 9 Feb.
	Brome, Richard	*The Northern Lass* (mistranscribed in Pepys as *The Northern Castle*, 1667)	lic. 29 July(?)
	Carlell, Lodowick	*The Deserving Favourite*	*c.* 1622–1629
	Clavell, J. ('Shakerly Marmion' in S.R., 1653)	*The Soddered Citizen*	*c.* 1629–1631
	Davenant, William	*The Just Italian*	lic. 2 Oct.
	Davenant, William	*The Siege* (Prob. same as *The Colonel*, lic. 22 July.)	1629(?)
	Dekker, Thomas	*Believe It Is So and 'Tis So* (Ment. by Hill.)	*c.* 1594–*c.* 1629
	Dekker, Thomas	*London's Tempe, or The Field of Happiness*	29 Oct.
	Dekker, Thomas	*The White Moor* (Ment. by Hill; see Supp. II, m.)	*c.* 1594–*c.* 1629
	Jonson, Ben	*The New Inn, or The Light Heart*	lic. 19 Jan.
	Massinger, Philip	*Minerva's Sacrifice* (*The Forced Lady*, alternative title, added in S.R., 1653, an independent Massinger play; see 1633.)	lic. 3 Nov.
	Massinger, Philip	*The Picture*	lic. 8 June
	Randolph, Thomas	*Praeludium*	Nov.(?)
	Randolph, Thomas	*The Prodigal Scholar* (S.R. 1660. May be same as following.)	*c.* 1623–1635
	Randolph, Thomas	*The Drinking Academy, or The Cheaters' Holiday* (May be same as preceding.)	1626–1631
	Shirley, James	*The Grateful Servant* (*The Faithful Servant*)	lic. 3 Nov.
	Anon. ('Reverardus')	*Hierarchomachia, or The Anti-Bishop*	1629(?)
1630	Brome, Richard	*The City Wit, or The Woman Wears the Breeches*	*c.* 1630
	Ford, John	*Beauty in a Trance* (S.R., 1653.)	28 Nov. (acted)
	Ford, John	*The Broken Heart*	*c.* 1630–1633
	Randolph, Thomas	*Amyntas, or The Impossible Dowry* (Revived as *The Wavering Nymph, or Mad Amyntas c.* 1683–4 when it was possibly altered by Aphra Behn.)	lic. 26 Nov.
	Randolph, Thomas	*The Muses' Looking Glass* (*The Entertainment*)	lic. 25 Nov.
	Sidnam, Jonathan	*Filli di Sciro, or Phillis of Scyros* (Trans. Bonarelli.)	*c.* 1630–*c.*1631
	Sidnam, Jonathan	*Il Pastor Fido* (Trans. Guarini.)	1630
	Wilson, Arthur	*The Inconstant Lady, or Better Late Than Never*	*c.* 1629–1630
	Anon.	*An Induction for the House*	Nov.

TYPE	AUSPICES	EARLIEST TEXTS	LATEST TEXTS
Latin Comedy	Trinity Col., Cambridge	1648★ & MSS	F
Comedy	King's	Lost	
Tragicomedy	Unknown	MS ('author-plot')	E
Comedy (?)	King's	Lost	
Comedy	King's	1632	C,T
Tragicomedy	King's	1629	E
Comedy	King's	MS	G
Comedy	King's	1630	C
Tragicomedy	King's (?)	1673★	C
Unknown	Unknown	Lost	
Civic Pageant	London	[1629]★	C
Tragicomedy (?)	Unknown	Lost	
Comedy	King's	1631	C,S
Tragedy (?)	King's	Lost	
Tragicomedy	King's	1630★	C,T
Dialogue	King's Revels (?)	MS	C
Comedy	Trinity Col., Cambridge (?)	Lost (?)	
Comedy	Westminster School (?)	MS	E
Tragicomedy	Queen Henrietta's	1630	C,T
'Comic Satire'	Unknown	MS	
Comedy	King's Revels (?) (Revived by Queen Henrietta's, 1637–9?)	1653★	C,T
Unknown	King's	Lost	
Tragedy	King's	1633★	E,M,B,S,C
Pastoral	King's Revels	1638	C
Comedy	King's Revels	1638	C
Pastoral	Closet	1655★★	
Pastoral	Closet	MS	
Comedy	King's	MSS	E,T
Curtain-raiser (?)	King's	Lost	

DATE	AUTHOR	TITLE	LIMITS
1631	Brome, Richard	*The Queen's Exchange* (*The Royal Exchange*, 1661.)	1629–1632(?)
	Dekker, Thomas	*Gustavus, King of Sweden* (S.R., 1660.)	1630(?)–1632
	Dekker, T. (& Day, J.?)	*The Wonder of a Kingdom* (Same as *Come See a Wonder* 1623?)	1619–1631
	Hausted, Peter	*Senile Odium*	*c.* 1627–1631
	Heywood, Thomas	*II The Fair Maid of the West, or A Girl Worth Gold*	*c.* 1630–1631
	Heywood, Thomas	*London's Jus Honorarium*	29 Oct.
	Jonson, Ben	*Chloridia: Rites to Chloris and Her Nymphs*	22 Feb.
	Jonson, Ben	*Love's Triumph through Callipolis*	9 Jan.
	Knevet, Ralph	*Rhodon and Iris*	3 May
	Mabbe, James	*The Spanish Bawd* (*Calisto and Meliboea*) (Trans. Roja's *Celestina*.)	1631
	Marmion, Shackerly	*Holland's Leaguer*	Dec. (acted)
	Massinger, Philip	*Believe as You List* (See *Sebastian, King of Portugal*, 1601.)	lic. 6 May
	Massinger, Philip	*The Emperor of the East*	lic. 11 Mar.
	Massinger, Philip	*Fast and Welcome* (S.R., 1660.)	*c.* 1613–1640
	Massinger, Philip	*The Unfortunate Piety*	lic. 13 June
	Shirley, James	*The Contention for Honour and Riches* (See *Honoria and Mammon*, 1658.)	*c.* 1625–1632
	Shirley, James	*The Humorous Courtier* (*The Duke*)	lic. 17 May
	Shirley, James	*Love's Cruelty*	lic. 14 Nov.
	Shirley, James	*The Traitor*	lic. 4 May
	Simons, Joseph	*Zeno sive Ambitio Infelix* (*Fratrum Concordia Saeva*)	7 Aug.
	Wilson, Arthur	*The Swisser*	1631
	Wright, Abraham	*The Reformation*	1629–1633
1632	'T.B.' (Brewer, Anth. or Th.?)	*The Country Girl*	1632–*c.* 1633
	Brome, Richard	*The Novella*	1632–1633
	Brome, Richard	*The Weeding of the Covent Garden, or The Middlesex Justice of Peace* (*The Covent Garden Weeded*)	1632
	Ford, John	*Love's Sacrifice*	1632–1633
	Ford, John	*'Tis Pity She's a Whore*	1615–1633
	Hausted, Peter	*The Rival Friends*	19 Mar.
	Heywood, Thomas	*Londini Artium et Scientiarum Scaturigo, or London's Fountain of Arts and Sciences*	29 Oct.
	Jonson, Ben	*The Magnetic Lady, or Humours Reconciled*	lic. 12 Oct.
	Massinger, Philip	*The City Madam*	lic. 25 May
	Percy, William	*Necromantes, or The Two Supposed Heads*	1632
	Pestell, Jr (?), Thomas	*Versipellis*	1631–1632
	Randolph, Thomas	*The Jealous Lovers*	20 Mar.
	Shirley, James	*The Ball* (Chapman's name associated with Shirley's prob. through error.)	lic. 16 Nov.

TYPE	AUSPICES	EARLIEST TEXTS	LATEST TEXTS
Tragicomedy	King's (?)	1657**	C
Foreign History	Unknown	Lost	
Comedy	Queen Henrietta's	1636*	C
Latin Comedy	Queens' Col., Cambridge	1633* & MS	E (text & trans.), F
Comedy	Queen Henrietta's	1631*	M,S,F
Civic Pageant	London	1631*	C
Mask	Court	[1631]	C
Mask	Court	1630[31]	C
Pastoral	Florists' Feast, Norwich	1631**	
Romance	Closet	1631** & MS	E
Comedy	Prince Charles's	1632*	C,T
Tragedy	King's	MS F	G,M,C
Tragicomedy	King's	1632*	C,T
Comedy	Unknown	Lost	
Tragedy (?)	King's	Lost	
Moral	Privately acted (?)	1633*	C
Comedy	Queen Henrietta's	1640*	C,T
Tragedy	Queen Henrietta's	1640*	C,T
Tragedy	Queen Henrietta's	1635	M,S
Latin Tragedy	St Omers	1648 & MSS	
Tragicomedy	King's	MS	E
Comedy	St John's Col., Oxford	Lost	
Comedy	King's (?)	1647*	
Comedy	King's	1653*	C
Comedy	King's (?)	1659*	C,T
Tragedy	Queen Henrietta's	1633*	B,M,T
Tragedy	Queen Henrietta's	1633**	B,M,S,F,C
Tragicomedy	Queens' Col., Cambridge	1632*	E
Civic Pageant	London	1632*	C
Comedy	King's	1641	C
Comedy	King's	1658 or 1659*	E,M,C,S
Comedy	Closet (?)	MSS	
Latin Comedy	Queens' Col., Cambridge	Lost	
Comedy	Trinity Col., Cambridge	1632	C
Comedy	Queen Henrietta's	1639*	C,T

DATE	AUTHOR	TITLE	LIMITS
	Shirley, James	*Changes, or Love in a Maze*	lic. 10 Jan.
	Shirley, James	*Hyde Park*	lic. 20 Apr.
	Tatham, John	*Love Crowns the End*	1632
	Townshend, Aurelian	*Albion's Triumph*	8 Jan.
	Townshend, Aurelian	*Tempe Restored*	14 Feb.
	Anon.	*The Invisible Knight* (Ment. in *The Bird in a Cage*, 1633. Ghost?)	c. 1632–1633
	Anon.	*The Ring* (Also ment. in above. Ghost?)	c. 1632–1633
1633	Blencowe, John	*Mercurius sive Literarum Lucta*	1629–1638(?)
	Brome, R.; Chapman, G.	*Christianetta, or Marriage and Hanging Go by Destiny* (Ment. by Hill; see Supp. II, m.)	c. 1623–1634
	Cokain, Aston	*Trappolin Creduto Principe, or Trappolin Supposed a Prince*	1633
	Cowley, Abraham	*Love's Riddle*	c. 1633–1636
	Drummond, William (?)	*The Entertainment at Edinburgh*	15 June
	Ford, J.	*Perkin Warbeck*	c. 1625–1634
	Hemming, William	*The Coursing of a Hare, or The Madcap*	Mar.
	Heywood, Thomas	*Londini Emporia, or London's Mercatura*	29 Oct.
	Heywood, Thomas	*A Maidenhead Well Lost*	c. 1625–1634
	Jonson, Ben	*The King's Entertainment at Welbeck* (*Love's Welcome at Welbeck*)	21 May
	Jonson, Ben	*A Tale of a Tub* (Revised version?)	lic. 7 May
	Marmion, Shackerly	*A Fine Companion*	1632–1633
	Massinger, Philip	*The City Honest Man* (S.R., 1653; see *The Guardian*, below.)	c. 1615–1641
	Massinger, Philip	*The Forced Lady* (King's list, 1641; see *Minerva's Sacrifice*, 1629.)	c. 1615–1641
	Massinger, Philip	*The Guardian* (Title coupled in S.R., 1653, with *The City Honest Man*, above.)	lic. 31 Oct.
	Milton, John	*Arcades* (Fragment.)	1630–1634
	Montague, Walter	*The Shepherd's Paradise*	9 Jan.
	Mountfort, Walter	*The Launching of the Mary, or The Seaman's Honest Wife*	lic. 27 June
	Nabbes, Thomas	*Covent Garden*	1633
	Rickets, John	*Byrsa Basilica sive Regale Excambium*	1633(?)
	Shirley, James	*The Bird in a Cage* (*The Beauties*)	lic. 21 June
	Shirley, James	*The Gamester*	lic. 11 Nov.
	Shirley, James	*The Young Admiral*	lic. 3 July
	Wilson, Arthur	*The Corporal*	lic. 14 Jan. (?)
	Anon.	*II The City Shuffler* (First part unknown.)	1633(?)

TYPE	AUSPICES	EARLIEST TEXTS	LATEST TEXTS
Comedy	'King's Revels' (Prince Charles's?)	1632*	C,T
Comedy	Queen Henrietta's	1637*	M,T
Pastoral	Bingham School, Notts.	1640**	C
Mask	Court	1631[32]*	C
Mask	Court	1631[32]*	C
Unknown	Unknown	Lost	
Unknown	Unknown	Lost	
Latin Comedy	St John's Col., Oxford (?)	MS	F
Comedy (?)	Unknown	Lost	
Comedy	Unknown	1658**	C
Pastoral	Unacted	1638	C
Royal Entertainment	Edinburgh	1633*	C
History	Queen Henrietta's	1634* & MS	B,M,S,C
Comedy	King's Revels	Lost	
Civic Pageant	London	1633*	C
Comedy	Queen Henrietta's	1634*	C,T
Royal Entertainment	Host: William Cavendish	1641 & MS	C
Comedy	Queen Henrietta's	1640	C
Comedy	Prince Charles's	1633*	C,T
Unknown	Unknown	Lost	
Tragedy	King's	Lost	
Comedy	King's	1655*	M,C,T
Entertainment	Harefield	1645 F & MS F	C
Pastoral Romance	Court	1629 [1659] or 1659* & MSS	
Comedy	Unknown	MS	G
Comedy	Queen Henrietta's	1638**	C
Latin Comedy	Jesus Col., Cambridge (?)	MS	B (trans.), E,F
Comedy	Queen Henrietta's	1633*	C,T
Comedy	Queen Henrietta's	1637*	C,T
Tragicomedy	Queen Henrietta's	1637*	C,T
Comedy	King's	MSS (frags.)	
Comedy (?)	King's Revels	Lost	

DATE	AUTHOR	TITLE	LIMITS
1634	Brome, R.; Heywood, T.	*The Late Lancashire Witches*	1634
	Brome, R. (?) & Heywood, T. (?)	*The Apprentice's Prize* (S.R., 1654.)	*c.* 1633–1641
	Brome, R.; Heywood, T.	*Sir Martin Skink* (S.R., 1654.)	*c.* 1633–1641
	Carew, Thomas	*Coelum Britannicum*	18 Feb.
	Carlell, Lodowick	*The Spartan Ladies* (*The Spartan Lady*)	1 May (acted)
	Davenant, William	*Love and Honour* (*The Courage of Love. The Nonpareilles, or The Matchless Maids*)	lic. 20 Nov.
	Davenant, William	*The Wits*	lic. 19 Jan.
	Glapthorne, Henry	*Albertus Wallenstein*	1634–1639
	Heywood, Thomas	*Love's Mistress, or The Queen's Mask* (*Cupid and Psyche, or Cupid's Mistress*)	1634
	Jonson, Ben	*Love's Welcome at Bolsover*	30 July
	Le Grys, Robert	*Nothing Impossible to Love* (S.R., 1660.)	b. 1635
	Lovelace, Richard	*The Scholars*	1634–1635(?)
	Massinger, Philip (reviser)	*Cleander* (*Lisander and Calista*) (Revision of *The Wandering Lovers*, 1623.)	lic. 7 May
	Massinger, Philip (reviser)	*A Very Woman, or The Prince of Tarent* (Poss. reworking of Fletcher and Massinger play of *c.* 1619–22.)	lic. 6 June
	Milton, John	*Comus* (*The Mask at Ludlow Castle*)	29 Sept.
	Nabbes, Thomas	*Tottenham Court*	1633–1634
	Peaps, [William?]	*Love in Its Ecstasy, or The Large Prerogative*	*c.* 1634
	Rutter, Joseph	*The Shepherds' Holiday*	1633–1635
	Shirley, James	*The Example*	lic. 24 June
	Shirley, James	*The Opportunity*	lic. 29 Nov.
	Shirley, James	*The Triumph of Peace*	3 Feb.
	Sparrow, Thomas	*Confessor*	*c.* 1630–1640(?)
	Taylor, John	*The Triumphs of Fame and Honour*	29 Oct.
	Anon.	*Doctor Lamb and the Witches* (An earlier play revived, with additions.)	lic. 16 Aug. (as old)
	Anon.	*The Entertainment at Chirke Castle* (*The Mask of the Four Seasons*)	1634(?)
	Anon.	*Love's Aftergame, or The Proxy*	lic. 24 Nov.
1635	Bristowe, Francis	*King Free-Will* (Trans. Francesco Negri Di Bassano's *Tragedia del libero arbitrio*.) (See Biog. Dram., I, 68.)	1635
	Brome, Richard	*The New Academy, or The New Exchange*	1635(?)
	Brome, Richard	*The Queen and Concubine*	1635–1639
	Brome, Richard	*The Sparagus Garden* (*Tom Hoydon o' Tanton Deane*)	1635
	Cartwright, William	*The Ordinary, or The City Cozener*	1634–1635
	Davenant, William	*News from Plymouth*	lic. 1 Aug.

TYPE	AUSPICES	EARLIEST TEXTS	LATEST TEXTS
Topical Play	King's	1634★	C,T
Comedy (?)	King's (?)	Lost	
History	King's (?)	Lost	
Mask	Court	1634	C,F
Tragicomedy (?)	King's	Lost	
Tragicomedy	King's	1649	E
Comedy	King's	1636	C,T
Foreign History	King's	1639 or 1640★	C
Classical Legend	Queen Henrietta's	1636	C,S
Royal Entertainment	Host: William Cavendish	1641 & MS	C
Tragicomedy (?)	Unknown	Lost	
Comedy	Gloucester Hall, Oxford (?), & Queen Henrietta's in 1637–42 (?)	Lost (Prol. and Epil. extant)	
Tragicomedy	King's	1647	C
Tragicomedy	King's	1655★	C
Moral Mask	Ludlow Castle	1637 F & MSS F	M
Comedy	Prince's Men, or King's Revels	1638★★	C
Pastoral Tragicomedy	Unacted	1649★	
Pastoral	Queen Henrietta's	1635★	D
Comedy	Queen Henrietta's	1637★	C,T
Comedy	Queen Henrietta's	1640★	C
Mask	Inns of Court at Court	1633[34]	M,C
Latin Comedy	St John's Col., Cambridge (?)	MS	F
Civic Pageant	London	1634★	
Topical Play	King's Revels	Lost	
Entertainment	Thomas Middleton's	MS	C
Comedy (?)	King's Revels	Lost	
Anti-Catholic Moral	Closet (?)	MS (lost?)	
Comedy	King's Revels (?)	1659★	C
Tragicomedy	King's Revels	1659★	C
Comedy	King's Revels	1640★	C,T
Comedy	Christ Church, Oxford (?)	1651★	C,D
Comedy	King's	1673★	C

DATE	AUTHOR	TITLE	LIMITS
	Davenant, William	*The Platonic Lovers*	lic. 16 Nov.
	Davenant, William	*The Temple of Love*	10 Feb.
	Davenport, Robert	*A Dialogue between Policy and Piety*	*c.* 1635
	Digby, Kenelm	*Amyntas* (Trans. Tasso's *Aminta*.)	*c.* 1630–1638
	Digby, Kenelm	*Il Pastor Fido* (Trans. Guarini.)	*c.* 1630–1638
	Ford, John	*The Fancies Chaste and Noble* (1631 play revised?)	1635–1636
	Glapthorne, Henry	*The Lady Mother*	lic. 15 Oct.
	Glapthorne, Henry	*The Noble Husbands*	*c.* 1633–1642
	Glapthorne, Henry	*The Noble Trial* (S.R., 1653.)	*c.* 1633–1642
	Henrietta Maria (?)	*Florimene*	21 Dec.
	Heywood, Thomas	*A Challenge for Beauty*	1634–1636
	Heywood, Thomas	*Londini Sinus Salutis, or London's Harbour of Health and Happiness*	29 Oct.
	Heywood, Thomas	*Pleasant Dialogues and Dramas* (A miscellany, including playlets, some of which may have been parts of lost dramas: *Amphrisa, or The Forsaken Shepherdess* [*Pelopaea and Alope*], *Apollo and Daphne* [from Ovid], *Jupiter and Io*.)	1635 (S.R.)
	Jones, John	*Adrasta, or The Woman's Spleen and Love's Conquest*	1635 (pub.)
	Jordan, Thomas	*Money Is an Ass* (*Wealth Outwitted*)	*c.* 1635(?)
	Killigrew, Henry	*The Conspiracy* (*Pallantus and Eudora*)	8 Jan.(?)
	Killigrew, Thomas	*The Prisoners*	1632–1636
	Kirke, John	*The Seven Champions of Christendom*	1634–1638
	Marmion, Shackerly	*The Antiquary*	1634–1636
	Massinger, Philip	*The Orator* (*The Noble Choice, or The Orator*, S.R., 1653. *The Noble Choice* may be an independent Massinger play.)	lic. 10 Jan.
	Nabbes, Thomas	*Hannibal and Scipio*	1635
	Richards, Nathaniel	*Messalina, the Roman Empress*	1634–1636
	Rider, William	*The Twins*	1630–1642
	Shirley, James	*The Coronation*	lic. 6 Feb.
	Shirley, James	*The Lady of Pleasure*	lic. 15 Oct.
	Speed, John	*Stonehenge* (Same as *The Converted Robber*, 1637?)	1635
	Wilde, George	*Eumorphus sive Cupido Adultus*	5 Feb.
	Anon.	*Icon Ecclesiastici*	1635–1637
	Anon.	*Love's Changelings' Change*	*c.* 1630–*c.* 1640(?)
	Anon.	*Truth's Triumphs* (Poss. subtitle of known play.)	Feb. (acted)
	Anon.	*Wit's Triumvirate, or The Philosopher*	1635 (MS date)
1636	Carlell, Lodowick	*I & II Arviragus and Philicia*	1635–1636
	Cartwright, William	*The Royal Slave*	30 Aug.
	Davenant, William	*The Triumphs of the Prince d'Amour*	23 or 24 Feb.

TYPE	AUSPICES	EARLIEST TEXTS	LATEST TEXTS
Comedy	King's	1636	C,T
Mask	Court	1634[35]	C,T
Moral Dialogue	Closet	MSS	
Pastoral	Closet	Lost	
Pastoral	Closet	MS (frag.)	C
Comedy	Queen Henrietta's	1638*	B,T
Tragicomedy	King's Revels	MS	G
Unknown	Unknown	Lost	
'Tragicomedy'	Unknown	Lost	
French Pastoral	Queen's Maids at Court	1635* (design)	
Tragicomedy	King's	1636*	C,T
Civic Pageant	London	1635*	C
Dialogues	Unacted (?)	1637*	B
Tragicomedy	Unacted	1635*	
Comedy	King's Revels (?)	1668**	
Tragicomedy	York House (?) & King's	1638	
Tragicomedy	Queen Henrietta's	1641	C,F
Heroical Romance	Prince Charles's (?)	1638*	E
Comedy	Queen Henrietta's	1641*	C,D
Unknown	King's	Lost	
Tragedy	Queen Henrietta's	1637*	C
Tragedy	King's Revels	1640*	B
Tragicomedy	King's Revels (?)	1655*	
Comedy	Queen Henrietta's	1640	C
Comedy	Queen Henrietta's	1637*	M,T
Pastoral	St John's Col.,	Lost (?)	M,T
Latin Comedy	St John's Col., Oxford	MS	E,F
Latin Comedy (Epigrams)	Unknown	MS	
Pastoral	Closet (?)	MS	
Unknown	Queen Henrietta's (?)	Lost (?)	
Comedy	Unknown	MS	S
Tragicomedy	King's	1639* & MSS	T
Tragicomedy	Christ Church, Oxford	1639 & MSS	C
Mask	Middle Temple	1635[36]	C

DATE	AUTHOR	TITLE	LIMITS
	Glapthorne, Henry	*The Hollander*	lic. 12 Mar.
	Killigrew, Thomas	*Claracilla (Claricilla, Clarasilla)*	1635–1636
	Killigrew, Thomas	*The Princess, or Love at First Sight*	1635–1637(?)
	Kynaston, Francis (?)	*Corona Minervae*	27 Feb.
	Massinger, Philip	*The Bashful Lover*	lic. 9 May
	May, Thomas	*The Old Couple*	lic. 1636
	More, Thomas	*Mr Moore's Revels*	1636
	Sackville, E. (?); & others	*The Entertainment at Richmond*	12 Sept.
	Shirley, James	*The Duke's Mistress*	lic. 18 Jan.
	Strode, William	*The Floating Island (Passions Calmed. Prudentius)*	29 Aug.
	Townshend, Aurelian	*A Pastoral Mask [with Anti-Mask of Man of Canada, Egyptians, Pantaloons, and Spaniards]*	*c.* 1632–1640
	Wilde, George	*Love's Hospital (Lovers' Hospital)*	30 Aug.
	Anon.	*Andronicus Comnenus*	*c.* 1636–1637
	Anon.	*The Presentment of Bushell's Rock*	23 Aug.
	Anon.	*A Projector Lately Dead* (Ghost title?)	1636 (ment.)
	Anon. (Hausted, P., now rejected)	*Senilis Amor*	1635–1636
	Anon.	*A Spanish Tragedy [of Petrus Crudelis]*	1626–1648(?)
1637	Berkeley, William	*The Lost Lady*	1637–1638
	Brome, Richard	*The English Moor, or The Mock Marriage*	1637
	Brome, Richard	*Wit in a Madness* (S.R., 1640.)	*c.* 1635–1640
	Carlell, Lodowick	*The Fool Would Be a Favourite, or The Discreet Lover*	*c.* 1625–1642
	Carlell, Lodowick	*Osmond the Great Turk, or The Noble Servant (Same as Osmond the Great Turk, 1622?)*	1622–*c.* 1638
	Cartwright, William	*The Lady Errant*	1628–1638
	Formido, Cornelius (?)	*The Governor (Same as The Governor, 1656?)*	16 or 17 Feb. (acted)
	Glapthorne, Henry	*The Ladies' Privilege (The Lady's Privilege)*	1637–1640
	Heywood, Thomas	*Londini Speculum, or London's Mirror*	30 Oct.
	Jonson, Ben	*Mortimer His Fall* (Left incomplete.)	1595–1637
	Jonson, Ben	*The Sad Shepherd, or A Tale of Robin Hood* (Left incomplete.)	*c.* 1612–1637
	Mayne, Jasper	*The City Match*	1637–1638(?)
	Nabbes, Thomas	*Microcosmus*	1637
	Nabbes, Thomas	*The Spring's Glory*	*c.* 1625–1638
	Neale, Thomas	*The Ward*	1637
	Rutter, J. (with Sackville, E. & R.?)	*I The Cid (The Valiant Cid)* (Trans. Corneille.)	1637–1638
	Shirley, James	*The Royal Master*	1637 (lic. 23 Apr. 1638, for Queen's)
	Speed, J. (Wilde, G., now rejected)	*The Converted Robber (Same as Stonehenge, 1635?)*	1637 (MS date)
	Suckling, John	*Aglaura*	1637
	Suckling, John	*The Sad One* (Left incomplete.)	*c.* 1637–1641

TYPE	AUSPICES	EARLIEST TEXTS	LATEST TEXTS
Comedy	Queen Henrietta's	1640*	C
Tragicomedy	Queen Henrietta's	1641 & MS	T,F
Tragicomedy	King's (?)	1664*	C,F
Academic Entertainment	Museum Minervae	1635[36]**	C
Tragicomedy	King's	1655*	C
Comedy	Unknown	1658*	D,T
Mask	Eastgate, Oxford	MS	
Comic Show	Courtiers at Richmond	1636*	B
Tragicomedy	Queen Henrietta's	1638*	C
Moral Allegory	Christ Church, Oxford	1655*	C
Mask	Court	[*c.* 1636?]* (frag.)	
Comedy	St John's Col., Oxford	MSS	T
Jesuit Neo-Latin Tragedy	Royal Col.	MS (?)	
Royal Entertainment	Host: Thomas Bushell	1636*	
Comedy	Unknown	Lost	
Latin Comedy	Trinity Col. (?), Cambridge	MS	E (text & trans.), F
Tragedy	Oxford	Lost	
Tragicomedy	King's	1638 & MS	D,T
Comedy	Queen's	1659* & MS	C,E
Comedy (?)	Queen's (?)	Lost	
Tragicomedy	Queen's (?)	1657*	E
Tragicomedy	Queen's (?)	1657*	E
Tragicomedy	Privately acted	1651*	E
Unknown	King's	Lost (?)	E
Tragicomedy	Beeston's Boys	1640*	C,T
Civic Pageant	London	1637*	C
History	Unacted	1641	C
Comic Pastoral	Unacted	1641	C,B
Comedy	King's	1639	D,T
Moral Mask	Queen's	1637*	C
Mask	Unacted (?)	1638**	C
Tragicomedy	Unacted	MS	E
Tragicomedy	Beeston's Boys	1637[38]	
Comedy	I Ogilby's Men & Queen's	1638* & MS (lost)	C
Pastoral	St John's Col., Oxford	MS	
Tragedy	King's	1638 & MSS	C,T,F
Tragicomedy (?)	Unacted	1659	C

DATE	AUTHOR	TITLE	LIMITS
1638	Baylie, Simon	*The Wizard*	*c.* 1620–*c.* 1640
	Brome, Alexander (?)	*The Cunning Lovers*	1632–1639
	Brome, Richard	*The Antipodes*	1636–1638
	Brome, Richard	*The Damoiselle, or The New Ordinary*	1637–1638(?)
	Carlell, Lodowick	*I & II The Passionate Lovers*	Pt. I – 10 July 1638, Pt. II – 2 Dec. 1638
	Cartwright, William	*The Siege, or Love's Convert*	1628–1638
	Cowley, Abraham	*Naufragium Joculare*	2 Feb.
	Davenant, William	*Britannia Triumphans*	lic. 8 Jan.
	Davenant, William	*The Fair Favourite*	lic. 17 Nov.
	Davenant, William	*Luminalia, or The Festival of Light*	6 Feb.
	Davenant, William	*The Unfortunate Lovers* (Same as *The Tragedy of Heildebrand?*)	lic. 16 Apr.
	Ford, John	*The Lady's Trial*	lic. 3 May
	Ford, John (?)	*The Royal Combat* (S.R., 1660.)	*c.* 1621–1642
	Glapthorne, Henry	*Argalus and Parthenia*	*c.* 1632–1638
	Glapthorne, Henry	*Wit in a Constable*	1636–1638 (revised 1639)
	Heywood, Thomas	*Porta Pietatis, or The Port or Harbour of Piety*	29 Oct.
	Johnson, William	*Valetudinarium*	6 Feb.
	Massinger, Philip	*The King and the Subject*	lic. 5 June
	May, Charles	*Grobiana's Nuptials*	1638(?)
	Mayne, Jasper	*The Amorous War*	*c.* 1628–1648
	Mead, Robert	*The Combat of Love and Friendship*	1634–1642
	Nabbes, Thomas	*The Bride*	Summer
	Nabbes, Thomas	*A Presentation for the Prince* (*Time and the Almanac-Makers*)	29 May (projected)
	Oldisworth, Gyles	*The Pattern of Piety*	1638
	'T.R.' (Randolph, T., completed by Brathwait, R.?)	*Cornelianum Dolium*	1638 (pub.)
	Rawlins, Thomas	*The Rebellion*	1637–1639
	Rutter, J. (with Sackville, E. & R.?)	*II The Cid* (Trans. Desfontaines' *La Vraie suite du Cid.*)	1637–1639
	Salusbury, Thomas	*Love or Money*	*c.* 1638–1642
	Shirley, James	*The Constant Maid* (*Love Will Find out the Way*)	1630(?)–1640
	Shirley, James	*The Doubtful Heir* (*Rosania, or Love's Victory*)	*c.* 1638 lic. 1 June 1640, (for King's)
	Suckling, John	*Aglaura* (Second version.)	1638
	Suckling, John	*The Goblins*	*c.* 1637–1641
	Anon.	*The Fairy Knight, or Oberon the Second* (Based on Westminster School Play by T. Randolph, 1623–4?)	1637(?)–1658(?)
	Anon. (Boyle, R.?)	*The General* (Poss. earlier version of Boyle's play, 1662.)	*c.* 1637–1640
	Anon.	*Hocus-Pocus*	1638 (acted)

TYPE	AUSPICES	EARLIEST TEXTS	LATEST TEXTS
Comedy	Unknown	MSS	B
Comedy	Beeston's Boys	1654*	
Comedy	Queen's	1640*	C,S
Comedy	Beeston's Boys (?)	1653*	C
Tragicomedy	King's	1655**	T
Tragicomedy	Unacted (?)	1651*	C
Latin Comedy	Trinity Col., Cambridge	1638	C,F
Mask	Court	1637[38]*	C
Tragicomedy	King's	1673*	C
Mask	Court	1637[38]*	C
Tragedy	King's	1643	C
Comedy	Beeston's Boys	1639*	B
'Comedy'	Unknown	Lost	
Tragicomedy	Beeston's Boys	1639*	C
Comedy	Beeston's Boys	1640*	C
Civic Pageant	London	1638*	C
Latin Comedy	Queens' Col., Cambridge	MSS	F
Unknown	King's	Lost	
Comedy	St John's Col., Oxford	MS	E
Comedy	Unknown	1648	
Tragicomedy	Christ Church, Oxford	1654*	
Comedy	Beeston's Boys	1640*	C,T
Mask	Court	1638**	C
Interlude	Westminster	MS	
Latin Comedy	Unknown	1638*	
Tragedy	King's Revels	1640**	D
Tragicomedy	Unacted (?)	1640*	
Comedy	Privately Acted	MS	
Comedy	I Ogilby's Men, Dublin (?)	1640	C
Tragicomedy	I Ogilby's Men, Dublin, & King's	1653*	
Tragicomedy	King's	1638	C,T
Comedy	King's	1646	C
Comedy	Unknown	MS	E
Unknown	I Ogilby's Men, Dublin	Lost (?)	
Comedy	Red Bull Company at Coventry	Lost	

DATE	AUTHOR	TITLE	LIMITS
	Anon.	*The Irish Gentleman*	1636–1640
	Anon.	*The Toy*	1636–1640
	Anon.	*The Wasp*	*c.* 1636–1640
1639	Brome, Richard	*The Lovesick Court, or The Ambitious Politic*	*c.* 1632–1640
	Brome, Richard	*A Mad Couple Well Matched*	1637(?)–1639
	Cokain, Aston	*The Obstinate Lady*	*c.* 1630–1642
	'T.D.' (Drue, Thomas?)	*The Bloody Banquet*	*c.* 1617–1639
	Davenant, William	*The Spanish Lovers* (*The Distresses*)	lic. 30 Nov.
	Freeman, Ralph	*Imperiale*	1639 (pub.)
	Glapthorne, Henry	*The Duchess of Fernandina* (S.R., 1660.)	*c.* 1633–1642
	Glapthorne, Henry	*The Vestal* (S.R., 1660.)	*c.* 1633–1642
	Hemming, William	*The Fatal Contract* (*The Eunuch* in 1687 ed.)	*c.* 1638–1639(?)
	Heywood, Thomas	*Londini Status Pacatus, or London's Peaceable Estate*	29 Oct.
	Lower, William	*The Phoenix in Her Flames*	*c.* 1622–1639 (pub.)
	Massinger, Philip	*Alexius, or The Chaste Lover* (or *Gallant*)	lic. 25 Sept.
	Nabbes, Thomas	*The Unfortunate Mother*	1639(?)
	Sharpe, Lewis	*The Noble Stranger*	1638–1640
	Shirley, James	*The Gentleman of Venice*	lic. 30 Oct. (for Queen's)
	Shirley, James	*The Politician*	*c.* 1639(?)
	Shirley, James	*I St Patrick for Ireland* (Second part unknown.)	*c.* 1637–1640
	Suckling, John	*Brennoralt, or The Discontented Colonel*	1639–1641
	Anon.	*The Cardinal's Conspiracy* (An old play revived.)	1639 (acted)
	Anon.	*The Conceited Duke*	1639 (Cockpit list)
	Anon. (Dekker, T.?)	*The Telltale*	1605–*c.* 1640
	Anon.	*The Whore New Vamped*	29 Sept. (ordered suppressed)
	Anon. (Middleton and Rowley?)	*The World* (Same as *The World Tossed at Tennis*, 1620?)	1639 (Cockpit list)
1640	Brome, Richard	*The Court Beggar*	1639–1640
	Brome, Richard	*The Jewish Gentleman*	1640 (S.R.)
	Burnell, Henry	*Landgartha*	1639–1640
	Cavendish, W.; Shirley, J.	*The Country Captain* (*Captain Underwit*)	*c.* 1639–*c.* 1640
	Chamberlain, Robert	*The Swaggering Damsel*	*c.* 1625–1640 (pub.)
	Cokain, Aston	*A Mask at Bretbie*	6 Jan.
	Davenant, William	*Salmacida Spolia*	21 Jan.

TYPE	AUSPICES	EARLIEST TEXTS	LATEST TEXTS
Unknown	I Ogilby's Men, Dublin	Lost	
Comedy (?)	I Ogilby's Men, Dublin	Lost	
'Comical History'	King's Revels	MS	S
Tragicomedy	Prince Charles's (?)	1659*	C,T
Comedy	Beeston's Boys (?)	1653*	C,T
Comedy	Unknown	1657	C
Tragedy	Beeston's Boys (in 1639)	1639* F	G
Comedy	King's	1673*	C
Tragedy	Closet (?)	1639 & MS	
Tragedy	Unknown	Lost	
Tragedy	Unknown	Lost	
Tragedy	Queen Henrietta's	1653	
Civic Pageant	London	1639*	C
Tragedy	Unacted (?)	1639*	
Comedy (?)	King's	Lost	
Tragedy	Unacted	1640*	C
Tragicomedy	Queen's	1640*	
Tragicomedy	I Ogilby's Men, Dublin (?), & Queen's	1655**	C,S,T
Tragedy	I Ogilby's Men, Dublin (?), & Queen's	1655**	C,T
Neo-miracle	I Ogilby's Men, Dublin	1640*	C,T
Tragedy	King's	[1642?]	C
Unknown	Red Bull Company at Fortune	Lost	
Comedy (?)	Beeston's Boys	Lost	
Tragicomedy	Unknown	MS (IV incomplete)	G
Topical Comedy	Prince Charles's	Lost	
Mask (?)	Beeston's Boys	Lost (?)	
Comedy	Beeston's Boys	1653*	C
Comedy (?)	Unknown	Lost	
Tragicomedy	I Ogilby's Men, Dublin	1641*	
Comedy	King's	1649** & MS	C
Comedy	Beeston's Boys (?)	1640**	
Mask	Earl of Chesterfield's	1658 or 1659**	C
Mask	Court	1639[40]*	C

DATE	AUTHOR	TITLE	LIMITS
	Day, John	*The Parliament of Bees*	*c.* 1634–1640
	Fane, Mildmay	*Raguaillo D'Oceano*	1640
	Glapthorne (?) ('George Chapman' on t.p., 'Henry Glapthorne' in S.R. Glapthorne prob. author rather than reviser.)	*Revenge for Honour* (*The Parricide, or Revenge for Honour*, S.R., 1653.)	1637–1641
	Gough, John	*The Strange Discovery*	1624–1640 (pub.)
	Habington, William	*The Queen of Aragon* (*Cleodora*)	9 Apr.
	Harding, Samuel	*Sicily and Naples, or The Fatal Union*	1640 (pub.)
	Heywood, Thomas	*Love's Masterpiece*	1640 (S.R.)
	Holles, William	*The Country Court*	1635–1643
	Jordan, Thomas	*Love Hath Found His Eyes, or Distractions* (Prol. and Epil. extant.)	*c.* 1640–1649
	Massinger, Philip	*The Fair Anchoress of Pausilippo* (See following.)	lic. 26 Jan.
	Massinger, Philip	*The Prisoner*[s] (Identified with above in S.R., 1653, but separately listed as a tragicomedy in S.R., 1660.)	*c.* 1613–1640(?)
	Sadler, John	*Masquerade du Ciel*	1640
	Sandys, George	*Christ's Passion* (Trans. Grotius's *Christus Patiens*.)	1640
	Shirley, James	*The Imposture* (*The Impostor*)	lic. 10 Nov.
	Shirley, James (?)	*The Arcadia* (An older play falsely ascribed?)	1640 (pub.)
	Snelling, Thomas	*Thibaldus sive Vindictae Ingenium* (*Pharamus sive Libido Vindex*, in 1650 issue.)	1634–1640
	Suckling, John	*A Mask at Witten*	*c.* 1637(?)–1641
	Anon.	*The Cyprian Conqueror, or The Faithless Relict*	b.1642
	Anon.	*The Ghost, or The Woman Wears the Breeches*	1640(?)
	Anon. (Dekker and Middleton?)	*The Roaring Girl, or The Catchpole* (Revision of *The Roaring Girl*, 1608?)	*c.* 1640(?)
1641	Brathwait, Richard	*Mercurius Britannicus, or The English Intelligencer* (*The Censure of the Judges, or The Court Cure*)	1641
	Brome, Richard	*A Jovial Crew, or The Merry Beggars*	1641
	Cavendish, W. (& Shirley, J.)	*The Variety*	1639–1642
	Denham, John	*The Sophy*	1641(?)
	Fane, Mildmay	*Candy Restored* (*Candia Restaurata*)	12 Feb.
	Jordan, Thomas	*The Walks of Islington and Hogsdon* (*Tricks of Youth*)	lic. 2 Aug.
	Killigrew, Thomas	*The Parson's Wedding* (Revised after closing of theatres.)	1640–1641
	Lovelace, Richard	*The Soldier*	1640–1642
	Quarles, Francis	*The Virgin Widow*	*c.* 1640–1642
	Salusbury, Thomas	*An Antimask of a Citizen and Wife*	29 Dec.

TYPE	AUSPICES	EARLIEST TEXTS	LATEST TEXTS
Dialogue	Closet	1641★ & MS	M,S,T
Mask	At Apthorpe	MS	B
Tragedy	Unknown	1654★★	C
Tragicomedy	Closet (?)	1640★	
Tragicomedy	Amateurs at Court, & King's	1640★★	D
Tragedy	Unacted (?)	1640★	T
Comedy	Unknown	Lost	
Comedy	Pembroke Col., Cambridge (?)	Lost	
Comedy	Unknown	Lost	
Unknown	King's	Lost	
Tragicomedy	Unknown	Lost	
'Mask'	Closet	1640★	
Neo-miracle	Closet	1640	C
Tragicomedy	King's	1653★	C,T
Pastoral Tragicomedy	'Queen Henrietta's'	1640★	C,T
Latin Tragedy	St John's Col., Oxford	1640★★	C,T,F
Mask	House of Lionel Cranfield (?)	Lost	
Comedy	Closet (?)	MS	
Comedy	Unknown	1653★	
Comedy	Red Bull Company (?)	Lost (?)	
Latin Political Comedy	Closet	[1641]★★	C
English Translation	....	1641	
Comedy	Beeston's Boys	1652	C,T,S
Comedy	King's	1649★	
Tragedy	King's	1642	C
Political Allegory	At Apthorpe	MSS	B
Comedy	Red Bull Company (?)	1657★★	
Comedy	King's	1664★	C,D,F
Tragedy	Unacted	Lost	
Tragicomedy	Privately acted (by 1649)	1649	C,T
Mask	Privately acted (Chirk Castle?)	MS	

DATE	AUTHOR	TITLE	LIMITS
	Salusbury, Thomas	*An Antimask of Gypsies*	30 Dec.
	Salusbury, Thomas	*A Mask at Knowsley*	6 Jan.
	Shirley, James	*The Brothers* (*The Politic Father*)	lic. 26 May
	Shirley, James	*The Cardinal*	lic. 25 Nov.
	Tatham, John (?)	*The Whisperer, or What You Please*	*c.* 1640–1650
	Taylor, John (describer)	*England's Comfort and London's Joy*	25 Nov.
	Taylor, John	*A Pedlar and a Romish Priest*	1641
	Wild, Robert	*The Benefice*	1641(?)
	Anon.	*Canterbury His Change of Diet*	1641
	Anon.	*Charles, Duke of Bourbon* (Poss. same as *Burben*, 1599 add.)	1641 (S.R.)
	Anon.	*The Doge and the Dragon*	lic. 23 June
	Anon.	*England's First Happiness*, or *The Life of St Austin*	1641 (S.R.)
	Anon.	*Five Most Noble Speeches*	1641
	Anon.	*King Charles His Entertainment, and London's Loyalty*	1641
	Anon.	*The Parroiall* (i.e. *Pareil? Parol?*) *of Princes*	1641 (S.R.)
	Anon.	*Read and Wonder*	1641
1642	Cowley, Abraham	*The Guardian* (See *Cutter of Coleman Street*, 1661.)	12 Mar.
	Fane, Mildmay	*The Change*	Dec. (written)
	Fane, Mildmay	*Time's Trick upon the Cards*	22 Feb.
	Jaques, Francis	*The Queen of Corsica*	1642
	'J.S.'	*Andromana, or The Merchant's Wife*	1642–1660
	Shirley, James	*The Court Secret* (Revised as *The Secret*, 1664?)	1642
	Shirley, James	*The Sisters*	lic. 26 Apr.
	Anon. (often assumed to be Kirke, J.)	*The Irish Rebellion*	lic. 8 June
	Anon.	*A Threefold Discourse between Three Neighbors, Algate, Bishopsgate, and John Heyden, the Late Cobler of Hounsditch, a Professed Brownist*	1642
1643	Fuller, T. (?) (Wilson, J., now rejected)	*Andronicus: Impiety's Long Success, or Heaven's Late Revenge*	*c.* 1642–1643 pub. 1661
	Anon.	*Bel and the Dragon*	1643 (acted)
	Anon.	*The Cruel War*	1643
	Anon.	*Fraus Pia*	*c.* 1643–1660(?)
	Anon. (Fane, M.?)	*Time's Triumph* (*Sight and Search. Juno in Arcadia, Juno's Pastoral. The Bonds of Peace, Time's Distractions.*)	1641?–1643
	Anon.	*Tyrannical Government Anatomized, or A Discourse Concerning Evil Counsellors* (Trans. Buchanan's *Baptistes sive Calumnia.*)	1643

TYPE	AUSPICES	EARLIEST TEXTS	LATEST TEXTS
Mask	Privately acted (Chirk Castle?)	MS	
Mask	Lord Strange's House	MS	E
Comedy	King's	1653★	C
Tragedy	King's	1653★	M,T,F
Comedy (?)	Red Bull Company (?)	Lost	
Royal Entertainment	London	1641★	
Polemical Religious Dialogue	Closet	1641★	
Comedy	Cambridge (?)	1689★ & MSS	
Political Dialogue	Closet	1641★ F	
Tragedy	Unknown	Lost	
Romance (?)	Prince Charles's	Lost	
Neo-miracle (?)	Unknown	Lost	
Royal Entertainment	York to London	1641★	
Royal Entertainment	London	1641★	
Unknown	Unknown	Lost	
Political Dialogue	Closet	1641★	
Comedy	Trinity Col., Cambridge	1650★★	C
Political Allegory	Unacted (?)	MS	
Moral	At Apthorpe (?)	MS	
Tragedy	Unacted (?)	MS	
Tragedy	Unacted (?)	1660★	D
Tragicomedy	Unacted	1653★ & MS	C,T
Comedy	King's	1653★	C
Topical Play	Prince Charles's (?)	Lost	
Political Dialogue	Closet	1642★	
Tragedy	Oxford (?)	1661★	
Puppet Show	Holborn Bridge	Lost	
Political Dialogue	Closet	1643★	
Latin Comedy	Unknown	MS	
Pastoral-Allegorical Entertainment	Closet (?)	MS	T
Political Allegory	Closet	1642[43]★	E

DATE	AUTHOR	TITLE	LIMITS
1644	Fane, Mildmay	*Virtue's Triumph*	1644
	Anon.	*Titus, or The Palm of Christian Courage*	1644
1645	Burkhead, Henry	*Cola's Fury, or Lirenda's Misery*	1645
	Cavendish, J.; Brackley, E.	*The Concealed Fancies*	1644–1646
	Cavendish, J.; Brackley, E.	*A Pastoral*	1644–1646
	Fane, Mildmay	*Don Phoebo's Triumph*	1645(?)
1646	Burroughs,–	*The Fatal Friendship*	1646 (S.R.)
	Killigrew, Thomas	*The Pilgrim*	1646(?)
	Llueyln (or Llewellyn), Martin	*The King Found at Southwell* (Mr Loyd on t.p.)	5 May
	Shirley, James	*The Triumph of Beauty*	1646 (pub.)
1647	Baron, Robert	*Deorum Dona*	1647
	Baron, Robert	*Gripsius and Hegio, or The Passionate Lovers*	1647
	Fanshawe, Richard	*Il Pastor Fido (The Faithful Shepherd)* (Trans. Guarini.)	1647
	Mason, John	*School Moderator, or The Combat of Caps (Princeps Rhetoricus)*	21 Dec.
	Nedham, Marchmont	*The Levellers Levelled, or The Independents' Conspiracy to Root out Monarchy*	1647
	Sheppard, Samuel	*I The Committee-Man Curried*	1647
	Sheppard, Samuel	*II The Committee-Man Curried*	1647
	Anon.	*News out of the West, or The Character of a Mountebank*	1647
	Anon.	*Ruff, Cuff, and Band* (Same as *Band, Cuff, and Ruff*, 1615?)	24 Feb. 1647 (acted?)
	Anon.	*The Scottish Politic Presbyter Slain by an English Independent, or The Independents' Victory over the Presbyterian Party*	1647
1648	Sherburne, Edward	*Medea* (Trans. Seneca.)	1648
	Anon.	*I Crafty Cromwell, or Oliver Ordering Our New State*	1648
	Anon.	*II Crafty Cromwell, or Oliver in His Glory as King*	1648
	Anon.	*The Cuckow's Nest at Westminster, or The Parliament between the Two Lady-Birds, Queen Fairfax and Lady Cromwell*	1648
	Anon.	*The Devil and the Parliament, or The Parliament and the Devil*	1648
	Anon.	*Ding-Dong, or Sir Pitiful Parliament on His Death-bed*	1648
	Anon.	*The Kentish Fair, or The Parliament Sold to Their Best Worth*	1648
	Anon.	*Marcus et Marcellianus*	1648

TYPE	AUSPICES	EARLIEST TEXTS	LATEST TEXTS
Moral	Closet (?)	MS	
Biblical Moral	Jesuit Col., Kilkenny	1644*	
Political Tragicomedy	Closet	1646*	
Comedy	Closet	MS	E
Pastoral Dialogues	Closet	MS	
Moral Mask	At Apthorpe	MS	
Tragedy	King's (?)	Lost	
Tragedy	English players at Paris (?)	1664*	C,F
Entertainment	Cavaliers at Oxford	1646* F	
Mask	Privately acted	1646*	C,F
Mask	Closet	1647**	
Pastoral	Closet	1647**	
Pastoral	Closet	1647	
Academic Allegory	Mason's School, Surrey	1648* (extracts)	
Political Dialogue	Closet	1647*	
Political Dialogue	Closet	1647*	
Political Dialogue	Closet	1647*	
Comic Interlude	Unknown	1647*	
Comic Dialogue	Oxford (?)	MS (1646)	
Political Dialogue	Closet	1647*	C
Tragedy	Closet	1648*	
Political Dialogue	Closet	1648*	
Political Dialogue	Closet	1648*	
Political Dialogue	Closet	1648*	
Political Dialogue	Closet	1648*	
Political Dialogue	Closet	1648*	
Political Dialogue	Closet	1648*	
Latin Tragedy	St Omers	MS	

DATE	AUTHOR	TITLE	LIMITS
	Anon.	*Mercurius Honestus, or News from Westminster*	1648
	Anon.	*Mistress Parliament Brought to Bed*	1648
	Anon.	*Mistress Parliament, Her Gossiping*	1648
	Anon.	*Mistress Parliament, Her Invitation of Mistress London*	1648
	Anon.	*Mistress Parliament Presented in Her Bed*	1648
1649	'T.B.'	*The Rebellion of Naples, or The Tragedy of Massenello*	1649
	Wase, Christopher	*Electra* (Trans. Sophocles.)	1649–1650 (pub.)
	Anon.	*A Bartholomew Fairing*	1649
	Anon.	*Charles I*	1649
	Anon.	*The Disease of the House, or The State Mountebank Administering Physic to a Sick Parliament*	1649
	Anon.	*A New Bull-Baiting, or A Match Played at the Town Bull of Ely by Twelve Mongrels*	1649
	Anon.	*I Newmarket Fair, or A Parliament Outcry of State Commodities, Set to Sale*	1649
	Anon.	*II Newmarket Fair, or Mistress Parliament's New Figaries*	1649
	Anon.	*Women Will Have Their Will, or Give Christmas His Due*	1649
1650	Cartwright, George	*The Heroic Lover, or The Infanta of Spain*	*c.* 1645–*c.* 1655
	Fane, Mildmay	*De Pugna Animi*	1650
	Flecknoe, Richard	*Love in Its Infancy* (Earlier version of *Love's Dominion*, 1654.)	1650
	Flecknoe, Richard	*Love Stripped from Suspicion of Harm* (Projected. Became the above?)	1650
	Garfield, Benjamin	*The Unfortunate Fortunate*	b.1650
	Killigrew, Thomas	*I & II Cicilia and Clorinda, or Love in Arms*	1649–1650
	Tatham, John	*The Distracted State*	1641–1650
	Anon.	*Love's Victory*	*c.* 1630–*c.* 1650
	Anon.	*The White Ethiopian*	*c.* 1640(?)– *c.* 1650(?)
1651	Denny, William	*The Shepherd's Holiday*	1651
	Johnson, Nathaniel	*Pyrander* (Trans. from French. De Boisrobert's *Pyrandre et Lisimène*?)	1633(?)–1663
	Prestwich, Edmund	*Hippolytus* (Trans. Seneca.)	1651
	'J.S.'	*The Prince of Prigs' Revels*	3 Sept.– 11 Nov.
	Sheppard, Samuel	*The Jovial Crew, or The Devil Turned Ranter*	1651
	Willan, Leonard	*Astraea, or True Love's Mirror*	1651
	Anon.	*Felix Concordia Fratrum sive Joannes et Paulus*	1651
	Anon.	*Fortunae Ludibrium sive Belisarius*	17 Aug.
	Anon.	*Marcus Tullius Cicero*	1651 (pub.)

TYPE	AUSPICES	EARLIEST TEXTS	LATEST TEXTS
Political Dialogue	Closet	1648★	
Political Dialogue	Closet	1648★	C
Political Dialogue	Closet	1648★	
Political Dialogue	Closet	1648★	
Political Dialogue	Closet	1648★	
Contemporary Foreign History	Closet	1649★	
Tragedy	Closet	1649[/50?]★	
Political Dialogue	Closet	1649★	
Topical Tragedy	Closet	1649	
Political Dialogue	Closet	1649★	
Political Dialogue	Closet	1649★	
Political Dialogue	Closet	1649	
Political Dialogue	Closet	1649	
Political Dialogue	Closet	1649★	
Rimed Tragicomedy	Closet	1661★	
Moral	Unacted (?)	MS	T
Pastoral Tragicomedy	Berseel: Duchess of Lorraine	Lost	
Pastoral Tragicomedy	Berseel	...	
Tragicomedy	Closet	Lost	
Tragicomedy	Closet	1664★ & MS	F
Tragedy	Unacted (?)	1651★	C
Pastoral	Closet (?)	MS	C (extracts) T
Tragicomedy	Closet (?)	MS	T
Pastoral	Closet	MS	C
Tragicomedy	Unknown	Lost	
Tragedy	Closet	1651★	
Comic Interlude	Unknown	1651★	
Political Dialogue	Closet	1651★	
Rimed Tragicomedy	Closet	1651★	
Latin Tragedy	St Omers	MS	
Latin Tragedy	St Omers	MS	
Tragedy	Closet (?)	1651★	

DATE	AUTHOR	TITLE	LIMITS
1652	Goldsmith, Francis	*Sophompaneas, or Joseph* (Trans. Grotius.)	1652
	Killigrew, Thomas	*I & II Bellamira Her Dream, or The Love of Shadows*	1650–1652
	Manuche, Cosmo	*The Just General*	1652 (pub.)
	Manuche, Cosmo	*The Loyal Lovers*	1652 (pub.)
	Tatham, John	*The Scots Figgaries, or A Knot of Knaves*	1652
	Anon. (prob. not Manuche, C.)	*The Bastard*	1652 (pub.)
	Anon.	*Simo* (Ment. in Hazlitt's *Manual.* Ghost title?)	1652 (pub.) (?)
1653	Cox, Robert (author or adapter)	*Actaeon and Diana*	*c.* 1650–1655
	Cox, Robert (author or adapter)	*John Swabber*	9 June
	Cox, Robert (author or adapter)	*Rural Sports, or The Birthday of the Nymph Oenone*	*c.* 1650–1655
	Cox, Robert (author or adapter)	*Simpleton the Smith*	*c.* 1650–1655
	Cox, Robert (adapter?)	*The Black Man* (A traditional piece.)	*c.* 1600–1673
	Cox, Robert (?)	*Diphilo and Granida*	*c.* 1650–1673
	Cox, Robert (?)	*King Ahasuerus and Queen Esther*	*c.* 1650–1673
	Cox, Robert (?)	*King Solomon's Wisdom*	*c.* 1650–1673
	Cox, Robert (?)	*Philetis and Constantia*	*c.* 1650–1673
	Cox, Robert (?)	*Venus and Adonis, or The Maid's Philosophy*	*c.* 1650–1673
	Pepys, Samuel	*Love a Cheat*	1650–1653
	Shirley, James	*Cupid and Death*	26 Mar.
	Stapylton, Robert	*The Royal Choice* (Same as the 'Pastor Stapilton' in Rogers and Ley's list, 1656?)	1653 (S.R.)
	Anon.	*S. Edoardus Confessor sive Mites Terram Possidebunt*	16 Aug.
1654	Fanshawe, Richard	*To Love Only for Love's Sake* (Trans. Mendoza's *Querer por solo querer.*)	1654
	Flecknoe, Richard	*Ariadne*	1654 (pub.)
	Flecknoe, Richard	*Love's Dominion* (See *Love's Kingdom*, 1664.)	1654
	Howell, James	*The Nuptials of Peleus and Thetis* (*The Great Royal Ball*)	1654
	Jordan, Thomas	*Cupid His Coronation* (See *Fancy's Festivals*, 1657.)	1654
	Killigrew, Thomas	*I & II Thomaso, or The Wanderer*	1654
	'T.R.'	*The Extravagant Shepherd* (Trans. T. Corneille's *Le Berger extravagant.*)	1654
	Anon.	*The New Brawl, or Turnmill Street against Rosemary Lane*	1654
	Anon.	*The True Tragicomedy* [*of Robert Carr and Francis Howard*]	*c.* 1654

TYPE	AUSPICES	EARLIEST TEXTS	LATEST TEXTS
Biblical Play	Closet	1652*	
Tragicomedy	Closet	1664*	F
Tragicomedy	Closet (?)	1652*	
Tragicomedy	Closet (?)	1652*	
Political Comedy	Closet	1652	C
Tragedy	Unknown	1652*	
Latin Comedy	Unknown	1652* (?)	
Pastoral	At Red Bull (?)	[1655?]**	C
Droll	By Cox at Red Bull	[1655?]	C
Pastoral	At Red Bull (?)	[1655?]	C
Droll	At Red Bull (?)	1656	C
Jig	Unknown	1673	C
Pastoral	Unknown	1673	C
Dialogue	Unknown	1673	C
Dialogue	Unknown	1673	C
Droll	Unknown	1673	C
Droll	Unknown	1673	C
Comedy (?)	Closet (?)	Lost	
Mask	'Gentlemen' for Portuguese Ambassador	1653 & MS	C
Pastoral (?)	Closet (?)	Lost	
Latin Tragedy	St Omers	MS	
Romance	Closet	1670 & MS	
Pastoral with Recitative	Unknown	1654*	
Tragicomedy	Closet	1654**	
Translation of French Royal Entertainment	Closet	1654*	
Mask	Girls' School, Spittle	MS	
Comedy	Closet	1664*	C,F
Pastoral	Closet	1654*	
'Mock Comedy' (Dialogue)	Closet	1654*	
Thesis Play	Closet	MS	

DATE	AUTHOR	TITLE	LIMITS
1655	Baron, Robert	Mirza	1655
	Gayton, Edmund (describer)	*Charity Triumphant, or The Virgin Show*	29 Oct.
	Lower, William	*Polyeuctes, or The Martyr* (Trans. Corneille's *Polyeucte*.)	1655
	Lower, William	*Scaevoli*	*c.* 1655–1656
	Manuche, Cosmo	*Love in Travail*	1642–1656
	Stanley, Thomas	*The Clouds* (Trans. Aristophanes.)	1655
	Anon.	*The Gossips' Brawl, or The Women Wear the Breeches*	1655 (pub.)
	Anon. ('P. Claretus')	*Homo Duplex sive Funestum Corporis et Animae Duellum*	July
1656	'I.B.' (Bulteel, John?)	*London's Triumph*	29 Oct.
	Davenant, William	*The Athenians' Reception of Phocion*	1656–1657
	Davenant, William	*The First Day's Entertainment at Rutland House*	23 May
	Davenant, William	*Satirical Declamations* (Same as above?)	1656–1657
	Davenant, William	*I The Siege of Rhodes*	Sept.
	Holland, Samuel	*Cupid and Psyche*	1656
	Holland, Samuel	*The Enchanted Grove*	1656(?)
	Holland, Samuel	*Venus and Adonis*	1656
	Lower, William	*Horatius* (Trans. Corneille's *Horace*.)	1656
	Anon.	*Crux Vindicata*	8 Aug.
	Anon. (Formido, C?)	*The Governor* (Same as *The Governor*, 1637?)	1656 (MS date)
	Anon. (wrongly assigned to Prestwich, E.)	*The Hectors, or The False Challenge*	1656
	Anon.	*Prodigality and Covetousness*	31 Jan. (acted)
1657	D'Ouvilley, George Gerbier	*The False Favourite Disgraced, and The Reward of Loyalty*	1657
	Jordan, Thomas	*Fancy's Festivals* (Incorporates *Cupid His Coronation*, 1654.)	1654–1657
	Lower, William	*Don Japhet of Armenia* (Trans. Scarron's *Don Japhet d'Arménie*.)	1657
	Lower, William	*The Three Dorothies, or Jodelet Boxed* (Trans. Scarron's *Les Trois Dorotées, ou le Jodelet soufflete*.)	*c.* 1655–1660
	Talbot, Gilbert	*Filli di Sciro* (Trans. Bonarelli.)	1657
	Tatham, John	*London's Triumphs*	29 Oct.
	Anon. (Davenant, W.?)	*The Countryman* (Prob. same as *The Countryman*, S.R., 1653; see Supp. II, a.)	5 Nov. (?) (acted)
1658	Cavendish, Margaret	*Plays* (Published in folio, in 1662, were the anomalous dramas of the Marchioness of Newcastle, mostly sketches of morals and comedies. The titles of these, most of	1653–1662

TYPE	AUSPICES	EARLIEST TEXTS	LATEST TEXTS
Tragedy	Closet	[1655]★	
Civic Pageant	London	1655★	
Tragedy	Closet	1655★	
Unknown	Closet (?)	Lost	
Comedy	Closet		
Unknown	Unknown	MS	
Comedy	Closet	1655	
Comic Interlude	Unknown	1655★	
Latin Moral	St Omers	MSS	
Civic Pageant	London	1656★	
Entertainment	Rutland House 'Opera'	Lost	
Disputation	Rutland House 'Opera'	1657	C
Disputations	Rutland House 'Opera'	Lost (?)	
Tragicomedy	Rutland House 'Opera'	1656	E,S
Burlesque Mask	Closet	Lost	
Mask	Unknown	MS (lost?)	
Burlesque Mask	Closet	1656★★	
Tragedy	Closet	1656★	
Latin Tragedy	St Omers	MS	
Tragicomedy	King's (?)	MS	
Comedy	Closet	1656★	
Moral Interlude	Schoolchildren in Forres	Lost	
Tragicomedy	Closet	1657★★	
Medley	Private Entertainment	1657★★	
Comedy	Closet	MS	
Comedy	Closet	MS	
Pastoral	Closet	MSS	
Civic Pageant	London	[1657]★	
Unknown	At Inner Temple	Lost	
Dialogues	Closet	1662★	

DATE	AUTHOR	TITLE	LIMITS
		which were probably written during the Interregnum, are as follows: *The Apocryphal Ladies*; *Bell in Campo*; *The Comical Hash*; *The Female Academy*; *The Lady Contemplation*; *Love's Adventures*; *The Matrimonial Trouble*; *Nature's Three Daughters – Beauty, Love, and Wit*; *The Public Wooing*; *The Religious*; *Several Wits*; *The Unnatural Tragedy*; *The Wits' Cabal*; *Youth's Glory and Death's Banquet*. For Lady Margaret's second flowering, see 1665.)	
	Cavendish, William	*A Pleasant and Merry Humour of a Rogue* (See *The Triumphant Widow*, 1674.)	*c.* 1655–1660(?)
	Chamberlaine, William	*Love's Victory*	1658
	Davenant, William	*The Cruelty of the Spaniards in Peru* (Same as *II Sir Francis Drake?*) (Included as Act IV of *The Playhouse to Be Let*, 1663.)	1658
	Davenant, William	*I Sir Francis Drake* (Included as Act III of *The Playhouse to Be Let*, 1663.)	1658–1659
	Fane, Mildmay	*Ladrones, or The Robber's Island*	*c.* 1656–*c.* 1660
	Fanshawe, Richard	*La Fida Pastora* (Trans. Fletcher's *The Faithful Shepherdess*.)	1658
	Lower, William	*The Enchanted Lovers*	1658 (pub.)
	Meriton, Thomas	*The Chaste Virgin*	*c.* 1658
	Meriton, Thomas	*Love and War*	1658
	Meriton, Thomas	*The Several Affairs*	*c.* 1658
	Meriton, Thomas	*The Wandering Lover*	1658
	Shirley, James	*The Contention of Ajax and Ulysses for the Armour of Achilles*	*c.* 1645–1658
	Shirley, James	*Honoria and Mammon* (Adapt. *The Contention for Honour and Riches*, 1631.)	1658 (pub.)
	Swinhoe, Gilbert	*The Unhappy Fair Irene*	1658 (pub.)
	Tatham, John	*London's Triumph, Presented by Industry and Honour*	29 Oct.
	Willan, Leonard	*Orgula, or The Fatal Error*	1658
1659	'H.B.' (Birkhead, Henry?)	*The Female Rebellion*	*c.* 1657–*c.* 1659
	'H.H.B.'	*The World's Idol, Plutus* (Trans. Aristophanes.)	1659
	Davenant, William	*II The Siege of Rhodes*	1657–*c.* 1659
	Flecknoe, Richard	*The Marriage of Oceanus and Britannia*	1659 (pub.)
	Kirkham, R. (?)	*Alfred, or Right Re-enthroned*	1659
	Jordan, Thomas	*An Eclogue, or Representation in Four Parts*	18 Dec.
	Lower, William	*The Amorous Fantasm* (Trans. Quinault's *Le Fantôme amoureux*.)	7 Nov.

TYPE	AUSPICES	EARLIEST TEXTS	LATEST TEXTS
Comic Interlude	See 1674	MS	E
Tragicomedy	Closet	1658*	E
Operatic Show	Cockpit 'Opera'	1658	C
Pseudo-history	Cockpit 'Opera'	1659	C
'Opera'	Unknown	MS (lost?)	
Latin Pastoral	Closet	1658**	E
Pastoral Tragicomedy	Unacted (?)	1658** & MS	C
'Romance'	Closet	Lost	
Tragedy	Unacted	1658*	
Comedy	Closet	Lost	
Tragicomedy	Privately acted	1658*	
Entertainment	Shirley's school (?)	[1658]**	C
Moral	Unacted (?)	[1658]	C
Tragedy	Unacted (?)	1658*	
Civic Pageant	London	1658*	
Tragedy	Unacted (?)	1658*	
Tragicomedy	Closet	MSS	E
Comedy	Closet	1659*	
Tragicomedy	Cockpit 'Opera' (?)	1663	E,S
Mask	Unknown	1659*	
Pseudo-history	Closet	MS	
Entertainment	London	1659**	C
Tragicomedy	Closet	1660**	

DATE	AUTHOR	TITLE	LIMITS
	Lower, William	*The Noble Ingratitude* (Trans. Quinault's *La Généreuse ingratitude.*)	1659
	Neville, Henry	*Shuffling, Cutting, and Dealing in a Game of Picquet*	1659
	Reymes, William	*Self-Interest, or The Belly Wager* (Trans. Secchi's *L'Interesse.*)	*c.* 1650–1660
	Tatham, John	*London's Triumph*	29 Oct.
	Anon. (Jordan, T.?)	*The Florentine Ladies*	*c.* 1659–1660
	Anon.	*Lady Alimony, or The Alimony Lady* (Revis. of Caroline play?)	1659 (revised?)
	Anon.	*The London Chanticleers*	1659 (pub.)
1660	Dancer, John	*Aminta* (Trans. Tasso.)	1660
	Forde, Thomas	*Love's Labyrinth, or The Royal Shepherdess*	1660
	Howard, Robert	*The Blind Lady*	1660
	Jordan, Thomas	*Bacchus' Festival, or A New Medley*	12 Apr.
	Jordan, Thomas	*The Cheaters Cheated* (In *Rosary of Rarities Planted in the Garden of Poetry*)	*c.* 1660 (pub.)
	Manuche, Cosmo	*The Banished Shepherdess*	1659–1660
	Pordage, Samuel	*Troades* (Trans. Seneca.)	1660
	Richards, William (preserver?)	*The Christmas Ordinary*	1633–1660
	Sadler, Anthony	*The Subject's Joy for the King's Restoration*	1660
	Tatham, John	*London's Glory Represented by Time, Truth, and Fame*	5 July
	Tatham, John	*The Royal Oak*	29 Oct.
	Tatham, John	*The Rump, or The Mirror of the Late Times*	June
	Thomson, Thomas	*The English Rogue*	1660–1668 (pub.)
	Anon.	*Le Ballet de la paix*	1660 (pub.)
	Anon.	*Cromwell's Conspiracy*	8 Aug. (MS date)
	Anon.	*England's Joy* (Descrip. of welcome of Charles II.)	1660
	Anon.	*The Life and Death of Mrs. Rump*	1660
	Anon.	*A Phanatique Play*	1660
	Anon.	*The Tragical Actors, or The Martyrdom of the Late King Charles*	1660
1661	'C.,J.'	*Q.F.F.Q.S. A New Fiction As We Were: A.I.M.E.I.M.I.D2.F.4*	1661
	Carpenter, Richard	*The Pragmatical Jesuit New Leavened*	*c.* 1660–1670
	Cowley, Abraham	*Cutter of Coleman Street* (Adapt. *The Guardian*, 1642.)	16 Dec. (Pepys)
	Flecknoe, Richard	*Erminia, or The Fair and Virtuous Lady*	1661 (pub.)
	Fountain, John	*The Rewards of Virtue* (See *The Royal Shepherdess*, 1669.)	1661
	Jordan, Thomas	*The New Medley* (In *Merry Drollerie.*)	1661 (pub.)

TYPE	AUSPICES	EARLIEST TEXTS	LATEST TEXTS
Pastoral Tragicomedy	Closet (?)	1659★★	
Political Dialogue	Closet	1659★	C
Comedy	Unacted (?)	MS	E
Civic Pageant	London	1659★	
Comedy	'at night by Gentlemen'	Lost	
Comedy	Rhodes' Company at Cockpit (?)	1659★	D
Comic Interlude	Acted out of London	1659★	D
Pastoral	Closet	1660★	
Pastoral Tragicomedy	Closet	1660	
Tragicomedy	Closet	1660★★	
Entertainment	Vintners' Hall	1660★	
Jig	Unknown	[*c.* 1660]	E
Political Allegory	Unknown	MS	
Tragedy	Closet	1660★	
Christmas Play	Trinity Col., Oxford (?)	1682★ & MS (frag.)	
Biblical Allegory	Closet	1660★	
Royal Entertainment	London	1660★★	C
Civic Pageant	London	1660★	C
Topical Comedy	Beeston's Company	1660★	C
Comedy	Privately acted (?)	1668★	
Ballet	Court	1660★	
History	Unknown	1660★	
Triumph	Dover to Westminster	1660	
Political Dialogue	Closet	1660★	
Political Dialogue	Closet	1660★★	
Political Dialogue	Closet	[1660]★	
Political Allegory	Closet	1661★	
Satirical Comedy	Unacted	[1661?]★	
Comedy	Duke's	1663	C,T
Tragicomedy	Unacted (?)	1661	
Tragicomedy	Unacted	1661★	
Jig	Acted 1671 in Civic Pageant	1661	C

DATE	AUTHOR	TITLE	LIMITS
	Kirkman, Francis (?)	*The Presbyterian Lash, or Noctroff's Maid Whipped*	1661
	Ogilby, John (describer)	*The Coronation Entertainment for Charles II*	22 Apr.
	Tatham, John	*London's Triumphs*	29 Oct.
	Tatham, John	*Neptune's Address* [to King Charles]	22 Apr.
	Anon.	*The Fall of Sodom and Gomorrah*	Aug.
	Anon.	*Hell's Higher Court of Justice, or The Trial of the Three Politic Ghosts*	1661
	Anon.	*Hewson Reduced, or The Shoemaker Returned to His Trade*	1661
	Anon.	*The Liar* (Same as *The Mistaken Beauty*, 1684?) (Anonymous translation of P. Corneille's *Le Menteur*.)	1661(?)–1664
	Anon.	*Lot Debauched*	Aug.
	Anon.	*Love's Quarrel* (Alternative title for earlier play revived? *The School of Compliment*?)	6 Apr. (Pepys)
	Anon. (poss. Cox, R?)	*The Merry Conceited Humors of Bottom the Weaver* (Adapt. of *A Midsummer-Night's Dream*.)	Apri. (?)
	Anon.	*Robin Hood and His Crew of Soldiers*	23 Apr.
1662	Bartley (Berkeley?), William	*Cornelia*	1 August
	Bayley, George	*Noah's Flood*	1662
	Clerke, William	*Marciano, or The Discovery*	27 Dec.
	Codrington, Robert	*Ignoramus* (Trans. Ruggle. Related to Parkhurst's trans.?)	1662 (pub.)
	Cokain, Aston	*Ovid*	1662 (pub.)
	Davenant, William	*The Law against Lovers* (Adapt. Shakespeare's *Measure for Measure* and *Much Ado about Nothing*.)	15 Feb.
	Howard, Robert	*The Committee*	27 Nov. (at Court) (poss. early performance mid-Nov.)
	Howard, Robert	*The Surprisal*	*c.* Apr.
	Killigrew, William	*Selindra*	3 Mar.
	Lawrence, William	*News from Geneva, or The Lewd Levite*	*c.* 1662
	Kirkman, Francis	*I The Wits, or Sport upon Sport*: A collection of drolls fashioned from comic scenes in older plays: *The Bouncing Knight, or The Robbers Robbed* (from *I Henry IV*); *The Bubble* (from Greene's *Tu Quoque*); *The Club-Men* (from *Philaster*); *The Doctors of Dull-Head College* (from *Monsieur Thomas*); *The Encounter* (from *The Knight of the Burning Pestle*); *An Equal Match* (from *Rule a Wife and Have a Wife*); *The False Heir and*	1662 (pub.)

TYPE	AUSPICES	EARLIEST TEXTS	LATEST TEXTS
Topical Comedy	Unacted	1661*	
Coronation Entertainment	London	1661	
Civic Pageant	London	1661*	
Entertainment	London	1661*	
Puppet Show	Bartholomew Fair	Current	
Political Dialogue	Closet	1661*	
Political Dialogue	Closet	1661*	
Comedy (?)	King's	1661* 1685 (*Mistaken Beauty*)	
Puppet Show	Bartholomew Fair	Current	
Tragicomedy (?)	Duke's	Lost	
Droll	King's (?)	1661	C
Dialogue	At Nottingham	1661*	
Tragicomedy (?)	King's	Lost	
Musical Show (or Mystery)	By Bayley in London (?)	Lost	
Tragicomedy	Holyrood House, Edinburgh	1663*	E
Comedy	Unacted (?)	1662*	
Tragedy	Unacted (?)	1662	C
Comedy	Duke's	1673*	C
Comedy	King's	1665 MS (copy of 1st printed ed.)	E
Comedy	King's	1665	
Tragicomedy	King's	1665	
Comedy	Unacted?	MS	E
Drolls	Offered for acting	1662	C

DATE	AUTHOR	TITLE	LIMITS
		Formal Curate (from *The Scornful Lady*); *Forced Valour* (from *The Humorous Lieutenant*); *The Grave-Makers* (from *Hamlet*); *The Humour of Bumpkin* (from Cox's *Actaeon and Diana*); *The Humour of Hobbinol* (from Cox's *Rural Sports*); *The Humour of John Swabbler* (from Cox's *Actaeon and Diana*); *The Humour of Simpleton* (from Cox's *Simpleton the Smith*); *The Humours of Monsieur Galliard* (from *The Variety*); *The Humours of Simpkin* (from Cox's *Actaeon and Diana*); *The Imperick* (from *The Alchemist*); *Invisible Smirk, or The Pen Combatants* (from *Two Merry Milkmaids*); *Jenkin's Love-Course and Perambulation* (from *Love Tricks*); *The Lame Commonwealth* (from *Beggars' Bush*); *The Landlady* (from *The Chances*); *The Loyal Citizens* (from *Cupid's Revenge*); *A Prince in Conceit* (from *The Opportunity*); *The Sexton, or The Mock Testator* (from *The Spanish Curate*); *The Stallion* (from *The Custom of the Country*); *The Surprise* (from *The Maid in the Mill*); *The Testy Lord* (from *The Maid's Tragedy*); *The Three Merry Boys* (from *The Bloody Brother*). For *II The Wits*, see 1673.	
	Neville, Robert	*The Poor Scholar*	1662 (pub.)
	Ogilby, John	*The Merchant of Dublin* (Poss. pre-Restoration.)	1662(?)– 1663(?)
	Parkhurst, Ferdinando	*Ignoramus, or The Academical Lawyer* (Three versions in MS.) (Trans. Ruggle.)	1 Nov. (at Court)
	Porter, Thomas	*The Villain*	18 Oct. (Pepys)
	Tatham, John	*Aqua Triumphalis*	23 Aug.
	Tatham, John	*London's Triumph*	29 Oct.
1663	Cary, (Henry, Lucius?)	*The Marriage Night*	16 Oct. (lic.)
	Davenant, William	*The Playhouse to Be Let* (One act from Moliere's *Sganarelle*. See *The Cruelty of the Spaniards in Peru* and *I Sir Francis Drake*, 1658.)	*c.* Aug.
	Digby, George	*Elvira, or The Worst Not Always True* (Adapt. Calderón's *No siempre lo peor es cierto*.)	1663–1664
	Dryden, John	*The Wild Gallant* (Revised for a revival before publication.)	5 Feb.
	Evelyn, John	*Thyrsander*	1663
	Filmer; Godolphin; Sackville, C.; Sedley; Waller	*Pompey the Great* (Trans. Corneille's *Pompée*.)	*c.* Dec. 1663– Jan. 1664?)

TYPE	AUSPICES	EARLIEST TEXTS	LATEST TEXTS
Comedy	Unacted (?)	1662★	
Unknown	II Ogilby's Men, Dublin (?)	Lost	
Comedy	Duke's	MSS	
Tragedy	Duke's	1663	
Royal Entertainment	London	1662	
Civic Pageant	London	1662★	
Tragicomedy	Duke's	1664★	D
Comic Medley	Duke's	1673★	C
Comedy	Duke's	1667 & MS	D
Comedy	King's	1669	C
Tragicomedy in verse	Unacted	MS	
Tragedy	Duke's	1664★★	

DATE	AUTHOR	TITLE	LIMITS
	Flecknoe, Richard	*Love's Kingdom* (Adapt. *Love's Dominion*, 1654.)	Autumn, 1663
	Green, Alexander	*The Politican Cheated*	1663
	Head, Richard	*Hic et Ubique, or The Humours of Dublin*	1663 (pub.)
	Hoole, Charles	*Comoedia Sex Anglo-Latinae* (Trans. Terence's *Adelphi, Andria, Eunuchus, Heautontimorumenos, Hecyra, Phormio.*)	1663
	Howard, Henry	*The United Kingdoms*	*c.* 1663
	Howard, James	*The English Monsieur*	30 July (acted)
	Killigrew, William	*Pandora, or The Converts*	1662–1663
	Philips, Katherine	*Pompey* (Trans. Corneille's *Pompée.*)	10 Feb.
	Porter, Thomas	*The Carnival*	1663–1664
	P., T.	*A Witty Combat, or The Female Victor*	June
	Rhodes, Richard	*Flora's Vagaries* (First produced at Christ Church, Oxford, 8 Jan. 1663.)	3 Nov.
	S[outhland?], T[homas?]	*Love à la Mode*	1662–1663
	Stanley, Thomas	*Aeschyli Tragoediae Septem* (The seven plays edited and translated.)	1663
	Stapylton, Robert	*The Slighted Maid*	23 Feb. (Pepys)
	Stapylton, Robert	*The Stepmother*	*c.* Nov.
	Tatham, John	*Londinium Triumphans*	29 Oct.
	Tuke, Samuel	*The Adventures of Five Hours* (Adapt. Coello's *Los Empeños de seis horas.*)	8 Jan. (Pepys)
	Wilson, John	*The Cheats*	lic. 6 Mar.
	Anon.	*Encyclochoria, or Universal Motion*	3 Jan.
	Anon.	*The Exposure*	*c.* Nov.
	Anon.	*The Four Hours Adventure*	Spring (?) 1663
	Anon.	*School-Play*	1663
	Anon.	*The Unfortunate Usurper*	1663
	Anon.	*The Wandering Whores' Complaint*	1663 (pub.)
1664	Banister, William	*Andronichus sive Aulae Byzantinae Vota*	1664
	Banister, William	*Jephte sive Christi Naturam Humanam Immolantis Expressa Figura*	1664
	Banister, William	*Perseus et Demetrius sive Discordia Omnis Pessima Imperii Lues*	7 Aug. (acted)
	Boyle, Roger	*The General* (Formerly acted in Dublin as *Altemira*; altered and published under the title of *Altemira.*)	14 Sept.
	Boyle, Roger	*Henry V*	Aug.
	Bulteel, John	*Amorous Orontus, or The Love in Fashion* (*The Amorous Gallant*, 1675) (Adapt. T. Corneille's *L'Amour à la mode.*) (Poss. same as *Love in and Love out of fashion*, 1689.)	1664

TYPE	AUSPICES	EARLIEST TEXTS	LATEST TEXTS
Tragicomedy	Duke's	1664**	
Comedy	Unacted	1663*	
Comedy	Acted privately	1663*	
Comedies	Closet	1663	
Tragedy (?)	Duke's (?)	Lost	
Comedy	King's	1674	
Comedy altered from Tragedy	Duke's	1664	
Tragedy	II Ogilby's Men, Dublin	1663	
Comedy	King's	1664*	
Comedy	Privately acted (?)	1663*	
Comedy	King's	1670	C
Comedy	Middlesex House	1663**	
Latin Tragedies	Closet	1663	
Tragicomedy	Duke's	1663	
Tragicomedy	Duke's	1664**	
Civic Pageant	London	1663*	
Tragicomedy	Duke's	1663	E,D
Comedy	King's	1664 & MS	E,T
Royal Entertainment	Lincoln's Inn	1662[63]*	
Pastoral	King's	Lost	
Unknown	Duke's (?)	MS (Prol. & Epil.)	
Academic Moral	A Middlesex School	1664*	
Tragedy	Unacted	1663*	
Comedy	Unacted (?)	1663*	
Latin Tragedy	St Omers	MS	
Latin Tragedy	St Omers	MS	
Latin Tragedy	St Omers	MS	
Tragicomedy	II Ogilby's Men, Dublin; King's in 1664	MSS	C
Tragicomedy	Duke's	1668 & MSS	C,F,T
Comedy	King's	1665	

DATE	AUTHOR	TITLE	LIMITS
	Carlell Lodowick	*Heraclius, Emperor of the East* (Trans. Corneille.)	9 Mar. (imprim.)
	Clarges, Thomas (translator)	*Heraclius* (Trans. Corneille.)	8 Mar. (Pepys)
	Davenant, William	*Macbeth* (Adapt. Shakespeare.)	5 Nov. (Pepys)
	Davenant, William	*The Rivals* (Adapt. Shakespeare & Fletcher's *The Two Noble Kinsmen*.)	1664
	Davenant, William and Ellis (?)	*The Secret* (revision of James Shirley's *The Court Secret*, 1642?)	*c.* 1663–1664?
	Digby, George	*'Tis Better Than It Was* (Adapt. Calderón's *Mejor está que estaba*.)	1662–1666
	Digby, George	*Worse and Worse* (Adapt. Calderón's *Peor está que estaba*.)	20 July (Pepys)
	Dryden, John	*The Rival Ladies*	1663–1664
	Etherege, George	*The Comical Revenge, or Love in a Tub*	Mar.
	Holden, J.	*The German Princess*	15 Apr. (Pepys)
	Howard, Edward	*The Usurper*	2 Jan. (Pepys)
	Howard, James	*Romeo and Juliet* (Adapt. Shakespeare; with happy ending.)	1664(?)
	Howard, Robert	*The Vestal Virgin, or The Roman Ladies* (With alternative endings.)	1664–1665
	Howard, R.; Dryden, J.	*The Indian Queen*	25 Jan.
	Killigrew, William	*Ormasdes, or Love and Friendship*	23 Aug. (imprim.)
	Lacy, John	*The Old Troop, or Monsieur Raggou*	1662–1664
	Tatham, John	*London's Triumphs*	29 Oct.
	Waller, Edmund	*The Maid's Tragedy* (Adapt. Beaumont & Fletcher; with happy ending.)	*c.* 1664
	Wilson, John	*Andronicus Comnenus*	1664
	Wilson, John	*The Projectors*	13 Jan. (imprim.)
	Anon.	*Irena*	1664
	Anon.	*Judith and Holofernes*	1664 (acted)
	Anon.	*Knavery in All Trades, or The Coffee-House*	'Christmas Holidays'
	Anon.	*The Labyrinth*	2 May (Pepys)
	Anon. (Southland, Thomas?)	*The Ungrateful Favourite*	11 May (imprim.)
1665	Boyle, Peter	*Mustapha, Son of Solyman the Magnificent*	3 Apr. (Pepys)
	Brathwait, Richard	*Regicidium*	1665
	Cavendish, Margaret	*Plays* (Composed between 1662–8; see above under 1658. Present volume	1662–1668

TYPE	AUSPICES	EARLIEST TEXTS	LATEST TEXTS
Tragedy	Unacted	1664*	
Tragedy	Duke's	Lost	
Dramatic Opera	Duke's	1674 & MS	E,C,F
Comedy	Duke's	1668**	C,F
Tragicomedy	King's?	Lost	
Comedy	Duke's (?)	Lost	
Comedy	Duke's	Lost	
Tragicomedy	King's	1664	C
Comedy	Duke's	1664	C
Comedy (?)	Duke's	Not printed	
Tragedy	King's	1668*	
Tragicomedy	Duke's	Lost	
Tragedy and Tragicomedy	King's	1665	
Tragicomedy	King's	1665	C
Tragicomedy	Unacted (?)	1665	
Comedy	King's	1672	C
Civic Pageant	London	1664*	
Tragicomedy	King's (Recorded performances from 1666)	1690	
Tragedy	Unacted	1664*	C,T
Comedy	Unacted (?)	1665*	C,T
Tragicomedy	Unacted	1664*	
Droll	Bartholomew Fair	Lost	
Comedy	'By Several Apprentices'	1664*	
Comedy (?)	King's	Lost	
Tragedy	Unacted	1664*	
Tragedy	Duke's	1668 & MSS	C,F
Latin Topical Play	Closet	1665*	
Dramatic Sketches	Closet	1668*	

DATE	AUTHOR	TITLE	LIMITS
		contains *The Bridals*; *The Convent of Pleasure*; *The Presence*; *The Sociable Companions, or The Female Wits*; and fragments.)	
	Cotton, Charles	*Horace* (Trans. Corneille.)	1665(?)
	Dryden, John	*The Indian Emperor, or The Conquest of Mexico by the Spaniards*	*c.* Apr.
	Holden, John	*The Ghosts*	17 Apr. (Pepys)
	Howard, James	*All Mistaken, or The Mad Couple* (mistakenly given title of *The Widow* and attributed to Roger Boyle)	1665(?)
	Killigrew, William	*The Siege of Urbin*	1665–1666
	Manuche, Cosmo	*The Feast* (Other MS plays attributed to Manuche, as yet undated, are *Agamemnon* [Tragedy, frag.]; *The Captives* [Comedy, frag.; trans. Plautus?]; *Lenotius, King of Cyprus* [Tragedy]; *The Mandrake* [Comedy]; *Mariamne* [Tragedy]; a titleless comedy and titleless tragedy.)	1664–*c.* 1665
	Stroude,-	*All Plot, or The Disguises*	1662–1671
1666	Hoadley, S. (?)	*The War of Grammar* (*Basileia seu Bellum Grammaticale*)	1666
	M., E.	*St Cecily, or The Converted Twins* ('E.M.' on t.p., but dedication signed by Medbourne, published.)	11 June (imprim.)
	Anon.	*Punchinello* (*Polichinello. Punch and Judy*)	1666 (lic.)
1667	Bailey, Abraham	*The Spiteful Sister*	10 Apr. (imprim.)
	Boyle, Roger	*The Black Prince*	19 Oct. (Pepys)
	Caryl, John	*The English Princess, or The Death of Richard III*	7 Mar. (Pepys)
	Cavendish, William (& Dryden? Davenant? or Shadwell?)	*The Humorous Lovers*	28 Mar.
	Davenant, William	*Greene's Tu Quoque* (Adapt. Cooke.)	12 Sept. (Pepys)
	Davenant, W.; Dryden, J.	*The Tempest, or The Enchanted Island* (Adapt. Shakespeare.)	7 Nov. (Pepys)
	Dover, John	*The Roman Generals, or The Distressed Ladies*	7 Nov. (imprim.)
	Dryden, John	*Secret Love, or The Maiden Queen*	2 Mar. (Pepys)
	Dryden, J. (adapting trans. by Cavendish, W.?)	*Sir Martin Mar-all, or The Feigned Innocence* (Adapt. Quinault's *L'Amant indiscret* and Molière's *L'Etourdi*.)	15 Aug. (Pepys)

TYPE	AUSPICES	EARLIEST TEXTS	LATEST TEXTS
Tragedy	Closet	1671★	
Tragedy	King's	1667 & MSS	C,F
Comedy (?)	Duke's	Lost	
Tragicomedy	King's	1672	D
Tragicomedy	Unacted (?)	1666★ & MS	T
Comedy	Unknown	MS	
Comedy	Duke's	Lost	
Academic Allegory	Cranebrook School	MS	
Tragedy	Unacted (?)	1666★★	
Puppet Show	Bartholomew Fair	Current	
Comedy	Unacted	1667★★	
Tragicomedy	King's	1669	C
Tragedy	Duke's	1667	
Comedy	Duke's	1677★ & MS	
Comedy	Duke's	Lost	
Comedy	Duke's	1670	C,F
Tragedy	Unacted	1667★	
Tragicomedy	King's	1668	C
Comedy	Duke's	1668	C

DATE	AUTHOR	TITLE	LIMITS
	Flecknoe, Richard	*The Damoiselles à la Mode* (Adapt. Molière's *Les Précieuses ridicules*, etc.)	15 May (imprim.)
	Howard, Edward	*The Change of Crowns*	15 Apr. (Pepys)
	Howard, Edward	*The London Gentleman*	1667 (S.R.)
	Lacy, John	*Sauny the Scot, or The Taming of the Shrew* (Adapt. Shakespeare.)	9 Apr. (Pepys)
	St Serfe, Thomas	*Tarugo's Wiles, or The Coffee-House* (Adapt. Moreto's *No puede ser guarda una mujer*.)	5 Oct. (Pepys)
	Villiers, George	*The Chances* (Adapt. Fletcher.)	1664–(?)1667
	Weston, John	*The Amazon Queen, or The Amours of Thalestris to Alexander the Great*	11 Feb. (imprim.)
	Anon.	*Queen Elizabeth's Troubles, and The History of Eighty Eight* (adaptation of T. Heywood's *If You Know Not Me You Know Nobody, or The Troubles of Queen Elizabeth?*)	17 Aug. (Pepys)
	Anon.	*Patient Grizill*	30 Aug. (Pepys)
	Anon.	*The Poetess*	7 Oct.
1668	Boyle, Roger	*Tryphon*	8 Dec. (Pepys)
	Davenant, William	*The Man's The Master* (Trans Scarron's *Jodelet, ou le maître valet*.)	26 Mar. (Pepys)
	Denham, J. (completing Philips, K.)	*Horace* (Trans. Corneille, K. Philips's trans. ends at Act IV, Sc. 6.)	4 Feb.
	Dryden, John	*An Evening's Love, or The Mock Astrologer*	12 June
	'Dryden' (Flecknoe, R.?)	*The Ladies à la Mode* (Same as *The Damoiselles à la Mode*, pub. by Flecknoe, 1667?)	14 Sept. (Pepys)
	Etherege, George	*She Would if She Could*	6 Feb. (Pepys)
	Howard, Robert	*The Great Favourite, or The Duke of Lerma* (*The Spanish Duke of Lerma*, 1623, revised?)	20 Feb. (Pepys)
	Sedley, Charles	*The Mulberry Garden* (*The Wandering Ladies*)	18 May (Pepys)
	Shadwell, Thomas	*The Sullen Lovers, or The Impertinents*	2 May (Pepys)
	Anon.	*Dick Whittington*	21 Sept. (Pepys)
	Anon.	*The Feigned Astrologer* (Adapt. T. Corneille's *Le Feint astrologue*.)	1668 (pub.)
	Anon.	*Merry Andrew*	29 Aug. (Pepys)
1669	Boothby, Mrs. Frances	*Marcelia, or The Treacherous Friend*	*c.* July
	Boyle, Roger	*Guzman*	15 Apr.
	Boyle, Roger	*Mr Anthony*	14 Dec.
	Carr, William	*Pluto Furens et Vinctus, or The Raging Devil Bound*	1669 (pub.)
	Cavendish, W. (assisted by Dryden, W.?)	*The Heiress*	29 Jan. (Pepys)

TYPE	AUSPICES	EARLIEST TEXTS	LATEST TEXTS
Comedy	Unacted (?) (see 1668)	1667★	
Tragicomedy	King's	MS	E
Comedy	King's (?)	Lost	
Comedy	King's	1698	C,F
Comedy	Duke's	1667★	T
Comedy	King's	1682	
Tragicomedy	Unacted	1667★	
History	King's	Lost	
Puppet Show	Bartholomew Fair	Lost	
Unknown (Burlesque?)	King's	Lost	
Tragedy	Duke's	1669 & MS	C
Comedy	Duke's	1669	C
Tragedy	Amateurs at Court (King's in 1669)	1669 (1st 4 acts, 1667) & MS	
Comedy	King's	1671	C
Comedy	King's	1667 (?)	
Comedy	Duke's	1668	C,S
Tragicomedy	King's	1668	E
Comedy	King's	1668	C
Comedy	Duke's	1668 & MS	C,M
Puppet Show	Southwark Fair	Lost	
Comedy	Unacted (?)	1668★	
Droll	Bartholomew Fair	Lost	
Tragicomedy	King's	1670★	
Comedy	Duke's	1693	C
Comedy	Duke's	1690★★	C
Satirical Dialogue	Unacted (?)	1669★	
Comedy	King's	Lost	

DATE	AUTHOR	TITLE	LIMITS
	Dancer, John	*Agrippa, King of Alba, or The False Tiberinus* (Adapt. Quinault's *Agrippa roy d'Albe.*)	1666–1669
	Dryden, John	*Tyrannic Love, or The Royal Martyr*	June
	Flecknoe, Richard	*The Physician against His Will* (Adapt. Molière's *Le Médecin malgré lui.*)	*c.* 1669–1670
	Howard, R.; Villiers, G.	*The Country Gentleman*	27 Feb. (projected)
	Killigrew, William	*The Imperial Tragedy* (Adapt. Simons' *Zeno.*)	1669 (pub.)
	Lacy, John	*The Dumb Lady, or The Farrier Made Physician* (Adapt. Moliere's *L'Amour médecin* and *Le Médecin malgré lui.*)	*c.* 1669
	Shadwell, Thomas	*The Hypocrite* (Adapt. Moliere's *Tartuffe?* or Scarron's *Les Hypocrites?*)	14 June
	Shadwell, Thomas	*The Royal Shepherdess* (Adapt. Fountain's *The Rewards of Virtue*, 1661.)	25 Feb. (Pepys)
	Stapylton, Robert	*Hero and Leander*	1669
	Taylor, Silas	*The Serenade, or The Disappointment*	1669
	Anon.	*The Island Princess, or The Generous Portugal* (Adapt. Fletcher.)	7 Jan.
	Anon.	*The Roman Virgin, or Unjust Judge* (adapt. of Webster's *Appius and Virginia*); produced by Betterton (with alterations)	12 May
1670	Behn, Aphra	*The Forced Marriage, or The Jealous Bridegroom*	20 Sept.
	Betterton, Thomas	*The Amorous Widow, or The Wanton Wife* (In part from Molière's *Georges Dandin.*)	15 Nov.– 9 Dec.
	Betterton, Thomas	*The Woman Made a Justice* (Poss. adapt. of Montfleury's *La Femme juge et partie.*)	19 Feb.
	Caryl, John	*Sir Salomon, or The Cautious Coxcomb* (Adapt. Molière's *L'Ecole des Femmes*, etc.)	9 May
	Dancer, John	*Nicomede* (Trans. Corneille.)	*c.* 1670
	Dryden, John	*I The Conquest of Granada*	Dec.
	Howard, Edward	*The Women's Conquest*	*c.* Nov.
	Howard, R.; Wilmot, J.	*The Conquest of China by the Tartars* (Only a frag. by Wilmot extant.)	*c.* 1670–*c.* 1680
	Joyner, William	*The Roman Empress*	*c.* Aug.
	Medbourne, Matthew	*Tartuffe, or The French Puritan* (Adapt. Molière.)	*c.* May
	Polwhele, Elizabeth	*The Faithful Virgins*	1670
	Shadwell, Thomas,	*The Humorists*	10 Dec.
	Thomson, Thomas	*The Life of Mother Shipton* (Passages from Massinger's *City Madam.*)	1668–1671 (pub.)
	Anon.	*She's Jealous of Herself* (Alternative title of known play?)	20 Oct.
1671	Arrowsmith, Joseph	*All is Mistaken*	4 Oct. (?) 1671
	Aubrey, John	*Country Revel, or The Revel of Aldford*	1671

TYPE	AUSPICES	EARLIEST TEXTS	LATEST TEXTS
Tragicomedy	II Ogilby's Men, Dublin	1675*	
Tragedy	King's	1670	C
Comedy	Unacted (?)	Lost	
Comedy	'Forbidden' (intended for King's)	MS	
Tragedy	Nursery Company (?)	1669*	
Comedy	King's	1672*	C
Comedy	Duke's	Lost	
Tragicomedy	Duke's	1669	C
Tragedy	Unacted	1669*	
Comedy (?)	Unacted (?)	Lost	
Tragicomedy	King's	1669*	
Tragedy	Duke's	Lost	
Tragicomedy	Duke's	1671	C
Comedy	Duke's	1706	
Comedy	Duke's	Lost	
Comedy	Duke's	1671**	
Tragicomedy	II Ogilby's Men, Dublin	1671*	
Tragicomedy	King's	1672	C,M
Tragicomedy	Duke's	1671*	
Tragedy (?)	Unacted	MS (frag.)	C
Tragedy	King's	1671* & MS	
Comedy	King's	1670	
Tragedy	Duke's	MS	
Comedy	Duke's	1671 & MS	C
Comedy	Unknown	[1668–71]*	
Comedy	Duke's	Lost (?)	
Comedy	Trinity Col., Cambridge	Lost	
Comedy	Unacted	MS (frag.)	C

DATE	AUTHOR	TITLE	LIMITS
	Behn, Aphra	*The Amorous Prince, or The Curious Husband*	24 Feb.
	Corye, John	*The Generous Enemies, or The Ridiculous Lovers*	*c.* July
	Crowne, John	*Charles VIII of France, or The Invasion of Naples by the French*	*c.* Nov.
	Crowne, John	*Juliana, or The Princess of Poland*	*c.* June
	Dryden, John	*II The Conquest of Granada (Almanzor and Almahide)*	3 or 10 Jan.
	Dryden, John	*Marriage à la Mode*	*c.* Dec. 1671–1672
	Howard, Edward	*The Six Days' Adventure, or The New Utopia*	6 Mar.
	Jordan, Thomas	*London's Resurrection to Joy and Triumph*	30 Oct.
	Milton, John	*Samson Agonistes*	1671
	Polwhele, Elizabeth	*The Frolicks, or The Lawyer Cheated*	1671
	Revet, Edward	*The Town Shifts, or The Suburb Justice*	15 Mar.
	Settle, Elkanah	*Cambyses, King of Persia*	10 Jan.
	S[herman?], T[homas?]	*Youth's Tragedy*	1671
	Villiers; with Clifford, M.? Sprat? Butler? and others	*The Rehearsal* (First drafted in *c.* 1663.)	7 Dec.
	Wycherley, William	*Love in a Wood, or St James's Park*	*c.* Mar.
	Anon.	*The Religious Rebel, or The Pilgrim Prince*	1671
1672	Boyle, Roger	*Herod the Great*	*c.* 1672
	Dryden, John	*Amboyna, or The Cruelties of the Dutch to the English Merchants*	1672–1673
	Dryden, John	*The Assignation, or Love in a Nunnery*	*c.* Nov.
	Jordan, Thomas	*London Triumphant, or The City in Jollity and Splendour*	29 Oct.
	Payne, Nevil	*The Fatal Jealousy*	3 Aug.
	Payne, Nevil	*The Morning Ramble, or The Town Humours*	4 Nov.
	Ravenscroft, Edward	*The Citizen Turned Gentleman (Mamamouchi)*	4 July
	Shadwell, Thomas	*Epsom Wells*	2 Dec.
	Shadwell, Thomas	*The Miser* (Adapt. Molière's *L'Avare*.)	Jan.
	Shipman, Thomas	*Henry III of France, Stabbed by a Friar, with the Fall of the Guise*	1672–*c.* July 1678; pub. 1678
	Tuke, Richard	*The Soul's Warfare (The Divine Comedian, or The Right Use of Plays)*	1672
	Wycherley, William	*The Gentleman Dancing-Master*	6 Feb.
	Anon.	*The Dutch Cruelties at Amboyna, with the Humours of the Valiant Welshman*	11 Nov.
	Anon.	*Emilia* (revision of Flecknoe's *Erminia* [1661] [?])	1672
	Anon.	*The Illustrious Slaves*	Nov.
	Anon.	*The Romantic Lady* (Cartwright's *The Lady Errant?*)	13 Mar.
	Anon.	*Wit à la Mode* (Alternative title of *Wit at Several Weapons?*)	28 Feb.

TYPE	AUSPICES	EARLIEST TEXTS	LATEST TEXTS
Comedy	Duke's	1671	C
Comedy	King's	1672★	
Tragedy	Duke's	1672	C
Tragedy	Duke's	1671★	C
Tragicomedy	King's	1672	C,M
Comedy	King's	1673	E,M,S
Comedy	Duke's	1671★	
Civic Pageant	London	1671	C
Tragedy	Closet	1671 F	C
Comedy	Unacted	MS	
Comedy	Duke's	1671★	
Tragedy	Duke's	1671	T
Moral	Closet	1671	
Burlesque	King's	1672	E
Comedy	King's	1672	C,M
Political Dialogue	Unacted	1671★	C,M
Tragedy	Unacted	1694	C
Tragedy	King's	1673	C
Comedy	King's	1673	C
Civic Pageant	London	1672	C
Tragedy	Duke's	1673★★ F	
Comedy	Duke's	1673★★	
Comedy	Duke's	1672	
Comedy	Duke's	1673	E
Comedy	King's	1672	C
Tragedy	King's	1678★★	
Moral	Unacted	1672★★	
Comedy	Duke's	1673	C,M,T
Droll	Booth at Charing Cross	Lost	
Tragicomedy	Unacted	1672★	
Tragedy	Unknown	MS	
Unknown	Duke's	Lost	
Comedy	Duke's	Lost (?)	

DATE	AUTHOR	TITLE	LIMITS
1673	Arrowsmith, Joseph	*The Reformation*	*c.* before Aug.
	Behn, Aphra	*The Dutch Lover*	6 Feb.
	Duffett, Thomas	*The Empress of Morocco*	*c.* June
	Duffett, Thomas	*The Spanish Rogue*	*c.* May
	Jordan, Thomas	*London in Its Splendour*	29 Oct.
	Kirkman, Francis (compiler)	*II The Wits, or Sport upon Sport*: A collection of drolls, etc., fashioned from comic scenes in older plays: *Bottom the Weaver* (from *A Midsummer-Night's Dream*; see 1661), *The Cheater Cheated* (from *The Dutch Courtesan*), *Oenone* (expansion of Cox's *Rural Sports*), *Wiltshire Tom* (from *The King and Queen's Entertainment at Richmond*), and six other pieces attributed to Robert Cox (?); see 1653. For *I The Wits*, see 1662.	1673 (pub.)
	Pordage, Samuel	*Herod and Mariamne* (Written 1661–2 according to Prol. First performance in 1671?)	28 Oct. (revived?)
	Ravenscroft, Edward	*The Careless Lovers*	12 Mar.
	Settle, Elkanah	*The Empress of Morocco*	3 July
	Anon.	*The Recovery* (Listed mistakenly by Summers and Nicoll as *The Rectory*.)	27 Sept.
1674	Carleton, R.	*The Concealed Royalty, or The May Queen*	1674
	Cavendish, W. (produced by Shadwell, T.)	*The Triumphant Widow, or The Medley of Humours* (An elaboration of *A Pleasant and Merry Humour of a Rogue*, 1658.)	26 Nov.
	Crowe, John (reviser)	*Andromache* (Trans. Racine.)	*c.* Aug.
	'J.D.' (Dover, John?)	*The Mall, or The Modish Lovers*	*c.* Jan.
	Duffett, Thomas	*The Mock Tempest, or The Enchanted Castle* (Songs and mask pub. sep. [1674?].)	19 Nov.
	Jordan, Thomas	*The Goldsmiths' Jubilee, or London's Triumphs*	29 Oct.
	Lee, Nathaniel	*Nero, Emperor of Rome*	16 May
	Payne, Nevil	*The Siege of Constantinople*	2 Nov.
	Perrin, Pierre	*Ariadne, or The Marriage of Bacchus* (*Ariane, ou le mariage de Bacchus*)	30 Mar.
	Rant, Humphrey	*Phormio* (Trans. Terence.)	1674
	Settle, Elkanah	*Love and Revenge* (Adapt. Hemming's *The Fatal Contract*.)	9 Nov.
	Shadwell, T. (?) (produced by Betterton, T.?)	*The Tempest, or The Enchanted Island* (Adapt. Shakespeare.) (Songs and mask pub. sep. [1674?].)	30 Apr.
	Wright, John	*Thyestes* (trans. Seneca) and *Mock Thyestes*	1674
	Anon. (produced by Duffett, T.?)	*The Amorous Old Woman, or 'Tis Well if It Take* (*The Fond Lady*)	*c.* Feb.–March
	Anon. (one scene by Dryden, J.)	*The Mistaken Husband* (Adapt. lost Brome comedy?)	*c.* Mar.

TYPE	AUSPICES	EARLIEST TEXTS	LATEST TEXTS
Comedy	Duke's	1673**	
Comedy	Duke's	1673	C
Burlesque	At Court	1674*	T
Comedy	King's	1674*	
Civic Pageant	London	1673*	
Drolls	Offered for acting	1673* (reprint of 1662 ed. with new material incorporated.)	C
Tragedy	Duke's	1673	
Comedy	Duke's	1673*	T
Tragedy	Duke's	1673	
Unknown	Duke's	Lost	
Pastoral	Acted privately (by Lord Bruce and his family)	MS	
Comedy	Duke's	1677	
Tragedy	Duke's	1675	
Comedy	King's	1674*	C
Burlesque	King's	1675*	C,T
Civic Pageant	London	1674*	C
Tragedy	King's	1675	C
Tragedy	Duke's	1675*	
Opera (French and English)	Royal Academy of Music	1674	
Comedy	Unacted	MS	
Tragedy	Duke's	1675** & MS	
Dramatic Opera	Duke's	1674	C,F
Tragedy and Burlesque	Closet	1674*	
Comedy	King's	1674**	
Comedy	King's	1675*	C

DATE	AUTHOR	TITLE	LIMITS
	Anon.	*Mock Pompey* (Act V, Davenant's *The Playhouse to be Let*)	1674 (ment.)
	Anon.	*The Sea Captains*	18 Mar.
1675	Barnes, Joshua	*The Academy, or The Cambridge Dons*	28 June
	Belon, Peter (?)	*The Mock Duellist, or The French Valet*	*c.* May
	Carleton, R.	*The Martial Queen*	*c.* 1675
	Crowne, John	*Calisto, or The Chaste Nymph*	15 Feb. (performed)
	Crowne, J.	*The Country Knight* (Same as *The Country Wit*, 1676?)	19 Mar.
	Dryden, John	*Aureng-Zebe*	17 Nov.
	Duffett, Thomas	*Psyche Debauched*	*c.* Aug.
	Fane, Francis	*Love in the Dark, or The Man of Business*	10 May
	Jordan, Thomas	*The Triumphs of London*	29 Oct.
	Lee, Nathaniel	*Sophonisba, or Hannibal's Overthrow*	30 Apr.
	Lesley, George	*Abraham's Faith*	1675
	Lesley, George	*Dives' Doom, or The Rich Man's Misery*	1675
	Lesley, George	*Fire and Brimstone, or The Destruction of Sodom* (*Sodom's Flames*)	1675
	Otway, Thomas	*Alcibiades*	22 Sept. (?)
	Settle, Elkanah	*The Conquest of China by the Tartars*	28 May (?)
	Shadwell, Thomas	*The Libertine*	12 June
	Shadwell, Thomas	*Psyche*	27 Feb.
	Wycherley, William	*The Country Wife*	12 Jan.
	Anon.	*The Armenian Queen* (Prol. and Epil. by T. Duffett extant.) (Alternative title for known work?)	*c.* 1673–1675
	Anon.	*Paradise*	1675
	Anon.	*Piso's Conspiracy* (Adapt. *Nero*, 1624.)	*c.* Aug.
	Anon.	*The Woman Turned Bully*	24 Mar.
1676	Bannister, John	*I Music, or A Parley of Instruments*	30 Oct. (imprim.)
	Behn, Aphra	*Abdelazer, or The Moor's Revenge* (Adapt. *Lust's Dominion*, 1600.)	*c.* Apr.
	Behn, Aphra	*The Town Fop, or Sir Timothy Tawdrey*	*c.* Sept.
	Boyle, Roger	*King Saul*	*c.* 1676–1679
	Crowne, John	*The Country Wit* (Same as *The Country Knight*, 1675?)	10 Jan.
	Dryden, John	*All for Love, or The World Well Lost*	1675–1677
	Duffett, Thomas	*Beauty's Triumph*	1675–1676
	D'Urfey, Thomas	*The Fool Turned Critic*	18 Nov.
	D'Urfey, Thomas	*Madam Fickle, or The Witty False One*	4 Nov.
	D'Urfey, Thomas	*The Siege of Memphis, or The Ambitious Queen*	*c.* Sept.
	Etherege, George	*The Man of Mode, or Sir Fopling Flutter*	11 Mar.
	Jordan, Thomas	*London's Triumphs*	30 Oct.
	Lee, Nathaniel	*Gloriana, or The Court of Augustus Caesar*	29 Jan.

TYPE	AUSPICES	EARLIEST TEXTS	LATEST TEXTS
Droll (?)	At Fairs (?)	Lost	
Unknown	Duke's	Lost	
Comedy	Emmanuel Col., Cambridge	MSS	
Comedy	King's	1675★	
Tragedy	Acted privately (by Lord Bruce and his family)	MSS	
Mask	Court	1675★	C
Comedy	Duke's	Lost (?)	
Tragedy	King's	1676	C,S,M
Burlesque	King's	1678★	T
Comedy	King's	1675★★	
Civic Pageant	London	1675★	
Tragedy	King's	1676	C
Religious Dialogue	Closet	1678	
Moral	Closet	1678	
Biblical Tragedy	Closet	1678	
Tragedy	Duke's	1675	C
Tragedy	Duke's	1676★	
Comedy	Duke's	1676	C,T
Dramatic Opera	Duke's	1675	C
Comedy	King's	1675	E,M,S,F
Unknown	King's (?)	Lost	
Scenic Display (?)	Hatton House, Holborn	Lost	
Tragedy	Duke's	1676★	
Comedy	Duke's	1675★	
Dialogues with Music	A Music School	1676★	
Tragedy	Duke's	1677	C
Comedy	Duke's	1677	C
Tragedy	Unacted	1703★	C
Comedy	Duke's	1675[76]	C
Tragedy	King's	1678 F	C,M,S,F
Mask	School at Chelsea	1676★	
Comedy	King's	1678★	
Comedy	Duke's	1677	
Tragedy	King's	1676★	
Comedy	Duke's	1676	C,S
Civic Pageant	London	1676★	
Tragedy	King's	1676	C

DATE	AUTHOR	TITLE	LIMITS
	Otway, Thomas	*Don Carlos, Prince of Spain*	8 June
	Ravenscroft, Edward	*The Wrangling Lovers, or The Invisible Mistress*	25 July
	Rawlins,–	*Tom Essence, or The Modish Wife*	*c.* Aug.
	Settle, Elkanah	*Ibrahim, the Illustrious Bassa*	*c.* Mar.
	Settle, Elkanah	*Pastor Fido, or The Faithful Shepherd* (Adapt. Guarini.)	*c.* Dec.
	Shadwell, Thomas	*The Virtuoso*	25 May
	Wycherley, William	*The Plain Dealer*	11 Dec.
	Anon.	*No Fool Like the Old Fool*	13 June
	Anon.	*Zoroastres*	1675–*c.* 1676
1677	Banks, John	*The Rival Kings, or The Loves of Oroondates and Statira*	*c.* June
	Behn, Aphra	*I The Rover, or The Banished Cavaliers* (Adapt. T. Killigrew's *Thomaso.*)	24 Mar.
	Behn, Aphra (?)	*The Debauchee, or The Credulous Cuckold* (Adapt. Brome's *A Mad Couple Well Matched.*)	*c.* Feb.
	Crowe, John	*I & II The Destruction of Jerusalem by Titus Vespasian*	Pt. I: 12 Jan. Pt. II: 18 Jan.
	Davenant, Charles	*Circe*	12 May
	Dryden, John	*The State of Innocence, and Fall of Man* (*The Fall of Angels, and Man in Innocence*)	1677
	D'Urfey, Thomas	*A Fond Husband, or The Plotting Sisters*	31 May
	Jordan, Thomas	*London's Triumphs*	29 Oct.
	Leanerd, John	*The Country Innocence, or The Chambermaid Turned Quaker* (Adapt. 'T.B.''s *The Country Girl.*)	*c.* Mar.
	Lee, Nathaniel	*The Rival Queens, or The Death of Alexander the Great*	17 Mar.
	Otway, Thomas	*Titus and Berenice, with The Cheats of Scapin* (Adapt. Racine's *Berenice* and Molière's *Les Fourberies de Scapin.*)	*c.* Jan.
	Pordage, Samuel	*The Siege of Babylon*	*c.* Sept.
	P., T.	*The French Conjurer*	*c.* Mar.–April
	Ravenscroft, Edward	*The English Lawyer* (Adapt. Ruggle's *Ignoramus.*)	*c.* Dec.
	Ravenscroft, Edward	*King Edgar and Alfreda* (Revision of play written *c.* 1667.)	*c.* Oct.
	Ravenscroft, Edward	*Scaramouch a Philosopher, Harlequin a School-boy, Bravo, Merchant, and Magician*	5 May
	Roche-Guilhen, Mlle de la	*Rare en tout*	29 May
	Rymer, Thomas	*Edgar, or The English Monarch*	13 Sept. (imprim.)
	Sedley, Charles	*Antony and Cleopatra* (Remodelled as *Beauty the Conqueror, or The Death of Marc Antony,* pub. 1702.)	12 Feb.

TYPE	AUSPICES	EARLIEST TEXTS	LATEST TEXTS
Tragedy	Duke's	1676	C,M
Comedy	Duke's	1677**	
Comedy	Duke's	1677*	
Tragedy	Duke's	1677	
Pastoral	Duke's	1677 & MS	
Comedy	Duke's	1676	C,T
Comedy	King's	1677	C,S
Comedy	King's	Lost	
Tragedy	Unacted	MS	C
Tragedy	King's	1677**	
Comedy	Duke's	1677	C,S
Comedy	Duke's	1677	C
Tragedy	King's	1677	C,A
Dramatic Opera	Duke's	1677	C,T
Dramatic Opera	Unacted	1677 & MSS	C,T
Comedy	Duke's	1677	T
Civic Pageant	London	1677*	
Comedy	King's	1677*	
Tragedy	King's	1677	C,F,S
Tragedy and Farce	Duke's	1677**	C
Tragedy	Duke's	1678*	
Comedy	Duke's	1678*	
Comedy	King's	1678**	
Tragicomedy	King's	1677*	
Imitation Commedia dell'Arte	King's	1677*	
French Comedy with Music and Dance	Court	1677*	
Tragedy	Duke's (?)	1678**	
Tragedy	Duke's	1677	C,F

DATE	AUTHOR	TITLE	LIMITS
	Smith, John	*Cytherea, or The Enamouring Girdle*	30 May (imprim.)
	Wilson, John	*Belphegor, or The Marriage of the Devil*	1677–1678
	Anon.	*The Captain, or Town Miss* (Adapt. Fletcher?)	2 Apr.
	Anon.	*The Constant Nymph, or The Rambling Shepherd*	*c.* July
	Anon. (Behn?)	*The Counterfeit Bridegroom, or The Defeated Widow* (Adapt. Middleton's *No Wit, No Help Like a Woman's*.)	*c.* Sept.
	Anon.	*Midnight's Intrigues*	1677
	Anon.	*The Politician, or Sir Popular Wisdom*	17 Nov.
	Anon.	*Wits Led by the Nose, or A Poet's Revenge* (Adapt. Chamberlaine's *Love's Victory*.)	16 or 18 June.
1678	Banks, John	*The Destruction of Troy*	*c.* Nov.
	Behn, Aphra	*Sir Patient Fancy*	17 Jan.
	Cooke, Edward	*Love's Triumph, or The Royal Union*	1678
	Dryden, John	*The Kind Keeper, or Mr Limberham*	11 Mar.
	Dryden, J.;	*Oedipus*	*c.* Sept.
	D'Urfey, Thomas	*Squire Oldsapp, or The Night Adventurers*	*c.* June
	D'Urfey, Thomas	*Trick for Trick, or The Debauched Hypocrite* (Adapt. Fletcher's *Monsieur Thomas*.)	*c.* Mar.
	Fishbourne, C. (?)	*Sodom, or the Quintessence of Debauchery*	*c.* 1678–1680
	Howard, Edward	*The Man of Newmarket*	*c.* Mar.
	Johns, William	*The Traitor to Himself, or Man's Heart His Greatest Enemy*	1678 (pub.)
	Jordan, Thomas	*The Triumphs of London*	29 Oct.
	Leanerd, John	*The Rambling Justice, or The Jealous Husbands* (Adapt. Middleton's *More Dissemblers Besides Women*.)	*c.* Mar.
	Lee, Nathaniel	*Mithridates, King of Pontus*	. Feb.
	Otway, Thomas	*Friendship in Fashion*	5 Apr.
	Rawlins,– (?)	*Tunbridge Wells, or A Day's Courtship*	*c.* Mar.
	Shadwell, Thomas	*Timon of Athens, the Man-Hater* (Adapt. Shakespeare.)	*c.* Jan.
	Shadwell, Thomas	*A True Widow*	21 Mar. (?)
	Shaw, Samuel	*Words Made Visible, or Grammar and Rhetoric Accommodated to the Lives and Manners of Men* (*Minerva's Triumphs, or Grammar and Rhetoric*) (In two parts.)	1678
	Shipman, Thomas	*Henry IV* [of France]	1672–1680
	Tate, Nahum	*Brutus of Alba, or The Enchanted Lovers*	*c.* July
	Wilmot, John	*Lucina's Rape, or Valentinian* (Adapt. Fletcher.) (See also 1684.)	1678–1679
	Anon. (ascribed to Leanerd, John)	*The Counterfeits*	28 May
	Anon. ('W.M.')	*The Huntingdon Divertisement*	20 June
	Anon.	*The Rival Mother* (Ghost? No extant copy known.)	1678

TYPE	AUSPICES	EARLIEST TEXTS	LATEST TEXTS
Comedy	Unacted	1677*	
Tragicomedy	Smock Alley, Dublin (United in 1690)	1691** & MS	C,T
Comedy	King's	Lost	
Pastoral	Duke's	1678*	
Comedy	Duke's	1677*	S
Comedy	Duke's (?)	Lost	
Comedy	Duke's	Lost	
Tragicomedy	King's	1678**	
Tragedy	Duke's	1679*	
Comedy	Duke's	1678	C
Tragedy	Unacted	1678*	
Comedy	Duke's	1680	C
Tragedy	Duke's	1679	C
Comedy	Duke's	1679*	
Comedy	King's	1678*	
Comedy	Unacted	1684 (?) & MSS	E
Comedy	King's	1678*	
Moral	School at Evesham	1678*	
Civic Pageant	London	1678*	C
Comedy	King's	1678	
Tragedy	King's	1678 & MS	C
Comedy	Duke's	1678	C
Comedy	Duke's	1678*	
Tragedy	Duke's	1678	C,F
Comedy	Duke's	1679	C,M
Academic Allegory	School at Ashby-de-la-Zouch	1678–9	
Tragedy	King's (?)	Lost	
Tragedy	Duke's	1678*	T
Tragedy	King's	MSS	
Comedy	Duke's	1679*	
Entertainment	Merchant Taylors Hall	1678*	
Comedy	Unacted	1678*(?)	

DATE	AUTHOR	TITLE	LIMITS
	Anon. (attribution to 'Joan Philips' highly suspect)	*Pair Royal of Coxcombs* (Prol., 2 songs, and Epil. printed in *Female Poems on Several Occasions*, 1679.)	*c.* 1678
1679	Bancroft, John	*Sertorius*	*c.* Mar.
	Bedloe, W. (?) or Walter, T. (?)	*The Excommunicated Prince, or The False Relique*	1679
	Behn, Aphra	*The Feigned Courtesans, or A Night's Intrigue* (Same as *Midnight's Intrigues*, 1677?)	*c.* Mar.
	Behn, Aphra	*The Young King, or The Mistake*	*c.* Sept.
	Crowne, John	*The Ambitious Statesman, or The Loyal Favourite*	*c.* Mar.
	Dryden, John	*Troilus and Cressida, or Truth Found Too Late* (Adapt. Shakespeare.)	*c.* Apr.
	D'Urfey, Thomas	*The Virtuous Wife, or Good Luck at Last*	*c.* Sept.
	Ecclestone, Edward	*Noah's Flood, or the Destruction of the World* (*The Cataclysm, or General Deluge of the World. The Deluge, or The Destruction of the World*)	. 1679
	Jordan, Thomas	*London in Lustre*	29 Oct.
	Lee, Nathaniel	*Caesar Borgia, Son of Pope Alexander VI*	1679
	Otway, Thomas	*Caius Marius* (Adapt. Shakespeare's *Romeo and Juliet*.)	*c.* Sept.
	Ravenscroft, Edward	*Titus Andronicus, or The Rape of Lavinia* (Adapt. Shakespeare.)	1679–1686
	Shadwell, Thomas	*The Woman Captain*	*c.* Sept.
	Sherburne, Edward	*Troades, or The Royal Captives* (Trans. Seneca.)	1679
	Tate, Nahum	*The Loyal General*	*c.* Dec.
1680	Barnes, Joshua	*Englebert*	*c.* 1680
	Behn, A. (?)	*The Revenge, or A Match in Newgate* (*The Vintner Tricked*) (Adapt. Marston's *The Dutch Courtesan*.)	*c.* June
	Crowne, John	*The Misery of Civil War* (*II Henry VI. The Miseries of Civil War*) (Adapt. Shakespeare's *III Henry VI*.)	*c.* Feb.
	Crowne, John	*Thyestes*	*c.* Mar.
	Dryden, John	*The Spanish Friar, or The Double Discovery*	*c.* Oct.
	Jordan, Thomas	*London's Glory*	29 Oct.
	Lee, Nathaniel	*Lucius Junius Brutus, Father of His Country*	8 Dec. (?)
	Lee, Nathaniel	*Theodosius, or The Force of Love*	*c.* Sept.
	Maidwell, Lewis	*The Loving Enemies*	*c.* Jan.
	Otway, Thomas	*The Orphan, or The Unhappy Marriage*	Feb.
	Otway, Thomas	*The Soldier's Fortune*	*c.* June
	Settle, Elkanah	*Fatal Love, or The Forced Inconstancy*	*c.* Sept.
	Settle, Elkanah	*The Female Prelate, Being the History of the Life and Death of Pope Joan*	31 May
	Tate, Nahum	*Richard II* (*The Sicilian Usurper*) (Adapt. Shakespeare.)	11 Dec.

TYPE	AUSPICES	EARLIEST TEXTS	LATEST TEXTS
Comedy	'Acted at a Dancing-School'	Lost	
Tragedy	King's	1679*	
Political Dialogue	Unacted	1679*	
Comedy	Duke's	1679	T,C
Tragicomedy	Duke's	1683	C
Tragedy	King's	1679**	C,E
Tragicomedy	Duke's	1679	C,F
Comedy	Duke's	1680*	T
Dramatic Opera	Unacted (?)	1679**	
Civic Pageant	London	1679*	
Tragedy	Duke's	1680	C
Tragedy	Duke's	1680	C,T,F
Tragedy	King's	1687	F
Comedy	Duke's	1680	C
Tragedy	Closet	1679	
Tragedy	Duke's	1680*	
Opera and Tragedy	Emmanuel Col., Cambridge (?)	MS	
Comedy	Duke's	1680*	T
Tragedy	Duke's	1680**	F
Tragedy	King's	1681*	C
Comedy	Duke's	1681 & MS	C,M
Civic Pageant	London	1680*	C
Tragedy	Duke's	1681	C,S
Tragedy	Duke's	1680	C
Comedy	Duke's	1680*	
Tragedy	Duke's	1680	C,M,S
Comedy	Duke's	1681	C,M
Tragedy	King's	1680*	
Tragedy	King's	1680	
Tragedy	King's	1681**	F

DATE	AUTHOR	TITLE	LIMITS
	Whitaker, William	*The Conspiracy, or The Change of Government*	*c.* Mar.
	Anon.	*The Coronation of Queen Elizabeth with the Restoration of the Protestant Religion, or The Downfall of the Pope*	Aug.
	Anon.	*The Cure of Pride, or Everyone in Their Way* (Adapt. Massinger's *The City Madam,* *c.* 1700.) (Songs and mask pub. sep. [1674?].)	*c.* 1675–87
	Anon.	*Fools Have Fortune, or Luck's All* (MS Prol. and Epil. extant.)	*c.* 1680
	Anon.	*Love Lost in the Dark, or The Drunken Couple* (From Massinger's *The Guardian.*)	1680
	Anon.	*Marriage Revived, or The Mistress Returned*	*c.* 1680(?)
	Anon.	*The Merry Milkmaid of Islington, or The Rambling Gallants Defeated* (From Nabbes' *Tottenham Court.*)	*c.* 1680
	Anon.	*The Politic Whore, or The Conceited Cuckold* (From Davenport's *The City Nightcap.*)	*c.* 1680
1681	Banks, John	*The Unhappy Favourite, or The Earl of Essex*	*c.* May
	Behn, Aphra	*The False Count, or A New Way to Play an Old Game*	*c.* Nov.
	Behn, Aphra	*The Roundheads, or The Good Old Cause* (Adapt. Tatham's *The Rump.*)	*c.* Nov.
	Behn, Aphra	*II The Rover* (Adapt. T. Killigrew's *Thomaso.*)	1680–1681
	Crowne, John	*Henry VI, the First Part, with the Murder of Humphrey Duke of Gloucester* (Adapt. Shakespeare's *II Henry VI.*)	*c.* Apr.
	D'Urfey, Thomas	*Sir Barnaby Whigg, or No Wit Like a Woman's*	*c.* Oct.
	Jordan, Thomas	*London's Joy*	29 Oct.
	Lee, Nathaniel	*The Princess of Cleve*	1680–1682
	'N.N.' (N. Nowel? printer rather than author)	*Rome's Follies, or The Amorous Friars*	1681–1682
	Ravenscroft, Edward	*The London Cuckolds*	Nov.
	Saunders, Charles	*Tamerlane the Great*	*c.* Mar
	Shadwell, Thomas	*The Lancashire Witches, and Tegue O'Divelly the Irish Priest*	1681
	Tate, Nahum	*The Ingratitude of a Commonwealth, or The Fall of Caius Martius Coriolanus* (Adapt. Shakespeare.)	*c.* Dec.
	Tate, Nahum	*King Lear* (Adapt. Shakespeare.)	*c.* Mar.
1682	Banks, John	*Virtue Betrayed, or Anna Bullen*	*c.* Mar.
	Behn, Aphra	*The City Heiress, or Sir Timothy Treatall*	*c.* May
	Behn, Aphra	*Like Father Like Son, or The Mistaken Brothers* (Adapt. Randolph's *The Jealous Lovers.*) (Prol. and Epil. extant.)	*c.* Nov.

TYPE	AUSPICES	EARLIEST TEXTS	LATEST TEXTS
Tragedy	Duke's	1680★	
Popular Chronicle	Bartholomew and Southwark Fairs	1680★	
Tragicomedy	Unknown	MS	
Comedy	Duke's	Lost	
Droll	Court at Newmarket (Robert Parker's Strollers?)	1680★	
Comedy	Oxford (?) Privately acted (?)	MS	
Droll	Court at Newmarket (Robert Parker's Strollers?)	1680★	
Droll	Court at Newmarket (Robert Parker's Strollers?)	1680★	
Tragedy	King's	1682	E
Comedy	Duke's	1682	C
Comedy	Duke's	1682	C
Comedy	Duke's	1681	C,S
Tragedy	Duke's	1681★	F
Comedy	King's	1681★	
Civic Pageant	London	1681★	
Tragedy	Duke's	1689	C
Political Dialogue	Privately acted (?)	1681★	
Comedy	Duke's	1682	C
Tragedy	King's	1681★	
Comedy	Duke's	1682	C
Tragedy	King's	1682★	F,T
Tragedy	Duke's	1681	C,S,F
Tragedy	Duke's	1682	E
Comedy	Duke's	1682	C
Comedy	Duke's	Lost	

DATE	AUTHOR	TITLE	LIMITS
	Blow, John	*Venus and Adonis*	1680–1682
	Dryden, J.; Lee, N.	*The Duke of Guise* (Prepared for July, but banned.)	28 Nov.
	D'Urfey, Thomas	*The Injured Princess, or The Fatal Wager* (Adapt. Shakespeare's *Cymbeline*.)	*c.* Mar.
	D'Urfey, Thomas	*The Royalist*	23 Jan. (?)
	Jordan, Thomas	*The Lord Mayor's Show*	30 Oct. (intended)
	Luttrell, N. (?) (owner rather than author?)	*Love's Metamorphosis, or The Disguised Lovers*	*c.* 1660–1682
	Otway, Thomas	*Venice Preserved, or A Plot Discovered*	9 Feb.
	Settle, Elkanah	*The Heir of Morocco, with the Death of Gayland*	11 Mar.
	Southerne, Thomas	*The Loyal Brother, or The Persian Prince*	4 Feb. (?)
	Anon.	*The Irish Evidence, The Humours of Teague, or The Mercenary Whore*	Aug.
	Anon.	*Mr Turbulent, or The Melancholics* (*The Factious Citizen, or The Melancholy Visioner*)	27 Jan. (?)
	Anon.	*The Prince's Ball, or The Conquest of Queen Judith* (Listed by Summers.)	Aug.
	Anon.	*Romulus and Hersilia, or The Sabine War*	10 Aug.
1683	Barnes, Joshua	*Landgartha, or The Amazon Queen of Denmark* (*Sigward the Famous King of Norway*)	1682–1683
	Crowne, John	*City Politiques*	19 Jan.
	Jordan, Thomas	*The Triumphs of London*	29 Oct.
	Lee, Nathaniel	*Constantine the Great*	12 Nov. (?)
	Otway, Thomas	*The Atheist, or The Second Part of the Soldier's Fortune*	*c.* July
	Ravenscroft, Edward	*Dame Dobson, or The Cunning Woman*	31 May (?)
	Anon.	*Mr Doolittle*	1682–1683(?)
1684	Banks, John	*The Island Queens, or The Death of Mary Queen of Scotland* (*The Albion Queens*)	1684
	Behn, Aphra (?) (alterer?)	*The Wavering Nymph, or Mad Amyntas* (Alteration Randolph's *Amyntas*.) (Two songs extant.)	*c.* 1683–1684
	D'Urfey, Thomas	*Cinthia and Endimion, or The Loves of the Dieties*	*c.* 1684–1694 perf. Dec. 1696–Jan. 1697
	Fane, Francis	*A Mask* (*Frightful Dream to Lucina*) (Written to be inserted into *Valentinian*; see Anon., below.)	Feb. (?)
	Horne, John	*Fortune's Task, or The Fickle Fair One*	1684
	Jordan, Thomas	*London's Royal Triumph*	29 Oct.
	Lacy, John	*Sir Hercules Buffoon, or The Poetical Squire*	June
	Southerne, Thomas	*The Disappointment, or The Mother in Fashion*	5 Apr. (?)
	Tate, Nahum	*A Duke and No Duke* (Adapt. Cokain's *Trappolin Creduto Principe*.)	18 Aug. (?)

TYPE	AUSPICES	EARLIEST TEXTS	LATEST TEXTS
Opera	Oxford (?)	MSS	E
Tragedy	United	1683	C
Tragicomedy	King's	1682*	
Comedy	Duke's	1682*	
Civic Pageant	London (not performed)	1682*	C
Comedy	Unacted (?)	MS	
Tragedy	Duke's	1682	C,M,S
Tragedy	King's	1682	
Tragedy	King's	1682**	C,E
Droll	Bartholomew Fair	Lost	E
Comedy	Duke's	1682**	
Droll	Bartholomew Fair	Lost	
Tragedy	Duke's	1683*	
Tragedy	Emmanuel Col. (?), Cambridge	MSS	
Comedy	United	1683	C,S
Civic Pageant	London	1683*	
Tragedy	United	1684	C
Comedy	United	1684	C
Comedy	United	1684*	
Comedy	Unknown	MS & MS (frag.)	
Tragedy	Unacted until 1704	1684	T
Pastoral	Unknown	Lost	
Dramatic Opera	Patent	1697	
Operatic Interlude	United (?)	1685*	
Pastoral	Oxford (?)	MS	
Civic Pageant	London	1684*	
Comedy	United	1684*	C
Comedy	United	1684	C
Farce	United	1685	C

DATE	AUTHOR	TITLE	LIMITS
	Anon.	*The Indian Empress*	*c.* 1684
	Anon.	*The Mistaken Beauty, or The Liar* (Revival of *The Liar*, 1661?) (Adapt. P. Corneille's *Le Menteur.*)	1661–*c.* Sept. 1684
	Anon.	*Valentinian* (Adapt. Wilmot's *Lucina's Rape.*)	11 Feb.
1685	Crowne, John	*Sir Courtly Nice, or It Cannot Be*	9 May (?)
	Dryden, John	*Albion and Albanius*	3 June
	D'Urfey, Thomas	*A Commonwealth of Women* (Adapt. Fletcher's *The Sea Voyage.*)	20 Aug. (?)
	Tate, Nahum	*Cuckolds Haven, or An Alderman No Conjurer* (Adapt. Jonson, *et al.*, *Eastward Ho.*)	*c.* June
	Taubman, Matthew	*London's Annual Triumph*	29 Oct.
	Tutchin, John	*The Unfortunate Shepherd*	1685
	Wharton, Anne (née Lee)	*Love's Martyr, or Wit above Crowns*	*c.* 1685 (S.R.)
	Anon.	*The Rampant Alderman, or News from the Exchange* (Adapt. Marmion's *A Fine Companion.*)	1685 (pub.)
	Anon.	*The Whore of Babylon, the Devil, and the Pope* (Adapt. of Dekker's *The Whore of Babylon.*)	Aug.
1686	Behn, Aphra	*The Lucky Chance, or An Alderman's Bargain* (*The Disappointed Marriage, or the Generous Mistress*)	*c.* Apr.
	D'Urfey, Thomas	*The Banditti, or A Lady's Distress*	*c.* Feb.
	Fane, Francis	*The Sacrifice*	1686
	Jevon, Thomas	*The Devil of a Wife, or A Comical Transformation*	4 Mar.
	Talbot, John	*Troas* (Trans. Seneca.)	1686
	Taubman, Matthew	*London's Yearly Jubilee*	29 Oct.
	Villiers, George (?)	*The Restoration, or Right Will Take Place* (Adapt. Beaumont and Fletcher's *Philaster.*) (Doubtful play printed in Villiers' *Works: The Battle, or The Rehearsal at Whitehall* [*Sedgemoor Fight*], 1704.)	*c.* 1685–1686(?)
	Anon.	*St George and the Dragon*	Aug.
	Anon.	*Vienna Besieged*	Aug.
1687	Behn, Aphra	*The Emperor of the Moon*	*c.* Mar.
	Sedley, C.	*Bellamira, or The Mistress* (Adapt. Terence's *Eunuchus.*)	12 May
	Tate, Nahum	*The Island Princess* (Adapt. Fletcher.)	25 Apr.
	Taubman, Matthew	*London's Triumph, or The Goldsmiths' Jubilee*	29 Oct.
	Anon.	*Augustus Caesar* (Alt. title for Nathaniel Lee's *Gloriana, or The Court of Augustus Caesar*, 1676?)	*c.* 1687
	Anon.	*The Critics* (Poss. Villiers' *The Rehearsal.*)	1687

TYPE	AUSPICES	EARLIEST TEXTS	LATEST TEXTS
Unknown	Acted privately	Lost	
Comedy	United	1685★	
Tragedy	United	1685 (i.e. '84)	C
Comedy	United	1685	C,T
Dramatic Opera	United	1685	C,M
Comedy	United	1686	C
Farce	United	1685★	
Civic Pageant	London	1685★	
Pastoral	Unacted	1685★	
Tragedy	Unacted	MS	
Farce	Unacted (?)	1685★	
Droll	Bartholomew Fair	MS altered, 1607 first quarto	
Comedy	United	1687	C,T
Comedy	United	1686★	
Tragedy	Unacted	1686	
Comedy	United	1686	
Tragedy	Closet	1686★	
Civic Pageant	London	1686★	
Tragicomedy	Unacted (?)	1714	
Droll	Bartholomew Fair	Lost	
Droll	Bartholomew Fair	Lost	
Farce	United	1687	C
Comedy	United	1687	C
Tragicomedy	United	1687★	
Civic Pageant	London	1687★	
Tragedy (?)	Unknown	Lost	
Comedy	Acted privately at Norwich	Lost (?)	

DATE	AUTHOR	TITLE	LIMITS
	Anon.	*Woman Rules* (Error for *The Women Turned Bully,* 1675; or *The Woman Captain,* 1680?)	1687
1688	Crowne, John	*Darius, King of Persia*	Apr.
	D'Urfey, Thomas	*A Fool's Preferment, or The Three Dukes of Dunstable* (Adapt. Fletcher's *The Noble Gentleman.*)	*c.* Apr.
	Finch, Anne	*The Triumphs of Love and Innocence*	*c.* 1685–1690
	Mountfort, William	*Doctor Faustus, with the Humours of Harlequin and Scaramouche* (Adapt. Marlowe.)	*c.* March
	Mountfort, William	*The Injured Lovers, or The Ambitious Father*	6 Feb.
	Shadwell, Thomas	*The Squire of Alsatia*	4 May
	Taubman, Matthew	*London's Anniversary Festival*	29 Oct.
1689	Behn, Aphra	*The Widow Ranter, or The History of Bacon in Virginia*	*c.* Nov.
	Carlisle, James	*The Fortune Hunters, or Two Fools Well Met*	*c.* Mar.
	Dryden, John	*Don Sebastian, King of Portugal*	*c.* Nov.
	Lee, Nathaniel	*The Massacre of Paris* (Prob. written *c.* 1679.)	7 Nov.
	Mountfort, William	*The Successful Strangers*	*c.* Dec.
	Shadwell, Thomas	*Bury Fair*	*c.* Apr.
	Singleton, Thomas	*Talpae sive Conjuratis Papistica* (Transcribed 1689.)	*c.* 1642–1689
	Tate, Nahum	*Dido and Aeneas*	*c.* Dec.
	Taubman, Matthew	*London's Great Jubilee*	29 Oct.
	Anon. (Bulteel, J.?)	*Love in and Love out of Fashion* (See *Amorous Orontus,* 1665.)	1689(?)
1690	Betterton, Thomas	*The Prophetess, or The History of Diocletian* (Adapt. Fletcher and Massinger.)	*c.* May
	'W.C.'	*The Rape Revenged, or The Spanish Revolution*	*c.* 1690
	Crowne, John	*The English Friar, or The Town Sparks* (Prol. and Epil., imprim., 17 Mar. 1689[90].)	*c.* Mar.
	Dryden, John	*Amphitryon, or The Two Socias*	*c.* Oct.
	Finch, Anne	*Aristomenes, or The Royal Shepherd* (Title altered from *The Queen of Cypress, or Love above Ambition.*)	1688–1691
	Harris, J. (one scene by Mountfort, W.)	*The Mistakes, or The False Report* (*All in Confusion,* possibly an abandoned second title.)	*c.* Dec.
	Mountfort, W. (?) (producer?) (often attributed to Bancroft, J.)	*Edward III, with the Fall of Mortimer* (Adapt. Davenport's *The Politic Queen?*)	*c.* Nov.
	Powell, George	*Alphonso, King of Naples*	*c.* Dec.
	Powell, George	*The Treacherous Brothers*	*c.* Jan.
	Settle, E. (one scene by Mountfort, W.)	*Distressed Innocence, or The Princess of Persia*	*c.* Oct.

TYPE	AUSPICES	EARLIEST TEXTS	LATEST TEXTS
Comedy (?)	Unknown	Lost	
Tragedy	United	1688**	C
Comedy	United	1688*	C
Tragicomedy	Closet	MS	C
Farce	United	1697	
Tragedy	United	1688	
Comedy	United	1688	C,M
Civic Pageant	London	1688*	
Tragicomedy	United	1690	C
Comedy	United	1689*	
Tragedy	United	1690	M,C
Tragedy	United	1690	C
Tragicomedy	United	1690	
Comedy	United	1689	C,M
Latin Tragicomedy	Hoxton Wells (1689)	MS	
Dramatic Opera	J. Priest's Boarding School, Chelsea	MS	
Civic Pageant	London	1689*	
Comedy	United	Lost (?)	
Dramatic Opera	United	1690	C
Tragedy	Unknown	MS	
Comedy	United	1690	C
Comedy	United	1690	C
Tragedy	Closet	1713 & MS	C
Tragicomedy	United	1691*	
Tragedy	United	1691	E
Tragedy	United	1691*	
Tragedy	United	1690	
Tragedy	United	1691*	

DATE	AUTHOR	TITLE	LIMITS
	Shadwell, Thomas	*The Amorous Bigot, with the Second Part of Tegue O'Divelly*	*c.* Mar.
	Shadwell, Thomas	*The Scowrers*	*c.* Dec.
	Southerne, Thomas	*Sir Anthony Love, or The Rambling Lady*	*c.* Dec.
	Walsh, William (?)	*The Gordian Knot United*	*c.* Nov.
	Anon.	*The Abdicated Prince, or The Adventures of Four Years*	1690
	Anon.	*The Banished Duke, or The Tragedy of Infortunatus*	1690
	Anon.	*The Bloody Duke, or The Adventures for a Crown*	1690
	Anon.	*The Folly of Priest-Craft (The Converts)*	1690
	Anon.	*The Late Revolution, or The Happy Change*	1690
	Anon.	*The Mystery of Iniquity, or The Revolution, Deduced to the Time of K.J. His Being Forced . . . to Retire from England.*	*c.* 1690
	Anon.	*The Royal Flight, or The Conquest of Ireland*	1690
	Anon.	*The Royal Voyage, or The Irish Expedition*	1690
1691	Dryden, John	*King Arthur, or The British Worthy*	*c.* May
	D'Urfey, Thomas	*Bussy D'Ambois, or The Husband's Revenge* (Adapt. Chapman.)	*c.* Mar.
	D'Urfey, Thomas	*Love for Money, or The Boarding School*	*c.* Jan.
	Mountfort, William	*Greenwich Park*	*c.* Apr.
	Pitcairne, Archibald	*The Assembly, or Scotch Reformation*	*c.* 1690–1692
	Popple, William	*The Cid* (Trans. Corneille.)	1691
	Settle, Elkanah	*The Triumphs of London*	29 Oct.
	Shaw, Samuel	*Poikilo-Phronesis, or The Different Humours of Men*	15 Dec.
	Smythe, J. (produced by Underhill, C.)	*Win Her and Take Her, or Old Fools Will Be Meddling*	1691
	Southerne, Thomas	*The Wives' Excuse, or Cuckolds Make Themselves*	Dec.
	Anon.	*The Braggadocio, or The Bawd Turned Puritan*	1691
	Anon.	*The Siege and Surrender of Mons*	1691
	Anon.	*Wit for Money, or Poet Stutter*	1691
1692	Bourne, Reuben	*The Contented Cuckold, or The Woman's Advocate*	1692
	Brady, Nicholas	*The Rape, or The Innocent Impostors*	Feb.
	Crowne, John	*Regulus*	June
	Dryden, J. (fifth act completed by Southerne, T.?)	*Cleomenes, The Spartan Hero*	Apr.
	D'Urfey, Thomas	*The Marriage Hater Matched*	*c.* Jan.
	Haynes, Joe	*A Fatal Mistake, or The Plot Spoiled*	1692
	Pix, Mary (?)	*Zelmane, or The Corinthian Queen*	b.1692(?)
	Popple, William	*Tamerlane the Beneficent*	1692
	'Mr Rivers'	*The Traitor* (Same as 1631 play of same name by Shirley; not by Jesuit Anthony Rivers, as often supposed.)	Mar.

TYPE	AUSPICES	EARLIEST TEXTS	LATEST TEXTS
Comedy	United	1690	C
Comedy	United	1691	C
Comedy	United	1691	C,T
Comedy	United	Lost	
Political Dialogue	Closet	1690	
Political Dialogue	Unacted	1690★	
Political Dialogue	Closet	1690★	
Political Dialogue	Closet	1690★★	
Political Dialogue	Closet	1690★	
Political Play	Closet	MS	
Political Dialogue	Closet	1690★	
Political Dialogue	Closet	1690★	
Dramatic Opera	United	1691	C
Tragedy	United	1691★	C,S
Comedy	United	1691	T
Comedy	United	1691	
Political Comedy	Closet	1722★ & MS	
Tragedy	Unacted	MS	
Civic Pageant	London	1691★	
Academic Allegory	School at Ashby-de-la-Zouch	1692★	
Comedy	United	1691★	
Comedy	United	1692	C,T
Comedy	Unacted	1691★	
Political Dialogue	Closet	1691★	
Critical Dialogue	Closet	1691★	
Comedy	Unacted	1692★	
Tragedy	United	1692★★	
Tragedy	United	1694★	
Tragedy	United	1692	C,T
Comedy	United	1692	
Burlesque	Unacted (?)	1692	
Tragedy	Unacted until 1704	1705	
Tragicomedy	Unacted	MS	
Tragedy	United	1692	

DATE	AUTHOR	TITLE	LIMITS
	Settle, Elkanah	*The Triumphs of London*	29 Oct.
	Shadwell, Thomas	*The Volunteers or The Stock Jobbers*	*c.* Nov.
	Anon.	*The Earthquake in Jamaica*	13 Sept. (acted)
	Anon. (Settle, E.?)	*The Fairy Queen* (Adapt. Shakespeare's *A Midsummer-Night's Dream*.)	2 May
	Anon. (adaptation by Bancroft, J.? of a lost MS by Davenport; produced by Mountfort, W.?)	*Henry II, King of England, with the Death of Rosamond* (Adapt. Davenport's *Henry II?*)	8 Nov.
	Anon.	*Piety and Valour, or Derry Defended* (Same as *The Siege of Derry*, below?)	1692
	Anon.	*The Rehearsal of Kings*	1692
	Anon.	*The Siege of Derry* (Same as *Piety and Valour, or Derry Defended*, above?)	1692
1693	Barnes, Joshua	*Plautus His Trinummi Imitated*	1693
	Congreve, William	*The Double Dealer*	Oct.–Nov.
	Congreve, William	*The Old Bachelor* (Written originally in 1689.)	Mar.
	D'Urfey, Thomas	*The Richmond Heiress, or A Woman Once in the Right*	*c.* Apr.
	Higden, Henry	*The Wary Widow, or Sir Noisy Parrot*	*c.* Mar.
	Keigwyn, John	*The Creation of the World, with Noah's Flood* (Trans. Jordan; see 1611.)	1693
	Powell, George	*A Very Good Wife*	*c.* Apr.
	Settle, Elkanah	*The New Athenian Comedy*	1693
	Settle, Elkanah	*The Triumphs of London*	30 Oct.
	Southerne, Thomas	*The Maid's Last Prayer, or Any Rather Than Fail*	*c.* Feb.
	Wright, Thomas	*The Female Virtuosos* (Adapt. Molière's *Les Femmes savantes*.)	*c.* May
	Anon.	*The Royal Cuckold, or Great Bastard*	1693
1694	Banks, John	*The Innocent Usurper, or The Death of the Lady Jane Grey*	1694 (pub.)
	Crowne, John	*The Married Beau, or The Curious Impertinent*	*c.* May
	Dryden, John	*Love Triumphant, or Nature Will Prevail*	*c.* Jan.
	D'Urfey, Thomas	*I & II The Comical History of Don Quixote*	*c.* May
	Echard, Lawrence	*Plautus's Comedies: Amphitryon, Epidicus, and Rudens Made English*	1694
	Echard, Lawrence	*Terence's Comedies Made English* (The six plays translated.)	1694
	Motteux, P.A. (words); Eccles, J. (music)	*The Rape of Europa by Jupiter*	1694
	Ravenscroft, Edward	*The Canterbury Guests, or A Bargain Broken*	*c.* Sept.

TYPE	AUSPICES	EARLIEST TEXTS	LATEST TEXTS
Civic Pageant	London	1692*	
Comedy	United	1693	E
Droll? Puppet Play?	Acted at Southwark Fair	Lost	
Opera	United	1692	
Tragedy	United	1693	
'Tragicomedy' (Political Dialogue?)	Closet (?)	1692* (extant?)	
Farce	United (?)	Lost	
'Tragicomedy' (Political Dialogue?)	Closet (?)	1692* (extant?)	
Comedy	Emmanuel Col., Cambridge (?)	MS	
Comedy	United	1694	C,M,F
Comedy	United	1693	C,M
Comedy	United	1693	T
Comedy	United	1693*	
Cornish Mystery	Closet	MSS	E
Comedy	United	1693	
Comedy (Satire)	Closet	1693*	
Civic Pageant	London	1693*	C
Comedy	United	1693	C
Comedy	United	1693	T
Political Dialogue	Closet	1693*	
Tragedy	Unacted (banned)	1694*	
Comedy	United	1694*	C
Tragicomedy	United	1694	C
Comedy	United	I: 1694 II: 1694**	
Comedies	Closet	1694*	
Comedies	Closet	1694	
'Mask'	United	1694*	
Comedy	United	1695*	T

DATE	AUTHOR	TITLE	LIMITS
	Settle, Elkanah	*The Ambitious Slave, or A Generous Revenge* (Written originally in 1681–2.)	21 Mar.
	Settle, Elkanah	*The Triumphs of London*	29 Oct.
	Southerne, Thomas	*The Fatal Marriage, or The Innocent Adultery*	Feb.
	Williams, Joseph	*Have at All, or The Midnight Adventures* (Same as *Midnight's Intrigues*, 1677?)	*c.* Apr.
	Anon.	*The Unhappy Marriage* (*Bateman or The Unhappy Marriage, with the Humours of Sparrow* – title varies.)	5 Sept.
1695	Banks, John	*Cyrus the Great, or The Tragedy of Love*	Dec.
	Congreve, William	*Love for Love*	30 Apr.
	Dilke, Thomas	*The Lover's Luck*	*c.* Dec.
	D'Oyley, E.	*Britannicus, or The Man of Honour*	1695
	D'Urfey, Thomas	*III The Comical History of Don Quixote, with the Marriage of Mary the Buxom*	*c.* Nov.
	Gould, Robert	*Innocence Distressed, or The Royal Penitents*	*c.* 1695–1708
	Gould, Robert	*The Rival Sisters, or The Violence of Love*	*c.* Oct.
	Granville, George	*The She Gallants* (*Once a Lover Always a Lover*)	*c.* Dec.
	Hopkins, Charles	*Pyrrhus, King of Epirus*	*c.* Aug.
	Keigwyn, John	*Origo Mundi*, etc. (Trans.; see 14th cent.)	1695
	Motteux, Peter	*The Taking of Namur, and His Majesty's Safe Return*	1695
	Scott, Thomas	*The Mock Marriage*	*c.* Sept.
	Settle, Elkanah	*Philaster, or Love Lies a-Bleeding* (Adapt. Beaumont and Fletcher.)	*c.* Dec.
	Settle, Elkanah	*The Triumphs of London*	29 Oct.
	Southerne, Thomas	*Oroonoko*	*c.* Nov.
	Trotter, Catherine	*Agnes de Castro*	*c.* Dec.
	Anon. (not Powell, G.)	*Bonduca, or The British Heroine* (Adapt. Fletcher.)	*c.* Sept.
	Anon.	*The Indian Queen* (Adapt. Dryden and Howard.)	1695
	Anon.	*The Marshal of Luxemburgh upon His Deathbed* (Trans. from French.)	1695
	Anon. ('Ariadne')	*She Ventures and He Wins*	Sept.
1696	Behn, Aphra	*The Younger Brother, or The The Amorous Jilt*	*c.* Feb.
	Cibber, Colley	*Love's Last Shift, or The Fool in Fashion*	Jan.
	Cibber, Colley	*Woman's Wit, or The Lady in Fashion*	*c.* Dec.
	Doggett, Thomas	*The Country Wake* (*Hob*)	*c.* Apr.
	Dryden, John, Jr	*The Husband His Own Cuckold*	*c.* Feb.
	D'Urfey, Thomas	*A Wife for Any Man*	1695–1697
	Gildon, Charles	*The Roman Bride's Revenge*	*c.* Nov.
	Harris, Joseph	*The City Bride, or The Merry Cuckold* (Adapt. Webster's *A Cure for a Cuckold*.)	*c.* Mar.
	Hughes, John	*Amalasont, Queen of the Goths, or Vice Destroys Itself*	1696

TYPE	AUSPICES	EARLIEST TEXTS	LATEST TEXTS
Tragedy	United	1694★	
Civic Pageant	London	1694★	
Tragicomedy	United	1694	C
Comedy	United	Lost	
Droll	Bartholomew Fair	Lost	
Tragedy	Betterton's	1696	
Comedy	Betterton's	1695	C,M,S,F
Comedy	Betterton's	1696★★	T
Comedy	Closet	MS	
Comedy	Patent	1696	
Tragedy	Unacted	1737★	
Tragedy	Patent	1696★	
Comedy	Betterton's	1696	
Tragedy	Betterton's	1695★	
Cornish Mystery	Closet	MSS	
'Musical Entertainment'	Betterton's	[1695?]★	
Comedy	Patent	1696★	
Tragicomedy	Patent	1695★	
Civic Pageant	London	1695★	
Tragedy	Patent	1696	C,S,T
Tragedy	Patent	1696★	C
Tragedy	Patent	1696★	
Dramatic Opera	Patent	MS	
Tragicomedy	Closet (?)	1695	Lost
Comedy	Betterton's	1696★	
Comedy	Patent	1696 & MS	C
Comedy	Patent	1696	C,T
Comedy	Patent	1697	
Comedy	Betterton's	1696	
Comedy	Betterton's	1696★	
Comedy	Patent (?) Rich's (?)	Lost	
Tragedy	Patent	1697★	C
Comedy	Betterton's	1696★ F	
Tragedy	Unacted	MS (lost?)	

DATE	AUTHOR	TITLE	LIMITS
	Manley, Mary de la Rivière	*The Lost Lover, or The Jealous Husband*	*c.* Mar.
	Manley, Mary de la Rivière	*The Royal Mischief*	*c.* May
	Motteux, Peter	*Love's a Jest*	*c.* June
	Motteux, Peter	*The Loves of Mars and Venus* (Performed with *The Anatomist*, below.)	14 Nov.
	Norton, [Richard?]	*Pausanious, the Betrayer of His Country*	*c.* Apr.
	Pix, Mary	*Ibrahim, the Thirteenth Emperor of the Turks*	*c.* June
	Pix, Mary	*The Spanish Wives*	*c.* Sept.
	Ravenscroft, Edward	*The Anatomist, or The Sham Doctor*	14 Nov.
	Vanbrugh, John	*I Aesop*	*c.* Dec.
	Vanbrugh, John	*The Relapse, or Virtue in Danger*	21 Nov.
	Anon. (produced by Powell, G.; Verbruggen, J.)	*Brutus of Alba, or Augusta's Triumph*	*c.* Oct.
	Anon. (produced by Powell, George?)	*The Cornish Comedy*	*c.* June
	Anon. ('W.M.')	*The Female Wits, or The Triumvirate of Poets at Rehearsal*	*c.* 1696? (pub.) (preface states 'acted some years since')
	Anon. (Doggett, T.?)	*Mad Tom of Bedlam, or The Distressed Lovers, with the Comical Humours of Squire Numskull*	*c.* 1696(?)–1730
	Anon. (prod. by Horden, Hildebrand)	*Neglected Virtue, or The Unhappy Conqueror*	1695–1696
1697	Browne, Thomas	*Physic Lies a-Bleeding, or The Apothecary Turned Doctor*	1697
	Congreve, William	*The Mourning Bride*	20 Feb. (?)
	Dennis, John	*A Plot and No Plot*	8 May
	Dilke, Thomas	*The City Lady, or Folly Reclaimed*	Jan.
	Drake, James	*The Sham Lawyer, or The Lucky Extravagant*	31 May
	D'Urfey, Thomas	*The Intrigues at Versailles, or A Jilt in All Humours*	*c.* Feb.
	Filmer, Edward	*The Unnatural Brother* (See *The Novelty*, below.)	*c.* Jan.
	Granville, George	*Heroic Love*	*c.* Dec.
	Hopkins, Charles	*Boadicea, Queen of Britain*	*c.* Nov.
	Motteux, Peter	*Europe's Revels for the Peace, and His Majesty's Happy Return*	Nov.
	Motteux; Oldmixon; Filmer	*The Novelty: Every Act a Play*: Consists of *Thyrsis* (Pastoral), by Oldmixon; *All without Money* (Comedy), by Motteux; *Hercules* ('Mask'), by Motteux; *The Unfortunate Couple* (Tragedy; alteration of *The Unnatural Brother*, above), by Filmer; *Natural Magic* (Farce), by Motteux.	*c.* June

TYPE	AUSPICES	EARLIEST TEXTS	LATEST TEXTS
Comedy	Patent	1696★	
Tragedy	Betterton's	1696★	
Comedy	Betterton's	1696★	
Dramatic Opera	Betterton's	1697★	
Tragedy	Patent	1696★	
Tragedy	Patent	1696★	C
Comedy	Patent	1696★	C,T
Farce	Betterton's	1697★★	C
Comedy	Patent	1697	C
Comedy	Patent	1697	C,M,S
Dramatic Opera	Patent	1697★★	
Comedy	Patent	1696★	
Burlesque	Patent	1697	
Droll	Bartholomew Fair	Lost	
Play	Patent	1696★	
Comedy	Closet	1697	
Tragedy	Betterton's	1697	C,M
Comedy	Patent	[1697]★	C
Comedy	Betterton's	1697★	
Comedy	Patent	1697★	
Comedy	Betterton's	1697	
Tragedy	Betterton's	1697★	
Tragedy	Betterton's	1698	
Tragedy	Betterton's	1697★	
Entertainment	Betterton's	1697★	
Comedy, etc.	Betterton's	1697★	

DATE	AUTHOR	TITLE	LIMITS
	Pix, Mary	*The Deceiver Deceived* (*The French Beau*) (Includes dialogues by D'Urfey [Act IV] and Motteux [Act V].)	*c.* Dec.
	Pix, Mary	*The Innocent Mistress*	*c.* June
	Powell, George	*The Imposture Defeated, or A Trick to Cheat the Devil* (Songs and Mask, *Endymion, the Man in the Moon*, in Act V, printed separately as *The Mask of Cynthia and Endimion*, 1697.)	*c.* Sept. (poss. first acted in summer, 1695)
	Ravenscroft, Edward	*The Italian Husband*	*c.* Nov.
	Scott, Thomas	*The Unhappy Kindness, or A Fruitless Revenge* (*The Unfortunate Kindness*) (Adapt. Fletcher's *A Wife for a Month*.)	*c.* July
	Settle, Elkanah	*The World in the Moon*	June
	Vanbrugh, John	*II Aesop*	*c.* Mar.
	Vanbrugh, John	*The Provoked Wife*	*c.* May
	Anon. (Southby?)	*Timoleon, or The Revolution*	1697
	Anon.	*The Triumphs of Virtue*	*c.* Jan.
	Anon. ('Ariadne'?)	*The Unnatural Mother* (*Love's Reward*)	*c.* Aug.
1698	Crowne, John	*Caligula*	*c.* Mar.
	Dennis, John	*Rinaldo and Armida*	*c.* Nov.
	Dilke, Thomas	*The Pretenders, or The Town Unmasked*	*c.* Mar.
	D'Urfey, Thomas	*The Campaigners, or The Pleasant Adventures at Brussels*	*c.* June
	Farquhar, George	*Love and a Bottle*	*c.* Dec.
	Gildon, Charles	*Phaeton, or The Fatal Divorce* (Adapt. Quinault.)	*c.* Mar.
	Motteux, Peter	*Beauty in Distress*	*c.* Apr.
	Oldmixon, John	*Amintas* (Trans. Tasso.)	1698
	Phillips, William	*The Revengeful Queen*	*c.* June
	Phillips, William	*Alcamenes and Menalippa*	*c.* 1698(?)
	Pix, Mary	*Queen Catharine, or The Ruins of Love*	*c.* June
	Settle, Elkanah	*Glory's Resurrection, Being the Triumphs of London Revived*	29 Oct.
	Trotter, Catherine	*Fatal Friendship*	*c.* May
	Vanbrugh, John	*The Country House* (Trans. Dancourt's *La Maison rustique*.)	18 Jan. (première?)
	Walker, William	*Victorious Love*	*c.* June
	Anon.	*The Fatal Discovery, or Love in Ruins*	*c.* Mar.
	Anon.	*The Fool's Expectation, or The Wheel of Fortune* (Prol. and Epil. only.)	18 Oct.
	Anon.	*Jephtha's Rash Vow, or The Virgin Sacrifice*	23 Aug. (acted)
	Anon.	*The Mad Wooing, or A Way to Win and Tame a Shrew* (From Shakespeare's *The Taming of the Shrew*.)	1698 (pub.)
	Anon.	*Puritanical Justice, or The Beggars Turned Thieves*	1698

TYPE	AUSPICES	EARLIEST TEXTS	LATEST TEXTS
Comedy	Betterton's	1698★★	C
Comedy	Betterton's	1697★★	C
Comedy	Patent	1698★★	
Tragedy	Betterton's	1698	
Tragedy	Patent	1697★	
Dramatic Opera	Patent	1697	T
Comedy	Patent	1697	C
Comedy	Betterton's	1697	C,M,S
Tragicomedy	Unacted (?)	1697★	
Tragicomedy	Patent	1697★	
Tragedy	Betterton's	1698★	
Tragedy	Patent	1698★	C
Dramatic Opera	Betterton's	1699★	C
Comedy	Betterton's	1698★	
Comedy	Patent	1698★	
Comedy	Patent	1699	C
Tragedy	Patent	1698★	S,F
Tragedy	Betterton's	1698★	
Pastoral	Patent	1698★	
Tragedy	Patent	1698★	
Tragedy	Patent (?)	Lost	
Tragedy	Betterton's	1698★	
Civic Pageant	London	1698★	
Tragedy	Betterton's	1698★	C
Farcical Comedy	Patent	1715	C
Tragedy	Patent	1698★	
Tragedy	Patent	1698★	
Lottery Show	Patent	1698★	C
Droll	Bartholomew Fair	Lost	
Droll	Unknown	1698★	
'Farce' (Political Dialogue?)	Closet	1698★	

DATE	AUTHOR	TITLE	LIMITS
	Anon.	*The Siege of Namur*	23 Aug. (acted)
	Anon.	*The Strollers*	b. 1698(?)
1699	Boyer, Abel	*Achilles, or Iphigenia in Aulis (The Victim, or Achilles and Iphigenia in Aulis)*	c. Dec.
	Cibber, Colley	*Richard III* (Adapt. Shakespeare.)	c. Dec.
	Cibber, Colley	*Xerxes*	c. Feb.
	Corye, John	*A Cure for Jealousy*	c. Dec.
	Dennis, John	*Iphigenia*	c. Dec. (première?)
	D'Urfey, Thomas	*I & II Massaniello, or A Fisherman a Prince*	c. May
	Farquhar, George	*The Constant Couple, or A Trip to the Jubilee*	28 Nov.
	Harris, Joseph	*Love's a Lottery and a Woman the Prize, with Love and Riches Reconciled*	c. Mar.
	Hopkins, Charles	*Friendship Improved, or The Female Warrior*	7 Nov.
	Maittaire, Michael (?)	*'Comoedia, Adoptivus'*	c. 1699(?)
	Maittaire, Michael (?)	*Dido* (Adapted from Virgil.)	c. 1699(?)
	Maittaire, Michael (?)	*Excidium Trojae* (Adapted from Virgil.)	c. 1699(?)
	Maittaire, Michael (?)	*Inferno Navigatio* (Adapted from Virgil.)	c. 1699(?)
	Motteux, Peter	*The Four Seasons, or Love in Every Age* (Included in following.)	c. Jan.
	Motteux, Peter	*The Island Princess, or The Generous Portuguese* (Adapt. Fletcher.)	c. Jan.
	Pix, Mary	*The False Friend, or The Fate of Disobedience*	c. May
	Settle, Elkanah	*The Triumphs of London*	30 Oct.
	Smith, Henry	*The Princess of Parma*	c. Apr.
	Anon.	*Bateman's Ghost*	30 Aug.
	Anon.	*The Devil of a Wife*	23 Aug.
	Anon.	*Feigned Friendship, or The Mad Reformer*	c. May
	Anon. (Doggett, T.?)	*Friar Bacon, or The Country Justice* (Performance listed for 1691, prob. error for 1699.)	23 Aug.
	Anon. (Penkethman, W.?)	*Love without Interest, or The Man Too Hard for the Master*	c. June
1700	Betterton, Thomas (producer)	*Henry IV, with the Humours of Sir John Falstaff* (Shakespeare, play altered for performance.)	9 Jan.
	Burnaby, William	*The Reformed Wife*	c. Mar.
	Centlivre, Susannah	*The Perjured Husband, or The Adventures of Venice*	c. Oct.
	Cibber, Colley	*Love Makes a Man, or The Fop's Fortune*	9 Dec.
	Congreve, William	*The Way of the World*	5 Mar. (?)
	Crauford, David	*Courtship à la mode*	9 July
	Crowne, John	*Justice Busy, or The Gentleman Quack* (2-3 songs extant.)	1699-1700
	Dryden, John	*The Secular Mask* (Incorporated in Vanbrugh's *The Pilgrim*.)	29 Apr.

TYPE	AUSPICES	EARLIEST TEXTS	LATEST TEXTS
Droll	Bartholomew Fair	Lost	
Comedy	Patent (?)	Lost	
Tragedy	Patent	1700	
Tragedy	Patent	[1700]	E,C,F
Tragedy	Betterton's	1699	
Comedy	Betterton's	1701★	
Tragedy	Betterton's	1700★	C
Tragedy	Patent	1700★	T
Comedy	Patent	1699	C,M
Comedy and Mask	Betterton's	1699★	
Tragedy	Betterton's	1700★	
Latin Comedy	Closet (?)	MS	
Latin Tragedy	Closet (?)	MS	
Latin Tragedy	Closet (?)	MS	
Latin Tragedy	Closet (?)	MS	
Musical Interlude	Patent	1699	
Opera	Patent	1699 & MS	C
Tragedy	Betterton's	1699	C
Civic Pageant	London	1699★	
Tragedy	Betterton's	1699★	
Droll	Bartholomew Fair	Lost	
Droll	Bartholomew Fair	Lost	
Comedy	Betterton's	[1699]★	
Droll	Bartholomew Fair	Lost	
Comedy	Patent	1699★	
Tragicomedy	Betterton's	1700★	
Comedy	Patent	1700	C
Tragedy	Patent	1700	C
Comedy	Patent	1701	C
Comedy	Betterton's	1700	C,M,S,F
Comedy	Patent	1700★	
Comedy	Betterton's	Lost	
Mask	Patent	1700	C

DATE	AUTHOR	TITLE	LIMITS
	Gildon, Charles	*Measure for Measure, or Beauty the Best Advocate* (Adapt. Shakespeare.)	*c.* Feb.
	Lister, Martin	*Eunuchus* (Trans. Terence.)	b.1700(?)
	Manning, Francis	*The Generous Choice*	*c.* Feb.
	Oldmixon, John	*The Grove, or Love's Paradise*	19 Feb. (première?)
	Phillips, William	*St Stephen's Green, or The Generous Lovers*	1699–1700
	Pix, Mary	*The Beau Defeated, or The Lucky Younger Brother* (Based on Dancourt's *Le Chevalier à la mode.*)	*c.* Mar.
	Rowe, Nicholas	*The Ambitious Stepmother*	*c.* Dec.
	Settle, Elkanah	*The Triumphs of London*	29 Oct.
	Sherburne, Edward	*Hippolytus* (Trans. Seneca.)	*c.* 1700(?)
	Southerne, Thomas	*The Fate of Capua*	*c.* Apr.
	Trotter, Catherine	*Love at a Loss, or The Most Votes Carry It*	Nov.
	Vanbrugh, John	*The Pilgrim* (Adapt. Fletcher.)	29 Apr.
	Waterhouse, David	*Cleophilus*	1700 (pub.)
	Wright, James	*La Mallad* (Trans. Molière's *Le Malade imaginaire.*)	b.1700(?)
	Anon.	*Hengist, the Saxon King of Kent* (Adapt. or revival of Middleton's *The Mayor of Queenborough?*)	3 June
	Anon.	*The Tempest, or The Distressed Lovers*	*c.* 1700

TYPE	AUSPICES	EARLIEST TEXTS	LATEST TEXTS
Comedy	Betterton's	1700*	C,F,T
Comedy	Closet	MS	
Comedy	Betterton's	1700*	
Opera	Patent	1700*	
Comedy	Smock Alley, Dublin	1700	
Comedy	Betterton's	[1700]*	C
Tragedy	Betterton's	1701	
Civic Pageant	London	1700*	
Tragedy	Closet	1701*	
Tragedy	Betterton's	1700	C
Comedy	Patent	1701*	C
Comedy	Patent	1700	C,T
Latin Comedy	Closet (?)	1700*	
Comedy	Closet (?)	MS	
Tragedy	Patent	Lost	
Droll	Bartholomew Fair	Lost	

SUPPLEMENTARY LIST I

The following are extant dramatic pieces omitted from the Chronology and Information section because of their uncertain date and identity. Most are in manuscript copies, the location of which may be found in the List of Extant Play Manuscripts, 975–1700: Their Locations and Catalogue Numbers.

Buchanan, George; Schonaeus, Cornelius; Plautus Bodleian MS. Rawlinson 1388–91 consists of anon. translations, of uncertain date, of the following plays: *Jephthes, The Baptist, Media, Alcestis* (all from the Latin plays of Buchanan); *Naamen, Tobit, Nehemiah, Saul, Joseph, Judith* (all from Terentius Christianus, 1592, of Schonaeus); *Bacchides, Mostellaria, Menaechmi, Pseudolus, Miles Gloriosus, Mercator* (all from Plautus).

Alice and Alexis. Anon. 17th-cent. tragicomedy. MS (frag.).

Alphonsus. Latin play, poss. by Dudley North. Notations on MS suggest connection with Cambridge U., *c.* 1617–19. MS.

Ananias, Azarias, Mesael. Anon. Latin St Omers play, 17 cent. MS.

Antipolargesis. Anon. Latin St Omers play, 17th cent. MS.

Antonio of Ragusa. Prose comedy, prob. late 17th cent., beginning 'Antonio, All this is most true', and featuring the characters Octavio and Allesandra, daughter of a Turk. The title has been assigned to it. MS.

Artaxerxes. Anon. Latin St Omers play, 17th cent. MS.

Ascanius. Anon. Latin religious play, prob. 17th cent., poss. Continental. MS.

Basilindus. Anon. Latin St Omers play, 17th cent. MS.

The Battle of the Vices against the Virtues. Moral, '*tempe* Charles I'. Ment. by Fleay (*Biog. Chron.*, II, 337) as extant in MS. Poss. Fane's *De Pugna Animi.*

Bila, Ariscancus, etc. Anon. Latin 15th-cent. MS frag., ed. J. Boete, [*Hermes*] xxi (1886): 313–318.

Britanniae Primitiae sive S. Albanus Protomartyr.

Anon. Latin St Omers play, 17th cent. MSS.

The Captive Lady. Anon. tragicomedy, 1618–*c.* 1625. MS.

Cinna. Anon. trans. Corneille. MS.

Death, a Comedy. By Robert Squire, trans. Drury's *Mors Comoedia*, first half of 17th cent. MS.

Diana's Grove, or The Faithful Genius. Anon. tragicomedy, 'never acted'. Prob. 17th cent. MS.

The Disloyal Favourite, or The Tragedy of Mettellus. Anon. tragedy of 17th cent. MS.

Don Pedro, the Cruel King of Castile. Anon. Latin play, 'early 17th cent.'. MS.

Don Sancho. Trans. attrib. to Cosmo Manuche of first act of Corneille's *Don Sancho D'Aragon.* MS.

An Elizabethan Jig. Frag. prob. dated end of 16th cent. MS.

The Emperor's Favourite. Title assigned. Court play with Roman characters Nero, Crispinus (a Buckingham-like courtier, the model for the play's title), Vologesus, Tiridates, Tigranes, Corbulus, and Locusta. In a 17th-cent. hand, the play is prob. dated between 1623 and 1628. Corrected MS.

Emperor Caracalla. Five act, untitled blank verse drama in a 17th-cent. hand, discovered among papers of Cosmo Manuche. MS.

The Fatal Marriage, or A Second Lucretia. Anon. tragedy, 1620–30? The name of its leading male character suggests a relation of the play with Henslowe's *Galiaso*, 1594. MS. Ed. for Malone Society in 1958.

Free-will. Trans. of Francesco Negri's *Tragedia del libero arbitrio*; first half of 17th cent., assigned incorrectly to Henry Cheke on title page, fly leaf ascription (erased) to Francis Bristowe. MS.

Gallomyomachia. A play in Greek. MS.

Gemitus Columbae. Anon. Latin St Omers play, 17th cent. MS.

Ghismonda and Guiscardo. Title assigned. Tragedy, 17th cent., recently attrib. to John Newdigate. MS is a revised version of *Glausamond and Fidelia*, below.

Glausamond and Fidelia. Title assigned. Early 17th cent. tragedy. One of the two MSS. (the other being *Ghismonda and Guiscardo*, above) of the British Library MS play ed. by Wright as *Tancred and Ghismonda*. Corrected MS.

The Great Cham. Anon. tragedy, 17th cent. MS (frag.).

Hannibal. Anon. Latin play later 16th cent. MS frag. (ed. C. Moore, *The Dramatic Works of Thomas Nabbes*, 1918).

Hercules Furens. Anon. trans. of Seneca, prob. later 17th cent. MS.

The Humorous Magistrate. Title assigned. Jonsonian farce with Mr Thrifty as the justice, Mrs Mumble as deaf, rich widow, Christopher Spruce as her son, and Mr Wellcome as her brother. Corrected MS. Prob. date of composition between 1625 and 1640, 1635 very likely.

The Hypochondriac, or The Turmoils of Love. Apparently 'notes for a play and odd speeches, rather than fragments of a once complete play' (Bentley, *J. &C. S.*, V, 1353). Mid-17th cent.? Adaptation of *Le Malade imaginaire*? MS fragment.

Jovis et Junonius Nuptiae. Anon. Latin Cambridge (?) play, prob. 17th cent. MS.

Jugurtha, or The Faithless Cousin German. Anon. tragedy, prob. late 17th cent. Poss. related to *Jugurth*, 1600. MS.

The Lover's Stratagem, or Virtue Rewarded. Anon. comedy, prob. late 17th cent. MS.

Lusiuncula. Latin play with same story as *Macbeth* (Hazlitt, *Manual*, p. 145). MS.

The Marriage Broker, or The Pander. Comedy dated 1635–42. Pub. as by 'M.W.' in *Gratiae Theatrales*, 1622 (ed. by W.M. Braille; repub. 1984 by Center for Medieval and Early Renaissance Studies). 'At least in part post-Restoration' (Greg, *Bibl.*, II, 922), and prob. a redaction of an older play, as appear to be the other two plays in the collection: *Thorney Abbey* (see below) and *Grim the Collier of Croydon* (see *The Devil and His Dame*, 1600).

Medea. Anon. rhymed verse trans. of Seneca, mid-17th-cent. hand; frag. includes three acts and part of a fourth. MS.

Mercurius Rusticans. Anon. Latin comedy. 'Scena Hyneksey vel Hincksie.' According to Madan, 'written in 1663' (*Summary Cat.*, vol II, pt. ii, 1183). MS.

The Merry Loungers. Anon. 'A farce as it was acted by a private company in Cambridge.' Before 1700? MS.

Montezuma sive Mexici Imperii Occasus. Anon. Latin St Omers play, 17th cent. MS.

Morus. Anon. Latin St Omers play, 17 cent. MS.

Mystery of Iniquity or The Revolution. Anon. metrical drama of nearly 2,000 lines written about the time of the Revolution (acc. to the preface). MS.

The New Moon. Anon. play in three acts. MS.

Nottola. Anon. Latin comedy. Earlier 17th cent.? MS.

Oedipus. Anon. tragedy, 'between 1583 and 1603', intended for performance at a school, poss. in Newcastle or Berwick. MS.

Oedipus. Anon. trans. Seneca, later 17th cent. MS.

Pelopidarum Secunda. Anon. English tragedy associated with Winchester School. Written during Elizabeth's reign? MS.

Perfidus Hetruscus. Anon. Latin tragedy, 17th cent.? MS.

Psyche et Filii ejus. Anon. Latin Valladolid play, 17th cent., poss. acted at St Omers in 1643 MS.

Publius Cornelius Scipio sui Victor. Anon. Latin play, prob. 17th cent. MS.

Pygmalion. Anon. Latin playlet; mid-17th cent.? MS (ed. R.H. Bowers, *Modern Philology*, XLVII [1949–50], 73–81).

The Review. Anon. comedy, 'probably though not certainly after 1700'. MS.

Rodogune. Anon. 'English verse translation of the tragedy [by Corneille], *c*. 1700?' MS.

Romanus. Two scenes and synopsis of English tragedy. Some evidence suggests poss. attrib. to James Cobb. MS frag.

S. Franciscus Xaverius. Anon. Latin St Omers play, 17 cent. MS.

S. Hermenigildus. Untitled play found among the

papers of Cosmo Manuche and attrib. to him. MS.

Sanguis Sanguinem sive Constans Fratricida. Anon. Latin tragedy, prob. St Omers. 'About A.D. 1600.' MS. Prob. not *Sanguis Sanguinem* acted at St Omers 14 Apr. 1640, but may be same as *Furor Impius sive Constans Fraticida* in Stonyhurst MS.

The Siege of Croya. Anon. tragedy, c. 1700? MS.

Sisigambis, Queen of Syracuse. Anon. tragedy, poss. Restoration. MS frag.

Speech of Delight. Extract from a morality, late 15th cent. MS.

Thorney Abbey, or The London Maid. History play prob. of early 17th cent. pub. as by 'T.W.' in *Gratiae Theatrales*, 1662 (ed. by W.M. Braille). Repub. 1984 by Center for Medieval and Early Renaissance Studies. Prob. a redaction of a 16th-cent. play. Some parts appear to be Elizabethan, 'others are considerably later, but not necessarily after the closing of the theatres' (Greg, *Bibl.*, II, 922).

Tragoedia Cyri Regis Persarum. Latin play trans. by Gregory Martin; said by Pitsius (*De Angliae Scriptoribus*, 1619) to be extant in library of St John's Col., Oxford. St John's claims no printed or MS copy, however.

Tragoedia Miserrima Pyrami et Thisbes fata enuncians. By 'N.R.'. One-act English tragedy, transcribed c. 1624–31 (?). MS (ed. G. Bullough, *Narrative and Dramatic Sources of Shakespeare*, I, 1957).

Troelus and Cresyd (Troilus and Cressida). Anon. Welsh closet tragedy, dated 1596–1612. MS.

Try Before You Trust. Anon. comedy. Before 1700? MS.

The Twice-changed Friar. Anon. comedy dated before 1650, reasonably dated 1624–27. Mentioned in Bullen as extant in a 17th-cent. MS vol. in a Warwickshire library. [See Anon.], 'The Twice chan'd friar: A comedie', *The Gentleman's Magazine*, CCC (1906), 285–90.

TITLELESS PLAYS AND FRAGMENTS

British Library MS Egerton 2623, ff. 37–38, ed. W.W. Greg, *MLQ* VII (1904): 148–55.

Comedy by Joseph Arrowsmith seen by Charles II, 4 Oct. 1671 on a Cambridge visit; prologue and epilogue by Isaac Barrow survive. [Milhous and Hume, 'Lost English Plays', *HLB* 25, No. 1 (Jan. 1977): 17; and Harold Love, 'A Lost Comedy by Joseph Arrowsmith', *N & Q* 212 (1967): 217–18.] British Library MS Add. 18220.

'Masque', c. 1625. Huntington Library MS. HM 22 (frag.).

'A pastoral' in five acts with scene 'the Isle of Scyros' and characters Xamolxis, Perindo, and Rascipolis, Cotys, Cleta, etc. Prob. late 17th cent. and poss. adapt. Sidnam's trans. (1655) of *Filli di Sciro*. Brit. Lib. Add MS. 29496.

'Fragment of a play'. Chief characters are Ethel[bert?], the Duch[ess] his wife, Os[wald], their son, Orina, Sir Ingram, Mousetrap, etc.; contains a Collier forgery. Brit. Lib. MS Egerton 2623, ff. 37–8.

Prologue, 15th-cent., to a moral play of a rich knight who loses his fortune; in northern dialect. Durham Dean and Chapter MS. Archia. Dunelm. 60 (ed. J. Cooling, *RES*, N.S., X [1959], 172–3).

'A Dramatic Fragment from a Caesar Augustus Play', c. 1500 (speech by a 'Secundus Miles'). Bodl. MS. Ashmolean 750 (ed. R.H. Robbins, *Anglia*, LXXII [1954], 31–4).

'A Sixteenth Century English Mystery Fragment' (Epil. only). Bodl. MS. Tanner 407 (ed. R.H. Robbins, *English Studies*, XXX [1949], 134–6).

'A Christmas Entertainment' in five acts, with characters Leonides, Ingenio, Roscius, Sapientia, Obligia, Charita, Justitia, etc. Bodl. MS. Rawlinson D. 1361, ff. 306–28.

'A comedy without a title', by 'R.M.' Characters are Wardho; Leyman; two English cavaliers; Bubble, a Frenchman; Grim; etc. Bodl. MS. Rawlinson C. 923.

'A dramatic fragment', c. 1620. *Dramatis personae* include Pilades and Horestes. Folger Shakespeare Lib. MS. X.d. 391, I f.

'Dramatic fragment in verse, *c.* 1630'. Characters Eusebius, Timotheus, Theopilus. Folger Shakespeare Lib. MS. X. d. 390, 2 ff.

'Fragment of a religious play in verse, *c.* 1550'. Folger Shakespeare Lib. MS. L.b. 554, 2 ff.

'Play in blank verse, the scene Samos and Thrace.' Anon. pastoral comedy, with principal characters shepherds Ellaenus, Syringus, Ormillus, Melarchus, Armissus, and Nanthus, and nymphs Chloris, Charia, Spinella, and Lyncida. Prob. 1610–*c.* 1630. Folger Shakespeare Lib. MS. V.b. 222, f. 63.

'An English Mystery Play Fragment Ante 1300.' Camb. Univ. Lib. MS. Mm. I. 18, f. 58a (ed. R.H. Robbins, *MLN*, XLV [1950], 30–35).

'A play of the 17th century, written by John Pallin, Chancellor of the Church of Lincoln.' MS cited in *Hist. MSS. Comm.*, I, 61 (MSS formerly at Helmingham Hall, Suffolk, now at Peckforton Castle, Tarporley, Cheshire [lib. of Lord Tollemache]).

Titleless English play in three acts, with characters Quadro, Rectangulum, Compasse, Line, Circulus, etc. 17th cent. English Col., Rome, Archives MS. Z. 141.

Titleless Latin play based on life of early Christians in Rome at time of Julian the Apostate. 17th-cent. frag. English Col., Rome, Archives MS. C. 17(v).

Fragment of a play in the Journal of Benjamin Greene, factor on the *Darling*, 1610. See William Foster, *Notes and Queries*, 23 July 1900, pp. 41–2.

Titleless play on the Gunpowder Plot, mentioned by Oliver Ormerod in *The Picture of a Papist* (entered 9 Dec. 1605).

Incomplete verse drama found among MSS in Essex Record Office, Chelmsford. Cat. D/DW25; MSS formed part of the papers of the Conyers and Wythes family of Copped Hall, Essex. Short description of the piece in F.G. Emmison's *Guide to the Essex Record Office*, 1969, p. 145.

Latin philosophical farce. Deals with Aristotelian and Platonic philosophy. Characters include Crobolus, Dromodotus, Pedantius, Panglossus, Ludio, Blebus, Lydia, and Tuscidellax. Late 17 cent. Included among papers of Kenyon of Peele Cooke in Lancashire Record Office, Preston, Lancs.

English play begun by Sir Thomas Salusbury. Includes characters named Isabella, Carlo, Aemilia, Barnardo, Claudio, Frederick, Mendoza, and Pancalier. Before 1643. MS (see *Salusbury* in MS listings).

Christmas pageant performed at Lincoln. Speakers include three senators. MS in Registers of Corporation of Lincoln, Vol. IV; printed in *History MSS. Comm.* 14th Report, Appendix, Pt. VIII, (1895): 58–60.

Fragment of an English play in which the Sexton of St Denys Church is a character. 16–17 cent. National Library of Wales MS, Peniarth 403D.

Fragment of a play, mid-17th cent. Characters include King, Prince Rupert, a tailor, apprentices, and True Wit. MS in collection of James M. Osborn, New Haven, Connecticut.

Fragment of untitled play in blank verse set in Ancient Greece. Characters include Pseudolon, Sophius, Callophilus. Discovered among papers of Cosmo Manuche. MS (see *Manuche* in MS listings).

'An unfinished indecent comedy.' The characters are a Quaker, Woodfall a lawyer, Sir Tho. Trueman, Capt. Mackforrest, Sally Salisbury, the Gaolkeeper at Newgate. The last three named suggest that this is an 18th-cent. play related to *The Beggar's Opera*. Bodl. MS. Rawlinson D. 1413.

'Duke of Florence'. Title assigned to a handwritten frag. of a final working draft of a prev. unknown Jacobean play. Discovered 1985 by Edward Saunders and Felix Pryor in Melbourne Hall. Stylistic evidence suggests Webster's authorship. The subject of the scene is a conversation between Alexander de Medici, the Duke of Florence, and the Duke's favourite, his kinsman Lorenzo. The frag. was placed on sale at the Bloomsbury Book Auction on 20 June 1986.

Comedy by Douglas Castilion. Untitled lost play composed in 1505 and performed 27–30 Aug. 1605 at Magdalen College, Oxford for Prince Henry. Included in *Reed* Oxford volume, forthcoming.

SUPPLEMENTARY LIST II

(The following are non-extant plays omitted from the Chronology because of their uncertain date and identity. Some of them may be extant under alternative titles.)

(a) On 9 Sept. 1653, Humphrey Moseley entered in the Stationers' Register a number of plays dating between 1600 and 1642. The following unidentified anonymous plays appear in the list: *The Countryman*; *The King's Mistress*; *The Politic Bankrupt, or Which Is the Best Girl?* (alternative title may be an independent play). Also listed is *The Jew of Venice*, 'by Tho: Decker'.

(b) On 29 Nov. [Dec.?] 1653, Richard Marriott entered a number of anonymous plays in the Stationers' Register; the titles of most of them suggest composition during the decade before 1642, but the list is otherwise a miscellaneous one. The titles of the unidentified plays are as follows: *The Black Wedding*; *The Bondwoman*; *Castara, or Cruelty without Hate*; *The Conceits*; *The Divorce*; *The Eunuch* ('a Tragedy'); *The Florentine Friend*; *The Law Case*; *The Noble Ravishers*; *Pity the Maid*; *Salisbury Plain* ('a comedy'; Speed's *The Converted Robber?*); *Supposed Inconstancy*; *The Woman's Law*; *The Woman's Masterpiece*.

(c) The following titles appear in Rogers and Ley's play-list of 1656: *Bays*; *Cleopatra* (possibly Daniel's or May's play); *Play of the Netherlands*; *Robin Conscience* (possibly *The Book in Meter of Robin Conscience*, 1550, non-dramatic dialogue).

(d) The following additional titles appear in Edward Archer's play-list of 1656, which is derived from that of Rogers and Ley; the majority of them probably do not represent lost plays: *Baggs Seneca* (Trag.); *Battle of Affliction* ('Trag.'; probably a misprint for *Battle of Affections*, alternative title of *Pathomachia*, 1617); *English Arcadia* ('Com.'; probably not a play, but Markham's romance); *Impatient Grissel* (Com.); *Mother Rumming* (Com.); *Ortenus* (Com.) or *Ortenas* (Trag.) [probably one play rather than two]; *The Owl* (Com.); *Virgil's Eclogues* (Trag.).

(e) The following plays were advertised as 'Books in the Press, and ready for Printing' in E. Phillips's *New World of English Words*, 1658, and in other such lists, 1658–62: *The Chaste Woman against Her Will* (Com.); *The Fair Spanish Captive* (Tragicom.); *The Fool Transformed* (Com.); *The History of Don Quixote, or The Knight of the Ill-Favoured Face* (Com.); *The History of Louis XI, King of France* (Tragicom.); *The Tooth-Drawer* (Com.). In *The Wits*, Part I, 1662, a comedy entitled *The French Schoolmaster* is advertised for sale.

(f) The following titles are mentioned by Malone (*Plays and Poems of Shakespeare* [1821], II, 438–9) as anonymous plays not known to have been printed: *Love Yields to Honour*; *The Noble Friend*; *The Tragedy of Heildebrand*.

(g) The following titles appear in the list of plays which were claimed by John Warburton to have been burned by his cook: *A Mask*, by R. Govell (*The Mask*, 1624, by R. Gunnell?); *The Flying Voice*, by Ra. Wood; *An Interlude*, by Ra. Wood; *Fairy Queen*; *The Lovers of Ludgate*; *Orpheus* (Com.); *The Spanish Purchase* (Com.). In the Warburton sale of 1759 appeared the title, not previously listed, *Demetrius and Marina* (or *Marsina*), or *The Imperial Impostor and Unhappy Heroine* (Trag.).

(h) Listed as extant in MS in Hazlitt's *Manual* are the following: *Otho*, translated from Corneille by Corbet Owen; *The Death of the Black Prince* (Trag.); *The Yorkshire Gentleman* (Trag.). The present whereabouts of these MSS is unknown. *Catilina Triumphans* (Latin Com.), also listed by Hazlitt, is probably an erroneous entry.

(*i*) The following are titles from books of masking airs. A few may indicate lost masks, but the majority probably derive from known masks or from independent dancing airs: From Brit. Mus. Add. MS. 10444: *Adson's Mask*; *The Amazonians' Mask*; *Are Mask*; *Bateman's Mask*; *Blackfriars Mask*; *Brox(burn)bury Mask*; *The Bull Mask*; *The Cuckolds' Mask*; *Durance Mask*; *Essex Antic Mask*; *The Fairy Mask*; *The Fools' Mask*; *The Goats' Mask*; *Gray's Inn Antic Mask*; *The Gypsies' Mask*; *Hampton Court Mask*; *The Haymakers' Mask*; *The Lady Lucy's Mask*; *Lincoln's Inn Mask*; *Mary Magdalene Mask*; *A Mask in Flowers*; *The Old Antic Mask*; *The Pages' Mask*; *Pearce His Mask*; *The Prince's Mask*; *The Queen's Mask*; *The Sailors' Mask*; *The Satyrs' Mask*; *The Shepherds' Mask* (MS date 1635); *Sir Jerome Poole's Mask*; *The Standing Mask*; *The Temple Antic Mask*; *York House Mask*. From Playford's *Musick's Handmaid*, 1678: *The Queen's Mask*. From Brit. Mus. Add. MS. 10338: *The Mask of Vices* (possibly part of Randolph's *Muses' Looking Glass*, 1630). Mentioned in Halliwell[-Phillipps]'s *Dictionary*: *Death of Dido*, by 'R. C.', 1621; *The Furies' Mask*, *c*. 1624; *All is Mistaken* (mentioned in *The Bulstrode Papers*, [ed. A. W. Thibaudeau: London, privately printed, 1897, p. 206]).

(*j*) The following are lost plays mentioned in various works: *Comoediae aliquot Sacrae* (attributed by Bishop Bale to Gawain Douglas, Bishop of Dunkeld); *Comoediae* (attributed by Bishop Bale to John Scogan, time of Edward IV); *Priscianus Vapulans* (Latin Com., mentioned by Peacham, *The Complete Gentleman*, 1622); *The Greeks and Trojans* [possibly Heywood's *Iron Age*] and *The Guelphs and Ghibellines* (mentioned by E. Gayton, *Pleasant Notes upon Don Quixote*, 1654); *The Famous History of Petronius Maximus* (Trag., by 'W. S.', 1619, described in Constable's *Edinburgh Magazine*, IX [July 1821], 3–8); *Kynes Redux* (attributed to W. Gager by M. L. Lee, ed., *Narcissus* [1893], p. xiv); *Pharaoh's Daughter* (mentioned by K.

L. Bates, *The English Religious Drama* [1893], p. 251); *The Revenge* (appearing among the titles of his plays in the engraving of Thomas Killigrew, frontispiece of his *Comedies and Tragedies*, 1664); *Saturnalia* (Com. attributed to John Edwards by M. J. Simmonds, *Merchant Taylor Fellows* [1930], p. 18); *The Secrets* (attributed to Davenant and Ellis by Summers, *Playhouse of Pepys*, p. 153); *The Guiltless Adulteress, or Judge in His Own Cause* (adaptation of *The Fatal Dowry*, supposedly by Davenant; MS in existence *c*. 1750; see J. F. Kermode, 'A Note on the History of Massinger's *The Fatal Dowry* in the Eighteenth Century', *Notes and Queries*, CXCII [1947], 186–7); *The Creation of the World*, *The Conspiracy of Gunpowder Treason under the Parliament House*, *The Destruction of Sodom and Gomorrha*, *The Story of Dives and Lazarus* ('strange sights', i.e. Motions, licensed by Sir George Buc to William Jones, William Selby, and Thomas Wrench on 16 July 1619; see B. M. Wagner, *Notes and Queries*, CLXIX [1935], 97–98); *The Chaos of the World*, *The Creation of the World* (Motions licensed by Herbert; see Adams, ed., *Dramatic Records of Sir Henry Herbert*, p. 47). *The Gordian Knot Untied*, mentioned in prologue of anonymous play, *Edward the Third* (1690) and first published in part in Henry Purcell's postumously published *A Collection of Ayres for the Theatre* (1697); A Wife for Any Man, mentioned in one source (Br. Lib. Add. MS 35043, F. 71) as a farce and in two anonymous songs with texts by Durfey attributed to this play in *Mercurius Musicus*, September–December, 1699, pp. 193–95; *The Match at Bedlam*, mentioned in *The British Union Catalogue of Early Music* entry for 'Amintors warmth declines. A Song in the Match at Bedlam . . . Sung by Mrs. Perrin and exactly engrav'd by Tho: Cross', where publication is assigned to *c*. 1700 (William J. Burling in 'Four More "Lost" Restoration Plays "found" in Musical Sources' in *Music and Letters*, 64: 45–47 (1984) assigns a 1696–98 performance date at Lincoln's Inn

Fields); *The Self-Conceit*; or, *The Mother Made a Property* mentioned in a song, 'Oh! the mighty power of love' which exists in single sheet form – a folio 'engrav'd by Tho: Cross' to be found at King's College, Cambridge, and Gresham College, London – and in two collections, *Wit and Mirth*; or, *Pills to Purge Melanchol* (1706) and *A Collection of the Choicest Songs and Dialogues* (*c.* 1715) and is assigned by William J. Burling (*supra*) to the period 1700–1703; *The Surprised Lovers*, mentioned in a song, 'When first I saw her charming face', dated *c.* 1700 by *The British Union Catalogue of Early Music* and between 1695 and 1706 by William J. Burling (*supra*).

(*k*) A number of plays of English origin are known through records of performances by English actors on the Continent, or through publication there of German versions of certain plays in the visitors' repertories. The principal English actors who headed Continental troupes were Robert Browne, active at intervals between 1590 and 1620, and his co-adjutor John Green, who made a last expedition in 1626. The activities of these two were usually associated with ruling houses of Hesse-Cassel and Brunswick. A third actor-manager of Continental troupes was John Spencer, patronized by the houses of Brandenburg and Saxony, and active abroad at intervals from 1603 to 1623. Those plays in the Continental repertories certainly of German origin are not included in the following list; a few of those which are included may not be of English origin. In Aug. 1593 Browne performed *Abraham and Lot* and *The Destruction of Sodom and Gomorrha* at Frankfurt. In Sept. 1603 *Susanna* (probably a Continental play) was performed by English actors at Stuttgart. In 1604 a company, probably English, performed at Rothenburg: *An Ancient Roman, Botzarius* (probably not English); *Celinde and Sedea* (also acted by Spencer at Nuremberg in 1613); *Lewis, King of Spain*; *Melone, King of Dalmatia*. In Jan. 1604 Eichelin, a German actor heading what seems to have been an English company, performed at Nördlingen: *Annabella, a Duke's Daughter of Ferrara* (usually identified as Marston's *Parasitaster* and probably the same play as *The Duke of Ferrara* acted by Green at Dresden in 1626); *Charles, Duke of Burgundy*; *Daniel in the Lions' Den*; *The Merchant's Disobedient Son* (*The London Prodigal*, 1604?); *Pyramus and Thisbe* (possibly from *Midsummer-Night's Dream*, since the repertory included also *Romeo and Juliet*). In 1607 the Browne-Green troupe performed at Cassel: *The King of England and the King of Scotland* (also performed by Green at Dresden in 1626); at Passau: *The Prodigal Son* (common in Continental records); at Gräz: *The King of England and the Goldsmith's Wife* (*Edward IV*, 1599?); at Passau: *The Jew* (variously identified as *The Jew of Malta*, *The Merchant of Venice*, and Dekker's *Jew of Venice*, and perhaps the same play as *Joseph the Jew of Venice* performed by Green at Dresden in 1626). In Feb. 1608 the Browne-Green troupe at Gräz performed: *Dives and Lazarus* (probably same as *The Rich Man* acted by Green at Dresden in 1626); *A Duke of Florence and a Nobleman's Daughter* (also acted by Green at Dresden in 1626); *King Louis and King Frederick of Hungary*; *A King of Cyprus and a Duke of Venice*; *A Proud Woman of Antwerp* (probably Day and Haughton's *Friar Rush*). In June 1613 Spencer at Nuremberg performed: *The Destruction of Constantinople*; *The Destruction of Troy* (Heywood's *Iron Age*?); *Philole and Mariana* (Machin's *Dumb Knight*?); *The Turk* (Mason's *The Turk*?). In May–July 1614 at Strassburg, Spencer repeated *The Destruction of Constantinople*, and performed also a play of *Government*. Between 31 May and 4 Dec. 1626 Green at Dresden performed: *Amphitruo* (Heywood's *Silver Age*? or an adaptation of Plautus?); *Christabella*; *The Clever Thief* (*The Winter's Tale*?); *The Count of Angiers*; *Crysella* (Dekker, Chettle, and Haughton's *Patient Grissil*?); *The Duke of Mantua and the Duke of Verona*; *The Godfather*; *Haman and Esther*; *The King of Aragon* (*Mucedorus*? or Greene's *Alphonsus, King of*

Aragon?); *The King of Denmark and the King of Sweden* (*Clyomon and Clamydes*, 1570? or Dekker's *Gustavus, King of Sweden*?); *The Martyr Dorothea* (*The Virgin Martyr*?). Additional plays, chiefly based on those of Shakespeare and Marlowe, were in Green's repertory: *Doctor Faustus*; *Fortunatus* (Dekker); *Hamlet*; *Hieronymo* (Kyd's *Spanish Tragedy*?); *The Jew of Malta*; *Julius Caesar*; *King Lear*; *Nobody and Somebody*; *Orlando Furioso* (Greene?); *Romeo and Juliet*. A few of the plays listed above survive in seventeenth-century German versions, the dates of which, however, are not necessarily the dates of performance indicated above. German scholars have printed from MSS: *The Duke of Ferrara* (based on Marston's *Parasitaster*); *Hamlet*; *The Merchant of Venice*; *Nobody and Somebody*; *Romeo and Juliet*. In *Engelische Comedien und Tragedien*, 1620, appeared, besides two farces and five jigs, *Esther and Haman*; *Fortunatus* (related to Dekker's *Old Fortunatus*); *Julio and Hyppolita* (related to *Two Gentlemen of Verona*); *A King's Son of England and a King's Daughter of Scotland* (same as *A King of England and a King of Scotland*, above?); *Nobody and Somebody*; *The Prodigal Son*; *Titus Andronicus* (related to Shakespeare's play); and an additional play of known German origin. In *Liebeskampff oder Ander Theil der Englischen Comödien und Tragödien*, 1630, appear two additional jigs and six additional plays. The plays of Shakespearean interest have been edited by A. Cohn, *Shakespeare in Germany*, 1865. For the jigs (edited by J. Bolte, 1893), see the reprints and discussion in C. R. Baskervill, *The Elizabethan Jig*, 1929.

(*l*) The following are lost anonymous plays written at the English Jesuit College of St Omers. The dates of these are known, and here indicated, but the plays have been omitted from their regular place in the Chronology because they were seldom more than academic exercises. See W. H. McCabe, 'The Play-List of the English College of St Omers (1592-1762)', *Revue de littérature comparée*, XVII (1937), 355-75:

Guido Varvicensis, 9 Feb. 1623; *Trebellius Bulgarorum Rex*, 2 May 1624; *Paulus Japonensis*, 11 June 1624; *Ovo Frisius*, 11 July 1624; *Astraea*, 9 Oct. 1625; *Syrgiannes*, 16 Aug. 1630; *Geminus Alcides*, 7 Feb. 1640; *Fratrum Discordia Felix sive Stanislaus Fuga Victor*, May 1640; *Gonsalvus Sylveira*, 1640; *Aloysius sive Saeculi Fuga*, Apr. 1640; *Sanguis Sanguinem* (probably not same as *Sanguis Sanguinem*, Supp. I), 14 Apr. 1640; *Haeresis Triumphata sive B. Ignatius Societatis Jesu Fundator*, Aug. (?) 1640; *Odoardus Varvici Comes*, 27 Feb. 1642; *Alexander et Aristobulus*, 24 July 1642; *Mors Valentiniani Imperatoris*, 16 Dec. 1642; *Nicephorus*, Autumn 1646; *Sigibertus*, 1647; *Joseph*, 1649; *Barlaam et Josaphat*, Aug. 1650; *Ferdinandus Rex Castellae*, 17 Feb. 1652; *S. Augustinus Angliae Apostolus*, 2 Oct. 1653; *S. Sigismundus*, 22 Jan. 1659; *Leontius, Hypatius, et Theodulus*, Aug. (?) 1659; *Leo Sapiens*, 10 Nov. 1659; *Rex Oswius*, 26 Jan. 1660; *S. Kenelmus Rex*, 1661; *Phoenix* (?), 1661; *Geaner et Hamarte*, Nov. 1661; *SS. Petrus et Paulus*, 1662; *Vincentius et Anastasius* (?), 22 Jan. 1663; *Constantinus*, 1665; *Catilina*, 1666; *S. Justus et S. Pastor*, 1666; *Valentinianus*, 31 Aug. 1667; *Abenner, Josaphat, et Barachias*, 1668; *Julianus et Celsus*, 1668; *Judicium Ultimum*, 8 Aug. 1669; *Crux Vindicata*, 1670 (revival? see Chronology, 1656); *Bellum Grammaticale*, 1676.

(*m*) The following are titles of plays once existing in a MS collection catalogued by Abraham Hill, probably at some time between 1677 and 1703. The collection also contained plays by known dramatists, and the titles of these have been incorporated in the foregoing chronological list. Most of the plays below probably were written before 1642, and in a greater number of instances than here indicated may be identical with works known under alternative titles. For a scholarly annotation of Hill's list, see J. Q. Adams, 'Hill's List of Early Plays in Manuscript', *Library*, N.S., XX (1939), 71-99: *Aleumista* (in Latin); *All Is Not Gold that Glisters* (Chettle's play?); *The Ambitious Brother* (by

'G. Buc'); *A Christmas Tale, or The Knight and the Cobbler* (by Philip Lane); *The Cloudy Queen and Singing Moor*; *A Court Purge*; *The False Friend* (the play of *c.* 1619?); *The Fatal Banquet*; *A Gentleman No Gentleman, a Metamorphosed Courtier* (Actors: Eustace, Frampole, Friswood, etc.); *Look on Me and Love Me, or Marriage in the Dark*; *Love's Infancy* (possibly same as Flecknoe's *Love in Its Infancy*, earlier version of *Love's Dominion*, 1654); *The Lover's Holiday*; *The Lover's Holiday, or The Bear* (another copy of the preceding?); *The Marriage Night* (Cary's play?); *A Match without Money, or The Wives' Prize*; *More Than Nine Days Wonder, Two Constant Women*; *Mull Sack, or The Looking Glass, the Bachelor, or the Hawk* (possibly the original of the Jack Cottington play, which was altered and published in 1640 as *The Knave in Grain New Vamped*); *Mustapha* (Greville's play? Boyle's play?); *Osman the Turk, or The Ottoman Custom* (possibly Carlell's *Osmond the Great Turk*); *The Painted Lady*; *Pandorae Pyxis* (in Latin); *Philip of Macedon*; *Roxolana, or The Ambitious Step-Dame* (possibly same as Boyle's *Mustapha*); *Spanish Preferment*; *Tereus with a Pastoral* (by 'M.A.'; actors: Agnostus, Eupathus, etc., Mufti, Nassuf, etc.; one play or two? *Tradeway's Tragedy*; *The Tragedy of Tomerania*; *The Triumph of Innocence*; *The Two Spanish Gentlemen*; *The Unfaithful Wife*; *Valentinian, or Rape's Revenge* (probably Fletcher's *Valentinian*, or Rochester's adaptation of it); *The Wandering Jew*; *A Way to Make a Knave Honest*; *The White Witch of Westminster, or Love in a Lunacy*; *The Widow Captain*; *The Wronged Widow's Tragedy*; *The Younger Brother, or Male Courtesan* (possibly same as *The Younger Brother*, 1617).

(*n*) The following items are bound into Volume III of the Family Letters of Sir William Herrick (1562–1653): Introduction by 'pore Amintas' to 'square play' performed by shepherd boys, *c.* 1570–90; Prologue introducing maskers dressed as sailors for a wedding mask, *c.* 1570–90.

(*o*) The following non-extant entertainments presented by the Children of St Paul's are listed by Trevor N. S. Lennan in *Sebastian Westcott, the Children of St Paul's, and the Marriage of Wit and Science* (1975): 55–73:

Winter, 1551/1552:	before Princess Elizabeth at Hatfield House
Spring, 1553?	before King Edward VI (on the state of Ireland [by William Baldwin; possibly *Nice Wanton?*])
July, 1553	pageant presented to Queen Mary during her progress through the city
December, 1554 or April, 1557	before Princess Elizabeth and Queen Mary at Hatfield House
7 August 1559	presented before Queen Elizabeth at Nonsuch House, Surrey
Christmas, 1561	presented before Queen Elizabeth at Whitehall
February, 1562	presented before Queen Elizabeth at Whitehall
Christmas, 1562	presented before Queen Elizabeth at Whitehall
Christmas, 1564	presented before Queen Elizabeth at Whitehall
2 February 1565	presented before Queen Elizabeth at Whitehall
Winter, 1565/66	three plays, two presented at Christmas before Queen Elizabeth at Whitehall and the third presented before Queen Elizabeth and Princess Cecilia of Sweden at Durham House in the Strand
Christmas, 1566	two plays presented before Queen Elizabeth at Whitehall
1 January 1569	presented before Queen Elizabeth at Hampton Court
28 December 1570	presented before Queen Elizabeth at Hampton Court
25–27 February 1571	presented by William Hunnis, Richard Farrant, and Sebastian Westcott and the Children of the Queen's Majesties, Chapel Royal of Windsor, and St Paul's before Queen Elizabeth at Whitehall
Christmas to Twelfth Night, 1572–1573	presented before Queen Elizabeth at Hampton Court
6 January 1576	presented before the Queen at Hampton Court

29 December 1577   an unknown play, but possibly *Cupid and Psyche* presented before
                                   Queen Elizabeth at Hampton Court
26 December 1581   presented before Queen Elizabeth at Whitehall

(*p*) The following plays presented by the Children of St Paul's are listed as lost by Reavley Gair in *The Children of Paul's: The Story of a Theatre Company, 1553–1608* (1982): 186–7:

1567–1568	*As Playne a Canne Be*
1567–1568	*The Paynfull Pillgrimage*
1567–1568	*Jack and Jyll*
	Wit and Will (this may be the same as
	The Marriage of Wit and Science)
	Orestes
	Tragedy of the King of Scots
	Six Fooles
1571/2	*Effiginia*
c. 1573	*Alkmeon*
1577	*The History of Error*
	The History of Titus and Gesippus
1579	*A Moral of the Marryage of Mynde and Measure*
1580	*Scipio Africanus*
1584	*Agamemnon and Ulysses*
1599	The Plays of William Stanley (?)
1606	*Abuses*

(*q*) The sixteenth-century account books kept by the Augustinian canons of Hickling Priory, in northeast Norfolk, includes among the entries on daily expenditures payments to visiting entertainers. Richard Beadle in 'Entertainments at Hickling Priory, Norfolk, 1510–1520' (*REEDN*, II [1980: 17–19]) transcribed entries found in Bodleian Library's Tanner MS 194 including the following (translated below from the Latin):

for a play on the Passion of Chirst, the men of Beccles (Suffolk); entered 29 September 1510 to 29 September 1511, f. 12v.

for a play performed on the next-to-last day in December by the men of Beccles and Washingham; entered 29 September 1512 to 29 September 1513, f. 75v.

for plays performed during the week of the Lord's birthday by: the men of Norwich, the men of Wumondham, the men of Northrepps; entered 29 September 1515 to 29 September 1516; f. 75v.

for the bear keeper of our Lord, the King, on the 12th of November; entered 29 September 1517 to 29 September 1518; f. 107v.

for those called the King's Players in Waiting [?];

entered 29 September 1517 to 29 September 1518; f. 107v.

for various interludes performed by diverse men at the time of the Lord's birthday; and to the Bear Keepers, namely those of our Lord, the King, and of the [ninth] Duke of Suffolk; entered 29 September 1518 to 29 September 1519; f. 117v.

for the Bear Keeper of the Bears of John DeVere, the Lord of Oxford; entered 29 September 1519 to 29 September 1520; f. 131.

for a performance by the players of Lord Prior [Robert Bronde, Prior of Holy Trinity, Norwich, 1504–1529]; entered 29 September 1519 to 29 September 1520; f. 131.

(*r*) Noted in the *Diary Journals of Richard Sackville*, Fifth Earl of Dorset is a brief citation, possibly relating to a dramatic presentation:
1659: *The Unreasonable and Insupportable Burthen*, by William Prinne [Prynne?]. Kent County Archives Office, Ref. U269 F3/6.

(*s*) The following entertainment found listed in Gibson's Revels accounts at the Public Record Office among accounts of King's Remembrancers, Exchequer of Receipts:

Henry VIII's Entertainment for the Queen of Scots, 20 May 1516. Accounting found at P.R.O. E101/418/7.

(t) An entry for *Tragico-Comoedia de Tarquinio Superbo*, 1632, by Richard Todkill is noted for 1632 in the Catholic Record Society's *The Douai College Diaries, Third, Fourth, and Fifth, 1598–1654*, volume 1, edited by Edwin H. Burton and Thomas L. Williams (London: privately printed, 1911), pp. 302, 303.

INDEX OF ENGLISH PLAYWRIGHTS

Of the more than 600 writers here listed, about two-thirds are noted in the *Dictionary of National Biography*. Many of the others are noticed in *Biographia Dramatica*, in *Alumni Oxonienses, Alumni Cantabrigienses*, and in the *Dictionary of Literary Biography*. When the dates given below differ from those in these five reference works, as happens in a number of instances, the reason is that recent research has yielded new biographical facts; in such instances the source of my information is that indicated in the prefatory essay. Initials of anonymous authors are listed, but not in cases where the authors have been satisfactorily identified. In library catalogues, it should be noted that (a) translated or adapted plays are sometimes listed under the name of the original author and not of the translator or adaptor, and (b) plays may be listed under the author's name alternatively spelled. Thus, Broke may appear as Brooke; Bellon as Belon; Corey as Corye; Crawford as Crauford; Stapleton as Stapylton; Sydserff as St Serfe, etc. When an author is cited in the Chronology more than once in any given year, the number of listings is indicated below in round brackets following the date. Each playwright entry also includes bibliographical citations of standard and comprehensive collections following the pertinent dates and record of listings. References to Nicoll are to *Early English Century Drama*, 3rd ed. (*A History of English Drama, 1660–1900*, Vol. II), 1952.

A., M., Supp. II, m.

A., R., 1612.

Admamson, William (Scottish poet), 1558.

Aethelwold, Bishop of Winchester (908?–984), 10th cent.

Ainsworth, William (*c.* 1607–71: clergyman), 1625.

A., G., 1566.

Alabaster, William (1567–1630: clergyman), 1592, Supp. I.

Alder, John (*c.* 1588–1609: student), 1608.

Alexander, Sir William, Earl of Stirling (*c.* 1568–1640): courtier), 1603, 1604, 1607(2). *The Dramatic Works of William Alexander*, L. Kastner and H. B. Charlton , eds, 1921.

Alley, William, Bishop of Exeter (*c.* 1510–70), 1560.

Amerie, Robert (d. 1613: Chester ironmonger), 1610.

Anton, Robert (satirist), 1612.

'Ariadne', 1695, 1697.

Armin, Robert (*c.* 1565–1615: actor), 1606, 1612.

Arrowsmith, Joseph (*c.* 1647–*c.* 1708: clergyman), 1673, Supp. I.

Artour, or Arthur, Thomas (*c.* 1495–1532: Cambridge Fellow), 1525(2).

Ascham, Roger (1515–68: tutor), 1543.

Ashton, Thomas (*c.* 1540–78: schoolmaster), 1561, 1566.

Aske, James (same as James Askew, *fl.* 1588–93?: stationer), 1588.

Atchelow, Thomas (unknown), may have written plays, *c.* 1589; see Chambers, *E. S.*, III, 211.

Atkinson, Thomas (1599–1639: Oxford proctor), 1618.

Attowell, George (*fl.* 1590–5: actor), 1593.

Aubrey, John (1626–97: antiquary), 1671.

Authinleck, Patrick (schoolmaster), 1574.

B., H., 1659.

B., H. H., 1659.

B., I., 1656.

B., R., 1564.

B., T., 1614.

B., T., 1632; adapt., 1677.

B., T., 1649.

Bacon, Francis (1561–1626: jurist), 1588, 1594, 1595. *The Works of Francis Bacon*, J. Spedding, R. L. Ellis, and D. D. Heath, eds, 1857–74.

Badger, John (*fl.* 1555–77: Oxford University beadle), 1575.

Bailey, Abraham (*fl.* 1667–70: Lincoln's Inn lawyer), 1667.

Baldwin, William (*fl.* 1547–71: proofreader, etc.), 1556.

Bale, John, Bishop of Ossory (1495–1563), 1536(3), 1537(5), 1538(8), 1545.
The Dramatic Writings of John Bale, Bishop of Ossory, John S. Farmer, ed., 1907; facsimile reprint ed., 1966.
The Complete Plays of John Bale, Peter Happi, ed., 2 vols, 1985.

Bancroft, John (d. 1696: surgeon), 1678, 1690, 1692.

Banister, William, *vere* Selby, William (1636–66: Master of St Omers), 1664(3).

Banks, John (*c.* 1650–1706: playwright), 1677, 1678, 1681, 1682, 1684, 1694, 1695.

Barjona, Laurentius, *see* Johnson, Laurence.

Barkstead, or Barstead, William (*fl.* 1607–16: actor), 1607.

Barnes, – (unknown), 1624.

Barnes, Barnabe (*c.* 1569–1609: poet), 1606, 1607.

Barnes, Joshua (1654–1712: Cambridge professor of Greek), 1675, 1680, 1683, 1693.

Baron, Robert (1630–58: poet), 1647(2), 1655.

Barry, Lording (1580–1629: adventurer), 1608.

Bartley, Sir William, *see* Berkeley, Sir William.

Bayley, George (strolling actor), 1662.

Baylie, Simon (unknown), 1638.

Beaumont, Sir Francis (1584 or 1585–1616: gentleman-playwright), 1606(3), 1607, 1608, 1609(2), 1610, 1611, 1612, 1613(4), 1615, 1616, 1617, 1621; adapt., 1662(6), 1664, 1686, 1695.
The Works of Beaumont and Fletcher, A. Glover and A. R. Waller, eds, 1905–12.
The Dramatic Works in the Beaumont and Fletcher Canon, Fredson Bowers, general ed., 5 vols, 1966–84.

Beaumont, Sir John (1582 or 1583–1627: courtier), 1625.

Bedloe, William (1650–80: sharper), 1679.

Behn, Aphra (1640?–89: playwright), 1670, 1671, 1673, 1676(2), 1677(3), 1678, 1679(2), 1680, 1681(3), 1682(2), 1684, 1686, 1687, 1689, 1696; *see* 1630.
The Works of Aphra Behn, M. Summers, ed., 1915.

Belchier, or Belcher, Daubridgecourt (1580?–1621: author), 1618.

Bellamy, Henry (1604–a. 1637: clergyman), 1626.

Bellenden, John (Scottish author), listed by Hazlitt as author of a dramatic allegory, in error? See *Manual*, p. 247.

Belon, Peter (physician), 1675.

Berkeley, Sir William (1606?–77): Governor of Virginia), 1637, 1662.

Bernard, Richard (1568?–1642: clergyman), 1598, 1604.

Bernard, Samuel (*c.* 1591–1657: schoolmaster), 1617, 1618, 1619.

Berners, Lord, *see* Bourchier, John.

Betterton, Thomas (1635?–1710: actor), 1669, 1670(2), 1674, 1690, 1700; for later plays, *see* Nicoll, pp. 297–8.

Bird, William (*fl.* 1597–1619: actor), 1592, 1601.

Birkhead, Henry (1617–1696: Oxford Fellow), 1659.

Blencowe, John (1609–a. 1648: Oxford Fellow), 1633.

Blow, John (1648–1708: composer), 1682.

Bonen, William (unknown), 1623(2).

Boothby, Mrs Frances (unknown), 1669.

Bourchier, John, 2nd Baron Berners (1467–1533), 1525.

Bourne, Reuben (lawyer?), 1692.

Bower, Richard (d. 1561: Master of Chapel), 1564.

Boyer, Abel (1667–1729: journalist), 1699.

Boyle, Roger, 1st Earl of Orrery (1621–79), 1638, 1662, 1664(2), 1665(2), 1667, 1668, 1669(2), 1672, 1676.

Boyle, William (unknown), 1600.

Brackley, *née* Cavendish, Lady Elizabeth (*c.* 1623–63), 1645(2).

Brady, Nicholas (1659–1726: clergyman), 1692.

Brandon, Samuel (unknown), 1598.

Brathwait, Richard (1588–1673: miscellanist), 1638, 1641, 1665.

Breton, Nicholas (*c.* 1552–*c.* 1626: poet), 1591.

Brewer, Anthony (d. 1624?: actor?), 1617, 1632.

Brewer, Thomas (*fl.* 1623: miscellanist), 1623, 1632.

Bridges, John, Bishop of Oxford (d. 1618), 1553.

Cecil T(homas? *c.* 1580?–1628: clergyman), 1615.

Centlivre, Mrs Susannah (*c.* 1670–1723: actress), 1700; for later plays, *see* Nicoll, pp. 303–6, 433.

The Dramatic Works of the Celebrated Mrs Centlivre, 1872.

The Plays of Susanna Centlivre, Richard C. Frushell, ed., 3 vols, 1982.

Chaloner, Sir Thomas (1521–65: diplomatist), 1552.

Chamberlain, Robert (1607–a. 1640: clerk), 1640.

Chamberlaine, William (*c.* 1619–89: physician), 1658; adapt. 1677.

Chamberleyn, Thomas (unknown), 15th cent.

Chapman, George (*c.* 1560–1634: playwright), 1594, 1596, 1597, 1598, 1599(3), 1600, 1601, 1602(4), 1603, 1604(2), 1605(3), 1608(2), 1610, 1611(2), 1612, 1613(2), 1632, 1633, 1640;·adapt. 1685, 1691.

The Plays of George Chapman: The Tragedies, T. M. Parrott, 2 vols, 1910.

The Plays of George Chapman: The Comedies, T. M. Parrott, 2 vols, 1913.

The Plays of George Chapman: The Comedies, G. Blakemore Evans, ed., Allan Holaday, gen. ed., 1970.

Chappell, John (*c.* 1590–a. 1632: clergyman), 1616.

Chettle, Henry (*c.* 1560–1607: printer and playwright), 1592, 1595, 1598(16), 1599(9), 1600(6), 1601(6), 1602(8), 1603(3), Supp. Iĩ, k.

Christopherson, John, Bishop of Chichester (*c.* 1520?–58), 1544.

Churchyard, Thomas (1520?–1604: poet), 1574, 1578, 1579, 1587.

Cibber, Colley (1671–1757: actor), 1696(2), 1699(2), 1700; for later plays, *see* Nicoll, pp. 306–13, 433–4.

The Plays of Colley Cibber, Rodney Hayle, ed., 1980.

'Claretus, Pater' (*fl.* 1623–55: Jesuit of St Omers), 1623, 1655.

Clarges, Thomas (d. 1695: politician), 1664.

Clavell, John (1601–43: ex-highwayman), 1629.

Clerke, or Clark, William (d.b. 1699: lawyer), 1662.

Clifford, George, 3rd Earl of Cumberland (1558–1605: author of tilting speeches as Knight of the Crown; *see* Chambers, *E.S.,* III, 268.

Clifford, Martin (*c.* 1625?–77: courtier), 1671.

Cobbes, James (unknown: translator, poet, playwright), Supp. I. (*See, Romanus*), 1619.

Codrington, Robert (1601–65: translator), 1662.

Cokain, or Cokayne, Sir Aston (1608–84: literary amateur), 1633, 1639, 1640, 1662; adapt., 1684.

The Dramatic Works of Sir Aston Cokain, J. Maidment and W. H. Logan, eds, 1874.

Compton, Thomas, *see* Carleton, Thomas.

Congreve, William (*c.* 1670–1729: playwright), 1693(2), 1695, 1697, 1700: for later compositions, *see* Nicoll, pp. 315, 434.

The Complete Works of William Congreve, M. Summers, ed., 1923.

The Comedies of William Congreve, N. Marshall, ed., 1948.

The Comedies of William Congreve, Anthony G. Henderson, ed., 1982.

Cooke, Edward (unknown), 1678.

Cooke, Jo[shua?] (unknown), 1602, 1611; adapt., 1662, 1667.

Cornish, William, Sr (d. by 1502: choirmaster at Westminster, 1480–90), 1494, 1501(2).

Cornish, William, Jr (*fl.* 1509–23: dramatist, choirmaster, Master of Children of Chapel), 1514, 1516(3), 1517, 1522.

Coyre, John (d.a. 1731?: actor?), 1671, 1699; for later plays *see* Nicoll, p. 316.

Cotton, Charles (1630–87: poet), 1665.

Cowley, Abraham (1618–67: poet), 1633, 1638, 1642, 1661, 1671.

The Complete Works in Verses and Prose of Abraham Cowley, (The Chertsey Worthies' Lib.), A. B. Grosart, ed., 1881; rpt. 1967.

The English Works of Abraham Cowley, A. Waller, ed., 1905–6.

Cox, Robert (1604?–1655?: strolling actor), 1653(10); adapt., 1662(5), 1673.

Crauford, David (1665–1726: Historiographer

Doggett, Thomas (d. 1721: actor), 1696(2), 1699.

Douglas, Gawain, Bishop of Dunkeld (1474–1522), Supp. II, j.

D'Ouvilley, George Gerbier (army officer), 1657.

Dover, John (1644–1725: clergyman), 1667, 1674.

D'Oyley, E. (unknown), 1695.

Drake, James (1667–1707: political writer), 1697.

Drayton, Michael (*c*. 1563–1631: poet), 1598(13), 1599(3), 1600, 1601, 1602, 1604.
The Works of Michael Drayton, J. William Hebel, ed., (intro., notes, variant readings by Kathleen Tillotson and B. H. H. Newdigate) 5 vols, 1931–41; corrected edition with revised biblio. by Bent Juel-Jensen, 1961.

Drue, or Drewe, Thomas (*fl.* 1624: actor?), 1620, 1624, 1639.

Drummond of Hawthornden, William (1585–1649: poet), 1633.
The Poetical works of Drummond of Hawthornden, L. E. Kastner, ed., 1913.

Drury, William (*fl.* 1616–41: teacher at Douai), 1619(3).

Dryden, John (1631–1700: poet), 1663, 1664(2), 1665, 1667(4), 1668(2), 1669(2), 1670, 1671(2), 1672(2), 1675(2), 1676, 1677, 1678(2), 1679, 1680, 1682, 1685, 1689, 1690, 1691, 1692, 1694, 1700; adapt., 1695.
The Works of John Dryden, G. Saintsbury, ed., 1882–93.
The Dramatic Works of John Dryden, M. Summers, ed., 1931–2.
Four Comedies, L. A. Beaurline and Fredson Bowers, eds, 1967.
Four Tragedies, L. A. Beaurline and Fredson Bowers, eds, 1967.

Dryden, John, Jr (1668–1701), 1696.

Duffett, Thomas (London milliner), 1673(2), 1674(2), 1675, 1676.

Dugdale, Gilbert (unknown), 1604.

Dunbar, William (*c*. 1460–1530?: poet), 1503.

D'Urfey, Thomas (1653–1723: playwright), 1676(3), 1677, 1678(2), 1679, 1681, 1682(2), 1684, 1685, 1686, 1688, 1691(2), 1692, 1693, 1694, 1695, 1696, 1697, 1698, 1699; for later

plays, *see* Nicoll, pp. 320, 435.

Dymock, or Dymmock, John (brother of following?), 1601.

Dymock, Tailbois (*fl.* 1584–1602), 1601.

Eccles, John (musician), 1694.

Ecclestone, Edward (unknown), 1679.

Echard, or Eachard, Lawrence (*c*. 1670–1730: historian), 1694(2).

Edes, Richard (1555–1604: clergyman), 1582, 1592.

Edward VI, King (1537–53), 1548.

Edwards, John (1600–a. 1648: Oxford Proctor), Supp. II, j.

Edwards, Richard (*c*. 1523–66: Master of Chapel), 1564, 1566.
The Dramatic Writings of Richard Edwards, Thomas Norton, and Thomas Sackvile, comprising 'Damon and Pithias' – 'Palamon and Arcyte' (Note) – 'Gorboduc' (or 'Ferrex and Porrex') – Note-Book and Word-List, John Stephen Farmer, ed., 1906; reprinted 1966.

Elizabeth I, Queen (1533–1603), 1561.

Essex, Earl of, *see* Devereux, Robert.

Etherege, Sir George (*c*. 1634–91: courtier), 1664, 1668, 1676.
The Dramatic Works of Sir George Etherege, (Percy Reprints, No. 6), H. F. B. Brett-Smith, ed., 1927.
The Plays of Sir George Etherege, Michael Cordner, ed., 1982.

Evelyn, John (1620–1706: virtuoso), 1663.

Falkland, Viscount, *see* Cary, Henry.

Falkland, Viscountess, *see* Cary, Elizabeth.

Fane, Sir Francis (d. 1691: courtier), 1675, 1684, 1686.

Fane, Mildmay (2nd Earl of Westmorland (1602–66), 1640, 1641, 1642(2), 1643, 1644, 1645, 1650, 1658.

Fane, Lady Rachel (d. 1654), 1626.

Fanshawe, Sir Richard (1608–66: diplomatist), 1647, 1654, 1658.

Farquhar, George (1678–1707: army officer), 1698, 1699; for later plays, *see* Nicoll, pp. 321–3, 435–6.
George Farquhar, Edited with Introduction and Notes,

William Archer, 1907?

The Complete Works of George Farquhar, 2 vols, Charles Stonehill, ed., 1930; reprinted 1967.

The Works of George Farquhar, Shirley Strum Kenny, ed., 1986.

Farrant, Richard (d. 1580: Master of Children of Windsor), 1588.

Ferebe, George (*c.* 1573–a. 1613: composer), 1613.

Ferrers, George (*c.* 1500–79: politician), 1553, 1575.

Field, Nathan (1587–1619 or 1620: actor), 1609, 1611, 1613, 1614, 1617(2), 1618, 1619, 1621.
The Plays of Nathan Field, Edited from the Original Quartos, William Peery, ed., 1950.

Filmer, Sir Edward (*c.* 1619–69: courtier), 1663.

Filmer, Edward (1652–a. 1707: lawyer), 1697(2).

Finch, Anne, Countess of Winchilsea (1661–1720), 1688, 1690.
The Poems of Anne, Countess of Winchilsea (Univ. of Chicago Decennial Pubs., 2nd Ser., vol. 5), M. Reynolds, ed., 1903.

Fishbourne, Christopher (*fl.* 1678–85), 1678.

Fisher, Jasper (1591–1643: clergyman), 1625.

Fisher, John (1469?–1535: Bishop of Rochester), 1558.

Flecknoe, Richard (d. 1678?: lay brother), 1650(2), 1654(2), 1659, 1661, 1663, 1667(2), 1668, 1669, 1672.

Fletcher, John (1579–1625: playwright), 1606(2), 1607, 1608(2), 1609(2), 1610, 1611(3), 1612, 1613(7), 1614(2), 1615(2), 1616(3), 1617(6), 1618(2), 1619(4), 1620(4), 1621(3), 1622(4), 1623(3), 1624(2), 1625, 1626, 1634; adapt. 1658, 1662(15), 1664(2), 1667, 1669, 1677, 1678, 1685, 1686, 1687, 1688, 1690, 1695(2), 1697, 1699, 1700.
The Works of Beaumont and Fletcher, A. Glover and A. R. Waller, eds, 1905–12.
The Dramatic Works in the Beaumont and Fletcher Canon, 5 vols, Fredson Bowers, gen. ed., 1966–85.

Fletcher, Phineas (1582–1650: clergyman), 1615.
The Poetical Works of Giles and Phineas Fletcher, F. S. Boas, ed., 1908–9.

Flower, Francis (lawyer?), 1588.

Ford, John (1586–a. 1639: playwright), 1612, 1619, 1621, 1623(4), 1624(5), 1626, 1628(2), 1630(2), 1632(2), 1633, 1635, 1638(2).
The Works of John Ford, 3 vols, William Gifford and Alexander Dyce, eds, 1869; reissued 1895, 1965.
Selected Plays of John Ford, Colin Givson, ed., 1986.

Forde, Thomas (*fl.* 1647–61: bookseller's assistant), 1660.

Formido, Sir Cornelius (unknown), 1637, 1656.

Forsett, Edward (*c.* 1553–*c.* 1630: political writer), 1581.

Fountain, John (d. *c.* 1667?), 1661; adapt., 1669.

Fowler, William (*fl.* 1581–1609: Scottish poet), 1594.

Fox, or Foxe, Richard, Bishop of Winchester, Lord Privy Seal (1448?–1528), 1501.

Foxe, John (1516–87; martyrologist), 1545, 1556.

Francis, Sir Henry (*fl.* 1377–1382: monk of St Werburgh), mentioned as possible author of *Chester Plays*, 14th cent.

Fraunce, Abraham (*c.* 1558–a. 1633: poet), 1579, 1582, 1591.

Freeman, Sir Ralph (*c.* 1590–1667: Master of the Mint), 1639.

Fulbeck, William (1560–1603?: historian), 1588.

Fuller, Thomas (1608–61: clergyman), 1643.

Fulwell, Ulpian (*c.* 1546–a. 1578: clergyman), 1568.
The Dramatic Writings of Ulpian Fulwell, J. S. Farmer, ed., 1906.

G., I., 1614.

Gager, William (1555–1622: clergyman), 1582, 1583(2), 1584, 1592(2), Supp. II, j.

Garfield, Benjamin (unknown), 1650.

Garnett, Jasper (Lancashire schoolmaster), 1621.

Garter, Bernard (*fl.* 1565–80: poet), 1578.

Garter, Thomas (poss. same as above), 1569.

Gascoigne, George (*c.* 1539–78: courtier), 1566(2), 1572, 1575(3).
The Complete Works of George Gascoigne, 2 vols, John W. Cunliffe, ed., 1907–10; reprinted 1969.

Gayton, Edmund (1608–66: scholar), 1655.

Geoffrey of Gorham (d. 1146: Abbot of St Albans), 11th cent.

Gildon, Charles (1665-1724: author), 1696, 1698, 1700; for later plays, *see* Nicoll, pp. 332-3, 437.
The Plays of Charles Gildon, Paula K. Backscheider, ed., 197.

Glapthorne, Henry (1610-a. 1643: poet), 1634, 1635(3), 1636, 1637, 1638(2), 1639(2), 1640.
The Plays and Poems of Henry Glapthorne, (Pearson Reprints), R. H. Shepherd, ed., 1874.

Godolphin, Sidney, 1st Earl of Godolphin (1645-1712), 1663.

Goffe, John, *see* Gough, John.

Goffe, or Gough, Thomas (*c.* 1591-1629: clergyman), 1617, 1618, 1619(3).

Golding, Arthur (1536-1606: scholar), 1575.

Goldingham, Henry (*fl.* 1575-*c.* 1587: nobleman's retainer), 1575, 1578.

Goldingham, William (*c.* 1540?-*c.* 1589: Cambridge Fellow), 1572.

Goldsmith, Francis (1613-55: lawyer?) 1652.

Goldwell, Henry (unknown), 1581.

Gomersall, Robert (1602?-1644?: clergyman), 1628.

Gosson, Stephen (1554-1624: actor? later clergyman), 1577(2), 1578.

Gough, or Goffe, John (*c.* 1610-61: clergyman), 1640.

Gould, Robert (d. *c.* 1709: upper servant), 1695(2).

Govell, R. (a 'ghost' name?), Supp. II, g.

Grafton, John (York schoolmaster), 1584.

Grafton, Richard (d. 1572?: chronicler), 1554.

Granville, George, Baron (1667-1735), 1695, 1697; for later plays, *see* Nicoll, pp. 333, 437.

Green, Alexander (unknown), 1663.

Greene, Robert (1558-92: playwright), 1587(2), 1588, 1589, 1590(2), 1591, 1592(2), 1594, Supp. II, k.
Complete Works, 15 vols, A. B. Grosart, ed., 1881-6, reprinted, 1964.
The Plays and Poems of Robert Greene, J. Chruton Collins, ed., 1905.
Robert Greene T. Fisher Unwin, ed., 1907.

Greville, Fulke, Lord Brooke (1554-1628), 1596, 1600, 1601.

The Poems and Dramas of Fulke Greville, G. Bullough, ed., 1939.

Grimald, Nicholas (1519-62: clergyman), 1540(2), 1547(6).
The Life and Poems of Nicholas Grimald, L. R. Merrill, ed., 1925.

Gunnell, Richard (d. 1634: actor), 1623, 1624(2), Supp. II, g.

Gwinne, Matthew (*c.* 1558-1627: physician), 1603, 1605(2).

Gwyn, Owen (*c.* 1570-1633: St John's, Oxford, Master), 1599, 1600, 1602, 1603.

Habington, William (1605-54: poet), 1640.

Hacket, John, Bishop of Coventry (1592-1670), 1623.

Halliwell, Edward (born *c.* 1514: Cambridge Fellow), 1564.

Harding, Samuel (*c.* 1616 or 1618-a. 1699?: clergyman), 1640.

Harris, Joseph (*fl.* 1661-1702: actor), 1690, 1696, 1699.

Harrison, John (High Master of St Paul's School, 1581-96) 1584, 1586.

Harrison, Stephen (architect), 1604.

Hathway, Richard (*fl.* 1597-1603: playwright), 1598(2), 1599(2), 1600(3), 1601(5), 1602(2), 1603(3).

Hatton, Sir Christopher (1540-91; statesman), 1566.

Haughton, William (*c.* 1575-1605: playwright), 1598, 1599(4), 1600(9), 1601(10), 1602, Supp. II, k.

Hausted, Peter (*c.* 1605?-1644: clergyman), 1631, 1632, 1636.

Hawkesworth, Walter (*c.* 1570?-1606: secretary), 1599, 1603.

Hawkins, William (*c.* 1602?-1637: schoolmaster), 1627.

Haynes, Joe (*c.* 1648-1701: actor), 1692.

Head, Richard (1637?-1686?: gambler), 1663.

Hemming, or Heminges, William (1602-b. 1653: playwright), 1626, 1633, 1639; adapt., 1674.

Henrietta Maria, Queen (1609-69), 1635.

Herbert, Mary, Countess of Pembroke (1561-1621), 1590, 1592.

1611(3), 1612, 1613(3), 1614, 1615, 1616(5), 1617, 1618(3), 1619, 1620(3), 1621, 1622, 1623, 1624(2), 1625, 1626, 1629, 1631(2), 1632, 1633(2), 1634, 1637(2); adapt., 1662, 1685.

Ben Jonson, Vols 1-5, C. H. Herford and Percy Simpson, eds; Vols 6-11, C. H. Herford, Percy Simpson, and Evelyn Simpson, eds, 1925-52; some volumes reprinted 1952-61.

The Yale Ben Jonson, Alvin B. Kernan and Richard B. Young, gen. eds, 1962-74.

The Works of Benjamin Jonson, 1616 Introduction, D. H. Brock; facsimile reprint of first folio of 1616, Scolar, 1976.

The Complete Plays of Ben Jonson, 4 vols, Gerald A. Wilkes, 1981-2 [modernized version of the texts of Vols 3-6 of the *Oxford Jonson*, ed. Herford and Simpson].

Jonson, 'Young' (unknown), 1623.

Jordan, Thomas (*c.* 1620-85?: actor), 1635, 1640, 1641, 1654, 1657, 1659(2), 1660(2), 1661, 1671, 1672, 1673, 1674, 1675, 1676, 1677, 1678, 1679, 1680, 1681, 1682, 1683, 1684.

Jordan William (Cornish priest?), 1611; trans., 1693.

Joyner, William (1622-1706: Oxford Fellow), 1670.

Katherine of Sutton (Abbess of Barking), 14th cent.

Keigwyn, John (1641-1716: scholar), 1693, 1695.

Kempe, William (d.b. 1608: actor), 1589, 1592, 1595(3).

Key, or Caius, Thomas (d. 1572: scholar), 1550.

Killigrew, Henry (1613-1700: clergyman), 1635.

Killigrew, Thomas (1612-83: courtier and playhouse manager), 1635, 1636(2), 1641, 1646, 1650, 1652, 1654, Supp. II, j; adapt., 1677, 1681.

Killigrew, Sir William (1606-95: courtier), 1662, 1663, 1664, 1665, 1669.

Kinwelmershe, Francis (d. 1580: lawyer), 1566.

Kirke, John (*fl.* 1629-42?: actor?) 1635, 1643.

Kirkham, R. (unknown), 1659.

Kirkman, Francis (*c.* 1632-a. 1680: printer), 1661, 1662, 1673.

Knevet, Ralph (1600-71: clergyman), 1631.

Kornyshe, William, *see* Cornish, William.

Kyd, Thomas (1558-94: playwright), 1587, 1589, 1591, 1594(2), 1599, 1604, Supp. II, k.

The Works of Thomas Kyd, Edited from the Original Texts with Introduction, Notes, and Facsimiles, Frederick S. Boas, 1901. Reprinted with *Supplement*, 1955; rpt. 1962.

Kyffin, Maurice (d. 1599: poet), 1588(2).

Kynaston, Sir Francis (1587-1642: virtuoso), 1636.

Kynder, Philip (1597-a. 1665: physician), 1615.

Lacy, John (d. 1681: actor), 1665, 1667, 1669, 1682.

The Dramatic Works of John Lacy, J. Maidment and W. H. Logan, eds, 1875.

Laingby, Robert (d. 1455: clergyman), 15th cent.

Lancaster, John (Gray's Inn Lawyer), 1588.

Lane, Philip (unknown), Supp. II, m.

Lansdowne, Lord, *see* Granville, George.

Lateware, Richard (1560-1601: scholar), 1588.

Lauder, William (1520?-1573: poet priest), 1554, 1558.

Lawrence, William (1635-97: diarist, lawyer), 1662.

Leanerd, John (unknown), 1677, 1678(2).

Lee, Sir Henry (1531-1611: courtier), 1575, 1590, 1592.

Lee, Nathaniel (1651-92: playwright), 1674, 1675, 1676, 1677, 1678(2), 1679, 1680(2), 1681, 1682, 1683, 1689.

The Works of Nathaniel Lee, T. B. Stroup and A. L. Cooke, eds, 1954-5.

Lee, Robert (*fl.* 1591-1623: actor), 1598.

Legge, Thomas (1535-1607: Cambridge professor), 1580, 1584.

Le Grys, Sir Robert (d. 1635: courtier), 1634.

Leland, John (1506?-1552: antiquary), 1533.

Lesley, or Leslie, George (d. 1701: clergyman), 1675(3).

Lindsay, Sir David (1486-1555: poet), 1538, 1540.

The Works of Sir David Lindsay of the Mount,

1638, 1639, 1642; adapt., 1662(2), 1675, 1680, 1690.

The Plays of Philip Massinger, 4 vols, William Gifford, 1805; 2nd ed., 1813.

The Plays of Philip Massinger, Francis Cunningham, ed. (prints Gifford's texts and adds his own edition of *Believe as You List*), 1871.

The Plays and Poems of Philip Massinger, 5 vols, P. Edwards and C. Gibson, eds, 1976.

Mathews, Toby (1546–1628; President of St John's; Dean of Christ Church; Archbishop of York), 1566.

May, Charles (unknown), 1638.

May, (Mey), John (d. 1598?: Bishop of Carlisle), 1554.

May, Thomas (*c.* 1595–1650: man of letters), 1616, 1620, 1626, 1627, 1628, 1636.

Maydiston, or Maidstone, Richard (d. 1396: Carmelite friar), 14th cent.

Maynard, Sir John (1592–1658: politician), 1623, 1624.

Mayne, Jasper (1604–72: clergyman), 1637, 1638.

Mead, Robert (*c.* 1616–53: diplomatist), 1638.

Mease, Peter (*c.* 1599–*c.* 1649: clergyman), 1622.

Medbourne, Matthew (d. 1679: actor, publisher), 1666, 1670.

Medcalf, *see* Carleton, Thomas.

Medwall, Henry (*fl.* 1490–1514: clergyman), 1496, 1497, 1514.

The Plays of Henry Medwall, Alan H. Nelson, ed., 1980.

Merbury, Francis (unknown), 1579.

Meriton, Thomas (born 1638: clergyman), 1658(4).

Mewe, William (*c.* 1602?–*c.* 1669: clergyman), 1626.

Mey (May), John (d. 1598?: Bishop of Carlisle), 1554.

Middleton, Thomas (1580–1627: playwright), 1601, 1602(2), 1603, 1604(3), 1605, 1606(6), 1607, 1611(3), 1613(5), 1614, 1615, 1616(3), 1617(2), 1618(2), 1619(2), 1620, 1621(4), 1622(4), 1623(2), 1624, 1626(2), 1640; adapt., 1677, 1678.

The Works of Thomas Middleton, 8 vols, A. H. Bullen, ed., 1885–6.

Thomas Middleton, Martin W. Sampson, ed., 1915.

The Canon of Middleton's Plays, David J. Lake, ed., 1975.

Milton, John (1608–74: poet), 1633, 1634, 1671.

John Milton, Dramatic Poems, G. and M. Bullough, eds, 1958.

Mitchell, Francis (Yorkshire gentleman's retainer), 1601.

Montague, Walter (1603?–1677: courtier, later Abbot), 1633.

Montgomery, or Montgomerie, Alexander (*c.* 1556–*c.* 1610: Scottish Poet Laureate), 1603.

More, Thomas (1611?–1685: Puritan polemicist and self-publicist), 1636.

More, Sir Thomas (1478–1535: Lord Chancellor), 1495(2), 1501.

Morrell, Roger (*c.* 1556?–1624: clergyman), 1597.

Motteux, Peter Anthony (1663–1718: librettist), 1694, 1695, 1696(2), 1697(2), 1698, 1699; for later works, *see* Nicoll, pp. 345–6; 441.

Mountfort, Walter (*fl.* 1615–35: officer in East India Co.), 1633.

Mountfort, William (1664?–1692: actor), 1688(2), 1689, 1690(3), 1691, 1692.

Mulcaster, Richard (*c.* 1530–1611: schoolmaster), 1575.

Munday, Anthony (1560–1633: actor), 1582, 1584, 1589, 1594, 1595, 1598(6), 1599(2), 1600(2), 1601, 1602(4), 1605, 1609, 1610, 1611, 1614, 1615, 1616, 1618, 1621.

Murgetrode, or Murgetroid, Michael, Archbishop (1551–1608), 1582.

N., N., 1681.

Nabbes, Thomas (*c.* 1605–41: playwright), 1633, 1634, 1635, 1637(2), 1638(2), 1639; adapt., 1680.

The Dramatic Works of Thomas Nabbes, (Old Eng. Plays, N.S.), A. H. Bullen, ed., 1887.

Naile, Robert (unknown), 1613.

Nashe, Thomas (1567–1601: nobleman's retainer), 1586(2), 1592, 1597.

plays, *see* Nicoll, pp. 349-50, 442.

The Plays of Mary Pix and Catherine Trotter, Edna L. Stevens, ed., 1982.

Polwhele, Elizabeth (unknown), 1671.

Popple, William (1638-1708: merchant), 1691, 1692.

Pordage, Samuel (1633-91?: poet), 1660, 1673, 1677.

Porter, Henry (d. 1599: playwright), 1588, 1598(3), 1599(3).

Porter, Thomas (1636-80: man about town), 1662, 1663(2), 1677.

Pound, Thomas (1538?-1616?: lawyer), 1566(2).

Powell, George (1659-1714: actor), 1690(2), 1693, 1695, 1696(2), 1697, 1698.

Preston, Thomas (unknown: probably not the Cambridge scholar, 1537-98), 1561, 1570.

Prestwich, Edmund (unknown), 1651, 1656.

Price, Daniel (1581-1631: clergyman), 1610.

Prinne (Prynne), William (1600-69: pamphleteer, Bencher of Lincoln's Inn), Supp. II, q.

Punt, William (unknown), 1548.

Puttenham (George, d. 1590, or Richard, d. *c.* 1601, or neither?) 1580(3).

Quarles, Francis (1592-1644: poet), 1641.

The Complete Works of Francis Quarles A. B. Grosart, ed., 1880-1.

Quarles, William (unknown), 1604.

R., N., Supp. I.

R., T., 1638.

R., T., 1654.

R., W., 1622.

Radcliff, Robert (Cambridge professor, translator), 1540.

Radcliffe, Ralph (1519?-1559: schoolmaster), 1546(4).

Radcliffe, Robert (Cambridge professor, translator), 1546.

Randolph, Thomas (1605-35: poet), 1626, 1627(3), 1629(3), 1630(2), 1632, 1638(2); adapt., 1682, 1684.

The Dramatic Works of Thomas Randolph, W. C. Hazlitt, ed., 1875.

Rankins, William (*fl.* 1587-1601: playwright), 1598, 1601(3).

Rant, Humphrey (same as Humphrey Rant of Cambridge and Gray's Inn, *c.* 1640-1726?, or H. R. of Yelverton, d. 1681?), 1674.

Rastell, John (*c.* 1475-1536: printer), 1510, 1517, 1522, 1527(3).

Ravenscroft, Edward (*c.* 1643-1707: playwright), 1672, 1673, 1676, 1677(3), 1679, 1681, 1683, 1694, 1696, 1697.

Rawlins, - (unknown), 1676, 1678.

Rawlins, Thomas (*c.* 1618-70: engraver), 1638.

Redford, John (d. 1547: Master of Paul's Boys), 1539.

Revet, Edward (unknown), 1671.

Reymes, William (1629-60), 1659.

Reynolds, Henry (*fl.* 1627-32: critic), 1628.

Rho, John, *see* Roo, John.

Rhodes, Richard (*c.* 1641?-1668: poet), 1663.

Richards, Nathaniel (*fl.* 1631-41: poet), 1635.

Richards, Thomas (*c.* 1553-1620: schoolmaster), 1570.

Richards, William (1643-1705: lecturer at St Andrew's, Newcastle), 1660.

Rickets, John (*c.* 1606-a. 1646: clergyman), 1633.

Rider, W[illiam?] (Master of Arts), 1635.

Ritwise, or Rightwise, John (1490-*c.* 1532: schoolmaster), 1527(2).

Roberts, Henry (*fl.* 1585-1616: Miscellanist), 1606(2).

Roberts, John (unknown), 1574.

Robinson, - (unknown), 1602.

Robinson, Gwiliam (*fl.* 1580: unknown), 1580.

Robinson, Nicholas, Bishop of Bangor (*c.* 1528?-1585), 1553.

Roche-Guilhen, Mlle de la (writer for a visiting French troupe), 1677.

Rochester, Earl of, *see* Wilmot, John.

Rollinson, Francis (born *c.* 1575?: clergyman), 1597, 1606.

Roo, or Rho, John (*fl.* 1506-26: Gray's Inn sergeant at law), 1526.

Rowe, Nicholas (1674-1718: playwright), 1700; for later plays, *see* Nicoll, pp. 351-3, 443.

Rowley, Samuel (d. 1624: actor) 1586, 1591, 1592, 1601, 1602(2), 1604, 1623(2), 1624, 1626.

Rowley, William (d. 1626: actor), 1599, 1607,

1612, 1613, 1619, 1625(2), 1626(3), 1628, 1629, 1631(4), 1632(3), 1633(3), 1634(3), 1635(2), 1636, 1637, 1638(2), 1639(3), 1640(3), 1641(3), 1642(2), 1646, 1653, 1658(2); adapt., 1662(2), 1692.

The Dramatic Works and Poems of James Shirley . . . With Notes by the Late William Gifford, Esq. and Additional Notes and Some Account of Shirley and His Writings, by the Rev. Alexander Dyce, 6 vols, 1833; reprinted 1966.

Sidman, Jonathan (unknown), 1630(2).

Sidney, Sir Philip (1554–86: poet), 1578, 1580.
The Works of Sir Philip Sidney, A. Feuillerat, ed., 1921–6.

Simons, Joseph, *vere* Lobb, Emmanuel (1594–1671: St Omers teacher), 1623(2), 1624(2), 1626, 1627, 1631; adapt., 1669.

Singer, John (*fl.* 1583–1603: actor), 1603.

Singleton, Thomas (1621–a. 1689: schoolmaster), 1689.

Skelton, John (1460?–1529: poet), 1504, 1515(4), 1533.

Smith, – (same as Wentworth or Will., or W. Smith?), 1623.

Smith, Henry (of Clifford's Inn), 1699.

Smith, John (*c.* 1620–83), 1677.

Smith, W. (same as Wentworth, or Will. Smith?), 1602, 1614.

Smith, Wentworth (*fl.* 1601–5: playwright), 1601(4), 1602(9), 1603(3), 1614.

Smith, Will. (unknown), 1623.

Smythe, or Smith, John (1563–1616: clergyman) 1584.

Smythe, John (born 1662: school usher), 1691.

Snelling, Thomas (born 1614: Latin poet), 1640.

Southby, – (unknown), 1697.

Southerne, Thomas (1660–1746: playwright), 1682, 1684, 1690, 1691, 1692, 1693, 1694, 1695, 1700; for later plays, *see* Nicoll, pp. 355–6.
The Works of Thomas Southerne, 2 vols, R. Jordan and H. Lowe, eds, 1988.

Southland, Thomas (gentleman), 1663, 1664.

Sparrow, Thomas (born *c.* 1614?: Bishop Williams scholar), 1634.

Speed, John (1595–1640: physician), 1623, 1635, 1637.

Spencer, – (priest, turned actor), 1539.

Spenser, Edmund (1552–99: poet), presumed author of 'nine English comedies' – closet plays of unknown title composed before 1580; but plays poss. contemplated only, never written: *see* A. Gilbert, *Mod. Lang. Notes, LXXIII* (1958), 241–3.

Sprat, Thomas, Bishop of Rochester (1635–1713), 1671.

Squire, John (City poet), 1620.

Stafford, Roderick (unknown), 1566.

Stanley, Thomas (1625–78: scholar), 1655, 1663.

Stanley, William, Earl of Derby (1561–1642), reputedly wrote plays *c.* 1599.

Stapylton, or Stapleton, Sir Robert (*c.* 1600?–1669: courtier), 1653, 1663(2), 1669.

Stephens, John (*fl.* 1611–17: author), 1613.

Stevenson, William (*c.* 1521–75: Cambridge Fellow), 1553.

Stirling, Earl of, *see* Alexander, Sir William.

Strode, William (1603–45: clergyman), 1636.
The Poetical Works of William Strode, B. Dobell, ed., 1907.

Stroude, – (unknown), 1665.

Stub, Stubbe, or Stubbes, Edmund (*c.* 1594–1659: clergyman), 1619.

Studley, John (*c.* 1545–*c.* 1590: scholar), 1566(3), 1567.

Suckling, Sir John (1609–42: courtier), 1637(2), 1638(2), 1639, 1640.
The Works of Sir John Suckling, A. H. Thompson, ed., 1910.
The Works of Sir John Suckling, 2 vols, Thomas Clyton and L. A. Beaurline, eds, 1971.

Swinhoe, Gilbert (unknown), 1658.

T., I., 1600.

Tailor, Robert (*fl.* 1613–15: poet), 1613.

Talbot, Sir Gilbert (unknown), 1657.

Talbot, John (unknown), 1686.

Tarlton, Richard (d. 1588: actor), 1585(2), 1586.

Tate, Nahum (1652–1715: playwright), 1678, 1679, 1680, 1681(2), 1684, 1685, 1687, 1689: for a later play, *see* Nicoll, p. 358.

Tatham, John (d.a. 1664: miscellanist), 1632, 1641, 1650, 1652, 1657, 1658, 1659, 1660(3),

Lucas, ed., 1927; American ed., 1937; reprinted 1967.

The Selected Plays of John Webster, Jonathan Dollimore and Alan Sinfield, 1983.

Wedderburn, James (1495?-1553: merchant), 1540(2).

Westmorland, Earl of, *see* Fane, Mildmay.

Weston, John (unknown), 1667.

Wever, R. (unknown), 1550.

Wharton, *née* Lee, Anne (1632?-1685: poet), 1685.

Whetstone, George (1544?-1587?: adventurer), 1578.

Whitaker, William (unknown), 1680.

White, Robert (schoolmaster at Ladies' Hall?), 1617.

Wilburne, Wibarn, or Wilbourne, Nathaniel (1573-1613: clergyman), 1597.

Wild, Robert (1615 or 1616-79: clergyman) 1641.

Wilde, George, Bishop of Derry (1610-64), 1635, 1636, 1637.

Wilkins, George (*fl.* 1604-8: pamphleteer), 1604, 1606, 1607, 1608.

Willan, Leonard (*fl.* 1649-70), 1651, 1658.

Williams, Joseph (*fl.* 1673-1700: actor), 1694.

Wilmot, John, 2nd Earl of Rochester (1647-80), 1670, 1678; adapt., 1684.

Collected Works of John Wilmot, Earl of Rochester, J. Hayward, ed., 1926.

Wilmot, Robert (*fl.* 1566-1608: clergyman), 1566.

Wilson, Arthur (1595-1652: secretary), 1630, 1631, 1633.

Wilson, John (1627-96: lawyer), 1643, 1663, 1664(2), 1677.

The Dramatic Works of John Wilson, J. Maidment and W. H. Logan, eds, 1874.

Wilson, Robert (*fl.* 1572-1600: actor; perhaps a synthesis of the careers of two men is here represented), 1579, 1581, 1588, 1590(2), 1592, 1598(10), 1599(3), 1600(2).

Winchilsea, Countess of, *see* Finch, Anne.

Wingfield, Anthony (*c.* 1550-1615: Cambridge Proctor), 1581.

Wood, Ra[lph?], (unknown), Supp. II, g.(2).

Woodes, Nathaniel (born *c.* 1550?: Norwich clergyman) 1572.

Worseley, Ralph (d. 1590: lawyer) 1555.

Wotton, Sir Henry (1568-1639: diplomatist), 1586.

Wren, Christopher, Sr (1591-1658: clergyman), 1609.

Wright, Abraham (1611-90: clergyman), 1631.

Wright, James (1643-1713: antiquary), 1700.

Wright, John (Middle Temple lawyer?), 1674.

Wright, Thomas (theatre mechanic), 1693.

Wyatt, Ralph (unknown), 1575.

Wycherley, William (1640-1715: playwright), 1671, 1672, 1675, 1676.

The Complete Works of William Wycherley, M. Summers, ed., 1924.

The Plays of William Wycherley, Peter Holland, ed., 1981.

Wylley, Thomas (clergyman), 1537(4).

Yarington, Robert (unknown), 1594.

Yelverton, Sir Christopher (*c.* 1535-1612: judge), 1588.

Zouche, Richard (1590-1661: Oxford professor), 1614.

INDEX OF ENGLISH PLAYS

A coded record of recent or 'last' editions follows the title and date of many of the plays listed in the Index below. The expanded entries incorporate the publications previously contained in a separate List of Editions and add bibliographical information on new publications. All of the publication data following a play's title are categorized, and each category is represented by an initial which corresponds to the initial found in the seventh column of the Chronology and Information section: C designating a comprehensive collection in which the play appears; S designating the publication of an edition as part of a scholarly series; E indicating a modern edition which was not part of a series; F indicating a facsimile edition; V designating the Shakespeare Variorum edition; VS representing the publication of a Shakespeare Variorum Supplement; and T indicating a thesis edition. Because of their number and the space constraints of this publication, editions of Shakespeare's plays as well as single editions and collections are omitted. When the editor of a thesis subsequently publishes an edition of the same play, the thesis entry is omitted. Titleless plays and unidentified manuscript fragments are listed in Supplementary List I.

Abdelazer, or The Moor's Revenge, 1676.

Abdicated Prince, The, or The Adventures of Four Years, 1690.

Abenner, Josaphat, et Barachias, Supp. II, 1.

Aberdeen Plays, 15th cent.

Abraham and Isaac (Brome), 14th cent.

Abraham and Isaac (Dublin), 15th cent.

Abraham and Isaac (St Dunstan's), 15th cent.

Abraham and Lot, 1599 add.

Abraham and Lot, Supp. II, k.

Abraham's Faith, 1675.

Abraham's Sacrifice, A Tragedy of, 1575.
  E A Tragedie of Abraham's Sacrifice, (Univ. of Toronto Philol. Ser.), M.W. Wallace, ed., 1907.

Absalom, 1540.
  S 'A Humanist's "True Imitation": Thomas Watson's "Absalom" ', Illinois Studies in Lang. and Lit. (52), 1964, J.H. Smith, ed. and trans.

Absalom (MS), 1540.

Absalom, 1602.

Absalom, see Ambitio Infelix, 1622.

Abuses, 1606, Supp. II, p.

Academical Lawyer, The, see Ignoramus, 1662.

Academy, The, or The Cambridge Dons, 1675.

Achademios, 1515.

Achilles, or Iphigenia in Aulis, 1699.

Achilles and Iphigenia in Aulis, see Achilles, 1699.

Acolastus, 1540.

Actaeon and Diana, 1653; adapt., 1662.
  C The Wits, or Sport Upon Sport, J. Elson, 1932.

Actaeons, A Mask of, 1560.

Adam, 12th cent.

Adam and Eve, 1528.

Adam and Eve (Reading), 15th cent. add.

Adam and Eve, see Norwich Plays, 15th cent.

Adam's Tragedy, probably not a play.

Adelphe, 1613.
  F Renaissance Latin Drama in England, Marvin Spevack, J.W. Binns, Hans-Jurgen Weckermann, gen. eds, 1982–6; prep. & intro., G. Schmitz.

Adelphi, 1598.

Adelphi, see Comoedia Sex Anglo-Latinae, 1663.

Adelphi, see Terence's Comedies Made English, 1694.

Adoratio Crucis, 10th cent.

Adrasta, or The Woman's Spleen and Love's Conquest, 1635.

Adrastus Parentans sive Vindicta, 1622
  F Renaissance Latin Drama in England, Marvin Spevack, J.W. Binns, Hans-Jurgen Weckermann, gen. eds, 1982–6; prep. & intro., J.C. Coldewey and B.F. Copenhaver.

Adson's Mask, Supp. II, i.

Adventures for a Crown, The, *see* Bloody Duke, The, 1690.

Adventures of Five Hours, The, 1663.
    E 1) A.E.H. Swaen, ed.
        2) B. Van Thal, ed., 1928.

Adventures of Four Years, The, *see* Abdicated Prince, The, 1690.

Adventures of Venice, The, *see* Perjured Husband, The, 1700.

Aegio, 1560.

Aemilia, 1615.

Aeneas and Dido, 1607.

Aeneas and Queen Dido, The History of, 1563.

Aeschyli Tragoediae Septem, 1663.

I Aesop, 1696.

II Aesop, 1697.

Aesop's Crow, 1552.

Aethelred Troper, *see* Quem Quaeritis, 10th cent.

Against Adulterators of the Word of God, 1537.

I Against Momi and Zoili, 1537.

II Against Momi and Zoili, 1537.

Against Scoffers and Backbiters, see I & II Against Momi and Zoili, 1537.

Against the Cardinals, 1533.

Against the Pope's Councillors, 1537.

Agamemnon, 1599.

Agamemnon, 1665.

Agamemnon, The Tragedy of, 1566.
    C Seneca His Tenne Tragedies Translated into English, (Tudor trans., 2nd ser.), 1927.

Agamemnon and Ulysses, 1584, Supp. II, p.

Aglaura, 1637.
    F Scolar (1971).
    T Chicago, L.A. Beaurline, 1959–60.

Aglaura (altered), 1638.

Agnes de Castro, 1695.
    C The Plays of Mary Pix and Catherine Trotter, Edna L. Steeves, ed., 1982.

Agrippa King of Alba, or The False Tiberinus, 1669.

Agrippina, *see* Julia Agrippina, 1628.

Ahasuerus and Queen Esther, King. 1653.
    C The Wits, or Sport Upon Sport, J.J. Elson, ed., 1932.

Ajax and Ulysses, 1572.

Ajax and Ulysses, The Contention of, 1658.

Ajax Flagellifer, 1564.

Ajax Flagellifer, 1605.

Alaham, 1600.

Alarum for London, *see* Larum for London, A, 1599.

Alba, 1605.

Albere Galles, 1602.

Albertus Wallenstein, The Tragedy of, 1634.

Albion, *see* Albion Knight, 1537.

Albion and Albanius, 1685.
    W California *Dryden*, Vol. XV, E. Miner, F.B. Zimmerman, G.R. Guffey, eds, 1976.

Albion Knight, 1537.

Albion Queens, The, or The Death of Mary Queen of Scotland, *see* Island Queens, The, 1684.

Albion's Triumph, 1632.

Albovine King of the Lombards, The Tragedy of, 1628.

Albumazar, 1615.
    E Albumazar: A Comedy, (Univ. of California Pubs. in Eng., XIII), H.G. Dick, ed., 1944.

Alcamenes and Menalippa, 1698.

Alcestis, 1541; *see also* Supp. I.

Alchemist, The, 1610; adapt., 1662.
    C Yale *Ben Jonson*, Alvin Kernan, ed., 1974.
    S 1) Fountainwell, S. Musgrove, ed., 1968.
        2) *New Mermaid*, D. Brown, ed., 1966.
        3) *Revels*, Francis H. Mares, ed., 1967.

Alcibiades, 1675.

Alcmaeon, 1573.

Alderman No Conjurer, An, *see* Cuckolds Haven, 1685.

Alderman's Bargain, An, *see* Lucky Chance, The, 1686.

Aleumista, Supp. II, m.

Alexander, Campaspe, and Diogenes, *see* Campaspe, 1584.

Alexander VI, The Tragedy of Pope, *see* Devil's Charter, The, 1607.

Alexander and Lodowick, 1597.

Alexander et Aristobulus, Supp. II, 1.

Alexander the Great, The Death of, *see* Rival Queens, The, 1677.

Alexandraean Tragedy, The, 1607.

Alexius Imperator, *see* Andronicus Comnenus, 1618.

Alexius (*or* Alexis, *or* Alexias), or The Chaste Gallant, *see* Alexius, 1639.

Alexius, or The Chaste Lover, 1639.

Alfonso, *see* Alphonsus Emperor of Germany, 1594.

Alfred, or Right Re-enthroned, 1659.

Alfredus, *see* Aluredus, 1619.

Alice and Alexis, Supp. I.

Alice Pierce, 1597.

Alimony Lady, The, *see* Lady Alimony, 1659.

Alkmeon, 1573, Supp. II, p.

All Fools, 1601.

    C The Plays of George Chapman: The Comedies; Gen. ed. Allan Holaday, G. Blakemore Evans, ed., 1970.

    S Regents, Frank Manley, ed., 1968.

All Fools but the Fool, 1599.

All for Love, or The World Well Lost, 1676.

    W John Dryden: Four Tragedies, L.A. Beaurline, Fredson Bowers, eds, 1967.

    S Regents, David M. Vieth, ed., 1972.

    F Scolar (1678).

All for Money, 1577.

    E 'All for Money', *Jahrbuch de deutschen Shakespeare Gesellschaft*, XL, 129–86, E. Vogel, ed., 1904.

All in Confusion, *see* Mistakes, The, 1690.

All is Mistaken, 1671, Supp. II, j.

All Is Not Gold That Glisters, 1601; *see also* Supp. II, m.

All Is True, *see* Henry VIII, 1613.

All Manner Weathers, A New and Very Merry Interlude of, *see* Play of the Weather, The, 1528.

All Mistaken, or The Mad Couple, 1665.

All Plot, or The Disguises, 1665.

All without Money, *see* Novelty, The, 1697.

All's Lost by Lust, 1619.

    E William Rowley, His All's Lost by Lust, and A Shoemaker, a Gentleman, (U. of Pa., Pabs. in Lit. and Philol., Vol. 13, C.W. Stork, ed., 1910.

All's One, or One of the Four Plays in One, *see* Yorkshire Tragedy, A., 1606.

All's Well That Ends Well, 1602. *V* 1963.

Allot, The Pageant for John, 1590.

Almains, A Mask of, 1543.

Almains, A Mask of, 1549.

Almains and Palmers, A Mask of, 1559.

Almains and Spaniards, 1510.

Almains, Pilgrims, and Irishmen, A Great Mask of, 1557.

Almanac, The, 1611.

Almanzor and Almahide, *see* II Conquest of Granada by the Spaniards, The, 1671.

Aloysius sive Saeculi Fuga, Supp. II, 1.

Alphonso King of Naples, 1690.

Alphonsus, Supp. I.

    F Renaissance Latin Drama in England, Marvin Spevack, J.W. Binns, Hans-Jurgen Weckermann, gen. eds, 1982-6; prep. & intro., Gotz Schmitz.

Alphonsus Emperor of Germany, The Tragedy of, 1594.

Alphonsus King of Aragon, The Comical History of, 1587; *see also* Supp. II, k.

    T 1) Birmingham, N.J. Sanders, ed., 1957-8.

    2) Saint Louis, Mary Jeanette Sulzman, ed., 1968.

Altemira, *see* General, The, 1662.

Althorp, A Particular Entertainment of the Queen and Prince Their Highness at, 1603.

Alucius, The History of, 1579.

Aluredus sive Alfredus, 1619.

Amalasont Queen of the Goths, or Vice Destroys Itself, 1696.

Amazon Queen, The, or The Amours of Thalestris to Alexander the Great, 1667.

Amazon Queen of Denmark, The, *see* Landgartha, 1683.

Amazonians' Mask, The, Supp. II, i.

Amazons, A Mask of, 1579.

Amazons, The Mask of, or The Ladies' Mask, 1618.

Amazons Women of War, A Mask of, 1551.

Ambitio Infelix sive Absalom, 1622.

Ambitio Infelix, *see* Zeno, 1631.

Ambitious Brother, The, Supp. II, m.

Ambitious Father, The, *see* Injured Lovers, The, 1688.

Ambitious Politic, The, *see* Lovesick Court, The, 1639.

Ambitious Queen, The, *see* Siege of Memphis, The, 1676.

Ambitious Slave, The, or A Generous Revenge, 1694.

Ambitious Statesman, The, or The Loyal Favourite, 1679.
  E Shivaji Sengupta, ed., 1979.

Ambitious Step-Dame, The, *see*, Roxolana, Supp. II, m.

Ambitious Stepmother, The, 1700.

Amboyna, or The Cruelties of the Dutch to the English Merchants, 1672.

Amends for Ladies, 1611.

Aminta (Reynolds), 1628.

Aminta (Dancer), 1660.

Aminta, *see also* Amyntas, 1635, *and* Phillis and Amyntas, 1591.

Amintas, 1698.

Amity, The Triumph of, *see* Friendship, Prudence, and Might, 1522.

Amity of Graius and Templarius, The, *see* Gesta Grayorum, 1594.

Amores Perinthi et Tyantes, 1596.

Amoris Imago, *see* Image of Love, The, 1538.

Amorous Bigot, The, with the Second Part of Tegue O'Divelly, 1690.

Amorous Fantasm, The, 1659.

Amorous Friars, The, *see* Rome's Follies, 1681.

Amorous Gallant, The, *see* Amorous Orontus, 1664.

Amorous Jilt, The, *see* Younger Brother, The, 1696.

Amorous Old Woman, The, or 'Tis Well If It Take, 1674.

Amorous Orontus, or The Love in Fashion, 1664.

Amorous Prince, The, or The Curious Husband, 1671.

Amorous War, The, 1638.

Amorous Widow, The, or The Wanton Wife, 1670.

Amours of Thalestris to Alexander the Great, The, *see* Amazon Queen, The, 1667.

Amphitruo, Supp. II, k.

Amphitryon, 1694.
  C California *Dryden*, Vol. XV, E. Miner, F.B. Zimmerman, G.R. Guffey, eds, 1976.

Amphitryon, or The Two Socias, 1690.

Amphrisa, or The Forsaken Shepherdess, *see* Pleasant Dialogues and Dramas, 1635.

Amurath I, *see* Courageous Turk, The, 1618.

Amurath, Third Tyrant of the Turks, The Tragedy of, *see* Courageous Turk, The, 1618.

Amyntas, 1635.

Amyntas, or The Impossible Dowry, 1630; adapt., 1684.
  C The Poems and Amyntas of Thomas Randolph, J.J. Parry, ed., 1917.

Amyntas' Pastoral, *see* Phillis and Amyntas, 1591.

Ananias, Azarias, Mesael, Supp. I.

Anatomist, The, or Sham Doctor, The, 1696.
  C Ten English Farces, 1948, L. Hughes and A.H. Scouten, eds, 1948.

Ancient Roman, Botzarius, An, Supp. II, k.

Andria, 1520.

Andria, 1588.

Andria, 1598.

Andria, *see* Andrian Woman, The, 1627.

Andria, *see* Comoedia Sex Anglo-Latinae, 1663.

Andria, *see* Terence's Comedies Made English, 1694.

Andrian Woman, The, 1627.

Andromache, 1674.

Andromana, or Merchant's Wife, The, 1642.

Andronichus sive Aulae Byzantinae Vota, 1664.

Andronicus: Impiety's Long Success, or Heaven's Late Revenge, 1643.

Andronicus Comnenius, 1664.
  T George Washington, Kathleen Menzie Lesko, ed., 1980.

Andronicus Comnenus, 1618.
  F Renaissance Latin Drama in England, Marvin Spevack, J.W. Binns, Hans-Jurgen Weckermann, gen. eds, 1982–6; prep. & intro., J. Klause.

Andronicus Comnenus, 1636.

Angel King, The, 1624.

Anglia Deformata et Anglia Restituta, 1553.

Anglorum Feriae, 1595.

Anna Bullen, 1680.

Anna Bullen, *see* Virtue Betrayed, 1682.

Annabella, a Duke's Daughter of Ferrara, Supp. II, k.

Anne Boleyn, *see* Coronation Triumph of - , The, 1533.

Annunciation Play, 14th cent.

Annus Recurrens, *see* Vertumnus, 1605.

Anthony and Vallia, *see* Antony and Vallia, 1599 add., *and* Antonio and Vallia, 1620.

Anti-Bishop, The, *see* Hierarchomachia, 1629.

'Antic Play and a Comedy', 1585.

Antigone, 1581.

    F Renaissance Latin Drama in England, Marvin Spevack, J.W. Binns, Hans-Jurgen Weckermann, gen. eds, 1982–6; prep. & intro., J.C. Coldewey and B.F. Copenhaver.

Antigone the Theban Princess, The Tragedy of, 1627.

    T Case Western Reserve, Edward J. Lautner, ed., 1970.

Antipodes, The, 1638.

    C Representative English Comedies, C.M. Gayley, ed., (1903–36), 1914.

    S Regents, Ann Haaker, ed., 1966.

Antipoe, 1604.

Antipolargesis, Supp. I.

Antiquary, The, 1635.

Antonii Vindictae, *see* Antonio's Revenge, 1600.

Antoninus Bassianus Caracalla, *see* Caracalla, 1618.

    F Renaissance Latin Drama in England, Marvin Spevack, J.W. Binns, Hans-Jurgen Weckermann, gen. eds, 1982–6; prep. & intro., J.W. Binns.

I Antonio and Mellida, 1599.

    S Regents, G.K. Hunter, ed., 1965.

    T Toronto, Kathyrn L. Schoonover, ed., 1976.

II Antonio and Mellida, *see* Antonio's Revenge, 1600.

Antonio and Vallia, 1620.

Antonio of Ragusa, Supp. I.

Antonio's Revenge, 1600.

    S 1) Regents, G.K. Hunter, ed., 1965, 1966.

       2) Revels, W. Reavley Gair, ed., 1978.

Antonius, 1590.

    E The Countess of Pembroke's Antonie, A. Luce, ed., 1897.

Antony, *see* Antonius, 1590.

Antony and Cleopatra (Greville), 1601.

Antony and Cleopatra (Sedley), 1677.

    F Cornmarket (1677).

Antony and Cleopatra (Shakespeare), The Tragedy of, 1607.

Antony and Cleopatra, *see also* All for Love, 1677.

Antony and Vallia, 1599 add.

Any Rather Than Fail, *see* Maid's Last Prayer, The, 1693.

Anything for a Quiet Life, 1621.

    T California, Berkeley, Nancy Ruth Katz, ed., 1975.

Aphrodisial, The, or Sea Feast, 1602.

Apocalypse, Interpretation of a Chapter, 1534.

Apocryphal Ladies, The, 1658.

Apollo and Daphne, *see* Pleasant Dialogues and Dramas, 1635.

Apollo, the Nine Muses, and Lady Peace, A Mask of, 1572.

Apollo et Musae Exules, 1561.

Apollo Shroving, 1627.

    E Wm. Hawkins' Apollo Shroving, H.G, Rhoads, ed., 1936.

Apothecary Turned Doctor, The, *see* Physic Lies a-Bleeding, 1697.

Appius and Virginia ('R.B.'), 1564.

Appius and Virginia (Webster), 1624; adapt., 1669.

Appius and Virginia, *see* Roman Virgin, The, or Unjust Judge, 1669.

Apprentice's Prize, The, 1634.

Aqua Triumphalis, 1662.

Ara Fortunae, *see* Christmas Prince, The, 1607.

    E F.S. Boas, ed., 1922.

Arabia Sitiens, or A Dream of a Dry Year, 1601.

Arcades, 1633.

Arcadia, The, 1640.

    T Michigan, Paul A. Ramsey, ed., 1975.

Arcadia Reformed, *see*, Queen's Arcadia, The, 1605.

Arcadian Virgin, 1599.

Archer, The, *see* Honourable Entertainments, 1621.

Arches of Triumph, 1604.

Archipropheta, 1547.

    C The Life and Poems of Nicholas Grimald, Yale

Studies in Eng., no. 69, L.R. Merrill, ed., 1925.

F *Renaissance Latin Drama in England*, Marvin Spevack, J.W. Binns, Hans-Jurgen Weckermann, gen. eds, 1982–6; prep. & intro., K. Tetzeli von Rosador.

Arcules with Mariners, A Mask of, 1554.

Arden of Faversham, 1591.

C *The Shakespeare Apocrypha*, C.F. Tucker Brooke, ed., 1908; reprinted 1967.

S Revels, M.L. Wine, ed., 1973.

F Scolar, 1971.

E *Arden de Faversham*, (Collection bilingue), F. Carriere, ed., 1950.

Are Mask, Supp. II, i.

Argalus and Parthenia, 1638.

Argus, A Mask of, 1551.

Ariadne, 1654.

Ariadne, or The Marriage of Bacchus, 1674.

Ariodante and Genevora, 1583.

Ariosto, *see* Supposes, The, 1566.

Ariscancus Bila, Supp. I.

Aristippus, or Jovial Philosopher, The, 1626.

Aristomenes, or Royal Shepherd, The, 1690.

Armenian Queen, The, 1675.

Arraignment, The, *see* Poetaster, 1601.

Arraignment of London, The, 1613.

Arraignment of Paris, The, 1581.

T Yale, R.M. Benlow, ed., 1950–51.

Arsenius, *see* Magister Bonus, 1614.

Artaxerxes, Supp. I.

Artenice, L', 1626.

C *Oeuvres complètes de Racan*, J.B.T. de Latour, ed., 1857.

Arthur, The Marriage of Prince, 1501.

Arthur, *see* Misfortunes of Arthur, The, 1588.

Arthur, King, or British Worthy, The, 1691.

Arthur and his Knights, *see* Corpus Christi Procession. (Dublin), 15th cent. add.

Arthur King of England, The Life of, 1598.

Arthur's Knights, King, 1539.

Arthur's Show, *see* Arthur King of England, 1598.

I Arviragus and Philicia, 1636.

T Pennsylvania, J.E. Ruoff, ed., 1954.

II Arviragus and Philicia, 1636.

T Pennsylvania, J.E. Ruoff, ed., 1954.

As Merry as May Be, 1602.

As Plain as Can Be, 1567, Supp. II, p.

As You Like It, 1599.

V 1965; 1977; Richard Knowles, ed.

Ascanius, Supp. I.

Ashby, The Entertainment at, 1607.

C *The Poems of John Marston*, A. Davenport, ed., 1887.

Assembly, The, or Scotch Reformation, 1691.

Assignation, The, or Love in a Nunnery, 1672.

W California *Dryden*, Vol. XI, J. Loftis, D.S. Rodes, V.A. Dearing, eds, 1978.

Assumption or Coronation of the Virgin, The, 15th cent.; *see also* Lincoln Plays, 15th cent.

Astiages, 1598.

Astraea, Supp. II, 1.

Astraea, or True Love's Mirror, 1651.

Astronomers, A Mask of, 1559.

Atalanta, 1612.

S Two University Latin Plays (with Atkinson's 'Homo'), Salzburg, W.E. Mahaney, W.K. Sherwin, eds, 1973.

F *Renaissance Latin Drama in England*, Marvin Spevack, J.W. Binns, Hans-Jurgen Weckermann, gen. eds, 1982–6; prep. & intro., H.-J. Weckermann.

Athanasius sive Infamia, 1547.

Atheist, The, or The Second Part of the Soldier's Fortune, 1683.

Atheist's Tragedy, The, or The Honest Man's Revenge, 1611.

S Revels, Irving Ribner, ed., 1964.

F Scolar (1611).

Athenians' Reception of Phocion, The, 1656.

C *A Poetical Rhapsody, 1602–1621*, H.E. Rollins, ed., 1929.

Attowell's Jig, 1593.

Augurs, The Mask of, 1622.

C *The Complete Masques* (Yale Ben Jonson), Stephen Orgel, ed., 1969.

Augusta's Triumph, *see* Brutus of Alba, 1696.

Augustus Caesar, 1687.

Augustus Caesar, The Court of, *see* Gloriana, 1676.

Aulae Byzantinae Vota, *see* Andronichus, 1664.

Auld Man and His Wife, *see* Satire of the Three Estates, 1540.

Aureng-Zebe, 1675.

C 1) *Dryden: Poetry and Plays*, Douglas Grant, ed., 1952.

C 2) *John Dryden: Four Tragedies*, L.A. Beaurline, Fredson Bowers, eds. 1967.

S Regents, Frederick Link, ed., 1971.

B. Ignatius Societatis Jesu Fundator, *see* Haeresis Triumphata, Supp. II, 1.

Babions, A Mask of, 1552.

Bacchides, Supp. I.

Bacchus, 1528.

Bacchus, The Marriage of, *see* Ariadne, 1674.

Bacchus' Festival, or A New Medley, 1660.

Bacon, *see*, Friar Bacon, 1699.

Bacon in Virginia, The History of, *see* Widow Ranter, The, 1689.

Bad Beginning Makes (*or* May Have) a Good Ending, A, 1612.

Bad May Amend, alternative title for II Worse (A)feared Than Hurt, 1598?   ·

Baggs Seneca, Supp. II, d.

Bagpipes, A Mask of, 1553.

Baiting of the Jealous Knight, The, *see* Fair Foul One, The 1623.

Bajazet II, *see* Raging Turk, The, 1618.

Ball, The, 1632.

T Illinois, Dana Gene McKinnon, ed., 1966.

Ballet de la Paix, Le, 1660.

Band, Cuff, and Ruff, A Merry Dialogue between, or Exchange Ware at the Second Hand, 1615.

C 1) *The Old Book Collector's Miscellany*, C. Hindley, ed., (1871–73), 1872.

2) Academic Entertainment in the Folger Manuscripts, T. Berger and S. Gossett, eds, forthcoming.

S Malone Society: Academic Entertainments in the Folger Manuscripts, T. Berger & S. Gossett, eds, forthcoming.

Banditti, The, or A Lady's Distress, 1686.

Banished Cavaliers, The, *see* I Rover, The, 1677.

Banished Duke, The, or The Tragedy of Infortunatus, 1690.

Banished Shepherdess, The, 1660.

I Baptism and Temptation, The, 1536.

II Baptism and Temptation, The, 1536.

Baptism of Prince Henry, The, 1594.

Baptist, The, Supp. I.

Baptistes sive Calumnia, 1540; *see also* 1643; and Supp. I.

E 'An English Translation of Buchanan's Baptistes Attributed to John Milton', *George Buchanan: Glasgow Quatercentenary Studies.*, J.T.T. Brown, ed., 1907.

T 'A Critical Edition of George Buchanan's *Baptistes* and of the Anonymous Tyrannical-Government Anatomized', S.B. Berkowitz, ed., Howard, 1986.

Barbarians, A Mask of, 1560.

Barbarous Terrine, 1563.

Bargain Broken, A, *see* Canterbury Guests, The, 1694.

Barlaam et Josaphat, Supp. II, 1.

Barnardo and Fiammetta, 1595.

Barnavelt, The Tragedy of Sir John van Olden, 1619.

Bartholomew Fair, 1614.

C Yale *Ben Jonson*, Eugene M. Waith, ed., 1963.

S 1) The New Mermaids, Maurice Hussey, ed., 1964.

2) New Mermaids, *Elizabethan and Jacobean Comedies*, Brian Gibbons, ed., 1984.

3) Regents, Edward Partridge, ed., 1964.

4) Revels, E.A. Horsman, ed., 1960.

Bartholomew Fairing, A, 1649.

Bashful Lover, The, 1636.

C *The Plays and Poems of Philip Massinger*, Vol. 4 of 5 Vols., Philip Edwards, Colin Gibson, eds, 1976.

Basileia seu Bellum Grammaticale, *see* War of Grammar, The, 1666.

Basilindus, Supp. I.

Bastard, The, 1652.

Bateman, or the Unhappy Marriage, with the Humours of Sparrow, 1694.

Bateman's Ghost, 1699.

Bateman's Mask, Supp. II, i.

Battle, The, or The Rehearsal at Whitehall, 1686.

Battle between the Spirit, the Soul, and the Flesh,   · The, 1542.

Battle of Affections, The, *see* Pathomachia, 1617.

Battle of Affliction, Supp. II, d.

Battle of Agincourt, The, *see* Henry V, The
Famous Victories of, 1586.

Battle of Alcazar, The, 1589.
*C Dramatic Documents from the Elizabethan
Playhouses*, W.W. Greg, ed., 1931.

Battle of Evesham, The, *an erroneous title for* Battle
of Hexham, The, 1607.

Battle of Hexham, The, 1607.

Battle of the Vices against the Virtues, The,
Supp. I.

Bawd Turned Puritan, The, *see* Braggadocio,
The, 1691.

Baxter's Tragedy, 1602.

Bays, Supp. II, c.

Bear, The, *see* Lover's Holiday, The, Supp. II,
m.

Bear a Brain, 1599.

Bearing Down the Inn, The, *see* Cuckqueans and
Cuckolds Errants, The, 1601.

Beau Defeated, The, or The Lucky Younger
Brother, 1700.
C The Plays of Mary Pix and Catherine Trotter, I,
Edna L. Steeves, ed., 1982.

Beauties, The, *see* Bird in a Cage, The, 1633.

Beauty, The Mask of, 1608.
C The Complete Masques (Yale *Ben Jonson*)
Stephen Orgel, ed., 1969.

Beauty and Good Properties of Women, The, as
Also Their Vices and Evil Conditions, *see*
Calisto and Melebea, 1527.

Beauty and Housewifery, A Comedy of, 1582.

Beauty and Venus, 1513.

Beauty in a Trance, 1630.

Beauty in Distress, 1698.

Beauty the Best Advocate, *see* Measure for
Measure, 1700.

Beauty the Conqueror, or The Death of Marc
Antony, *see* Antony and Cleopatra, 1677.

Beauty's Triumph, 1676.

Becket, Thomas, *see* Knaveries of Thomas
Becket, The, 1538.

Becket Procession, St Thomas à (Norwich), 15th
cent.

Beech's Tragedy, *see* Thomas Merry, 1599.

Beggars, The, 1641.

Beggars Turned Thieves, The, *see* Puritanical
Justice, 1698.

Beggars' Bush, 1622; adapt., 1662.
E The Hague, J.H. Dorenkamp, ed., 1968.

Beheading of John the Baptist, The, 1540.

Bel and the Dragon, 1643.

Belial, 15th cent.

Believe as You List, 1631.
C The Plays and Poems of Philip Massinger, vol. 3
of 5 vols, Philip Edwards, Colin Gibson,
eds, 1976.

Believe It Is So and 'Tis So, 1629.

Belin Dun, *see* Bellendon, 1594.

Belinus, Brennus, 1610.

Belisarius, *see* Fortunae Ludibrium, 1651.

Bell in Campo, 1658.

Bellamira, or The Mistress, 1687.

I Bellamira Her Dream, or The Love of Shadows,
1652.
F Blom, *Comedies and Tragedies*, 1664.

II Bellamira Her Dream, or The Love of
Shadows, 1652.
F Blom, *Comedies and Tragedies*, 1664.

Bellendon, 1594.

Bellman of London, The, *see* Arraignment of
London, The, 1613.

Bellman of Paris, The, 1623.

Bellum Grammaticale, Supp. II, 1.

Bellum Grammaticale sive Nominum Verbor-
umque Discordia Civilis, 1582.
E Andrea Guarnas, *Bellum Grammaticale und
Seine Nachahmungen*, J. Bolte, ed., 1908.
F Renaissance Latin Drama in England,
Marvin Spevack, J.W. Binns, Hans-Jurgen
Weckermann, gen. eds, 1982–6; prep. &
intro., L. Cerny.

Bellum Grammaticale, *see* War of Grammar,
The, 1666.

Belly Wager, The, *see* Self-Interest, 1659.

Belphegor, or The Marriage of the Devil, 1677.
T George Washington, Kathleen Menzie
Lesko, ed., 1980.

Belyn Dun, The Life and Death of, *see* Bellendon,
1594.

Bendo (*or* Byndo) and Richardo, 1599 add.

Benefice, The, 1641.

Bergeries, Les, *see* Artenice, L', 1626.

Berowne, *see* Biron, 1602.

Berwick, Speech to King James I at, 1603.

Bottom the Weaver, The Merry Conceited Humours of, 1661; *see also* 1673.

Botzarius, *see* Ancient Roman, An, Supp II, k.

Bouncing Knight, The, or The Robbers Robbed, 1662.

Bourbon, *see* Burbon, 1599 add.

Boys, A Mask of, 1577.

Braggadocio, The, or The Bawd Turned Puritan, 1691.

Brandimer, 1599 add.

Branhowlte, 1597.

Brazen Age, The, 1611.

    T Vanderbilt, Rose Ann Marie Cacciola, ed., 1969.

Brennoralt, or The Discontented Colonel, 1639.

Brennus, *see* Belinus, 1610.

Bretbie, A Mask Presented at, 1640.

Bridals, The, 1665.

Bride, The, 1638.

    T Michigan, Donna Jean Barcy Lurie, ed., 1974.

Bridegr[oom], The, 1619.

Bridegroom and the Madman, The, *see* Bridegr[oom], The, 1619.

Bristol, The Entertainment at, 1613.

    C *The Progresses, Processions, and Magnificent Festivities of King James The First. . . .*, J. Nichols, ed., 1828.

Bristow, The Queen's Entertainment at, 1574.

Bristow Merchant, The, 1624.

Bristow Tragedy, 1602.

Britain's Burse, Entertainment at, for James I, 1609.

Britannia Triumphans, 1638.

Britanniae Primitiae sive S. Albanus Proto-martyr, Supp. I.

Britannia's Honour, 1628.

Britannicus, or The Man of Honour, 1695.

British Heroine, The, *see* Bonduca, 1695.

British Worthy, The, *see* Arthur, King, 1691.

Broken Heart, The, 1630.

    C *Selected Plays of John Ford*, Colin Gibson, ed., 1986.

    S 1) New Mermaid, B.R. Morris, ed., 1965.
       2) Regents, Donald K. Anderson, ed., 1968.
       3) Revels, T.J.B. Spencer, ed., 1980.

    E *Le Coeur Brisé* (Collection bilingue), R. Davril, ed., 1954.

Brome Abraham and Issac, 14th cent.

Broom-Man, The, 1595.

Brothers, The, 1626.

Brothers, The, 1641.

    C *The Works of the British Dramatists*, J.S. Keltie, ed., 1870.

Brougham Castle, The Entertainment at, 1618.

Brox(burn) bury Mask, Supp. II, i.

Brunhild, *see* Branhowlte, 1597.

Brute, *see* I Conquest of Brute, 1598.

Brute Greenshield, *see* II Conquest of Brute, 1598.

Brutus of Alba, or Augusta's Triumph, 1696.

Brutus of Alba, or The Enchanted Lovers, 1678.

    T Rhode Island, Robert Russell Craven, ed., 1976.

Bubble, The, 1662.

Buck Is a Thief, The, 1623.

Buckingham, 1599 add.

Buckingham's Mask, The Duke of, 1627.

Buenas Noches, *see* Bonos Nochios, 1609.

Bugbears, The, 1564.

    S Garland, James Drummond Clark, ed., 1979.

Building of the Royal Exchange, The, *see* II If You Know Not Me You Know Nobody, 1605.

Bull Mask, The, Supp. II, i.

Bumpkin, The Humour of, 1662.

Burbon, 1599 add.

Burial and Resurrection, The, 1536.

Burial and Resurrection of Christ, The, 15th cent.

Burley, The Mask at, 1624.

Burone, *see* Biron, 1602.

Bury Fair, 1689.

Bury St Edmunds Fragment, 14th cent.

Bury St Edmunds Plays, or Dumb Shows, 15th cent.

Bussy D'Ambois, 1604.

II Bussy D'Ambois, *see* Revenge of Bussy D'Ambois, The, 1610; adapt., 1691.

Bussy D'Ambois, or The Husband's Revenge, 1691.

    C *Five Restoration Theatrical Adaptations* (Eighteenth-Century English Drama Series)

(Facsimile Reproduction), Edward A. Langhans, ed., 1979.

S 1) New Mermaid, Maurice Evans, ed., 1966.

2) Regents, Robert J. Lordi, ed., 1964.

3) Revels, Nicholas Brooke, ed., 1964.

E *Bussy D'Ambois* (Collection bilingue), J. Jacquot, ed., 1960.

Byndo and Richardo, *see* Bendo and Richardo, 1599 add.

I Byron, Charles Duke of, *see* Conspiracy and Tragedy of Charles Duke of Byron, The, 1608.

II Byron, Charles Duke of, *see* Conspiracy and Tragedy of Charles Duke of Byron, The, 1608.

Byron's Conspiracy, *see* Conspiracy and Tragedy of Charles Duke of Byron, The, 1608.

Byron's Tragedy, *see* Conspiracy and Tragedy of Charles Duke of Byron, The, 1608.

Byrsa Basilica sive Regale Excambium, 1633.

E *Byrsa Basilica, Materials for the Study of the Old English Drama*, H. de Vocht, gen. ed., R.H. Bowers, ed. and trans., 1939.

F *Renaissance Latin Drama in England*, Marvin Spevack, J.W. Binns, Hans-Jurgen Weckermann, gen. eds, 1982–6; prep. & intro., Sabine V. Bŭckmann de Villegas.

I Caesar and Pompey, 1594.

II Caesar and Pompey, 1595.

Caesar and Pompey, 1605.

Caesar and Pompey, The History of, 1581.

Caesar and Pompey, The Tragedy of, or Caesar's Revenge, 1595.

E 'The Tragedie of Caesar and Pompey, or Caesars Reuenge', Jahrbuch der deutschen Shakespeare Geselleschaft, XLVII, 132–55 and XLVIII, 37–80, W. Muhlfeld, ed., 1911–12.

Caesar Borgia, Son of Pope Alexander VI, 1679.

Caesar Interfectus, 1582.

Caesar's Fall, 1602.

Caesar's Revenge, *see* Caesar and Pompey, The Tragedy of, 1595.

Caiphas, 14th cent.

E C. Brown, 'Caiphas as a Palm-Sunday Prophet', *Kittredge Anniversary Papers*, ed. F.N. Robinson *et al.*

Caius Marius, The History and Fall of, 1679.

C *Five Restoration Theatrical Adaptations* (Eighteenth-Century English Drama Series) (Facsimile Reproductions) Edward L. Langhans, ed., 1979.

F Cornmarket (1680).

T Denver, J.E. Spring, ed., 1951–3.

Calais, The Manner of the Triumphs at, 1532.

Caligula, 1698.

Calisto, or The Chaste Nymph, 1675.

Calisto, or The Escapes of Jupiter, 1625.

S Malone Society, (From the Autograph MS Egerton, 1994), H.D. Janzen, ed., 1976.

Calisto and Melebea, 1527.

Calisto and Meliboea, *see* Spanish Bawd, The, 1631.

Calistus, 1580.

Callidamus et Callanthia, *see* Fraus Honesta, 1619.

Calthrop, The Pageant for Martin, 1588.

Cambises, A Lamentable Tragedy of, 1561.

T Illinois, Robert Carl Johnson, ed., 1964.

Cambridge Dons, The, *see* Academy, The, 1675.

Cambyses King of Persia, 1671.

T Southern California, Richard Barsam, ed., 1967.

Campaigners, The, or The Pleasant Adventures at Brussels, 1698.

Campaspe, 1583.

T Toronto, Herbert Joseph Batt, ed., 1975.

Campbell, or The Ironmongers' Fair Field, 1609.

Cancer, 1612.

F *Renaissance Latin Drama in England*, Marvin Spevack, J.W. Binns, Hans-Jurgen Weckermann, gen. eds, 1982–6; prep. & intro., T.W. Best.

Candia Restaurata, *see* Candy Restored, 1641.

Candlemas Day and the Killing of the Children of Israel, *see* Massacre of Innocents, The, 15th cent.

Candy Restored, 1641.

Canterbury Guests, The, or A Bargain Broken, 1694.

T Rochester, Edmund Henry, ed., 1976.

Canterbury His Change of Diet, A New Play Called, 1641.

Canterbury Plays, 15th cent.

Canute, *see* Hardicanute, 1599 add.

Captain, The, 1612; adapt.?, 1677.

Captain, The, or Town Miss, 1677.

Captain Mario, 1577.

Captain Thomas Stukeley, 1596.

   C *School of Shakespeare*, Richard Simpson, ed., 1878; reprinted 1973.

   S Malone Society, Judith C. Levinson, ed., 1970.

Captain Underwit, *see* Country Captain, The, 1640.

Captiva Religio, 1612.

Captive Lady, The, Supp. I.

   S Malone Society (From the Ms. Osborn Collection, Yale U. Library), A.R. Braunmuller, ed., 1982.

Captives, The, 1665.

Captives, The, or The Lost Recovered, 1624.

Capture of Stuhlweissenburg, The, 1602.

Caracalla, Antoninus Bassianus, 1618.

Caradoc the Great, The True Chronicle History of the Life and Valiant Deeds of, *see* Valiant Welshman, The, 1612.

Cardenio, 1613.

Cardenno, *see* Cardenio, 1613.

Cardinal, The, 1641.

   S Revels, E.M. Yearling, ed., 1986.

   F C.R. Forker, ed., 1964.

Cardinal Wolsey, *see* Wolsey, 1601.

Cardinal's Conspiracy, The, 1639.

Cards, The Play of, *see* Game of the Cards, A, 1582.

Careless Lovers, The 1673.

   T Rochester, Edmund Henry, ed., 1976.

Careless Shepherdess, The, 1619.

Cariclea, *see* Theagenes and Chariclea, 1572.

Carnival, The, 1663.

Carwidgeon, The, *see* Hengist King of Kent, 1618.

Case Is Altered, The, 1597.

Castara, or Cruelty without Hate, Supp. II, b.

Castle Dangerous, The, 1512.

Castle of Perseverance, The, 15th cent.

   C 1) *Perseverance, Wisdom, Mankind, 1972*

(A Facsimile Edition with Facing Transcriptions), David Bevington, ed., 1972.

   2) *The Macro Plays* (EETS 262), Mark Eccles, ed., 1969.

   T *A Critical Edition*, Toronto, D.M. Parry, ed., 1983.

Castle of Security, The, 1570.

Cataclysm, The, or General Deluge of the World, *see* Noah's Flood, 1679.

Catchpole, The, *see* Roaring Girl, The, 1640.

Catherine, Queen, *see* Queen Catherine, 1698.

Catilina, Supp. II, 1.

Catilina Triumphans, Supp. II, h.

Catiline, *see* Catiline's Conspiracy, 1598.

Catiline, *see* Short and Sweet, 1579.

Catiline, *see* Sylla Dictator, 1588.

Catiline His Conspiracy, 1611.

   S Regents, W.F. Bolton, Jane F. Gardner, eds, 1973.

Catiline's Conspiracies, 1578.

Catiline's Conspiracy, 1598.

Cats, A Mask of, 1553.

Cautious Coxcomb, The, *see* Sir Salomon, 1670.

Cawsome, The Entertainment at, 1613.

Cecil House, The Entertainment at, 1602.

   C *The Poems of John Davies* (Early Eng. Poets), A.B. Grosart, ed., 1876.

   C *The Progress and Public Processions of Queen Elizabeth*, J. Nichols, ed., 1823.

Celestina, 1598.

Celestina, *see* Calisto and Melebea, 1527.

Celestina, *see* Spanish Bawd, The, 1631.

Celinde and Sedea, Supp. II, k.

Cenofalles, The History of the, *see* Cynocephali, The 1577.

Censure of the Judges, The, or The Court Cure, *see* Mercurius Britannicus, 1641.

Cephalus et Procris, 1627.

   F *Renaissance Latin Drama in England*, Marvin Spevack, J.W. Binns, Hans-Jurgen Weckermann, gen. eds, 1982–6; prep. & intro., B. Nugel.

Ceres, 1528.

Certain Devices and Shows Presented to Her Majesty at Greenwich, *see* Misfortunes of Arthur, The, 1588.

Chabot Admiral of France, The Tragedy of, 1612.

Challenge at Tilt, A, 1613.
   C The Complete Masques (Yale *Ben Jonson*), Stephen Orgel, ed., 1969.

Challenge for Beauty, A. 1635.
   T Duke, W.W. Powell, ed., 1958.

Chambermaid Turned Quaker, The, *see* Country Innocence, The, 1677.

Chance Medley, 1598.

Chances, The, 1617, adapt., 1667.

Change, The, 1642.

Change Is No Robbery, or The Bearing Down of the Inn, *see* Cuckqueans and Cuckolds Errants, The, 1601.

Change of Crowns, The, 1667.
   E F.S. Boas, ed., 1949.

Change of Government, The, *see* Conspiracy, The, 1680.

Changeling, The, 1622.
   S 1) New Mermaids, Patricia Thompson, ed., 1964.
     2) Regents, George Walton Williams, ed., 1966, 1967.
     3) Revels, N.W. Bawcutt, ed., 1958; rev. ed. 1961 (paper 1970).
   T Wisconsin, R.G. Laurence, ed., 1956.

Changes, or Love in a Maze, 1632.
   T Chicago, Henrietta Louise Herod, ed., 1942.

Chaos of the World, The, Supp. II, j.

Character of the Mountebank, The, *see* News out of the West, 1647.

Chariclea, 1572.

Chariclea, *see* Queen of Ethiopia, The, 1578.

Charity Triumphant, or The Virgin Show, 1655.

Charlemagne, or The Distracted Emperor, 1604.
   S Malone Society, (Egerton MS 1994), J. Johnson, ed., 1938.

Charles Duke of Bourbon, 1641.

Charles Duke of Burgundy, Supp. II, k.

Charles Duke of Byron, 1608.

Charles His Entertainment and London's Loyalty, King, 1641.

Charles I, The Entertainment of King, *see* Edinburgh, The Entertainment of King Charles into, 1633.

Charles I, The Famous Tragedy of King, 1649.

Charles I, The Martyrdom of the Late King, *see* Tragical Actors, The, 1660.

Charles II, The Coronation Entertainment for, *see* Coronation, The Relation of . . . , 1661.

Charles II, *see* Presentation for the Prince on His Birthday, A, 1638.

Charles V, The Welcome for Emperor, 1522.

Charles VIII of France, The History of, or The Invasion of Naples by the French, 1671.

Chaste Gallant, The, *see* Alexius, 1639.

Chaste Lady, The, *see* Erminia, 1661.

Chaste Lady, The, *see* Toy to Please Chaste Ladies, A, 1595.

Chaste Lover, The, *see* Alexius, 1639.

Chaste Maid in Cheapside, A, 1613.
   S 1) Fountainwell, C. Barber, ed., 1969.
     2) New Mermaids, A. Brissenden, ed., 1968.
     3) Revels, R.B. Parker, ed., 1969.
   F Scolar (1630).
   T Michigan, R.J. Wall, ed., 1958.

Chaste Nymph, The, *see* Calisto, 1675.

Chaste Virgin, The, 1658.

Chaste Woman against Her Will, The, Suppl. II, e.

Chastity and Time, 1564.

Cheater and the Clown, The, *see* Hengist King of Kent, 1618.

Cheater Cheated, The, 1673.

Cheaters Cheated, The, 1660.
   C The Elizabethan Jig, G.R. Baskerville, ed. 1929.

Cheaters' Holiday, The, *see* Drinking Academy, The, 1629.

Cheats, The, 1663.
   E John Wilson's The Cheats, M.C. Nahum, ed., 1935.
   T George Washington, Kathleen Menzie Lesko, ed., 1980.

Cheats of Scapin, The, *see* Titus and Berenice, 1677.

Chelmsford Play, 15th cent. add.

Chester Corpus Christi Play, 15th cent. add.

Chester Plays, 14th cent., *see* List of Medieval Plays.

T 1) 'An Edition of Plays XI through XV of the Chester Cycle', Chicago, Allen D. Goldhamer, ed., 1971.

2) 'A Tentative Edition of Plays XVII through XXI of the Chester Cycle Based upon a Preliminary Reconsideration of the Manuscripts and the Editorial Method They Require', Chicago, Irene Skala, 1970.

Chester Tragedy, *see* Randall Earl of Chester, 1602.

Chester's Triumph, 1610.

E *Chester's Triumph in Honor of Her Prince* . . . (Chetham Soc. Pubs., III), T. Corser (?), ed., 1844.

Chief Promises of God unto Man, A Tragedy or Interlude Manifesting the, *see* God's Promises, 1538.

Child Hath Found His Father, The, *see* Birth of Merlin, The, 1608.

Chinon of England, 1596.

Chirke Castle, The Entertainment at, 1634.

C *Inigo Jones, a Life; and Five Court Masques*, P. Cunningham and J.P. Collier, 1848.

Chiswick, The Entertainment at, 1602.

Chloridia: Rites to Chloris and Her Nymphs, 1631.

C *The Complete Masques* (Yale *Ben Jonson*) Stephen Orgel, ed., 1969.

Christ and the Doctors, 1536.

Christ Jesus Triumphant (Day, J. & R.), not dramatic.

Christ's Burial and Resurrection, *see* Burial and Resurrection of Christ, The, 15th cent.

Christ's Passion (Anon.), 1618.

Christ's Passion (Sandys), 1640.

Christ's Resurrection, *see* Resurrection of Our Lord, The, 1545.

Christabella, Supp. II, k.

Christi Descensus ad Inferos, 15th cent.

Christian Turned Turk, A, or The Tragical Lives and Deaths of the Two Famous Pirates, Ward and Dansiker, 1610.

C 'Robert Daborne's Plays', *Anglia*, XX, 153–256, and XXI, 373–440, A.E.H. Swaen, 1898–9.

Christiana Fortitudo, *see* Vitus, 1623.

Christianetta, or Marriage and Hanging Go by Destiny, 1633.

Christmas Comes but Once a Year, 1602.

Christmas His Mask, 1616.

C *The Complete Masques* (Yale *Ben Jonson*), Stephen Orgel, ed., 1969.

Christmas His Show, *see* Christmas His Mask, 1616.

'Christmas Messe, A', 1619.

S Malone: *Academic Entertainments in the Folger Manuscripts*, T. Berger and S. Gossett, eds, forthcoming.

T ' "A Christmas Messe", "Giganto-machia", "Heteroclitanomalonomia": Three Hitherto Unpublished Jacobean Dramatic Works of Probable University Origin', Bowling Green State, David Lee Russell, 1979.

Christmas Ordinary, The, 1660.

Christmas Prince, The, 1607 and 1608.

E F.S. Boas, ed., 1922.

F *Renaissance Latin Drama in England*, Marvin Spevack, J.W. Binns, Hans-Jurgen Weckermann, gen. eds, 1982–6; prep. & intro., E.J. Richards.

Christmas Tale, A., or The Knight and the Cobbler, Supp. II, m.

Christus Nascens, 1540.

Christus Redivivus, 1540.

F *Renaissance Latin Drama in England*, Marvin Spevack, J.W. Binns, Hans-Jurgen Weckermann, gen. eds, 1982–6; prep. & intro., K. Tetzeli von Rosador.

Christus Triumphans, 1556.

F *Renaissance Latin Drama in England*, Marvin Spevack, J.W. Binns, Hans-Jurgen Weckermann, gen. eds, 1982–6; prep. & intro., J.H. Smith.

Chrysanaleia: The Golden Fishing, or Honour of Fishmongers, 1616.

E *The Fishmongers' Pageant on Lord Mayor's Day, 1616*, 1869.

Chryso-Thriambos, 1611.

F J.H.P. Pafford, 1962.

C *The Lord Mayor's Pageants*, F.W. Fairholt, ed., 1844.

Cicero, Marcus Tullius, That Famous Roman

Cloudy Queen and Singing Moor, The, Supp. II, m.

Clowns, A Mask of, 1560.

Club Law, 1599.

    E G.C. Moore Smith, ed., 1907.

Club-Men, The, 1662.

Clyomon and Clamydes, 1570; *see also* Supp. II, k.

    E The Hague: Mouton, Betty J. Littleton, ed., 1968.

Clytophon, 1625.

    F Renaissance Latin Drama in England, Marvin Spevack, J.W. Binns, Hans-Jurgen Weckermann, gen. eds, 1982–6; prep. & intro., M.J. Arnold.

Cobbler (of Queenhithe), The, 1597.

Cobbler's Prophecy, The, 1590.

    T University of Illinois, Sarah T. Sisson, ed., 1942.

Cock, The, *see* Honourable Entertainments, 1621.

Cockle de Moye, *see* Dutch Courtesan, The, 1604.

Coelum Britannicum, 1634.

    F Poems, 1640.

Coffee-House, The, *see* Knavery in All Trades, 1664.

Coffee-House, The, *see* Tarugo's Wiles, 1667.

Cola's Fury, or Lirenda's Misery, 1645.

Coleoverton, A Mask Presented at, 1618.

    E Die Englischen Maskenspiele, R. Brotanek, ed., 1902.

College of Canonical Clerks, The, 1567.

Collier, The History of the, 1576.

Colonel, The, *see* Siege, The 1629.

Columbus, a title now believed to be a Collier forgery.

Combat of Caps, The, *see* School Moderator, 1647.

Combat of Love and Friendship, The, 1638.

Combat of the Tongue and Five Senses for Superiority, The, *see* Lingua, 1607.

Come See a Wonder, 1623.

Come to My Country House, *see* Cra[fty?] Merchant, The, 1623.

Comedy in Disguises, A, *see* Welsh Ambassador, The, 1623.

Comedy of Errors, The, 1592.

Comedy of Humours, The, *see* Humorous Day's Mirth, An, 1597.

Comical Hash, The, 1658.

Comical Revenge, The, or Love in a Tub, 1664.

Comical Transformation, A, *see* Devil of a Wife, The, 1686.

Committee, The, 1662.

    E Sir Robert Howard's Comedy, 'The Committee', C.N. Thurber, ed., 1921.

I Committee-Man Curried, The, 1647.

II Committee-Man Curried, The, 1647.

Common Conditions, 1576.

    E Common Conditions (Yale Elizabethan Club Reprints), C.F.T. Brooke, ed., 1915.

Commonwealth of Women, A, 1685.

    C Bibliothica Curiosa, E. Goldsmed, ed., 1886.

'Comoedia, Adoptivus', 1699.

Comoedia Sex Anglo-Latinae, 1663.

'Comoediae', Supp. II, j.

'Comoediae aliquot Sacrae', Supp. II, j.

'Comoediolae', 1495.

Complaint of the Satyrs, *see* Althorp, A Particular Entertainment . . . at, 1603.

Comus, 1634.

Comus the Great Sir of Feasts, *see* Honourable Entertainments, 1621.

Concealed Fancies, The, 1645.

    E 'The Concealed Fansyes: A Play by Lady Jane Cavendish and Lady Elizabeth Brackley', PMLA, XLVI, 802–38, N.C. Starr, ed., 1931.

Concealed Royalty, The, or The May Queen, 1674.

Conceited Cuckold, The, *see* Politic Whore, The, 1680.

Conceited Duke, The, 1639.

Conceited Pedlar, The, 1627.

Conceits, The, Supp. II, b.

Concessus Animalium, *see* Synedrii, 1555.

Concordia Regularis, *see* Regularis Concordia, 10th cent.

Conference between a Gentleman Huisher and a Post, A, probably part of Cecil House, The Entertainment at, 1602.

Confessor, 1634.

    F Renaissance Latin Drama in England,

Marvin Spevack, J.W. Binns, Hans-Jurgen Weckermann, gen. eds, 1982–6; prep. & intro., Sabine V. Bŭckmann de Villegas.

Conflict of Conscience, The, 1572.

Conjuratis Papistica, *see* Talpae, 1689.

Connan Prince of Cornwall, 1598; related, 1623.

Conquerors, A Mask of, 1559.

Conqueror's Custom, The, or The Fair Prisoner, 1626.

I Conquest of Brute, with the First Finding of the Bath, The, 1598.

II Conquest of Brute, The, 1598.

Conquest of China by the Tartars (Howard), The, 1670.

Conquest of China by the Tartars (Settle), The, 1675.

I Conquest of Granada by the Spaniards, The, 1670.
   C California *Dryden*, Vol. XI, J. Loftis, D.S. Rodes, V.A. Dearing, eds, 1978.

II Conquest of Granada by the Spaniards, The, 1671.
   C California *Dryden*, Vol. XI, J. Loftis, D.S. Rodes, V.A. Dearing, eds, 1978.

Conquest of Ireland, The, *see* Royal Flight, The, 1690.

Conquest of Lady Scorn, The, 1522.

Conquest of Mexico by the Spaniards, The, *see* Indian Emperor, The, 1665.

Conquest of Queen Judith, The, *see* Prince's Ball, The, 1682.

Conquest of Spain by John of Gaunt, The, 1601.

Conquest of the West Indies, The, 1601.

Conspiracy, The, 1635.

Conspiracy, The, or The Change of Government, 1680.

Conspiracy and Tragedy of Charles Duke of Byron, The, 1608.
   T Rochester, G.W. Ray, III, ed., 1966.

Conspiracy of Gunpowder Treason under the Parliament House, Supp. II, j.

Constans Fratricida, *see* Sanguis Sanguinem, Supp. I.

Constans in Aula Virtus, *see* Theoctistus, 1624.

Constant Couple, The, or A Trip to the Jubilee, 1699.

Constant Maid, The, (Love Will Find out the Way), 1638.

Constant Nymph, The, or The Rambling Shepherd, 1677.

Constantine, 1599 add.

Constantine the Great, 1683.

Constantinus, Supp. II, 1.

Contented Cuckold, The, or The Woman's Advocate, 1692.

Contention between Eteocles and Polynices, The, *see* Destruction of Thebes, The, 1569.

Contention between Liberality and Prodigality, The, 1601.

Contention betwixt a Wife, a Widow, and a Maid, A, *see* Cecil House, The Entertainment at, 1602.

I Contention betwixt the Two Famous Houses of York and Lancaster, The, *see* II Henry VI, 1591. For the second part, *see* III Henry VI, 1591.

Contention for Honour and Riches, The, 1631.

Contention of Ajax and Ulysses for the Armour of Achilles, The, 1658.

I Contention of the Two Famous Houses, York and Lancaster, The, *see* II Henry VI, 1591.

II Contention of the Two Famous Houses, York and Lancaster, The, *see* III Henry VI, 1591.

Contra Adulterantes Dei Verbum, *see* Against Adulterators of the Word of God, 1537.

Contract Broken Justly Revenged, A, *see* Noble Spanish Soldier, The, 1626.

Convent of Pleasure, The, 1665.

Conversion of St Paul, The, 15th cent.

Converted Conjurer, The, *see* Two Noble Ladies, The, 1622.

I Converted Courtesan, The, *see* I Honest Whore, The, 1604.

II Converted Courtesan, The, *see* II Honest Whore, The, 1605.

Converted Robber, The, 1637.

Converted Twins, The, *see* St Cecily, 1666.

Converts, The, *see* Folly of Priest-Craft, The, 1690.

Converts, The, *see* Pandora, 1663.

Coridon and Phyllida, *see* Elvetham, The Entertainment to the Queen at, 1591.

Corinthian Queen, The, *see* Zelmane, 1692.

Coriolanus, The Fall of Caius Martius, *see* Ingratitude of a Commonwealth, The, 1681.

Coriolanus, The Tragedy of, 1608; adapt., 1681.

Cornelia (Kyd), 1594.

Cornelia (Bartley), 1662.

Cornelianum Dolium, 1638.

Cornish Comedy, The, 1696.

Cornish Ordinalia, *see* Ordinalia, 14th cent.

Corona Minervae, 1636.

Coronation, The, 1635.

Coronation Entry of Queen Mary, 1553.

Coronation of King Edward VI, The, 1547.
> *C De Rebus Collectanea*, J. Leland, comp., 1774.

Coronation of Queen Elizabeth with the Restoration of the Protestant Religion, The, or The Downfall of the Pope, 1680.

Coronation of the Virgin, The, *see* Assumption of the Virgin, The, 15th cent.

Coronation Triumph, The, 1604; *see also* Arches of Triumph, 1604.

Coronation Triumph of Anne Boleyn, The, 1533.

Coronation Triumph of Henry VIII, The, 1509.

Coronation Triumph of Queen Elizabeth, The, 1559.
> *C An English Garner*, E. Arber, ed., 1903.

Coronation, The Relation of His Majesty's Entertainment Passing through the City of London to His, 1661.

Corporal, The, 1633.

Corpus Christi Pageant (Bungay), 15th cent. add.

Corpus Christi Play (Heybridge), 15th cent. add.

Corpus Christi Play (Dunmow), 15th cent. add.

Corpus Christi Play (Chester), 15th cent. add.

Corpus Christi Play (Chelmsford), 15th cent. add.

Corpus Christi Play (Kendal), 15th cent. add.

Corpus Christi Play (Doncaster), 15th cent. add.

Corpus Christi Plays or Pageants (Hereford), 15th cent.

Corpus Christi Plays, *see* Beverley Plays, 14th cent.; Bury St Edmunds Plays, 15th cent.; Canterbury Plays, 15th cent.; Chester plays, 14th cent.; Coventry Plays, 14th cent.; Hereford Plays, 15th cent.; Ipswich Plays, 14th cent.; Lincoln Plays, 15th cent.; Ludus Coventriae, 15th cent.; Newcastle Plays, 15th cent.; Wakefield Plays, 14th cent.; Worcester Plays, 15th cent.; York Plays, 14th cent.

Corpus. Christi Procession (King's Lynn), 15th cent.

Corpus Christi Procession (Norwich), 15th cent.

Corpus Christi Procession (Coventry), 15th cent.

Corpus Christi Procession (Dublin), 15th cent. add.

Corruptiones Legum Divinarum, *see* Three Laws of Nature, Moses, and Christ, A Comedy Concerning, 1538.

Cosmo, The Comedy of, 1599 add.

Costly Whore, The, 1620.
> *C Old English Plays*, A.H. Bullen, ed., (1882–5), 1885.

Council of Bishops, The, 1536.

Count of Angiers, The, Supp. II, k.

Counter Scuffle, The, the Second Part, *see* New Droll, A.

Counterfeit Bridegroom, The, or The Defeated Widow, 1677.
> *S* Salzburg (JDS 94), M.S. Balch, ed., 1980.

Counterfeits, The, 1678.

Country Captain, The, 1640.
> *C Old English Plays*, A.H. Bullen, ed., (1882–85), 1883.

Country Court, The, 1640.

Country Gentleman, The, 1669.

Country Girl, The, 1632; adapt., 1677.

Country House, The, 1698.

Country Innocence, The, or The Chambermaid Turned Quaker, 1677.

Country Justice, The, *see* Friar Bacon, 1699.

Country Knight, The, 1675.

Country Revel, or The Revel of Aldford, 1671.
> *C* John Aubrey, *Brief Lives*, A. Clark, ed., 1898.

Country Tragedy in Vacunium, A, or Cupid's Sacrifice, 1602.

Country Wake, The, 1696.

Country Wife, The, 1675.
> *E* *The Country Wife by William Wycherley* (Smith Coll. Stud. in Mod. Lang., vol. XII), U. Todd-Naylor, ed., 1931.
> *S* 1) New Mermaids (Based on First Quarto,

1675), John D. Hunt, ed., 1973.

2) Regents, Thomas H. Fujimura, ed., 1965.

3) Revels, David Cook, John Swannell, eds, 1975.

  F Scolar, (1675).

Country Wit, The, 1676.

Countryman, The, 1657.

Countryman, The, Supp. II, a.

Courage, Kindness, Cleanness, 1539.

Courage of Love, The, *see* Love and Honour, 1634.

Courageous Turk, The, or Amurath I, 1619.

  S Malone Society, (From the editions of 1631 and 1632). Carnegie, ed., 1968.

  T Tulane, Susan Gushee O'Malley, ed., 1973.

Coursing of a Hare, The, or The Madcap, 1633.

Court Beggar, The, 1640.

Court Cure, The, *see* Mercurius Britannicus, 1641.

Court of Augustus Caesar, The, *see* Gloriana, 1676.

Court of Comfort, The, 1578.

Court Purge, A, Supp. II, m.

Court Secret, The, 1642.

  T Iowa, Linda Kay Ward Ellinger, ed., 1979.

Courtship à la Mode, 1700.

Covent Garden, 1633.

Covent Garden Weeded, The, *see* Weeding of the Covent Garden, The, 1632.

Coventry Hock-Tuesday Play, *see* Princely Pleasures at Kenilworth, The, 1575.

Coventry Plays, 14th cent.

Covetous Men, A Mask of, 1552.

Cowdray, The Speeches and Entertainment of the Queen at, 1591.

Cox of Collumpton, 1599.

Coxcomb, The, 1609.

Crack Me This Nut, 1595.

Cradle of Security, The, *see* Castle of Security, The, 1570.

Craft upon Subtlety's Back, 1570 add.

I Crafty Cromwell, or Oliver Ordering Our New State, 1648.

II Crafty Cromwell, or Oliver in His Glory as King, 1648.

Cra[fty?] Merchant, The, or Come to My Country House, 1623.

Creation of Eve with the Expelling of Adam and Eve out of Paradise, The, *see* Norwich Plays, 15th cent.

Creation of Prince Henry, The, 1610.

  C The Progresses Processions and Magnificent Festivities of King James the First, J. Nichols, ed., 1828.

Creation of the World, The, Supp. II, j.

Creation of the World, The, *see* Origo Mundi, 14th cent.

Creation of the World with Noah's Flood, The, 1611; trans., 1693.

  E Gwreans an Bys. The Creation of the World (Trans. of the Philol. Soc.), W. Stokes, ed., 1864.

Creation of the World with Noah's Flood, The, 1693.

  E The Creation of the World, with Noah's Flood, D. Gilbert, ed., 1827.

Creation of White Knights of the Order of Aristotle's Well, The, *see* Christmas Prince, The, 1608.

Crede Quod Habes et Habes, *see* City Nightcap, The, 1624.

Credulous Cuckold, The, *see* Debauchee, The, 1677.

Creed Play (York), 15th cent.

Cripple of Fenchurch, The, *see* Fair Maid of the Exchange, The, 1602.

Crispin and Crispinianus, 1528.

Critics, The, 1687.

Croesus, 1604.

Cromwell, Thomas Lord, 1600.

  C The Shakespeare Apocrypha, C.F.T. Brooke, ed., 1908.

Cromwell's Conspiracy, 1660.

Croxton Play of the Sacrament, The, *see* Sacrament, The Play of the, 15th cent.

Cruel Brother, The, 1627.

Cruel Debtor, The, 1565.

Cruel War, The, 1643.

Cruelties of the Dutch to the English Merchants, The, *see* Amboyna, 1672.

Cruelty of a Stepmother, The, 1578.

Cruelty of the Spaniards in Peru, The, 1658.

Cruelty without Hate, *see* Castara, Supp. II, b.

Crumena Perdita, *see* De Crumena Perdita, 1555.

Crumenaria, *see* De Crumena Perdita, 1555.

Crux Vindicata, 1656.

Crux Vindicata, Supp. II, 1.

Crysella, Supp. II, k.

Cuckolds Haven, or An Alderman No Conjurer, 1685.

Cuckolds Make Themselves, *see* Wives' Excuse, The, 1691.

Cuckolds' Mask, The, Supp. II, i.

Cuckow's Nest at Westminster, The, or The Parliament between the Two Lady-Birds Queen Fairfax and Lady Cromwell, 1648.
> C *The Harleian Miscellany*, W. Oldys & T. Park, ed., (1808–13), 1810.

Cuckqueans and Cuckolds Errants, The, or The Bearing Down the Inn, 1601.
> E J. Haslewood, introd., *The Cuck-Queanes and Cockolds Errants . . . The Faery Pastorall . . . By W.P. Esq.* (Roxburghe Club), 1936.

Cunning Lovers, The, 1638.

Cunning Woman, The, *see* Dame Dobson, 1683.

Cupid, The Mask of, 1614.

Cupid and Death, 1653.
> C *A Book of Masques in Honour of Allardyce Nicoll*, T.J.B. Spencer, S.W. Wells, *et al.*, eds, 1967.

Cupid and Psyche (Anon.), 1581.

Cupid and Psyche (Chettle *et al.*), 1600.

Cupid and Psyche (Holland), 1656.

Cupid and Psyche, or Cupid's Mistress, *see* Love's Mistress, 1634.

Cupid, Chastity, and Time, 1564.
> C *History of the Affairs of Church and State in Scotland*, (Spottiswoode Soc.) R. Keith, ed., (1844–50) 1845.

Cupid His Coronation, 1654.

Cupid, Venus, and Mars, A Play or Triumph of, 1553.

Cupid's Banishment, 1617.
> C *The Progresses, Processions and Magnificent Festivities of King James the First*, J. Nichols, ed., 1828.

Cupid's Festival, 1614.

Cupid's Mistress, *see* Love's Mistress, 1634.

Cupid's Revenge, 1608; adapt., 1662.

> T Chicago, J.E. Savage, ed., 1942.

Cupid's Sacrifice, *see* Country Tragedy in Vacunium, A, 1602.

Cupid's Vagaries, *see* Hymen's Holiday, 1612.

Cupid's Whirligig, 1607.

Cupido Adultus, *see* Eumorphus, 1635.

Cure for a Cuckold, A, 1625; adapt., 1696.

Cure for Jealousy, A, 1699.

Cure of Pride, The, or Everyone in Their Way, 1680.

Curialis Curia, *see* Mercurius Britannicus, 1641.

Curious Husband, The, *see* Amorous Prince, The, 1671.

Curious Impertinent, The, *see* Married Beau, The, 1694.

Custom of the Country, The, 1620; adapt., 1662.

Cutlack, 1599 add.

Cutter of Coleman Street, 1661.
> C 1) *Representative English Comedies*, C.M. Jayley, ed., (1903–36) 1936.
> C 2) *The Complete Works in Verse and Prose of Abraham Cowley Now For the First Time Collected and Edited*, Alexander B. Grosart, ed., 1881, reprinted 1967.
> T Southern Mississippi, Darlene Johnson Gravett, ed., 1979.

Cutting Dick, 1602.

Cutwell, 1577.

Cymbeline, King of Britain, 1609; adapt., 1682.

Cynocephali, The, 1577.

Cynthia and Ariadne, *see* Ashby, The Entertainment at, 1607.

Cynthia and Endimion, The Mask of, *see* Imposture Defeated, The, 1697.

Cynthia's Revels, or The Fountain of Self-Love, 1600.

Cynthia's Revenge, or Maenander's Ecstasy, 1613.
> T Texas Tech. Mainelle Cole, ed., 1977.

Cyprian Conqueror, The, or The Faithless Relict, 1640.

Cyrus, *see* Wars of Cyrus, The, 1588.

Cyrus the Great, or The Tragedy of Love, 1695.

Cytherea, or The Enamouring Girdle, 1677.

D,G, and T[om], 1539.

Dame Dobson, or The Cunning Woman, 1683.

Death of Richard III, The, *see* English Princess, The, 1667.

Death of Robert Earl of Huntingdon, The, 1598.
  S Malone Society, J.C. Meagher, ed., 1965.

Death of the Black Prince, The, Supp. II, h.

Death of the Duke of Guise, The, *see* Massacre at Paris, The, 1593.

Death of the Lady Jane Grey, The, *see* Innocent Usurper, The, 1694.

Death of the Lord of Kyme, The, 1601.

Deaths of the Apostles, The, 1528.

Debauched Hypocrite, The, *see* Trick for Trick, 1678.

Debauchee, The, or The Credulous Cuckold, 1677.

Deceiver Deceived, The, 1697.
  C The Plays of Mary Pix and Catherine Trotter, Edna L. Steeves, ed., 1982.

Defeated Widow, The, *see* Counterfeit Bridegroom, The, 1677.

Defiance of Fortune, A, a romance sometimes listed as a play.

Delight, A Comedy Called, 1580.

Delight, A Speech of, *see* Speech of Delight, A, Supp. I.

Deliverance of the Pope, The, *see* Heretic Luther, 1527.

Deliverer Set Forth in His Proper Colours, The, *see* Belgic Hero Unmasked, The, 1686.

Delphrygus and the King of Fairies, 1570 add.

Deluge, The, *see* Noah's Flood, 1679.

Demetrius and Enanthe, *see* Humorous Lieutenant, The, 1619.

Demetrius and Marina (or Marsina), or The Imperial Impostor and Unhappy Heroine, Supp. II, g.

Denmark, The Welcome of the King of, etc., 1606.

Deorum Dona, 1647.

Deorum Judicium, non-dramatic dialogue in Pleasant Dialogues and Dramas, 1635.

Deposing of Richard II, The, *see* Richard II, 1595.

Depositio Crucis (Winchester), 10th cent.

Depositio Crucis (Barking), 14th cent.

Depositio Crucis (Dublin), 14th cent.

Depositum, *see* Reparatus, 1619.

Derry Defended, *see* Piety and Valour, 1692.

Descensus Astrae, 1591.

Deserving Favourite, The, 1629.
  E Lodowick Carliell . . . and 'The Deserving Favourite', C.H. Gray, ed., 1905.

Destruction of Constantinople, The, Supp. II, k.

Destruction of Jerusalem (Legge), The, 1584.

Destruction of Jerusalem (Smythe), The, 1584.

I Destruction of Jerusalem by Titus Vespasian, The, 1677.

II Destruction of Jerusalem by Titus Vespasian, The, 1677.

Destruction of Sodom, The, *see* Fire and Brimstone, 1675.

Destruction of Sodom and Gomorrha, The, Supp. II, j.

Destruction of Sodom and Gomorrha, The, Supp. II, k.

Destruction of the World, The, *see* Noah's Flood, 1679.

Destruction of Thebes, The, 1569.

Destruction of Troy, The, 1678.

Destruction of Troy, The, Supp. II, k.

Devices for Nottingham Castle, 1562.
  C Early English Classical Tragedies, J.S. Cunliffe, ed., 1897.

'Devices of war and a play at Osterley, The', 1579.

Devil and Dives, The, 1570 add.

Devil and His Dame, The, 1600.
  C Five Anonymous Plays (4th ser.), J.S. Farmer, ed., 1908.

Devil and the Parliament, The, or The Parliament and the Devil, 1648.

Devil Is an Ass, The, 1616.

Devil of a Wife, The, 1699.

Devil of a Wife, The, or A Comical Transformation, 1686.

Devil of Dowgate, The, or Usury Put to Use, 1623.

Devil Turned Ranter, The, *see* Jovial Crew, The, 1651.

Devil's Charter, The, or The Tragedy of Pope Alexander VI, 1606.
  S Garland, Jim C. Pogue, ed., 1980.

Devil's Law Case, The, 1619.
  S Regents, Frances A. Shirley, ed., 1972.

Dialogue Between Two Shepherds, A, 1580.

Dialogue of Dives, The, 1570 add.

Dialogues Between Gelasimus and Spudaeus, Eda and Agna, and Wisdom and Will, 1558.

Dialogues of Creatures Moralized, non-dramatic dialogues formerly included in *Annals*.

Diana and Six Nymphs Huntresses, A Mask of, 1560.

Diana Pallas, *see* Juno and Diana, 1565.

Diana's Grove, or The Faithful Genius, Supp. I.

Diccon of Bedlam, *see* Gammer Gurton's Needle, 1553.

Dick of Devonshire, 1626.

Dick Whittington, 1668.

Dido (Ritwise), 1527.

Dido (Halliwell), 1564.

Dido (Gager), 1583.
   C *The Works of Christopher Marlowe*, (frag.) A. Dyce, ed., 1858.
   T 'William Gager and the Dido Tradition in English Drama of the Renaissance', Delaware, 1969, H.B. Schramm, ed. and trans., 1969.
   F *Renaissance Latin Drama in England*, Marvin Spevack, J.W. Binns, Hans-Jurgen Weckermann, gen. eds, 1982–6; J.W. Binns, ed.

Dido (Maittaire), 1699.

Dido and Aeneas (Anon.), 1598.

Dido and Aeneas (Tate), 1689.

Dido Queen of Carthage, The Tragedy of, 1586.
   S Revels, H.J. Oliver, ed., 1968.
   T Denver, Patricia Ann Brandt Romo, ed., 1979.

Different Humours of Men, The, *see* Poikilo-Phronesis, 1691.

Digby Mysteries, *see* Conversion of St Paul, The, 15th cent.; Mary Magdalene, 15th cent.; Massacre of Innocents, The, 15th cent.
   T London, V.M. Devlin, ed., 1965–6.

Ding-Dong, or Sir Pitiful Parliament on His Death-Bed, 1648.

Diocletian, 1594.

Diocletian, The History of, see Prophetess, The, 1690.

Diogenes, *see* Campaspe, 1584.

Dionysius the Tyrant, History of, 1540.

Diphilo and Granida, 1653.
   C *The Wits, or Sport Upon Sports*, J.J. Elson, ed., 1932.

Disappointed Marriage, The, or The Generous Mistress, *see* Lucky Chance, The, 1686.

Disappointment, The, *see* Serenade, The, 1669.

Disappointment, The, or The Mother in Fashion, 1684.
   C *The Works of Thomas Southerne*, vol. 1, R. Jordan and H. Lowe, eds, 1988.

Discontented Colonel, The, see Brennoralt, 1639.

Discourse between Three Neighbors, Algate, Bishopsgate, and John Heyden, the Late Cobbler of Hounsditch, a Professed Brownist, 1642.

Discourse Concerning Evil Counsellors, A, *see* Tyrannical Government Anatomized, 1643.

Discourse of the World, A, *see* Way of Life, The, 1556.

Discovery, The, *see* Marciano, 1662.

Discreet Lover, The, *see* Fool Would Be a Favourite, The, 1637.

Disease of the House, The, or The State Mountebank Administering Physic to a Sick Parliament, 1649.

Disguised Lovers, The, *see* Love's Metamorphosis, 1682.

Disguises, or Love in Disguise, a Petticoat Voyage, 1595.

Disguises, The, *see* All Plot, 1665.

Disguises, The, *see* Disguises, 1595.

Disloyal Favourite, The, or The Tragedy of Mettellus, Supp. I.

Disobedience, Temperance, and Humility, *see* Temperance and Humility, 1535.

Disobedient Child, The, 1560.
   C *The Dramatic Writings of Richard Wever and Thomas Ingelend*, J.S. Farmer, ed., 1905.

Distracted Emperor, The, *see* Charlemagne, 1600.

Distracted State, The, 1650.

Distractions, *see* Love Hath Found His Eyes, 1640.

Distressed Innocence, or The Princess of Persia, 1690.

Distressed Ladies, The, *see* Roman Generals, The, 1667.

Distressed Lovers, The, *see* Cardenio, 1613.

Distressed Lovers, The, *see* Mad Tom of Bedlam, 1696.

Distressed Lovers, The, *see* Tempest, The, 1700.

Distresses, The, *see* Spanish Lovers, The, 1639.

Dives and Lazarus, 1570 add.

Dives and Lazarus, Supp. II, k.

Dives and Lazarus, The Story of, Supp. II, j.

Dives' Doom, or The Rich Man's Misery, 1675.

Divine Comedian, The, or The Right Use of Plays, *see* Soul's Warfare, The, 1672.

Divorce, The, Supp. II, b.

Doctor Dodypoll, *see* Wisdom of Doctor Dodypoll, The, 1599.

Doctor Faustus, The Tragical History of, 1592; *see also* Supp. II, k.
 S 1) Fountainwell, Keith Walker, ed., 1973.
  2) New Mermaids, Roma Gill, ed., 1965.
  3) Revels, John D. Jump, ed., 1962 (paper, 1968).
 F Scolar (1604 and 1616).

Doctor Faustus with the Humours of Harlequin and Scaramouche, The Life and Death of, 1688.

Doctor Lamb and the Witches, 1634.

Doctors of Dull-Head College, The, 1662.

Doge and the Dragon, The, 1641.

Dolorous Castle, The, 1512.

Don Carlos Prince of Spain, 1676.

Don Horatio, 1599 add.

Don Japhet of Armenia, 1657.

Don Pedro the Cruel King of Castile, Supp. I.

Don Phoebo's Triumph, 1645.

I Don Quixote, The Comical History of, 1694.

II Don Quixote, The Comical History of, 1694.

III Don Quixote with the Marriage of Mary the Buxom, The Comical History of, 1695.

Don Quixote, The History of, or The Knight of the Ill-Favoured Face, Supp. II, e.

Don Sancho, Supp. I.

Don Sebastian King of Portugal, 1689.
 C *Dryden: Poetry and Plays*, Douglas Grant, ed., 1952.
 C 1) *John Dryden: Four Tragedies*, L.A. Beaurline, Fredson Bowers, ed., 1967.

  2) California *Dryden*, vol. XV, E. Miner, F.B. Zimmerman, G.R. Guffey, eds, 1976.

Doolittle, Mr, 1683.

Double Dealer, The, 1693.
 C 1) *The Complete Plays*, Herbert Davis, ed., 1967.
  2) *The Comedies of William Congreve*, Anthony G. Henderson, ed., 1982.
 F Scolar (1694), 1973.

Double Discovery, The, *see* Spanish Friar, The, 1680.

Double Falsehood, or The Distressed Lovers, *see* Cardenio, 1613.

Double Marriage, The, 1620.

Double Mask, A, 1572.

Doublet, Breeches, and Shirt, 1620.

Doubtful Heir, The, 1638.

Downfall of the Pope, The, *see* Coronation of Queen Elizabeth, The, 1680.

Downfall of Robert Earl of Huntingdon, The, 1598.
 S Malone Society, John C. Meagher, ed., 1965.
 T Mississippi, G.C. Pittman, ed., 1967.

Drake, *see* Sir Francis Drake, 1658.

Dramatic Pastimes for Children, 1626.

Dream of a Dry Year, A, *see* Arabia Sitiens, 1601.

Drinking Academy, The, or The Cheaters' Holiday, 1629.
 E S.A. Tannenbaum and H.E. Rollins, ed., 1930.

Droichis [Dwarf's] Part of the Play, The, 1503.
 C *The Poems of William Dunbar*, W.M. Mackenzie, ed., 1932.

Drunken Couple, The, *see* Love Lost in the Dark, 1680.

Drunken Mask, A, 1552.

Dublin Abraham and Isaac, 15th cent.

Duchess of Fernandina, The, 1639.

Duchess of Malfi, The, 1614.
 S 1) New Mermaid, Elizabeth Brenna, ed., 1964.
  2) Revels, J.R. Brown, ed., 1964 (paper: 1969).
 F Scolar (1623).
 E F.L. Lucas, ed., 1959.
 T Washington, R.B. Carey, ed., 1969.

Duchess of Suffolk, The, 1624.

   T Delaware, Robert A. Raines, ed., 1968.

Duke, The, *see* Humorous Courtier, The, 1631.

Duke and No Duke, A, 1684.

   C *Ten English Farces*, L. Hughes and A.H. Scouten, eds, 1948.

Duke Humphrey, 1613.

Duke Moraud, *see* Dux Moraud, 14th cent.

Duke of Ferrara, The, Supp. II, k.

Duke of Florence and a Nobleman's Daughter, A, Supp. II, k.

Duke of Guise (Shirley), The, 1623.

Duke of Guise (Dryden & Lee), The, 1682.

Duke of Lerma, The, *see* Great Favourite, The, 1668.

Duke of Lerma, *see also* Spanish Duke of Lerma, The, 1623.

Duke of Mantua and the Duke of Verona, The, Supp. II, k.

Duke of Milan, The, 1621.

   C *The Plays and Poems of Philip Massinger*, vol. 1 of 5 vols., Philip Edwards, Colin Gibson, eds, 1976.

   E T.W. Baldwin, ed., 1918.

Duke of Milan and the Marquis of Mantua, The, 1579.

Duke's Mistress, The, 1636.

Dumb Bawd, The, 1623; *see also* 1628.

Dumb Bawd of Venice, The, 1628.

Dumb Knight, The, 1608; *see also* Supp. II, k.

Dumb Lady, The, or The Farrier Made Physician, 1669.

Duns Furens, 1586.

Durance Mask, Supp. II, i.

Dutch Courtesan, The, 1605; adapt., 1673, 1680.

   S 1) Fountainwell, P. Davison, ed., 1968.

     2) Regents, M.L. Wine, ed., 1965.

Dutch Cruelties at Amboyna, with the Humours of the Valiant Welshman, The, 1672.

Dutch Lover, The, 1673.

Dutch Painter, and the French Branke, The, 1622.

Dux Moraud, 14th cent.

   C *Non-Cycle Plays and Fragments* (EETS, Supplementary Series, 1), N. Davis, ed., 1970.

Dyccon of Bedlam, *see* Gammer Gurton's Needle, 1553.

I Earl Godwin and His Three Sons, 1598.

II Earl Godwin and His Three Sons, 1598.

Earl of Essex, The, *see* Unhappy Favourite, The, 1681.

Earl of Gloucester, *see* Gloucester.

Earl of Hertford, The, 1602.

Easter Play (Kingston-on-Thames), 15th cent. add.

Easter Play (Morebath), 15th cent. add.

Easter Play, *see also* Quem Quaeritis.

Eastward Ho, 1605; adapt., 1685.

   S 1) New Mermaids, C.G. Petter, ed., 1973.

     2) New Mermaids, *Elizabethan and Jacobean Comedies*, Brian Gibbons, ed., 1984.

     3) Revels, R.W. Van Fossen, ed., 1979.

     4) Scolar (1605).

Earthquake in Jamaica, The, 1692.

Ebrauk with All His Sons, King, 1589.

Ecclesia, or A Governance of the Church, 1540.

Ecologue or Representation in Four Parts, An, 1659.

   C *A Royal Arbor of Loyal Poesie* (Illus. of Old Eng. Lit., vol. 3, no. 7), J.P. Collier, ed., 1866.

Edgar, or The English Monarch, 1677.

Edgar and Alfreda, King, 1677.

Edinburgh, The Entertainment of King Charles into, 1633.

Edinburgh Entertainment for Queen Mary, The, 1554.

Edinburgh Entertainments, *see* 1554, 1561, 1579, 1590, 1633.

Edmond Ironside, or War Hath Made All Friends, 1595.

   C *Six Early Plays Related to the Shakespeare Canon*, Anglistica, Vol. 14 (1965), Ephraim B. Everitt, ed. (with R.L. Armstrong).

   E *Shakespeare's Lost Play: Edmund Ironside*, Eric Sams, ed., 1985.

Edoardus Confessor, Sanctus, 1653.

Edward I, The Famous Chronicle of King, 1591.

Edward II, *see* Troublesome Reign and Lamentable Death of Edward II, The, 1592.

Edward III, The Reign of King, 1590.

C 1) *Six Early Plays Related to the Shakespeare Canon*, Anglistica, Vol. 14, 1965, R.L. Armstrong, ed. (with E.B. Everitt).
2) *The Shakespeare Apocrypha*, C.F. Tucker Brooke, ed., 1908; 1967.

S New Mermaids, W.M. Merchant, ed., 1967.

T 1) Rutgers, Frederick Robert Lapides, ed., 1966.
2) Delaware, Frederick D. Horne, ed., 1974.

Edward III with the Fall of Mortimer Earl of March, King, 1690.

   E *King Edward the Third with the Fall of Mortimer Earl of March, 1691*, J. Cadwalder, ed., 1949.

I Edward IV, 1599; *see also* Supp. II, k.
   T Wisconsin, Yu-Cheng Lo, ed., 1954.

II Edward IV, 1599; *see also* Supp. II, k.
   T Wisconsin, Yu-Cheng Lo, ed., 1954.

Edward VI, *see* Coronation of Edward VI, The, 1547.

Effiginia, 1571, Supp. II, p.

Eglemour and Degrebelle, 15th cent.

Egyptian Women, A Mask of, 1545.

Elckerlijc, *see* Summoning of Every Man, The, 1495.

Elder Brother, The, 1625.

Electra, 1649.

Elevatio Crucis (Winchester), 10th cent.

Elevatio Crucis (Dublin), 14th cent.

Elevatio Crucis (Barking), 14th cent.

Elizabeth, and the French Ambassadors, Shows . . . before Queen, *see* Fortress of Perfect Beauty, The, 1581.

Elizabeth, The Coronation of Queen, *see* Coronation of Queen Elizabeth, The, 1680.

Elizabeth, Play of Queen, *see* I & II If You Know Not Me, 1604 and 1605.

Elizabeth, Reception for Queen at Greenwich, 1580.

Elizabeth, The Troubles of Queen, *see* I If You Know Not Me You Know Nobody, 1604; The Famous Victory of Queen, *see* II If You Know Not Me, 1605.

II Elizabeth's Troubles, Queen, *see* II If You Know Not Me, 1605.

Elizabetha Triumphans, *see* Queen's Visit to Tilbury, The, 1588.

Elizabethan Jig, An, Supp. I.
   S *Malone Society Collections*, IX (1977 for 1971). J.M. Nosworthy, ed.

Elstrid, *see* Locrine, 1591.

Eltham, A Mumming at, 15th cent.

Eltham Pageant of a Castle, The, 1516.

Elvetham, The Entertainment to the Queen at, 1591.

Elvira, or The Worst Not Always True, 1663.

Embassage from Lubber-Land, The, *see* Christmas Prince, The, 1608.

Emilia, 1672.

Emma Angliae Regina, 1620.

Emperor Caracalla, Supp. I.

Emperor Charles V, The Entertainment of, 1522.

Emperor of the East, The, 1631.
   C *The Plays and Poems of Philip Massinger*, vol. 3 of 5 vols., Philip Edwards, Colin Gibson, eds, 1976.
   T Denver, Donald Frank Peel, ed., 1970.

Emperor of the Moon, The, 1687.
   C *Ten English Farces*, L. Hughes and A.M. Scouten, eds, 1948.

Emperor's Favourite, The, Supp. I.

Empress of Morocco (Duffett), The, 1673.
   T 1) Illinois, Anne Therese Doyle, ed., 1963.
2) (with the Mock-Tempest, Psyche Debauch'd): 'An Edition of the Burlesque Plays of Thomas Duffett', Iowa, Ronald E. Di Lorenzo, ed., 1968.

Empress of Morocco (Settle), The, 1673.

Enamouring Girdle, The, *see* Cytherea, 1677.

Enchanted Castle, The, *see* Mock Tempest, The, 1674.

Enchanted Grove, The, 1656.

Enchanted Island, The, *see* Tempest, The, 1667.

Enchanted Island, The, *see* Tempest, The, 1674.

Enchanted Lovers, The, 1658.

Enchanted Lovers, The, *see* Brutus of Alba, 1678.

Enchiridion Christiados, work by John Cayworth, called 'Mask', but not dramatic.

Encounter, The, 1662.

Encyclochoria, or Universal Motion, 1663.

Endymion the Man in the Moon, 1588.

T Rochester, Donald James Edge, ed., 1974.

Endymion the Man in the Moon, *see* Imposture Defeated, The, 1697.

England's Comfort and London's Joy, 1641.

England's Farewell to the King of Denmark, 1606.

   C *The Progresses, Processions, and Magnificent Festivities, of King James the First* . . . , J. Nichols, ed., 1828.

England's First Happiness, or The Life of St Austin, 1641.

England's Joy, 1602.

   C *Dramatic Documents from the Elizabethan Playhouses*, W.W. Greg, ed., 1931.

England's Joy for the Coming in of . . . Charles II, 1660.

England's Welcome, *see* Entertainment of the Two Kings . . . , The, 1606.

Englebert, 1680.

English Arcadia, Supp. II, d.

English Friar, The, or The Town Sparks, 1690.

English Fugitives, The, 1600.

English Intelligencer, The, *see* Mercurius Britannicus, 1641.

English Lawyer, The, 1677.

English Monarch, The, *see* Edgar, 1677.

English Monsieur, The, 1663.

English Moor, The, or The Mock Marriage, 1637.

   E (Critical edition of Litchfield Ms. 68), Sara Jayne Steen, ed., 1983.

English Princess, The, or The Death of Richard III, 1667.

English Profit [Prophet?], The, *see* Richard III, 1623.

English Rogue, The, 1660.

English Traveller, The, 1627.

   F Da Capo (1633), 1973.

   T New York, Robert Jackson Hudson, ed., 1962.

Englishmen for My Money, or A Woman Will Have Her Will, 1598.

   E A.C. Baugh, ed., 1917.

Enough Is as Good as a Feast, 1560.

   S (With: *The Longer Thou Livest*) Regents, R. Mark Benbow, ed., 1967.

Entertainment, The, *see* Muses' Looking Glass, The, 1630.

Entertainment at Bunhill on the Shooting Day, The, *see* Honourable Entertainments, 1621.

Entertainment at Sir Francis Jones's at Christmas, The, *see* Honourable Entertainments, 1621.

Entertainment at Sir Francis Jones's at Easter, The, *see* Honourable Entertainments, 1621.

Entertainment at Sir Francis Jones's Welcome, The, *see* Honourable Entertainments, 1621.

Entertainment at Sir William Cokayne's in Easter Week, The, *see* Honourable Entertainments, 1621.

Entertainment at Sir William Cokayne's upon Simon and Jude's Day, The, *see* Honourable Entertainments, 1621.

Entertainment at the Conduit Head, The, *see* Honourable Entertainments, 1621.

Entertainment at Greenwich for Mary, Queen of Scots, 1516.

Entertainment at the Theatre Royal at the Drawing of the Lottery, *see* Wheel of Fortune, The, 1698.

Entertainment at Wanstead, The, *see* Lady of May, The, 1578.

Entertainment at –, *see also under next word in such titles*.

Entertainment for Queen Mary, The, 1554.

Entertainment for the General Training, The, *see* Honourable Entertainments, 1621.

Entertainment of the Ambassadors, The, 1510.

Entertainment of the Emperor's Ambassadors, The, 1521.

Entertainment of the Flemish Ambassadors, *see* Betrothal of Mary and Archduke Charles, 1508.

Entertainment of the French Ambassadors, The, 1518.

Entertainment of the Hostages, The, 1519.

Entertainment of the Lords of the Council by Sheriff Allen, The, *see* Honourable Entertainments, 1621.

Entertainment of the Lords of the Council by Sheriff Ducie, The, *see* Honourable Entertainments, 1621.

Entertainment of the Scottish Ambassadors, The, 1524.

Entertainment of the Two Kings of Great Britain and Denmark, The, 1606.

Entertainments, Early Tudor, 1510, 1518, 1519, 1521, 1522, 1524.

Epicoene, or The Silent Woman, 1609.
> *W* Yale *Ben Jonson*, Edward Partridge, ed., 1971.
> *S* Regents, L.A. Beaurline, ed., 1966.

Epidicus, 1694.

Epiphany Mask, An, 1512.

Epithalamion on the Marquis of Huntly's Marriage, An, 1588.
> *C* *The Poems of James VI of Scotland* (Scottish Text Soc. Pubs., 3rd Ser., Nos. 22, 26 1955–58), J. Craigie, ed., 1958.

Epsom Wells, 1672.
> *E* *Epsom Wells, and The Volunteers, or The Stock-Jobbers*, D.M. Walmsley, ed., 1930.

Equal Match, An, 1662.

Eramus, *see* St Erasmus.

Erga Momos et Zoilos, *see* I & II Against Momi and Zoili, 1537.

Erminia, or The Fair and Virtuous Lady, 1661.

Error, The History of, 1577.

Errors, *see* Comedy of Errors, The, 1592.

Escapes of Jupiter, The, or Calisto, 1625.
> *S* Malone Society, (From the Autograph MS Egerton 1994), H.D. Janzen, ed., 1976.

Essex, The Earl of, *see* Unhappy Favourite, The, 1681.

Essex Antic Mask, Supp. II, i.

Essex Entertainment, The, *see* Love and Self-Love, 1595.

Eteocles and Polynices, The Contention between, *see* Destruction of Thebes, The, 1569.

Eumorphus sive Cupido Adultus, 1635.
> *E* Salzburg, 1973.
> *F* *Renaissance Latin Drama in England*, Marvin Spevack, J.W. Binns, Hans-Jurgen Weckermann, gen. eds, 1982–6; prep. & intro., H.J. Vienken.

Eunuch, The, 1627.

Eunuch, The (Tragedy), Supp. II, a.

Eunuch, The, *see* Fatal Contract, The, 1639.

Eunuch, The, *see* Terence's Comedies Made

English, 1694.

Eunuchus (Kyffin?), 1588.

Eunuchus (Bernard), 1598.

Eunuchus (Lister), 1700.

Eunuchus, *see* Comoedia Sex Anglo-Latinae, 1663.

Euribates Pseudomagus, 1616.
> *F* *Renaissance Latin Drama in England*, Marvin Spevack, J.W. Binns, Hans-Jurgen Weckermann, gen. eds, 1982–6; prep. & intro., J.C. Coldewey and B.F. Copenhaver.

Euriolus (*i.e.*, Euryalus) and Lucretia, sometimes incorrectly listed as a play.

Europe's Revels for the Peace and His Majesty's Happy Return, 1697.

Evangelical Tragedy, An, or A Harmony of the Passion of Our Lord, sometimes incorrectly listed as a play.

Evening Adventure, An, or A Night's Intrigue, probably a ghost title.

Evening's Love, An, or The Mock Astrologer, 1668.
> *C* 1) *John Dryden: Four Comedies*. (Curtain Playwrights). L.A. Beurline, Fredson Bowers, eds, 1967.
> 2) California Dryden, M.E. Novak, G.R. Guffey, eds, 1970.

Every Act a Play, *see* Novelty, The, 1697.

Every Man in His Humour, 1598.
> *C* Yale *Ben Jonson*, Gabriele Bernhard Jackson, ed., 1969.
> *S* 1) New Mermaids, M. Seymour Smith, ed., 1967.
> 2) Regents, (A Parallel-Text Edition of the 1601 Quarto & 1616 Folio), J.W. Lever, ed., 1971.
> *F* Scolar (1601).

Every Man out of His Humour, 1599.

Every Woman in Her Humour, 1607.
> *C* *Old English Plays*, A.H. Bullen, ed., 1882–5.
> *S* Garland, Archie Mervin Tyson, ed. 1980.
> *T* Pennsylvania, A.M. Tyson, ed., 1952.

Everyone in Their Way, *see* Cure of Pride, The, 1700.

Evoradanus Prince of Denmark, a romance, sometimes listed as a play.

Example, The, 1634.
   T Denver, William Frederick Jones, ed., 1978.
Excellency of Her Sex, The, *see* Queen, The, 1628.
Exchange Ware at the Second Hand, *see* Band, Cuff, and Ruff, 1615.
Excidium Trojae, 1699.
Excommunicated Prince, The, or The False Relique, 1679.
Exposure, The, 1663.
Extravagant Shepherd, The, 1654.
Ezekias, 1539.

Fabii, The, *see* Four Sons of Fabius, The, 1580.
Factious Citizen, The, or The Melancholy Visioner, *see* Mr Turbulent, 1682.
Fair Anchoress of Pausilippo, The, 1640.
Fair and Virtuous Lady, The, *see* Erminia, 1661.
I Fair Constance of Rome, 1600.
II Fair Constance of Rome, 1600.
Fair Em the Miller's Daughter of Manchester, with the Love of William the Conqueror, 1590.
   C *The Shakespeare Apocrypha*, C.F. Tucker Brooke, ed., 1908; 1967.
   T 1) Illinois, R.W. Barzak, ed., 1959.
      2) Harvard, Standish Henning, 1960 (not listed in DAI).
Fair Favourite, The, 1638.
Fair Foul One, The, or The Baiting of the Jealous Knight, 1623.
Fair Maid of Bristow, The, 1604.
   E *The Faire Maide of Bristow* (Univ. of Pennsylvania Pubs. in Philol., Lit., and Archaeol.), A.H. Quinn, ed., 1902.
Fair Maid of Clifton, The, *see* Vow Breaker, The, 1625.
Fair Maid of Italy, The, 1599 add.
Fair Maid of London, The, 1598.
Fair Maid of the Exchange, The, 1602.
   S 1) Malone Society, Peter H. Davison, Arthur Brown, eds, 1963 (for 1962).
      2) Garland, Karl R. Synder, ed., 1980.
Fair Maid of the Inn, The, 1626.
I Fair Maid of the West, The, or A Girl Worth Gold, 1604.
   S 1) Salzburg, Brownell Salomon, ed., 1975.

      2) Regents, Robert K. Turner, Jr, ed., 1967.
      3) '*A Woman Killed with Kindness*' *and* '*The Fair Maid of the West*' (Belles-Lettres Ser.), K.L. Bates, ed., 1917.
   F Da Capo, (1631) 1973.
II Fair Maid of the West, The, or A Girl Worth Gold, 1631.
   S Regents, Robert K. Turner, Jr, ed., 1967.
   F Da Capo, (1631) 1973.
Fair Prisoner, The, *see* Conqueror's Custom, The, 1626.
Fair Quarrel, A, 1617.
   S 1) New Mermaids, Roger V. Holdsworth, ed., 1974.
      2) Regents, George R. Price, ed., 1976.
   T Alabama, Gerald David Johnson, ed., 1972.
Fair Spanish Captive, The, Supp. II, e.
Fair Star of Antwerp, The, 1624.
Fairy Chase, The, or A Forest of Elves, *see* Fairy Pastoral, The, 1603.
Fairy Knight, The, 1624.
Fairy Knight, The, or Oberon the Second, 1638.
   E *The Fairy Knight, or Oberon the Second*, F. Bowers, ed., 1942.
Fairy Mask, The, Supp. II, i.
Fairy Pastoral, The, or Forest of Elves, 1603.
   E *The Cuck-Queanes and Cockholds Errants . . . The Faery Pastorall . . .* (Roxburghe Club), By W.P. Esq.; J. Haslewood, Intro., 1824.
Fairy Queen, Supp. II, g.
Fairy Queen, The, 1692.
   F Cornmarket (1692).
Faithful Friends, The, 1621.
   S Malone Society (From the MS Dyce 10), G.M. Pinciss, G.R. Proudfoot, eds, 1970.
Faithful Genius, The, *see* Diana's Grove, Supp. I.
Faithful Irishman, The, *see* Committee, The, 1662.
Faithful Servant, The, *see* Grateful Servant, The, 1629.
Faithful Shepherd, The, *see* Pastor Fido, II.
Faithful Shepherdess, The, 1608.
   T Northwestern, Florence A. Kirk, ed., 1944.

Faithful Virgins, The, 1670.

Faithless Cousin German, The, *see* Jugurtha, Supp. I.

Faithless Relict, The, *see* Cyprian Conqueror, The, 1640.

Fall of Angels and Man in Innocence, The, *see* State of Innocence, The, 1677.

Fall of Caius Martius Coriolanus, The, *see* Ingratitude of a Commonwealth, The, 1681.

Fall of Mortimer, The, *see* Mortimer His Fall, 1637.

Fall of Sodom and Gomorrha, The, 1661.

Fallacy, or The Troubles of Great Hermenia, *see* Sophister, The, 1614.

False Challenge, The, *see* Hectors, The, 1656.

False Count, The, or A New Way to Play an Old Game, 1681.

False Favourite Disgraced, The, and The Reward of Loyalty, 1657.

False Friend, The, 1619; *see also* Supp. II, m.

False Friend, The, or The Fate of Disobedience, 1699.
> *C The Plays of Mary Pix and Catherine Trotter*, 1982. Edna L. Steeves, ed., 1982.

False Heir and Formal Curate, The, 1662.

False One, The, 1620.

False Relique, The, *see* Excommunicated Prince, The, 1679.

False Report, The, *see* Mistakes, The, 1690.

False Tiberinus, The, *see* Agrippa King of Alba, 1669.

Falstaff, The Humours of Sir John, *see* Henry IV, 1700.

Falstaff, Sir John, *see* Merry Wives of Windsor, The, 1600.

Fama, 1547.

Fame and Honour, The Triumphs of, 1634.

Family of Love, The 1603.
> *S* Nottingham, Simon Shepherd, ed., 1979.
> *T* New York, Andrew Dillon, ed., 1968.

Famous Victories of Henry V, The, 1586.
> *C Narrative and Dramatic Sources of Shakespeare*, G. Bullough, ed., 1962.
> *T* Stanford, W.S. Wells, ed., 1935.

Famous Wars of Henry I and the Prince of Wales, The, 1598.

Fancies Chaste and Noble, The, 1635.

> *S* Renaissance Imag., v. 12, J. Dominick and J. Hart, eds, 1985.
> *T* U.C.L.A., Nadine S. St Louis, ed., 1972.

Fancy's Festivals, 1657.

Far Fetched and Dear Bought Is Good for Ladies, 1566.

Farrier Made Physician, The, *see* Dumb Lady, The, 1669.

Fast and Welcome, 1631.

Fast Bind, Fast Find, mentioned 1539 as by John Heywood, probably not a play.

Fatal and Deserved End of Disloyalty and Ambition, The, *see* Andromana, 1642.

Fatal Banquet, The, Supp. II, m.

Fatal Brothers, The, 1623.

Fatal Contract, The, 1639; adapt., 1674.

Fatal Discovery, The, or Love in Ruins, 1698.

Fatal Divorce, The, *see* Phaeton, 1698.

Fatal Dowry, The, 1619; adapt., Supp. II, j.
> *C The Plays and Poems of Philip Massinger*, vol. 1 of 5 volumes, Philip Edwards, Colin Gibson, eds, 1976.
> *E* C.L. Lockert, Jr, ed., *The Fatal Dowry*, 1918.
> *S* 1) Fountainwell, T.A. Dunn, ed., 1969.
> 2) Salzburg, Carol Bishop, ed., 1976.

Fatal Embarrassment, The, *see* Labyrinth, The, 1664.

Fatal Error, The, *see* Orgula, 1658.

Fatal Friendship, 1698.

Fatal Friendship, The, 1646.
> *C The Plays of Mary Pix and Catherine Trotter*, II, Edna L. Steeves, ed., 1982.

Fatal Jealousy, The, 1672.

Fatal Love, or The Forced Inconstancy, 1680.

Fatal Marriage, The, or The Innocent Adultery, 1694.
> *C The Works of Thomas Southerne*, Vol. II, R. Jordan and H. Lowe, eds, 1988.

Fatal Marriage, The, or A Second Lucretia, Supp. I.

Fatal Mistake, A, or The Plot Spoiled, 1692.

Fatal Union, The, *see* Sicily and Naples, 1640.

Fatal Wager, The, *see* Injured Princess, The, 1682.

Fate of Capua, The, 1700.
> *C The Works of Thomas Southerne*, Vol. II, R. Jordan and H. Lowe, eds, 1988.

Floating Island, The, 1636.

Flora's Figgaries, *see* Flora's Vagaries, 1663.

Flora's Servants, *see* Honourable Entertainments, 1621.

Flora's Vagaries, 1663.
  T Pennsylvania, Andress Taylor, ed., 1963.

Flora's Welcome, *see* Honourable Entertainments, 1621.

Florence, The Great Duke of, 1627.

Florentine Friend, The, Supp. II, b.

Florentine Ladies, The, 1659.

Florimene, The Pastoral of, 1635.

Flowers, The Mask of, 1614.
  C 1) *English Masques*, M.A. Evans, ed., 1897.
     2) *A Book of Masques in Honour of Allardyce Nicoll*, T.J.B. Spencer, S.W. Wells, *et al.*, eds, 1967.

Flowers for Latin Speaking (Udall), phrases from Terence, included in previous edition of *Annals*, but non-dramatic.

Flying Voice, The, Supp. II, g.

Focas, *see* Phocasse, 1596.

Folly of Priest-Craft, The, 1690.

Folly Reclaimed, *see* City Lady, The, 1697.

Fond Husband, A, or The Plotting Sisters, 1677.
  T Denver, J.A. Vaughn, ed., 1964.

Fond Lady, The, *see* Amorous Old Woman, The, 1674.

Fool and Her Maidenhead Soon Parted, A, 1625.

Fool in Fashion, The, *see* Love's Last Shift, 1696.

Fool Transformed, The, Supp. II, e.

Fool Turned Critic, The, 1676.

Fool without Book, The, 1613.

Fool Would Be a Favourite, The, or The Discreet Lover, 1637.
  E *The Fool Would Be a Favourite or The Discreet Lover* (1657) By Lodowick Carlell, 1926.

Fool's Expectation, The, or The Wheel of Fortune, 1698.
  C *Rare Prologues and Epilogues, 1642–1700*, A.N. Wiley, ed., 1940.

Fool's Fortune, 1619.
  C *Lost Plays of Shakespeare's Age*, C.J. Sisson, ed., 1936.

Fools Have Fortune, or Luck's All, 1680, Supp. I.

Fool's Preferment, A, or The Three Dukes of Dunstable, 1688.
  C *A Study of the Plays of Thomas Durfey . . . and The Fool's Preferment* (Western Reserve Stud., vol. I), R.S. Forsythe, 1971.

Fools' Mask, The, Supp. II, i.

Fop's Fortune, The, *see* Love Makes a Man, 1700.

For the Honour of Wales, 1618.
  C *The Complete Masques* (Yale *Ben Jonson*), Stephen Orgel, ed., 1969.

Force of Love, The, *see* Theodosius, 1680.

Forced Inconstancy, The, *see* Fatal Love, 1680.

Forced Lady, The, 1633.

Forced Marriage, The, or The Jealous Bridegroom, 1670.

Forced Valour, 1662.

Forces of Hercules, The, 1586.

Forest of Elves, *see* Fairy Pastoral, The, 1603.

Forest Tragedy in Vacunium, A, or Love's Sacrifice, *see* Country Tragedy in Vacunium, A, 1602.

Foresters or Hunters [with Wild Men?], A Mask of, 1574.

Forlorn Son, The, 1574.

Forsaken Shepherdess, The, *see* Pleasant Dialogues and Dramas, 1635.

Fortewn Tenes, The, 1600.

Fortress of Perfect Beauty, The, 1581.
  C *The Progresses and Public Processions of Queen Elizabeth*, J. Nichols, ed., 1823.
  T Colorado at Boulder, Alan Lee Blankenship, ed., 1978.

Fortunae Ludibrium sive Belisarius, 1651.

Fortunate Isles and Their Union, The, 1625.
  C *The Complete Masques* (Yale *Ben Jonson*), Stephen Orgel, ed., 1969.

Fortunatus, 1599 add.

Fortunatus, Supp. II, k.

Fortune, The Play of, 1572.

Fortune by Land and Sea, 1609.
  T Pennsylvania, Herman Herbert Doh, Jr, 1962.

Fortune Hunters, The, or Two Fools Well Met, 1689.

Fortune's Task, or The Fickle Fair One, 1684.

II Fortune's Tennis, 1602.

Fuimus Troes, 1625.

I & II Fulgens and Lucrece, 1497.

   C   The Plays of Henry Medwall, M.E. Moeslin, ed., 1981.

Fulgens, Senator of Rome, *see* Fulgens and Lucrece, 1497.

Fulgius and Lucrell, *probably same as* Fulgens and Lucrece.

Funeral of Richard Coeur de Lion, The, 1598.

Funestum Corporis et Animae Duellum, *see* Homo Duplex, 1655.

Furies' Mask, The, Supp. II, i.

Furor Impius sive Constans Fratricida, *see* Sanguis Sanguinem, Supp. I.

Galfrido and Bernardo, a forged title.

Galiaso, 1594.

Gallant Cavaliero Dick Bowyer, This, *see* Trial of Chivalry, The, 1601.

Gallathea, 1585.

   *S   Regents, Anne Begor Lancashire, ed., 1969.

Gallomyomachia, Supp. I.

Game at Chess, A, 1624.

   *S   New Mermaids, J.W. Harper, ed., 1966.

   *E   R.C. Bald, ed., 1929.

   *T   ' "A Game at Chess": A Textual Edition Based on the Manuscripts Written by Ralph Crane', Michigan State, Milton A. Buettner, ed., 1972.

Gamester, The, 1633.

   *T   Chicago, S.H. Ronay, ed., 1948.

Gammer Gurton's Needle, 1553.

   E   Gammer Gurtons Nedle (Percy Reprints, No. 2), H.F.B. Brett-Smith, ed., 1920.

   *S   New Mermaids, *Three Sixteenth-Century Comedies*, Charles Walters Whitworth, ed., 1984.

Garden of Esperance, The, 1517.

Garden of Pleasure, The, 1511.

Garlic, 1612.

Geaner et Hamarte, Supp. II, l.

Gelasimus and Spudaeus, Eda and Agna, and Wisdom and Will, Three Dialogues Between, 1558.

Geminus Alcides, Supp. II, l.

Gemitus Columbae, Supp. I.

General (Anon.), The, 1638.

General (Boyle), The, 1664.

General Deluge of the World, *see* Noah's Flood, 1679.

Generous Choice, The, 1700.

Generous Enemies, *see* Humorous Lieutenant, The, 1619.

Generous Enemies, The, or The Ridiculous Lovers, 1671.

Generous Lovers, The, *see* St Stephen's Green, 1700.

Generous Mistress, The, *see* Lucky Chance, The, 1686.

Generous Portugal, The, *see* Island Princess, The, 1669.

Generous Portuguese, The, *see* Island Princess, The, 1699.

Generous Revenge, A, *see* Ambitious Slave, The, 1694.

Genius, The, *see* Theobalds, The Entertainment of the King and Queen at, 1607.

Gentle Craft, The, *see* Shoemaker's Holiday, The, 1599.

Gentleman and a Husbandman, A Proper Dialogue between a, included in previous edition of *Annals*, but not dramatic.

Gentleman and a Priest, A Dialogue between a, included in previous edition of *Annals*, but not dramatic.

Gentleman Dancing-Master, The, 1672.

   *T   Stanford, D.S. Rodes, ed., 1968

Gentleman No Gentleman, a Metamorphosed Courtier, A, Supp. II, m.

Gentleman of Venice, The, 1639.

   *S   Salzburg, Wilson F. Engel, ed., 1976.

   *T   Wisconsin-Madison, Wilson Farnsworth Engel, III, ed., 1975.

Gentleman of Venice, The, *see* Renegado, The, 1624.

Gentleman Quack, The, *see* Justice Busy, 1700.

Gentleman Usher, The, 1602.

   C   The Plays of George Chapman: The Comedies, Alan Holaday, gen. ed., Robert Ornstein, ed., 1970.

   *S   Regents, John Hazel Smith, ed., 1970.

I Gentleness and Nobility, 1527.

II Gentleness and Nobility, 1527.

Genus Humanum, 1553.

George a Greene, the Pinner of Wakefield, 1590.

   T Illinois, Urbana-Champaign, Charles A. Pennel, ed., 1962.

George Scanderbarge, The True History of, 1601.

German Princess, The, (adapt. of The Witty Combat), 1664.

Gesta Grayorum, 1594.

   C Law Sports at Gray's Inn, (1594) B. Brown, ed., 1921.

Ghismonda, (Tancred and Ghismond), 1623.

Ghismonda and Guiscardo, Supp. I.

Ghost, The, or The Woman Wears the Breeches, 1640.

Ghosts, The, 1665.

Gigantomachia, or Work for Jupiter, 1613.

   S Malone, *Academic Entertainments in the Folger Manuscripts*, T. Burger & Suzanne Gossett, eds, forthcoming.

   T In: 'A Christmas Messe, Gigantomachie, Heteroclitanomalonomia: Three Hitherto Unpublished Jacobean Dramatic Works of Probable University Orgin', Bowling Green State, David Lee Russell, ed., 1979

Gillian of Brentford and Friar Fox, *see* Friar Fox, 1599.

Giraldo the Constant Lover, 1623.

I Girl Worth Gold, A, *see* I Fair Maid of the West, The, 1610.

II Girl Worth Gold, A, *see* II Fair Maid of the West, The, 1631.

Gismond of Salerne, 1567.

   T 'A Comparison of the Two Versions of "Gismond of Salerne" ', Yale, Kyoko Iriye Selden, ed., 1965.

Gismond of Salerne in Love, *see* Gismond of Salerne, 1567.

   C Early English Classical Tragedies, J.W. Cunliffe, ed., 1912.

Give a Man Luck and Throw Him into the Sea, 1600.

Give Christmas His Due, *see* Women Will Have Their Will, 1649.

Glass of Government, The, 1575.

Glausamond and Fidelia, Supp. I.

Gloriana, or The Court of Augustus Caesar, 1676.

Glory's Resurrection, Being the Triumphs of London Revived, 1698.

Gloucester, *see* Duke Humphrey, 1613; *see also* Henry VI, 1591, 1592, 1681.

Goats' Mask, The, Supp. II, i.

Goblins, The, 1638.

God Speed the Plough, 1599 add.

God's Promises, 1538.

   E Emrys E. Jones, ed., Erlangen, 1909.

Goddesses, Huntresses, with Turkish Women, A Mask of, 1555.

Godfather, The, Supp. II, k.

Godfrey of Boulogne, with the Conquest of Jerusalem, *see* Jerusalem, 1599 add.; *also* I & II Godfrey of Boulogne, 1594.

I & II Godfrey of Boulogne, 1594.

Godly Queen Hester, 1527.

   C Six Anonymous Plays (1st Ser.), J.S. Farmer, ed., 1906.

I Godwin and His Three Sons, Earl, 1598.

II Godwin and His Three Sons, Earl, 1598.

Golden Age, The, or The Lives of Jupiter and Saturn, 1610.

Golden Age Restored, The, 1615.

   C The Complete Masques (Yale *Ben Jonson*), Stephen Orgel, ed., 1969.

Golden Ass, The, *see* Cupid and Psyche, 1600.

Golden Fishing, The *see* Chrysanaleia, 1616.

Golden Fleece, The, 1525.

Goldsmiths' Jubilee, The, or London's Triumphs, 1674.

Goldsmiths' Jubilee, The, *see also* London's Triumph, 1687.

   C The Lord Mayor's Pageants, F.W. Fairhold, ed., 1844.

Goldsmiths' Mumming, *see* Mumming for the Goldsmiths of London, A, 15th cent.

Gonsalvus Sylveira, Supp. II, l.

Good Beginning May Have a Good End, A, Warburton's title, probably for Bad Beginning Makes a Good Ending, A, 1612.

Good Luck at Last, *see* Virtuous Wife, The, 1679.

Good Old Cause, The, *see* Roundheads, The, 1681.

Good Order, 1515.

Good Order, *see* Old Christmas, 1533.

Goosecap, *see* Sir Giles Goosecap, 1602.

Gorboduc, 1562.

   S   Regents, Irby B. Cauthen, ed., 1970.

   F   Scolar (1570).

   T   St Louis, Maureen Walsh, ed., 1964.

Gordian Knot, Untied, The, 1690, Supp. II, j.

Gossips' Brawl, The, or The Women Wear the Breeches, 1655.

Governance of the Church, A, *see* Ecclesia, 1546.

Government, Supp. II, k.

Governor (Formido?), The, 1637.

Governor (Anon.), The, 1656.

Gown, Hood, and Cap, 1623.

   S   Malone: *Academic Entertainments in the Folger Manuscripts*, T. Berger and S. Gossett, eds, forthcoming.

Gowry, 1604.

Graius and Templarius, *see* Gesta Grayorum, 1594.

Gramercy Wit, 1621.

Grammar and Rhetoric, *see* Words Made Visible, 1678.

Grateful Servant, The, 1629.

   T   Michigan, Jack R. Ramsey, ed., 1972.

Grave-Makers, The, 1662.

Gray's Inn, The Mask at, *see* First Anti-Mask of Mountebanks, The, 1618.

Gray's Inn Antic Mask, Supp. II, i.

Great Bastard, *see* Royal Cuckold, The, 1693.

Great Cham, The, Supp. I.

Great Duke, The, *see* Great Duke of Florence, The, 1627.

   C   *The Plays and Poems of Philip Massinger*, vol. 3 of 5 vols., Philip Edwards, Colin Gibson, eds, 1976.

   E   *The Great Duke of Florence*, J.M. Stochholm, ed., 1905.

Great Favourite, The, or The Duke of Lerma, 1668.

   E   *Dryden and Howard, 1664–1668; the Text of 'An Essay of Dramatic Poesy'* . . . *and 'The Duke of Lerma'*, D.D. Arundell, ed., 1929.

Great Man, The, 1612.

Great Mask of Almains, Pilgrims, and Irishmen, A, 1557.

Great Royal Ball, The, *see* Nuptials of Peleus and Thetis, The, 1654.

Grecian Comedy, The, *see* Love of a Grecian Lady, The, 1599 add., *and* Turkish Mahomet and Hiren the Fair Greek, The, 1588.

Greek Maid, A Pastoral or History of a, 1579.

Greek Worthies, A Mask of, 1553.

Greeks and Trojans, The, Supp. II, j.

Greene's Tu Quoque, 1667.

Greene's Tu Quoque, or The City Gallant, 1611; adapt., 1662, 1667.

Greenwich, A Reception for Queen Elizabeth at, 1580.

Greenwich Park, 1691.

Gresham, Sir Thomas, with the Building of the Royal Exchange, The Life and Death of, *see* II If You Know Not Me You Know Nobody, 1605.

Gresham, Sir Thomas, *see also* Byrsa Basilica, 1633.

Grim the Collier of Croydon, or The Devil and His Dame, *see* Devil and His Dame, The, 1600.

Gripsius and Hegio, or The Passionate Lovers, 1647.

Griselda, *see* Rare Patience of Chaucer's Griselda, The, 1546.

Grobiana's Nuptials, 1638.

   E   *Grobianus in England, Palaestra*, XXXVIII, 164–91, E. Ruhl, ed., 1904.

Grove, The, or Love's Paradise, 1700.

Guardian (Massinger), The, 1633.

   C   *The Plays and Poems of Philip Massinger*, vol. 4 of 5 vols., Philip Edwards, Colin Gibson, eds, 1976.

   T   Brandeis, Carol A.M. Parssinen, ed., 1971.

Guardian, The, (Cowley), 1642; adapt. 1661, *see* Cutter of Coleman Street, 1661.

   C   *The English Writings of Abraham Cowley*, vol. 2 A.R. Waller, ed., 1905–6

Guelphs and Ghibellines, Supp. II, j.

Guido, 1597.

Guido Varvicensis, Supp. II, l.

Guildless Adulteress, The, or Judge in His Own Cause, Supp. II, j.

Guise, *see* Duke of Guise, The, 1623 *and* 1682.

Guise, 1615.

Hecyra, *see* Terence's Comedies Made English, 1694.

Hedon Plays, 14th cent.

Hegge Plays, *see* Ludus Coventriae, 15th cent.

Heildebrand, The Tragedy of, 1638, Supp. II, f.

Heir, The, 1620.

Heir of Morocco with the Death of Gayland, The, 1682.

Heiress, The, 1669.

Heliogabalus, The Life and Death of, 1594.

Hell's Higher Court of Justice, or The Trial of the Three Politic Ghosts, viz. Oliver Cromwell, King of Sweden, and Cardinal Mazarin, 1661.

Helmet, The Mask of the, *see* Gesta Grayorum, 1594.

Hemetes the Hermit, *see* Queen's Entertainment at Woodstock, The, 1575.

Hemidos and Thelay, The Rueful Tragedy of, entered S.R., 1570, probably not a play.

Hengist, 1599 add.

Hengist King of Kent, or The Mayor of Queenborough, 1618, adapt., 1700.
   E Hengist, King of Kent; or The Mayor of Queenborough, R.C. Bald, ed., 1938.

Hengist the Saxon King of Kent, The History of, 1700.

Henrico 8°, 1623.

Henrietta's Mask, Queen, 1626.

Henrietta's Mask, Queen, 1627.

Henrietta's Pastoral, *see* Artenice, L', 1626.

Henry I, The History of, 1624.

Henry I, The Life and Death of, 1597.

Henry I and the Prince of Wales, The Famous Wars of, 1598.

Henry II, 1624.

Henry II King of England, with the Death of Rosamond, 1692.

Henry III of France Stabbed by a Friar, with the Fall of the Guise, 1672.

Henry IV, 1623.
   E Shakespeare's Play of King Henry IV, Printed from a Contemporary Manuscript, J.O. Hallowell-[Phillips], ed., 1845.
   F Henry IV (Adaptation of I and II Henry IV), 1623, *The History of King Henry the Fourth as Revised by Sir Edward Dering*. Folger

Facsimile Ms. Ser. I, G.W. Williams, G.B. Evans, eds, 1974.

I Henry IV, (The History of Henry the Fourth), 1597; adapt., 1623, 1662.
   V S.B. Hemingway, ed., 1936.
   VS A Bibliography to Supplement the New Variorum Edition of 1936, Michael Kiernan, compiler, 1977.

II Henry IV (the Second Part of Henry the Fourth), 1597; adapt., 1623, 1662.
   V Mathias A. Shaaber, ed., 1940.
   VS A Bibliography to Supplement the Variorum Edition of 1940, M.A. Shaaber, compiler, 1977.

Henry IV [of France], 1678.

Henry IV, with the Humours of Sir John Falstaff, 1700.

Henry V, 1595.

Henry V, The Life of, 1599.

Henry V, The Famous Victories of, 1586.

Henry V, The History of, 1664.
   F Cornmarket (1668).
   T in: *'Henry V': A Textual Edition of the First Quarto*, Michigan State, Jonathan Harold Spinner, ed., 1973.

Henry V, The Reception of, 15th cent.

I Henry VI, 1590.
   F with the Murder of Humphrey, Duke of Gloucester. Cornmarket (1681).

II Henry VI, with the Death of the Good Duke Humphrey (the First Part of the Contention of the Two Famous Houses of York and Lancaster), 1590; adapt., 1681.
   T In: 'The First Part of the Contention Betwixt the Two Famous Houses of Yorke and Lancaster, with the Death of the Good Duke Humphrey: And the Banishment and Death of the Duke of Suffolke and The Tragicall end of the Proud Cardinall of Winchester . . .' Yale, 1953. Arleigh D. Richardson, III, ed., 1953.
   F Malone, John Pitcher, ed., 1594 (1985).

III Henry VI, with the Death of the Duke of York, (the True Tragedy of Richard Duke of York and the Good King Henry the Sixth), 1591; adapt., 1680.

Henry VI, The Reception of, 15th cent.

Henry VI, *see* Innocentia Purpurata, 1623.

II Henry VI, *see* Misery of Civil War, The, 1680.

Henry VI, the First Part, with the Murder of Humphrey Duke of Gloucester, 1681.

Henry VI, the Second Part, *see* Misery of Civil War, The, 1680.

Henry VII, The Coronation of, 1485.

Henry VII's Provincial Progress, 15th cent.

   C De Rebus Britannicis Collectanea, J. Leland, comp., 1774.

   T Toronto, Christopher E. McGee, ed., 1978.

Henry VIII, *see* I & II Upon Both Marriages of the King, 1538.

Henry VIII, The Coronation Triumph of, 1509.

Henry VIII, The Famous Chronicle History of, *see* When You See Me You Know Me, 1604.

Henry VIII, The Famous History of the Life of King, 1613.

Henry, Prince, *see* Creation of Prince Henry, The, 1610.

II Henry Richmond, 1599.

Henry the Una . . ., 1619.

Henry's Barriers, Prince, 1610.

   C The Complete Masques (Yale *Ben Jonson*), Stephen Orgel, ed., 1969.

Henry's Welcome to Winchester, Prince, 1603.

Heraclius, 1664.

Heraclius Emperor of the East, 1664.

Herbert Mask, *see* Wedding Mask for Sir Philip Herbert, The, 1604.

I Hercules, 1595.

II Hercules, 1595.

Hercules, *see* Novelty, The, 1697.

Hercules Furens, 1561.

   C Seneca His Tenne Tragedies Translated into English, (Tudor Trans., 2nd Ser.), 1927.

Hercules Furens, Supp. I.

Hercules Oetaeus (Elizabeth I), 1561.

   C H. Walpole, *A Catalogue of the Royal and Noble Authors of England, Scotland, and Ireland*, Vol. I, T. Park, ed., 1806.

   E Poems, E.L. Bradner, ed., 1964.

Hercules Oetaeus (Studley), 1566.

   C Seneca His Tenne Tragedies Translated into English (Tudor Trans. 2nd. Ser.), 1927.

Hereford Plays, 15th cent.

Heretic Luther, 1527.

Hermophus, erroneous title for Eumorphus, 1636.

Hero and Leander, The Tragedy of, 1669.

Herod and Antipater, with the Death of Fair Mariam, 1622.

   T Florida, Gordon N. Ross, ed., 1969.

Herod and Mariamne, 1673.

Herod the Great, 1672.

Herodes, 1572.

   F Renaissance Latin Drama in England, Marvin Spevack, J.W. Binns, Hans-Jurgen Weckermann, gen. eds, 1982–6; prep. & intro., C. Upton.

Heroes, Mask of, *see* Inner Temple Mask, The, 1619.

Heroic Love, 1697.

Heroic Lover, The, or The Infanta of Spain, 1650.

Herpetulus the Blue Knight and Perobia, 1574.

Hertford, The Earl of, 1602.

Hertford, A Mumming at, 15th cent.

Hester, *see* Godly Queen Hester, 1527.

Hester and Ahasuerus, 1599 add.

Heteroclitanomalonomia, 1613.

   S Malone: *Academic Entertainments in the Folger Manuscripts*, T. Berger and S. Gossett, eds, forthcoming.

   T In: ' "A Christmas Messe", "Gigantomachia", "Heteroclitanomalonomia": Three Hitherto Unpublished Jacobean Dramatic Works of Probable University Origin', Bowling Green State, 1979. David Lee Russell, ed., 1979.

Hewson Reduced, or The Shoemaker Returned to His Trade, 1661.

Hey for Honesty, Down with Knavery, *see* Plutophthalmia Plutogamia, 1627.

   T New York, Phyllis Brooks Toback, ed., 1971.

Hic et Ubique, or The Humours of Dublin, 1663.

Hick Scorner, 1513.

   S Revels, Ian Lancashire, ed., 1980.

Hierarchomachia, or the Anti-Bishop, 1629.

Hieronimo, The First Part of, or The Spanish Comedy, 1599 add.

S Regents, Andrew S. Cairncross, ed., 1967 (with The Spanish Tragedy, or Hieronimo is Mad Again).

Hieronimo Is Mad Again, *see* Spanish Tragedy, The, 1587.

Highgate, The Entertainment of the King and Queen at, 1604.

Highway to Heaven, The, 1570 add.

Himatia-Poleos: The Triumphs of Old Drapery, or The Rich Clothing of England, 1614.

Hippolytus (Studley), 1567.
  C *Seneca His Tenne Tragedies Translated into English*, (Tudor Trans. 2nd. Ser.) 1927.

Hippolytus (Anon.), 1604.

Hippolytus (Prestwich), 1651.

Hippolytus (Sherburne), 1700.

Hispanus, 1597.
  F *Renaissance Latin Drama in England*, Marvin Spevack, J.W. Binns, Hans-Jurgen Weckermann, gen. eds, 1982-6; prep. & intro., A.J. Cotton.

Historia de Daniel Repraesentanda, *see* Daniel, 12th cent.

History of Error, 1577, Supp. II, p.

History of Love and Fortune, The, *see* Rare Triumphs of Love and Fortune, The, 1582.

History of the Cenofalles, *see* Cynocephali, The, 1577.

Histriomastix, *see* Fucus, 1623.

Histriomastix, or The Player Whipped, 1599.

Hit Nail o' the Head, 1570 add.

Hob, *see* Country Wake, The, 1696.

Hobbinol, The Humour of, 1662.

Hobby-Horses, A Mask of, 1574.

Hock-Tuesday Play, *see* Princely Pleasures at Kenilworth, The, 1575.

Hocus-Pocus, 1638.

Hoffman, The Tragedy of, or A Revenge for a Father, 1602.
  T Princeton, E.J. Schlochauer, ed., 1948.

Hog Hath Lost His Pearl, The, 1613.
  S Malone Society (from the Edition of 1614), D.F. McKenzie, ed., 1967.

Holland's Leaguer, 1631.
  T Michigan, Dean Stanton Barnard, Jr, ed., 1963.

Hollander, The, 1636.

Holofernes, 1564.

Holophernes, The Play of, 1556.

Homo, 1618.
  S In: Two University Latin Plays (With Parsons' Atalanta), EDS 16, Salzburg, W.E. Mahaney, W.K. Sherwin, eds, 1973.
  F *Renaissance Latin Drama in England*, Marvin Spevack, J.W. Binns, Hans-Jurgen Weckermann, gen. eds, 1982-6; prep. & intro., H.-J. Weckermann.

Homo Duplex, sive Funestum Corporis et Animae Duellum, 1655.

Honest Lawyer, The, 1615.

Honest Man's Fortune, The, 1613.
  E J. Gerritsen, ed., 1952.

Honest Man's Revenge, The, *see* Atheist's Tragedy, The, 1609.

I Honest Whore, The, with the Humours of the Patient Man and the Longing Wife, 1604.

II Honest Whore, The, with the Humours of the Patient Man, the Impatient Wife, 1605.

Honoria and Mammon, 1658.

Honour, The Triumph of, *see* Four Plays or Moral Representations in One, 1612.

Honour and Industry, The Triumphs of, 1617.

Honour and Virtue, The Triumphs of, 1622.

Honour in the End, 1624.

Honour of Fishmongers, *see* Chrysanaleia, 1616.

Honour of Wales, For the, 1618.

Honour of Women, The, 1628.

Honour of Young Ladies, The, *see* Lovesick Maid, The, 1629.

Honour Triumphant (by J. Ford, 1606), not dramatic.

Honour's Academy, or The Famous Pastoral of the Fair Shepherdess Julietta, sometimes incorrectly listed as a play.

Honourable Entertainment of the King of Denmark, 1606.
  C *The Progresses, Processions, and Magnificent Festivities of King James the First . . .*, J. Nichols, ed., 1828.

Honourable Entertainments, 1621.

Horace (Cotton), 1665.

Horace (Denham & Philips), 1668.

Horatius, 1656.

the Building of the Royal Exchange, and the Famous Victory of Queen Elizabeth, 1605.

Ignoramus, 1615; adapt., 1662, 1677.

   E J.S. Hawkins, ed., 1787.

   F Renaissance Latin Drama in England, Marvin Spevack, J.W. Binns, Hans-Jurgen Weckermann, gen. eds, 1982–6; prep. & intro., E.F.J. Tucker.

Ignoramus (Codrington), 1662.

Ignoramus, or The Academical Lawyer (Parkhurst), 1662.

Ill Beginning Has a Good End, An, *see* Bad Beginning Makes a Good Ending, A, 1612.

Ill (Jill?) of a Woman, The, *see* Fount(ain) of New Fashions, The, 1598.

Illustrious Slaves, The, 1672.

Image of Love, The, 1538.

Image of St Nicholas, The, *see* St Nicholas, 12th cent.

Impatient Poverty, 1547.

   S The Tudor Interludes: Nice Wanton and Impatient Poverty, Renaissance Imag., vol. 10, Leonard Tennenhouse, ed., 1984.

Imperial Impostor and Unhappy Heroine, The, *see* Demetrius and Marina, Supp. II, g.

Imperial Tragedy, The, 1669.

Imperiale, 1639.

Imperick, The, 1662.

Impertinents, The, *see* Sullen Lovers, The, 1668.

Impiety's Long Success, *see* Andronicus, 1643.

Impossible Dowry, The, *see* Amyntas, 1630.

Impostor, The, *see* Imposture, The, 1640.

Imposture, The, 1640.

   T Toronto, Bruce Michael Salvatore, ed., 1972.

Imposture Defeated, The, or A Trick to Cheat the Devil, 1697.

In Duc Reducem, or A Welcome from the Isle of Rhé, satiric verses previously included in *Annals*.

Inconstant Lady, The, or Better Late Than Never, 1630.

   E The Inconstant Lady, A Play, P. Bliss, ed., 1814.

   T Delaware, Linda V. Itzoe, ed., 1979.

Independents' Conspiracy to Root out

Monarchy, The, *see* Levellers Levelled, The, 1647.

Independents' Victory over the Presbyterian Party, The, *see* Scottish Politic Presbyter Slain by an English Independent, The, 1647.

Indian Emperor, The, or The Conquest of Mexico by the Spaniards, 1665.

   C 1) John Dryden: *Four Tragedies*, L.A. Beaurline, Fredson Bowers, eds, 1967.

     2) California *Dryden*, Vol. IX, John Loftis, Vinton A. Dearing, eds, 1966.

   F (1667) 1971.

Indian Empress, The, 1684.

Indian Queen, The, 1664; adapt., 1695.

   C California *Dryden*, Vol. VIII, J.H. Smith, D. Macmillan, V.A. Dearing, eds, 1974.

Indian Queen, The, 1695.

Indictment Against Mother Messe, The, 1548.

   F Scolar, in: *Three Tudor Dialogues*, 1928.

Induction for the House, An, 1630.

Induction to Four Plays in One, *see* Four Plays or Moral Representations in One, 1612.

Industry and Honour, *see* London's Triumph, 1658.

Infanta of Spain, The, *see* Heroic Lover, The, 1650.

Inferno Navigatio, 1699.

Infortunatus, The Tragedy of, *see* Banished Duke, The, 1690.

Ingratitude of a Commonwealth, The or the Fall of Caius Martius Coriolanus, 1681.

   F Cornmarket (1682).

   T Illinois, Ruth E. McGugan, ed., 1965.

Injured Lovers, The, or The Ambitious Father, 1688.

Injured Princess, The, or The Fatal Wager, 1682.

Inner Temple and Gray's Inn, The Mask of the, 1613.

   C A Book of Masques in Honour of Allardyce Nicoll, T.J.B. Spencer, S.W. Wells, *et al.*, eds, 1967.

Inner-Temple Mask, The, or Mask of Heroes, 1619.

   C A Book of Masques in Honour of Allardyce Nicoll, T.J.B. Spencer, S.W. Wells, *et al.*, eds, 1967.

Inner-Temple Mask, *see* Ulysses and Circe, 1613.

Innocence Distressed, or The Royal Penitents, 1695.

Innocent Adultery, The, *see* Fatal Marriage, The, 1694.

Innocent Impostors, The, *see* Rape, The, 1692.

Innocent Mistress, The, 1697.
  C The Plays of Mary Pix and Catherine Trotter, Edna L. Steeves, ed., 1982.

Innocent Usurper, The, or the Death of the Lady Jane Grey, 1694.

Innocentia Purpurata, 1623.

Insatiate Countess, The, 1607.
  S Revels, Giorgio Melchiori, ed., 1984.

Integrity, The Triumphs of, 1623.

Interludium de Clerico et Puella, 14th cent.
  C Early Middle English Texts, B. Dickins and R.M. Wilson, eds, 1951.

Interludium de Corpore Christi, 14th cent.

Intrigues at Versailles, The, or A Jilt in All Humours, 1697.

Invasion of Naples by the French, The, *see* Charles VIII of France, The History of, 1671.

Invention for the Service of the Right Honourable Edward Barkham, Lord Mayor, An, 1622.
  T (With 'The Sun in Aries',: 'The Triumphs of Integrity', 'The Triumphs of Health and Prosperity'; British Columbia, Christina Jean Burridge, ed., 1978.

Invisible Knight, The, 1632.

Invisible Mistress, The, *see* Wrangling Lovers, The, 1676.

Invisible Smirk, or The Pen Combatants, 1662.

Iphigenia, 1571.

Iphigenia, 1579.

Iphigenia, 1699.
  C The Plays of John Dennis, J.W. Johnson, ed., 1980.

Iphigenia in Aulis, 1558.
  C 'Lady Lumley's Übersetzung von Euripides' Iphigenie in Aulis', *Jahrbuch der deutschen Shakespeare Gesellschaft*, XLVI, 28–59, G. Becker, ed., 1910.

Iphigenia in Aulis, *see* Achilles, 1699.

Iphis, 1626.
  F Renaissance Latin Drama in England,

Marvin Spevack, J.W. Binns, Hans-Jurgen Weckermann, gen. eds, 1982–6; prep. & intro., B. Nugel.

Iphis and Ianthe, or A Marriage without a Man, 1613.

Ipswich Corpus Christi Procession and Plays, 14th cent.

Ira Seu Tumulus Fortunae, *see* Christmas Prince, The, 1608.

Irena, 1664.

Irish Evidence, The, The Humours of Teague, or The Mercenary Whore, 1682.

Irish Expedition, The, *see* Royal Voyage, The, 1690.

Irish Gentleman, The, 1638.

Irish Knight, The, 1577.

Irish Mask, The, 1613.
  C The Complete Masques (Yale *Ben Jonson*), Stephen Orgel, ed., 1969.

Irish Rebellion, The, 1642.

I Iron Age, The, 1612, *see also* Supp. II, k.
  T 1) Florida State, Marvin Russell Evans, ed., 1968.
     2) Brandeis, Arlene Weitz Weiner, ed., 1971.

II Iron Age, The, 1612.

Ironmongers' Fair Field, The, *see* Campbell, 1609.

Irus, *see* Blind Beggar of Alexandria, The, 1596.

Island Princess, The, 1621; adapt., 1669, 1687, 1699.

Island Princess, The, 1687.

Island Princess, The, or The Generous Portugal, 1669.

Island Princess, The, or The Generous Portuguese, 1699.
  C Five Restoration Theatrical Adaptations (Eighteenth-Century English Drama Series; Facsimile Reproductions), Edward L. Langhans, ed., 1979.

Island Queens, The, or The Death of Mary Queen of Scotland, 1684.
  T Pennsylvania, J.J. Devlin, ed., 1957–8.

Isle of Dogs, The, 1597.

Isle of Gulls, The, 1606.
  T Pennsylvania, Raymond Stephen Burns, ed., 1963.

It Cannot Be, *see* Sir Courtly Nice, 1685.

Italian Husband, The, 1697.

Italian Nightpiece, The, *see* Unfortunate Piety, The, 1631.

Italian Tragedy, The, 1603.

Italian Tragedy of – , The, 1600.

Italian Women, A Mask of, 1560.

Ite in Vineam, or The Parable of the Vineyard, 1525.

Ivychurch, The Countess of Pembroke's, *see* Phillis and Amyntas, 1591.

Jack and Jill, 1567, Supp. II, p.

Jack Drum's Entertainment, 1600.

Jack Juggler, 1555.

Jack Straw, The Life and Death of, 1591.

Jacob and Esau, The History of, 1554.

James I, Entertainment at Britain's Burse for, 1609.

James I, Entertainment at Salisbury House for, 1608.

James IV, The Scottish History of, 1590.
  S 1) New Mermaids, J.A. Lavin, ed., 1967.
       2) Revels, Norman Sanders, ed., 1970.
  T St Louis, Charles H. Stein, ed., 1968.

Jane Grey, *see* I & II Lady Jane, 1602, *and* Innocent Usurper, The, 1694.

Jane Grey, The Death of Lady, *see* Innocent Usurper, The, 1694.

[Jane] Shore, The Book of, 1603.

Janus, A Mask of, 1573.

Jealous Bridegroom, The, *see* Forced Marriage, The, 1670.

Jealous Comedy, The, 1593.

Jealous Husband, The, *see* Lost Lover, The, 1696.

Jealous Husbands, The, *see* Rambling Justice, The, 1678.

Jealous Lovers, The, 1632; adapt., 1682.
  C Poetical and Dramatic Works of Thomas Randolph, Vol. 1, William C. Hazlett, ed., 1875.

Jenkin's Love-Course and Perambulation, 1662.

Jephte sive Christi Naturam Humanam Immolantis Expressa Figura, 1664.

Jephtha's Rash Vow, or The Virgin Sacrifice, 1698.

Jephthah, 1544.
  E F.H.Forbes, ed. and trans., 1928.

Jephthah, 1602.

Jephthes, Supp. I.
  F Renaissance Latin Drama in England, Marvin Spevack, J.W. Binns, Hans-Jurgen Weckermann, gen. eds, 1982–6; prep. & intro., C. Upton.

Jephthes sive Votum, 1541; *see also* Supp. I.

I Jeronimo with the Wars of Portugal, 1604; *see also* Supp. II, k.
  S Regents, (Kyd's 'The First Part of Hieronimo and the Spanish Tragedy'); Andrew S. Cairncross, ed., 1967.

Jeronimo, The Comedy of, *see* Don Horatio, 1599 add.

Jerusalem, 1599 add.

Jesuits' Comedy, The, 1607.

Jew, The, 1578.

Jew, The, Supp. II, k.

Jew of Malta, The, 1589; *see also* Supp. II, k.
  S 1) New Mermaids, Thomas W. Craik, ed., 1966.
       2) Regents, Richard Van Fossen, ed., 1964.
       3) Revels, N.W. Bawcutt, ed., 1978.
  F Scolar (1633).

Jew of Venice, The, Supp. II, a; *see also* Supp. II, k.

Jeweller of Amsterdam, The, or The Hague, 1617.

Jewish Gentleman, The, 1640.

Jews' Tragedy, The, 1626.

Jilt in All Humours, A, *see* Intrigues at Versailles, The, 1697.

Joan as Good as My Lady, 1599.

Joannes et Paulus, *see* Felix Concordia Fratrum, 1651.

Job, *see* De Iobi, 1546.

Job, History of, 1587.

Job, The Tragedy of, *see* Job, History of, 1587.

Job the Saint, *see* Jube the Sane, 1549.

Jocasta, 1566.
  T Vanderbilt, C.F.W. Forssberg, Jr, 1968.

Joconda and Astols[f?]o, 1624.

Jodelet Boxed, *see* Three Dorothies, The, 1657.

Johan, King, *see* I & II John, King, 1538.

Julianus et Celsus, Supp. II, l.

Julio and Hyppolita, Supp. II, k.

Julius Caesar (Anon.), 1562.

Julius Caesar (Alexander), 1607; *see also* Supp. II, k.

Julius Caesar (May), 1616.

Julius Caesar (Shakespeare), The Tragedy of, 1599.
> *VS Bibliography to the Supplement Variorum Edition of 1913*, John W. Velz, compiler, 1977.

Julius Caesar, *see also* Caesar.

Julius et Gonzaga, 1617.

Juno and Diana, 1565.

Juno and Hymenaeus, *see* Wedding Mask for Sir Philip Herbert, The, 1604.

Juno in Arcadia, *see* Time's Triumph, 1643.

Juno's Pastoral, *see* Time's Triumph, 1643.

Jupiter and Io, *see* Pleasant Dialogues and Dramas, 1635.

Jupiter and Saturn, The Lives of, *see* Golden Age, The, 1610.

Just General, The, 1652.

Just Italian, The, 1629.

Justice Busy, or The Gentleman Quack, 1700.

Katherine and Pasquil, *see* Jack Drum's Entertainment, 1600.

Katherine of Aragon, The Welcome for, 1502.

Keep the Widow Waking, *see* Late Murder in White Chapel, The, 1624.

Kendal Corpus Christi Play, 15th cent. add.

Kenilworth, The Princely Pleasures at, 1575.

Kentish Fair, The, or The Parliament Sold to Their Best Worth, 1648.

Key to the Cabinet of Parliament, A, 1648.

Kind Keeper, The, or Mr Limberham, 1678.

King Alfred, King John, etc., *see* Alfred, John, etc.

King and No King, A, 1611.
> *S* Regents, Robert A. Turner, ed., 1963.

King and the Subject, The, 1638.

King Arthur's Knights, 1539.

King Found at Southwell, The, 1646.

King John, The Life and Death of, 1591.

King John and Matilda, 1628.

King Louis and King Frederick of Hungary, Supp. II, k.

King of Aragon, *see* Alphonsus, 1587.

King of Aragon, The, Supp. II, k.

King of Cyprus and the Duke of Venice, A, Supp. II, k.

King of Denmark and the King of Sweden, The, Supp. II, k.

King of Denmark's Welcome, The, 1606.
> *C The Progresses, Processions and Magnificent Festivities of King James the First . . .*, J. Nichols, ed., 1828.

King of England and the Goldsmith's Wife, The, Supp. II, k.

King of England and the King of Scotland, The, Supp. II, k.

King of Fairies, The, 1570 add.

King of Numidia, *see* Jugurth, 1600.

King of Scots, The Tragedy of the, 1568, Supp. II, p.

King of Spain and the Portuguese Ambassador, The, Supp. II, k.

King of Sweden, *see* Gustavus, 1631.

'King Play' (Hascombe), 15th cent. add.

King Robert of Sicily (Lincoln), 15th cent.

King Robert of Sicily (Chester), 15th cent. add.

King Robert of Sicily, 1623.

King's Entertainment at Welbeck, The, 1633.

King's Mistress, The, Supp. II, a.

King's Son of England and a King's Daughter of Scotland, A, Supp. II, k.

Kings of Cologne (Reading), 15th cent. add.

Kitchen Stuff Woman, The, 1595.

Knack to Know a Knave, A, 1592.
> *S* Malone Society, G.R. Proudfoot, ed., 1964 (for 1963).
> *T* Univ. of Pennsylvania, P.E. Bennett, ed., 1952.

Knack to Know an Honest Man, A, 1594.

Knave in Grain New Vamped, The, 1625.

Knave in Print, A, or One for Another, 1613.

Knaveries of Thomas Becket, The, 1538.

Knavery in All Trades, or The Coffee-House, 1664.

Knavery in All Trades, *see* Knaves in Grain New Vamped, The, 1639.

I Knaves, The, 1613.

II Knaves, The, 1613.

Knight and the Cobbler, The, *see* Christmas Tale, A, Supp. II, m.

'Knight cleped Florence, A', 15th cent.

Knight in the Burning Rock, The, 1579.

Knight of Malta, The, 1618.

    T Bryn Mawr, Marianne Brock, ed., 1944.

Knight of Rhodes, The, *mentioned in* Merry Conceited Jests of Peele, 1627; probably a fictitious title.

Knight of the Burning Pestle, The, 1607; adapt., 1662.

    S 1) Regents, John Doebler, ed., 1967.

       2) Revels, Sheldon P. Zitner, ed., 1985.

    F 1) Scolar (1613), 1973.

       2) Theatrum Orbis Terrarum (Amsterdam), De Capo (1613).

    E *Le Chevalier de Pardent pilon* (Collection bilingue), M.T. Jones-Davies, ed., 1958.

Knight of the Golden Shield, *see* Clyomon and Clamydes, 1570.

Knight of the Ill-Favoured Face, The, *see* Don Quixote, The History of, Supp. II, e.

Knights, A Mask of, 1579.

Knights of India and China, A Mask of the, 1604.

Knights of the Helmet, A Mask of, *see* Gesta Grayorum, 1594.

Knot of Fools, A, 1623.

Knot of Fools, The, 1612.

Knot of Knaves, A, *see* Histriomastix, 1599.

Knot of Knaves, A, *see* Scots Figgaries, The, 1652.

Knowsley, A Mask at, 1641.

    E 'A Masque at Knowsley', *Trans, of the Historic Soc. of Lancashire and Cheshire*, N.S., XLI, 1–17, R.J. Broadbent, ed., 1926.

Kynes Redux, Supp. II, j.

Labyrinth, The, 1664.

Labyrinthus, 1603.

    F *Renaissance Latin Drama in England*, Marvin Spevack, J.W. Binns, Hans-Jurgen Weckermann, gen. eds, 1982–6; prep. & intro., S. Brock.

Ladies à la Mode, The, 1668.

Ladies and Boys, A Mask of, 1583.

Ladies' Mask, The, *see* Amazons, The Mask of, 1618.

Ladies' Privilege, The, 1637.

    T Maryland, Robert Milton Brown, ed., 1977.

Ladrones, or The Robber's Island, 1658.

Lady Alimony, or The Alimony Lady, 1659.

Lady Amity, 1604.

Lady Barbara, 1571.

Lady Contemplation, The, 1658.

Lady Errant, The, 1637.

Lady in Fashion, The, *see* Woman's Wit, 1696.

I Lady Jane, 1602.

II Lady Jane, 1602.

Lady Jane Grey, The Death of, *see* Innocent Usurper, The, 1694.

Lady Lucy's Mask, The, Supp. II, i.

Lady Mother, The, 1635.

Lady Nature, *See* Histriomastix, 1599; *also* Nature, 1495.

Lady of May, The, 1578.

    E 'The Helmingham Hall MS of Sidney's The Lady of May: A Commentary & Transcription', *Renaissance Drama*, N.S., I, 103–19, R. Kimbrough and P. Murphy, eds, 1968.

Lady of Pleasure, The, 1635.

    S Revels, Ronald Huebert, ed., 1986.

    T Iowa, Marilyn D. Papousek, ed., 1971.

Lady of the Lake, The, *see* Henry's Barriers, Prince, 1610.

Lady of the Lake, The, *see* Princely Pleasures at Kenilworth, The, 1575.

Lady Peace, *see* Mask of Apollo, the Nine Muses, and Lady Peace, A, 1572.

Lady's Distress, A, *see* Banditti, The, 1686.

Lady's Privilege, The, *see* Ladies' Privilege, The, 1637.

Lady's Trial, The, 1638.

Laelia, 1595.

    E G.C. Moore Smith, ed., *Laelia*, 1910.

    F *Renaissance Latin Drama in England*, Marvin Spevack, J.W. Binns, Hans-Jurgen Weckermann, gen. eds, 1982–6; prep. & intro., Horst-Dieter Blume.

Lame Commonwealth, The, 1662.

Lancashire Witches, The, and Tegue O'Dively, the Irish Priest, 1681.

Lance Knights, A Mask of, 1573.

Landgartha, 1640.

Landgartha, or The Amazon Queen of Denmark, 1683.

Landlady, The, 1662.

Large Prerogative, The, *see* Love in Its Ecstasy, 1634.

Larum for London, A, or The Siege of Antwerp, 1599.

Lascivious Knight, The, *see* Histriomastix, 1599.

Lascivious Queen, The, *see* Lust's Dominion, 1600.

Late Lancashire Witches, The, 1634.
   T Michigan, L.H. Barber, Jr, ed., 1962.

Late Murder in White Chapel, The, or Keep the Widow Waking 1624.

Late Murder of the Son upon the Mother, The, *see* Late Murder in White Chapel, The, 1624.

Late Revolution, The, or The Happy Change, 1690.

Launching of the Mary, The, or The Seaman's Honest Wife, 1633.

Launching of the May, The, *an error for* Launching of the Mary, The, 1633.

Law against Lovers, The, 1662.

Law Case, The, Supp. II, b.

Law Tricks, or Who Would Have Thought It, 1604.

Laws of Candy, The, 1619.

Lawyer Cheated, The, *see* Frolic, The, 1671.

Lazarus, *see* De Lazaro, 1546.

Lazarus, *see* Raising of Lazarus, The, 12th cent., *and* 1536.

Leander, 1599.
   F Renaissance Latin Drama in England, Marvin Spevack, J.W. Binns, Hans-Jurgen Weckermann, gen. eds, 1982–6; prep. & intro., S. Brock.

Lear, The History of King, 1681 (adaptation by Tate, 1681).
   C 1) *Shakespeare Adaptations*, M. Summers, ed., 1922.
      2) *Five Restoration Adaptations of Shakespeare*, C. Spencer, ed., 1965.
   S Regents, James Black, ed., 1975.
   F Cornmarket (1681).

Lear, The Tragedy of King, 1605; adapt., 1681; *see also* Supp. II, k,

V 1965.

Leicester Passion Play, 15th cent.

Leicester's Service in Flanders, 1587.

Leir, The True Chronicle History of King, 1590.
   E Quellen zu Konig Lear, R. Fischer, ed., 1914.
   C 1) *Six Early Plays Related to the Shakespeare Canon*, Anglistica, Vol. 14, E.B. Everitt, R.L. Armstrong, eds, 1965.
      2) *Shakespeare and His Sources*, Joseph Satin, ed., 1966.
   T 1) Michigan–Madison, Donald Michael Michie, ed., 1979.
      2) Brown, Cordelia Caroline Sherman, ed., 1981.

Lenotius King of Cyprus, 1665.

Leo Armenus, 1627.

Leo Sapiens, Supp. II, l.

Leontius, Hypatius, et Theodulus, Supp. II, l.

Lerma, *see* Great Favourite, The, 1668, *and* Spanish Duke of Lerma, The, 1623.

Lethe, The Mask of, *see* Lovers Made Men, 1617.

Levellers Levelled, The, or The Independents' Conspiracy to Root out Monarchy, 1647.

Lewd Levite, The, *see* News from Geneva, 1662.

Lewis King of Spain, Supp. II, k.

Liar, The, 1661.

Liar, The, *see* Mistaken Beauty, The, 1684.

Liberality and Prodigality, *see* Contention between Liberality and Prodigality, The, 1601.

Libertine, The, 1675.
   T Stanford, Helen Taylor Pellegrin, ed., 1978.

Libido Vindex, *see* Thibaldus, 1640.

Life and Death of Mrs Rump, The Famous Tragedy of the, 1660.

Life and Death of Sir Thomas Gresham with the Building of the Royal Exchange, The *see* II If You Know Not Me You Know Nobody, 1605.

Life and Repentance of Mary Magdalene, The, 1558.
   E The Life and Repentaunce of Marie Magdalene (univ. of Chicago Decennial Pubs., 2nd. Ser., Vol. I), F.I. Carpenter, ed., 1904.

Life of Cardinal Wolsey, The, 1601.

Life of Mother Shipton, The, 1670.

Light Heart, The, *see* New Inn, The, 1629.

London's Tempe, or The Field of Happiness, 1629.

London's Triumph, 1656.

London's Triumph, 1659.

London's Triumph, 1662.

London's Triumph, or The Goldsmiths' Jubilee, 1687.

London's Triumph, Presented by Industry and Honour, 1658.

London's Triumphs, 1657.

London's Triumphs, 1661.

London's Triumphs, 1664.

London's Triumphs, 1676.

London's Triumphs, 1677.

London's Triumphs, *see* Goldsmiths' Jubilee, The, 1674.

London's Yearly Jubilee, 1686.

Long Meg of Westminster, 1595.

Longbeard, *see* William Longbeard, 1599.

Longer Thou Livest the More Fool Thou Art, The, 1559.

   S Regents, R. Mark Benbow, ed., 1967.

   E 'The Longer Thou Livest, the More Fool Thou Art', *Jahrbuch der deutschen Shakespeare Gesellschaft*, XXXVI, 1–64., A. Brandl, ed., 1900.

Longshanks, 1595.

Longsword, *see* William Longbeard, 1599.

Look About You, 1599.

   E *A Pleasant Commodie Called Looke About You*, Richard S.M. Hirsh, ed., 1980.

   T Harvard, Anne Charlotte Begor, ed., 1965.

Look on Me and Love Me, or Marriage in the Dark, Supp. II, m.

Look to the Lady, 1619.

Looking Glass for London and England, A, 1588.

   T 1) Michigan, G.A. Glugston, ed., 1966.
       2) Kent State, T. Hyashi, ed., 1968.

Looking Glass, the Bachelor, or the Hawk, The, *see* Mull Sack, Supp. II, m.

Lord Governance and Lady Public Weal, 1526.

Lord Mayor's Show, The, 1535.

Lord Mayor's Show, The, 1682.

   C *Lord Mayor's Pageants of the Merchant Taylors' Company in the XVth, XVIth, and XVIIth Centuries*, R.T.D. Sayle, ed., 1931.

Lord Mendall, The, *see* Peaceable King, The, 1623.

Lord's Supper and Washing the Feet, The, 1536.

Lord's Mask, The, 1613.

   C *A Book of Masques in Honour of Allardyce Nicoll*, T.J.B. Spencer, S.W. Wells, *et al.*, eds, 1967.

Lost Lady, The, 1637.

   T New Brunswick, Donald F. Rowan, ed., 1967.

Lost Lover, The, or The Jealous Husband, 1696.

Lost Muse, A Mask of the, 1600.

Lost Recovered, The, *see* Captives, The, 1624.

Lot Debauched, 1661.

Louis XI King of France, The History of, Supp. II, e.

Louis and King Frederick of Hungary, King, Supp. II, k.

Love, A Play of, 1533.

Love, The Triumph of, *see* Four Plays or Moral Representations in One, 1612.

Love a Cheat, 1653.

Love à la Mode, 1663.

Love above Ambition, *see* Aristomenes, 1690.

Love and a Bottle, 1698.

Love and Antiquity, The Triumphs of, 1619.

Love and Beauty, The Triumph of, 1514.

Love and Fortune, *see* Rare Triumphs of Love and Fortune, The, 1582.

Love and Friendship, *see* Ormasdes, 1664.

Love and Honour, 1634.

   E 'Love and Honour' and 'The Siege of Rhodes' (Belles-Lettres Ser.), J.W. Tupper, ed., 1909.

Love and Life, *see* Way to Life, The, 1556.

Love and Revenge, 1674.

Love and Riches, A Dialogue of, 1527.

Love and Self-Love, 1595.

Love and War, 1658.

Love at a Loss, or The Most Votes Carry It, 1700.

   C *The Plays of Mary Pix and Catherine Trotter, II*, Edna L. Steeves, ed., 1982.

Love at First Sight, *see* Princess, The, 1636.

Love Crowns the End, 1632.

Love Feigned and Unfeigned, 1550.

Love for Love, 1695.

C *The Plays of Colley Cibber*, Rodney Hayley, ed., 1980.

T New York, Byrne, R.S. Fone, ed., 1966.

Love's Loadstone, *see* Pathomachia, 1617.

Love's Martyr, or Wit above Crowns, 1685.

Love's Masterpiece, 1640.

Love's Metamorphosis, 1590.

T 'Critical Editions of John Lyly's "Endymion" and "Love's Metamorphosis" ', Rochester. Donald James Edge, ed., 1974.

Love's Metamorphosis, or The Disguised Lovers, 1682.

Love's Mistress, or The Queen's Mask, 1634.

C *Bibliotheca Curiosa*, E. Goldsmid, ed., 1886.

S Salzburg, Raymond C. Shady, ed., 1977.

Love's Paradise, *see* Grove, The, 1700.

Love's Pilgrimage, 1616.

Love's Quarrel, 1661.

Love's Reward, see Unnatural Mother, The, 1697.

Love's Riddle, 1633.

Love's Sacrifice, 1632.

T Columbia, Herbert Wilson Hoskins, Jr, ed., 1963.

Love's Sacrifice, *see* Country Tragedy in Vacunium, A, 1602.

Love's Trial, *see* Hollander, The, 1636.

Love's Triumph, or The Royal Union, 1678.

Love's Triumph through Callipolis, 1631.

C *The Complete Masques* (Yale *Ben Jonson*), Stephen Orgel, ed., 1969.

Love's Victory (Anon.), 1650.

C *A Brief Description of Ancient and Modern Manuscripts Preserved in the Public Library of Plymouth*, J.O. Halliwell-Phillipps, ed., 1853.

T Stanford, Helena Maxwell, ed., 1933.

Love's Victory (Chamberlaine), 1658; adapt., 1677.

E C.K. Meschter, ed., 1914.

Love's Victory, *see* Doubtful Heir, The, 1638.

Love's Welcome at Bolsover, 1634.

Love's Welcome at Welbeck, *see* King's Entertainment at Welbeck, The, 1633.

Lover's Holiday, The, Supp. II, m.

Lover's Holiday, The, or The Bear, Supp. II, m.

Lover's Luck, The, 1695.

Lover's Melancholy, The, 1628.

S Revels, R.F. Hill, ed., 1985.

T 'An old-spelling, Critical Edition of John Ford's The Lover's Melancholy', Tennessee, J.M. Blackburn, ed., 1986.

Lover's Stratagem, The, or Virtue Rewarded, Supp. I.

Lovers Made Men, 1617.

C 1) *The Complete Masques* (Yale *Ben Jonson*), Stephen Orgel, ed., 1969.
   2) *A Book of Masques in Honour of Allardyce Nicoll*, T.J.B. Spencer, S.W. Wells, *et al.*, eds, 1967.

Lovers of Ludgate, The, Supp. II, g.

Lovers' Hospital, *see* Love's Hospital, 1636.

Lovers' Progress, The, *see* Wandering Lovers, The, 1623.

Loves of Mars and Venus, The, 1696.

Loves of Oroondates and Statira, The, *see* Rival Kings, The, 1676.

Loves of the Deities, The, *see* Cinthia and Endimion, 1696.

Lovesick Court, The, or The Ambitious Politic, 1639.

T Missouri-Columbia, Allan Burnam MacLeod, ed., 1977.

Lovesick King, The, 1617.

Lovesick Maid, The, or The Honour of Young Ladies, 1629.

Loving Enemies, The, 1680.

Loyal Brother, The, or The Persian Prince, 1682.

C *The Works of Thomas Southerne*, Vol. I, R. Jordan and H. Lowe, eds, 1988.

E *Thomas Southern's 'Loyal Brother': A Play on the Popish Plot*, (Bibliothèque de la Faculté de philosophie et lettres de l'Université de Liège, facs. xx), P. Hamelius, ed.

Loyal Brother, The, sometimes erroneously cited as alternative title for Revenger's Tragedy, The, 1606.

Loyal Citizens, The, 1662.

Loyal Favourite, The, *see* Ambitious Statesman, The, 1679.

Loyal General, The, 1679.

Loyal Lovers, The, 1652.

Loyal Subject, The, 1618.

Loyalty and Beauty, 1579.

Loyola, 1623.

Lucina's Rape, or The Tragedy of Valentinian, 1678.

Lucius Junius Brutus, Father of His Country, 1680.

    S Regents, John Loftis, ed., 1967.

Luck's All, *see* Fools Have Fortune, 1680.

Lucky Chance, The, or An Alderman's Bargain, 1686.

    T. Miami, Jean Alexander Coakley, ed., 1981.

Lucky Extravagant, The, *see* Sham Lawyer, The, 1697.

Lucky Younger Brother, The, *see* Beau Defeated, The, 1700.

Lucretia, 1605.

Lud, King, 1599 add.

Ludi Domini Regis, 14th cent.

Ludlow Castle, The Mask at, *see* Comus, 1634.

Ludus Coventriae, 15th cent.

Ludus de Bellyale, *see* Belial, 15th cent.

Ludus de Sancta Katerina, *see* St Katherine, 11th cent.

Ludus Filiorum Israelis, 14th cent.

Ludus super Iconia Sancti Nicolai, *see* St Nicholas, 12th cent.

Luminalia, or The Festival of Light, 1638.

Lusiuncula, Supp. I.

Lust's Dominion, or The Lascivious Queen, 1600; adapt., 1676.

    C *The Dramatic Works of Thomas Dekker*, Vol. 4, Fredson Bowers, ed., 1961.

Lusty Juventus, 1550.

    S 1) Garland, H.S. Thomas, ed., 1982.
       2) Malone Society, (from an undated edition of Abraham Vele), J.M. Nosworthy, ed., 1966.

    T 'A Critical Edition of Three Tudor Interludes: "Impatient Poverty", "Lusty Juventus", and "Nice Wanton" ', Rochester, Leonard W. Tennenhouse, ed., 1970.

Lusty London, 1580.

Luther, *see* Heretic Luther, 1527.

Macbeth, 1664.

    C *Davenant's Macbeth from the Yale Manuscript* (Yale Stud. in Eng., No. 146), C. Spencer, ed., 1961.

    C *Five Restoration Adaptations of Shakespeare*, C. Spencer, ed., 1965.

    F Cornmarket (1674).

Macbeth, The Tragedy of, 1606; adapt., 1664.

    V 1963.

Machiavel, 1599 add.

Machiavel and the Devil, 1613.

Machiavellus, 1597.

    F *Renaissance Latin Drama in England*, Marvin Spevack, J.W. Binns, Hans-Jurgen Weckermann, gen. eds, 1982-6; prep. & intro., A.J. Cotton.

Mack, The, 1595.

Macro Morals, *see* Castle of Perseverance, The; Mankind; Mind, Will, and Understanding.

Mad Amyntas, *see* Wavering Nymph, The, 1684.

Mad Couple, The, *see* All Mistaken, 1665.

Mad Couple Well Matched, A, 1639; adapt., 1677.

    T North Carolina, Chapel Hill, Holst Steen Spove, ed., 1973.

Mad Lover, The, 1617.

Mad Priest of the Sun, The, 1587.

Mad Reformer, The, *see* Feigned Friendship, 1699.

Mad Tom of Bedlam, 1696.

Mad Wooing, The, or A Way to Win and Tame a Shrew, 1698.

Mad World My Masters, A, 1606.

    S Regents, Standish Henning, ed., 1965.

    T 1) Birmingham, M.J. Taylor, ed., 1963.
       2) George Washington, R.H. Lane, ed., 1946.
       3) Wisconsin, G.J. Eberle, ed., 1945.

Madam Fickle, or The Witty False One, 1676.

Madcap, The, 1624.

Madcap, The, *see* Coursing of a Hare, The, 1633.

Madman's Morris, The, 1598.

Madon King of Britain, The History of, 1606.

Maenander's Ecstasy, *see* Cynthia's Revenge, 1613.

Magister Bonus sive Arsenius, 1614.

Magnetic Lady, The, or Humours Reconciled, 1632.

Magnificence, a Goodly Interlude, 1515.

S Revels, Paula Neuss, ed., 1980.

Magnificent Entertainment Given to King James, The, 1604.

Mahomet, 1599 add.; *see also* Turkish Mahomet, The, 1588.

Mahomet and Hiren, *see* Turkish Mahomet, The, 1588.

Mahomet and His Heaven, or Epimethea, Grand Empress of the Deserts of Arabia, or A Dream of a Dry Summer, or The Weather-Woman, *see* Arabia Sitiens, 1601.

Mahomet's Poo [Pow], *see* Alphonsus King of Aragon, 1587.

Maid, a Widow, and a Wife, A Dialogue between a , *part of* Cecil House, The Entertainment at, 1602.

Maid in the Mill, The, 1623; adapt., 1662.

Maid of Honour, The, 1621.

 C *The Plays and Poems of Philip Massinger*, vol. 1 of 5 vols, Philip Edwards, Colin Gibson, eds, 1976.

 E E.A.W. Byrne, ed., 1931.

Maid's Last Prayer, The, or Any Rather Than Fail, 1693.

 C *The Works of Thomas Southerne*, Vol. I, R. Jordan and H. Lowe, eds, 1988.

Maid's Metamorphosis, The, 1600.

Maid's Philosophy, The, *see* Venus and Adonis, 1653.

Maid's Revenge, The, 1626.

Maid's Tragedy, The, 1610; adapt., 1662, 1664.

 S 1) Fountainwell, A. Gurr, ed., 1969.

 2) Regents, Howard B. Norland, ed., 1968.

 3) Revels, T. M. Craik, ed., 1987.

 T 1) Chicago, A. H. Carter, ed., 1940.

 2) Florida, Frances Woy Terhune, ed., 1976.

 E C. Morley, ed., 1932.

Maid's Tragedy, The, 1664.

Maiden Queen, The, *see* Secret Love, 1667.

Maiden's Holiday, The, 1593.

Maidenhead Well Lost, A, 1633.

 T St Louis, Khalid Mahir Tikriti, ed., 1971.

Mak, *see* Wakefield Plays, 14th cent.

Malcolm King of Scots, 1602.

Malcontent, The, 1604.

 S 1) Fountainwell, B. Harris, ed., 1967.

 2) Regents, M.L. Wine, ed., 1964.

 3) Revels, George K. Hunter, ed., 1975.

 4) New Mermaids, Elizabethan and Jacobean Comedies, Brian Gibbons, ed., 1984.

 F Scolar (1604).

Male Courtesan, *see* Younger Brother, The, Supp. II, m.

Malfi, *see* Duchess of Malfi, The, 1614.

Mall, The, or The Modish Lovers, 1674.

Mallad, La, 1700.

Mamamouchi, *see* Citizen turned Gentleman, The, 1672.

Mamillia, 1573.

Man-Hater, The, *see* Misanthropos.

Man in the Moon Drinks Claret, The, 1621.

Man of Business, The, *see* Love in the Dark, 1675.

Man of Honour, The, *see* Britannicus, 1695.

Man of Mode, The, or Sir Fopling Flutter, 1576.

 S 1) Fountainwell, John Conaghan, ed., 1973.

 2) Regents, W.B. Carnochan, ed., 1966-7.

Man of Newmarket, The, 1678.

Man Too Hard for the Master, The, *see* Love without Interest, 1699.

Man's Heart His Greatest Enemy, *see* Traitor to Himself, The, 1678.

Man's the Master, The, 1668.

Man's Wit, 1570 add.

Mandeville, Sir John, 1599 add.

Mandrake, The, 1665.

Manhood and Desert, *see* Norwich, The Entertainment at, 1578.

Manhood and Misrule, 1570 add.

Manhood and Wisdom, *see* Manhood and Misrule, 1570 add.

Mankind, 15th cent.

 C 1) *The Macro Plays: The Castle of Perseverance, Wisdom, Mankind*, (A facsimile edition with facing transcriptions), David Bevington, ed., 1972.

 2) (With Castle of Perseverance, Wisdom), (EETS 262), M. Eccles, ed., 1969.

 T Michigan State, G.R. Fattic, ed., 1972.

Manner of the Crying of a Play, The, *see* Droichis

[Dwarf's] Part of the Play, 1503.

Manningtree Moralities, 15th cent. add.

Marcelia, or The Treacherous Friend, 1669.

Marciano, or The Discovery, 1662.
  E Marciano; or, The Discovery. A Tragi-comedy, by William Clark, Advocate, W.H. Logan, ed., 1871.

Marcus et Marcellianus, 1648.

Marcus Geminus, 1566.

Marcus Tullius Cicero That Famous Roman Orator His Tragedy, 1651.

Margaret, Princess, *see* Welcome for Princess Margaret, The, 1503.

Margaret, Queen, *see* Welcome for Queen Margaret, The, 1511.

Mariam the Fair Queen of Jewry, 1604.

Mariamne, 1665.

Marie de Lorraine, *see* Welcome for Marie de Lorraine, The, 1538.

Mariners, A Mask of, 1543.

Mariners, A Mask of, 1554.

Mariners, A Mask of, 1559.

Mariners, A Mask of, 1574.

Marius and Scilla, *see* Wounds of Civil War, The, 1588.

Market of Mischief, The, 1546.

Marquis d'Ancre, 1617.

Marriage à la Mode, 1671.
  C 1) *John Dryden: Four Comedies,* L.A. Beaurline, Fredson Bowers, ed., 1967.
    2) California *Dryden,* Vol. XI, J. Loftis, D.S. Rodes, V.A. Dearing, eds, 1978.
  S Regents, Mark S. Auburn, ed., 1981.
  E Marriage à la Mode (Temple Dramatists), J.R. Sutherland, ed., 1935.

Marriage and Hanging Go By Destiny, *see* Christianetta, 1633.

Marriage between Wit and Wisdom, A Contract of a, 1579.
  S Malone Society, (From the MS add. 26792), T.N.S. Lennam, ed., 1966).

Marriage Broker, The, or The Pander, Supp. I.

Marriage Entertainment for Lord James Stuart, The, 1562.

Marriage Hater Matched, The, 1692.

Marriage in the Dark, *see* Look on Me and Love Me, Supp. II, m.

Marriage Night, The, 1663; *see also* Supp. II, m.

Marriage of a Farmer's Son, The, 1618.

Marriage of Bacchus, The, *see* Ariadne, 1674.

Marriage of Frederick and Elizabeth, The, 1613.
  C The Progresses, Processions, and Magnificent Festivities of King Edward the First . . ., J. Nichols, ed., 1828.

Marriage of Mind and Measure, A Moral of the, 1579, Supp. II, p.

Marriage of Oceanus and Britannia, The, 1659.

Marriage of Prince Arthur, The, 1501.
  C A Collection of Rare Tracts, J. Somers, comp., 1807–9.

Marriage of Queen Mary, The, 1558.

Marriage of the Devil, The, *see* Belphegor, 1677.

Marriage of the Thames and the Rhine, The, *see* Inner Temple and Gray's Inn, The Mask of the, 1613.

Marriage of Wit and Science, The, 1658.
  S Malone Society, (From the undated edition of Thomas Marshe, ?1569), A. Brown, J.W. Crow, F.P. Wilson, eds, 1960.
  E Sebastian Westcott, The Children of Paul's and 'The Marriage of Wit and Science', Trevor Lennam, ed., 1975.

Marriage Revived, or The Mistress Returned, 1680.

Marriage without a Man, A, *see* Iphis and Ianthe, 1613.

Marriages of the Arts, The, *see* Technogamia, 1618.

Married Beau, The, or The Curious Impertinent, 1694.

Marshal of Luxemburgh upon His Death-bed, The, 1695.

Marshal Osric, 1602.

Martial Maid, The, *see* Love's Cure, 1606; rev. 1625.

Martial Queen, The, 1675.

Martin Calthrop, The Pageant for, 1588.

Martin Swart, Life and Death of, 1597.

Martyr, The, *see* Polyeuctes, 1655.

Martyr Dorothea, The, Supp. II, k.

Martyrdom of the Late King Charles, The, *see* Tragical Actors, The, 1660.

Martyred Soldier, The, 1618.

C *Old English Plays*, A.H. Bullen, ed. (1882–5), 1882.

Mary and Archduke Charles, Betrothal of, (also, Entertainment of the Flemish Ambassadors), 1508.

Mary Magdalene (Lynn?), 15th cent.
> T 1) Arizona State, Robert Barry Donovan, ed., 1977.
> 2) Wisconsin–Madison, L. Lewis, ed., 1963.
> 3) ('A Critical Edition of the Legend of Mary Magdalene from Caxton's Golden Legend of 1483'), Rochester, D.A. Mycoff, ed., 1984.

Mary Magdalene, The Life and Repentance of, 1558.

Mary Magdalene (Thetford), St, 15th cent. add.

Mary Magdalene (Oxford), St, 1507.

Mary Magdalene Mask, Supp. II, i.

Mary, The Coronation Entry of Queen, *see* Coronation Entry of Queen Mary, The, 1553.

Mary, The Marriage of Queen, 1558.

Mary Queen of Scotland, The Death of, *see* Island Queens, The, 1684.

Masculine Bride, The, *see* Whimsies of Señor Hidalgo, The, Supp. I.

Mask, A, 1684.

Mask, A, Supp. II, g.

Mask, The, 1624.

Mask in Flowers, A, Supp. II, i.

Masquerade du Ciel, 1640.

Massacre at Paris with the Death of the Duke of Guise, The, 1593.
> S Revels, (with, *Dido Queen of Carthage*) H.J. Oliver, ed., 1968.

Massacre of France, The, *see* Massacre at Paris, The, 1593.

Massacre of Innocents, The, 15th cent.

Massacre of Paris, The, 1689.

I Massaniello, The Famous History of the Rise and Fall of, 1699.
> T Tennessee, Nancy Grayson Holmes, ed., 1980.

II Massaniello, The Famous History and Fall of, or A Fisherman a Prince, 1699.

Massenello, The Tragedy of, *see* Rebellion of Naples, The, 1649.

Massinissa and Sophonisba, 1565.

Match at Bedlam, The, Supp. II, j.

Match at Midnight, A, 1622.

Match in Newgate, A, *see* Revenge, The, 1680.

Match Me in London, 1611.

Match or No Match, A, 1624.

Match Played at the Town Bull of Ely by Twelve Mongrels, A, *see* New Bull-Baiting, A, 1649.

Match without Money, A, or The Wives' Prize, Supp. II, m.

Matchless Maids, The, *see* Love and Honour, 1634.

Matrimonial Trouble, The, 1658.

Matrons, A Mask of, 1552.

May-Day, 1602.
> C *The Plays of George Chapman: The Comedies*, Allan Holaday, gen. ed., Robert F. Welsh, ed., 1970.

May Lady, The, *see* Lady of May, The, 1578.

May Lord, The, 1613.

May Queen, The, *see* Concealed Royalty, The, 1674.

Mayor of Queenborough, The, *see* Hengist King of Kent, 1618; adapt., 1700.

Measure for Measure, 1604; adapt., 1662, 1700.
> V 1980, Mark Eccles, ed.

Measure for Measure, or Beauty the Best Advocate, 1700.
> C *The Plays of Charles Gildon*, Paula R. Backscheider, ed., 1979.
> F Cornmarket (1700).
> T Denver, Edward Alan Cairns, ed., 1971.

Medea (Buchanan), 1540; *see also* Supp. I.

Medea (Studley), 1566.
> C *Seneca His Tenne Tragedies Translated into English* (Tudor Trans., 2nd Ser.), 1927.

Medea (Hobbes), 1602.

Medea (Sherburne), 1648.

Medea, Supp. I.

Medicine for a Curst Wife, A, 1602.

Medioxes, A Mask of, 1553.

Medley of Humours, The, *see* Triumphant Widow, The, 1674.

Melancholics, The, *see* Mr Turbulent, 1682.

Melancholy Visioner, The, *see* Mr Turbulent, 1682.

Melanthe Fabula Pastoralis, 1615.

Marvin Spevack, J.W. Binns, Hans-Jurgen Weckermann, gen. eds, 1982–6; prep. & intro. J. Mulryan.

Microcosmus (Nabbes), 1637.

Midas, 1589.
> S   Regents, Anne B. Lancashire, ed., 1969.

Middle Temple, The Mask at the, 1617.

Middle Temple, A Mask of the, 1621.

Middle Temple and Lincoln's Inn, The Mask of the, 1613.
> C   *The Plays of George Chapman: The Comedies*; Allan Holaday, ed., 1970.

Middlesex Justice of the Peace, The, *see* Weeding of the Covent Garden, The, 1632.

Midnight Adventures, The, *see* Have at All, 1694.

Midnight's Intrigues, 1677.

Midsummer Show (Chester), 15th cent. add.

Midsummer Show, 1584.

Midsummer Watch (London), 15th cent. add.

Midsummer-Night's Dream, A, 1596; adapt., 1661, 1692; *see also* 1673, Supp. II, k.
> V   1966.

Milan, *see* Duke of Milan.

Miles Gloriosus, Supp. I.

Miller, The, 1598.

Mind, Will, and Understanding, 15th cent.
> C   1)   *The Macro Plays: The Castle of Perseverance, Wisdom, Mankind*, (Facsimile Edition with Facing Transcriptions), David Bevington, ed., 1972.
> 2)   *The Macro Plays* (EETS 262), 1969.

Minds, An Interlude of, 1574.

Minerva's Sacrifice, 1629.

Minerva's Triumphs, or Grammar and Rhetoric, *see* Words Made Visible, 1678.

Mingo (or Myngs), 1577.

Mirror of the Late Times, The, *see* Rump, The, 1660.

Mirth and Drollery, *see* Muse of Newmarket, The, 1680.

Mirza, 1655.

Misanthropos, or The Man-Hater, non-dramatic dialogue in Pleasant Dialogues and Dramas, 1635.

Miser, The, 1672.

Miseries of Civil War, The, *see* Misery of Civil War, The, 1680.

Miseries of Enforced Marriage, The, 1606.
> S   Malone Society (from edition of 1607), G.H. Blayney, ed., 1963.
> T   New York, G.B. Dickson, ed., 1934.

Misery of Civil War, The, 1680.
> F   Cornmarket (1680).

Misfortunes of Arthur, The, 1588.
> C   *Early English Classical Tragedies*, J.W. Cunliffe, ed., 1912.

Misogonus, 1571.
> S   Garland, Lester E. Barber, ed., 1979.

Mistake, The, *see* Young King, The, 1679.

Mistaken Beauty, The, or The Liar, 1684.

Mistaken Brothers, The, *see* Like Father Like Son, 1682.

Mistaken Husband, The, 1674.

Mistakes, The, or The False Report, 1690.

Mr Anthony, 1669.

Mr Doolittle, 1683.

Mr Limberham, *see* Kind Keeper, The, 1678.

Mr Turbulent, or The Melancholics, 1682.

Mistress, The, *see* Bellamira, 1687.

Mistress Parliament Brought to Bed, 1648.

Mistress Parliament Her Gossiping, 1648.

Mistress Parliament Her Invitation of Mistress London, 1648.

Mistress Parliament Presented in Her Bed, 1648.

Mistress Parliament's New Figaries, *see* II Newmarket Fair, 1649.
> C   *The Antiquarian Repertory*, F. Grose, comp. (1807–09), 1808.

Mistress Returned, The, *see* Marriage Revived, 1680.

Mitcham, The Entertainment at, 1598.
> E   *Queen Elizabeth's Entertainment at Mitcham*, L. Hotson, ed., 1953.

Mites Terram Possidebunt, *see* S. Edoardus Confessor, 1653.

Mithridates King of Pontus, 1678.

Mock Astrologer, The, *see* Evening's Love, An, 1668.

Mock Duellist, The, or The French Valet, 1675.

Mock Marriage, The, 1695.

Mock Marriage, The, *see* English Moor, The, 1637.

'Mock Mass' before Queen Elizabeth, 1564.
> E   'Anti-Catholic Masques Performed before

Queen Elizabeth I', *N&O*, ns 33. Marion Colthorpe, ed., 1986.

Mock Pompey, 1674.

Mock Tempest, The, or The Enchanted Castle, 1674.

    C *Shakespeare Adaptations*, M. Summers, ed., 1922.

    T 'An Edition of the Burlesque Plays of Thomas Duffett', Iowa, Ronald E. DiLorenzo, ed., 1968.

Mock Testator, The, *see* Sexton, The, 1662.

Mock Thyestes, *see* Thyestes, 1674.

Modish Lovers, The, *see* Mall, The, 1674.

Modish Wife, The, *see* Tom Essence, 1676.

Moll Cutpurse, *see* Roaring Girl, The, 1608.

Money Is an Ass, 1635.

Monsieur D'Olive, 1605.

    C *The Plays of George Chapman: The Comedies*, Allan Holaday, gen. ed.; Alan Holaday, ed., 1970.

Monsieur Galliard, The Humours of, 1662.

Monsieur Raggou, *see* Old Troop, The, 1664.

Monsieur Thomas, 1615; adapt., 1662, 1678.

    T Toronto, Nanette Cleri Clinch, ed., 1979.

Montacute, The Mask for Lord, 1572.

    C *The Complete Works of George Gascoigne* J.W. Cunliffe, ed. (1907–10), 1907.

Montague Mask, The, *see* Montacute, The Mask for Lord, 1572.

Montezuma sive Mexici Imperii Occasus, Supp. I.

Monuments of Honour, 1624.

Moor's Mask, The, *see* Moore's Mask, 1636.

Moor's Revenge, The, *see* Abdelazer, 1676.

Moore's Mask, 1636.

Moors, A Mask of, 1559.

Moors and Amazons, A Mask of, 1551.

More, The Book of Sir Thomas, 1595.

More Dissemblers Besides Women, 1615; adapt., 1678.

    T Michigan State, Frank Tolle Mason, ed., 1974.

More Than Nine Days Wonder: Two Constant Women, Supp. II, m.

Morning Ramble, The; or The Town Humours, 1672.

Morris Mask, A, 1579.

Mors Comoedia, 1619.

    T ('Robert Squire's Death, A Comedie; A Seventeenth Century Translation of William Drury's *Mors*: A Critical Edition'), Syracuse, M. Sicinolf, ed., 1983.

Mors Valentiniani Imperatoris, Supp. II, l.

Mortimer His Fall, 1637.

Morus, Supp. I; *see also* Thomas Morus, 1612.

Most Firm Friendship of Titus and Gisippus, The, 1546.

Most Virtuous and Godly Susanna, The, 1569.

Most Votes Carry It, The, *see* Love at a Loss, 1700.

Mostellaria, Supp. I.

Mother Bombie, 1591.

Mother in Fashion, The, *see* Disappointment, The, 1684.

Mother Messe, *see* Indictment Against Mother Messe, An, 1548.

Mother Redcap, 1598.

Mother Rumming, Supp. II, d.

Mother Shipton, The Life of, 1670.

Motions, Supp. II, j.

Mountebanks, The First Anti-Mask of, 1618.

Mourning Bride, The, 1697.

    C *Congreve: The Complete Plays*, Herbert Davis, ed., 1967.

Mucedorus (and Amadine), 1590; *see also* Supp. II, k.

    C *The Shakespeare Apocrypha* C.F. Tucker Brooke, ed., 1908; 1967.

    T 1) Denver, Norman P. Boyer, ed., 1969.
        2) Kentucky, Arvin H. Jupin, ed., 1978.

Much Ado about Nothing, 1598; adapt., 1662.
    V 1966.

Mulberry Garden, The, 1668.

Mull Sack, or The Looking Glass, the Bachelor, or the Hawk, Supp. II, m.

Mulleasses the Turk, *see* Turk, The, 1607.

Mulmutius Dunwallow, 1598.

Muly Molloco, 1599 add.

Mumming at –, *see under next word in such titles*.

Mumming before the Great Estates of the Land, A, *see* London, A Mumming at, 15th cent.

Mumming for the Goldsmiths of London, A, 15th cent.

Mumming for the Mercers of London, A, 15th cent.

Mundus et Infans, *see* World and the Child, 1508.

Mundus Plumbeus, 1525.

Murder Will Out, *see* Politic Queen, The, 1623.

Murderous Michael, The History of, 1579.

Muse of Newmarket, The, or Mirth and Drollery, a collection of three drolls listed under 1680.

Muses' Looking Glass, The, 1630.

I Music, or A Parley of Instruments, 1676.

Mustapha, 1596; *see also* Supp. II, m.

Mustapha, Son of Solyman the Magnificent, 1665; *see also* Supp. II, m.
  F Cornmarket (1668).

Mutius Scaevola, The History of, 1577.

Myngs, *see* Mingo, 1577.

Mystère d'Adam, Le, *see* Adam, 12th cent.

Mystery of Iniquity, or The Revolution, 1690.

N. Town Plays, *see* Ludus Coventriae, 15th cent.

Naamen, Supp. I.

Narcissus, The Play of, 1572.

Narcissus, a Twelfth Night Merriment, 1603.
  E M.L. Lee. ed., 1893.

Nativity Play, *see* Aberdeen Plays, 15th cent.

Nativity Play, *see also* Quem Quaeritis, Stella, Pastores.

Nativity Play *and* Resurrection Play, 15th cent. add.

Natura Naturata, *see* Nature of the Four Elements, The, 1517.

Natural Magic, *see* Novelty, The, 1697.

I Nature, A Goodly Interlude of, 1495.
  C 1) *Recently Recovered 'Lost' Tudor Plays*, J.S. Farmer, ed., 1907.
  T 2) North Carolina at Chapel Hill, M.E. Moeslein, ed., 1968.

II Nature, A Goodly Interlude of, 1495.
  C 1) *Recently Recovered 'Lost' Tudor Plays*, J.S. Farmer, ed., 1907.
  T 2) North Carolina at Chapel Hill, M.E. Moeslein, ed., 1968.

Nature of the Four Elements, The, 1517.
  C *Six Anonymous Plays* (1st Ser.), J.S. Farmer, ed., 1905.

Nature Will Prevail, *see* Love Triumphant, 1694.

Nature's Three Daughters, Beauty, Love, and Wit, 1658.

Naufragium Joculare, 1638.
  C *The Complete Works in Verse and Prose of Abraham Cowley*, Vol. 1, Alexander B. Grosart, ed., 1881; reprinted 1967.
  F *Renaissance Latin Drama in England*, Marvin Spevack, J.W. Binns, Hans-Jurgen Weckermann, gen. eds, 1982–6; prep. & intro. H.-J. Weckermann.

Nebuchadnezzar, 1596.

Necromancer, The, *see* Nigramansir, The, 1504.

Necromantes, or The Two Supposed Heads, 1632.

Necromantia, translation of dialogue by Lucian previously included in *Annals*; not dramatic.

Nectar et Ambrosia, 1578.

Neglected Virtue, or The Unhappy Conqueror, 1696.

Nehemiah, Supp. I.

Neptune's Address, 1661.

Neptune's Triumph for the Return of Albion, 1624.
  C *The Complete Masques* (Yale *Ben Jonson*), Stephen Orgel, ed., 1969.

Nero (Gwinne), 1603.
  F *Renaissance Latin Drama in England*, Marvin Spevack, J.W. Binns, Hans-Jurgen Weckermann, gen. eds, 1982–6; prep. & intro. H.-D. Leidig.

Nero (Anon.), The Tragedy of, 1619; adapt., 1675.
  S 1) Garland, Elliott McNeal Hill, ed., 1979.
    2) Mermaids: "Nero" and Other Plays,'' H.P. Horne, *et al.*, eds., 1883, 1888, 1904.
  T Illinois, Stephen James Teller, ed., 1967.

Nero Emperor of Rome, The Tragedy of, 1674.

Nero, Claudius Tiberius, 1607.
  T North Carolina, Chapel Hill, John Francis Abbick, ed., 1968.

Netherlands, Play of the, Supp. II, c.

New Academy, The, or The New Exchange, 1635.

New Athenian Comedy, The, 1693.

New Brawl, The, or Turnmill Street against Rosemary Lane, 1654.

New Bull-Baiting, A, or A Match Played at the

Town Bull of Ely by Twelve Mongrels, 1649.

New Custom, 1571.

   C Anonymous Plays (3rd. Ser.), 1906.

New Droll, A, or The Counter Scuffle, the Second Part, not dramatic.

New Exchange, The, *see* New Academy, The, 1635.

New Guise, *see* New Custom, 1571.

New Inn, The, or The Light Heart, 1629.

   S Revels, Michael Hattaway, ed., 1984.

New Medley, A, *see* Bacchus' Festival, 1660.

New Medley, The, 1661.

   C The Elizabethan Jig, G.R. Baskerville, ed., 1929.

New Moon, The, Supp. I.

New Ordinary, The, *see* Damoiselle, The, 1638.

New River, The Entertainment at the Opening of the, 1613.

New Trick to Cheat the Devil, A, 1625.

New Utopia, The, *see* Six Days' Adventure, The, 1671.

New Way to Pay Old Debts, A, 1625.

   C The Plays and Poems of Philip Massinger, vol. 2 of 5 vols, Philip Edwards, Colin Gibson, eds, 1976.

   S New Mermaids, T.W. Craik, ed., 1964.

   F Scolar (1633).

   E M.S.C. Byrne, ed., 1949.

New Way to Play an Old Game, A, *see* False Count, The, 1681.

New Way to Please You, A, *see* Old Law, The, 1618.

New Wonder, a Woman Never Vexed, A, 1611.

   T Tennessee, George Dayton Cheatham, Jr, ed., 1982.

New World's Tragedy, The, 1595.

Newcastle, The Entertainment at, *see* Blackfriars, The Entertainment at, 1620.

Newcastle Plays, 15th cent.

   C Non-Cycle Plays and Fragments (EETS, Supplementary Series 1), N. Davis, ed., 1970.

I Newmarket Fair, or A Parliament Out-Cry of State Commodities Set to Sale, 1649.

II Newmarket Fair, or Mistress Parliament's New Figaries, 1649.

News from Geneva, or The Lewd Levite, 1662.

   E The Diary of William Lawrence, G.E. Aylmer, ed., 1961.

News from Plymouth, 1635.

News from the Exchange, *see* Rampant Alderman, The, 1685.

News from the New World Discovered in the Moon, 1620.

   C The Complete Masques (Yale *Ben Jonson*), Stephen Orgel, ed., 1969.

News from Westminster, *see* Mercurius Honestus, 1648.

News out of the West, or The Character of a Mountebank, 1647.

Nice Valour, The, or The Passionate Madman, 1616.

Nice Wanton, A Pretty Interlude Called, 1550.

   S (*The Tudor Interludes 'Nice Wanton' and 'Impatient Poverty'*) Renaissance Imag., Vol. 10, Leonard Tennenhouse, ed., 1984.

Nicephorus, Supp. II, 1.

Nicomede, 1670.

Night Adventurers, The, *see* Squire Oldsapp, 1678.

Night Walker, The, or The Little Thief, 1611.

Night's Intrigue, A, *see* Feigned Courtesans, The, 1679.

Nigramansir, The, 1504.

Nine Hierarchies of Angels, The, 1510.

Nine Passions, A Mask of the, 1598.

Nine Worthies, The, 1541.

Nine Worthies, *see* Corpus Christi Procession (Dublin), 15th cent. add.

Nineveh's Repentance, 1570 add.

Ninus and Semiramis the First Monarchs of the World, The Tragedy of, 1595.

No Fool Like the Old Fool, 1676.

No Wit Like a Woman's, *see* Sir Barnaby Whigg, 1681.

No Wit, No Help Like a Woman's, 1611 adapt., 1677.

   S 1) Regents, Lowell E. Johnson, ed., 1976.
      2) Salzburg (JDS # 94), M.S. Balch, ed., 1980.

Noah Play by the Guild of Master Mariners (Hull), 15th cent.

Noah's Ark, *see* Newcastle Plays, 15th cent.

Noah's Flood, 1662.

Noah's Flood, or The Destruction of the World, 1679.

Noah's Flood, *see* Creation of the World, The, 1693.

Noah's Ship, *see* Newcastle Plays, 15th cent.

Noble Bondman, The, *see* Bondman, The, 1623.

Noble Choice, The, *see* Orator, The, 1635.

Noble Enemy, The, *see* Humorous Lieutenant, The, 1619.

Noble Friend, The, Supp. II, f.

Noble Gentleman, The, 1606, rev. b. 1625; lic. 1626, adapt., 1688.

Noble Grandchild, The, 1614.

Noble Husbands, The, 1635.

Noble Ingratitude, The, 1659.

Noble Ravishers, The, Supp. II, b.

Noble Servant, The, *see* Osmond the Great Turk, 1637.

Noble Soldier, The, or A Contract Broken Justly Revenged, *see* Noble Spanish Soldier, The, 1622.

Noble Spanish Soldier, The, 1622.

Noble Stranger, The, 1639.

Noble Trial, The, 1635.

Nobleman, The, 1612.

Nobody and Somebody, with the True Chronicle History of Elydure, 1605; *see also* Supp. II, k.
  C *The School of Shakespeare*, R. Simpson, ed., 1931; reprinted 1973.
  S Garland, David L. Hay, ed., 1980.

Noctroff's Maid Whipped, *see* Presbyterian Lash, The, 1661.

Nonesuch, The, 1623.

Nonpareilles, The, or The Matchless Maids, *see* Love and Honour, 1634.

Norfolk and Suffolk, The Entertainment in, 1578.

Northern Lass, The, 1629.
  T New York, H. Fried, ed., 1959.

Northward Ho, 1605.

Norwich, The Entertainment at, 1578.
  C *The Progresses and Public Processions of Queen Elizabeth*, J. Nichols, ed., 1823.

Norwich Plays, 15th cent.
  C *Non-Cycle Plays and Fragments* (EETS, Supplementary Series 1), N. Davis, ed., 1970.

Nothing Impossible to Love, 1634.

Nottingham Castle, Devices for, 1562.

Nottola, Supp. I.

Novella, The, 1632.

Novelty, The, Every Act a Play, 1697.

Nugize, *see* New Custom, 1571.

Nuptials of Peleus and Thetis, The, 1654.

Nurture and Kind, Dialogue between, previously included in *Annals*; not dramatic.

Nusquams with Turkish Commoners, A Mask of, 1559.

Oberon, the Fairy Prince, 1611.
  C 1) *A Book of Masques in Honour of Allardyce Nicoll*, T.J.B. Spencer, S.W. Wells, *et al.*, gen. eds, Richard Hosley, ed.,1967.
    2) *The Complete Masques* (Yale *Ben Jonson*), Stephen Orgel, ed., 1969.

Oberon the Second, *see* Fairy Knight, The, 1638.

Obstinate Lady, The, 1639.

Octavia (Nuce), 1566.
  C *Seneca His Tenne Tragedies Translated into English* (Tudor Trans., 2nd. Ser.), 1927.

Octavia (Anon.), 1591.

Odoardus Varvici Comes, Supp. II, l.

Oedipus (Neville), 1563.
  C *Seneca His Tenne Tragedies Translated into English*, (Tudor Trans., 2nd Ser.), 1927.

Oedipus (Gager), 1584.
  E R.H. Bowers, *Stud. in Philol.*, XLVI, 141–53, 1949.
  F *Renaissance Latin Drama in England*, Marvin Spevack, J.W. Binns, Hans-Jurgen Weckermann, gen. eds, 1982–6; J.W. Binns, ed.

Oedipus (Dryden & Lee), 1678.

Oedipus, Supp. I.

Oedipus, A Tragedy Called, Supp. I.

Oenone, 1673.

Oenone, *see* Rural Sports, 1653.

Of a King How He Should Rule His Realm, 1537.

Officium Pastorum, *see* Pastores.

Officium Peregrinorum, *see* Peregrini.

Officium Resurrectionis, *see* Quem Quaeritis (of Easter), or Visitatio Sepulchri.

Old Antic Mask, The, Supp. II, i.

Osmond the Great Turk, or The Noble Servant, 1637.

 E The Tragedy of Osmond the Great Turk, or The Noble Servant (1657), A. Nicoll, ed., 1926.

Osric, 1599 add.

Osric, *see* Marshal Osric, 1602.

Osterley Device, 1579.

Othello the Moor of Venice, The Tragedy of, 1604.

 V 1965.

Otho, Supp. II, h.

Ottoman Custom, The, *see* Osman the Turk, Supp. II, m.

Overthrow of Rebels, The, *see* I Lady Jane, 1602.

Ovid, The Tragedy of, 1662.

Ovo Frisius, Supp. II, l.

Owen Tudor, 1600.

Owl, The, 1614.

Owl, The, Supp. II, d.

Owls, The Mask of, 1624.

 C The Complete Masques (Yale *Ben Jonson*), Stephen Orgel, ed., 1969.

Page of Plymouth, 1599.

Pageant for John Allot, The, 1590.

 C Narrative and Dramatic Sources of Shakespeare, G. Bullough, ed., 1960.

Pageant for Martin Calthrop, The, 1588.

Pageant of a Mountain, A, 1511.

Pageant of a Wagon, A, 1520.

Pages' Mask, The, Supp. II, i.

Painful Pilgrimage, The, 1567, Supp. II, p.

Painted Lady, The, Supp. II, m.

Painter, The, 1626.

Painter's Daughter, The, 1576.

Pair Royal of Coxcombs, 1678.

Palamedes, 1513.

I Palamon and Arcite, 1566.

II Palamon and Arcite, 1566.

Palamon and Arcite, 1594.

Pallantus and Eudora, *see* Conspiracy, The, 1635.

Pallas, *see* Honourable Entertainments, 1621.

Palm of Christian Courage, The, *see* Titus, 1644.

Palmers, A Mask of, 1518.

Palsgrave Prime Elector, The, *see* Hector of Germany, The, 1614.

I, II, III, & IV Pammachii, 1538.

Pan's Anniversary, or The Shepherds' Holiday, 1620.

 C The Complete Masques (Yale *Ben Jonson*), Stephen Orgel, ed., 1969.

Pander, The, *see* Marriage Broker, The, Supp. I.

Pandora, or The Converts, 1663.

Pandorae Pyxis, Supp. II, m.

Panecia, 1574.

Panegyre, A., 1604.

Panniculus Hippolyto Assutus, 1592.

 F Renaissance Latin Drama in England, Marvin Spevack, J.W. Binns, Hans-Jurgen Weckermann, gen. eds, 1982–6; prep. & intro., J.W. Binns.

Papists, 1559.

Parable of the Vineyard, The, *see* Ite in Vineam, 1525.

Paradise, 1675.

Paradox, 1596.

Parasitaster, or The Fawn, 1604.

 S 1) Regents, Gerald A. Smith, ed., 1965.

   2) Revels, David A. Blostein, ed., 1978.

 T Michigan, Philip W. London, ed., 1964.

Pardoner and the Friar, the Curate, and Neighbour Pratte, A Merry Play between the, 1519.

 C John Heywood, Entertainer, R. De la Bere, 1937.

Paria, 1628.

 F Renaissance Latin Drama in England, Marvin Spevack, J.W. Binns, Hans-Jurgen Weckermann, gen. eds, 1982–6; prep. & intro., S. Berkowitz.

Paris and Vienne, 1572.

Parliament and the Devil, The, *see* Devil and the Parliament, The, 1648.

Parliament between the Two Lady-Birds Queen Fairfax and Lady Cromwell, The, *see* Cuckow's Nest at Westminster, The, 1648.

Parley of Instruments, A, *see* I Music, 1676.

Parliament of Bees, The, 1640.

 S Garland, Stephen Orgel, William T. Cocke, eds, 1979.

 T Vanderbilt, W.T. Locke, III, ed., 1967.

Parliament of Love, The, 1624.

 C The Plays and Poems of Philip Massinger, vol. 2

of 5 vols., Philip Edwards, Colin Gibson, eds, 1976.

Parliament Out-cry of State Commodities Set to Sale, A, *see* I Newmarket Fair, 1649.

Parliament Sold to Their Best Worth, The, *see* Kentish Fair, The, 1648.

Parnassus, *see* Pilgrimage to –, The, 1599; Return from –, The, 1600 *and* 1603.

Parricide, The, 1624.

Parricide, The, *see* Revenge for Honour, 1640.

Parroiall of Princes, The, 1641.

Parson's Wedding, The, 1641.

   C Restoration Comedies, M. Summers, ed., 1921.

   F Blom, *Comedies and Tragedies*, 1664.

Part of Poor, The, 1618.

Parthenia, 1626.

   F Renaissance Latin Drama in England, Marvin Spevack, J.W. Binns, Hans-Jurgen Weckermann, gen. eds, 1982–6; prep. & intro. M.J. Arnold.

Partial Law, The, 1625.

   E B. Dobell, ed., 1908.

Pasquil and Catherine, The Comedy of, *see* Jack Drum's Entertainment, 1600.

Passio Domini, *see* Origo Mundi, 14th cent.

I Passion of Christ, The, 1536.

II Passion of Christ, The, 1536.

Passion of Christ, The (Grey Friars), 1557.

Passion of Christ, The, 1561.

Passion of the Saviour, The, 1528.

Passion Play (London), 15th cent. add.

Passion Play, *see* Aberdeen Plays, 15th cent.

Passion Play and Resurrection Play (New Romney), 15th cent.

I Passionate Lover(s), The, 1638.

II Passionate Lover(s), The, 1638.

   T Rice, Gene Stephenson Enton, ed., 1963.

Passionate Lovers, The, *see* Gripsius and Hegio, 1647.

Passionate Madman, The, *see* Nice Valour, The, 1616.

Passions Calmed, *see* Floating Island, The, 1636.

Pastor Fido (Sidnam), Il, 1630.

Pastor Fido (Digby), Il, 1635.

   C Poems from Sir Kenelm Digby's Papers, in the Possession of Henry A. Bright, 1877.

Pastor Fido (Fanshawe), Il, 1647.

Pastor Fido, Il, or The Faithful Shepherd (Dymock?), 1601.

Pastor Fido, or The Faithful Shepherd (Settle), 1676.

Pastor Fidus, 1604.

   F Renaissance Latin Drama in England, Marvin Spevack, J.W. Binns, Hans-Jurgen Weckermann, gen. eds, 1982–6; prep. & intro. M.J. Arnold.

'Pastor Stapilton', *see* Royal Choice, The, 1653.

Pastoral, *see* Royal Choice, The, 1653.

Pastoral, A, 1645.

Pastoral Dialogue, *see* Dialogue between Two Shepherds, A, 1580.

Pastoral Mask, A, 1636.

Pastoral Tragedy, A, 1599.

Pastores (Lichfield), 12th cent.

Pastores (York), 13th cent.

Pastores, *see* Shrewsbury Fragments, 14th cent.

Pastorum Secunda, *see* Wakefield Plays, 14th cent.

Pater, Filius, et Uxor, or The Prodigal Son, 1530; *see also* Supp. II, k.

Pater Noster Play (Lincoln), 14th cent.

Pater Noster Play (York), 14th cent.

Pater Noster Play (Beverley), 15th cent.

Pater Noster Play, 1536.

Pathomachia, or The Battle of Affections, 1617.

   E P.E. Smith, ed., 1942.

Patient and Meek Grissil, The Comedy of, 1559.

Patient Grissil, 1600; *see also* Supp. II, k.

Patient Grizill, 1667.

Patriarchs, A Mask of, 1560.

Pattern of Piety, The, 1638.

Paulo Giordano Ursini, The Tragedy of, *see* White Devil, The, 1612.

Paulus Japonensis, Supp. II, l.

Pausanious the Betrayer of His Country, 1696.

Peaceable King, The, or The Lord Mendall, 1623.

Pearce His Mask, Supp. II, i.

Pedantius, 1581.

   F Renaissance Latin Drama in England, Marvin Spevack, J.W. Binns, Hans-Jurgen Weckermann, gen. eds, 1982–6; prep. & intro. E.F.J. Tucker.

Pedlar, The, *see* Conceited Pedlar, The, 1627.

Pedlar and a Romish Priest, A., 1641.

Pedlar's Mask, The, 1574.

Pedlar's Prophecy, The, 1561.

   T Nebraska, Margaret M. Chapman Peek, ed., 1972.

Pelopaea and Alope, *see* Pleasant Dialogues and Dramas, 1635.

Pelopidarum Secunda, Supp. I.

Pen Combatants, The, *see* Invisible Smirk, 1662.

Penates, The, *see* Highgate, The Entertainment . . . at, 1604.

Penelope's Wooers, *see* Christmas Prince, The, 1608.

Peregrini (Lichfield), 12th cent.

Peregrini (Lincoln), 14th cent.

Peregrini, *see* Shrewsbury Fragments, 14th cent.

Perfidus Hetruscus, Supp. I.

Periander, *see* Christmas Prince, The, 1608.

Pericles Prince of Tyre, 1608.

Perjured Husband, The, or The Adventures of Venice, 1700.

Perjured Nun, The, *see* Lovesick King, The, 1617.

Perkin Warbeck (Anon.), 1619.

Perkin Warbeck (Ford), 1633.

   C Cambridge, *Selected Plays of John Ford*, Colin Gibson, ed., 1986.

   S 1) Regents, Donald K. Anderson, Jr, 1965.

      2) Revels, Peter Ure, ed., 1968 (paper, 1973).

Perseus and Andromeda, 1574.

Perseus et Demetrius sive Discordia Omnis Pessima Imperii Lues, 1664.

Persian Prince, The, *see* Loyal Brother; The, 1682.

Petronius Maximus, The Famous History of, Supp. II, j.

Phaedra, 1700.

Phaeton, 1598.

   C *The Plays of Charles Gildon*, Paula R. Backscheider, ed., 1979.

Phaeton, or The Fatal Divorce, 1698.

Phanatique Play, A, 1660.

Pharamus sive Libido Vindex, *see* Thibaldus, 1640.

Pharoah's Daughter, Supp. II, j.

Phedrastus, 1574.

Phigon and Lucia, 1574.

Philander King of Thrace, 1628.

   E 'The Author-Plot of an Early Seventeenth Century Play', *Library*, 4th Ser., XXVI, 17–27, J.Q. Adams, ed., 1945.

Philaster, or Love Lies a-Bleeding, 1609; adapt., 1662, 1686, 1695.

   S 1) Regents, Dora J. Ashe, ed., 1968.

      2) Revels, Andrew Gurr, ed., 1969.

   F 1) Scolar (1620).

      2) Theatrum Orbis Terrarum (Amsterdam) and De Capo Press (1620).

Philaster, or Love Lies a-Bleeding, 1695.

Philemon and Philecia, 1574.

Philenzo and Hypollita, 1620.

Philetis and Constantia, 1653.

   C *The Wit, or Sport Upon Sports*, J.J. Elson, ed., 1932.

Philip of Macedon, Supp. II, m.

Philip of Spain, 1602.

Philipo and Hippolito, 1594; *see also* Philenzo and Hypollita, 1620.

Phillis and Amyntas, 1591.

Phillis of Scyros, *see* Filli di Sciro, 1630.

Philoctetes, 1543.

Philole and Mariana, Supp. II, k.

Philomathes, *see* Christmas Prince, The, 1608.

Philomathes' Dream, 1584.

Philomathes' Second Dream, 1586.

Philomela, or Tereus and Progne, *see* Christmas Prince, The, 1607.

Philosophaster, 1606.

   E P. Jordan-Smith, ed. and trans., 1931.

   F *Renaissance Latin Drama in England*, Marvin Spevack, J.W. Binns, Hans-Jurgen Weckermann, gen. eds, 1982–6; prep. & intro. M. Spevack.

Philosopher, The, *see* Wit's Triumvirate, 1635.

Philotas (Lateware), 1588.

Philotas (Daniel), The Tragedy of, 1604.

   E (Yale Stud. in Eng., No. 110), L. Michel, ed., 1949.

Philotus, 1603.

   C *Miscellany Volume* (Scottish Text Soc.), A.J. Mill, ed., 1933.

Phocas, 1619.

Phocas (C. Wren, Sr), previously included in *Annals*; ghost entry.

Phocasse, 1596.

Phoebus's Knights *see* Hay's Mask, 1607.

Phoenissae, 1619.

Phoenix, Supp. II, l.

Phoenix, The, 1604.

 T Pennsylvania, John B. Brooks, ed., 1965.

Phoenix in Her Flames, The, 1639.

Phormio (Bernard), 1598.

Phormio (Rant), 1674.

Phormio, *see* Comoedia Sex Anglo-Latinae, 1663.

Phormio, *see* Terence's Comedies Made English, 1694.

Phyllida and Corin, 1584.

Physic Lies a-Bleeding, or The Apothecary Turned Doctor, 1697.

Physician against His Will, The, 1669.

Physiponomachia, 1609.

 F *Renaissance Latin Drama in England*, Marvin Spevack, J.W. Binns, Hans-Jurgen Weckermann, gen. eds, 1982-6; prep. & intro. H.-J. Weckermann.

Picture, The, 1629.

 C *The Plays and Poems of Philip Massinger*, vol. 3 of 5 vols., Philip Edwards, Colin Gibson, eds, 1976.

 T Cornell, G.E. Dawson, ed., 1931.

Pierce, Alice, 1597.

Pierce of Exton, 1598.

Pierce of Winchester, 1598.

Pietas Coronata, *see* Mercia, 1624.

Piety and Valour, or Derry Defended, 1692.

Pilgrim (Fletcher), The, 1621; adapt., 1700.

Pilgrim (Killigrew), The, 1646.

 F Blom, *Comedies and Tragedies*, 1664.

Pilgrim (Vanbrugh), The, 1700.

 T Maryland, Nancy G. Smith, ed., 1981.

Pilgrim Prince, The, *see* Religious Rebel, The, 1671.

Pilgrimage to Parnassus, The, 1599.

 C *The Three Parnassus Plays*, J.B. Leishman, ed., 1949.

Pinner of Wakefield, The, *see* George a Greene, 1590.

Pirate, The, 1626.

Piscator sive Fraus Illusa, 1539.

Piscatory, A., *see* Sicelides, 1615.

Piso's Conspiracy, 1675.

Pity the Maid, Supp. II, b.

Place Perilous, The, 1515.

Placidas, alias Sir Eustace, 1534.

Placidas, Sir, a Collier forgery.

Plain Dealer, The, 1676.

 C *Representative English Comedies*, C.M. Gayley, gen. ed., (1903-36), 1936.

 S Regents, Leo Hughes, ed., 1967-8.

Plantation of Virginia, A Tragedy of the, 1623.

Platonic Lovers, The, 1635.

 T 1) Florida, A.S. Johnston, Jr, ed., 1951.

  2) (old-spelling edition) Texas Tech., Wendell Wright Broom, Jr, ed., 1984.

Plautus His Trinummi Imitated, 1693.

Plautus's Comedies: Amphitryon, Epidicus, and Rudens Made English, 1694.

Play of Love, A, 1534.

 S 1) Garland, Franke La Rosa, ed., 1979.

  2) Malone Society (from the edition of 1534), A.B. Somerset, ed., 1977.

Play of Plays and Pastimes, The, 1582; *see also* Delight, 1580.

Play of the Weather, The, *see* Weather, The Play of, 1528.

Player Whipped, The, *see* Histriomastix, 1599.

Playhouse to Be Let, The, 1663, 1674.

Pleasant Adventures at Brussels, The, *see* Campaigners, The, 1698.

Pleasant and Merry Humour of a Rogue, A, 1658; *see also* Triumphant Widow, The, 1674.

 E 'A Pleasante & Merrye Humor off a Roge', *Welbeck Miscellany*, No. I., F. Needham, ed., 1933.

Pleasant Dialogues and Dramas, 1635.

Pleasure Reconciled to Virtue, 1618.

 C 1) *A Book of Masques in Honour of Allardyce Nicoll*, T.J.B. Spencer, S.W. Wells, *et al.*, eds, 1967.

  2) *The Complete Masques* (Yale *Ben Jonson*), Stephen Orgel, ed., 1969.

Plenum Reconciled to Kulum, *error for* Pleasure Reconciled to Virtue, 1618.

Plot and No Plot, A, 1697.

C *The Plays of John Dennis*, J.W. Johnson, ed., 1980.

Plot Discovered, A, *see* Venice Preserved, 1682.

Plot Spoiled, The, *see* Fatal Mistake, A, 1692.

Plotting Sisters, The, *see* Fond Husband, A, 1677.

Pluto Furens et Vinctus, or The Raging Devil Bound, 1669.

Plutophthalmia Plutogamia, A Pleasant Comedy Entitled, 1627.
    C *The Dramatic Works of Thomas Randolph*, W.C. Hazlitt, ed., 1875.

Plutus the God of Wealth, *see* World's Idol Plutus, The, 1659.

Poet, Painter, and Musician, *see* Mitcham, The Entertainment at, 1598.

Poet Stutter, *see* Wit for Money, 1691.

Poet's Revenge, A, *see* Wits Led by the Nose, 1677.

Poetaster, or The Arraignment, 1601.
    S Nottingham, George Parfitt, ed., 1979.

Poetess, The, 1667.

Poetical Squire, The, *see* Sir Hercules Buffoon, 1682.

Poikilo-Phronesis, or The Different Humours of Men, 1691.

Polanders, A Mask of, 1552.

Polichinello, *see* Punchinello, 1666.

Policy and Piety, A Dialogue between, 1635.

Politic Bankrupt, The, or Which Is the Best Girl?, Supp. II, a.

Politic Father, The, *see* Brothers, The, 1641.

Politic Queen, The, or Murder Will Out, 1623.

Politic Whore, The, or The Conceited Cuckold, 1680.

Politician, The, 1639.
    T 1) Duke, E. Huberman, ed., 1934.
       2) Missouri, R.J. Fehrenback, ed., 1968.

Politician, The, or Sir Popular Wisdom, 1677.

Politician Cheated, The, 1663.

Politique Father, The, *see* Brothers, The, 1641.

Polyeuctes, or The Martyr, 1655.

Polyhymnia, 1590.

Polyphemus, The Tragedy of, *see* Troy's Revenge, 1599.

Pompae Deorum in Nuptiis Mariae, 1565.

Pompae Deorum Rusticorum, 1566.

Pompae Equestres, 1565.

Pompey, 1663.

Pompey, A. Story of, 1581, Supp. II, p.

Pompey and Caesar, The Wars of, *see* Caesar and Pompey, 1605.

Pompey the Great, 1663.

Pompey the Great His Fair Cornelia's Tragedy, *see* Cornelia, 1594.

Pontius Pilate, 1597.

Poor, The Part of, 1618.

Poor Man and the Pardoner, The, *see* Satire of the Three Estates, 1540.

Poor Man's Comfort, The, 1617.
    T Pennsylvania, Sister Marie E. McIlvaine, ed., 1934.

Poor Man's Paradise, The, 1599.

Poor Northern Man, The, a Collier forgery.

Poor Scholar, The, 1662.

Pope Alexander VI, The Tragedy of, *see* Devil's Charter, The, 1606.

'Pope, Cardinals, Friars', 1598.

Pope Joan, 1599 add.

Pope Joan, *see* Female Prelate, The, 1680.

Pope's Councillors, *see* Against the Pope's Councillors, 1537.

Port of Harbour of Piety, The, *see* Porta Pietatis, 1638.

Porta Pietatis, or The Port or Harbour of Piety, 1638.

Portia, 1594.

Portio and Demorantes, 1580.

Practice of Parasites, The, *see* Jew, The, 1578.

Praeludium, 1629.

Pragmatical Jesuit New Leavened, The, 1661.

Praise at Parting, 1577.

Predor and Lucia, 1573.

Presbyterian Lash, The, or Noctroff's Maid Whipped, 1661.

Presence, The, 1665.

Presentation for the Prince on His Birthday, A, 1638.

Presentation of Bushell's Rock, The, 1636.

Prester John, A Mask of, 1547.

Pretenders, The, or The Town Unmasked, 1698.

Pretestus, 1574.

Pretty Complaint of Peace that Was Banished out of Diverse Countries, A, 1538.

Pride of Life, The, 14th cent.

Priest the Barber, 1611.

Priests were Railed on and Called Knaves, An Interlude Wherein, 1541.

Prince D'Amour, The Triumphs of the, 1636.

Prince in Conceit, A, 1662.

Prince of Prigs' Revels, The, 1651.

Prince of Tarent, The, *see* Very Woman, A, 1634.

Prince's Ball, The, or The Conquest of Queen Judith, 1682.

Prince's Mask, The, Supp. II, i.

Princely Pleasures at Kenilworth, The, 1575.

Princeps Rhetoricus, *see* School Moderator, 1647.

Princess, The, or Love at First Sight, 1636.
    F Blom, *Comedies and Tragedies*, 1664.

Princess of Cleve, The, 1681.

Princess of Parma, The, 1699.

Princess of Persia, The, *see* Distressed Innocence, 1690.

Princess of Poland, The, *see* Juliana, 1671.

Priscianus Vapulans, Supp. II, j.

Prisoner[s] (Massinger), The, 1640.

Prisoners (Killigrew), The, 1635.
    F Blom, *Comedies and Tragedies*, 1664.

Processus Satanae, 1575.

Prodigal Child, The, *see* Histriomastix, 1599.

Prodigal Scholar, The, 1629.

Prodigal Son, The, Supp. II, k.

Prodigal Son, The, *see* Pater, Filius, et Uxor, 1530.

Prodigality, 1567, 1575.

Prodigality and Covetousness, 1656.

Proditiones Papistarum, *see* I & II On Sects Among the Papists, 1537.

Progne, 1566.

Progress to Parnassus, The, *see* II Return from Parnassus, The, 1603.

Projector Lately Dead, A, 1636.

Projectors, The, 1664.
    T George Washington, Kathleen Menzie Lesko, ed., 1980.

I Promos and Cassandra, The History of, 1578.
    T Arkansas, G.W. Amos, ed., 1968.

II Promos and Cassandra, The History of, 1578.
    C *Narrative and Dramatic Sources of Shakespeare*, G. Bullough, ed., 1958.
    T Arkansas, G.W. Amos, ed., 1968.

Prophetess, The, 1622; adapt., 1690.

Prophetess, The, or The History of Diocletian, 1690.
    C *Five Restoration Theatrical Adaptations* (Eighteenth-Century English Drama Series), Edward L. Langhans, ed., 1979.

Proteus and the Rock Adamantine, A Mask of, *see* Gesta Grayorum, 1594.

Protomartyr, 1547.

Proud Heart and a Beggar's Purse, A, *see* Histriomastix, 1599.

Proud Maid's Tragedy, The, 1612.

Proud Woman of Antwerp, A, Supp. II, k.

Proud Woman of Antwerp, The, *see* Friar Rush, 1601.

Provoked Wife, The, 1697.
    C *Representative English Comedies*, C.M. Gayley, gen. ed., (1903–36) 1936.
    S 1) New Mermaids, James L. Smith, ed., 1974.
       2) Regents, Curt A. Zimansky, ed., 1969.

Proxy, The, *see* Love's Aftergame, 1634.

Prudentius, *see* Floating Island, The, 1636.

Pseudolus, Supp. I.

Pseudomagia, 1626.
    E John C. Caldewey and Brian P. Copenhaver, eds & trans., 1979.
    F *Renaissance Latin Drama in England*, Marvin Spevack, J.W. Binns, Hans-Jurgen Weckermann, gen. eds, 1982–6; prep. & intro. J.C. Coldewey.

Psyche, 1675.
    C *Five Restoration Theatrical Adaptations* (Eighteenth-Century English Drama Series), (Facsimile Reproductions) Edward L. Langhans, ed., 1979.

Psyche Debauched, 1675.
    T 'An Edition of the Burlesque Plays of Thomas Duffett', Iowa, Ronald E. DiLorenzo, ed., 1986.

Psyche et Filii ejus, Supp. I.

Ptolome, 1578.

Public Wooing, The, 1658.

Publii Ovidii Nasonis Meleager, 1580.

Publius Cornelius Scipio sui Victor, Supp. I.

Puer Vapulans, 1582.

Punch and Judy, *see* Punchinello, 1666.

Punchinello, 1666.

Punishment of the Vices, The, *see* Satire of the Three Estates, 1540.

Puritan, The, or The Widow of Watling Street, 1606.
　　C 1) *The Shakespeare Apocrypha*, C.F. Tucker Brooke, ed., 1967, 1980.
　　　 2) *Lost Plays of Shakespeare's Age*, C.J. Sisson, ed., 1908.
　　E (Garrick Playbooks) Sidney Heaven, ed.
　　T Wisconsin, D.F. Kaiser. ed., 1966.

Puritan Maid, Modest Wife, and Wanton Widow, The, 1623.

Puritan Widow, The, *see* Puritan, The, 1606.

Puritanical Justice, or The Beggars Turned Thieves, 1698.

Pygmalion, Supp. I.

Pyrami et Thisbes, *see* Tragoedia Miserrima, Supp. I.

Pyramus and Thisbe, Supp. II, k.

Pyrander, 1651.

Pyrrhus King of Epirus, 1695.

Pythagoras, 1596.

Q.F.F.Q.S. A New Fiction As We Were: A.I.M.E.I.M.I.D2.F.4, 1661.

Queen, The, or The Excellency of Her Sex, 1628.
　　T Vanderbilt, J.A. Sutfin, ed., 1964.

Queen and Concubine, The, 1635.

Queen Ann, The Welcome for, 1590.

Queen Catharine, or The Ruins of Love, 1698.
　　C *The Plays of Mary Pix and Catherine Trotter, I.*, Edna L. Steeves, ed., 1982.

Queen Hester, *see* Hester.

Queen of Aragon, The, 1640.

Queen of Corinth, The, 1617.

Queen of Corsica, The, 1642.

Queen of Cypress, The, or Love above Ambition, *see* Aristomenes, 1690.

Queen of Ethiopia, The, 1578.

Queen Henrietta's Masks, 1626, 1627.

Queen's Arcadia, The, 1605.
　　T State University of New York, L.H. Butrick, ed., 1968.

Queen's Entertainment at Bristow, The, 1574.
　　C 'Churchyard's Chippes', Illustrations of

Early English Poetry, II, J.P. Collier, ed., (1866–70) 1867.

Queen's Entertainment at Theobalds, The, 1594.
　　C *The Progresses and Public Processions of Queen Elizabeth*, J. Nichols, ed., 1823.

Queen's Entertainment at Woodstock, The, 1575.
　　E *The Queen's Majesty's Entertainment at Woodstock*, 1575, A.W. Pollard, ed., 1910.

Queen's Exchange, The, 1631.

Queen's Mask (two entries), The, Supp. II, i.

Queen's Mask, The, *see* Love's Mistress, 1634.

Queen's Pastoral, The, *see* Artenice, L', 1626.

Queen's Visit to Tilbury, The, 1587.
　　C *The Progresses and Public Processions of Queen Elizabeth*, J. Nichols, ed., 1823.

Queen's Wake, The, *see* Tethys' Festival, 1610.

Queens, The Mask of, 1609.

Quem Quaeritis (of Easter), *or* Visitatio Sepulchri, *see following.*

Quem Quaeritis (Winchester), 10th cent.
　　C *Regularis Concordia*, D.T. Symons, ed., 1953.

Quem Quaeritis (Lichfield), 12th cent.

Quem Quaeritis (Dublin), 14th cent.

Quem Quaeritis (Barking), 14th cent.

Quem Quaeritis (Bath), 15th cent.

Quem Quaeritis (Leicester), 15th cent.

Quem Quaeritis (Magdalen College), 15th cent.

Quem Quaeritis, *see* Shrewsbury Fragments, 14th cent.

Quid pro Quo, 1578.

Quintessence of Debauchery, The, *see* Sodom, 1678.

Quintus Fabius, 1574.

Radcliffe Wedding Mask, The, 1566.

Raging Devil Bound, The, *see* Pluto Furens et Vinctus, 1669.

Raging Turk, The, or Bajazet II, 1618.
　　S Malone Society (From the editions of 1631 and 1632), D. Carnegie, ed., 1967.
　　T West Virginia, Alam-El-Deon, Ahmed Abd-El-Majeed, ed., 1984.

Raguaillo D'Oceano, 1640.

Raising of Lazarus, The, 12th cent.

Raising of Lazarus, The, 1536.

II Return from Parnassus, The, or The Scourge of Simony, 1603.
   C *The Three Parnassus Plays*, J.B. Leishman, ed., 1949.
Reunited Britannia, The Triumphs of, 1605.
Revel of Aldford, The, *see* Country Revel, The, 1671.
'Revels called a Maskalyn', 1519.
Revenge, The, Supp. II, j.
Revenge, The, or A Match in Newgate, 1680.
   T Pennsylvania State, Douglas R. Butler, ed., 1982.
Revenge for a Father, A, *see* Hoffman, The Tragedy of, 1602.
Revenge for Honour, 1640.
Revenge of Bussy D'Ambois, The, 1610.
   S Salzburg, Robert J. Lordi, ed., 1977.
   F Scolar (1613), 1968.
Revengeful Queen, The, 1698.
Revenger's Tragedy, The, 1606.
   S 1) New Mermaids, Brian Gibbons, ed., 1967.
      2) Regents, Lawrence J. Ross, ed., 1966.
      3) Revels, R.A. Foakes, ed., 1966 (paper: 1975).
   E 1) Rutherford, 1983.
      2) H. Fluchere, ed., *La Tragédie du vengeur* (Collection bilingue), 1958.
Reverent Receiving of the Sacrament, A, 1537.
Review, The, Supp. I.
Revolution, The, *see* Mystery of Iniquity, Supp. I.
Revolution, The, *see* Timoleon, 1697.
Reward of Loyalty, The, *see* False Favourite Disgraced, The, 1657.
Rewards of Virtue, The, 1661; adapt., 1669.
Rex Diabole, 1538.
Rex Oswius, Supp. II, l.
Rhodon and Iris, 1631.
Rich Man, The, Supp. II, k.
Rich Man's Misery, The, *see* Dives' Doom, 1675.
Rich Mount, The, 1513.
Richard II, 1611.
I Richard II, or Thomas of Woodstock, 1592.
   C *Six Early Plays Related to the Shakespeare Canon, Anglistica*, Vol. 14. E.B. Everitt (with R.L. Armstrong), ed., 1965.

   E *Woodstock*, A.P. Rossiter, ed., 1946.
Richard II, The History of King, 1680.
   F Cornmarket (1681).
Richard II, The Tragedy of, 1595; adapt., 1680.
   V M.W. Black, ed., 1955.
   S *Bibliography to Supplement the Variorum Edition of 1955*, W. Black, G. Herold Metz, compilers, 1977.
Richard II, The Visit to, 14th cent.
Richard II's Reconciliation with the City of London, 14th cent.
   E *De Concordia inter Ric II et Civitatem London* (Camden Soc., No. 3) T. Wright, ed., 1835.
Richard III, The Death of, *see* English Princess, The, 1667.
Richard III, A Tragedy of, or The English Profit, 1623.
Richard III, The Tragedy of King, 1592; adapt., 1699.
Richard III, The Tragical History of King, 1699.
   C 1) *Five Restoration Adaptations of Shakespeare*, C. Spencer, ed., 1965.
      2) *The Plays of Colley Cibber*, Rodney Hayley, ed., 1980.
   E (Oxberry's New Eng. Drama, No. 7), 1918.
   F Cornmarket (1700).
Richard III, The True Tragedy of, 1591.
Richard III, The Tragedy of King, 1592.
Richard Crookback, 1602.
Richard Duke of York, and the Death of Good King Henry VI, with the Whole Contention between the Two Houses Lancaster and York, The True Tragedy of, *see* III Henry VI, 1591.
Richard the Confessor, 1599 add.
Richard Whittington, The History of, 1605.
Richardus Tertius, 1580.
   C *Shakespeare's Library*, W.C. Hazlitt, ed., 1875.
   F *Renaissance Latin Drama in England*, Marvin Spevack, J.W. Binns, Hans-Jurgen Weckermann, gen. eds, 1982-6; prep. & intro., R.J. Lordi and R. Ketterer.
   T Illinois, R.J. Lordi, ed. and trans., 1957-8.

Riches and Youth, 1552.

Richmond, The King and Queen's Entertainment at, 1636; adapt., 1673.

Richmond Heiress, The, or A Woman Once in the Right, 1693.
    T Pennsylvania, R.A. Biswanger, Jr, ed., 1950-1.

Ridiculous Lovers, The, *see* Generous Enemies, The, 1671.

Right Re-enthroned, *see* Alfred, 1659.

Right Use of Plays, The, *see* Soul's Warfare, The, 1672.

Right Will Take Place, *see* Restoration, The, 1686.

Right Woman, A., 1615.

Rinaldo and Armida, 1698.
    C The Plays of John Dennis, J.W. Johnson, ed., 1980.

Ring, The, 1632.

Rising of Cardinal Wolsey, The, 1601.

Risus Anglicanus, 1620.
    F Renaissance Latin Drama in England, Marvin Spevack, J.W. Binns, Hans-Jurgen Weckermann, gen. eds, 1982-6; prep. & intro., M.M. Brennan.

Rites to Chloris and Her Nymphs, *see* Chloridia, 1631.

Rival Friends, The, 1632.
    E Peter Hausted's The Rival Friends (Indiana U. Pubs., Humanities Ser., XXIII), L.J. Mills, ed., 1951.

Rival Kings, The, or The Loves of Oroondates and Statira, 1677.

Rival Ladies, The, 1664.

Rival Mother, The, 1678.

Rival Queens, The, of The Death of Alexander the Great, 1677.
    S Regents, P.F. Vernon, ed., 1970.

Rival Sisters, The, or The Violence of Love, 1695.

Rivales, 1583.

Rivals, The, 1664.
    F Cornmarket (1668).

Roaring Girl, The, or Moll Cutpurse, 1611.
    S Revels, Paul Mulholland, ed., 1986.

Roaring Girl, The, or The Catchpole, 1640.

Robber's Island, The, *see* Ladrones, 1658.

Robbers Robbed, The *see* Bouncing Knight, The, 1662.

Robert II King of Scots, 1599.

Robert of Sicily (Lincoln), King, 15th cent.

Robert of Sicily (Chester), King, 15th cent. add.

Robert of Sicily, King, 1623.

Robert Earl of Huntingdon, The Death of, 1598.

Robert Earl of Huntingdon, The Downfall of, 1598.

Robin Conscience, Supp. II, c.

Robin Conscience, The Book in Meter of, dialogue previously included in *Annals*; not dramatic. *See* Robin Conscience, Supp. II, c.

Robin Goodfellow, of 1602, a Collier forgery.

Robin Goodfellow, 1604.

I Robin Hood, *see* Robert Earl of Huntingdon, The Downfall of, 1598.

II Robin Hood, *see* Robert Earl of Huntingdon, The Death of, 1598.

Robin Hood, The Play of, 1560.

Robin Hood, A Tale of, dialogue previously included in *Annals*; not dramatic.

Robin Hood, A Tale of, *see* Sad Shepherd, The, 1637.

Robin Hood and His Crew of Soldiers, 1661.

Robin Hood and Little John, A Pastoral Comedy of, 1594.

Robin Hood and the Friar, *see* Robin Hood, The Play of, 1560.

Robin Hood and the Potter, *see* Robin Hood, The Play of, 1560.

Robin Hood and the Sheriff of Nottingham, 15th cent.

Robin Hood Procession or Play (Wells), 15th cent. add.

Robin Hood Plays (St Albans), 15th cent.

Robin Hood's Feast, 1515.

Robin Hood's Men, 1510.

Robin Hood's Pennyworths, 1601.

Rock of Amity, The, 1518.

Roderick, 1599 add.

Rodogune, Supp. I.

Roffensis, 1612.

Roister Doister, *see* Ralph Roister Doister, 1552.

Rollo Duke of Normandy, *see* Bloody Brother, The, 1619.

Roman Actor, The, 1626.

C   *The Plays and Poems of Philip Massinger*, vol. 3 of 5 vols, Philip Edwards, Colin Gibson, ed., 1976.

E   W.L. Sandidge, ed., *The Roman Actor*, 1929.

Roman Bride's Revenge, The, 1696.

C   *The Plays of Charles Gildon*, Paula R. Backscheider, ed., 1979.

Roman Empress, The, 1670.

Roman Generals, The, or The Distressed Ladies, 1667.

Roman Ladies, The, *see* Vestal Virgin, The, 1664.

Roman Virgin, The, or Unjust Judge, 1669.

Romantic Lady, The, 1672.

Romanus, Supp. I.

Rome's Follies, or The Amorous Friars, 1681.

Romeo and Juliet, 1561.

Romeo and Juliet, The Most Excellent and Lamentable Tragedy of, 1596, adapt., 1664, 1679; *see also* Supp. II, k.

Romeo and Juliet, 1664; *see also* Caius Marius, 1679.

Romeus et Julietta, 1615.

Romulus and Hersilia, or The Sabine War, 1682.

Rosa Candida et Rubicunda, *see* Innocentia Purpurata, 1623.

Rosania, or Love's Victory, *see* Doubtful Heir, The, 1638.

Roundheads, The, of The Good Old Cause, 1681.

I Rover, The, or The Banished Cavaliers, 1677.
   S   Regents, Frederick M. Link, ed., 1967.

II Rover, The, 1681.

Rowland, 1589.

Rowland and the Sexton, *see* Rowland, 1589.

Rowland's Godson, 1590.

C   *The Elizabethan Jig*, G.R. Baskerville, 1929.

Roxana, 1592.

F   *Renaissance Latin Drama in England*, Marvin Spevack, J.W. Binns, Hans-Jurgen Weckermann, gen. eds, 1982–6; prep. & intro. J.C. Coldewey, and B.F. Copenhaver.

T   'Roxana: A Critical Ed. of the English Version with Parallel Latin Text', Harvard, Ethel R. Kaplan, ed., 1980.

Roxolana, or The Ambitious Step-Dame, Supp. II, m.

Royal Captives, The, *see* Troades, 1679.

Royal Choice, The, 1653.

Royal Combat, The, 1638.

Royal Cuckold, The, or Great Bastard, 1693.

Royal Exchange, The, *see* Queen's Exchange, The, 1631.

Royal Flight, The, or The Conquest of Ireland, 1690.

Royal King and the Loyal Subject, The, 1602.

E   K.W. Tibbals, ed., *The Royal King and the Loyal Subject* (1637) (Univ. of Pennsylvania Pubs. in Philol., Lit., and Archaeol.), 1906.

Royal Martyr, The, *see* Tyrannic Love, 1669.

Royal Master, The, 1637.

C   *Representative English Comedies* C.M. Gayley, gen. ed., [1903–36], 1914.

Royal Mischief, The, 1696.

Royal Oak, The, 1660.

C   *Lord Mayor's Pageants of the Merchant Taylors' Company in the XVth, XVIth, and XVIIth Centuries*, R.T.D. Sayle, ed., 1931.

Royal Penitents, The, *see* Innocence Distressed, 1695.

Royal Shepherd, The, *see* Aristomenes, 1690.

Royal Shepherdess, The, 1669.

Royal Shepherdess, The, *see* Love's Labyrinth, 1660.

Royal Slave, The, 1636.

Royal Union, The, *see* Love's Triumph, 1678.

Royal Voyage, The, or The Irish Expedition, 1690.

Royal Widow of England, The History of a, 1602.

Royalist, The, 1682.

Rubum Quem Viderat, 15th cent.

Rude Commonalty, A, 1537.

Rudens, 1694.

Ruff, Cuff, and Band, 1647; *see also* Band, Cuff, and Ruff, 1615.

Rufus (*i.e.*, Henry) I with the Life and Death of Belyn Dun, The True Tragical History of King, *see* Bellendon, 1594.

Ruins of Love, The, *see* Queen Catherine, 1698.

Rule a Wife and Have a Wife, 1624; adapt., 1662.

St Tewdricus (Carnarvon), 15th cent. add.

St Thomas (from Peregrini?), 14th cent.

St Thomas à Becket Pageant (Canterbury), 15th cent. add.

St Thomas à Becket Procession (Norwich), 15th cent.

St Thomas à Becket, *see also* Becket, Thomas.

S. Thomas Cantuariis, 1613.

St Thomas the Apostle, 1536.

St Thomas the Martyr, 14th cent.

St Tobias (Lincoln), 15th cent. add.

Sts Feliciana and Sabina, *see* Shrewsbury Plays, 15th cent. add.

SS Petrus et Paulus, Supp. II, l.

Salisbury House, Entertainment at for James I, 1608.

Salisbury Plain, Supp. II, b.

Salmacida Spolia, 1640.

   C A Book of Masques in Honour of Allardyce Nicoll, T.J.B. Spencer, S.W. Wells, *et al.*, eds, 1967

Samson, 1567.

Samson, 1602.

Samson Agonistes, 1671.

   C John Milton Dramatic Poems, G. and M. Bullough, eds, 1958.

Sanguis Sanguinem, Supp. II, l.

Sanguis Sanguinem sive Constans Fratricida Tragaedia, Supp. I.

Sapientia Solomonis, 1560.

Sapientia Solomonis, 1566.

   *E (Yale Stud. in Eng., No. 89), E.R. Payne, ed. and trans., 1938.

Sappho and Phao, 1583.

Sarpedon, The History of, 1580.

Sarum Sepulchrum, *see* Depositio Crucis.

Satire of the Three Estates in Commendation of Virtue and Vituperation of Vice, A, 1540.

   E Ane Satyre of the Thrie Estaits, J. Kinsley, ed., 1954.

   *F Theatrum Orbis Terrarum (Amsterdam), De Capo Press Fascimile, 1602 edition.

Satirical Declamations, 1656.

Satiromastix, or The Untrussing of the Humorous Poet, 1601.

Saturnalia, Supp. II, j.

Saturnalia, *see* Christmas Prince, The, 1607.

   *E F.S. Boas, ed., 1922.

Satyr, The, *see* Althorp, A Particular Entertainment . . . at, 1603.

Satyrs and Tilters, A Mask of, 1565.

Satyrs' Mask, The, Supp. II, i.

Saul, Supp. I.

Saul, King, 1577.

Saul, King, 1676.

Sauny the Scot, or The Taming of the Shrew, 1667.

   *F Cornmarket (1698).

Savage Man and Echo, The, *see* Princely Pleasures at Kenilworth, The, 1575.

Scaevoli, 1655.

Scanderbarge, *see* George Scanderbarge, 1602.

Scaramouch a Philosopher, Harlequin a Schoolboy, Bravo, Merchant, and Magician, 1677.

Scholar Turned to School Again, The, 1619.

Scholars, The, 1634.

Scholars of Dame Pallas and Knights of Diana, The, 1509.

School Moderator, or The Combat of Caps, 1647.

School of Compliment, The, 1625; adapt., 1662.

   *T Pennsylvania, Nixon Mumper, ed., 1959.

School-Play, 1663.

Scipio, *see* Publius Cornelius Scipio, Supp. I.

Scipio Africanus, 1580.

Scoffers and Backbiters, Against, 1538.

Scogan and Skelton, 1601.

Scornful Lady, The, 1613; adapt., 1662.

Scot's Tragedy, The, *see* Robert II King of Scots, 1599.

Scotch Figgaries, The, *see* Scots Figgaries, The, 1652.

Scotch Reformation, *see* Assembly, The, 1691.

Scots, A Mask of, 1604.

Scots Figgaries, The, or A Knot of Knaves, 1652.

Scottish History of James IV, The, 1590.

   *S 1) New Mermaids, J.A. Lavin, ed., 1967.
      2) Revels, Norman Sanders, ed., 1970.

   *T St Louis, Charles H. Stein, ed., 1968.

Scottish Politic Presbyter Slain by an English Independent, The, or The Independents' Victory over the Presbyterian Party, 1647.

   C The Harleian Miscellany, W. Oldys and T. Park, (1808–13) 1811.

II Seven Deadly Sins, The, *see* Three Plays in One, 1585.

Seven Dialogues (Sun and the Moon, etc.), dialogues previously included in *Annals*; not dramatic.

Seven Ladies, A Mask of, 1574.

Seven Sins, On the, 1536.

Seven Warriors, A Mask of, 1574.

Seven Wise Masters, The, 1600.

Several Affairs, The, 1658.

Several Wits: The Wise Wit, the Wild Wit, the Choleric Wit, the Humble Wit, 1658.

Sexton, The, or The Mock Testator, 1662.

Sforza, The Tragedy of Lodovick, 1628.

Sham Doctor, The, *see* Anatomist, The, 1696.

Sham Lawyer, The, or The Lucky Extravagant, 1697.

Shank's Ordinary, 1624.

She Gallants, The, 1695.

She Saint, The, 1614.

She Ventures and He Wins, 1695.

She Would if She Could, 1668.
    S Regents, Charlene Taylor, ed., 1971-3.

She's Jealous of Herself, 1670.

Shearmen and Tailors' Pageant, *see* Coventry Plays, 14th cent.

Shepherd's Holiday, The, 1651.
    C Inedited Poetical Miscellanies, 1584-1700, W.C. Hazlitt, ed., 1870.

Shepherd's Paradise, The, 1633.

Shepherd's Song, The, 1613.

Shepherds' Holiday, The, 1634.

Shepherds' Holiday, The, *see* Pan's Anniversary, 1620.

Shepherds' Mask, The, Supp. II, i.

Ship, The, 1611.

Ship of Fame, The, 1511.

Shipmen and Country Maids, A Mask of, 1559.

Shoemaker a Gentleman, A, 1608.
    E William Rowley, His All's Lost by Lust, and A Shoemaker, a Gentleman (Univ. of Pennsylvania Pubs. in Lit. and Philol., Vol. 13), C.W. Stork, ed., 1910.

Shoemaker Returned to His Trade, The, *see* Hewson Reduced, 1661.

Shoemaker's Holiday, The, or The Gentle Craft, 1599.

S 1) Fountainwell, Paul C. David, ed., 1968.
    2) Revels, R.L. Smallwood, Stanley Wells, eds, 1979.
    3) New Mermaids, *Elizabethan and Jacobian Comedies*, Brian Gibbons, ed., 1984.
F Scolar (1600), 1971.

Shore, The Book of [Jane], 1603.

Short and Sweet, 1579.

Shrewsbury Fragments, 14th cent.

Shrewsbury Plays, 15th cent. add.

Shuffling, Cutting, and Dealing in a Game of Picquet, 1659.
    C The Harleian Miscellany, W. Oldys and T. Park, eds, (1808-13) 1810.

Sicelides, 1615.
    C Giles and Phineas Fletcher, Poetical Works, Vol. 1, F.S. Boas, ed., 1908-9.

Sicilian Usurper, The, *see* Richard II, The History of King, 1680.

Sicily and Naples, or The Fatal Union, 1640.
    T Cincinnati, Joan Warthling Roberts, ed., 1975.

Siderothriambos, or Steel and Iron Triumphing, 1618.

Siege, The, 1629.

Siege, The, or Love's Convert, 1638.

Siege and Surrender of Mons, The, 1691.

Siege of Antwerp, The, *see* Larum for London, A, 1599.

Siege of Babylon, The, 1677.

Siege of Constantinople, The, 1674.

Siege of Croya, The, Supp. I.

Siege of Derry, The, 1692.

Siege of Dunkirk with Alleyn the Pirate, The, 1603.

Siege of Edinburgh Castle, The, 1571.

Siege of London, The, 1599 add.

Siege of Memphis, The, or The Ambitious Queen, 1676.

Siege of Namur, The, 1698.

I Siege of Rhodes, The, 1656.

II Siege of Rhodes, The, 1659.
    S Act Universitatis Upsalionsis, Studia Anglistica Upsaliensia, 1973, Ann-Mari Hedback, ed.
    E Love and Honour and *The Siege of Rhodes,*

(Belles-Lettres Ser.), J.W. Tapper, ed., 1909.

Siege Of Urbin, The, 1665.

   T Pennsylvania, I.E. Taylor, ed., 1941–2.

Sight and Search, *see* Time's Triumph, 1643.

Sigibertus, Supp. II, l.

Sigward the Famous King of Norway, *see* Landgartha, 1683.

Silent Woman, The, *see* Epicoene, 1609.

Silvanus, 1597.

   F *Renaissance Latin Drama in England*, Marvin Spevack, J.W. Binns, Hans-Jurgen Weckermann, gen. eds, 1982–6; prep. & intro. A.J. Cotton.

Silvanus, *see* Princely Pleasures at Kenilworth, The, 1575.

Silver Age, The, 1611; *see also* Supp. II, k.

Silver Mine, The, 1608.

Silvia, 1615.

Simo, 1652.

Simon the Leper, 1536.

Simpkin, *see* Singing Simpkin, 1595.

   C *The Wits, or Sport upon Sports*, J. Elson, ed., 1932.

Simpkin, The Humours of, 1662.

Simpleton, The Humour of, 1662.

Simpleton the Smith, 1653; *see also* 1662.

   C *The Wits, Sport upon Sports*, J.J. Elson, ed., 1932.

Singer's Voluntary, 1603.

Singing Simpkin, 1595.

Sir Anthony Love, or The Rambling Lady, 1690.

   C *The Works of Thomas Southerne*, Vol. I, R. Jordan and H. Lowe, eds, 1988.

   T U.C.L.A., Ronald D. Scheer, ed., 1971.

Sir Barnaby Whigg, or No Wit Like a Woman's, 1681.

Sir Clyomon and Sir Clamydes, *see* Clyomon and Clamydes, 1570.

Sir Courtly Nice, or It Cannot Be, 1685.

   C *Restoration Comedies*, M. Summers, ed., 1921.

   T Brown, Charlotte Bradford Hughes, 1959–60.

Sir Fopling Flutter, *see* Man of Mode, The, 1676.

Sir Francis Bacon's Mask, *see* Inner Temple and Gray's Inn, The Mask of the, 1613.

I Sir Francis Drake, The History of, 1658.

II Sir Francis Drake, The History of, *see* Cruelty of the Spaniards in Peru, The, 1658.

Sir Giles Goosecap, 1602.

   F Students (1606).

   T Illinois, John F. Hennedy, ed., 1965.

Sir Hercules Buffoon, or The Poetical Squire, 1684.

Sir Jerome Poole's Mask, Supp. II, i.

Sir John Falstaff, *see* Merry Wives of Windsor, The, 1600.

Sir John Mandeville, 1599 add.

I Sir John Oldcastle, 1599.

   C *The Shakespeare Apocrypha*, C.F. Tucker Brooke, ed., 1908, 1967.

   T Toronto, Jonathan Charles Rittenhouse, ed., 1980.

II Sir John Oldcastle, 1599.

Sir John van Olden Barnavelt, The Tragedy of, 1619.

   S Malone Society, (From the MS add. 18653), T.H. Howard-Hill, ed., 1979.

   E W.P. Frijlinck, ed., 1922.

   T Cornell, David Buchbinder, ed., 1973.

Sir Martin Mar-all, or The Feigned Innocence, 1667.

   C 1) *John Dryden: Four Comedies*, 1967. L.A. Beurline, Fredson Bowers, eds. 2) California *Dryden*, Vol. IX, John Loftis, Vinton A. Dearing, eds, 1966.

Sir Martin Skink with the Wars of the Low Countries, The Life and Death of, 1634.

Sir Noisy Parrot, *see* Wary Widow, The, 1693.

Sir Patient Fancy, 1678.

Sir Pitiful Parliament on His Death-bed, *see* Ding-Dong, 1648.

Sir Popular Wisdom, *see* Politician, The, 1677.

Sir Salomon, or The Cautious Coxcomb, 1670.

Sir Thomas Gresham, *see* Byrsa Basilica, 1633.

Sir Thomas Gresham, The Life and Death of, *see* II If You Know Not Me, 1605.

Sir Thomas More, The Book of, 1595.

   C *The Shakespeare Apocrypha*, C.F. Tucker Brooke, ed., 1908; 1967.

   T Michigan, B.W. Black, ed., 1953.

Sir Thomas Wyatt, 1602.

Sir Timothy Tawdrey, *see* Town Fop, The, 1676.

Sir Timothy Treat-all, see City Heiress, The, 1682.

Sisigambis Queen of Syracuse, Supp. I.

Sisters, The, 1642.

I Six Clothiers, The, 1601.

II Six Clothiers, The, 1601.

Six Days' Adventure, The, or The New Utopia, 1671.

Six Fools, 1567, Supp. II, p.

Six Pedlars, A Mask of, 1574.

Six Sages, A Mask of, 1574.

Six Seamen, A Mask of, 1583.

Six Shepherds, 1563.

Six Virtues, A Mask of, 1574.

Six Worthies, The, 1557.

Six Yeomen of the West, The, 1601.

II Six Yeomen of the West, The, see II Tom Dough, 1601.

Skinners' Well Plays, 14th cent.

Sleaford Ascension Play, 15th cent.

Slighted Maid, The, 1663.

Slip, The, see Ship, The, 1611.

Slippers, The, 1595.

Sociable Companions, The, or The Female Wits, 1665.

Soddered Citizen, The, 1629.

Sodom, or The Quintessence of Debauchery, 1678.

    E L.S.A.M. von Romer, Rochester's *Sodom*, 1904.

Sodom and Gomorrha, The Destruction of, Supp. II, j.

Sodom's Flames, see Fire and Brimstone, 1675.

Sodomo et Gomorre Incendio, De, 1546.

Soldan and the Duke of – , The History of the, 1580.

Soldier, The, 1641.

Soldier, and a Miser, and Sym the Clown, A, see Singing Simpkin, 1595.

Soldier's Fortune, The, 1680.

Soldier's Fortune, The Second Part of the, see Atheist, The, 1683.

Soldiers, A Mask of, 1552.

Solemn, Magnificent, and Memorable Receiving of Sir John Swinnerton, The, see Troia Nova Triumphans, 1612.

Soliman and Perseda, 1592.

    T N.Y. Univ., J.J. Murray, ed., 1959.

Solitary Knight, The History of the, 1577.

Solomon, 1501.

Solomon and the Queen of Sheba, 1606.

Solomon's Wisdom, King, 1653.

    C The Wits, or Sport upon Sports, J.J. Elson, ed., 1932.

Solymitana Clades, see Destruction of Jerusalem.

    F Renaissance Latin Drama in England, Marvin Spevack, J.W. Binns, Hans-Jurgen, Weckermann, gen. eds, 1982–6; prep. & intro. R.J. Lordi and R. Ketterer.

Solymannidae, 1582.

Somebody and Others, or The Spoiling of Lady Verity, see Somebody, Avarice, and Minister, 1550.

Somebody, Avarice, and Minister, 1550.

Somerset's Marriage, The Mask at the Earl of, 1613.

    F Scolar (1614), 1973.

Somnium Fundatoris, see Christmas Prince, The, 1608.

Son of Pope Alexander VI, see Caesar Borgia, 1679.

Sophister, The, 1614.

Sophomorus, 1620.

Sophompaneas, or Joseph, 1652.

Sophonisba, or Hannibal's Overthrow, 1675.

Sophonisba, The Tragedy of, see Wonder of Women, The, 1605.

Sophy, The, 1641.

Soul's Warfare, The, 1672.

Southampton Wedding Mask, The, 1566.

    C The British Bibliographer, II, 612–7, E. Brydges, ed., 1812.

Spaniard's Night Walk, The, see Blurt Master Constable, 1601.

Spanish Bawd, The, 1631.

    E H.W. Allen, ed., Celestina; or, The Tragicomedy of Calisto and Melibea, 1908.

Spanish Comedy, see Don Horatio, 1599 add.

Spanish Contract, The, 1624.

Spanish Curate, The, 1622; adapt., 1662.

Spanish Duke of Lerma, The, 1623.

Spanish Fig, The, 1602.

Spanish Friar, The, or The Double Discovery, 1680.

C *Dryden: Poetry and Plays*, Douglas Grant, ed., 1952.

Spanish Gypsy, The, 1623.

C *Representative English Comedies*, C.M. Gayley, ed., (1903–36) 1914.

T Northwestern, Kate P. Smith, ed., 1944.

Spanish Lovers, The, 1639.

Spanish Maze, The Tragedy of the, 1605.

Spanish Moor's Tragedy, The, 1600.

Spanish Preferment, Supp. II, m.

Spanish Purchase, The, Supp. II, g.

Spanish Revolution, The, *see* Rape Revenged, The, 1690.

Spanish Rogue, The, 1673.

Spanish Tragedy, The, 1587; *see also* Supp. II, k.

   S 1) Fountainwell, T.W. Ross, ed., 1968.

      2) New Mermaids, B. Joseph, ed., 1964.

      3) New Mermaids, J.R. Mulryne, 1970.

      4) (with the first part of Hieronimo) Regents, Andrew S. Cairncross, ed., 1967.

      5) Revels, Philip Edwards, ed., 1959.

   F Scolar, 1966

Spanish Tragedy [of Petrus Crudelis], A, 1636.

Spanish Viceroy, The, 1624.

Spanish Wives, The, 1696.

   C *The Plays of Mary Pix and Catherine Trotter, I*, Edna L. Steeves, ed., 1982.

   T Yale, Paula Louise Barbour, ed., 1975.

Sparagus Garden, The, 1635.

   T 1) 'Richard Brome's "The Weeding of Covent Garden" and "The Sparagus Garden": A Critical Edition', Vanderbilt, Donald S. McClure, ed., 1971.

      2) Kent State, L.L. Panek, ed., 1968.

Spartan Ladies, The, 1634.

Spartan Lady, The, *see* Spartan Ladies, The, 1634.

Speech Made to His Excellency (Monk) . . . at Drapers' Hall, A, 1660, previously included in *Annals*; not dramatic.

Speech Made to His Excellency . . . at Fishmongers' Hall, A, 1660, *see above*.

Speech Made to His Excellency . . . at Goldsmiths' Hall, A, 1660, *see above*.

Speech Made to His Excellency . . . at Skinners' Hall, A, 1660, *see above*.

Speech Made to the Lord General Monk at

Clothworkers' Hall, A, 1660, *see above*.

Speech of Delight, Supp. I.

Speech to King James I at Berwick, 1603.

Spencers, The, 1599.

Spiteful Sister, The, 1667.

Spoiling of Lady Verity, The, *see* Somebody, Avarice, and Minister, 1550.

I Sport upon Sport, *see* I Wits, The, 1662.

II Sport upon Sport, *see* II Wits, The, 1673.

Spring's Glory, The, 1637.

   C *A Book of Masques in Honour of Allardyce Nicoll*, T.J.B. Spencer, S.W. Wells, *et al.*, 1967.

Spurius, 1617.

Squire of Alsatia, The, 1688.

Squire Oldsapp, or The Night Adventurers, 1678.

Squire, Proteus, Amphitrite, and Thamesis, Dialogue between the, *see* Gesta Grayorum, 1594.

Squires, The Mask of, *see* Somerset's Marriage, The Mask at the Earl of, 1613.

Stallion, The, 1662.

Standing Mask, The, Supp. II, i.

Stanislaus Fuga Victor, *see* Fratrum Discordia Felix, Supp. II, l.

Staple of News, The, 1626.

   S Regents, Devra R. Kifer, ed., 1975.

   T 'A Critical Edition of Ben Jonson's *The Staple of News*', Toronto, A.N. Parr, ed., 1984.

Stark Flattery, *see* Sturgflaterey, 1598.

State Mountebank Administering Physic to a Sick Parliament, The, *see* Disease of the House, The, 1649.

State of Innocence and Fall of Man, The, 1677.

   T Virginia, M.H. Hamilton, ed., 1951–2.

State of Ireland, The, 1553.

Steel and Iron Triumphing, *see* Siderothriambos, 1618.

Stella (Salisbury), 13th cent.

Stella, or Tres Reges (York), 13th cent.

Stella, or Tres Reges (Lincoln), 14th cent.

Stephen, The History of King, 1613.

Stepmother, The, 1663.

Stepmother's Tragedy, The, 1599.

Stirling Revels, *see* Three Christians, The, 1594.

Stock Jobbers, The, *see* Volunteers, The, 1692.

Stoicus Vapulans, 1618.

   F Renaissance Latin Drama in England, Marvin Spevack, J.W. Binns, Hans-Jurgen Weckermann, gen. eds, 1982–6; prep,. & intro. J. Mulryan.

Stonehenge, 1635.

Stonyhurst Pageants, 1617.

   E C. Brown, ed., *The Stonyhurst Pageants, Hesperia*, 1920.

Strange Discovery, The, 1640.

Strange Flattery, *see* Sturgflaterey, 1598.

Strange News out of Poland, 1600.

Strollers, The, 1698.

Strowd, Tom, *see* I, II, & III Blind Beggar of Bednal Green, The, 1600, 1601.

Strylius, 1553.

Stuart, The Marriage Entertainment for Lord James, 1562.

Stukeley, *see* Captain Thomas Stukeley, 1596.

Sturgflaterey, 1598.

Subject's Joy for the King's Restoration, The, 1660.

Suburb Justice, The, *see* Town Shifts, The, 1671.

Successful Strangers, The, 1689.

Sudeley, The Entertainment at, 1592.

Suffolk, *see* Duchess of Suffolk, The, 1624.

Suffolk and Norfolk, The Queen's Entertainment in, *see* Norwich, The Entertainment at, 1578.

Sullen Lovers, The, or The Impertinents, 1668.

Sultanici in Aegypto Imperii Eversio, *see* Tomumbeius, 1590.

'Summer and Lust,' etc., 1519.

Summer's Last Will and Testament, 1592.

   T 'A Critical Modern Spelling Edition,' P.A. Posluszny, Bowling Green State, 1986.

Summoning of Every Man, The, 1519.

Sun and the Moon, *see* Seven Dialogues.

Sun in Aries, The, 1621.

   T (with 'The Triumphs of Integrity', 'The Triumph of Health and Prosperity', 'An Invention Performed For . . . Edward Barkham'), British Columbia, Christian Jean Burridge, ed., 1978.

Sun's Darling, The, 1624.

Super Oratione Dominica, *see* Pater Noster Play, 1536.

Super Utroque Regis Coniugio, see I & II Upon Both Marriages of the King, 1537.

Supposed Inconstancy, Supp. II, b.

Supposes, 1566.

   T Vanderbilt, S.F.W. Forssberg, Jr, ed., 1968.

Surprisal, The, 1662.

Surprise, The, 1662.

Surprised Lovers, The, Supp. II, j.

Susanna, Supp. II, k.

Susanna, The Comedy of the Most Virtuous and Godly, 1569.

Susanna's Tears, 1570 add.

Suscitacio Lazari, *see* Raising of Lazarus, The, 12th cent.

Susenbrotus, or Fortunia, 1616.

   F Renaissance Latin Drama in England, Marvin Spevack, J.W. Binns, Hans-Jurgen Weckermann, gen. eds, 1982–6; prep. & intro. J.C. Coldewey and B.F. Copenhaver.

Suspencio Iude, *see* Wakefield Plays, 14th cent.

Swaggering Damsel, The, 1640.

Swart Rutters, A Mask of, 1559.

Swetnam the Woman-Hater Arraigned by Women, 1618.

   E A.B. Grosart, ed., 1880.

   F Tudor, 1914.

   T Purdue, Coryl Crandall, ed., 1969.

Swisser, The, 1631.

   E A. Feuillerat, ed., 1904.

Sword, Rapier, and Dagger, A Merry Dialogue between, *see* Work for Cutlers, 1615.

Sycophant, The, 1613.

Sylla Dictator, 1588.

Sylvanus, *see* Silvanus.

Synedrii sive Concessus Animalium, 1555.

Synedrium, 1555.

Syrgiannes, Supp. II, l.

Tactus, see Lingua, 1607.

Taking of Namur and His Majesty's Safe Return, The, 1695.

Tale of a Tub, A, 1596.

Tale of a Tub (revised), A, 1633.

Talpae sive Conjuratis Papistica, 1689.

I Tamar Cham, 1592, 1596.

C   *The Theatre of Apollo*, W.W. Greg, ed., 1926.

Thebais (Browne), 1558.

Thebais (Forsett), 1581.

C   *Seneca His Tenne Tragedies Translated into
English* (Tudor Trans., 2nd Ser.), 1927.

Thenot and Piers in Praise of Astraea, 1592.

C   *A Poetical Rhapsody, 1602–21*, H.E. Rollins,
ed., 1931–2.

Theobalds, The Entertainment at, 1603.

Theobalds, The Entertainment of the King and
Queen at, 1607.

Theobalds, The Entertainment of the Two Kings
at, *see* Entertainment of the Two Kings of Great
Britain and Denmark, The, 1606.

C   *An English Garner*, E. Arber, ed., 1903.

Theobalds, Queen Elizabeth's Welcome at,
1591.

Theobalds, The Queen's Entertainment at, 1594.

Theoctistus sive Constans in Aula Virtus, 1624.

Theodosius, or The Force of Love, 1680.

Theomachia, 1618.

Thersites, A New Interlude Called, 1537.

C   *Six Anonymous Plays*, J. S. Farmer, ed.,
1905.

Thibaldus sive Vindictae Ingenium, 1640.

F   *Renaissance Latin Drama in England*, Marvin
Spevack,   J.W.   Binns,   Hans-Jurgen
Weckermann, gen. eds, 1982–6; prep. &
intro. L. Cerny.

Thierry and Theodoret, 1617.

This Gallant Cavaliero Dick Bowyer, *see* Trial of
Chivalry, The, 1601.

Thomas Lord Cromwell, 1600.

C   *The Shakespeare Apocrypha*, C.F. Tucker
Brooke, ed., 1908, 1967.

Thomas Merry, 1599.

Thomas Morus, 1612.

Thomas of Woodstock, see I Richard II, 1592.

Thomas Randolph's Salting, 1627.

I Thomaso, or The Wanderer, 1654; adapt.,
1677.

F   Blom, *Comedies and Tragedies*, 1664.

II Thomaso, or The Wanderer, 1654; adapt.,
1681.

F   Blom, *Comedies and Tragedies*, 1664.

Thorney Abbey, or The London Maid, Supp. I.

Tracian Wonder, The, 1599.

Three (or Two) Brothers, The, 1602.

Three Christians, The, 1594.

Three   Dialogues   between   Gelasimus   and
Spudaeus, Eda and Agna, and Wisdom and
Will, 1558.

Three Dorothies, The, or Jodelet Boxed, 1657.

Three Dukes of Dunstable, The, *see* Fool's Preferment, A, 1688.

Three Estates, Ane Pleasant Satire of the, 1540.

Three Kings of Cologne (Canterbury), 15th cent.
add.

Three Kings of Cologne (Holbeach), 15th cent.
add.

Three Kings of Cologne, *see* Shrewsbury Plays,
15th cent. add.

Three Ladies of London, The, 1581.

T   Birmingham, H.S.D. Mithal, ed., 1958–9.

Three Laws of Nature, Moses, and Christ Cor-
rupted by the Sodomites, Pharisees, and
Papists, A Comedy Concerning, 1538.

Three London Prentices, The, *see* Four London
Prentices, The, 1591.

Three Lords and Three Ladies of London, The,
1588.

Three Merry Boys, The, 1662.

Three Neighbors, Algate, Bishopsgate, and John
Heyden, the Late Cobbler of Hounsditch, a
Professed Brownist, 1642.

Three Plays in One, 1585.

C   *Dramatic Documents from the Elizabethan Playhouses*, W.W. Greg, ed., 1931.

Three Sisters of Mantua, The, 1578.

Three Vices Overcome Truth and Chastity, The,
see Satire of the Three Estates, 1540.

Threefold Discourse between Three Neighbors,
Algate, Bishopsgate, and John Heyden, the
Late Cobbler of Hounsditch, a Professed
Brownist, 1642.

Thyestes, 1560.

C   *Seneca, His Tenne Tragedies Translated into
English*, (Tudor Trans., 2nd. Ser.), 1927.

Thyestes, 1680.

Thyestes, Supp. I.

Thyestes, and Mock Thyestes, 1674.

Thyrsander, 1663.

Thyrsis, *see* Novelty, The, 1697.

Tide Tarrieth No Man, The, 1576.

E 'The Tide Taryeth No Man', *Jahrbuch der deutschen Shakespeare Gesellschaft*, XLIII, I-52, E. Ruhl, ed., 1907.

Tilbury, The Queen's Visit to, 1588.

Time, The Triumph of, *see* Four Plays or Moral Representations in One, 1612.

Time and the Almanac-Makers, *see* Presentation for the Prince on His Birthday, A, 1638.

Time Triumphant, *see* Welcome into England, The, 1603.

Time Triumphant, The, 1604.
C *An English Garner*, E. Arber, ed., 1903.

Time Vindicated to Himself and to His Honours, 1623.
C *The Complete Masques* (Yale *Ben Jonson*), Stephen Orgel, ed., 1969.

Time's Complaint, The Comedy of, *see* Christmas Prince, The, 1608.

Time's Trick upon the Cards, 1642.

Time's Triumph, 1643.
T 1) Birmingham, R.C. Elsely, ed., 1950.
2) 'A Critical Edition of an Anonymous, Title-Less Play, Dated 1643, in British Museum Ms. Egerton 1994', Ohio State, Diane Weltner Strommer, ed., 1969.

Time's Triumph and Fortus (i.e., Fortune's ?), 1599 add.

Timoclea at the Siege of Thebes by Alexander, 1574.

Timoleon, or The Revolution, 1697.

Timon, 1586.
C *Shakespeare's Library*, 2nd. ed., vol. 6., William C. Hazlitt, ed., 1875.

Timon, 1602.
C *Shakespeare's Library*, W.C. Hazlitt, ed., 1875.
S Malone Society (From the MS Dyce 52), J.C. Bulman, J.M. Nosworthy, G.R. Proudfoot, eds, 1980.

Timon of Athens, The Life of, 1607; adapt., 1678.

Timon of Athens the Man-Hater, The History of, 1678.
F Cornmarket (1678).

Tinker of Totness, The, 1596.

'Tis Better Than It Was, 1664.

'Tis Good Sleeping in a Whole Skin, 1563.

'Tis No Deceit to Deceive the Deceiver, 1598.

'Tis Pity She's a Whore, 1632.
C Cambridge, *Selected Plays of John Ford*, Colin Gibson, ed., 1986.
S 1) New Mermaids, B. Morris, ed., 1968.
2) Regents, N.W. Bawcutt, ed., 1966.
3) Revels, Derek Roper, ed., 1975.
F Scolar (1633).

'Tis Well if It Take, *see* Amorous Old Woman, The, 1674.

Titirus and Galathea, *see* Galathea, 1585.

Titleless Plays, Supp. I.

Titleless Tragedy, 1665.

Titus, or The Palm of Christian Courage, 1644.

Titus and Andronicus, *see* Titus Andronicus, 1594.

Titus and Berenice with the Cheats of Scapin, 1677.

Titus et Gisippus (Foxe), 1545.
F *Renaissance Latin Drama in England*, Marvin Spevack, J.W. Binns, Hans-Jurgen Weckermann, gen. eds, 1982-6; prep. & intro. J.H. Smith.

Titus and Gisippus, The History of, 1577, Supp. II, p.

Titus and Gisippus, The Most Firm Friendship of, 1546.

Titus and Vespasian, 1592.

Titus and Vespasian, 1619.

Titus Andronicus, The Tragedy of, (The Most Lamentable Tragedy of Titus Andronicus), 1594; adapt., 1679; *see also* Supp. II, k.

Titus Andronicus, or The Rape of Lavinia, 1679.
F Cornmarket (1687), 1969.

To Love Only for Love's Sake, 1654.

Tobias, 15th cent. add.

Tobias, 1602.

Tobit, Supp. I.

II Tom Dough, 1601.

Tom Essence, or The Modish Wife, 1676.

Tom Hoydon o' Tanton Deane, *see* Sparagus Garden, The, 1635.

Tom of Bedlam, the Tinker, 1618.

I, II, III Tom Strowd, *see* I, II, & III Blind Beggar of Bednal Green, The, 1600, 1601.

Tom Tyler and His Wife, 1561.

Tomerania, The Tragedy of, Supp. II, m.

Tomumbeius sive Sultanici in Aegypto Imperii
    Eversio, 1590.
Too Good to Be True, 1602.
Tooly, 1576.
Tooth-Drawer, The, Supp. II, e.
Torrismount, 1608.
Tottenham Court, 1634.
Tournay, The Mask at, 1514.
Tower of Babylon, The, 1548.
Town Fop, The, or Sir Timothy Tawdrey, 1676.
Town Humours, The, *see* Morning Ramble,
    The, 1672.
Town Miss, *see* Captain, The, 1677.
Town Shifts, The, or The Suburb Justice, 1671.
Town Sparks, The, *see* English Friar, The, 1690.
Town Unmasked, The, *see* Pretenders, The,
    1698.
Towneley Plays, *see* Wakefield Plays, 14th cent.
Toy, The, 1638.
Toy to Please Chaste Ladies, A, 1595.
Tradeway's Tragedy, Supp. II, m.
Tragedies of Euripides, 1550.
Tragedy of Caesar and Pompey, The, *see*
    Caesar's Revenge, 1605.
Tragedy of Love, The, *see* Cyrus the Great, 1695.
Tragedy of Tomerania, The, Supp. II, m.
Tragical Actors, The, or The Martyrdom of the
    Late King Charles, 1660.
Tragoedia Cyri Regis Persarum, Supp. I.
Tragoedia Miserrima Pyrami et Thisbes fata
    enuncians, Supp. I.
Tragoediae et Comoediae Vulgares, Supp. II, j.
Traitor, The, 1631; adapt., 1692.
    S Regents, John Stewart Carter, ed., 1965.
Traitor, The, 1692.
Traitor to Himself, The, or Man's Heart His
    Greatest Enemy, 1678.
Transformation of the King of Trinidadoes' Two
    Daughters, 'comedy' attrib. by Nashe to
    Anthony Chute; prob. not a play.
Trappolin Creduto Principe, or Trappolin
    Supposed a Prince, 1633; adapt., 1684.
Trappolin Supposed a Prince, *see* Trappolin
    Creduto Principe, 1633.
Travelling Mask, *see* 'Running' Mask, 1620.
Travels of the Three English Brothers, The,
    1607.

C 1) 'The Mohammedan World in English
    Literature, 1580–1642: Illustrated by a
    Text of "The Travailes of the Three
    English Brothers"', Duke, F. Sha'Ban,
    ed., 1965.
    2) Nebraska, Abdul Rahman Mohammed
    Ridha, ed., 1973.
I Treacheries of the Papists, 1537.
II Treacheries of the Papists, 1537.
Treacherous Brothers, The, 1690.
Treacherous Friend, The, *see* Marcelia, 1669.
Treatise How the High Father of Heaven
    Sendeth Death to Summon Every Creature, A,
    see Summoning of Every Man, The, 1495.
Trebellius Bulgarorum Rex, Supp. II, l.
Tres Reges, *see* Stella, 13th cent., 14th cent.
Tres Sibyllae, 1605.
    F *Renaissance Latin Drama in England*, Marvin
    Spevack, J.W. Binns, Hans-Jurgen
    Weckermann, gen. eds, 1982–6; prep. &
    intro. A. Cizek.
Trial of Chivalry, The, 1601.
    C *Old English Plays*, A.H. Bullen, ed.,
    (1882–85) 1884.
Trial of the Three Politic Ghosts, The, *see* Hell's
    Higher Court of Justice, 1661.
Trial of Treasure, The, 1567.
    C *Anonymous Plays* (3rd Ser.), J.S. Farmer,
    ed., 1906.
Triangle or (Triplicity) of Cuckolds, The, 1598.
Trick or Trick, or The Debauched Hypocrite,
    1678.
Trick to Catch the Old One, A, 1605.
    S 1) Fountainwell, C. Barber, ed., 1968.
    2) New Mermaids, G.J. Watson, ed.,
    1969.
    3) New Mermaids, *Elizabethan and Jacobean
    Comedies*, Brian Gibbons, ed., 1984.
    F Scolar (1607).
Trick to Cheat the Devil, A, *see* Imposture
    Defeated, The, 1697.
Tricks of Youth, *see* Walks of Islington and
    Hogsdon, The, 1641.
Trip to the Jubilee, A, *see* Constant Couple, The,
    1699.
Triplicity of Cuckolds, The, *see* Triangle of
    Cuckolds, The, 1598.

Tristram de Lyons, 1599.

Triumph and Play at the Marriage of the Queen's [Mary's] Grace, 1558.

Triumph at Calais and Boulogne, The, 1532.
  C An English Garner, E. Arber, ed., 1903.

Triumph of All the Founders of Colleges in Oxford, The, *see* Christmas Prince, The, 1608.

Triumph of Amity, The, *see* Friendship, Prudence, and Might, 1522.

Triumph of Beauty, The, 1646.
  F Scolar, *in Poems*, 1646.

Triumph of Death, The, *see* Four Plays or Moral Representations in One, 1612.

Triumph of Honour, The, *see* Four Plays or Moral Representations in One, 1612.

Triumph of Innocence, The, Supp. II, m.

Triumph of Love, The, *see* Four Plays or Moral Representations in One, 1612.

Triumph of Love and Beauty, The, 1514.

Triumph of Peace, The, 1634.
  C English Masques, H.A. Evans, ed., 1897.

Triumph of Temperance, The, *see* Honourable Entertainments, 1621.

Triumph of the Cross, The, 1613.

Triumph of Time, The, *see* Four Plays or Moral Representations in One, 1612.

Triumphant Widow, The, or The Medley of Humours, 1674.

Triumphs of Ancient Drapery, The, *see* Metropolis Coronata, 1614.

Triumphs of Fame and Honour, The, 1634.

Triumphs of Gold, The, *see* Chryso-Thriambos, 1611.

Triumphs of Health and Prosperity, The, 1626.
  T British Columbia, (with 'The Sun in Aries', 'The Triumphs of Integrity', 'An Invention Performed for . . . Edward Barkham'), Christina Jean Burridge, ed., 1978.

Triumphs of Honour and Industry, The, 1617.

Triumphs of Honour and Virtue, The, 1622.

Triumphs of Integrity, The, 1623.
  T British Columbia, (with 'The Sunne in Aries', 'The Triumphs of Health and Prosperity', 'An Invention Performed for . . . Edward Barkham'), Christina Jean Burridge, 1978.

Triumphs of London, The, 1675.

Triumphs of London, The, 1678.
  C The Lord Mayor's Pageants, F.W. Fairholt, ed., 1844.

Triumphs of London, The, 1683.

Triumphs of London, The, 1691.

Triumphs of London, The, 1692.

Triumphs of London, The, 1693.
  C Lord Mayor's Pageants of the Merchant Taylors' Company in the XVth, XVIth, & XVIIth Centuries, R.T.D. Sayle, ed., 1931.

Triumphs of London, The, 1694.

Triumphs of London, The, 1695.

Triumphs of London, The, 1699.

Triumphs of London, The, 1700.

Triumphs of London Revived, *see* Glory's Resurrection, 1698.

Triumphs of Love and Antiquity, The, 1619.

Triumphs of Love and Innocence, The, 1688.

Triumphs of Old Drapery, The, *see* Himatia-Poleos, 1614.

Triumphs of Peace, The, *see* Tes Irenes Trophoea, 1620.
  C A Book of Masques in Honour of Allardyce Nicoll, T.J.B. Spencer, S.W. Wells, *et al.*, eds, 1967.

Triumphs of Reunited Britannia, The, 1605.
  C R.T.D. Sayle, ed., *Lord Mayor's Pageants of the Merchant Taylors' Company in the XVth, XVIth, and XVIIth Centuries*, 1910.

Triumphs of the Prince D'Amour, The, 1636.

Triumphs of Truth, The, 1613.

Triumphs of Virtue, The, 1697.

Triumvirate of Poets at Rehearsal, The, *see* Female Wits, The, 1696.

Troades, 1660.

Troades, or The Royal Captives, 1679.

Troas, 1559.
  C Seneca His Tenne Tragedies Translated into English (Tudor Trans., 2nd Ser.), 1927.

Troas, 1686.

Troelus and Cresyd (Anon.), Supp. I.
  T Michigan, H.P. Tremaine, ed. and trans., 1965.

Troia Nova Triumphans, 1612.

Troilus and Cressida (Chettle & Dekker), 1599.
  C Dramatic Documents from the Elizabethan Playhouses, W.W. Grey, ed., 1931.

Troilus and Cressida (Shakespeare), The Tragedy of, 1602; adapt., 1679.
   V 1953; Harold N. Hullebrand, T.W. Baldwin, eds.
Troilus and Cressida, or Truth Found Too late, 1679.
   F Cornmarket (1679).
Troilus and Pander, The Story of, 1516.
Troilus ex Chaucero, *see* Troilus, from Chaucer, 1547.
Troilus, from Chaucer, 1547.
Troubles of Queen Elizabeth, The, *see* I If You Know Not Me, 1604.
Troubles of Great Hermenia, The, *see* Sophister, The, 1614.
Troublesome Reign and Lamentable Death of Edward II, King of England, with the Tragical Fall of Proud Mortimer, The, 1592.
   S New Mermaids, W. Moelwyn Merchant, ed., 1965.
Troublesome Reign of King John, The, 1591.
   C *Six Early Plays Related to the Shakespeare Canon, Anglistica*, Vol. 14, E.B. Everitt, R.L. Armstrong, ed., 1965.
   S Garland, J.W. Sider, ed., 1979.
   T Michigan State, Joseph Francis Dominic, ed., 1969.
Troy, 1596.
Troy's Revenge, with the Tragedy of Polyphemus, 1599.
True Coventry Plays, *see* Coventry Plays, 14th cent.
True Love's Mirror, *see* Astraea, 1651.
True Tragedy of Richard III, The, 1591.
True Tragedy of Richard Duke of York, The (*i.e.*, II Contention betwixt the Two Famous Houses of York and Lancaster, The), *see* III Henry VI, 1591.
True Tragicomedy [of Robert Carr and Francis Howard], The, 1654.
True Trojans, The, *see* Fuimus Troes, 1625.
True Widow, A, 1678.
Truth, The Triumphs of, 1613.
Truth, Faithfulness, and Mercy, 1574.
Truth Found Too Late, *see* Troilus and Cressida, 1679.
Truth's Supplication to Candlelight, 1600.

Truth's Triumphs, 1635.
Try before You Trust, Supp. I.
Tryphon, 1668.
Tu Quoque, *see* Greene's Tu Quoque, 1611.
Tumblers, A Mask of, 1553.
Tunbridge Wells, or A Day's Courtship, 1678.
Turk, The, 1607.
Turk, The, Supp. II, k.
Turk's Too Good for [Him?], A, 1619.
Turkish Mahomet and Hiren the Fair Greek, The, 1588.
Turks, A Mask of, 1559.
Turks Magistrates with Turks Archers, A Mask of, 1555.
Turmoils of Love, The, *see* Hypochondriac, The, Supp. I.
Turnholt, 1599.
Turnmill Street against Rosemary Lane, *see* New Brawl, The 1654.
Twelfth Night, or What You Will, 1601.
   V 1966.
   VS *A Bibliography to Supplement the New Varorium of 1901*, William C. McAuoy, compiler, 1984.
Twelfth Night's Revels, The, *see* Blackness, The Mask of, 1605.
Twelve Labours of Hercules, The, 1570 add.
Twelve Months, The Mask of the, 1611.
   C *Five Court Masques*, J.P. Collier, ed., 1848.
Twice-Changed Friar, The, Supp. I.
Twins, The, 1635.
Twins' Tragedy, The, 1612.
I Two Angry Women of Abingdon, The, 1598.
   T California, Berkeley, Karen Miller Wood, ed., 1979.
II Two Angry Women of Abingdon, The, 1599.
Two Brothers, The, *see* Three Brothers, The, 1602.
Two Famous Pirates Ward and Dansiker, The Tragical Lives and Deaths of the, *see* Christian Turned Turk, A, 1610.
Two Fools Well Met, *see* Fortune Hunters, The, 1689.
Two Gentlemen of Verona, The, 1593; *see also* Supp. II, k.
Two Italian Gentlemen, *see* Fedele and Fortunio, 1584.

Two Kings in a Cottage, 1623.

Two Lamentable Tragedies, 1594.

   C *Old English Plays*, A.H. Bullen, ed., (1882–85) 1883.

   T Michigan, Anne Weston Patenaude, ed., 1978.

Two Maids of More-Clacke, The, 1606.

   C *Choice Rarities of English Poetry*, A.B. Grosart, ed.

   S Garland, Alexander S. Liddie, ed., 1979.

Two Merry Milkmaids, The, or The Best Words Wear the Garland, 1619; adapt., 1662.

   S Garland, G. Harold Metz, ed., 1979.

Two Merry Women of Abingdon, 1599.

Two Noble Kinsmen, The, 1613; adapt., 1664.

   C *The Shakespeare Apocrypha*, C.F. Tucker Brooke, ed., 1908; 1967.

   S Regents, G.R. Proudfoot, ed., 1970.

   T Chicago, F.O. Waller, ed., 1957.

Two Noble Ladies and the Converted Conjurer, The, 1622.

Two Shapes, *see* Caesar's Fall, 1602.

Two Shepherds, A Dialogue between, 1580.

Two Sins of King David, The, 1562.

Two Socias, The, *see* Amphitryon, 1690.

Two Spanish Gentlemen, The, Supp. II, m.

Two Supposed Heads, The, *see* Necromantes, 1632.

Two the Most Faithfullest Friends, *see* Damon and Pithias, 1565.

Two Tragedies in One, *see* Two Lamentable Tragedies, 1594.

Two Wise Men and All the Rest Fools, 1619.

Tyrannic Love, or The Royal Martyr, 1669.

   C California *Dryden*, Vol. X, M.E. Novak, G.R. Guffey, ed., 1970.

Tyrannical Government Anatomized, or A Discourse Concerning Evil Counsellors, 1643.

   E 'An English Translation of Buchanan's *Baptistes* Attributed to John Milton's *George Buchanan*': *Glasgow Quartercentenary Studies*, 1907.

   T 'A Critical Edition of George Buchanan's *Baptistes and of the Anonymous Tyrannicall – Government Anatomiz'd*', Harvard, S.B. Berkowitz, 1986.

Tyrant, The, 1628.

Tyrant King of Crete, The, an adaptation of H. Killigrew's Pallantus and Eudora, included in Sedley's Works, 1722.

Tyrant of Sicily, The, *see* Richard II, The History of King, 1680.

Ultio Divina, *see* Leo Armenus, 1627.

Ulysses and Circe, 1615.

   C *A Book of Masques in Honour of Allardyce Nicoll*, T.J.B. Spencer, S.W. Wells, *et al.*, eds, 1967.

   E G. Jones, ed., *Ulysses and Circe*, 1954.

Ulysses Redux, 1592.

   F *Renaissance Latin Drama in England*, Marvin Spevack, J.W. Binns, Hans-Jurgen Weckermann, gen. eds, 1982–6; prep. & intro. J.W. Binns.

   T Facsimile ed., Florida State, E.F. Henley, ed. and trans., 1962.

Unfaithful Wife, The, Supp. II, m.

Unfortunate Couple, The, *see* Novelty, The, 1697.

Unfortunate Fortunate, The, 1650.

Unfortunate General, The, 1603.

Unfortunate Kindness, The, *see* Unhappy Kindness, The, 1697.

Unfortunate Lovers, The, 1638.

   C *Miscellanies of the Fuller Worthies' Library* A.B. Grosart, ed., (1872–76) 1872.

Unfortunate Mother, The, 1639.

Unfortunate Piety, The, 1631.

Unfortunate Shepherd, The, 1685.

Unfortunate Usurper, The, 1663.

Ungrateful Favourite, The, 1664.

Unhappy Conqueror, The, *see* Neglected Virtue, 1696.

Unhappy Fair Irene, The, Tragedy of the, 1658.

Unhappy Favourite, The, or The Earl of Essex, 1681.

   E *The Unhappy Favourite, or, The Earl of Essex*, by *John Banks*, T.M.H. Black, ed., 1939.

Unhappy Kindness, The, or A Fruitless Revenge, 1697.

Unhappy Marriage, The, 1694.

Unhappy Marriage, The, *see* Orphan, The, 1680.

Unhappy Marriage, with the Humours of Sparrow, The, *see* Bateman, 1694.

United Kingdoms, The, 1663.

Universal Motion, *see* Encyclochoria, 1663.

University Pedlar, The, *see* Conceited Pedlar, The, 1627.

Unjust Judge, *see* Appius and Virginia, 1669.

Unjust Usurped Primacy of the Bishop of Rome, A Tragedy or Dialogue of the, previously included in *Annals*; not dramatic.

Unnatural Brother, The, 1697.

Unnatural Combat, The, 1624.

    C *The Plays and Poems of Philip Massinger*, vol. 2 of 5 vols, Philip Edwards, Colin Gibson, eds, 1976.

    E R.S. Telfer, ed., 1932.

Unnatural Mother, The, 1697.

Unnatural Tragedy, The, 1658.

Unreasonable and Insupportable Burthen, The, Supp. II, q.

Untrussing of the Humorous Poet, The, *see* Satiromastix, 1601.

I Upon Both Marriages of the King, 1537.

II Upon Both Marriages of the King, 1537.

Usurper, The, 1664.

Usurping Tyrant, The, *see* Second Maiden's Tragedy, The, 1611.

Usury Put to Use, *see* Devil of Dowgate, The, 1623.

Uther Pendragon, 1597.

Valentine and Orson (Anon.), 1595.

Valentine and Orson (Hathway & Munday), 1598.

Valentinian, 1614; adapt., 1678, 1684.

Valentinian, 1684.

Valentinian, *see* Lucina's Rape, 1678.

Valentinian, or Rape's Revenge, Supp. II, m.

Valentinianus, Supp. II, l.

Valetudinarium, 1638.

    F *Renaissance Latin Drama in England*, Marvin Spevack, J.W. Binns, Hans-Jurgen Weckermann, gen. eds, 1982–6; prep. & intro., H.J. Weckermann.

Valiant Cid, The, *see* I Cid, The, 1637.

Valiant Scholar, The, 1622.

Valiant Scot, The, 1626.

    S Garland, George F. Byers, ed., 1980.

Valiant Welshman, The, or The True Chronicle History of the Life and Valiant Deeds of Caradoc the Great, 1612.

    E *The Valiant Welshman, by R.A. Gent.*, V. Kreb, ed., 1902.

Vallia (and Antony), *see* Antony and Vallia, 1599 add.

Valteger, *see* Vortigern, 1596.

Variety, The, 1641; adapt., 1662.

Vayvode, 1598.

Venetian Comedy, The, 1594.

Venetian Senators, A Mask of, 1554.

Venice Preserved, or A Plot Discovered, 1682.

    S Regents, Malcolm Kelsall, ed., 1969.

Venus and Adonis (Holland), 1656.

Venus and Adonis (Blow), 1682.

    E *Venus and Adonis* (Editions de l'oiseau lyre), A. Lewis, ed., 1949.

Venus and Adonis, or The Maid's Philosophy, 1653.

    C *The Wits, or Sport upon Sports*, J.J. Elson, ed., 1932.

Venus and Mars, *see* Cupid, Venus, and Mars, 1553.

Venus, Cupid, Six Damsels, and Six Old Men, A Mask of, 1527.

Venuses with Cupids, A Mask of, 1554.

Verily, *see* Re Vera, 1599.

Versipellis, 1632.

Vertumnus sive Annus Recurrens, 1605.

    F *Renaissance Latin Drama In England*, Marvin Spevack, J.W. Binns, Hans-Jurgen Weckermann, gen. eds, 1982–6; prep. and intro., A. Cizek.

Very Good Wife, A., 1693.

Very Woman, A., or The Prince of Tarent, 1634.

    C *The Plays and Poems of Philip Massinger*, Philip Edwards, Colin Gibson, eds, 1976.

Vestal, The, 1639.

Vestal Virgin, The, or The Roman Ladies, 1664.

Vice, A New Interlude of, 1567.

Vice Destroys Itself, *see* Amalasont Queen of the Goths, 1696.

Vices, The Mask of, Supp. II, i.

Victim, The, or Achilles and Iphigenia in Aulis, *see* Achilles, 1699.

Victoria, 1582.

    F *Renaissance Latin Drama in England*, Marvin

Wandering Ladies, The, *see* Mulberry Garden, The, 1668.

Wandering Lover, The, 1658.

Wandering Lovers, The, 1623.

Wandering Lovers, The, or The Painter, *see* Dutch Painter and the French Branke, The, 1623.

Wandering Whores' Complaint, The, 1663.

Wanstead, The Entertainment of Her Majesty at, *see* Lady of May, The, 1578.

Wanton Wife, The, *see* Amorous Widow, The, 1670.

War Hath Made All Friends, *see* Edmond Ironside, 1595.

War of Grammar, The, 1666.

War without Blows and Love without Suit (or Strife), 1599.

Warbeck, *see* Perkin Warbeck.

Ward, The, 1637.

   E *The Warde by Thomas Neale*, J.A. Mitchell, ed., 1937.

Ward and Dansiker, *see* Christian Turned Turk, A, 1610.

Warlamchester, 1599 add.

Warning for Fair Women, A, 1599.

   C The School of Shakespeare, R. Simpson, 1878 [reprinted, 1973].

   E 'A Warning for Fair Women: A Critical Edition', Charles Dale Cannon, ed., 1975.

   T Radcliffe, Dorothy Cohen, ed., 1957.

Warriors, A Mask of, 1619.

Wars of Cyrus King of Persia against Antiochus King of Assyria, with the Tragical End of Panthaea, The, 1588.

   E *The Wars of Cyrus* (Univ. of Illinois Stud. in Lang. and Lit., vol. XXVIII, nos. 3-4), J.P. Brawner, ed., 1942.

Wars of Pompey and Caesar, The, *see* Caesar and Pompey, 1605.

Wary Widow, The, or Sir Noisy Parrot, 1693.

Wasp, The, 1638.

   S Malone Society, (From the MS Alnwick Castle 507), J.W. Lever, G.R. Proudfoot, eds, 1974.

Water Nymph, The, *see* Honourable Entertainments, 1621.

Wavering Nymph, The, or Mad Amnyntas, 1684.

Way of the World, The, 1700.

   C 1) *Congreve: The Complete Plays*, Herbert Davis, ed., 1967.

      2) *The Comedies of William Congreve*, Anthony G. Henderson, ed., 1982.

   S 1) Fountainwell, John Michael Barnard, ed., 1972.

      2) New Mermaids, Brian Gibbons, ed., 1971.

      3) Regents, Kathleen M. Lynch, ed., 1965.

   F Scolar (1700).

Way to Content All Women, The, or How a Man May Please His Wife, 1624.

Way to Life, The, 1556.

Way to Make a Knave Honest, A, Supp. II, m.

Way to Win and Tame a Shrew, A, *see* Mad Wooing, The, 1698.

Weakest Goeth to the Wall, The, 1600.

   C *Six Early Plays Related to the Shakespeare Canon, Anglistica*, 14 E.B. Everitt, R.L. Armstrong, eds, 1965.

   S Garland, Jill Levenson, ed., 1980.

Wealth and Health, 1554.

   E *An Enterlude of Welth and Helth* (Englische Textbibliothek, XVII), F. Holthausen, ed., 1922.

Wealth Outwitted, *see* Money Is an Ass, 1635.

Weather, The Play of the, 1528.

   S Malone Society, (from the edition of 1533), T.N.S. Lennam, ed., 1971.

   T State University of New York, Vicki Knudsen Robinson, ed., 1979.

Weavers' Pageant, *see* Coventry Plays, 14th cent.

Wedding, The, 1626.

   T 'A Critical Modern-Spelling Edition of the 1629 Quarto of "The Wedding" by James Shirley', Wisconsin, Sister Martin Flavin, ed., 1972.

Wedding Mask for Sir Philip Herbert, The, 1604.

Weeding of the Covent Garden, The, or The Middlesex Justice of Peace, 1632.

   T 'Richard Brome's "The Weeding of Covent Garden" and "The Sparagus

Garden'': A Critical Edition', Donald S. McClure, ed., Vanderbilt, 1971.

Welbeck, The King's Entertainment at, 1633.

Welcome for Emperor Charles V, The, 1522.

    C 1) *English Pagentry* (excerpts), R. Withington, (1918-20) 1918.

    2) 'William Lyly's Verse for the Entry of Charles V. into London', *Huntington Library Bulletin*, IX, 1-14., C.R. Baskervill, ed., 1936.

Welcome for James VI, The, 1579.

    C Mediaeval Plays in Scotland, (Univ. of St Andrews Pubs. No. XXVI), 1927.

Welcome for Katherine of Aragon, The, 1501.

    C The Antiquarian Repertory, F. Grose, comp., (1807-9) 1808.

Welcome for Margaret of Anjoy, The, 15th cent.

Welcome for Marie de Lorraine, The, 1538.

Welcome for Princess Margaret, The, 1503.

Welcome for Queen Anne, The, 1590.

    C Mediaeval Plays in Scotland, (Univ. of St Andrews Pubs., No. XXVI), A.J. Mill, ed., 1927.

Welcome for Queen Margaret, The, 1511.

Welcome for Queen Mary, The, 1561.

    C Mediaeval Plays in Scotland, (Univ. of St Andrews Pubs., No. XXVI), A.J. Mill, ed., 1927.

Welcome from the Isle of Ree, A, *see* In Duc Reducem.

Welcome into England, The, 1603.

    C An English Garner, E. Arber, ed., 1903.

Wells Plays, 14th cent.

Welsh Ambassador, The, or A Comdey in Disguises, 1623.

Welsh Traveller, The,, 1622.

Welshman, The, 1599 add.

Welshman's Prize, The, *see* Famous Wars of Henry I and the Prince of Wales, The, 1598.

Westward Ho, 1604.

What Mischief Worketh in the Mind of Man, 1578.

What Will Be Shall Be, *see* That Will Be Shall Be, 1596.

What You Please, *see* Whisperer, The, 1641.

What You Will, 1601.

What You Will, *see* Twelfth Night, 1601.

Wheel of Fortune, The, *see* Fool's Expectation, The, 1698.

When You See Me You Know Me, 1604.

When Woman Go to Law the Devil Is Full of Business, *see* Devil's Law Case, the, 1617.

Whibble, The, *see* Hengist King of Kent, 1618.

Which Is the Best Girl, *see* Politic Bankrupt, The, Supp. II, a.

Whimsies of Señor Hidalgo, The, or The Masculine Bride, Supp. I.

Whirligig, The, *see* Hengist King of Kent, 1618.'

Whisperer, The, or What You Please, 1641.

White Devil, The, 1612.

    S 1) Fountainwell, Clive Hart, ed., 1970.

    2) New Mermaids, Elizabeth M. Brennan, ed., 1966.

    3) Regents, J.R. Mulryne, ed., 1969.

    4) Revels, J.R. Brown, ed.; rev. ed., 1966; paper, 1968.

    F Scolar (1612), 1970.

White Ethiopian, The, 1650.

    T Florida, A.D. Matthews, ed., 1951.

White Moor, The, 1629.

White Tragedy, The, or the Green Knight, *mentioned* 1599 by Nashe in Lenten Stuff, and possibly a play or plays.

White Witch of Westminster, The, or Love in a Lunacy, Supp. II, m.

Whitsun Plays, *see* Chester Plays, 14th cent. *and* Norwich Plays, 15th cent.

Who Would Have Thought It, *see* Law Tricks, 1604.

Whole Contention, The, *see* II & III Henry VI, 1591.

Whore in Grain, The, 1624.

Whore New Vamped, The, 1639.

Whore of Babylon, The, 1606.

    T Pennsylvania, Marrianne, G. Riely, ed., 1953.

Whore of Babylon, The, *see* De Meretrice Babylonica, 1548.

Whore of Babylon, the Devil and the Pope, The, 1685.

Widkirk Plays, *see* Wakefield Plays, 14th cent.

Widow (Middleton), The, 1616.

    S Salzburg, R.T. Levine, ed., 1975.

Widow (Boyle?), The, 1665.

Widow Captain, The, Supp. II, m.

Widow of Watling Street, The, see Puritan, The, 1606.

Widow Ranter, The, or The History of Bacon in Virginia, 1689.

Widow's Apron Strings, The, see Histriomastix, 1599.

Widow's Charm, The, 1602.

Widow's Prize, The, or The Woman Captain, 1625.

Widow's Tears, The, 1604.
  C The Plays of George Chapman: The Comedies, Allan Holaday, gen. ed., Robert Ornstein, ed., 1970.
  S 1) Regents, Ethel M. Smeak, ed., 1966.
     2) Revels, Akihiro Yamada, ed., 1975.

Wife for a Month, A, 1624; see also Unhappy Kindness, The, 1697.
  E David Rush Miller, ed., Amsterdam, 1983.

Wife for Any Man, A, 1696, Supp. II, j.

Wild Gallant, The, 1663.
  C California Dryden, Vol. VIII, J.H. Smith, D. Macmillan, V.A. Dearing, eds, 1974.

Wild Goose Chase, The, 1621.
  T Toronto, Rotraud Lister, ed., 1971.

Wild Goose Chase, The, see Hengist King of Kent, 1618.

Wild Knight and the Black Lady, The Joust of the, 1507.

Wild Men, see Place Perilous, The, 1515.

Will of a Woman, The, an error for Ill of a Woman, The; see Fount(ain) of New Fashions, The, 1598.

William Cartwright, 1602.

William Longbeard, 1599.

William Longsword, see William Longbeard, 1599.

William the Conqueror, 1599 add.

Wiltshire Tom, 1673.

Wily Beguiled, 1602.
  S Malone Society, H. Hart, ed., 1912.

Win Her and Take Her, or Old Fools Will Be Meddling, 1691.

Winchester, Prince Henry's Welcome to, 1603.

Winchester Troper, see Quem Quaeritis, 10th cent.

Windsor, A Mumming at, 15th cent.

Wine, Beer, Ale, and Tobacco Contending for Superiority, see Wine, Beer, and Ale Together by the Ears, 1625.
  E 'Wine, Beer, Ale, and Tobacco', Stud. in Philol., XII, 1-54, J.H. Hanford, ed., 1915.

Wine, Beer, and Ale Together by the Ears, 1625.

Winter's Tale, The, 1610; see also Supp. II, k.
  V 1966.

Wisdom of Doctor Dodypoll, The, 1600.
  C Old English Plays, A.H. Bullen, ed., (1882-85) 1884.
  S 1) Malone Society, M.N. Matson, ed., 1965.
     2) Garland, M.N. Matson, ed., 1980.

Wisdom That Is Christ, The, see Mind, Will, and Understanding, 15th cent.

Wise and Foolish Virgins, A Mask of, 1561.

Wise Man of West Chester, The, 1594.

Wise Woman of Hogsdon, The, 1604.
  T Southern California, Michael H. Leonard, ed., 1967.

Wit à la Mode, 1672.

Wit above Crowns, see Love's Martyr, 1685.

Wit and Folly, see Witty and Witless, 1533.

Wit and Science, 1539.
  T 'A Critical Edition of John Redford's Play "Wyt and Science"', Toronto, Linda Beamer, ed., 1973.

Wit and Science, see Marriage of Wit and Science, The, 1568.

Wit and Will, 1568, Supp. II, p.

Wit and Wisdom, see Marriage between Wit and Wisdom, A Contract of a, 1579.

Wit at Several Weapons, 1613, adapt., 1672.

Wit for Money, or Poet Stutter, 1691.

Wit in a Constable, 1638.

Wit in a Madness, 1637.

Wit at Several Weapons, 1672.

Wit of a Woman, The, 1604.

Wit without Money, 1614.

Wit's Triumvirate, or The Philosopher, 1635.
  S Salzburg, A Critical Edition of 'Wit's Triumvirate', or 'The Philosopher', Cathryn A. Nelson, ed., 1975.

Witch, The, 1612.

Witch of Edmonton, The, 1621.

T Brown, Etta Soicef, ed., 1953.

Witch of Islington, The, 1599 add.

Witch Traveller, The, *an error for* Welsh Traveller, The, 1622.

Wits, The 1634.

   I Florida, A.S. Johnson, Jr, ed., 1951.

I Wits, The, or Sport upon Sport, 1662.

   C *The Wits, or Sport upon Sport*, J.J. Elson, ed., 1932.

II Wits, The, or Sport upon Sport, 1673.

   C *The Wits, or Sport upon Sport*, J.J. Elson, ed., 1932.

Wits Led by the Nose, or A Poet's Revenge, 1677.

Wits' Cabal, The, 1658.

Witten, A Mask at, 1640.

Witty and Witless, 1533.

Witty Combat, A, or The Female Victor, 1663 (adapt., as The German Princess, 1664).

Witty Fair One, The, 1628.

   T Chicago, Esther M. Power, ed., 1942.

Witty False One, The, *see* Madam Fickle, 1676.

Wives' Excuse, The, or Cuckolds Make Themselves, 1691.

   C *The Works of Thomas Southerne*, Vol. I, R. Jordan and H. Lowe, eds, 1988.

   T Pennsylvania, Ralph Thornton, ed., 1966.

Wives' Prize, The, *see* Match without Money, A, Supp. II, m.

Wizard, The, 1638.

Wolsey, The Life of Cardinal, 1601.

Wolsey, The Rising of Cardinal, 1601.

Woman, The Play of a, *see* Woman's Tragedy, The, 1598.

Woman Captain, The, 1679, *see* Woman Rules, 1687.

Woman Captain, The, *see* Widow's Prize, The, 1625.

Woman Hard to Please, A, 1597.

Woman Hater, The, 1606.

Woman in the Moon, The, 1593.

Woman Is a Weathercock, A, 1609.

Woman Is Too Hard for Him, The, 1621.

Woman Killed with Kindness, A, 1603.

   S 1) Revels, R.W. Van Fossen, ed., 1961.
      2) New Mermaids, Brian W.M. Scobie, ed., 1985.

F Scolar (1607), 1971.

Woman Made a Justice, The, 1670.

Woman Never Vexed, A, *see* New Wonder, A, 1625.

Woman on the Rock, The, 1537.

Woman Once in the Right, A, *see* Richmond Heiress, The, 1693.

Woman Rules, 1687.

Woman the Prize, *see* Love's a Lottery, 1699.

Woman Turned Bully, The, 1675, *see* Woman Rules, 1687.

Woman Wears The Breeches, The, *see* City Wit, The, 1630.

Woman Wears the Breeches, The, *see* Ghost, The, 1640.

Woman Will Have Her Will, A, *see* Englishmen for My Money, 1598.

Woman's Advocate, The, *see* Contented Cuckold, The, 1692.

Woman's Law, The, Supp. II, b.

Woman's Masterpiece, The, Supp. II. b.

Woman's Mistaken, The, 1620.

Woman's Plot, The, 1621.

Woman's Prize, The, or The Tamer Tamed, 1611.

   T Illinois, G.B. Ferguson, ed., 1962–3.

Woman's Spleen and Love's Conquest, The, *see* Adrasta, 1635.

Woman's Tragedy, The, 1598.

Woman's Wit, or The Lady in Fashion, 1696.

Women, A Mask of, 1543.

Women, Two Masks of, 1548.

Women Beware Women, 1621.

   S 1) New Mermaids, Roma Gill, ed., 1968.
      2) Revels, J.R. Mulryne, ed., 1975.

   T Wisconsin, Elizabeth R. Jacobs, ed., 1941.

Women, in Defence of the Sex, Dialogue Concerning, previously included in *Annals*; not dramatic.

Women of Diana, A Mask of, 1552.

Women Pleased, 1620.

Women Wear the Breeches, The, *see* Gossips' Brawl, The, 1655.

Women Will Have Their Will, or Give Christmas His Due, 1649.

Women's Conquest, The, 1670.

Wonder of a Kingdom, The, 1631.

Wonder of a Woman, The, 1595.

Wonder of Women, The, or The Tragedy of Sophonisba, 1605.
   T South Carolina, James W. Kemp, Jr, ed., 1970.

Woodcock of Our Side, *see* Hengist King of Kent, 1618.

Woodkirk Plays, *see* Wakefield Plays, 14th cent.

Woodstock, The Queen's Entertainment at, 1575.

Woodstock, The Tragedy of Thomas of, *see* I Richard II, 1592.

Woodstock Entertainment, The Second, 1592.

Wooer, The, 1580.

Wooing of Death, The, 1600.

Wooing of Nan, The, 1598.
   C *The Elizabethan Jig*, G.K. Baskervill, 1929.

Woolstone Dixie, The Pageant before, 1585.

Worcester, The Entertainment at, 1575.

Worcester Plays, 15th cent.

Words Made Visible, or Grammar and Rhetoric Accommodated to the Lives and Manners of Men, 1678.

Work for Cutlers, or A Merry Dialogue between Sword, Rapier, and Dagger, 1615.
   E *Worke for Cutlers*, A.F. Sieveking, ed., 1904.

Work for Jupiter, *see* Gigantomachia, 1613.

World, The, 1639.

World and the Child, A Proper New Interlude of the, 1508.
   C *Six Anonymous Plays* (1st Ser.), J.S. Farmer, ed., 1905.

World in the Moon, The, 1697.
   T Missouri, Loren D. Reser, ed., 1974.

World Runs on Wheels, The, *see* All Fools but the Fool, 1599.

World Tossed at Tennis, The, 1620.

World Well Lost, The, *see* All for Love, 1677.

World's Idol Plutus, The, 1659.

I Worse (A)feared Than Hurt, *see* I Hannibal and Hermes, 1598.

II Worse (A)feared Than Hurt, 1598.

Worse and Worse, 1664.

Worst Not Always True, The, *see* Elvira, 1663.

Wounds of Civil War, The, or Marius and Scilla, 1588.
   S Regents, Joseph W. Houppert, ed., 1969.

Wangling Lovers, The, or The Invisible Mistress, 1676.

Wronged Widow's Tragedy, The, Supp. II, m.

Wyatt, Sir Thomas, 1604.

Wylie Beguylie, 1567.

Xerxes, 1699.

Xerxes, King, 1575.

Year's Funeral, The, *see* Honourable Entertainments, 1621.

York House, The Mask at, 1623.

York House Mask, Supp. II, i.

York Plays, 14th cent.; *see also* Wakefield Plays, 14th cent.

Yorkshire Gentleman, The, Supp. II, h.

Yorkshire Gentlewoman and Her Son, A, 1613.

Yorkshire Tragedy, A, 1606.
   C *The Shakespeare Apocrypha*, C.F. Tucker Brooke, ed., 1908; 1967.
   S 1) Malone Society (from the edition of 1608), S.D. Feldman, G.R. Proudfoot, eds, 1969.
     2) Revels, A.C. Cawley and Barry Gaines, eds, 1986.

Young Admiral, The, 1633.
   T Rice University, Kenneth J. Ericksen, ed., 1967.

Young King, The, or The Mistake, 1679.

Young Moors, A Mask of, 1548.

Younger Brother, The, 1617.

Younger Brother, The, or Male Courtesan, Supp. II, m.

Younger Brother, The, or The Amorous Jilt, 1696.

Your Five Gallants, 1607.
   S Garland, C.L. Colegrove, ed., 1979.

Youth, The Interlude of, 1514.
   C *Six Anonymous Plays*, (1st. Ser.), J.S. Farmer, ed., 1906.
   S Revels, Ian Lancashire, ed., 1980.
   E A. Gowans, trans., 1922.

Youth's Comedy, or The Soul's Trials and Triumph, previously included in *Annals*; not dramatic.

Youth's Glory and Death's Banquet, 1658.

Youth's Tragedy, 1671.

Yuletide, *see* Christmas Prince, the, 1608.

Zabeta, *see* Princely Pleasures at Kenilworth, The, 1575.

Zelmane, or The Corinthian Queen, 1692.

Zelotypus, 1606.

    F *Renaissance Latin Drama in England*, Marvin Spevack, J.W. Binns, Hans-Jurgen Weckermann, gen. eds., 1982–6; prep. &

intro., J.C. Coldewey and B.F. Copenhaver.

Zeno sive Ambitio Infelix, 1631; adapt., 1669.

Zenobia, 1599 add.

Zoroastres, 1676.

    C *Dramatic Works of Roger Boyle*, W.S. Clark, II, ed., 1937.

Zulziman, *see* Soliman and Perseda, 1592.

SELECTIVE LIST OF MEDIEVAL DRAMA TEXTS

The volumes in this listing update and supplement citations in the Harbage-Schoenbaum original List of Editions.

LUDUS COVENTRIAE

(1) Block, K.S., ed., *Ludus Coventriae: Or, The Plaie Called Corpus Christ*. Published for the Early English Text Society, 1922 (reprinted 1960).

The Creation of Heaven and the Angels; Fall of Lucifer
The Creation of the World and Man; Fall of Man
Cain and Abel
Noah
Abraham and Isaac
Moses
The Prophets
Mary in the Temple
The Betrothal of Mary
The Salutation and Conception
Joseph's Return
The Visit to Elizabeth
The Trial of Joseph and Mary
The Birth of Jesus
The Adoration of the Shepherds
The Adoration of the Magi
The Purification
The Massacre of the Innocents; The Death of Herod
Christ and Doctors
The Baptism
The Temptation
The Woman Taken in Adultery
The Raising of Lazarus
The Passion Play. I
The Last Supper
The Betrayal
The Passion Play. II (King Herod; Trial before Annas and Caiaphas)
The Death of Judas; The Trial before Pilate;

The Trial before Herod
Pilate's Wife's Dream; The Trial of Christ and the Thieves before Pilate
The Procession to Calvary; The Crucifixion
The Descent into Hell
The Burial; The Guarding of the Sepulchre
The Harrowing of Hell; The Resurrection
The Announcement to the Three Maries
The Appearance to Mary Magdalen
The Appearance to Cleophas and Luke; The Appearance to Thomas
The Ascension
The Day of Pentecost
The Assumption of the Virgin
Doomsday

(2) Craig, Hardin, ed., *Two Coventry Corpus Christi Plays*. London: published for the Early English Text Society (1902; 2nd edition, 1957; reprinted 1967).

The Shearmen and Tailors' Pageant
The Weavers' Pageant

(3) Davis, R.T., *The Corpus Christi Play of the Middle Ages*. 1972.

CHESTER

(1) Deimling, Hermann, *The Chester Plays*. Part I re-edited from the MSS by the Late Dr Hermann Deimling. Part II re-edited from the MSS by Dr Matthews. 2 vol. Published for the Early English Text Society. 1892–1916 (reprinted, 1935, 1959, 1968).

The Fall of Lucifer
The Creation
The Deluge
The Sacrifice of Isaac
Balaam and Balak

The Nativity
Adoration of the Shepherds
Adoration of the Magi
The Magi's Oblation
Slaying of the Innocents
Purification
The Temptation
Christ. The Adulteress. Chelidonius
Christ's Visit to Simon the Leper
Christ's Betrayal
Christ's Passion
Christ's Descent into Hell
Christ's Resurrection
Christ Appears to Two Disciples
Christ's Ascension
The Sending of the Holy Ghost
The Prophets and Antichrist
The Coming of Antichrist
The Last Judgment

(2) Hussey, Maurice, *The Chester Mystery Plays.* Sixteen Pageant Plays from the Chester Craft Cycle, 1960.
The Fall of Lucifer
The Creation of Man: Adam and Eve
Noah's Deluge
Abraham and Isaac
The Nativity
The Adoration of the Shepherds
The Adoration of the Magi
The Magi's Oblation
The Slaying of the Innocents
Simon the Leper
The Betrayal of Christ
Christ's Passion
Christ's Resurrection
Christ's Ascension
Antichrist
The Last Judgment

(3) Lumiansky, R.M. and David Mills, eds, *The Chester Mystery Cycle.* Published for the Early English Text Society, 1974–86, Facsimiles.
The Fall of Lucifer – The Tanners
Adam and Eve; Cain and Abel – The Drapers

Noah's Flood – The Waterleaders and Drawers of Dee
Abraham, Lot, and Melchysedeck; Abraham and Isaac – The Barbers
Moses and the Law; Balaack and Balaam – The Cappers
The Annunciation and the Nativity – The Wrights
The Shepherds – The Painters
The Three Kings – The Vintners
The Offerings of the Three Kings – The Mercers
The Slaughter of the Innocents – The Goldsmiths
The Purification; Christ and the Doctors – The Blacksmiths
The Temptation; the Woman Taken in Adultery – The Butchers
The Blind Chelidonian; the Raising of Lazarus – The Glovers
Christ at the House of Simon the Leper; Christ and the Money-lenders; Judas' Plot – The Corvisors
The Last Supper; the Betrayal of Christ – The Bakers
The Trial and Flagellation – The Fletchers, Bowyers, Coopers, and Stringers
The Passion – The Ironmongers
The Harrowing of Hell – The Cooks
The Resurrection – The Skinners
Christ on the Road to Emmaus; Doubting Thomas – The Saddlers
The Ascension – The Tailors
Pentecost – The Fishmongers
The Prophets of Antichrist – The Clothworkers
Antichrist – The Dyers
The Last Judgment – The Websters

TOWNELEY – WAKEFIELD

(1) Cawley, A.C., ed., The *Wakefield Pageants in the Towneley Cycle*, 1958 (reprinted 1963, 1968).
Mactacio Abel
Processus Noe Cum Filiis
Prima Pastorum

Secunda Pastorum
Magnus Herodes
Coliphizacio

(2) England, George, ed., *The Towneley Plays*.
Re-edited from the Unique MS. With
Side-notes and Introduction by Alfred W.
Pollard. Published for Early English Text
Society, 1897 (reprinted, 1907, 1925,
1952, 1966).
The Creation
Killing of Abel
Noah and the Ark
Abraham
Isaac
Sequitur Jacob
The Prophets
Pharaoh
Caesar Augustus
The Annunciation
The Salutation of Elizabeth
Shepherds' Play, I
Shepherds' Play, II
Offering of the Magi
The Flight into Egypt
Herod the Great
The Purification of Mary
The Play of the Doctors
John the Baptist
The Conspiracy
The Buffeting
The Scourging
The Crucifixion
The Talents
The Deliverance of Souls
The Resurrection of the Lord
The Pilgrims
Thomas of India
The Lord's Ascension
The Judgment
Lazarus
The Hanging of Judas

(3) Rose, Martial, ed., *The Wakefield Mystery
Plays*. 1961.
Part I:
The Creation
The Killing of Abel

Noah
Abraham
Isaac
Jacob
Pharaoh
The Procession of the Prophets
Caesar Augustus
Part 2:
The Annunciation
The Salutation of Elizabeth
The First Shepherds' Plays
The Second Shepherds' Play
The Offering of the Magi
The Flight Into Egypt
Herod the Great
The Purification of Mary
The Play of the Doctors
Part 3:
John the Baptist
Lazarus
The Conspiracy
The Buffeting
The Scourging
The Hanging of Judas
The Crucifixion
Part 4:
The Talents
The Deliverance of Souls
The Resurrection
The Pilgrims
Thomas of India
The Ascension of the Lord
The Judgment

YORK

(1) Beadle, R., *The York Plays*. London: Edward
Arnold, 1982.
The Fall of the Angels
The Creation
The Creation of Adam and Eve
Adam and Eve in Eden
The Fall of Man
The Expulsion
Cain and Abel
The Building of the Ark
The Flood
Abraham and Isaac

Moses and Pharaoh
The Annunciation and the Visitation
Joseph's Trouble about Mary
The Nativity
The Shepherds
Herod/The Magi
The Purification
The Flight into Egypt
The Slaughter of the Innocents
Christ and the Doctors
The Baptism
The Temptation
The Marriage at Cana
The Transfiguration
Jesus in the House of Simon the Leper
The Woman Taken in Adultery/The Raising
    of Lazarus
The Entry into Jerusalem
The Conspiracy
The Last Supper
The Agony in the Garden and the Betrayal
Christ before Annas and Caiaphas
Christ before Pilate 1: The Dream of Pilate's
    Wife
Christ before Herod
The Remorse of Judas
Christ before Pilate 2: The Judgment
The Road to Calvary
The Crucifixion
The Death of Christ
The Harrowing of Hell
The Resurrection
Christ's Appearance to Mary Magdalene
The Supper at Emmaus
The Incredulity of Thomas
The Ascension
Pentecost
The Death of the Virgin
The Funeral of the Virgin ('Fergus')
The Assumption of the Virgin
The Coronation of the Virgin
The Coronation of the Virgin (later
    fragment)
The Last Judgment

(2) Beadle, Richard, and Pamela M. King, *York
    Mystery Plays*. Oxford, 1974.
    The Fall of the Angels

The Fall of Man
The Building of the Ark
The Flood
Moses and Pharaoh
Joseph's Trouble about Mary
The Nativity
Herod and the Magi
The Flight into Egypt
The Slaughter of the Innocents
The Temptation
The Conspiracy
Christ before Annas and Caiaphas
Christ before Pilate (1): The Dream of
    Pilate's Wife
Christ before Herod
Christ before Pilate (2): The Judgment
The Crucifixion
The Death of Christ
The Harrowing of Hell
The Resurrection
The Last Judgment

(3) Purvis, J.S., *The York Cycle of Mystery Plays: A
    Complete Version*. London: S.P.C.K., 1962,
    1971.
    The Creation, and The Fall of Lucifer
    The Creation, to the Fifth Day
    God Creates Adam and Eve
    God Puts Adam and Eve in the Garden of
        Eden
    Man's Disobedience and fall from Eden
    Adam and Eve Driven from Eden
    Sacrificium Cayne and Abell
    The Building of the Ark
    Noah and His Wife, the Flood and its
        Waning
    Abraham's Sacrifice of Isaac
    The Departure of the Israelites from Egypt,
        the Ten Plagues, and the Passage of the
        Red Sea
    The Annunciation, and Visit of Elizabeth to
        Mary
    Joseph's Trouble about Mary
    The Journey to Bethlehem; the Birth of Jesus
    The Angels and the Shepherds
    The Coming of the Three Kings to Herod
    The Coming of the Three Kings to Herod;
        the Adoration

The Flight into Egypt

The Purification of Mary; Simeon and Anna Prophesy

The Massacre of the Innocents

Christ with the Doctors in the Temple

The Baptism of Jesus

The Temptation of Jesus

The Transfiguration

The Woman Taken in Adultery

The Entry into Jerusalem upon the Ass

The Conspiracy to Take Jesus

The Last Supper

The Agony and the Betrayal

Peter Denies Jesus: Jesus examined by Caiaphas

The Dream of Pilate's Wife: Jesus before Pilate

Trial before Herod

Second Accusation before Pilate; Remorse of Judas, and Purchase of Field of Blood

The Second Trial before Pilate Continued; the Judgment of Jesus

Christ led up to Calvary

Crucifixio Christi

Mortificacio Christi (and Burial of Jesus)

The Harrowing of Hell

The Resurrection; Fright of the Jews

Jesus Appears to Mary Magdalene after the Resurrection

The Travellers to Emmaus Meet Jesus

The Incredulity of Thomas

The Ascension

The Descent to the Holy Spirit

The Death of Mary

The Appearance of Our Lady to Thomas

The Assumption and Coronation of the Virgin

The Judgment Day

A Fragment? of a Coronation

(4) Smith, Lucy Toulmin, ed., *York Plays. The Plays Performed by the Crafts or Mysteries of York on the Day of Corpus Christi in the 14th, 15th, and 16th Centuries*. Now First Printed from the Unique Manuscript in the Library of Lord Ashburnham, 1885 (reissued, 1963).

The Creation and the Fall of Lucifer

The Creation, to the Fifth Day

God Creates Adam and Eve

God Puts Adam and Eve in the Garden of Eden

Man's Disobedience and Fall from Eden

Adam and Eve Driven from Eden

Sacrificium Cayne and Abell

The Building of the Ark

Noah and His Wife, the Flood and its Waning

Abraham's Sacrifice of Isaac

The Departure of the Israelites from Egypt, the Ten Plagues, and The Passage of the Red Sea

The Annunciation, and Visit of Elisabeth to Mary

Joseph's Trouble about Mary

The Journey to Bethlehem; the Birth of Jesus

The Angels and the Shepherds

The Coming of the Three Kings to Herod

The Coming of the Three Kings to Herod; the Adoration

The Flight into Egypt

The Massacre of the Innocents

Christ with the Doctors in the Temple

The Baptism of Jesus

The Temptation of Jesus

The Transfiguration

The Woman Taken in Adultery. The Raising of Lazarus

The Entry into Jesusalem upon the Ass

The Conspiracy to Take Jesus

The Last Supper

The Agony and the Betrayal

Peter Denies Jesus. Jesus Examined by Caiaphas

The Dream of Pilate's Wife: Jesus Before Pilate

Trial before Herod

Second Accusation before Pilate: Remorse of Judas, and Purchase of Field of Blood

The Second Trial before Pilate continued: Judgment of Jesus

Christ Led up to Calvary

Crucifixio Cristi

Mortificacio Cristi (and Burial of Jesus)

The Harrowing of Hell

The Resurrection; Fright of the Jews

Jesus Appears to Mary Magdalene after the Resurrection

The Travellers to Emmaus Meet Jesus

The Purification of Mary: Simeon and Anna Prophesy

The Incredulity of Thomas

The Ascension

The Descent of the Holy Spirit

The Death of Mary

The Appearance of our Lady to Thomas

The Assumption and Coronation of the Virgin

The Judgment Day

LITURGICAL

(1) Young, Karl, *The Drama of the Medieval Church.* 2 vols, 1933 (reprint ed. 1951).

VOLUME I: PLAYS ASSOCIATED WITH THE RESURRECTION AND THE PASSION

Dramatic Tropes of the Mass of Easter

The Easter Introit Trope in Transition

The Visit to the Sepulcre: First Stage

The Visit to the Sepulchre: First Stage (continued)

The Visit to the Sepulchre: Second Stage

The Visit to the Sepulchre: Second Stage (continued)

The Visit to the Sepulchre: Third Stage

The Ludus Paschalis

Other Plays of the Easter Season: The Journey to Emmaus – The Ascension – Pentecost

VOLUME II: PLAYS ASSOCIATED WITH THE NATIVITY

The Shepherds at the Holy Manger

The Coming of the Magi

The Coming of the Magi (continued)

The Slaughter of the Innocents

The Procession of Prophets

The Christmas Play from Benedikteuern

PLAYS UPON OTHER SUBJECTS FROM THE BIBLE

Plays from the New Testament: The Raising of Lazarus – The Conversion of Saint Paul

Plays of the Blessed Virgin Mary: The Presentation in the Temple – The Annunciation – The Purification – The Assumption

Plays on Subjects from the Old Testament: Isaac and Rebecca – Joseph and His Brethren – Daniel

The Miracle Plays of Saint Nicholas

Plays on Subjects from Eschatology: The Wise and Foolish Virgins – Antichrist

MACRO

(1) Bevington, David, ed., *The Macro Plays: The Castle of Perseverance, Wisdom, Mankind.* A facsimile edition with facing transcriptions. Folger Facsimiles Manuscript Series, Vol. 1, 1972.

(2) Eccles, Mark, ed., *The Macro Plays: The Castle of Perseverance, Wisdom, Mankind.* Published for the Early English Text Society, 1969.

DIGBY 133 & E MUSEO 160

Baker, Donald, E., J.L. Murphy, and L.B. Hall, eds, *The Late Medieval Religious Plays of Bodleian Manuscripts Digby 133 and e Museo 160.* Published for the Early English Text Society, 1982.

The Conversion of St Paul

Mary Magdalen

Killing of the Children

Wisdom

Christ's Burial

Christ's Resurrection

(1) Adams, Joseph Quincy, ed., *Chief Pre-Shakespearean Dramas: A Selection of Plays Illustrating the History of the English Drama from Its Origin Down to Shakespeare.* 1924.

I Sources of the Liturgical Drama
   The Wordless 'Alleluia' Sequence
   The 'Quem Quaeritis' Trope

The Easter Sepulchre ('Depositio Crucis, Elevatio Crucis')
Semi-Dramatic Trope (Easter)

II   Liturgical Plays Dealing with the Story of Christ
Sepulchrum (The Visit of the Marys)
Sepulchrum (The Visit of the Marys, and the Race of Peter and John)
Sepulchrum (The Visit of the Marys, The Race of Peter and John, and The Appearance to Mary Magdalene)
Peregrini
Pastores
Magi
Herodes
Prophetae

III Liturgical Plays Dealing with Miscellaneous Biblical Stories and with the Legends of the Saints
Conversio Beati Paul Apostoli
Ludus Super Iconia Sancti Nicolai
Tres Clerici
Adeodatus

IV   The Introduction of the Vernacular
The Sepulchre
The Wayfarers
The Shepherds

V   The Craft Cycles
Banns (N. Towne)
The Fall of Lucifer (N. Towne)
The Creation of Eve, with the Expelling of Adam and Eve out of Paradise (Norwich)
The Killing of Abel
Noah (Wakefield)
The Deluge (Chester)
The Sacrifice of Isaac (Brome)
Pharaoh (Wakefield)
The Prophets (Chester)
The Salutation and Conception (N. Towne)
The Birth of Jesus (York)
The Shepherds (Wakefield)
The Magi, Herod, and the Slaughter of the Innocents (Coventry)
Christ's Ministry (Chester)
The Betraying of Christ (N. Towne)
The Trial of Christ (N. Towne)
The Harrowing of Hell (Chester)
The Resurrection of Christ (Wakefield)
The Judgment Day (York)

VI   Non-Cycle Plays
Dux Moraud
The Conversion of St Paul
Mary Magdalene
The Play of the Sacrament

VII Moralities
The Castle of Perseverance
Everyman
Mankind
Wyt and Science

VIII Folk Plays
Robin Hood and the Sheriff of Nottingham
Robin Hood and the Friar
Shetland Sword Dance
Oxfordshire St George Play
Leicestershire St George Play
The Revesby Sword Play

IX   Farces
The Plays Called the Foure PP
The Merry Play betwene Johan Johan the Husbande, Tyb His Wyfe, and Syr Johan the Preest
The Play of the Wether

X   The Court Drama
Damon and Pithias

XI   Plays of the Professional Troupes
Cambises

(2) Bentley, Gerald Eades, ed., *The Development of English Drama*. 1950.
Brome: Abraham and Isaac
Chester: Deluge or Noah's Flood

Towneley: Second Shepherds' Play
The summoning of Everyman

(3) Bevington, David., ed., *Medieval Drama*. 1975.

PART ONE

A Dramatic Elements in the Liturgy of the Church
  1 Concerning Tragedies (Honorius of Autun)
  2 A Palm Sunday Procession in Fourth-Century Jerusalem (The Lady Etheria)
  3 The Service for the Consecration of a Church (Bishop of Metz)
  4 Adoration of the Cross (*Regularis Concordia*)
  5 The Interment of the Cross in the Sepulchre (*Regularis Concordia*)
  6 The Raising of the Host from the Sepulchre (St Gall)
  7 Antiphons for Easter Vespers
  8 Antiphons with Responses for the Vigil of the Most Holy Easter

B Tenth-Century Versions of the Visit to the Sepulchre
  9 Trope for Easter (Limoges)
  10 Of the Resurrection of the Lord (St Gall)
  11 The Visit to the Sepulchre (*Regularis Concordia*)
  12 The Visit to the Sepulchre (Winchester)

C Eleventh- and Twelfth-Century Easter Drama
  13 The Visit to the Sepulchre (Aquileia?)
  14 The Visit to the Sepulchre (St Lambrecht)
  15 [The Service] for Representing the Scene at The Lord's Sepulchre (Fleury)
  16 The Service [for Representing] the Pilgrim, at Vespers of the Second Holy Day of Easter [Easter Monday] (Beauvais)

D Eleventh- and Twelfth-Century Christmas Drama
  17 For the Mass of Our Lord (Limoges)
  18 The Service for Representing Herod (Fleury)
  19 [The Service for Representing] the Slaughter of the Innocents (Fleury)

PART TWO

  1 The Service for Representing Adam
  2 The Holy Resurrection
  3 The Play of Daniel (Beauvais)
  4 The Raising of Lazarus (Hilarius)
  5 [The Service] for Representing the Conversion of the Blessed Apostle Paul (Fleury)
  6 [The Service] for Representing How Saint Nicholas Freed the Son of Getron (Fleury)
  7 The Christmas Play (Benediktbeuern)
  8 The Passion Play (Benediktbeuern)

PART THREE

The Banns (N Town)
The Creation and the Fall of the Angels (Wakefield)
The Fall of Man (York)
The Killing of Abel (Wakefield)
Noah (Wakefield)
The Sacrifice of Isaac (Brome)
Pharaoh (Wakefield)
The Ten Commandments, Balaam and Balak, and the Prophets (Chester) 337
The Annunciation (Wakefield)
The Salutation of Elizabeth (Wakefield)
The Birth of Jesus (York)
The Shepherds (York)
The Second Shepherds' Pageant (Wakefield)
The Offering of the Magi (Wakefield)
The Flight into Egypt (York)
Herod the Great (Wakefield)
The Death of Herod (N Town)
The Woman Taken in Adultery (N Town)
The Raising of Lazarus (Wakefield)
The Passion Play (N Town)
The Buffeting (Wakefield)
The Scourging (Wakefield)
The Crucifixion of Christ (York)

Christ's Death and Burial (York)
The Harrowing of Hell (Wakefield)
The Resurrection of the Lord (Wakefield)
Christ Appears to the Disciples (Chester)
The Last Judgment (Wakefield)

PART FOUR

The Conversion of St Paul (Digby)
Mary Magdalene (Digby)
The Play of the Sacrament (Croxton)

PART FIVE

The Castle of Perseverance
Mankind
Everyman

PART SIX

A Merry Play Betwene Johan Johan the
    Husbande, Tib His Wife, and Sir Johan
    the Preest (John Heywood)
The Play of the Weather (John Heywood)
Wit and Science (John Redford)

(4) Cawley, A.C., ed., *Everyman and Medieval
    Miracle Plays,* 1959 (reprinted, 1974).
    Brome: Abraham and Isaac
    Chester: Noah's Flood
            The Harrowing of Hell
    Cornwall: The Death of Pilate
    Coventry: The Annunciation
    Ludus Coventriae: Cain and Abel
                    The Woman Taken in
                    Adultery
    Wakefield: The Second Shepherds' Pageant
            Herod the Great
    York: The Creation, and the Fall of Lucifer
        The Creation of Adam and Eve
        The Fall of Man
        The Crucifixion
        The Resurrection
        The Judgment
    Everyman

(5) Davis, Norman, ed., *Non-cycle Plays and
    Fragments.*
    Edited on the basis of the edition by Osborn
        Waterhouse. Published for the Early

English Text Society, 1970.
The Shrewsbury Fragments
    Officium Pastorum
    Officium Resurrectionis
    Officium Peregrinorum
The Norwich Grocers' Play (The Creation
    of Eve and the Fall)
The Newcastle Play (Noah's Ship)
Abraham's Sacrifice (Northampton and
    Brome)
The Play of the Sacrament (Croxton)
The Pride of Life
Dux Moraud
The Cambridge Prologue
The Rockinghall (Bury St Edmunds)
    Fragment
The Durham Prologue
The Ashmole Fragment
The Reuynes Extracts

(6) Franklin, Alexander, ed., *Seven Miracle
    Plays,* 1963.
    Cain And Abel (Towneley)
    Noah's Flood (Chester)
    Abraham and Isaac (Non-cycle mystery)
    The Shepherds (Chester)
    The Three Kings (York)
    King Herod (Chester)
    Adam and Eve (Non-cycle mystery)

(7) Happe, Peter, ed., *English Mystery Plays,*
    1975.
    The Fall of Lucifer [Chester I]
    The Creation, and Adam and Eve [Ch. 2]
    The Killing of Abel [Towneley 2]
    Noah [T. 3]
    Noah [Ch. 3]
    Abraham and Isaac [Ch. 4]
    Abraham and Isaac [Brome]
    Moses [York II]
    Balaam, Balak and the Profets [Ch. 5]
    The Parliament of Heaven, the Salutation
        and Conception [Ludus Coventriae II]
    Joseph [L.C. 12]
    The Nativity [L.C. 15]
    The First Shepherds' Play [T. 12]
    The Second Shepherds' Play [T. 13]
    Introduction to The Three Kings [Y. 16]

The Adoration [Y. 17]

The Flight into Egypt [T. 15]

The Purification, and Christ with the Doctors [Ch. 11]

The Death of Herod [L.C. 20]

The Shearmen and Tailors' Play [Coventry]

John the Baptist [Y. 21]

The Temptation of Christ, and the Woman Taken in Adultery [Ch. 12]s

Lazarus [T. 31]

The Passion Play I

The Council of the Jews [L.C. 26]

The Last Supper [L.C. 27]

The Betrayal [L.C. 28]

The Buffeting [T. 21]

The Dream of Pilate's Wife [Y. 30]

The Scourging [T. 22]

The Crucifixion [Y. 35]

The Death and Burial [Y. 36]

The Harrowing of Hell [Y. 37]

The Resurrection [T. 26]

Christ's Appearances to the Disciples [L.C. 38]

The Ascension [Ch. 20]

Pentecost [Y. 44]

The Assumption and Coronation of the Virgin [Y. 47]

Judgment Day [Y. 48]

(8) Hemingway, Samuel Burdett, ed., *English Nativity Plays*. 1909 (Yale Studies in English, XXXVIII), (reprinted 1964).

Chester:

Nativity

Shepherds' Play

Ludus Coventriae:

Incarnation

Joseph

Visitation

Nativity

Shepherds

Towneley:

Annunciation

Salutacio Elizabeth

First Shepherds' Play

Second Shepherds' Play

York:

Prophets, Annunciation, Visitation

Joseph

Nativity

Shepherds

(9) Schell, E.T., J.D. Shucter, eds, *English Morality Plays and Moral Interludes*. 1969.

The Castle of Perseverance

Everyman

The Interlude of Youth

The World and the Child

Wit and Science

Republica

The Tide Tarrieth No Man

Enough Is as Good as a Feast

All for Money

The Conflict of Conscience

(10) Thomas, R.G., ed., *Ten Miracle Plays*. 1966.

The Proclamation (Ludus Coventriae)

The Murder of Abel (Towneley Play II)

Noah (Ludus Coventriae IV)

Balaam and Balak (Chester Plays V)

The Annunciation (York Plays XII)

Herod and the Slaying of the Innocents (Coventry Pageants)

The Woman Taken in Adultery (Ludus Coventriae XXIV)

The Conspiracy (Towneley Play XX)

Christ's Passion (Chester Plays XVI)

The Harrowing of Hell (York Plays XXXVII)

Doomsday (Ludus Coventriae XLII)

(11) Wickham, G., ed., *English Moral Interludes*. 1976.

Mankind

Henry Medwall: Fulgens and Lucres

The Conversion of Saint Paul

John Bale: The Temptation of our Lord

Nice Wanton

Francis Merbury: The Marriage Between Wit and Wisdom

The Interlude of the Student and the Girl

John Lydgate: Mumming at Hertford

Mumming at Bishopswood

INDEX OF FOREIGN PLAYWRIGHTS

(The intention here is to list only those foreign playwrights one or more of whose plays were translated or frankly adapted by English playwrights, and to exclude those whose plays simply furnished an occasional scene or a 'source'. The distinction may not be consistently maintained, because it is not always maintained by my authorities.)

DUTCH

Dorlant, Peter, or Peter Dorlandus (1454–1507), 1495.

FRENCH

Beza, Theodore (1519–1605), 1575.

Boisrobert, François le Metel de (1592–1662), 1651.

Bueil, Honorat de, Seigneur de Racan (1589–1670), 1626.

Corneille, Pierre (1606–84), 1637, 1655, 1656, 1661, 1663(2), 1664(2), 1668, 1670, 1684, 1691, Supp. I, Supp. II, h.

Corneille, Thomas (1625–1709), 1654, 1664(2), 1665, 1668.

Dancourt, Florent Carton (1661–1725), 1698, 1700.

Desfontaines, – (fl. 1637–47), 1638.

Estienne, Charles (1504 or 1505–64), 1595.

Garnier, Robert (1534–90), 1590, 1594(2).

Molière, or Jean Baptiste Poquelin (1622–73), 1663, 1667(3), 1669(2), 1670(3), 1672, 1677, 1693, 1700, Supp. I.

Quinault, Philippe (1635–88), 1659, 1660, 1667, 1669, 1698.

Racine, Jean (1639–99), 1674, 1677.

Scarron, Paul (1610–60), 1657(2), 1668, 1669.

GREEK

Aeschylus (525–456 BC), 1663.

Aristophanes (c. 444–c. 380 BC), 1627, 1655, 1659.

Euripides (480–406 BC), 1543(2), 1550, 1558, 1579, 1602, Supp. I.

Sophocles (495–406 BC), 1543, 1564, 1581, 1649.

ITALIAN

Ariosto, Lodovico (1474–1533), 1566.

Bonarelli della Rovere, Guido (1563–1608), 1613, 1630, 1657.

Dolce, Lodovico (1508–68), 1566.

Grazzini, Antonfrancesco, or Il Lasca (1503–83), 1564.

Groto, Luigi, or Il Cieco d'Adria (1541–85), 1592, 1626.

Guarini, Giovanni Battista (1537–1612), 1601, 1604, 1630, 1635, 1647, 1676.

Negri, Francesco (1500-c. 60), 1550, 1635.

Pasqualigo, Luigi (fl. 1563–81), 1582, 1584.

Porta, Giovanni Battista della (1538–1615), 1599, 1603, 1615.

Salviati, Leonardo (1540–89), 1612.

Secchi, Niccolò (fl. c. 1549), 1659.

Tasso, Torquato (1544–95), 1591, 1628, 1635, 1660, 1698.

Textor, Ravisius (fl. 1500–46), 1546

LATIN

Plautus, Titus Maccius (c. 254–184 BC), 1555, 1577, 1592, 1604, 1665, 1694, Supp. I.

Seneca, Lucius Annaeus (4 BC?–AD 65), 1558, 1559, 1560, 1561, 1563, 1566, 1567, 1581, 1648, 1651, 1660, 1674, 1679, 1686, 1700, Supp. I.

Terentius Afer, Publius (c. 190–159 BC), 1520, 1588(2), 1598, 1613, 1627(2), 1663, 1674, 1687, 1694, Supp. I.

NEO-LATIN

Birck, Sixt, or Xystus Betulius (1501–54), 1560, 1566.

Corraro, Gregorio (1411–64), 1566.

De Groot, Hugo, or Hugo Grotius (1583–1645), 1640, 1652.

Kirchmayer, Thomas, or Naogeorgus (1511–78), 1538.

Schoepper, Jacob (c. 1514–54), 1547.

Tissier de Ravisy, Jean, or J. Ravisius Textor (c. 1480–1524), 1530, 1537.

Van Langeveldt, George, or Macropedius (c. 1475–1558), 1550.

INDEX OF FOREIGN PLAYS TRANSLATED OR ADAPTED

(See note to preceding index.)

INDEX OF DRAMATIC COMPANIES

Companies whose repertories are wholly unknown or include no new play are omitted from this index. Such companies, all minor ones, and for the most part purely provincial, are treated in John Tucker Murray, *English Dramatic Companies*, 2 vols, 1910. See also G.E. Bentley, *Jacobean and Caroline Stage* (1941), I, 260-9, for an account of the King and Queen of Bohemia's Company, not previously recognized; the repertory of this company, which was active between 1626 and 1631, and which probably played at the Fortune Theatre, is wholly unknown. For the English actors in Germany, see Supplementary List II,k.

ADMIRAL'S MEN, 1587-9, 1592, 1594-9, 1599 add. 1600-03

> *Active*: 1585-1603, and one of the two leading companies 1594-1603. *Patron*: Charles Howard, 2nd Baron Howard of Effingham, Earl of Nottingham, Lord High Admiral (1536-1624). *Principal actor*: Edward Alleyn (1566-1626). *Landlord and financier*: Philip Henslowe (d. 1616). *Theatres*: the Theatre, 1590-1; Newington Butts, *c*. 1591 (?); Rose, 1594-1600; Fortune, 1600-3. Continued after 1603 as Prince Henry's Men.

BATH'S MEN, 1578

> *Active*: 1542-79 intermittently. *Patrons*: John and William Bourchier, Earls of Bath. A provincial company.

BEESTON'S BOYS, 1637-41

> *Active*: 1637-42. *Patrons*: Charles I and Henrietta Maria. *Managers*: Christopher and (afterwards) William Beeston, 1637-40; William Davenant, 1640-1; William Beeston, 1641-2. *Theatre*: Cockpit. A troupe of boy actors (with several adults), otherwise called the King and Queen's Young Company.

BERKELEY'S MEN, 1578

> *Active*: 1578-1610 intermittently. *Patron*: Henry Fitzharding Berkeley, Baron Berkeley (d. 1611). A provincial company.

BETTERTON'S COMPANY, 1695-1700

> *Active*: 1695- a. 1700. *Manager*: Thomas Betterton. *Theatre*: Lisle's Tennis Court in Lincoln's Inn Fields. A company formed of the actors who seceded from the United Company.

CHAMBERLAIN'S MEN, 1582 (as Hunsdon's), 1589, 1594 (?), 1595-9, 1599 add., 1600-2

> *Active*: 1564-90 chiefly in provinces as Lord Hunsdon's Men; 1594-1603 newly organized and one of the chief London companies. *Patrons*: Henry Carey, 1st Lord Chamberlain (d. 1596); George Carey, 2nd Lord Hunsdon, Lord Chamberlain (1547-1603). *Chief playwright*: William Shakespeare. *Chief actor*: Richard Burbage (d. 1619). *Theatres*: Newington Butts, 1594; the Theatre, 1594-August, 1597; Curtain, Autumn, 1597-April, 1600; Globe, May, 1600-3. Continued after 1603 as King's Men.

CHAPEL ROYAL (Gentlemen of the Chapel) 1547, 1553 (Chapel Boys) 1514, 1516, 1560, 1565, 1567, 1568, 1572, 1577, 1579, 1581, 1582, 1587, 1601, 1602, (Oxford's Boys) 1584.

> *Active*: b. 1496-1603 intermittently, the gentlemen and choir boys of the royal establishment of the chapel together before 1553, the boys alone under various masters after 1553. *Theatres*: 1st Blackfriars, 1577-80 (with Windsor Boys); 1st Blackfriars, 1583-4 (with Windsor and

Paul's Boys under the name of 'Oxford's Boys'); 2nd Blackfriars, 1600–3. Continued after 1603 as Queen's Revels.

CLINTON'S MEN, 1574

Active: 1566–77, and as a provincial company 1599–1609 intermittently. *Patrons*: Edward Fiennes de Clinton, 1st Earl of Lincoln (d. 1585); Henry Fiennes de Clinton, 2nd Earl of Lincoln (d. 1616).

COURT INTERLUDERS, 1514, 1552, 1599

Active: b. 1493–1559, and thereafter intermittently in the provinces until 1573. An adult company forming before *c*. 1559 a part of the royal household.

I DERBY'S MEN, 1580, 1582

Active: 1563–70 in provinces as Strange's Men; 1574–82 in London and provinces. *Patron*: Henry Stanley, 4th Earl of Derby, Lord Strange (d. 1593).

II DERBY'S MEN, 1593, 1599, 1601

Active: 1594–1618 chiefly in the provinces. *Patron*: William Stanley, 6th Earl of Derby, Lord Strange (d. 1642).

DUDLEY'S MEN, *see* LEICESTER'S MEN

DUKE'S MEN, 1661–5, 1667–82

Active: 1660–82. *Patron*: James, Duke of York, afterwards King James II. *Managers*: Sir William Davenant, Lady Mary Davenant, Charles Davenant (with aid of Thomas Betterton). *Theatres*: Cockpit, 1660 (during temporary amalgamation with King's Men); Salisbury Court, 1660–1661; Lisle's Tennis Court in Lincoln's Inn Fields, 1661–71; Dorset Garden, 1671–82. After 1682 merged with King's Men to form United Company.

ELECTOR PALATINE'S MEN, *see* PALSGRAVE'S MEN

ETON BOYS, 1537, 1539

Students of The King's College of Our Lady of Eton beside Windsor. There are records of isolated performances under Udall before Cromwell, 1538–39, and at Court, 1573.

HOWARD'S MEN, 1576–8

Active: 1576–9. *Patron*: Charles Howard, 2nd Baron Howard of Effingham, later Earl of Nottingham and Lord High Admiral, patron of Admiral's Men.

HUNSDON'S MEN, *see* CHAMBERLAIN'S MEN

KING AND QUEEN'S YOUNG COMPANY, *see* BEESTON'S BOYS

I KING'S MEN, 1603–42

Active: 1603–42. *Patrons*: King James I (d. 1625), King Charles I (d. 1649). *Theatres*: Globe, 1603–42; 2nd Blackfriars, 1608–42. (Began production in Autumn, 1609.) Company a continuation of Chamberlain's Men.

II KING'S MEN, 1661–5, 1667–82

Active: 1660–82. *Patron*: King Charles II. *Manager*: Thomas Killigrew. *Theatres*: Cockpit, 1660 (during temporary amalgamation with Duke's Men); Red Bull, 1660; Gibbon's Tennis Court, 1660–3; Theatre Royal in Bridges Street, 1663–72; Lisle's Tennis Court in Lincoln's Inn Fields, *c*. 1672–3; Theatre Royal in Drury Lane, 1674–82. After 1682 merged with Duke's Men to form United Company.

KING'S REVELS (Boys), 1607, 1608; *see also* 1602.

Active: *c*. 1607–8. *Manager*: Martin Slater. *Theatre*: Whitefriars, from *c*. 1607–9.

KING'S REVELS (Men), 1630–6
>*Active*: 1629–37; *Patron*: King Charles I. *Theatres*: Salisbury Court, 1630–1; Fortune, 1631–4
>(?); Salisbury Court, 1634–6. Merged into Queen's Company, 1637.

LADY ELIZABETH'S MEN, 1611–15, 1622–5
>*Active*: 1611–16 in London, and 1616–22 in provinces; reorganized 1622, active in London
>1622–25. The company was revived in 1628 as the Queen of Bohemia's Players, and in
>existence until *c*. 1641. *Patron*: Lady Elizabeth, daughter of King James I and afterwards
>Queen of Bohemia (1596–1662). *Theatres*: Whitefriars, 1613–14; Hope, 1614–15; Porter's
>Hall, 1615 (?) (in combination with Prince's Men and Queen's Revels?); Swan, 1611–
>*c*. 1615; Cockpit, 1622–5.

LANE'S MEN, 1571, 1572
>*Active*: 1570–2. *Patron*: Sir Robert Lane (born *c*. 1528).

LEICESTER'S MEN, 1573, 1574, 1576–80, 1583
>*Active*: *c*. 1559–88. *Patron*: Robert Dudley, Earl of Leicester (*c*. 1532–88). *Theatre*: the
>Theatre, 1576–83.

LINCOLN'S MEN, *see* CLINTON'S MEN

MERCHANT TAYLORS BOYS, 1574, 1583
>Students of the Merchant Taylors Grammar School (founded 1561) performed occasionally
>at Court under the first headmaster, Richard Mulcaster, who resigned 1586.

NURSERY COMPANY, 1669
>*Active*: *c*. 1661–82 (?). *Manager*: George Jolly and others. *Theatres*: see under Nursery Theatres
>in List of Theatres. A company of young actors in training maintained by the King's Men
>and the Duke's Men as a subsidiary, and permitted to give public performances.

I & II OGILBY'S COMPANY, DUBLIN, 1638–40, 1662, 1663, 1669, 1670, 1700
>*Active*: 1637–41 under sponsorship of the Earl of Strafford, reorganized 1661 and active
>thereafter. *Manager*: John Ogilby, 1637–41, 1661–76, succeeded by Joseph Ashbury, who
>had long acted as his deputy. *Theatres*: Werburgh Street, 1637–41; Smock Alley, 1662–
>a. 1700.

OPERA COMPANY, 1656, 1658, 1659
>*Active*: 1656–*c*. 1659. *Manager*: Sir William Davenant. *Theatres*: Rutland House, 1656–8;
>Cockpit, 1658–9; and possibly others.

OXFORD'S BOYS, 1584
>*Active*: *c*. 1583–4. *Patron*: Edward de Vere, 17th Earl of Oxford (1550–1604). *Managers*: Henry
>Evans and John Lyly (?). *Theatre*: 1st Blackfriars. A separate company which amalgamated
>for some occasions with Paul's, Chapel, and Windsor Boys.

OXFORD'S MEN, 1600, 1601
>*Active*: 1547–1563 intermittently in provinces; 1580–1602 intermittently in London and
>provinces. *Patrons*: John de Vere, 15th Earl of Oxford (d. 1562), Edward de Vere, 17th Earl
>of Oxford (d. 1604). *Theatre*: Boar's Head, 1602.

PEMBROKE'S MEN, 1592–94, 1597, 1599 add.
>*Active*: *c*. 1592–1600. *Patron*: Henry Herbert, 1st Earl of Pembroke (d. 1601). *Theatre*: Swan,
>1597.

PRINCE CHARLES'S MEN, 1631, 1633–5, 1639, 1642
>*Active*: 1631–42. *Patron*: Prince Charles, afterwards King Charles II. *Theatres*: Salisbury
>Court, 1631–b. 1634; Red Bull, 1634–40; Fortune, 1640–2.

PRINCE HENRY'S MEN, 1604–6, 1608, 1611
> *Active*: 1603–12. *Patron*: Henry, Prince of Wales (1594–1612). *Theatre*: Fortune, 1603–12. A continuation of Admiral's Men. Continued as Palsgrave's Men.

PRINCE'S MEN, 1612, 1613, 1619, 1629, 1621, 1623–5
> *Active*: 1608–25, at first in provinces as Duke of York's Men. *Patron*: Charles, Duke of York, who became Prince of Wales at his elder brother Henry's death in 1612; afterwards King Charles I. *Theatres*: Porter's Hall, 1616 (?) (with Lady Elizabeth's Men and Queen's Revels?); Hope, 1615–17; Red Bull, 1617–19 (?); Cockpit, 1620–21, apparently occasionally at Swan, *c.* 1619–21; Curtain, 1622–23; Red Bull, 1623–5.

QUEEN ANNE'S MEN, 1604, 1605, 1607–12, 1615–18
> *Active*: 1603–19, and its provincial subsidiary until 1625. *Patron*: Queen Anne, Consort of King James I (1574–1619). *Theatres*: Boar's Head, *c.* 1595–1605; Curtain, 1603–5; Red Bull, summer, 1605–17; Cockpit, 1617–19. (Sometimes, apparently, still played Red Bull.) A continuation of Worcester's Men. Continued after 1619 as Red Bull (Revels) Company in London and as Late Queen's Men in provinces.

QUEEN HENRIETTA'S MEN, 1625–29, 1631–6; *see also* 1612, 1621, 1630
> *Active*: 1625–36. *Patron*: Queen Henrietta Maria. *Manager*: Christopher Beeston. *Theatre*: Cockpit, 1625–36.

QUEEN OF BOHEMIA'S COMPANY, *see* LADY ELIZABETH'S MEN

QUEEN'S MEN, 1546
> Various provincial companies so-called were active 1509–82.

QUEEN'S MEN, 1584–6, 1588, 1590–2, 1595, 1599 add.
> *Active*: 1583–94. *Patron*: Queen Elizabeth. *Chief Actor*: Richard Tarlton (d. 1588). *Theatres*: Bull Inn and Bell Inn, 1583 and perhaps until 1588; Bel Savage Inn, 1588; the Theatre, 1583–91; Curtain, 1585–92 (?); Rose, 1594. The chief company before the rise of the Admiral's Men and the Chamberlain's Men.

QUEEN'S MEN, 1637–9
> *Active*: 1637–42. *Patron*: Queen Henrietta Maria. (For her first company, see above.) *Manager*: Richard Heton. *Theatre*: Salisbury Court, 1637–42.

QUEEN'S REVELS, 1604–11, 1613
> *Active*: 1604–*c.* 1615. *Patron*: Queen Anne. *Theatres*: 2nd Blackfriars, 1604–8; Whitefriars, 1609–13; Porter's Hall, 1615 (?). A boys' company, formerly the Chapel Royal, otherwise known as Blackfriars or Whitefriars Children, or simply Revels Company. Effectively merged with Lady Elizabeth's Men in 1615.

RED BULL (REVELS) COMPANY, 1619–22
> *Active*: 1619–*c.* 1623. *Theatre*: Red Bull, 1619–23. A remnant of Queen Anne's Men which continued active after the death of their patron in 1619 and later recruited boys.

RED BULL COMPANY, 1638, 1639, 1641
> *Active*: *c.* 1626–*c.* 1642. *Theatres*: Red Bull, 1625–34; Fortune, 1634–40; Red Bull, 1640–2. A troupe probably formed of the remnant of the Prince's Men, joined to a provincial King's company.

RHODES'S COMPANY, 1659
> A company of 'young actors', under the direction of John Rhodes, active at the Cockpit Theatre in 1659–60.

RICH'S MEN, 1567

Active: 1564–70. Patrons: Richard, 1st Baron Rich (d. 1567); Robert, 2nd Baron Rich (d. 1581).

SALISBURY COURT COMPANY, 1660

A company of unknown personnel occupying Salisbury Court Theatre for a few months in 1660.

SHEFFIELD'S MEN, 1578

Active: 1578–86. Patron: Edmund, Baron Sheffield. A provincial company.

STRANGE'S MEN, 1587–93, 1599 add.

Active: 1577 (?)–1594. Patron: Ferdinando Stanley, Lord Strange, 5th Earl of Derby (d. 1594). Theatres: Cross Keys Inn, 1589 and 1594, and perhaps in the interim as a winter house; the Theatre, 1590–1; Rose, 1592–3; Newington Butts, 1594. This company is conjectured to have amalgamated with Admiral's intermittently c. 1588–94, and thereafter to have split up into sections merging with Admiral's, Chamberlain's, and II Derby's.

SUSSEX'S MEN, 1574, 1576–80, 1590, 1594, 1599 add.

Active: c. 1569–94 intermittently; 1602–18 intermittently in provinces. Patrons: Thomas Radcliffe, 3rd Earl of Sussex (d. 1583); Henry Radcliffe, 4th Earl of Sussex (d. 1593); Robert Radcliffe, 5th Earl of Sussex (d. 1629). Theatre: Rose, 1593–4.

UNITED COMPANY, 1683–94

Active: 1682–95. Patron: Held both royal patents. Manager: Thomas Betterton, until supplanted by Christopher Rich. Theatres: Theatre Royal in Drury Lane, and, occasionally, Dorset Garden, 1682–95.

WARWICK'S MEN, 1576–80

Active: 1559–65, 1575–80, 1592 (?). Patron: Ambrose Dudley, Earl of Warwick (d. 1590). Theatre: the Theatre, 1576–80. Company transferred its service to Oxford in 1580.

WESTMINSTER BOYS, 1564, 1566, 1572, 1574

The students of the grammar school of the Abbey of Westminster acted plays in early Tudor times, and later performed occasionally before Queen Elizabeth.

WINDSOR BOYS, 1572, 1574, 1575, 1577

Choir boys of the Chapel Royal of Windsor acted plays at Court 1567–77 under the mastership of Richard Farrant (master, 1564–80), and perhaps thereafter in combination with Chapel Royal Boys until 1580. May have formed part of the union of boys known as Oxford's Boys in 1584. Theatre: 1st Blackfriars, 1577–80, 1583–4 (?).

WORCESTER'S MEN, 1602, 1603

Active: 1555–85 intermittently in provinces; 1590–1603 intermittently in provinces and London. Patrons: William Somerset, 3rd Earl of Worcester (d. 1589); Edward Somerset, 4th Earl of Worcester (d. 1628). Theatres: Boar's Head, apparently from c. 1595 on 1602; Rose, 1602–3. Continued after 1603 as Queen Anne's Men.

LIST OF THEATRES

Theatres are listed in the order of their appearance. The list includes all the houses where plays are known to have been professionally presented before 1700.

CARPENTERS' HALL

An inn in Shoreditch where an interlude was 'openly played' in 1541.

JOHN WYLKYNSON'S DWELLING HOUSE

Wylkynson, a courier, was enjoined (27 May 1549) from suffering and maintaining 'interludes playes to be made and kept within his dwellyng house in London.'

BOAR'S HEAD INN

An inn in Whitechapel, probably in existence since the 1520s, where the play 'A Sackful of News' was suppressed in 1557 before it could be acted. Most important as the site of the Boar's Head Theatre, listed below.

SARACEN'S HEAD

An inn in Islington where plays were purported to have been performed in 1557.

RED LION INN

Built by John Brayne, probably the first permanent building to provide regular performance of plays. Originally a farm known by the name of 'The Sign of the Red Lion' in the parish of Stepney (eastern suburbs), records giving details of construction suggest that the theatre was not to be a conversion but an entirely new building situated on the south side of the garden belonging to the farm house. In 1567 the play *Samson* was performed on a stage which measured approximately 40 feet by 30 feet.

PAUL'S PLAYHOUSE

A playhouse established in 1575 by Sebastian Wescott. It was first fitted up in a 'private house', probably situated in one corner of the garth of the Cloister of St Paul's Cathedral. The size of the house is unknown. May have been used first for rehearsals and later for commercial purposes. The 'commercial' play period was in effect 1575–90 or 1591, then again by *c*. 1596 or 1599–1606.

BULL INN

An inn on Bishopsgate Street, London, probably altered for theatrical purposes. It was used for plays from before 1575 until after 1594. The Queen's Men acted here in 1583 and perhaps until 1588.

BELL INN

An inn in Gracious (Gracechurch) Street, London, probably altered for theatrical purposes. It was used for plays from before 1576 until after 1583. The Queen's Men acted here in 1583 and perhaps later.

BEL SAVAGE INN

An inn in Ludgate Hill, probably altered for theatrical purposes. It was used for plays from before 1576 until after 1588. It was occupied by the Queen's Men in 1588.

CROSS KEYS INN

An inn in Gracious (Gracechurch) Street, London, probably altered for theatrical purposes. It was used as a playhouse from before 1579 until some time before 1596. Strange's Men performed here in 1589 and 1594, and perhaps in the interim during the winter seasons.

THEATRE

Built in 1576 by St Leonard's Parish, Shoreditch (northern suburbs), by James Burbage, the first public playhouse in London and the first to be independent of other buildings. A radially framed, open-air theatre, probably black and white and having a tile roof, it measured approximately 100 feet in diameter and was topped by a cupola or tower which suggested a flagstaff. It was occupied by Leicester's Men, Warwick's Men, and others before 1583; by Queen's Men and others, 1583–91; by Strange's and Admiral's Men, 1590–1; by Chamberlain's Men, 1594–c. 1597. In the Christmas season of 1598, the structure was torn down and the timbers used in building the Globe.

FIRST BLACKFRIARS

An enclosed or so-called 'private' theatre, in type a medium-sized (26 feet wide, internal measure) hall forming part of one of the priory buildings – the Old Buttery. The priory buildings, formerly in the possession of the Dominican Monks, or Black Friars, were within the city, but not at this time subject to city control. The theatre was used by Chapel (and perhaps Windsor) Boys, 1577–1580, and by Oxford's Boys, 1583–1584. It was reconverted into lodgings after 1584.

NEWINGTON BUTTS

Erected or adapted from a standing building at Newington, a village one mile south of London Bridge, some time before 1580, possibly as early as 1576. Archery contests were frequently held at the site. Warwick's Men may have been the first to occupy the theatre. Newington Butts was used by Strange's Men c. 1591; and by the Admiral's and the Chamberlain's Men for a time in 1594. After 1599, it was no longer used.

CURTAIN

Built in 1577 in Moorfields, Shoreditch (near the Theatre in the northern suburbs), by an unknown enterpriser, this open-air radially framed theatre was occupied by Arundel's Men, 1584 (?); as an 'easer' for the Theatre, 1585–92, by various companies, probably including the Queen's Men; by Chamberlain's Men, Autumn 1597–April 1599; by Queen Anne's Men, 1603–c. 1605; and by Prince's Men, 1620–1, 1622–3. The structure was still standing in 1627.

BANQUETING HOUSE

Temporary structures for plays and masks at Court were erected, 1559, 1572, 1581, near Whitehall. A permanent one, also used only for masks, was erected from the designs of Inigo Jones in 1622 and still stands. Usually, the professional companies at Court played in the great hall of Whitehall Palace (approximately 39 feet, internal measure).

ROSE

Built in 1587 in the Clink on the Bankside by Philip Henslowe in partnership with John Cholmley. A radially framed, open-air theatre, it was occupied by Strange's Men, 1592–3 (?); Sussex's Men, 1593–4; Queen's Men, 1594; Admiral's Men, 1594–1600; Worcester's Men, 1602–3. It is referred to as 'the late playhouse' in 1606.

BOAR'S HEAD THEATRE

A rectangularly shaped playhouse constructed on the grounds of the Boar's Head Inn, Whitechapel. Constructed first in the summer of 1598 by Oliver Woodliffe, in partnership with Richard Samwell, Sr, the playhouse was an immediate financial success. To capitalize on the popularity of the theatre, the partners completely rebuilt the structure in the summer of 1599 at about ten times the original cost. The yard of the playhouse was roughly square at about 55 feet a side. Above it in the later playhouse were single galleries on the north and south and a double one in the west. A single gallery was above and behind the stage on the east. Spectators occupied all the galleries and the space under those in the north, south, and east. The same stage was used in both playhouses. It was 39 feet, 7 inches wide and about 25 feet deep. In the first playhouse, the stage was in the middle of the yard, but in the second playhouse, the stage adjoined the tiring house. Because of the unique arrangement of the playhouse, an audience of 1,000 people could be closer to the stage than the theatregoers in the remote sections of the larger playhouses. Derby's Men played there, 1599–1601; Worcester's, 1601–2; Derby's again 1602–3; and perhaps Prince Charles's from 1604. In

1616, at the termination of the original site lease between Woodliffe and Jane Poley, the playhouse was reacquired by Jane Poley and her son, Sir John Poley, who thereafter sold off the property in pieces, a process well under way by 1621.

SWAN

Built in 1595 or 1596 on the Bankside near Paris Stairs by Francis Langley, this radially framed, open-air theatre of approximately 100 feet in diameter was used by Pembroke's Men in 1597, by Lady Elizabeth's Men, 1611–c. 1615, and Prince's Men, 1619–25. The structure was still standing and in use in 1635.

SECOND BLACKFRIARS

Adapted by James Burbage in 1597 from the Great Hall in the precinct of Blackfriars (see First Blackfriars, above). The playhouse was built in a room (part of the Great Hall) measuring 66 by 46 feet, with several galleries. It is the third known 'private' theatre (after the First Blackfriars and Paul's Playhouse). It was used by the Chapel Royal Boys, 1600–3; Queen's Revels, 1604–8; King's Men, 1609–42. The interior was dismantled in 1655.

GLOBE

Built in 1599, destroyed by fire in 1613; rebuilt and reopened in 1614. A radially framed, open-air theatre, 100 feet in diameter on the Bankside, built by a syndicate consisting mostly of members of Chamberlain's Men, it was occupied by Chamberlain's Men, May 1560–1603, and by King's Men, 1603–42 (after 1608 intermittently as a summer theatre). It was torn down in 1644.

FORTUNE

Built in 1600 in the Parish of St Giles without Cripplegate (northwest suburbs) by Philip Henslowe and Edward Alleyn. An open-air theatre, originally square, measuring 80 feet on the outside and 55 feet on the inside of the auditorium. It was destroyed by fire in 1621, was rebuilt in the traditional radially framed shape or polygonal shape, and reopened in 1623. It was used by the Admiral's Men, 1600–3; Prince Henry's Men, 1603–12; Palsgrave's Men, 1612–1621, 1623–5; King and Queen of Bohemia's Company, 1626–31 (?); King's Revels, 1631–4 (?); Red Bull Company, 1634–40; Prince Charles's Men, 1640–2; and occasionally for surreptitious performances during the Commonwealth Period. The structure was 'totally demolished' by 1662.

THEATRE AT CHRIST CHURCH, OXFORD

The design of the hall at Christ Church, Oxford, for the visit of James I in August 1605 is the earliest English theatre design to be identified and is thought possibly to be early enough to be contemporary with the first Globe, the Swan, and the Fortune. The plan for the auditorium calls for a hall 115 feet long and 40 feet wide internally, a space 33 feet deep for the stage, and two entrance doors at the lower end of the hall. The designer called for a flat forestage with a raked stage beyond, the first record of a raked stage in England. Notes on the audience capacity suggest that the seating capacity was 550 persons with room for another 260 to stand behind the seating area. For further information, those interested may refer to British Library Add. Ms. 15505, folio 21.

RED BULL

Built c. 1605 in Upper St John's Street, St James, Clerkenwell (northwest suburbs), by Aaron Holland. A rectangularly-shaped, open-air theatre, it was renovated and enlarged by 1633, possibly c. 1625. It was used by Queen Anne's Men, c. 1605–17; Red Bull (Revels) Company, 1619–23; Prince's Men, 1623–25; Red Bull Company, 1625–34; Prince Charles's Men, 1634–40; Red Bull Company, 1640–42; occasionally for surreptitious performances during the Commonwealth period; Mohun and others, 1660. The structure was still standing in 1664.

WHITEFRIARS

Built c. 1606 by Thomas Woodford cooperating with Michael Drayton. A 'private' theatre on the model of the Second Blackfriars, it consisted of a hall, the size of which is uncertain, adapted from a refectory of the former priory of the Carmelites, or White Friars. It was located to the west of Salisbury Court and Blackfriars, and like the latter was not fully subject to city control until 1608. It was used by King's Revels, 1607–8 or early 1609; Queen's Revels, 1609–13; Lady Elizabeth's Men, 1613–14 – Queen's Revels and Lady Elizabeth's Men having merged by early 1613, both were at Whitefriars. The end of its career as a regular theatre seems to have come about 1614.

COCKPIT, OR PHOENIX

Built in 1609 by John Best as a cockpit and converted 1616–17 by Christopher Beeston into a theatre of the enclosed or 'private' type. It was located in St Giles in the Fields, adjoining Drury Lane, subsequently the regular theatrical district. Occupied by Queen Anne's Men, 1617–19; possibly the Prince's Men, 1619–22; Lady Elizabeth's Men, 1622–4 (perhaps as early as 1619); Queen Henrietta's Men, 1625–36; Beeston's Boys, 1637–42; Opera Company, 1658–9; Rhodes and his actors, 1659–60; King's and Duke's Men before their division, 1660; Jolly's Troupe at intervals, 1661–5. The interior had been razed in 1649, but subsequently repaired.

HOPE

Built in 1614 on the Bankside by Philip Henslowe in partnership with Jacob Meade. It was a circular, open-air theatre, 100 feet in diameter – like the first Globe, the second Globe, the Swan, and the Theatre and as opposed to such rectangularly framed playhouses as the Boar's Head, the Fortune, and the Red Bull. It had a removable stage so that it could be used for the performance of plays as well as for bear-baiting. It was occupied by Lady Elizabeth's Men, 1614–15, probably in a loose merger with Prince's Men, 1615–17. After 1617, the structure was used mostly for bear-baiting. It was razed in 1656.

PORTER'S HALL, or PUDDLE WHARF, or ROSSETER'S BLACKFRIARS

A theatre in the precinct of Blackfriars, begun in 1615 by Philip Rosseter. Although left incomplete because of the intervention of the authorities, it appears to have been used even after the order of September 1615, until January 1617, by Lady Elizabeth's and Prince's Men (in coalition with the disbanded Queen's Revels.

SALISBURY COURT

Built by Richard Gunnell and William Blagrove and opened in 1630 near Whitefriars and Salisbury Court, Fleet Street. Salisbury Court was a brick, enclosed or 'private' theatre on a plot of ground 140 feet by 42 feet. It was occupied by King's Revels, c. 1630–1; Prince Charles's Men, 1631–b. 1635; King's Revels, 1635–6; Queen's Men, 1637–42; Duke's Men, 1660–1; Jolly's Troupe, 1661. It was also used irregularly during the Commonwealth period and by William Beeston in 1663 and 1664. The inside had been razed in 1649 and repaired by Beeston in 1660. The structure was destroyed in the fire of 1666.

COCKPIT-IN-COURT

A cockpit in Whitehall used occasionally when the actors brought plays to Court in the reign of King James. It was converted in c. 1630 by Inigo Jones into a regular Court theatre. It was a small, elegant theatre on Italian lines with the interior decorated with gilded and painted wainscoting, carvings, and architectural and heraldic detail.

FRENCH PLAYERS' THEATRE

A temporary theatre for the French company under Josias de Soulas, alias Floridor, was fitted up in M. Le Febure's riding school, Drury Lane, and used 1635–6.

WERBURGH-STREET THEATRE, DUBLIN

Built by John Ogilby in Dublin in 1637 and used for performances between 1637 and 1641 by Ogilby's company. In type it probably resembled contemporary 'private' theatres of London. It fell into decay during the Interregnum.

RUTLAND HOUSE

A nobleman's mansion near Charterhouse Yard was occupied by Sir William Davenant, and a narrow hall in the building was used for entertainments by his Opera Company, 1656–8.

GIBBON'S TENNIS COURT, OR THEATRE ROYAL IN VERE STREET

Built in 1634 as an enclosed tennis court near Lincoln's Inn Fields and converted into a theatre in 1660 by Thomas Killigrew. As converted, it probably resembled the Elizabethan 'private' theatres. It was occupied by King's Men, 1660-3, and by Nursery Company, *c.* 1669-71. The structure was burnt down in 1809.

LISLE'S TENNIS COURT, or DUKE'S HOUSE, or LINCOLN'S INN FIELD

Built in 1656 near Lincoln's Inn Field by Anne Tyler and James Hooker as an enclosed tennis court and converted into a theatre in 1661 by Sir William Davenant. It is sometimes described as the first modern theatre with a 'picture-frame' stage; it was semi-modern in that it had a scene room for movable scenery and a proscenium arch, but retained a modification of the platform stage of the older theatres in its 'apron', which extended before the arch into the auditorium. It was used by Duke's Men, 1661-71; King's Men, 1672-4; Betterton's Company, 1695-a. 1700. The structure was demolished in 1848.

SMOCK ALLEY THEATRE, DUBLIN

Built in 1662 by John Ogilby and used by his company and that of his deputy and successor, Joseph Ashbury, 1662-a. 1700. In type it probably resembled Lisle's Tennis Court.

THEATRE ROYAL IN BRIDGES STREET

Built in 1663 near Lincoln's Inn Fields by Thomas Killigrew and a syndicate. Of the same type as Lisle's Tennis Court, it was used by the King's Men until 1672, when it burnt down.

NURSERY THEATRES

The Nursery Company occupied Gibbon's Tennis Court, *c.* 1669-71 and at other times certain houses of which little is known: a theatre or 'booth' in Hatton Garden, b. 1667-1669; another in Bunhill, 1671; and a playhouse of a more elaborate order erected by Lady Mary Davenant in the Barbican in 1671 and occupied until *c.* 1682.

DORSEY GARDEN

Built in 1671 fronting the Thames near the former Salisbury Court Theatre by Lady Mary Davenant and a syndicate. In type an elaborate theatre (possibly designed by Christopher Wren) on the model indicated by Lisle's Tennis Court. It was occupied by Duke's Men, 1671-82; United Company, 1682-95 occasionally; Patent Company, 1695-a. 1700 occasionally. The house was pulled down in 1709.

THEATRE ROYAL IN DRURY LANE

Built in 1674 by Thomas Killigrew and a syndicate. In type resembling Dorset Garden (and also possibly designed by Christopher Wren), but less ambitious and more practical. It was used by King's Men, 1674-82; United Company, 1682-a. 1700. It remained in use as a theatre until 1791, when it was demolished and rebuilt.

LIST OF EXTANT PLAY MANUSCRIPTS, 975–1700: THEIR LOCATIONS AND CATALOGUE NUMBERS

Titleless manuscripts and unidentified fragments are listed at the end of Supplementary List I. The Latin plays in the following list are marked (L), but no further description is offered. For alternative attributions of authorship and other information, see the Chronology, above.

AETHELWOLD, BISHOP OF WINCHESTER
  Regularis Concordia, containing directions for the *Quem Quaeritis (of Easter)*, *Depositio Crucis*, and *Elevatio Crucis* (L). (1) Brit. Lib. MS Cotton Tiberius A. III, f. 177 (dated *c.* 1025). (2) Ibid., Cotton Faustina B. III, ff. 159a–98a (an inferior version dated *c.* 1000).

ALABASTER, WILLIAM
  Roxana (L). (1) Camb. Univ. Lib. MS Ff. 2.9. (2) Lambeth Palace MS 838, Art. 3. (3) Emmanuel Col., Camb., MS 185 (3.1. 17). (4) Trinity Col., Camb., MS R. 17.10. (5) Folger Shakespeare Lib. MS. V.b. 222 (English trans.) (6) Yale U. Lib. MS Vault/Shelves/Plays, Item 5.

ARROWSMITH, JOSEPH
  Titleless comedy composed on occasion of Charles II's visit to Cambridge, 4 Oct. 1671. Four pieces of verse, among them a prologue and an epilogue survive in commonplace book of John Watson; Brit. Lib. MS Add. 18220.

ATKINSON, THOMAS
  Homo (L). Brit. Lib. MS Harleian 6925, Art. I.

AUBREY, JOHN
  The Country Revel. Bodl. MS Aubrey 21.

B., H. (Burkhead, or Birkhead, Henry?)
  The Female Rebellion. (1) Bodl. MS Tanner 466, ff. 174 seq. (2) Glasgow Univ. MS Hunterian 635.

BACON, FRANCIS
  Gesta Grayorum. Fragments by Bacon (?) and Francis Davison appear in Brit. Lib. MS Harleian 541, f. 138; Inner Temple MS Petyt 583.43, f. 294; Folger Shakespeare Lib. MS. V.a. 190 (Letter of Henry, Prince of Purpoole, to the Great Turk, Dec. 17 –).

BALE, JOHN
  King John. Huntington Lib. MS HM 3.

BANISTER, JOHN
  I Music, or *A Parley of Instruments*. Brit. Lib. Shelfmark 11621, f. 31.

BANISTER, vere SELBY, WILLIAM
  Andronichus (L). Brit. Lib. Add. MS 15204
  Jephte (L), Ibid.
  Perseus et Demetrius (L), Ibid.

BARNES, BARNABE
  The Battle of Hexham. MS 'sold among Isaac Reed's books in 1807' (Hazlitt, *Manual*, p. 23). Extant?

BARNES, JOSHUA
  The Academy. Emanuel Col., Camb., MS III. I.4 (2 copies).
  Englebert. Ibid, III. I.2.
  Landgartha. Ibid.
  Plautus His Trinummi Imitated. Ibid., III. I.4.
  Sigward, the Famous King of Norway (an earlier draft of *Landgartha*). Ibid.

BAYLIE, SIMON
  The Wizard. (1) MS in Durham Cathedral Lib. (2) Brit. Lib. Add. MS 10306.

BEAUMONT, FRANCIS, *see* Fletcher, John

BEAUMONT, SIR JOHN
  The Theatre of Apollo. Brit. Lib. MS Royal 18 A.LXX.

BEHN, APHRA
  The Younger Brother. Bodl. MS Rawlinson, poet. 195.

BELLAMY, HENRY
  Iphis (L). Bodl. MS Lat. misc. e. 17 (formerly Malone MS 43).

BERKELEY, SIR WILLIAM

The Lost Lady. Folger Shakespeare Lib. MS J.b. 4 (last 298 11. missing).

BERNARD, RICHARD

The Birth of Hercules. Brit. Lib. Add. MS 28722.

BLENCOWE, JOHN

Mercurius (L). St John's Col., Oxford, MS 218.

BLOW, JOHN

Venus and Adonis. (1) Brit. Lib. Add. MS 22100. (2) MS in Westminster Chapel Lib. (3) MS in Christ Church Lib., Oxford.

BOYLE, ROGER, EARL OF ORRERY

The General (Altemira). (1) MS in Worcester Col, Oxford. (2) MS, present location unknown, printed by Halliwell [Phillipps] in 1853.

Henry V. (1) Huntington Lib. MS EL 11642 (from the Bunbury MSS? see *Hist. MSS Comm.,* III 241). (2) Ibid., HM 20. (3) Ibid., HM 599. (4) Bodl. MS Rawlinson, poet. 2. (5) Ibid., poet. 180. (6) Folger Shakespeare Lib. MS V.b. 133. (7) Ibid., V.a. 220.

Mustapha. (1) Huntington Lib. MS EL 11641 (from the Bunbury MSS? see *Hist. MSS Comm.,* III, 241). (2) Brit. Lib. Add. MS 29280. (3) Bodl. MS Rawlinson, poet. 5. (4) Ibid., Rawlinson, poet. 27. (5) Folger Shakespeare Lib. MS V.b. 133. (6) Ibid., V.a. 220.

Tryphon. (1) Bodl. MS Malone II. (2) Bodl. MS. Rawlinson, poet. 39.

Zoroastres. Brit. Lib. MS Sloane 1828, ff. 46a–80a.

BROME, RICHARD

The English Moor. MS in Lichfield Cathedral Lib.

BROOKE, SAMUEL

Adelphe (L). (1) Trinity Col., Camb., MS R. 3.9, ff. 109–38v. (2) Ibid., R. 10.4. (3) Brit. L. Add. 44963, ff. 41–81v.

Melanthe (L). Folger Shakespeare Lib. MS. J.a. 2.

Scyros (L). (1) Camb. Univ. Lib. MS Ee.V. 16. (2) Emmanuel Col., Camb., MS 185 (3.1.17). (3) Trinity Col., Camb. MS R. 3.9. (4) Ibid., R. 3.37. (5) Ibid., R. 10.4. (6) Ibid., R. 17.10. (7) Ibid., 0.3.4. (8) Yale U. Lib. MS Vault/Shelves/Plays, Item 4.

BROWNE, WILLIAM

Ulysses and Circe. (1) Emmanuel Col., Camb.,

MS 68. (2) MS in the collection of H.C. Pole-Gell (see Chambers, *E.S.,* IV, 406).

BUCHANAN, GEORGE

Cupid, Chastity, and Time. MS verses sent by Thomas Randolph to Sir William Cecil (see Keith, *Hist. of the Affairs of Church and State in Scotland,* II. 220).

BURTON, ROBERT

Philosophaster (L). (1) Folger Shakespeare Lib. MS. V.a. 315. (2) MS in Harvard College Lib. (3) Harvard Univ. MS Thr. 10.1, ff. 48–56 (an actor's part).

C., W.

Rape Revenged. Brit. Lib. Add. MS 28807.

CARLELL, LODOWICK

Arviragus and Philicia. (1) Bodl. MS Eng. misc. d. II. (2) MS in Lord Leconfield's lib. at Petworth (see *Hist. MSS Comm.,* VI. 312; also B.M. Wagner, *TLS,* 4 Oct. 1934, p. 675). See also J.E. Ruoff, *Notes and Queries* (Jan. 1955), pp. 21-2. (3) MS in Sotheby ale Catalogue, 1-4, July, 1889.

CARLETON, R.

The Concealed Royalty. Bodl. MS Eng. poet. d. 2.

The Martial Queen. (1) Bodl. MS Rawlinson, poet. 126. (2) Bodl. MS Eng. poet. d. 2.

CARLETON, THOMAS

Fatum Vortigerni (L). Brit. Lib. MS Lansdowne 723, ff. 1-42.

CARTWRIGHT, WILLIAM

The Royal Slave. (1) Brit. Lib. Add. MS 41616 (from the Petworth collection). (2) Bodl. MS Arch. Seld. B. 26. (3) MS in the lib. of the Duke of Bedford. (4) Folger Shakespeare Lib. MS V.b. 212. (5) Heber MS 1043. Extant?

CAVENDISH, JANE, AND ELIZABETH BRACKLEY

The Concealed Fancies. Bodl. MS Rawlinson. poet. 16.

A Pastoral. Ibid.

CAVENDISH, WILLIAM, DUKE OF NEWCASTLE

The Country Captain. Brit. Lib. MS Harleian 7650 (formerly Add. 5001)

The Humorous Lovers. Brit. Lib. MS Harleian 7367, Art. I.

A Pleasant and Merry Humour of a Rogue. MS in the lib. of the Duke of Portland, Welbeck Abbey.

'Various drafts and fragments.' Ibid.

CECIL, ROBERT

The Queen's Entertainment at Theobalds, 1594. Bodl. MS Rawlinson D. 692, f. 106 (frag.)

CHAPMAN, GEORGE

The Twelve Months. MS formerly in the possession of J.P. Collier, but not now among his papers in the Brit. Lib. MS Egerton 2623. Extant?

MSS of *The Gentleman Usher and Monsieur D'Olive* are mentioned in Hazlitt, *Manual*, *passim*, but see Chambers, *E.S.*, III, 253.

CHAPPELL, JOHN

Susenbrotus (L). (1) Bodl. MS Rawlinson, poet. 195, ff. 79 seq. (2) MS at the Huntington (Calif.), titled 'Fortunia' – EL 1125 (Bridgewater modern shelfmark 35 B 67).

CHETTLE, HENRY AND THOMAS DEKKER

Troilus and Credssida. Brit. Lib. Add. MS 10449, f. 5 ('plot' only).

CHRISTOPHERSON, JOHN

Jephthes (Greek) [*Jephthah* (Latin version)]. (1) Trinity Col., Camb., MS 0.1.37. (2) St John's Col., Camb. MS 287. H. 19.

Jephthes (Latin version). Bodl. MS. Tanner 466, ff. 126–53.

'CLARETUS, PATER'

Homo Duplex (L). (1) Stonyhurst MS A.VII. 50 (2), ff. 33–62. (2) English Col., Rome, Archives MS C. 17 (ii) (frag.)

Innocentia Purpurata (L). Stonyhurst MS A.VII. 50 (2) ff. 2–31.

CLAVELL, JOHN

The Soddered Citizen. MS in the private collection of Lt. Col. E.G. Troyte-Bullock of Zeals House, Mere, Wilts.

COBBES, JAMES

Romanus. Brit. Lib. MS Harleian 4628, Art. 14., ff. 272–82v (frag.)

CORNISH, WILLIAM, JR

Entertainment at Greenwich (by Henry VIII for Mary Queen of Scots, 20 May, 1516. Mentioned in Chambers account, P.R.O. E 36/215 and Brit. Lib. Add. MS 21481.

CROWTHER, JOSEPH

Cephalus et Procris (L). St John's Col., Oxford, MS 217 P. 3587.

CRUSO, AQUILA

Euribates (L). Emmanuel Col., Camb. MS 185 (3.1.17), Art. 3.

DABORNE, ROBERT

The Poor Man's Comfort. Brit. Lib. MS. Egerton 1994, ff. 268–93.

DANIEL, SAMUEL

Hymen's Triumph. Edinburgh Univ. MS Drummond.

DAVENANT, WILLIAM

Macbeth. MS in Yale University Lib.

II The Siege of Rhodes. Public Lib., Douai, MS 7.87.

DAVENPORT, ROBERT

A Dialogue between Policy and Piety. (1) Folger Shakespeare Lib. MS V.a. 313. (2) MS reported to be once in the collection of John Withorn of Broomhead (see J.G. McManaway, *Notes and Queries*, CLXX [1936], 295).

See also *The Enchanted Lovers* and *The City Nightcap*, below, under ANONYMOUS.

DAVIES, JOHN

The Entertainment at Cecil House, 1602 (*A Conference between a Gentleman Huisher and a Post*). Brit. Mus. MS Harleian 286, f. 248. (For further fragments, see MS Hatfield XII. 568.)

The Entertainment at Harefield, 1602. Fragments in Brit. Lib. MS Harleian 5353, f. 95; Col. of Arms MS Talbot K, f. 43; Brit. Mus. MS Birch 4173; Folger Shakespeare Lib. MS X. d. 172. (See further Chambers, *E.S.*, IV, 68.)

DAVISON FRANCIS, *see* BACON, FRANCIS

DAY, JOHN

The Parliament of Bees. Brit. Lib. MS Lansdowne 725.

DEKKER, THOMAS

The Welsh Ambassador. MS in the Cardiff Public Lib.

The Whore of Babylon. First quarto, 1607, at Worcester College Library, Oxford, Play 3.13.

DENNY, SIR WILLIAM

The Shepherd's Holiday. Brit. Lib. Add. MS 34065.

DERING, SIR EDWARD

Henry IV (Shakespeare's two parts combined into one play). Folger Shakespeare Lib. MS V.b. 34.

DIGBY, GEORGE

Elvira. MS, item 251, in H.F. House sale at Sotheby's, 21 Jan. 1924.

DIGBY, KENELM
Il Pastor Fido. MS found among papers of Sir Kenelm Digby, once in the possession of Henry Bright (see *Poems from Sir Kenelm Digby's Papers*, 1877, pp. 4–5).

D'OYLEY, E.
Britannicus. Folger Shakespeare Lib. MS V.b. 219.

DRYDEN, JOHN
The Fall of Angels, and Man in Innocence (The State of Innocence). (1) Brit. Lib. Add. MS 37158. (2) Bodl. MS Rawlinson C. 146. (3) MS in the Harvard College Lib. (4) Huntington Lib. MS EL 11640. (5) Ibid. (6) Folger Shakespeare Lib. MS V.a. 225. (7) Ibid., V.b. 235.
The Indian Emperor. (1) Trinity Col., Camb., MS. R. 3.10. (2) Public Lib., Douai, MS. 7.87.
The Indian Queen (altered as an opera, in score by H. Purcell.) Brit. Lib. Add. MS 31449.

DUNBAR, WILLIAM
The Droichis Part of the Play. (1) Auchinleck, Ayrshire, MS Asloan. (2) Advocates' Lib., Edinburgh, MS Bannatyne.

EDES, RICHARD
Caesar Interfectus. Epil. Bodl: MS Top. Oxon e. 5.
The Second Woodstock Entertainment. Brit. Lib. Add. MS 41499A, ff. 12–16 (frag). For further MS fragments, see Chambers, E.S., III, 404.

ELIZABETH I, QUEEN
Hercules Oetaeus. Bodl. MS. E. Museo. 55, f. 48 (frag.).

EVELYN, JOHN
Thyrsander. Lib. of Christ Church, Oxford, Evelyn MS 41.

FANE, MILDMAY, EARL OF WESTMORLAND
Candy Restored. (1) Huntington Lib. MS HM 771. (2) Brit. Lib. Add. MS 34221, ff. 1ᵛ–18ᵛ.
The Change. Brit. Lib. Add. MS 34221, ff. 50ʳ–68ᵛ.
Don Phoebo's Triumph. Huntington Lib. MS HM 770.
Ladrones. MS, item 1054, in sale at Sotheby's, 17 July 1888.
De Pugna Animi. Brit. Lib. Add. MS 34221, ff. 124ᵛ–47ʳ.

Raguaillo D'Oceano. Ibid., ff. 107ᵛ–23ʳ.
Time's Trick upon the Cards. Ibid., ff. 19ᵛ–49ᵛ.
Virtue's Triumph. Ibid., ff. 69ᵛ–106ᵛ.

FANE, LADY RACHEL
Dramatic Pastimes for Children. Kent County Archives U269 F38/3. (Title added to volume in 17th-cent. hand, poss. by cataloguer. Small volume includes short note referring to a mask, a pastoral mask, two poems, and a plan for a second pastoral mask.)

FANSHAWE, SIR RICHARD
To Love Only for Love's Sake. Brit. Lib. Add. MS 32133.

FINCH, ANNE, COUNTESS OF WINCHILSEA
Aristomenes. Folger Shakespeare Lib. MS N.b. 3
Triumphs of Love and Innocence. Ibid.

FLETCHER, JOHN, and Others
Beggars' Bush. Folger Shakespeare Lib. MS J.b. 5.
Bonduca. Brit. Lib. Add. MS 36758.
The Elder Brother. Brit. Lib. MS Egerton 1994, ff. 2–30.
The Faithful Friends. See below, under ANONYMOUS
The Honest Man's Fortune. Victoria and Albert Mus. MS Dyce 9.
The Humorous Lieutenant (Demetrius and Emanthe). Brogyntyn MS 42, Library of Lord Harlech at Brogyntyn, Oswestry.
The Woman's Prize. Folger Shakespeare Lib. MS J.b. 3.

FLETCHER, PHINEAS
Sicelides. (1) Bodl. MS Rawlinson, poet. 214. (2) Brit. Lib. Sloane MS. 4453.

FORD, JOHN
Perkin Warbeck. Bodl. MS Rawlinson, poet. 122 (c. 1700?).

FORSETT, EDWARD
Pedantius (L). (1) Gonville and Caius Col., Camb., MS 62. (2) Trinity Col., Camb., MS R. 17.9. (3) Huntington Lib. MS EL 34. B. 13.

FOX, RICHARD
The Welcome for Katherine of Aragon. (1) Brit. Lib. MS Harleian 69, ff. 37 seq. (2) Ibid., Cotton Vitellius C.xi, ff. 117 seq. (3) Ibid., Cotton Vitellius A. xvi, ff. 184 seq. (4) MS printed in *Antiq. Rep.*, II, pp. 248 seq.

FOXE, JOHN
Christus Triumphans (L). Brit. Lib. MS Lansdowne 1045.

Titus et Gissipus (L). Brit. Lib. MS Lansdowne 388.

FRAUNCE, ABRAHAM

Hymenaeus (L). (1) St John's Col., Camb., MS S. 45. (2) Gonville and Caius Col., Camb. MS 125/62.

Victoria (L). (1) MS reported in *Hist. MSS Comm.*, III, 230 (MSS of Lord de L'Isle and Dudley at Penshurst). (2) Maidstone, Kent Archives Office, U1475/Z15.

FREEMAN, SIR RALPH

Imperiale. Brit. Lib. MS Egerton 2948.

GAGER, WILLIAM

Dido (L). (1) Brit. Lib. Add. MS 22583 (frag.). (2) Christ Church, Oxford, MS 486.

Oedipus (L). Brit. Lib. Add. MS 22583, ff. 31–4.

GASCOIGNE, GEORGE

Jocasta. Brit. Lib. Add. MS. 34063.

The Queen's Entertainment at Woodstock (The Tale of Hemetes the Hermit). (1) Brit. Lib. MS Royal 18A. XLVII, 27. (2) Ibid., Add. MS 41499A, ff. 4–5[b] (frag.).

GLAPTHORNE, HENRY

The Lady Mother. Brit. Lib. MS. Egerton 1994, ff. 186–211.

GOFFE, THOMAS

The Tragedy of Amurath. (1) MS in lib. of John Leicester-Warren, Esq., Tabley House, Knutsford, Cheshire (*Hist. MSS Comm.* I, 49). (2) Harvard Univ. MS Thr. 10.1, ff. 57–71 (an actor's part).

GOLDINGHAM, WILLIAM

Herodes (L). Camb. Univ. Lib. MS Mm I.24.

GRAFTON, RICHARD

Entry of Philip and Mary, August 1554. (1) Inner Temple MS Petyt 535, vol. II, ff. 61 seq. (2) Brit. Lib. MS Harleian 194. (3) STC #7552: John Elder, *The Copie of a Letter sent in to Scotlande* (London, 1555).

GREENE, ROBERT

John of Bordeaux. MS in the Duke of Northumberland's lib. at Alnwick.

Orlando Furioso. Dulwich Col. MS 1.138 (an actor's part).

GREVILLE, FULKE

Alaham. MS at Warwick Castle, Vol. D.

Mustapha. (1) MS at Warwick Castle, Vol. D. (2) Camb. Univ. Lib. MS Ff. 2.35.

(3) Folger Shakespeare Lib. MS V.b. 223 ('*c.* 1609').

GRIMALD, NICHOLAS

Archipropheta (L). Brit. Lib. MS Royal 12A. XLVI.

HACKET, JOHN

Loyola (L). (1) Brit. Lib. Add. MS 26709. (2) Trinity Col., Camb. MS R. 17.9. (3) Ibid., R. 17.10 (imperf.). (4) MS in Durham Cathedral Lib., Hunter 26, Item 1. (5) Folger Shakespeare Lib. MS. V.b. 222 (cast-list only). (6) Yale U. Lib. MS Vault/Shelves/Plays, Item 3.

HADTON, 'DOMINUS'

St Meriasek (Cornish). Hengwrt MS of Mr Wynne at Peniarth.

HAUSTED, PETER

Senile Odium (L). MS of Marquis of Bath (see *Hist. MSS Comm.*, III, 200), Longleat: 255A.

HAWKESWORTH, WALTER

Labyrinthus. (1) Bodl. MS. Douce 315, Art. 3. (2) Lambeth Palace MS 838. (3) Camb. Univ. Lib. MS Ee. 5.16. (4) St John's Col., Camb., MS. J. 8. (5) Trinity Col., Camb., MS R. 3.9. (6) Warwick County Record Office, MS Newdigate CR 136/B. 761. (7) Yale U. Lib. MS Vault/Shelves/Plays, Item 2.

Leander (L). (1) Lambeth Palace MS 838. (2) Camb. University Lib. MS Ee. V. 16. (3) Bodl. MS Rawlinson D. 341. (4) St John's Col., Camb., MS J. 8. (5) Emmanuel Col., Camb. MS I. 2 30. (6) Brit. Lib. MS Sloane 1762 (1602 version). (7) Trinity Col., Camb., MS R. 3.8 (1602 version). (8) MS in Hodgson Sale Catalogue 89, 29 Mar. 1951.

HEYWOOD, JOHN

Witty and Witless. Brit. Lib. MS Harleian 367.

HEYWOOD, THOMAS

The Captives. Brit. Lib. MS Egerton 1994, ff. 52[a]–73[a].

HILARIUS

Daniel. Bibliothèque Nationale. Paris, MS lat. 11331, XII, 9–10.

The Raising of Lazarus. Ibid., lat. 11331, XII, 11–12.

St Nicholas. Ibid., lat. 11331, XII, 12–16.

HOADLEY, SAMUEL
> *The War of Grammar.* Brit. Lib. Add. MS 22725.

HOLLAND, SAMUEL
> *The Enchanted Grove.* MS formerly in Lord Northampton's lib. at Castle Ashby (see A. Watkin-Jones, TLS, 15 Nov. 1934, p. 795). Extant?

HORNE, JOHN
> *Fortune's Task.* Huntington Lib. MS. HM II.

HOWARD, EDWARD
> *The Change of Crowns.* MS formerly in the possession of R.A. Austen-Leigh.

HOWARD, ROBERT
> *The Committee.* Clark Lib. H851M2 C734, 1664. A literal copy of the first printed edition in late 17th-century hand.

HUGHES, JOHN
> *Amalasont, Queen of the Goths.* MS once in the possession of the Rev. John Duncombe; see Halliwell-Phillips, *Dict.*, p. 13. Extant?

JAMES I, KING
> *'Wedding Masque'.* (1) Bodl. MS 165, ff. 60^r-64^v. (2) Brit. Lib. Add. MS 24195, ff. 52^r-55^v.

JAQUES, FRANCIS
> *The Queen of Corsica.* Brit. Lib. MS Lansdowne, 807, ff. 2-28.

JEFFERE, JOHN
> *The Bugbears.* Brit. Lib. MS Lansdowne 807, ff. 57 seq.

JOHNSON, LAURENCE
> *Misogonus.* Huntington Lib. MS. HM 542.

JOHNSON, WILLIAM
> *Valetudinarium* (L). (1) Camb. University Lib. MS Dd. III. 73. (2) St John's Col., Camb., MS S. 59. (3) Emmanuel Col., Camb., MS 52, 1.2.32.

JONSON, BEN
> *Christmas His Mask.* (1) Folger Shakespeare Lib. MS J.a. 1. (2) Bodl. MS Rawlinson, poet. 160, ff. 173-4 (song of Christmas only). (3) Brit. Lib. MS Harleian 4955, ff. 46-7 (song of Christmas only).
> *The Entertainment at the Earl of Newcastle's in Blackfriars.* Brit. Lib. MS Harleian 4955, ff. 48-52.
> *The Entertainment of the Two Kings of Great Britain and Denmark.* Brit. Lib. MS Egerton 2877,

f. 162b (speech of Eumone, Dice, and Irene).
> *The Gypsies Metamorphosed.* (1) Huntington Lib. MS HM 741. (2) Brit. Lib. MS Harleian 4955, ff. 2-30. (3) MS (frag.) in Conway papers in Public Record Office (S.P.D., James I, CXXII, art. 58). (4) Bodl. MS. Tanner 306, f. 252 (frag.). (5) Bodl. MS Rawlinson, poet. 172, f. 78 (frag.).
> *The King's Entertainment at Welbeck.* Brit. Lib. MS Harleian 4955, ff. 194-8.
> *Love's Welcome at Bolsover.* Ibid., ff. 199-202.
> *The Mask of Blackness.* Brit. Lib. MS Royal 17B. XXXI.
> *The Mask of Queens.* Ibid., Royal 18A. XLV.
> *Pleasure Reconciled to Virtue.* MS in Duke of Devonshire's collection at Chatsworth.
> *The Vision of Delight.* Brit. Lib. MS Harleian 4955, ff. 40-1 (frag.).
> *Volpone.* MS said to be extant by J.S. Farmer in Introduction to *Believe as You List*, but see Chambers, *E.S.*, III, 368.

JORDAN, THOMAS
> *Cupid His Coronation.* Bodl. MS Rawlinson B. 165, ff. 109-13.

JORDAN, WILLIAM
> *The Creation of the World, with Noah's Flood* (Cornish). (1) Bodl. MS. 219. (2) Bodl. MS. Corn. e. 2 (transcript of Bodl. MS. 219); includes Keigwin's English prose trans.). (3) Brit. Lib. MS. Harleian 1867. (4) MS belonging to J.C. Hotten, bookseller, in 1864 (see Chambers, *M.S.*, II, 435); same as Brit. Lib. Add. MS 28554?

JOYNER, WILLIAM
> *The Roman Empress.* MS at Worcester Col., Oxford.

KATHERINE OF SUTTON
> *Quem Quaeritis (of Easter)*, with directions for *Depositio Crucis* and *Elevatio Crucis* (L). University Col., Oxford, MS 169, XV, 108-9, 119-24.

KEIGWIN, JOHN
> *The Creation of the World, with Noah's Flood* (trans. of Jordan, W.). (1) Bodl. MS Corn. e. 2. (2) Brit. Lib. MS Harleian 1867. (3) Brit. Lib. Add. MS 28554. (4) National Library of Wales MS. Llanstephan 97.
> *Origo Mundi* (trans.). Bodl. MS. Corn. e. 3.

KILLIGREW, THOMAS

I and II Cicilia and Clorinda. Folger Shakespeare Lib. MS. V.b. 208–9.

Clarasilla. MS formerly in Castle Howard Lib.; now in Houghton Lib., Harvard Univ.

KILLIGREW, SIR WILLIAM

The Siege of Urbin. Bodl. MS Rawlinson, poet. 29.

KIRKHAM, R.

Alfred. Bodl. MS Rawlinson, poet. 80.

KYTTON, W.

'Mock Mass'. Camb. University Lib. MS F.R. 5.14.

LAWRENCE, WILLIAM

News from Geneva, or the Lewd Levite. In the possession of J. Stevens Cox, Beaminster, Dorset.

LEE, SIR HENRY, *see* GASCOIGNE, GEORGE: *The Queen's Entertainment at Woodstock.*

LEE, NATHANIEL

Mithridates, King of Pontus. Public Lib., Douai, MS 7.87.

Theodosius. MS, item 1322, in Joseph Haselwood's sale, 1833, to Thorpe. Extant?

LEGGE, THOMAS

Richardus Tertius (L). (1) Bodl. Lat. misc. e. 16. (2) Camb. Univ. Lib. MS Mm. IV. 40. (3) Folger Shakespeare Lib. MS V.a. 310. (4) Huntington Lib. MS HM 179. (5) Clare Col., Camb., MS Kk. 3.12 (dated Jan. 1583). (6) Gonville and Caius Col., Camb., MS 125. 62 (dated, prob. erroneously, 1573). (7) Emmanuel Col., Camb., MS I.3.19 (*c.* 1628). (8) Bodl. MS. Tanner 306, f. 42 (Part I only; dated, prob. erroneously, 17 Mar. 1582). (9) Finch-Hatton MS 320 in Northamptonshire Record Office. (10) Brit. (Lib.) MS Harleian 2412 (dated 1588). (11) Ibid., Harleian 6926, Art. I (dated 1586).

Solymitana Clades, or Destruction of Jerusalem. Camb. U. Lib. Add. 7958.

LINDSAY, DAVID

A Satire of the Three Estates. (1) Brit. Lib. MS. Reg. 7. C. XVI, ff. 136–9 (descrip. of version of 1540). (2) Advocates' Lib., Edinburgh, MS Bannatyne, ff. 164^a–210^a (version of 1552).

LISTER, MARTIN

Eunuchus (trans. Terence). Bodl. MS Lister 23.

LOWER, SIR WILLIAM

Don Faphet of Armenia. Brit. Lib. Add. MS 28723.

The Enchanted Lovers. See below, under ANONYMOUS.

The Three Dorothies. MS formerly in the collection at Skeffington Hall. Extant?

LUTTRELL, NARCISSUS

Love's Metamorphosis. Clark Library MS. FL 8975M2 (includes: 1931 transcription by Noel Broadbent; correspondence between Broadbent and Percy Simpson; typewritten analysis dated 1948 by John Harrington Smith).

LYDGATE, JOHN

The Mumming at Bishopswood. Bodl. MS Ashmolean 59, ff. 62–4.

A Mumming at Eltham. (1) Trinity Col., Camb., MS R. 3.20, ff. 37–40. (2) Brit. Lib. Add. MS 29729, ff. 135^b–6^b.

A Mumming at Hertford. (1) Trinity Col., Camb., MS R. 3. 20, ff. 40–8. (2) Brit. Lib. Add. 29729, ff. 136^b–40^n.

A Mumming at London (A Mumming before the Great Estates of the Land). (1) Trinity Col., Camb., MS R. 3.20, ff. 55–65. (2) Brit. Lib. Add. MS 29729, ff. 140^a–4^a.

A Mumming at Windsor. (1) Trinity Col., Camb., MS R. 3.20, ff. 71–4. (2) Brit. Lib. Add. MS 29729, ff. 144^a–5^b.

A Mumming for the Goldsmiths of London. (1) Trinity Col., Camb., MS R. 3.20, ff. 175–8. (2) Brit. Lib. Add. MS 29729, ff. 134^a–5^b.

A Mumming for the Mercers of London. (1) Trinity Col., Camb., MS R. 3.20, ff. 171–5. (2) Brit. Lib. Add. MS 29729, ff. 132^b–4^a.

The Reception of Henry VI. Brit. Lib. MS Cotton. Julius B. II, ff. 89–100.

LYLY, JOHN

The Entertainment at Chiswick. Finch-Hatton MS 2414.

MABBE, JAMES

The Spanish Bawd. MS, prob. of this play, reported at Alnwick Castle, *Hist. MSS. Comm.*, III, 119.

MAITTAIRE, MICHAEL

Excidium Trojae (L). Bodl. MS Rawlinson, D. 284.

Dido (L). Ibid.

Inferno Navigatio (L). Ibid.

MANUCHE, COSMO

The Banished Shepherdess. (1) Huntington Library MS EL 8395. (2) British Library Add. MS 60273.

The Feast. (1) MS at Worcester Col., Oxford. (2) Brit. Lib Add. MS 60274.

Love in Travail. Brit. Lib. Add. MS 60275.

Saint Hermenigildus. Brit. Lib. Add. MS 60276.

Agamemnon and *Hercules Furens* (blank verse translations of Seneca). Brit. Lib. Add. MS 60276.

Agamemnon and *Hercules Furens* (fair copy translations of Seneca, in folio). Brit. Lib. Add. MS 60277.

The Mandrake (*La Mandragola*), by Machiavelli (a draft of a translation).

Don Sancho (*Don Sancho D'Aragon*) by Corneille (the first act).

Leontius, King of Cyprus (a portion of the first act). Three preceding works contained in Brit. Lib. Add. MS 60278.

Leontius, King of Cyprus (folio MS of a fair copy in blank verse). Brit. Lib. Add. MS 60279.

Mariamne: the Wife of Herod the Great (folio MS of rough draft). Brit. Lib. Add. MS 60280.

The Reign of the Emperor Caracalla (title assigned) (untitled, blank verse drama in five acts). Brit. Lib. Add. MS 60281.

The Captives by Plautus (two ½ page fragments of an English translation of Act II). Brit. Lib. Add. MS 60281.

Untitled play in blank verse set in Greece (3 leaves). Brit. Lib. Add. MS 60281.

(See William P. Williams, 'The Castle Ashby Manuscripts: A Description of the Volumes in Bishop Percy's List'. *The Library*, 6th series II, no. 4, Dec. 1980: 391–412.)

MARLOWE, CHRISTOPHER

The Massacre at Paris. Folger Shakespeare Lib. MS J.b. 8 (frag.).

MARSTON, JOHN

The Entertainment at Ashby. (1) Huntington Lib. MS EL 34 B. 9. (2) Brit. Lib. MS Sloane 848, f. 9 (frag.).

City Pageant Brit. Lib. MS Royal 18A, xxxi.

MARTIN, GREGORY

Tragoedia Cyri Regis Persarum St John's College, Oxford.

MASSINGER, PHILIP

Believe as You List. Brit. Lib. MS Egerton 2828.

The Parliament of Love. Victoria and Albert Mus. MS Dyce 39 (frag.).

The Renegado. Bodl. MS Rawlinson poet. 20 (altered transcript of 1630 quarto).

Sir John van Olden Barnavelt. Brit. Lib. Add. MS 18653.

See also *The Cure of Pride* under ANONYMOUS, and *Beggars' Bush, The Elder Brother,* and *The Honest Man's Fortune,* above, under FLETCHER, JOHN.

MAY, CHARLES

Grobiana's Nuptials. St John's Col. MS text (Bodl. MS 30).

MAY, THOMAS

Cleopatra. Brit. Lib. MS Royal 18C. VII.

Julius Caesar (L). MS extant? See Hazlitt, *Manual,* p. 124, and Bentley, *J & C.S.,* IV, 838.

MAYDISTON, RICHARD

Richard II's Reconciliation with the City of London. (1) Bodl. MS Ashmolean 793. (2) Bodl. MS E. Museo. 94.

MEASE, PETER

Adrastus Parentans (L). Brit. Lib. Add. MS 10417.

MERBURY, FRANCIS

A Marriage between Wit and Wisdom. Brit. Lib. Add. MS 26782.

MEWE, WILLIAM

Pseudomagia (L). (1) Emmanuel Col., Camb., MS I.3.16 (item 3). (2) Trinity Col., Camb., MS R. 17.10. (3) Folger Shakespeare Lib. MS V.b. 222.

MIDDLETON, THOMAS

A Game of Chess. (1) Bodl. MS Malone 25. (2) Trinity Col., Camb. MS 0.2.66. (3) Brit. Lib. MS Lansdowne 690. (4) Huntington Lib. MS EL 34 B. 17. (5) Folger Shakespeare Lib. MS V.a. 231. (6) Ibid., V.a. 342.

Hengist, King of Kent (*The Mayor of Queenborough*). (1) Folger Shakespeare Lib. MS J.b.6. (2) MS in the lib. of the Duke of Portland, Welbeck Abbey.

An Invention. MS in Conway papers in Public Record Office (S.P.D., James I, CXXIX, art. 53).

The Witch. Bodl. MS Malone 12.

MILTON, JOHN

Arcades. MS (frag.) at Trinity Col., Camb. *Comus.* (1) MS at Bridgewater House,

London. (2) MS at Trinity Col., Camb. (3) Brit. Lib. Add. MS 11518 (songs only).

MITCHELL, FRANCIS

Michael and Francis. MS in Public Record Office, Star Chamber, Proceedings, 5. S. 30/16.

MONTAGUE, WALTER

The Shepherd's Paradise. (1) Brit. Lib. MS Sloane 3649. (2) Brit. Lib. MS Stowe 976. (3) Brit. Lib. Add. MS 41617. (4) Folger Shakespeare Lib. MS V.b. 203. (5) Ibid., V.b. 204.

MORE, THOMAS

Mr Moore's Revels. Bodl. MS Ashmole 47.

MORRELL, ROGER

Hispanus (L). Bodl. MS Douce 234, ff. 15 seq.

MOTTEUX, PETER

The Island Princess. Brit. Lib. Add. MS 15318.

MOUNTFORT, WALTER

The Launching of the Mary. Brit. Lib. MS Egerton 1994, ff. 318 seq.

MUNDAY, ANTHONY

John a Kent and John a Cumber. Huntington Lib. MS HM 500.

Sir Thomas More. Brit. Lib. MS Harleian 7368, Art. I.

NEALE, THOMAS

The Ward. Bodl. MS Rawlinson, poet. 79.

NEWDIGATE, JOHN

See listings below in Anonymous Plays listings under *Ghismonda*.

OLDISWORTH, GYLES

The Pattern of Piety. Bodl. MS Rawlinson C. 422.

PARKHURST, FERDINANDO

Ignoramus. Two copies of close, one of paraphrastical, trans. of Ruggle, MS reported in *Hist. MSS Comm.*, III, 215 (MSS of Marquis of Westminster, Eaton Hall, Chester).

PARKINSON

Speech to James I at Berwick, 1603. Folger Shakespeare Lib. MS V.b. 75.

PARSONS, PHILIP

Atalanta (L). Brit. Lib. MS Harleian 6924.

PEELE, GEORGE

Anglorum Feriae. Brit. Lib. Add. MS 21432.

The Battle of Alcazar. Brit. Lib. Add. MS 10449, f. 3 ('plot' only).

Polyhymnia. St John's Col., Oxford, MS 216.

PERCY, WILLIAM

The Aphrodisial. (1) Huntington Lib. MS HM 4. (2) Alnwick Castle MS 509.

Arabia Sitiens. (1) Huntington Lib. MS HM 4. (2) Alnwick Castle MS 508. (3) Ibid., 509.

A Country Tragedy in Vacunium. (1) Huntington Lib. MS HM 4. (2) Alnwick Castle MS 508 (frag.). (3) Ibid., 509 (dated 1646).

The Cuckqueans and Cuckolds Errants. (1) Huntington Lib. MS HM 4. (2) Alnwick Castle MS 508. (3) Ibid., 509.

The Fairy Pastoral. (1) Huntington Lib. MS HM 4. (2) Alnwick Castle MS 508. (3) Ibid., 509.

Necromantes. (1) Huntington Lib. MS HM 4. (2) Alnwick Castle MS 509.

PHILIPS, KATHERINE

Horace. Folger Shakespeare Lib. MS V.b. 231.

Pompey. (1) Folger Shakespeare Lib. MS V.b. 231. (2) National Lib. of Wales MS 21867B.

PITCAIRNE, ARCHIBALD

The Assembly. Brit. Lib. Add. MS 11503.

POLWHELE, ELIZABETH

The Faithful Virgins. Bodl. MS Rawlinson, poet. 95, ff. 49–78.

The Frolicks, or *The Lawyer Cheated.* Cornell University Library MS BD Rare P P77.

POPPLE, WILLIAM

The Cid. Brit. Lib. Add. MS 8888.

Tamerlane the Beneficent. Ibid.

POUND, THOMAS

Two Mask Orations. Bodl. MS Rawlinson, poet. 108, ff. 24, 29^v (formerly MS 14601).

PRYNNE [PRINNE], WILLIAM

The Unreasonable and Insupportable Burthen. 1659. Kent County Archives Office, Ref. U269 F3/6. Noted in *Diary Journals of Richard Sackville, Fifth Earl of Dorset.*

RADCLIFF, ROBERT

A Governance of the Church (One of *Three Dialogues*). National Library of Wales MS Brogyntyn 24, pp. 1–64. *See* entry under 'Textor, Ravisius'.

RANDOLPH, THOMAS

Aristippus. (1) Brit. Lib. MS Sloane 2531, ff. 124^a–140^b. (2) Folger Shakespeare Lib. V.b. 320.

The Conceited Pedlar. (1) Brit. Lib. Add. MS 27406, ff. 121-7ᵛ. (2) Edinburgh Univ. MS Laing III, 493, ff. 49–56ᵛ. (3) (*The University Pedlar.*) MS formerly in the possession of Richard West, then of the Rev. Mr Collins of Knaresborough: *teste* J. Hunter, *Cho. Vatum,* and R. West. Extant?

The Drinking Academy. Huntington Lib. MS HM91.

Praeludium. Brit. Lib. Add. MS 37425, ff. 54–5.

'*Thomas Randolph's Salting*'. MS, item 1488, in sale at Maggs Brothers, 1934 (Catalogue 598).

RANT, HUMPHREY

Phormio. Brit. Lib. MS Sloane, 1145, ff. 41–84.

REDFORD, JOHN

Courage, Kindness, Cleanness. Brit. Lib. Add. MS 15233, f. 28 (frag.).

D, G, and T[om]. Ibid., f. 38 (frag.).

Wit and Science. Ibid., ff. 11–27 (frag.).

REYMES, WILLIAM

Self-Interest. Folger Shakespeare Lib. MS V.b. 128.

RICHARDS, THOMAS, see JOHNSON, LAURENCE.

RICHARDS, WILLIAM

The Christmas Ordinary. Brit. Lib. MS Sloane 1458, ff. 36ᵛ–42ʳ.

RICKETS, JOHN

Byrsa Basilica (L). Bodl. MS Tanner 207.

ROBINSON, GWILIAM

Sailors' Mask. Description may be found among the 'Heyricke' papers preserved at Beaumanor in Leicestershire. (See John Gough Nichols, 'An Elizabethan Marriage', *N & Q,* 2nd series X, 11 Aug. 1960, 101–2.)

RUGGLE, GEORGE

Club Law. St John's Col., Camb., MS S. 62.

Ignoramus (L). (1) MS at Clare Hall, Camb. (2) Camb. U. Lib. Add. 7958, ff. 49–74. (3) Brit. Lib. MS Egerton 2982, Art. 5 (frag.). (4) Brit. Lib. MS Harleian 6869, ff. 57 seq. (frag.). (5) Brit. Lib. MS Sloane 2531. (6) Bodl. MS Douce 43. (7) Bodl. MS Tanner 306 (2 copies). (8) Bodl. MS Rawlinson 1361, ff. 129–84.

SALTERNE, GEORGE

Tomumbeius (L). Bodl. MS Rawlinson, poet. 75.

SALUSBURY, SIR THOMAS

An Antimask of a Citizen and Wife. National Lib. of Wales MS 5390D, ff. 59–67.

An Antimask of Gypsies. Ibid., MS 5390D, ff. 50-5.

Love or Money. Ibid. MS 5390D, ff. 69–109.

A Mask at Knowsley. Ibid. MS 5390D, ff. 35–45.

Isabela and the Friar (title assigned). Ibid. MS 5390D (frag.).

SANSBURY, JOHN.

Periander (part of *The Christmas Prince,* for MS of which see, below, ANONYMOUS). Folger Shakespeare Lib. MS J.a. I, ff. 134ʳ–57ᵛ.

SETTLE, ELKANAH

Love and Revenge. Brit. Lib. MS Harleian 6903, Art. I.

Pastor Fido. Bodl. MS Rawlinson, poet. 8.

SHADWELL, THOMAS

The Humorists. MS in the lib. of the Duke of Portland, Welbeck Abbey.

The Sullen Lovers. Ibid.

SHAKESPEARE, WILLIAM

Henry IV. (1) Brit. Lib. Add. MS 64078. Recently discovered anon. MS containing extracts corresponding to approx. 62 lines of the Oxford Standard Author's text of *Henry IV* (*c.* 1594–*c.* 1603). Other extracts, containing notes in Latin on metaphysics and theology, attrib. to Thomas Harriot. (2) See above, under DERING, SIR EDWARD.

Julius Caesar (transcript, with alterations, from MS based on Second Folio). Folger Shakespeare Lib. V.a. 85.

The Merry Wives of Windsor (transcript from Second Folio). (1) Folger Shakespeare Lib. V.a. 73. (2) Ibid., V.b. 240 (portion of III.5; IV. 1–5).

Sir Thomas More. See above, under MUNDAY, ANTHONY.

Titus Andronicus. MS in the possession of the Marquis of Bath at Longleat (frag. and illustration).

As You Like It, The Comedy of Errors, Julius Caesar, Macbeth, Romeo and Juliet, and *Twelfth Night* appear in MS 7.87, a volume dated 1694-5, Public Lib. of Douai, as do Lee's *Mithridates,* Dryden's, *The Indian Emperor,* and Davenant's *The Siege of Rhodes,* Pt. II. All the plays are transcripts from printed texts, or from MSS based on printed texts (the Second Folio for Shakespeare). See B.M. Wagner,

TLS, 4 Oct. 1934, p. 675, and G.B. Evans, 'The Douai Manuscript – Six Shakespearean Transcripts (1694–5)', *Phil. Quarterly*, XLI (1962), 158–72.

SIDNAM, JONATHAN
    Il Pastor Fido. Brit. Lib. Add. MS 29493.

SIDNEY, SIR PHILIP
    The Lady of May. Brit. Lib. Add. MS 61821.

SIMONS, JOSEPH, *vere* LOBB, EMMANUEL
    Leo Armenus (L). (1) Camb. Univ. Lib. MS Ii. VI. 35. (2) St John's Col., Camb., MS 504. (3) Stonyhurst MS B. VI. 25.
    S. Damianus (L). (1) St John's Col., Camb., MS. 504. (2) Stonyhurst MS B. VI. 25.
    Zeno (L). (1) Camb. Univ. Lib. MS Ii. VI. 35. (2) Brit. Lib. MS Harleian 5024, Art. I. (3) Stonyhurst MS B. VI. 25. (4) St John's Col., Camb., MS 504.

SINGLETON, THOMAS
    Talpae (L). Bodl. MS Rawlinson D. 288.

SPARROW, THOMAS
    Confessor (L). Bodl. MS Rawlinson, poet. 77.

SPEED, JOHN
    The Converted Robber. Brit. Lib. Add. MS 14047.

STUB, EDMUND
    Fraus Honesta (L). (1) Emmanuel Col., Camb., MS 185 (3.1.17), Art. 6. (2) Trinity Col., Camb., MS R. 17.9. (3) Ibid., R. 17.10. (4) Brit. Lib. MS Harleian 2296, Art. 29, f. 151–67ᵛ.

SUCKLING, SIR JOHN
    Aglaura. (1) Brit. Lib. MS Royal 18C. XXV. (2) Brit. Lib. MS Harleian 3889, ff. 28–31ᵛ (I.L and part of II.2)

TALBOT, SIR GEORGE
    Filli di Sciro. (1) Bodl. MS Rawlinson, poet. 130. (2) Brit. Lib. Add. MS 12128.

TATE, NAHUM.
    Dido and Aeneas. MS at St Michael's Col., Tenbury (score).

TEXTOR, RAVISIUS
    Ecclesia or *A Governance of the Church*. National Lib. of Wales Brogyntyn MS (second sequence) 10. Trans. by Robert Radcliff.

UDALL, NICHOLAS
    The Coronation Triumph of Anne Boleyn. Brit. Lib. MS Royal 18A. LXIV (frags.).
    Respublica. Carl H. Pforzheimer Lib. MS 40A.

VERNEY, FRANCIS
    Antipoe. Bodl. MS 31041.

VILLIERS, GEORGE
    The Country Gentleman. Folger Shakespeare Lib. MS V.b. 228.

VINCENT, THOMAS
    Paria (L). (1) Emmanuel Col., Camb., MS 68 (1.3.16). (2) Folger Shakespeare Lib. MS V.b. 222, f. 100–26ᵛ.

WARD, ROBERT
    Fucus sive Histriomastix (L). (1) Lambeth Palace. MS 828, ff. i + 1–25. (2) Bodl. MS Rawlinson, poet. 21, Art. 1.

WATSON, THOMAS
    Absalom (L). Brit. Lib. MS Stowe 957.

WHARTON, *née*, LEE, ANNE
    Love's Martyr. Brit. Lib. Add. MS 28693.

WHITE, ROBERT
    Cupid's Banishment. Pierpont Morgan Library MS M.A. 1296 (formerly MS V.9.c.).

WILBURNE, NATHANIEL
    Machiavellus (L). Bodl. MS Douce 234.

WILD, ROBERT
    The Benefice. (1) Brit. Lib. MS Lansdowne 807, Art. 4 (frag.). (2) Folger Shakespeare Lib. MS V.a. 232. Entire text edited by C.E. McGee for *Renaissance Drama*, N.S. XIX, 1988, pp. 227–64.

WILDE, GEORGE
    Eumorphus (L). Brit. Lib. Add. MS 14047, ff. 60–96.
    Love's Hospital. (1) Brit. Lib. Add. MS 14047, ff. 1–39ʳ. (2) Folger Shakespeare Lib. MS J.b. 7 (frags.).

WILMOT, JOHN, EARL OF ROCHESTER
    The Conquest of China. (1) Brit. Lib. Add. MS 28692, ff. 70–5 (one scene). (2) Folger Shakespeare Lib. MS V.b. 233 (one scene).
    Lucina's Rape. (1) Brit. Lib. Add. MS 28692. (2) Folger Shakespeare Lib. MS V.b. 233.
    Sodom. (1) MS in the Bibliothèque Nationale, Paris; see *Nouvelles acquisitions du département des manuscrits, 1891–1916, Manuscrits anglais, 1884–1910*. (2) Brit. Lib. MS Harleian 7312. (3) MS in the Hague Lib. (4) MS in the Hamburger Staats-und Universitäts-Bibliothek. (5) Victoria and Albert Mus. MS Dyce 43. (6) Princeton University Lib. MS 14401. (7) Ibid. (abridged version).

WILMOT, ROBERT, and others
    Gismond of Salerne. (1) Brit. Lib. MS Hargrave

205. (2) Brit. Lib. MS Lansdowne 786. (3) Folger Shakespeare Lib. MS V.a. 198. (frag.).

WILSON, ARTHUR

The Corporal. (1) Victoria and Albert Mus. MS Forster 638 (frag.). (2) Bodl. MS Douce C. 2 (frag.). (3) Bodl. MS Rawlinson, poet. 9, f. 45ʳ (title and *dramatis personae* only).

The Inconstant Lady. (1) Bodl. MS Rawlinson, poet. 9. (2) Ibid., 128. (3) Folger Shakespeare Lib. MS J.b.I.

The Swisser. Brit. Lib. Add. MS 36759.

WILSON, JOHN

Belphegor. Folger Shakespeare Lib. MS V.b. 109.

The Cheats. MS at Worcester Col., Oxford.

WORSELEY, RALPH

Synedrium (both versions) (L). Trinity Col., Camb., MS 0.3.25.

WREN, CHRISTOPHER, SR.

Physiponomachia (L). Bodl. MS 30, ff. 2 seq. (formerly 27639).

WRIGHT, JAMES

La Mallad (trans.). Folger Shakespeare Lib. MS V.b. 220.

WROTH, MARY (?)

Love's Victory. Huntington Lib. MS HM 600.

ZOUCHE, RICHARD

Fallacy. Brit. Lib. MS Harleian 6869, Art. 2, ff. 24ᵛ–56ᵛ.

ANONYMOUS

Abraham and Isaac (Brome). MS formerly at Brome Manor, Suffolk; now at Ipswich and East Suffolk Record Office, Ipswich.

Abraham and Isaac (Dublin). Trinity Col., Dublin. MS D. IV. 18.

Absalom (L). See under WATSON, THOMAS, above.

Adam (*Le Mystère d'Adam*), Lib. of the City of Tours MS 927.

Alcestis. See under BUCHANAN, GEORGE, Supp. I.

Alice and Alexis. Bodl. MS Douce 171, ff. 48⁶–70 (frag.).

Allesandro and Lorenzo de'Medici (frag.). Discovered in 1985 among the papers of Sir John Coke at Melbourne Hall, Derbyshire;

single MS sheet of 143 lines on 4 pages. Poss. the work of Webster or perhaps Shirley, who dramatized the story in *The Traitor*, 1631.

Alphonsus. By Dudley North (?). Harvard U. Lib. Houghton MS. Latin 329.

Ambitio Infelix sive Absalom (L). Stonyhurst MS A. VII. 50 (2).

Ananias, Azarias, Mesael (L). Stonyhurst MS B.VI. 10.

Andronicus Comnenus (L). Brit. Lib. MS Sloane, 1767, ff. 18–66. Possibly the work of Samuel Bernard; MS in hand of another.

Anna Bullen. Huntington MS HM 973. (derivative adaptation of Banks' play, *Virtue Betrayed*, 1682). MS lacks prol. or epil. No evidence that it was ever performed. Probably dates from early 18th century.

Antipolargesis (L). Stonyhurst MS A. VII. 50 (1).

Antoninus Bassianus Caracalla (L). (1) Bodl. MS Rawlinson C. 590. (2) Harvard Univ. MS Thr. 10.1, ff. 8–19 (an actor's part).

Antonio of Ragusa. Bodl. MS Rawlinson, poet. 93.

Ara Fortunae (L). See *The Christmas Prince*, below.

Artaxerxes (L). Stonyhurst MS. A. VII. 50 (1).

Ascanius (L). Bodl. MS. Add. B. 73.

Bacchides. See under BUCHANAN, GEORGE, Supp. I.

Baiazet (*Bajazet*). Arbury House, Warwick, C.R.O. microfilm No. M1 351/5, item no. 22. MS in several hands of the early 17th century. Probably to be identified with Thomas Goffe's *The Raging Turk*, or *Bajazet II*, first printed in 1631.

Band, Cuff, and Ruff (*Ruff, Band, and Cuff*). (1) Brit. Lib. Add. MS 23723. (2) MS reported in *Hist. MSS Comm.*, III, 295 (MSS at Ashton Hall, York). (3) Folger Shakespeare Lib. MS J.a.2, f. 25ʳ–25ᵛ (4) Bodl. Lyell 37, pp. 124–6, 139 (Speakers Bande, Cuffe, Ruffe) (5) Bradford, West Yorkshire Archive Service: Hopkinson 32D 86/17, pp. 1–6.

The Baptist. See under BUCHANAN, GEORGE, Supp. I.

Basilindus (L). Stonyhurst MS. A. VII 50 (I).

Betrothal of Mary and Archduke Charles (also *The Entertainment of the Flemish Ambassadors*). (1) Brit. Lib. Add. MS 21382, f. 19.

(2) Letter from Flemish ambassadors to Lady Margaret. P.R.O. LC950, ff. 149–53.

Bila, Ariscancus, etc. (L). Brit. Lib. Add. MS 27569, f. I.

Blurt, Master Constable. Folger Shakespeare Lib. 17876 (transcript of H2^r–4^v supplied in defective copy of 1602 Quarto).

Boot and Spur. Folger Shakespeare Lib. MS J.a. 1, ff. 19^r–23^r.

Britanniae Primitiae (L). (1) Stonyhurst MS A.VII. 50 (2). (2) Bodl. MS. Rawlinson, poet. 215 (frag.).

The Burial and Resurrection of Christ. Bodl. MS. E. Museo. 160.

Bury St Edmunds Fragment. MS attached to a roll of Rickinghall Manor, Suffolk, formerly property of Abbey of Bury St Edmunds, acquired by Brit. Lib. 1921 (Add. MS Charter 63481B [roll]).

Caiphas. Brit. Lib. MS Sloane 2478, f. 43^r.

Cancer (L). Folger Shakespeare Lib. MS J.a. 2, ff. 26^r–47^r.

Captiva Religio (L). (1) English Col., Rome, Archives MS Lib. 321. (2) Ibid., C. 17 (iv).

The Captive Lady. MS in the collection of James M. Osborn, New Haven, Connecticut.

The Castle of Perseverance. Macro MS in the Folger Shakespeare Lib., V.a. 354, ff. 38–75.

Charlemagne. Brit. Lib. MS Egerton 1994, ff. 119–36.

Chester Plays. (1) MS Peniarth 399, National Lib. of Wales. (2) Huntington Lib. MS HM2 (frag.). (3) Brit. Lib. Add. MS 10305. (4) Brit. Lib. MS Harleian 2013. (5) Ibid., 2124. (6) Bodl. MS 175. (7) MS in Manchester Free Lib. (frag.).

A Christmas Messe. Folger Shakespeare Lib. MS J.a.I, ff. 105^r–15^v.

The Christmas Prince. (Contains following Lat. pieces: *Ara Fortunae, Philomela, Philomathes, Saturnalia,* the last poss. by Owen Vertue. Contains also English *Periander,* for another MS of which see SANSBURY, JOHN, above.) St John's Col., Oxford, MS 52.

Cinna. Oxford MS Exoniensis, saec. XVII.

Clytophon (L) (William Ainsworth ?). Emmanuel Col., Camb., MS 185 (3.1.17), Art. 5.

The Conversion of St Paul. Bodl. MS Digby 133, ff. 37–50.

The Coronation Entry of Queen Mary. (1) Brit. Lib. MS Cotton Vitellius, F.v.: building preparations. (2) Brit. Lib. MS Harleian 194 (fullest account). (3) Brit. Lib. MS Harleian 540 (includes locations of pageants). (4) Palais de Justice, Bruges, West Flanders MS. (5) 'Copie d'une lettre en Français excrite de Londres par un témoin oculaire . . . 1553', in *Publications of the Caxton Society* A (1849); rept. N.Y.: 1967. (6) Holinshed, *Chronicles* (1586), IV: 6–7.

The Coronation of King Edward VI. MS 'formerly belonging to William Le Neve Norroy' (see Leland, *Collect.,* IV, pp. 310 seq.).

The Coronation of Henry VII. Brit. Lib. MS Egerton 985, f. 47.

The Country Gentleman. Folger Shakespeare Lib. MS. V.b. 228.

Crux Vindicata (L). Stonyhurst MS A. VII. 50 (2).

The Cure of Pride. Huntington Lib. MS HM95, *c.* 1675–80?

The Cyprian Conqueror. Brit. Lib. MS Sloane 3709.

The Dead Man's Fortune. Brit. Lib. Add. MS 10449, f. 1 ('plot' only).

Death: A Comedie. Newberry Library Case MS 5A.7.

Description of the Pageants Made in the City of London at the Receiving of . . . Charles V and Henry VIII . . . Corpus Christi Col., Camb., MS 298, No. 8.

Devices to Be Shown before the Queen at Nottingham Castle after the Meeting of the Queen of Scots. Brit. Lib. MS Lansdowne 5, item 38.

Diana's Grove, or *The Faithful Genius.* (1) MS cited by M. Summers, *Playhouse of Pepys,* p. 449, from Dobell catalogue of 1918. (2) MS, formerly item 361 in H.F. House sale at Sotheby's, 21 Jan. 1924 (*The Faithful Genius*), now in the collection of James M. Osborn, New Haven, Connecticut.

Dick of Devonshire. Brit. Lib. MS Egerton 1994, ff. 30–52.

The Disloyal Favourite. Bodl. MS Rawlinson D. 1361, ff. 285–306.

Don Pedro, the Cruel King of Castile (L). MS, item 482, in Sotheby's sale, 13 Dec. 1938.

Duke of Florence (title assigned). Fragment of a final working draft of a prev. unknown Jacobean play discovered in 1985. Stylistic

evidence suggests John Webster's authorship. Bloomsbury Book Auction, 20 June
1986.

Dux Moraud. Bodl. MS Eng. poet. f. 2(R).

Edmond Ironside. c. 1590. Brit. Lib. MS Egerton
1994, ff. 96–119.

The Enchanted Lovers (Lower) and *The City Nightcap* (Davenport). Adapted and combined.
Folger Shakespeare Lib: MS J.b. 2.

An Elizabeth an Jig. MS Peniarth 403. National
Lib. of Wales.

'The Emperor's Favourite.' (title assigned by
T.H. Howard-Hill). Arbury House, Nuneton, Warwicks. Warwickshire C.R.O.
microfilm number M1 351. Characters
include Nero, Crispinus his favourite,
Vologesus King of Parthia, Tiridates his
brother, Triganes, Corbulus, Locusta
mother to Crispinus. In a 17th-century
hand. Probably dated 1623–8.

The Entertainment at Chirke Castle. Brit. Lib. MS
Egerton 2623, ff. 20–23 (speeches of Genius,
Orpheus, and Winter).

The Entertainment at Mitcham. Brit. Mus. Add.
MS. 12497, ff. 253–62ᵛ.

The Essex Entertainment, 1595. Fragments
appear in Lambeth Palace MSS V. 118;
VIII, 274; Northumberland MS Burgoyne
55, ff. 47–53; S.P.D. Elizabeth, CCLIV,
67, 68; Folger Shakespeare Lib. MS V.b.
213 (speeches for a Squire, Hermit, Soldier,
and Secretary).

The Fairy Knight. Folger Shakespeare Lib. MS
V.a. 128.

The Faithful Friends. Victoria and Albert Mus.
MS Dyce 10.

The Faithful Virgins. Bodl. MS. Rawlinson,
poet. 195.

The Fatal Marriage. Brit. Lib. MS Egerton
1994, ff. 136–61.

Felix Concordia Fratrium (L). Stonyhurst MS
A.VII.50 (2).

Fenisa. MS, item 251, in H.F. House sale at
Sotheby's, 21 Jan. 1924.

The First Anti-Mask of Mountebanks. (1) Hunt-
ington Lib. MS HM 21. (2) Brit. Lib. Add.
MS 5956, ff. 72–84. (3) Bodl. MS
Rawlinson D. 1021. (4) MS in Gray's Inn
Lib.

Fool's Fortune. MS. in Public Record Office,
Star Chamber, Proceedings, 8. 250/31.

Fools Have Fortune, or *Luck's All.* Huntington
Lib. MS EL 8924 (prologue and epilogue).

Fortunae Ludibrium (L). Stonyhurst MS A.
VII.50 (2).

'II Fortune's Tennis.' MS once identified with
this play. Brit. Lib. Add. MS 10449, f. 4
('plot' only).

The Four Hours Adventure. Bodl. MS Rawlinson,
poet. 84. (prologue and epilogue).

Fraus Pia (L). Brit. Lib. MS Sloane 1855,
ff. 71–84.

Frederick and Basilea. Brit. Lib. Add. MS 10449,
f. 2 ('plot' only).

Free-Will. Folger Shakespeare Lib. MS V.b.
221, 1635.

Furor Impius sive Constans Fratricida (L). Bodl.
MS. Rawlinson, poet. 215. (May be same as
Sanguis Sanguinem sive Constans Fratricida,
below.)

Gallomyomachia (Greek). Brit. Lib. MS
Harleian 5664, Art. 5.

Gemitus Columbae (L). Stonyhurst MS A.VII.
50 (2).

Ghismonda (Tancred and Ghismonda). (1) Brit.
Lib. Add. MS 34312, f. 139. (2) Warwick
County Record Office, Newdigate MS CR
136/B766. Assigned the title of *Glausamond
and Fidelia* by T.H. Howard-Hill. May be a
partial draft of *Ghismonda.* (3) Arbury
House, Nuneton, Warwicks. Warwickshire
C.R.O. microfilm number M1 351 (Significantly revised version assigned the title
Ghismonda and Guiscardo. Authorship recently
identified as John Newdigate. (4) See entry
under NEWDIGATE, JOHN, in Supp. I.

Ghismonda and Guiscardo. (title assigned by T.H.
Howard-Hill). Arbury House, Nuneton,
Warwicks. Warwickshire C.R.O. M1 351.
17th-century tragedy, recently attri. to John
Newdigate. MS is a revised version of
Glausamond and Fidelia, below.

Gigantomachia. Folger Shakespeare Lib. MS
J.a. 1 ff. 186ʳ–200ʳ.

Glausamond and Fidelia. (title assigned by T.H.
Howard-Hill). Warwick County Record
Office, Newdigate MS CR 136/B766. Early
17th-century tragedy. One of the two MSS
(the other being *Ghismonda and Guiscardo,*
above) of the Brit. Lib. MS play edited by
Wright as *Tancred and Ghismonda.* Corrected
MS. Warwick.

The Governor. Brit. Lib. Add. MS 10419.

Gown, Hood, and Cap. Folger Shakespeare Lib. MS J.a. 2, ff. 43ᵛ–49ʳ.

The Great Cham. Folger Shakespeare Lib. MS X.d.259.

Hannibal (L). Bodl. MS Malone 531 (frag.).

The Harrowing of Hell. (1) Advocates' Lib., Edinburgh, MS Auchinleck W. 4, 1. (2) Bodl. MS Digby 86, ff. 119–20. (3) Brit. Lib. MS Harleian, 2253, ff. 55–6.

Henry VII, Coronation of. Brit. Lib. MS Egerton 985, f. 47ᵛ.

Henry VII's Provincial Progress. Brit. Lib. MS Cotton Julius B. xii.

Hercules Furens. (1) Bodl. MS Rawlinson, poet. 76. (2) Brit. Lib. Add. MS 60276 (blank verse translations by Cosmo Manuche?).

Heteroclitanomalonomia. Folger Shakespeare Lib. MS J.a. 1, ff. 119ʳ–133ʳ.

Hierachomachia. English Col., Rome, Archives MS C. 17 (i).

The Humorous Magistrate. (title assigned by T.H. Howard-Hill). Arbury House, Nuneton, Warwicks. Warwickshire County Record Office, M1 351. Jonsonian farce with Mr Thrifty as the justice; Mrs Mumble as a deaf, rich widow; Christopher Spruce as her son; and Mr Wellcome as her brother. Corrected MS. Prob. date of composition between 1625 and 1640; 1635 very likely.

The Hypochondriac. Brit. Lib. MS Sloane 1863, ff. 44ᵃ–69ᵇ (frag.).

Icon Ecclesiastici (L). Brit. Lib. MS Sloane 1767, ff. 2–17.

The Illustrious Slaves. Brit. Lib. Add. MS 32094, ff. 274 seq.

Interludium de Clerico et Puella. Brit. Lib. Add. MS 23986.

Jephthes. See under BUCHANAN, GEORGE, Supp. I.

Joseph. See under BUCHANAN, GEORGE, Supp. I.

Jovis et Junonis Nuptiae (L). Trinity Col., Camb., MS R. 10.4.

Judith. National Lib. of Wales MS Peniarth 508 (frag.).

Judith. See under BUCHANAN, GEORGE, Supp. I.

Jugurtha. Bodl. MS. Rawlinson, poet. 195.

Juli and Julian. Folger Shakespeare Lib. MS V.a. 159.

Laelia (L). Lambeth Palace MS 838.

'Locus, Corpus, Motus,' etc. Bodl. MS Tanner 306 (frag.).

Love and Self-Love. See *The Essex Entertainment*, above.

Love Feigned and Unfeigned. A fragment written on first and last leaves of J. Herolt's *Sermones Discipuli*, pub. 1492, Brit. Lib. MS I.B. 2172 (fac.).

Love's Changelings' Change. Brit. Lib. MS Egerton 1994, ff. 293–318.

The Lover's Stratagem. Bodl. MS Rawlinson, poet. 18.

Ludus Coventriae. Brit. Lib. MS Cotton Vespasian D. VIII.

Lusiuncula (L). Extant? See Hazlitt, *Manual*, p. 145.

Magister Bonus sive Arsenius (L). Stonyhurst MS A. VII. 50 (2).

Mankind. Macro MS in the Folger Shakespeare Lib. V.a. 354, ff. 1–13.

Marcus et Marcellianus (L). Stonyhurst MS B. VI. 22.

The Marriage of Frederick and Elizabeth. Brit. Lib. Add. MS 5767.

The Marriage of Prince Arthur. College of Arms MS 1st M. 13.

Marriage Revived. MS in Harvard Col. Lib.

Mary Magdalene, The Mystery Play of. Bodl. MS Digby 133, ff. 95–145.

The Masculine Bride. See *The Whimsies of Señor Hidalgo*, below.

A Mask Presented at Coleoverton. Victoria and Albert Mus. MS Dyce 36.

The Mask of Flowers. MS in Gray's Inn Library.

Mask of Sailors. MS of metrical epistle among Herrick papers preserved at Beaumanor in Leicestershire.

The Massacre of Innocents. Bodl. MS Digby 133, ff. 146–57.

Medea. (1) Brit. Lib. MS Sloane 911, ff. 100–15. (2) Bodl. MS Eng. poet. e. 34. (3) See under BUCHANAN, GEORGE, Supp. I.

Menaechmi. See under BUCHANAN, GEORGE, Supp. I.

Mercator. See under BUCHANAN, GEORGE, Supp. I.

Mercurius Rusticans (L). Bodl. MS Wood D. 18, part 2.

The Merry Loungers. Brit. Lib. Add. MS 6402, f. 84.

'Microcosmus' (L). Trinity Col., Camb., MS R. 10.4, ff. 66–82ᵛ (Art 4).

Miles Gloriosus. See under BUCHANAN, GEORGE, Supp. I.

Mind, Will, and Understanding. (1) Macro MS in the Folger Shakespeare Lib. V.a. 354, ff. 14–37. (2) Bodl. MS Digby 133, ff. 158–69 (large frag.).

Mr Doolittle. (1) Brit. Lib. MS Sloane 1828, ff. 1–45ᵇ. (2) Ibid., Sloane 1911–1913, ff. 203–04 (frag.).

Mock Mass. See entry under KYTTON, W..

Montezuma (L). Stonyhurst MS B.VI.10.

Morus (L). Stonyhurst MS A.VII. 50 (1).

Mostellaria. See under BUCHANAN, GEORGE, Supp. I.

The Mystery of Iniquity. National Lib. of Scotland MS 2093, ff. 1–26.

Naamen. See under BUCHANAN, GEORGE, Supp. I.

Narcissus. Bodl. MS Rawlinson, poet. 212.

Nehemiah. See under BUCHANAN, GEORGE, Supp. I.

Nero, The Tragedy of. (1) Brit. Lib. MS Egerton 1994, ff. 245–68. (2) Excerpts in Samuel Butler's commonplace book; see item 135 in A.S.W. Rosenbach catalogue, Oct. 1941.

The New Moon. English Col., Rome, Archives MS Z. 142.

Nottola (L). Bodl. MS Douce 47.

Oedipus. MS in the possession of Stevens Cox of Dorset.

Oedipus. Bodl. MS Rawlinson, poet. 76.

Origo Mundi, etc. (1) Bodl. MS 791. (2) Bodl. MS Corn, e. 3 (transcript of Bodl. MS 791.) (3) National Lib. of Wales, MS Peniarth 428E.

The Part of Poor. Harvard Univ. MS Thr. 10.1, ff. 21–46 (an actor's part).

Parthenia (L). Emmanuel Col., Camb., MS 68 (1.3.16).

The Partial Law. Folger Shakespeare Lib. MS V.a. 165.

Pastor Fidus (L). (1) Camb. Univ. Lib. MS Ff. 2.9. (2) Trinity Col., Camb., MS R.3.37, ff. 35–87ᵛ.

Pathomachia. (1) Brit. Lib. MS Harleian 6869, Art. I. (2) Bodl. MS Eng. misc. e. 5.

Pelopidarum Secunda. Brit. Lib. MS Harleian 5110, Art. 4.

Perfidus Hetruscus (L). Bodl. MS Rawlinson C. 787.

Philander, King of Thrace. Folger Shakespeare Lib. MS X.d.206.

The Pilgrimage to Parnassus. Bodl. MS Rawlinson D. 398.

Preist the Barber. Folger Shakespeare Lib. MS J.a.2, ff. 48ᵛ–49ʳ.

The Pride of Life. MS in the Public Record Office, Dublin.

'Processus Satanae'. MS in the lib. of the Duke of Portland at Welbeck Abbey (an actor's part).

Pseudolus. See under BUCHANAN, GEORGE, Supp. I.

Psyche et Filii ejus (L). Bodl. MS Rawlinson, poet. 172, f. 60.

Publius Cornelius Scipio sui Victor (L). Folger Shakespeare Lib. MS V.a. 227.

Pygmalion (L). Bodl. MS Rawlinson D.317, ff. 190–5.

The Queen's Welcome at Theobalds. (1) MS formerly in the collection of Frederic Ouvry (frag.). Extant? (2) MS formerly in the possession of J.P. Collier (frag.) Extant?

Quem Quaeritis in *Winchester Troper* (L). (1) Bodl. MS 775. X, 17 (dated 978–980?). (2) Christ's Col., Camb., MS 473, XI, 26 (dated *c*. 1050).

Quem Quaetitis (*of Easter*) of the Church of St John the Evangelist, Dublin (L). (1) Bodl. MS Rawlinson, Liturg. d. IV, XIV, 68–70, 85–6, 127–32. (2) Lib. of Archbishop Marsh, Dublin, MS Z.4.2.20.

Quem Quaeritis. See also under AETHELWOLD, KATHERINE OF SUTTON.

The Rape Revenged. Brit. Lib. Add. MS 28807.

Reception for Queen Elizabeth at Greenwich. Brit. Lib. Egerton MS 2877, f. 182.

The Renegado. See MASSINGER, above.

The Resurrection of Our Lord. Folger Shakespeare Lib. MS V.b. 192.

I The Return from Parnassus. Bodl. MS Rawlinson D. 398.

II The Return from Parnassus (*The Progress to Parnassus*). Folger Shakespeare Lib. MS V.a.355 (the Halliwell-Phillips MS).

The Review (prob. after 1700). Folger Shakespeare Lib. MS W.a.114.

I Richard II. Brit. Lib. MS Egerton 1994, ff. 161–86.

Risus Anglicanus (L). Folger Shakespeare Lib. MS J.a.I, ff. 24ʳ–43ᵛ.

Robin Hood and the Sheriff of Nottingham. MS at Trinity Col., Camb., (frag.).

Rodogune. Folger Shakespeare Lib. MS V.b.227.

Roffensis (L). English Col., Rome, Archives MS Lib. 321.

Romanus. Brit. Lib. MS Harleian 4628, Art. 14, ff. 272–282ᵛ (frag.); see entry under COBBES, JAMES, above.

Romeus et Julietta (L). Brit. Lib. MS Sloane 1775, f. 242 (frag.).

Rowland's Godson. Bodl. MS Rawlinson, poet. 85, ff. 15ᵛ–19ʳ.

Sacrament, The Croxton Play of the. Trinity Col., Dublin, MS F.IV.20.

S. Edoardus Confessor (L). (1) Magdalen Col., Oxford, MS C.2.22. (2) Harvard University Lib. MS Lat. 32, ff. 83–115ᵛ.

S. Franciscus Xaverius (L). Stonyhurst MS B.VI.10.

S. Pelagius Martyr (L). Stonyhurst MS B.VI.10.

S. Thomas Cantuariis (L). English Col., Rome, Archives MS. Lib. 321.

Sanguis Sanguinem sive Constans Fratricida (L). Stonyhurst MS A.VII. 50 (2). (May be same as *Furor Impius sive Constans Fratricida*, above.)

Sapientia Solomonis (L). (1) Brit. Lib. Add. MS 20061. (2) Folger Shakespeare Lib. MS V.a. 212.

Saul. See under BUCHANAN, GEORGE, Supp. I.

The Second Maiden's Tragedy. Brit. Lib. MS Lansdowne 807, ff. 28–56.

La Seinte resureccion (Anglo-Norman). (1) Bibliothéque Nationale, Paris, MS fr. 902 (frag.). (2) Brit. Lib. Add. MS 45103 (frag.).

Senilis Amor (L). Bodl. MS Rawlinson, poet. 9, ff. 46–80ᵛ.

II The Seven Deadly Sins. Dulwich Col. MS XIX ('plot' only).

Shrewsbury Fragments (Lat. and Eng.). Shrewsbury School MS. Mus. III. 42.

The Siege of Croya. Bodl. MS Rawlinson, poet. 119.

Silvanus (L). Bodl. MS Douce 234, ff. 1–15ᵛ.

Sisigambis, Queen of Syracuse. Bodl. MS Rawlinson, poet. 167.

Solymannidae (L). Brit. Lib. MS Lansdowne 723.

Sophomoros comoedia (L). MS, item 240, in Robinson sale catalogue 76.348, 3 May 1946.

A Speech of Delight. Bodl. MS Tanner 407, ff. 43–4.

Stonyhurst Pageants. Stonyhurst MS A.VI.33.

Tancred and Ghismonda. see *Ghismonda*, above.

The Telltale, Dulwich Col. MS XX.

Thomas Morus (L). English Col., Rome, Archives MS Lib. 321. (Same play as *Morus*, above?)

Thyestes. Bodl. MS Rawlinson, poet. 76.

Time's Triumph. Brit. Lib. MS Egerton 1994, ff. 212–45.

Timon. Victoria and Albert Mus. MS Dyce D25, f. 48.

Tobias (L). Harvard U. Lib. MS Lat. 32, ff. 57–82.

Tobit. See under BUCHANAN, GEORGE, Supp. I.

Towneley Plays. See *Wakefield Plays.*

Tragoedia Miserrima Pyrami et Thisbes fata enuncians. Brit. Lib. Add. MS 15227, ff. 56ᵛ–61ʳ.

Troelus a Chresyd (*Troilus and Cressida*). National Library of Wales, MS Peniarth 106.

The True Tragicomedy Formerly Acted at Court, etc. Brit. Lib. Add. MS 25348.

The Twice Chang'd Friar. Arbury House, Nuneton, Warwicks. Warwickshire County Record Office, M1 351. Early 17th-century comedy based on the *Decameron*, 4th day, novella 2, with Friar Albert, Lisetta, and two courtesans, Dianora and Oretta. Corrected MS, prob. dated 1624–7.

Try before You Trust. Brit. Lib. Add. MS 37158, f. 17.

The Two Noble Ladies and the Converted Conjurer. Brit. Lib. MS Egerton 1994, ff. 224–45.

Wakefield Plays. Huntington Lib. MS HM 1.

The Wasp. MS in the Duke of Northumberland's lib. at Alnwick, MS 507.

The Welcome for Emperor Charles V. Corpus Christi, Camb., MS 298 (no. 8), pp. 132 seq.

The Welcome for James VI. Advocates' Lib., Edinburgh, Hist. MSS. 35.4.2, vol. II, f. 524 (Johnston's MS History of Scotland).

The Welcome for Katherine of Aragon. (1) College of Arms MS 1st M. 13, ff. 27–74. (2) Brit. Lib. Cotton MS Vitellius A. XVI.

(3) Guildhall MS 3313 (*Great Chronicle*).

The Welcome for Princess Margaret. (See J. Leland, *Collectanea*, ed. T. Hearne, London, 1774, IV, 288ff.)

The Welcome for Queen Mary. (1) MS formerly in the possession of Sir John Maxwell of Pollock (*Diurnal of Remarkable Occurrents*). (2) Advocates' Lib., Edinburgh, Hist. MSS. 35.4.2., vol. II, f. 356 (Johnston's MS History of Scotland).

The Whimsies of Señor Hidalgo. Brit. Lib. MS Harleian 5152, Art. I.

The White Ethiopian. Brit. Lib. MS Harleian 7313, Art. I.

Wine, Beer, and Ale. Univ. of Edinburgh MS Laing. III. 493.

Wit's Triumvirate. Brit. Lib. Add. MS 45865.

The Wooing of Nan. Dulwich Col. MS Vol. I, f. 272 (no. 139).

York Plays. Brit. Lib. Add. MS 35290.

Zelotypus (L). (1) Trinity Col., Camb., MS R.3.9. (2) Emmanuel Col., Camb., MS 185 (3.1.17). (3) MS in Durham in Cathedral Lib., Hunter 76, item 6.